THIRD EDITION

INSIDE XEROX VENTURA PUBLISHER

The Complete Learning and Reference Guide

James Cavuoto
Jesse Berst

VENTANA PRESS

INSIDE XEROX VENTURA PUBLISHER
The Complete Learning and Reference Guide, Third Edition

Library of Congress Cataloging-in-Publication Data

Cavuoto, James.
Inside Xerox Ventura publisher: the complete learning and reference guide / by James Cavuoto and Jesse Berst. — 3rd ed.
p. cm.
Includes index.
ISBN 0-940087-61-8
1. Ventura publisher (Computer program) 2. Desktop publishing.
I. Berst, Jesse. II. Title
Z286.D47C38 1990 90-43955
686.2'2544536—dc20 CIP

Third Edition, First Printing
Printed in the United States of America
Ventana Press, Inc.
P.O. Box 2468
Chapel Hill, NC 27515
919/942-0220
FAX 919/942-1140

Cover Design: Nancy Frame, Durham, NC
Cover Illustration: © Gary Palmer, 1990

Limits of Liability and Disclaimer of Warranty

Table of Contents

Chapter One

Introduction to Desktop Publishing

Welcome to the revolution. A movement has been underway for several years, a movement that is revolutionizing the way businesspeople produce printed pages. This book will show you how to profit from that trend using a remarkable software program called Xerox Ventura Publisher.

To gain perspective, let's harken back to an earlier revolution and an event that dramatically illustrates the power of the printed word. In January 1776, Thomas Paine published *Common Sense*, a vivid call for the formation of a republic. His 50-page pamphlet led directly to the Declaration of Independence a few months later.

Common Sense was an immediate bestseller (120,000 copies in three months — equivalent to 10 million today). Paine's problems lay not with the writing and selling, but with the printing and production, which delayed him and cost more than expected.

Sound familiar?

Two hundred years after Paine's manifesto, the printing process was more sophisticated, but it wasn't any simpler. Two hundred years later, printing and production were still bottlenecks that delayed our important documents.

Until desktop publishing came along.

Which brings us back to our modern-day revolution. Desktop publishing has transformed the process of producing pages. If Thomas Paine were alive today, we think he would have been one of the first to use it. That cantankerous rebel could not

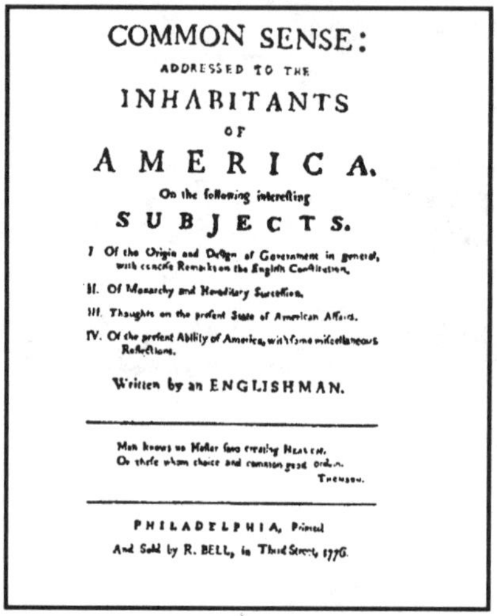
COMMON SENSE:
ADDRESSED TO THE
INHABITANTS
OF
AMERICA,
On the following interesting
SUBJECTS.

I. Of the Origin and Design of Government in general, with concise Remarks on the English Constitution.
II. Of Monarchy and Hereditary Succession.
III. Thoughts on the present State of American Affairs.
IV. Of the present Ability of America, with some miscellaneous Reflections.

Written by an ENGLISHMAN.

Man knows no Master save creating Heaven,
Or those whom choice and common good ordain.
THOMSON.

PHILADELPHIA, Printed
And Sold by R. BELL, in Third Street, 1776.

Figure 1-1. Thomas Paine's Common Sense as it appeared originally (left) and how it might have appeared if Ventura Publisher had been available (right).

have resisted the freedom it provides and the control it allows. Paine could have saved time. He could have gained the control to experiment until he got things right (Figure 1-1). And he could have saved money — something the penniless writer certainly would have appreciated.

It's too late for Thomas Paine. But those of us who are around today can cash in on desktop publishing, thanks to Xerox Ventura Publisher, a product that gives an inexpensive personal computer the power of a print shop.

Desktop publishing defined

We're anxious to show you how Ventura Publisher can pay off. First you need to understand where this exceptional product fits into the scheme of things.

Let's begin by defining the term desktop publishing. Put simply, it's the use of a personal computer for most or all the stages of publishing. Both desktop and traditional publishing have the same basic steps: creation (of text and pictures), assembly (into pages), and printing. But the traditional method is a tedious, detail-oriented process involving expensive equipment and highly trained personnel (Table 1-1).

Table 1-1. Traditional publishing versus desktop publishing.

Stage	Traditional Publishing	Desktop Publishing
Writing	Authors create text on typewriter.	Authors create text in word processor.
Editing	Editors make red pencil marks to typed copy. Typists retype pages if changes are extensive. Several iterations may occur.	Editors make changes to text file in word processor.
Typesetting	Typesetting machine operator rekeys the manuscript into the typesetter, following the editor's instructions about size and selection of typefaces. The text is typeset into long galleys, which are the proper column width, but not the right length. Galleys are proofread and corrections reset.	Editor applies generic labels to elements of text file such as headline. Text elements automatically take on proper type specifications.
Illustration	An artist creates charts, graphs, or drawings using pens and other tools.	An artist creates charts, graphs, or drawings using graphics software programs.
Page Design	Designer creates blank layouts on paste-up boards, using blue pencil to mark location of text columns.	Designer creates a style sheet for publication. This task need only be performed once.
Paste-up	Paste-up artist cuts galleys lengthwise into strips one column wide, then applies adhesive to back of galley. Artist begins process of applying galleys to columns on paste-up boards. Artist leaves "windows" on boards to fit drawings and photographs after computing how much space must be left and what scale factors should be used.	Designer flows text file into document using existing style sheet. Designer creates frames to hold artwork and then loads the graphic files into the frames. The graphics are scaled automatically. Designer outputs pages on laser printer or high-resolution imagesetter.
Negatives	Camera operator shoots a negative image of each page. Blank spaces appear on negatives where artwork is to appear. Camera operator then shoots negatives of the artwork, using the scale factors specified by the paste-up artist.	Camera operator shoots one negative of each page, with all elements in place.
Stripping	Prepress specialist assembles negatives of artwork into position on pages.	Prepress specialist need only position elements not included during page layout.
Printing	Combined negatives are grouped into a "signature" of 4, 8, or 16 pages and a large plate is made. The publication is printed onto large sheets, which are then trimmed, cut, folded, collated, and bound to make a finished product.	Same.

Desktop publishing had its beginnings in the 1970s, when Xerox Corporation introduced the Star workstation. This computer was the first to offer a high-resolution display that could integrate text and pictures on screen. It also incorporated a revolutionary device called a mouse, which let users move around the screen by sliding a hand-held controller. Other manufacturers subsequently borrowed this interface. It's evident in products such as the Apple Macintosh, Microsoft Windows, Digital Research Inc.'s GEM environment, and the Documenter system from Xerox itself.

The second major component of desktop publishing was the laser printer, first put to use by Xerox in the 1970s. Just as the Star workstation offered the ability to merge text and graphics on screen, laser printers offered the capability to merge text and graphics on the printed page.

Prices have fallen in the years since Xerox's pioneering efforts. The capabilities present in the early Star/laser printer system are now available for less than $5,000.

How to benefit from desktop publishing

Desktop publishing offers a host of benefits to the savvy businessperson. We've listed a few examples below.

Saving money

Desktop publishing saves on equipment and labor. Even low-end typesetters cost $25,000 to $50,000. Many cost more than $100,000. And labor costs continue to climb for the skilled personnel required to manually lay out, illustrate, code, paste up, and print. It takes significantly fewer man-hours to produce a page on a personal computer than it does using traditional methods. Desktop publishing also cuts paper costs when compared to typewritten pages. Typesetting fits up to 30 percent more on a page. Merging graphics with text also saves space (a picture's worth a thousand words, remember?).

When you add it all up, desktop publishing can cut costs almost in half. Now consider that American corporations spend an estimated $200 billion to produce 2.5 *trillion* pages each year. Desktop publishing is an easy computer application to cost-justify. Table 1-2 gives an example of how much money one company saved on a 24-page in-house monthly newsletter. (As the EPA likes to say, your actual mileage may vary.)

Table 1-2. Typical cost savings from desktop publishing.

Task	Before DTP	After DTP	Savings per Issue	Savings per Year
Writing	$126	$110	$16	$192
Editing	$75	$18	$57	$684
Keyboarding	$34	0	$34	$408
Proofreading	$31	$6	$25	$300
Typesetting	$35	0	$35	$420
Revisions	$15	0	$15	$180
Illustrations	$150	0	$150	$1800
Halftones	$15	$15	0	0
Paste up	$19	0	$19	$228
Corrections	$14	0	$14	$168
Total	**$514**	**$149**	**$365**	**$4380**

Saving time

Many desktop publishing installations can pay for themselves in less than a year through reduced labor costs alone. But there's another side to saving time that's difficult to quantify.

Often, getting a document out sooner provides a competitive advantage. A newsletter publisher, for instance, can wait right up to deadline before assembling the final pages. News is fresher and more timely. Result: satisfied customers and more subscriptions. Likewise, contractors might gain an edge by being the first to submit a professional-looking bid; scientists by getting a monograph out ahead of time; managers by getting a report to top brass before their rivals; consultants by beating the competition to the punch with a top-notch proposal.

More control

Now, for the first time, you govern when your work gets done and how it will look. That translates to freedom. Freedom from high-priced type shops that charge a lot for simple jobs. Freedom from artists and layout people who don't understand what you want. Freedom from outside companies who have no motivation to get it done right and on time. It also translates to fewer mistakes. Traditional publishing can involve as many as 10 different people — one for each stage discussed in Table 1-1.

With a personal computer, a laser printer, and Xerox Ventura Publisher, one person can take the place of these experts. Okay — one ambitious, hard-working person. But you get the point: The fewer people in the middle, the fewer the errors.

More power to persuade

There's a big difference between a typewritten document and one that's been professionally produced (see Figure 1-2). This difference means you'll have more *power to persuade*. Power to grab the reader's attention and keep it. Power to influence through words, graphics, and design. Power to create documents that look important, professional, expensive.

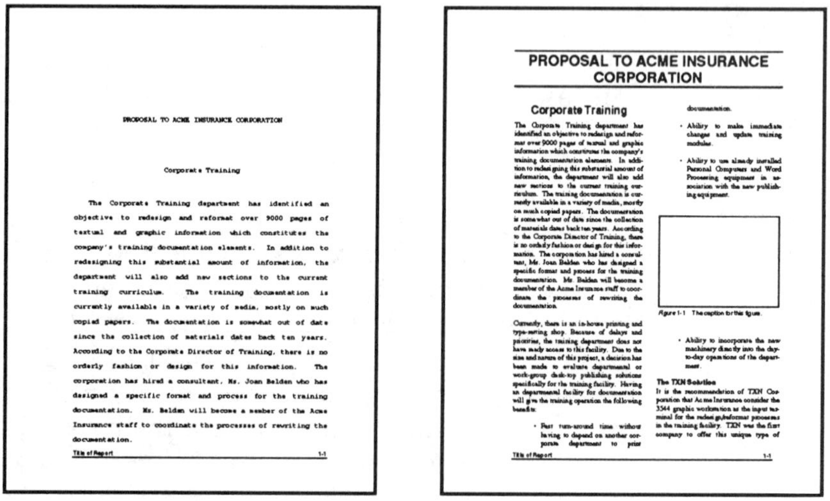

PROPOSAL TO ACME INSURANCE CORPORATION

Corporate Training

The Corporate Training department has identified an objective to redesign and reformat over 9000 pages of textual and graphic information which constitutes the company's training documentation elements. In addition to redesigning this substantial amount of information, the department will also add new sections to the current training curriculum. The training documentation is currently available in a variety of media, mostly on much copied papers. The documentation is somewhat out of date since the collection of materials dates back ten years. According to the Corporate Director of Training, there is no orderly fashion or design for this information. The corporation has hired a consultant, Ms. Joan Belden who has designed a specific format and process for the training documentation. Ms. Belden will become a member of the Acme Insurance staff to coordinate the processes of rewriting the documentation.

Title of Report 1-1

PROPOSAL TO ACME INSURANCE CORPORATION

Corporate Training

The Corporate Training department has identified an objective to redesign and reformat over 9000 pages of textual and graphic information which constitutes the company's training documentation elements. In addition to redesigning this substantial amount of information, the department will also add new sections to the current training curriculum. The training documentation is currently available in a variety of media, mostly on much copied papers. The documentation is somewhat out of date since the collection of materials dates back ten years. According to the Corporate Director of Training, there is no orderly fashion or design for this information. The corporation has hired a consultant, Ms. Joan Belden who has designed a specific format and process for the training documentation. Ms. Belden will become a member of the Acme Insurance staff to coordinate the processes of rewriting the documentation.

Currently, there is an in-house printing and type-setting shop. Because of delays and priorities, the training department does not have ready access to this facility. Due to the size and nature of this project, a decision has been made to evaluate departmental or work-group desk-top publishing solutions specifically for the training facility. Having an departmental facility for documentation will give the training operation the following benefits:

- Fast turn-around time without having to depend on another corporate department to prior documentation.
- Ability to make immediate changes and update training modules.
- Ability to use already installed Personal Computers and Word Processing equipment in association with the new publishing equipment.

Figure 1-1 The caption for this figure.

- Ability to incorporate the new machinery directly into the day-to-day operations of the department.

The TXN Solution

It is the recommendation of TXN Corporation that Acme Insurance consider the 3544 graphic workstation as the input terminal for the redesign/reformat processes in the training facility. TXN was the first company to offer this unique type of

Title of Report 1-1

Figure 1-2. The typewritten document on the left lacks the power and impact of the Ventura document on the right.

People judge you by what you produce. The old way of doing things discouraged experimentation. With desktop publishing you see the results immediately, right on the screen. You preview multiple options in seconds. You have the time to try things out until everything looks right. If you put words on paper — reports, proposals, memos, viewgraphs, presentations, whatever — desktop publishing can help you create a better image.

A competitive edge

Millions use desktop publishing already. They have an advantage over those who don't. Their proposals look better. Their reports appear more polished. Their brochures and advertisements have a sophisticated veneer. Put simply, they have a jump on the competition.

Versatility

Many users originally get into desktop publishing because they have one or two document types they want to produce. Once they get the equipment and the skills, however, they soon expand their horizons. They learn that Ventura Publisher can create any type of document, from simple one-page flyers to complex engineering documents.

The shortcomings of desktop publishing

We wouldn't be doing our job if we didn't warn you that current desktop technology has several limitations. It doesn't provide as many typestyles as a phototypesetter (although this limitation is rapidly disappearing). It doesn't do a good job with halftones (photos), which usually need to be stripped in the old-fashioned way. And it often relies on laser printing, which is not adequate for some jobs.

Not all problems arise from the technology. Some of them come from human limitations. Desktop publishing software has a learning curve. Then there's the "temptation curve." You'll probably be less productive for a brief period because you'll be tempted to fiddle with every document until it is "just right."

(We know about this problem first-hand). And finally, be aware that buying desktop equipment won't turn you into a graphic designer. Beginners will be wise to study and imitate professionally prepared pages. Otherwise, they may find that desktop publishing does nothing more than make them a lot faster at producing very ugly documents.

Ventura Publisher vs. other programs

Given that desktop publishing provides the benefits outlined above, why choose Xerox Ventura Publisher? Several features distinguish this product from the rest of the pack:

- A "What You See Is What You Get" display.
- Compatibility with the inexpensive IBM PC/XT (some other brands require costly 386 or Macintosh computers).
- Compatibility with leading software. Ventura works seamlessly with your favorite word processing and graphics programs. It even uses the same files, avoiding space-wasting duplication.
- Long document capabilities. Format and print hundreds of pages in one pass. Xerox Ventura Publisher is ideally suited for books, catalogs, reports, technical manuals, and other long documents.
- Style sheets that store reusable formats in an electronic file.

Style sheets are important enough to deserve additional comment. A style sheet is a separate file containing format rules. A different style sheet creates a different look. It's a simple idea, but one that's extremely powerful.

If you know how — and we'll show you — you can reformat a document in seconds by loading a new style sheet. You can even build a library of styles, then try out dozens of design alternatives with a few clicks of the mouse (see Figure 1-3).

But perhaps the single greatest selling point of Xerox Ventura Publisher is its amazing combination of simplicity and power. Make no mistake — Ventura is a feature-packed program that

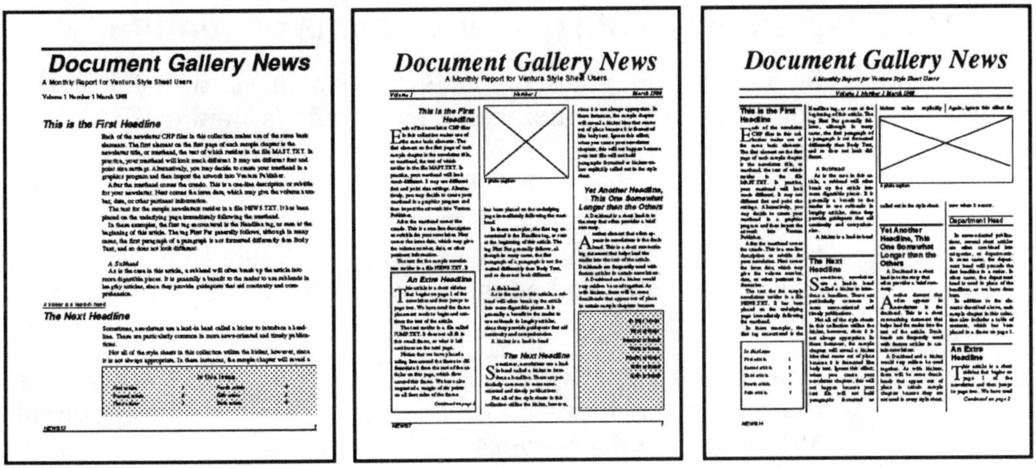

Figure 1-3. You can instantly change the look of a Ventura Publisher document simply by loading a new style sheet.

takes many hours to master completely. Yet almost anyone can learn to format simple documents in a few minutes. (We'll prove it to you in Chapter Two.)

Despite this ease of use, Ventura can create almost any kind of document. Today, many corporations produce pages in a dozen different ways, from hand-lettering to typewriters to press-on lettering all the way to phototypesetting. Ventura Publisher is so flexible and cost-efficient that most corporations can abandon this mish-mash of approaches. This one program can accomplish most publishing tasks:

- Advertisements
- Brochures
- Directories
- Financial Reports
- Instruction Manuals
- Memos
- Overhead Transparencies
- Press Releases
- Reports
- Books
- Catalogs
- Documentation
- Forms
- Labels
- Newsletters
- Parts Lists
- Proposals
- Technical Manuals

For those experienced with earlier versions of Ventura

Some of you may already be familiar with Ventura 1.1 or 2.0. You are probably anxious to learn what's new in DOS Version 3. (The official name of the new product is Ventura Publisher Gold Series, DOS/GEM Edition. In this book, we'll just refer to it as DOS Version 3 to distinguish it from the Windows and OS/2 versions.) You'll be happy to know that DOS Version 3 fixes bugs and adds new capabilities without abandoning the interface you already know.

Probably the most valuable new feature in DOS Version 3 is that it now includes all of the features of the Professional Extension and the Network Server, which formerly were additional-cost options.

In addition, this DOS-compatible version can still run on XT- and AT-class computers (although expanded memory is recommended). Table 1-3 summarizes the new features. If you are in a hurry, use this table with the index to zero in on key subject areas.

Table 1-3. Summary of new features in DOS Version 3.

Enhancements included	All features of the Professional Extension and Network Server products are now included in DOS Version 3.
Longer footnotes	Footnotes can now flow from page to page.
Improved HPGL converter	HPGL line art images now match plotter output more precisely.
New import filters	Macintosh PICT II images and Microsoft Word version 5 text files can now be imported.
Duplex printing	Automatic two-sided printing can now take place with printers such as the HP LaserJet IID that support duplex printing.

For those new to publishing

Some of you may be new to print production as well as to Ventura. Throughout this book, we occasionally use words from the graphic arts, or refer to traditional methods. If you are unfamiliar with any of these phrases, turn to the glossary at the back.

How to use this book

The best way to use this book depends on your level of expertise. Novices should start from the beginning and work their way through. They'll find it much easier to follow along if they complete the guided tour in Chapter Two before they attempt any tasks. Most of the other chapters start out with basic concepts and build up to advanced techniques. Beginners may prefer to read only the basic material, and return to the chapters later for the power tips. Experienced users, on the other hand, can plunge right in wherever they need help.

We could continue for many more pages on Ventura's advantages. Instead, we'd prefer to start showing you how to put it to work. The first step is to gain a general understanding of Ventura Publisher and the way it approaches page makeup. That's precisely what we'll do in the next chapter.

Chapter Two

Introduction to Ventura Publisher

Chapter One explained desktop publishing. Now we're going to give you an understanding of Xerox Ventura Publisher. Don't worry about details yet. Later chapters provide in-depth particulars, but first you need to get the big picture. Here are some things you'll learn in this chapter:

- how to get a simple application up and running
- how to understand the user interface
- how to apply the Ventura Formula to every document you create

We'll begin with a brief test drive. You might be overwhelmed if we plunged right into explanations of Ventura's commands. So we're going to start with a quick, hands-on tryout. After you've experienced the *what* of Ventura, the second half of this chapter explains the *how* and *why*.

Before you begin

Ventura Publisher runs on a wide range of MS-DOS computer systems. A hard disk drive is essential. You can get by with as little as five megabytes (MB) available, but we recommend 20 or more MB if you intend to do long documents.

For the moment, it doesn't matter what hardware you own, or what additional software you may plan to use with Ventura. We will conduct the test-drive using sample files that were copied to your hard disk when you installed Ventura. We have assumed that you have already installed Ventura. If not, do so now. Refer to the Ventura Publisher Reference Guide that came with Ventura for complete instructions. Ventura supports incremental installation. If you later want to change something (to add a different printer, for instance) answer "No" when VPPREP asks if this is the first time you have installed it. Then you can add only the files you need without stepping through the entire installation.

A word to newcomers

Our guided tour assumes that you understand the basic terminology of page design (margins, columns, etc.). If you're new to that topic, refer to the Glossary at the back of the book. It defines the most important computer, graphic arts, and Ventura words.

A word to the worried

Our test drive shows sample screens, so you can see what happens as you follow our instructions. Don't worry if your screen varies slightly from the ones you see on the page. Different monitors and graphics boards create different displays. You should be able to follow along despite these minor discrepancies.

A word to users of the Professional Extension

If you are using Ventura's Professional Extension, some of your dialog boxes and menus have extra choices. For now, ignore those additional options. The Professional Extension has the same core features as the base product, so the techniques you learn in this chapter still apply. We will mention these features as we go along, and we will cover them in detail in Chapter Eleven, "The Professional Extension."

A word to the adventurous

Although you can easily finish the test-drive in 15 minutes, feel free to take longer. Explore on your own. Experiment. When you're ready, come back to the second half of the chapter for an explanation of what you've seen.

Fifteen minutes to Ventura Publisher

The purpose of this brief tutorial is to experience the features and ideas explained later in the chapter. Don't worry if you don't grasp all the details yet. And don't be disturbed if you make a mistake and the tutorial doesn't go as planned. Simply try to get a feel for Ventura and the way it operates.

Starting the program

To load Ventura, go to the root directory of your hard disk. Most users can do this by getting to the C: prompt, then typing CD\. Now type VP (for the base product) or VPPROF (for the EMS version). Press Enter. The built-in batch program takes over, automatically loading the program files. When the program has finished loading, you have a blank Workspace with no text and no pictures. The active style sheet (shown in the title bar) will be the same one that was active when you quit Ventura the last time. Don't worry about the style sheet yet; we will change it as part of the test drive.

Start by looking around and getting comfortable with the Ventura environment. Use the nearby picture (Figure 2-1) to identify the following five key elements:

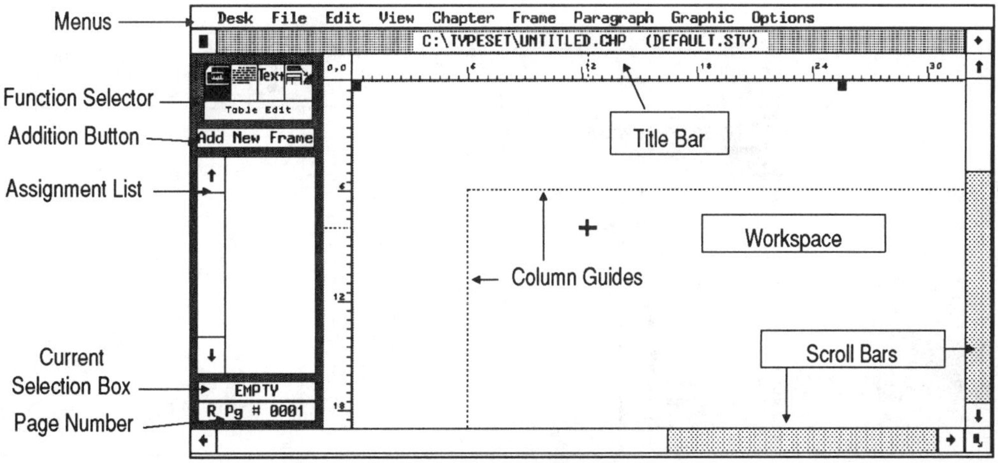

Figure 2-1. The key elements of the Ventura screen.

- the menus
- the scroll bars
- the Workspace
- the Title Bar
- the Side-Bar (which contains the Function Selector, the Assignment List, the Addition button, the Current Selection Box, and the Page Number Box)

You'll do four things to turn the blank Workspace into a real document:

- Load a text file
- Load a picture
- Load a new style sheet (a new format)
- Apply the new style sheet to the text

An important safety precaution

The first action you should take is to *save the document under a new name.* We made this the first step of the test drive, because we recommend it as the first step for every document. It is far too easy to destroy an old document by copying a new

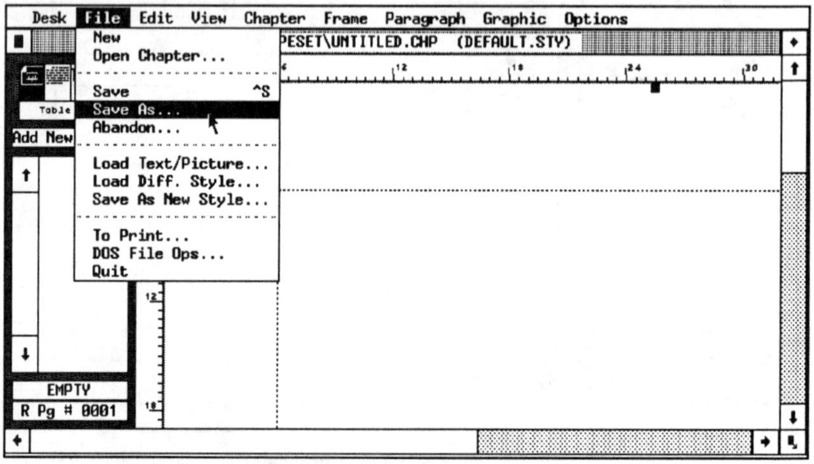

Figure 2-2. To select Save As, move the cursor down the File menu until Save As is highlighted by a black bar. Then click the mouse button.

variation on top. To prevent such calamities, always rename documents immediately. Here are the steps you should take:

- Touch the mouse cursor to the File menu at the top left of the screen. The menu drops down.
- Move the cursor down the list until Save As is highlighted (Figure 2-2).
- Click the mouse button once.

The process you just completed is called *selecting* a menu option. When you click the mouse, Ventura completes the function you asked for. In this case, it brings up a dialog box called an *Item Selector* to allow you to give this chapter (this document) a new name.

➥*NOTE: The discussion that follows assumes that you are in the \TYPESET subdirectory. This is Ventura's default condition when first installed. If you have already worked with Ventura, a different subdirectory may appear in the Item Selector. If so, move the cursor to the Directory line. Backspace to erase the current subdirectory name. Type "C:\TYPESET*.CHP" and press Enter.*

If your hard disk is D: rather than C:, you would type "D:\TYPESET*.CHP" instead. Every time the Item Selector appears, make sure it is in the \TYPESET subdirectory before

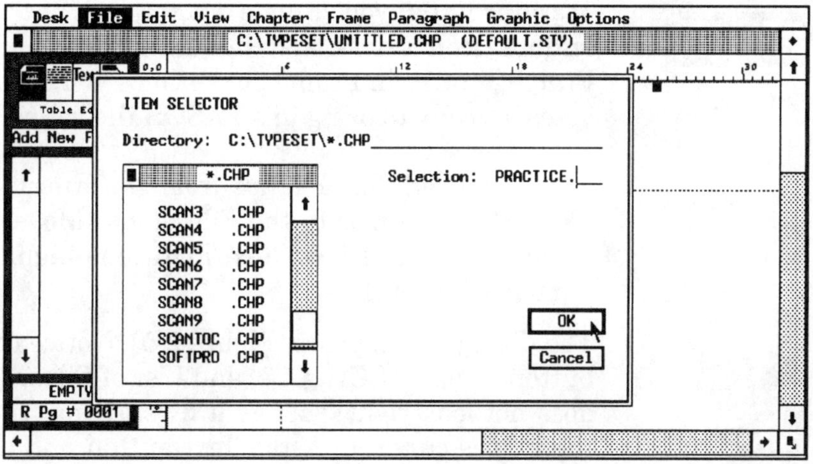

Figure 2-3. Save the chapter under a new name by typing that name onto the Selection line and clicking OK.

proceeding. If you have difficulty with this process, refer to the section titled "Changing directories and disk drives" later in this chapter for complete instructions.

- When the Item Selector appears (Figure 2-3), type in the new chapter name on the line labeled Selection. We suggest using the name PRACTICE. Backspace to correct any errors, or press Esc to clear the line and start over. When you have correctly typed the name, click on the OK button.

When you click OK, Ventura saves the chapter, and automatically appends the extension CHP. (The full name, therefore, is PRACTICE.CHP.) With the document safely renamed, you are ready to proceed.

Loading text

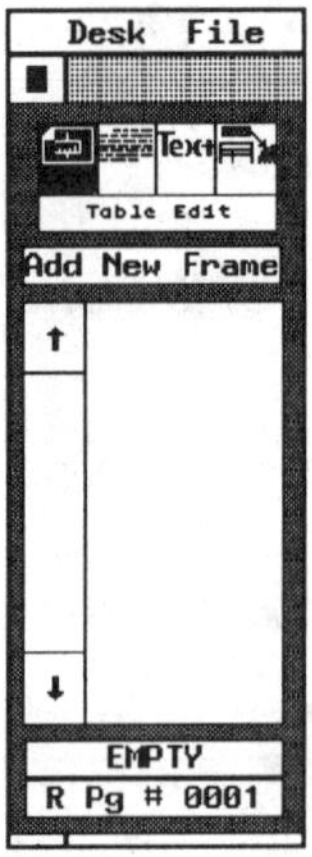

Figure 2-4.

Adding text takes place in two stages: (1) loading the text file and (2) placing it on the page. First make sure you are in the correct mode. Ventura's modes are represented by the icons in the Function Selector at the top of the Side-Bar. Ventura's base version has four modes and four icons. The EMS version has five modes and five icons. The fifth function, present only in the EMS version, is the Table Edit function (Figure 2-4).

To load and place a text file, switch to Frame mode:

- Click once on the leftmost icon in the Function Selector.

To confirm that you've done it right, look at the Side-Bar. If the leftmost icon is dark, and the Addition Button reads "Add New Frame," you're in Frame mode. Once you're in the right mode, you are ready to bring in an ASCII file called SAMPLE.TXT.

- Select Load Text/Picture from the File menu. (Reminder: Touch the cursor to the File menu. Move the cursor down the menu until Load Text/Picture is highlighted. Click the mouse button.)

The dialog box appears (Figure 2-5). Notice the four darkened buttons, Text, ASCII, One, and List of Files. If your dialog box does not look right, change it by starting from the top. Move the mouse cursor over the Text button and click once (this is called *choosing* a dialog box option). Once you choose Text, you will see the other options, including ASCII, One, and List of

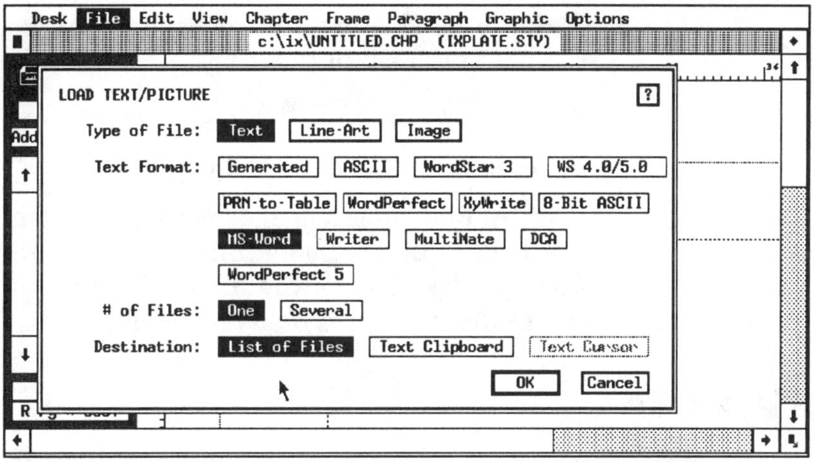

Figure 2-5. To load a text file for the test drive, make the Load Text/Picture dialog box match the one shown here.

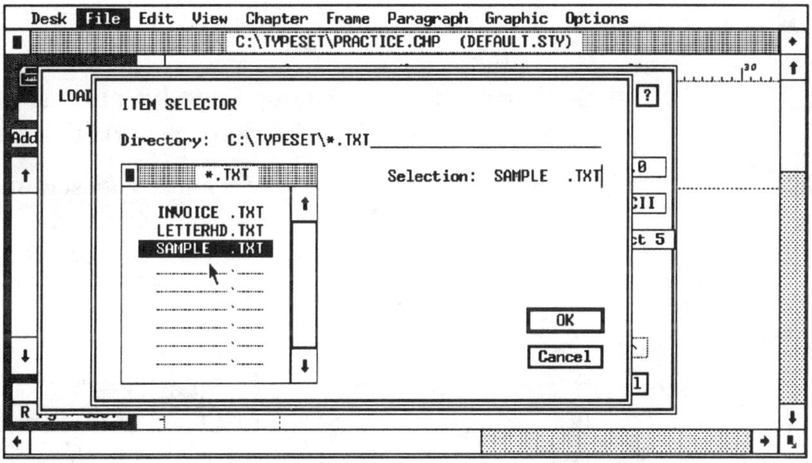

Figure 2-6. Select the file SAMPLE.TXT from the list and click OK to load the file into the chapter.

Files. Choose them as well. Once the dialog box looks like Figure 2-5, move the cursor to OK and click once.

An Item Selector appears (Figure 2-6). You will use this Item Selector to locate and choose the file you want.

- If the Item Selector does not show the subdirectory \TYPESET, move to the Directory line, type in "C:\TYPESET*.TXT" and press Enter.
- Click on the downward arrow at the lower right side of the Item Selector. The list of files scrolls down one line.

- Continue clicking and scrolling until you can see the file SAMPLE.TXT on the list.
- Click once on SAMPLE.TXT to select it.
- Click once on the OK button.

Ventura Publisher responds with a screen message telling you it is loading and hyphenating the file. When it has finished, it displays the name of the file in the Assignment List — your signal that the file is ready to be placed.

Placing text

NOTE: If you select the Underlying Page before you load the file, Ventura automatically places SAMPLE.TXT without any intervening steps. Otherwise, you have to place it on the Underlying Page, by telling Ventura where you want it to appear:

- Select the Underlying Page by moving the mouse cursor anywhere onto the Workspace and clicking once.

After clicking on the Workspace, the screen looks similar to Figure 2-7. Notice the small black handles at the top of the Workspace (sometimes called *selection buttons*). They tell you that the Page has been selected and is ready to accept text or graphics.

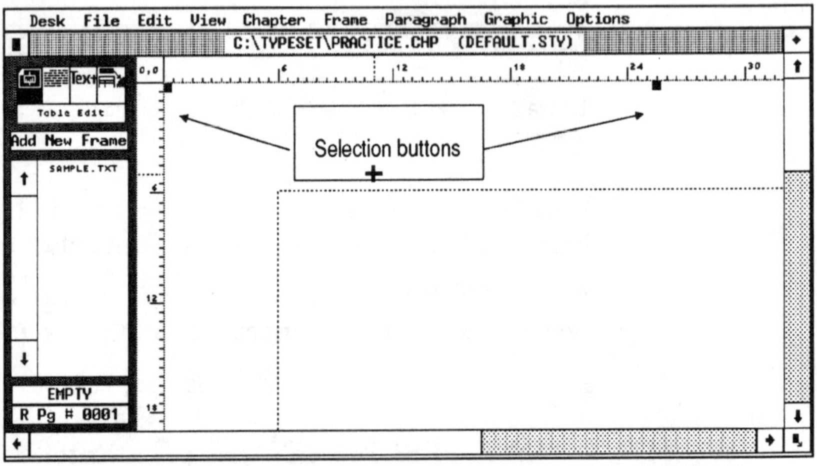

Figure 2-7. Tell Ventura where to place the text file by clicking on the Workspace (the Underlying Page) to select it.

To pour SAMPLE.TXT onto the page:

- Move the mouse cursor until it touches the name SAMPLE.TXT in the Assignment List. Click once.

The file flows onto the page (Figure 2-8). If you like, take a few moments to try moving around. Use the scroll bars at the right and bottom of the screen. To move down, move the cursor to the gray area below the scroll bar and click once. The display moves down one screen. You can move up and sideways in the same fashion.

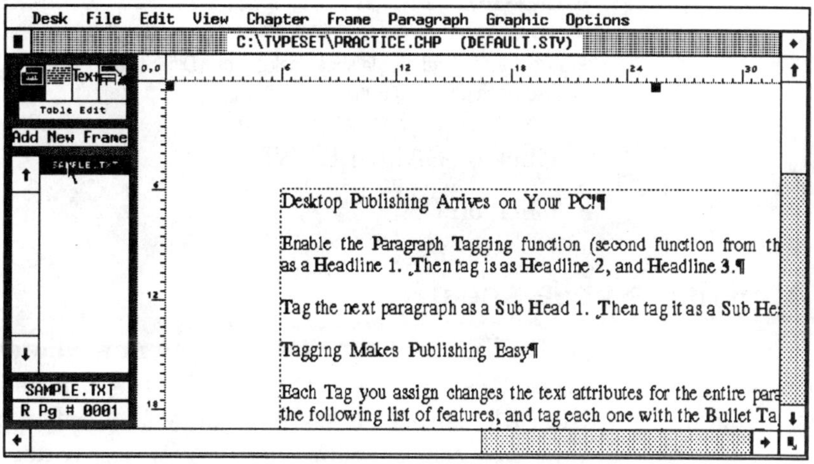

Figure 2-8. Your screen will look something like this once you place the text file.

> WARNING: Your screen may look different depending on the style sheet active at the time you place the text. In a moment, you will load a new style sheet, which will make your document match more closely.

Loading a style sheet

Now that you have text, let's give it a format (a style sheet):

- Select Load Diff. Style from the File menu. Ventura displays an Item Selector (Figure 2-9).
- Make sure the Item Selector displays \TYPESET*.STY on the Directory line. If not, type in this subdirectory and press Enter.
- Scroll in the Item Selector until you see SAMPLE1.STY.

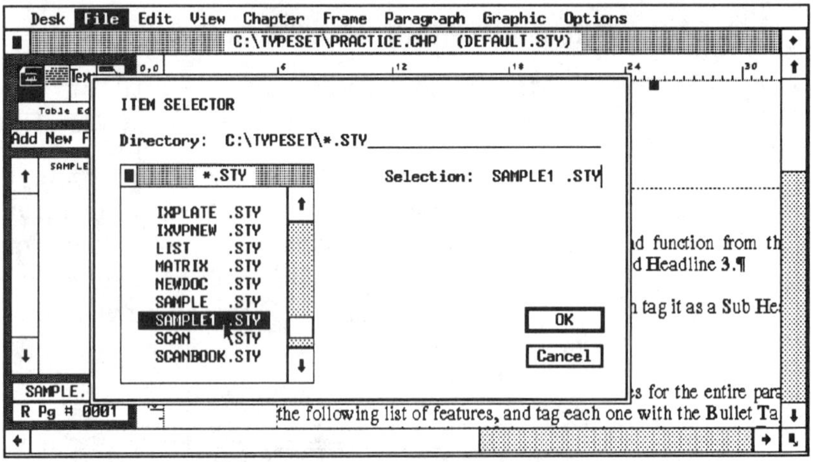

Figure 2-9. To load a style sheet, select Load Diff. Style and use the resulting Item Selector to choose whch ones you want.

- Click on SAMPLE1.STY.
- Click on OK.

Applying a style sheet

By loading a new style sheet, you immediately change overall attributes such as margins, columns, and headers. But to see the full result of a style sheet, you must apply it to the text. This process is called *tagging*. To tag a document, switch to Paragraph mode:

- Click on the second icon at the top of the Side-Bar.

You'll know you're in the proper mode if the icon turns dark, the Addition button reads "Add New Tag," and the Assignment List shows names like Headline 1 and Sub Head 1. Once you're in Paragraph mode, tagging is a simple two-step process: (1) click on the paragraph and (2) click on the tag name in the Assignment List.

This is a good place to define the word *paragraph* as used by Ventura. In common usage, a paragraph is a collection of sentences, usually set off by indenting the first line. As used by Ventura, it is any separate text element set off by carriage returns. It can be a single word, or hundreds of words. A Ventura paragraph, no matter how short or how long, is ended by placing a return after the final character (by pressing

Enter). Anytime you place a return, you are telling Ventura to start a new paragraph.

To apply the style sheet, simply tell Ventura which paragraphs should use which tags. For instance, here's how to apply the Headline 1 tag to the first paragraph of the document.

- Move the cursor until it touches any part of the first line. Click once to select the paragraph. You know you've succeeded if the entire paragraph is highlighted by a black box (Figure 2-10).
- Move to the Assignment List. Click once on the word Headline 1. Ventura immediately applies the Headline 1 format to the first line (Figure 2-11).

The sample text file contains instructions for tagging different sections of the text. If you wish, take a few moments to follow the directions on the screen. Experiment to see the results of different choices and combinations. Whenever you're ready, continue on to learn how to bring in a picture.

Loading and placing a picture

You learned earlier to use Frame mode to place text files. You also use that mode to draw frames for pictures and place picture files inside. Switch back to Frame mode now:

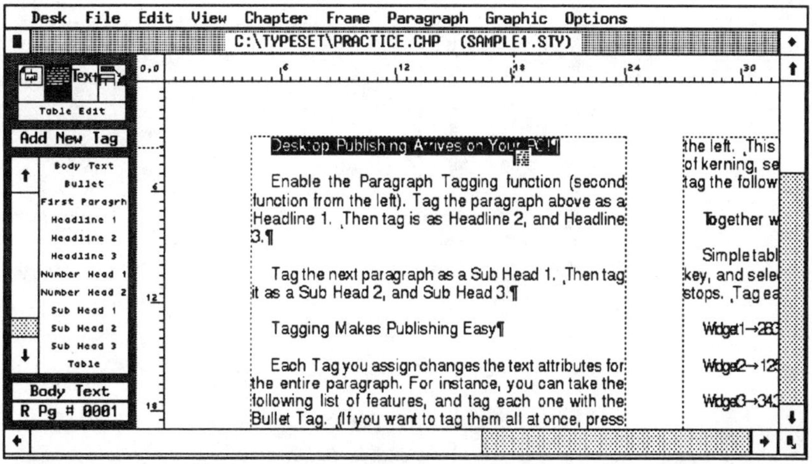

Figure 2-10. Ventura highlights the paragraph in reverse video to confirm that it has been selected.

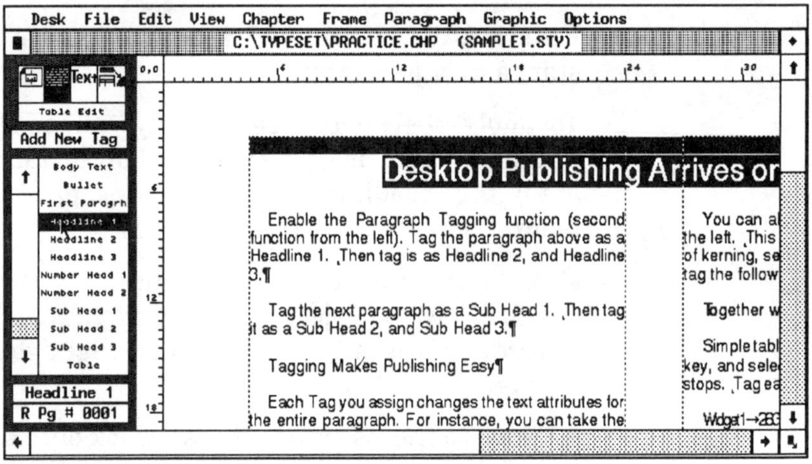

Figure 2-11. As soon as you click on the tag name, Ventura applies the format to the paragraph.

■ Select the leftmost icon from the Side-Bar.

Now move to Reduced View to see the entire page (Figure 2-12).

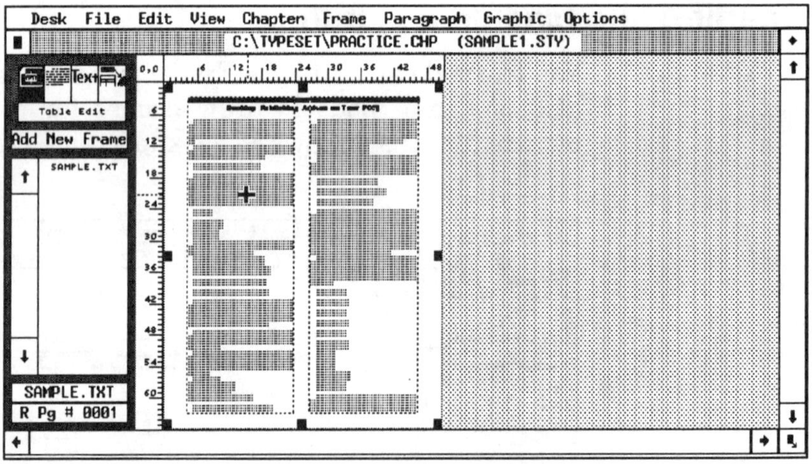

Figure 2-12. Reduced View shrinks the page to fit the size of the screen.

■ Select Reduced View from the View menu.

Before you can place a picture file, you need a frame in which to put it. To create a frame:

- Move to the Side-Bar. Click on the Addition button (which reads "Add New Frame.")
- Move the cursor to the left center of the page.
- Press the mouse button down until it changes to a pointing hand. Without releasing the button, drag the mouse diagonally downward as illustrated in Figure 2-13.

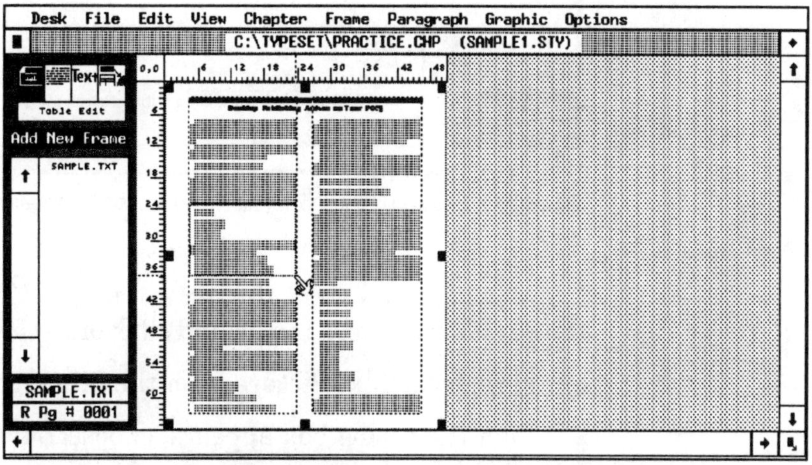

Figure 2-13. Hold the button while dragging the mouse to stretch the new frame to its intended size. Then release the button.

- Release the button when you've created a new frame about the size of the one shown. The precise size and position aren't important for this exercise.

As you can see, text automatically flows around this new frame.

Let's change back to Normal View. Here's a tip before you switch. Ventura uses the cursor position to decide where to put the upper left corner of the display area. If you want to be sure the new frame will show up, position the cursor at the upper left of the frame *before* you switch. (If you forget and get another part of the page, use the scroll bars to move.)

Now change the display to Normal View. (Hint: use the View menu or press Ctrl-N.) Make sure you can see the new frame as shown in Figure 2-14.

Now place a picture into this blank space. Check to make sure that the new frame has handles around the edges, so Ventura

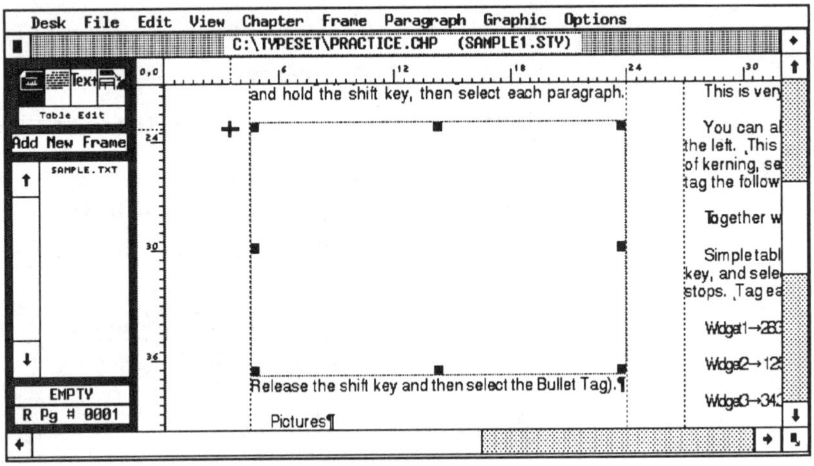

Figure 2-14. Switch to Normal View (Ctrl-N) and position the screen so you can see the new frame.

knows where you want the picture to go. (If it does not, place the cursor anywhere inside and click once to select the frame.)

- Select Load Text/Picture from the File menu.
- When the dialog box appears, choose Line-Art, GEM, One, and OK, in that order.

An Item Selector appears. As you have done previously, select the name of the file you wish to load:

- Make sure the Item Selector shows "\TYPESET*.GEM" on the Directory line. If not, type it in and press Enter.
- Scroll in the Item Selector until the filename COLUMBIA.GEM appears.
- Click once on COLUMBIA.GEM.
- Click OK.

Ventura loads the picture file and places it in the previously blank frame. A Reduced View of the page now looks something like Figure 2-15. (Hint: Press Ctrl-R and Ctrl-N to cycle between Reduced and Normal View.) Notice that the picture file appears on the Assignment List with the text file.

You've finished the test-drive. To save the document, choose Save from the File menu. To print out the first page, turn on your printer, select To Print from File menu, and press Enter. To start over with a blank page, select New. To stop using the

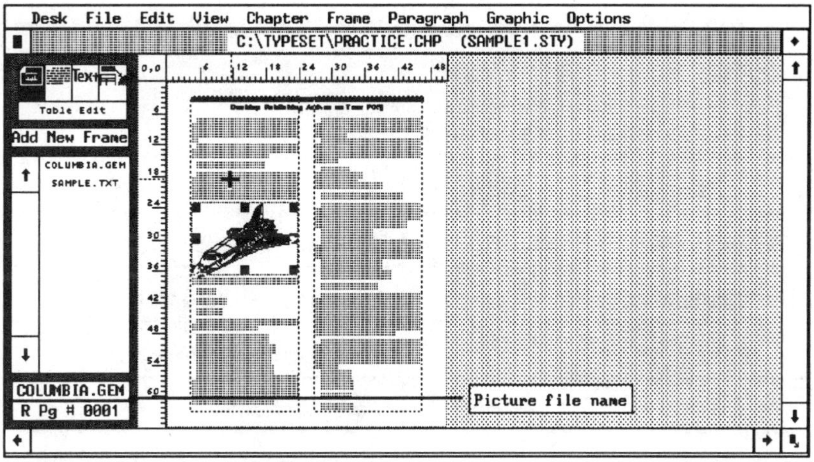

Figure 2-15. As soon as you click on the file name, Ventura places the picture into the frame you selected.

program, choose Quit. To reload this chapter another time, use Open Chapter and select PRACTICE.CHP from the Item Selector.

Understanding Ventura Publisher

Now you've seen Ventura Publisher for yourself. In a few short minutes you've done publishing tasks that would require hours using manual techniques. (And you've only experienced a fraction of Ventura's power and versatility!) Let's spend some time exploring and explaining what you saw on the screen.

The Ventura user interface

The *user interface* is the means by which the user and the program communicate. If you understand Ventura's rules, you'll have an easier time putting its power to work.

Ventura's screen symbols

During the test drive you had a chance to meet Ventura's main screen. In addition, Ventura uses special symbols inside the

Workspace. Table 2-1 shows what these symbols look like and what they mean.

Table 2-1. Screen symbols and their meaning.

Name	Symbol	Purpose
Paragraph End	¶	Shows end of paragraph.
Line Break	↵	Starts new line without starting a new paragraph.
Horizontal Tab	→	Shows location of tab character.
End Of File	□	Shows end of text file.
Special Spaces	␣	Shows location of special space characters: non-breaking spaces, em spaces, en spaces, figure spaces, and thin spaces. Does not display for normal spaces.
Special Items	°	Shows location of special items such as frame anchors, index entries, footnotes, markers, and cross-references.
Column Guides	⬚	Shows location of margins and columns.
Non-printing Screen Borders	⋮	Shows location of frames and graphics, even if they do not have rules around them when printed. Not visible in Paragraph mode.

Ventura and the mouse

Each time you move the mouse, the cursor moves on the screen. The cursor shape changes according to the part of the screen and the mode you're in. Table 2-2 shows the different shapes. Notice that each mode has a main cursor shape. Usually it also has one or more secondary shapes that indicate special functions.

Selecting with the mouse

The main function of the mouse is to select. This is always done in the same fashion: by highlighting the item and pressing the mouse button once. (If the mouse has more than one button, Ventura Publisher uses the left one.) In menus, the item turns dark the moment the cursor touches it. In Item Selectors and dialog boxes, choices darken after you press the mouse button. In Text mode, choices are highlighted after you drag the mouse over the phrase and release the button.

Table 2-2. Cursor shapes and their meaning.

Mode or Location	Main Shape	Secondary Shape(s)	Purpose
Side-Bar or Menus		(none)	Select modes and tools from the Side-Bar and options from the menus.
Frame			Create/modify frame; assign text/graphics to frames.
Paragraph Tagging		(none)	Assign paragraph styles to text.
Text			Create or modify text; change font attributes.
Graphics			Create or modify Ventura's graphics.
Table Edit			Create or modify tables.

Dragging with the mouse

A secondary use of the mouse is to draw, move, and resize objects on the screen. When we use the term *drag*, we mean the process of moving the mouse *while holding the button down*. After you finish the movement, release the button.

Moving around the page with the mouse

The mouse also moves you around the page, with the help of the scroll bars at the right edge and bottom edge of the screen (Figure 2-16). To move one line at a time, move the cursor to the arrow box and click. To move a screen at a time, put the cursor anywhere in the gray area and click. To move a distance of your choosing, place the cursor on the white scroll bar and drag it to the new position.

Besides the scroll bars on the side of the screen, you'll also see scroll bars in the Side-Bar, and in the Item Selectors. These smaller scroll bars operate in the same manner to move you up and down a list.

While we're talking about moving around, let's discuss moving to another page. You can press the PgUp and PgDn keys to

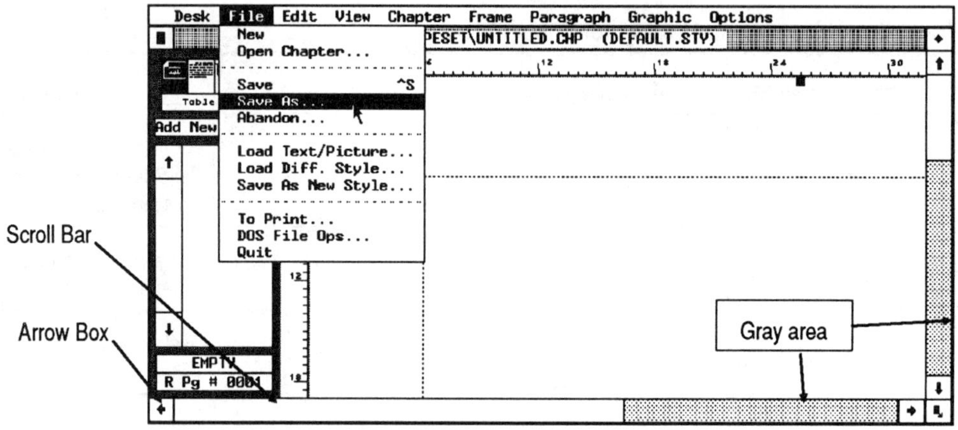

Figure 2-16. You can move around the page with the mouse and the scroll bars.

move one page at a time or use Go To Page from the Chapter menu, which jumps you directly to the page number you type.

Ventura and its menus

Ventura has an abundance of features scattered amongst its nine menus. Learning what they control is one of the challenges to mastering the program. Table 2-3 gives you a general idea of where to find things. Later chapters go into depth about menus and their functions.

Table 2-3. Menus and their functions.

Desk	Used only for program info.
File	Opening, loading and saving files, chapters, and style sheets.
Edit	Cutting, copying, and pasting text, pictures, and special items. Also contains certain file functions.
View	Selecting views and modes.
Chapter	Settings that apply throughout the chapter.
Frame	Settings that apply to a single frame (including the Underlying Page).
Paragraph	Settings that apply to the text.
Graphic	Settings that apply to drawing tools.
Options	Settings that alter Ventura to suit your preferences or expand its utility.

As you move through the menus, you'll notice items listed in gray. This means they're not currently available. If, for example, you are *not* in Graphic mode but you pull down the Graphic menu, you'll find the items in gray. You will be unable to select any of them. Change to Graphic mode and the menu items now show in black because they are available for use.

Ventura and the keyboard

Although you can do most things with the mouse and the menus, Ventura does assign special functions to certain keys. In addition, Ventura provides keyboard shortcuts for some menu functions. As an on-screen reminder, Ventura shows some shortcuts along the right-hand sides of the menus. Table 2-4 lists Ventura's key assignments for general functions.

In addition, Table 2-5 lists other keyboard shortcuts. Although you may not feel you are ready to start using shortcuts, we wanted to make this table available from the start. Some users like to photocopy it and keep it near the keyboard for quick reference.

Finally, Table 2-6 shows you the typographic characters you can enter using keyboard shortcuts. Beginners may not be familiar with typographic characters. We'll cover them more thoroughly in Chapters Three and Eleven. In those later sections, we also show you how to enter any character, even if it doesn't have a keyboard shortcut.

Table 2-4. Key assignments and their functions.

Type of Function	Keys	Purpose
Movement	Arrow keys	Moves text cursor without erasing.
	Backspace	Deletes characters to left of text cursor.
	End	Jumps to last page of document.
	Home	Jumps to first page of document.
Editing	Del	Deletes the frame or graphic currently selected. Deletes selected text.
	Esc	Deletes all characters on line in dialog box. Also halts printing and go to page functions. Redraws screen.
	Ins	Pastes the frame, text, or graphic.
	Shift-Del	Copies the selected frame, text, or graphic to Clipboard.
	Tab	In Text mode, inserts tab character. In dialog boxes, jumps to the next field where text could be inserted.
Special Functions	Alt	Used with mouse or other keys. In Frame mode, press while dragging to crop images. In Text mode, press while typing numeric equivalents of nonkeyboard characters.
	Ctrl	Used with mouse or other keys. In Frame and Graphic modes, press and hold while clicking to select objects hidden behind others. Also used for keyboard shortcuts (see Table 2-5).
	Shift	Used with mouse or other keys. Press while clicking to select more than one object in Frame, Paragraph, Graphic, and Table modes. Press while clicking to define selection range in Text mode. Hold while drawing to keep tool enabled in Frame and Graphic modes.
	Function keys	Assign names to function keys for one-key tagging in Paragraph and Text modes. Select options from Insert/Edit Special Item menu in Text mode.

Table 2-5. Keyboard shortcuts.

Type of Function	Key	Purpose
Changing Modes	Ctrl-U	Frame Setting
	Ctrl-I	Paragraph Tagging
	Ctrl-O	Text Editing
	Ctrl-P	Graphic Drawing
Viewing Options	Ctrl-E	Enlarged View
	Ctrl-N	Normal View
	Ctrl-R	Reduced View
	Ctrl-T	Show/Hide Tabs & Returns
	Ctrl-W	Show/Hide Side-Bar
Moving Around	Ctrl-G	Go to Page
	PgUp	Go to Previous Page
	PgDn	Go to Next Page
	End	Go to Last Page
	Home	Go to First Page
Editing	Ctrl-B	Renumber Chapter
	Ctrl-C	Insert Special Item
	Ctrl-D	Edit Special Item
	Del	Delete Text
	Ins	Paste
	Shift-Del	Copy
Dialog Boxes	Tab	Move to Next Field
	Shift-Tab	Move to Previous Field
	Esc	Clear Field Entry
	Ctrl-X	Cancel
	Enter	OK
Graphic Drawing	Ctrl-Z	Send to Back
	Ctrl-A	Bring to Front
	Ctrl-L	Line Attributes
	Ctrl-F	Fill Attributes
	Ctrl-Q	Select All Graphics
General Functions	Ctrl-K	Update Tag List
	Ctrl-S	Save Chapter
	Ctrl-X	Recall Previous Dialog Box
	Ctrl-2	Addition Button

Table 2-6. Keys for special characters.

Character Name	Symbol	Key Combination
Copyright mark	©	Ctrl-Shift-C
Discretionary hyphen	- (only appears w/ Show Tabs & Returns selected)	Ctrl-Hyphen
Em dash	—	Ctrl-]
Em space	⎵	Ctrl-Shift-M
En dash	–	Ctrl-[
En space	⎵	Ctrl-Shift-N
Figure Space	⎵	Ctrl-Shift-F
Non-breaking space	⎵	Ctrl-space
Open quote	“	Ctrl-Shift-[
Close quote	”	Ctrl-Shift-]
Registered trademark	®	Ctrl-Shift-R
Thin space	none	Ctrl-Shift-T
Trademark	™	Ctrl-Shift-2

Dialog boxes

Ventura is a rich, full-featured program with many options. Dialog boxes choose and control those options. They appear after you make a selection from a menu. As with Ventura's menus, gray type inside a dialog box means the item is not currently available for selection.

Dialog boxes contain several features that provide Ventura with power and flexibility:

- buttons
- pop-up menus
- selection lines
- units of measurement
- help box

Buttons

Ventura uses buttons for either/or choices. To select the choice represented by a button, move the mouse anywhere over the button and click once. The button becomes dark to show that your command was accepted. (Watch closely; sometimes it only stays dark for a brief moment.)

Pop-Up menus

Ventura uses pop-up menus to control multiple choices. You can spot a pop-up menu by the special symbol that appears to the right of a word (Figure 2-17). When you see this symbol, you can access a pop-up menu. Place the cursor *anywhere to the left of the symbol* on the same line (you do not have to be directly on top of the symbol). Press and hold the mouse button. The menu pops up. Move the cursor to highlight the choice you want. When you release the button, the choice is made.

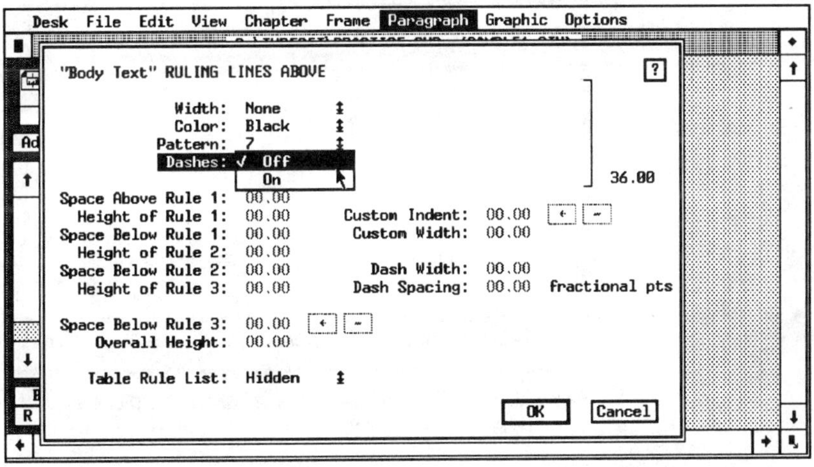

Figure 2-17. To use a pop-up menu, place the cursor on the line and press the mouse button. Move to the choice you want and release the button.

You can only choose one item from a pop-up menu; you cannot choose more than one at a time.

Selection lines

Sometimes Ventura needs to know more information than you

can supply with the mouse. For those situations, it lets you type onto a selection line. You can move from line to line with the mouse (click on the line), with the arrow keys, or with the Tab key. Pressing Tab jumps forward to the next line. Pressing Shift-Tab jumps backward. Pressing Esc clears the line of any existing numbers or letters. Pressing Backspace deletes the character to the left of the cursor.

Units of measurement

To change the units of measurement touch the name with the mouse cursor and click once (Figure 2-18). Click again, and the units change again. For example, click on the word "Inches" and it changes to "Centimeters." Usually, the measuring units you see apply to everything inside the dialog box, not just the nearest selection. At any time, you can cycle between these four choices:

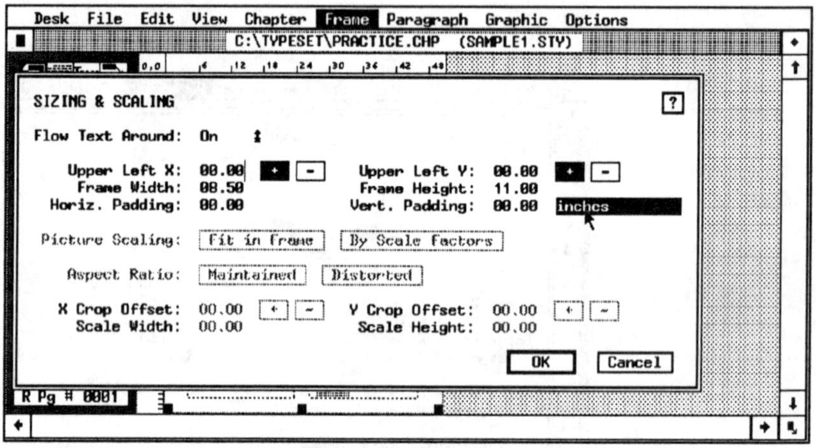

Figure 2-18. Move the mouse cursor anywhere on top of the unit of measurement and click once to change to different units.

- Inches
- Centimeters
- Picas & Points
- Fractional Points

When you reach the end, the cycle starts over. As you change, Ventura automatically recalculates values. Inches are converted to centimeters; centimeters to picas & points, etc. You may see the tilde character (~). The measurement has not been lost. It is simply too big, or too small, to display in the space. Convert to different units to see it reappear.

Help box

Dialog boxes have a help box, signaled by a question mark in the upper right. To get help, click and hold the question mark (Figure 2-19). A pop-up menu appears that allows you to get a brief explanation of the dialog box and its functions. Click OK to return to the original dialog box.

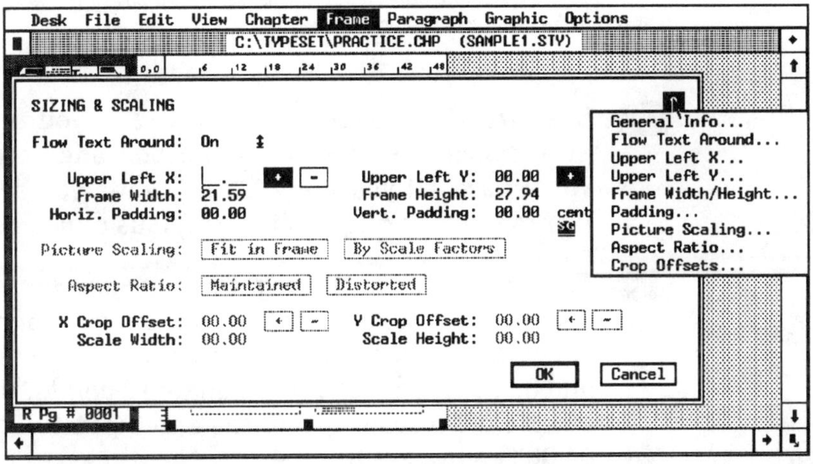

Figure 2-19. Help screens provide basic information about a dialog box and its features.

Tips for working with dialog boxes

TIP *You can start entering information* as soon as the box appears on the screen. Normally the text cursor is already blinking on the first line in the dialog box.

TIP *Use Enter as a shortcut for the OK Button.* If you press Enter, the program assumes you are finished using the dialog box.

TIP *If you change your mind,* click on the Cancel button to return to where you were. Don't worry about clearing the settings—if you select Cancel, Ventura ignores any changes made in the dialog box.

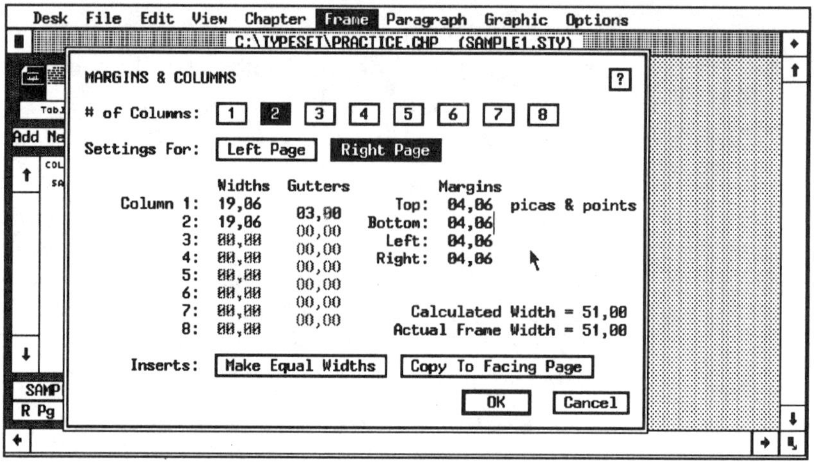

Figure 2-20. Take extra care when entering picas & points. To specify four and one-half picas, for instance, you must enter 04,06.

TIP *Use Ctrl-X as a shortcut for Cancel.* If you press Ctrl-X while in a dialog box, it cancels the box and returns you to the Workspace. (If you press Ctrl-X while you are already in the Workspace, it brings up the previous dialog box.)

TIP *Be careful when entering picas & points.* Consider, for example, the measurement 4½ picas. You might be tempted to enter 04,50. In actuality, Ventura interprets this as 4 picas and 50 points. Since 1 pica equals 12 points, the correct way to enter 4 1/2 picas is as 4 picas and 6 points. This is written as 04,06 (Figure 2-20).

Ventura's Item Selectors

Dialog boxes choose options and enter measurements. To choose *files*, Ventura uses an *Item Selector*. When you see the phrase "Item Selector," think "File Selector" instead and you'll be on the right track. An Item Selector shows up any time Ventura needs to know which file you want to use. To use Item Selectors, you must understand four concepts: (1) how to choose files with the mouse, (2) how to choose files directly by typing their names, (3) how to filter files, and (4) how to change subdirectories and disk drives.

Choosing a file with the mouse

Make sure the file name appears on the Item Selector list. If you don't see it, use the scroll bar or scroll buttons until it shows. Select it by clicking on the name. Notice how the file name appears in the previously blank selection line when you click. This is your confirmation that you've chosen the correct file. Once you've got the right file, click OK.

Choosing files directly

To bypass the mouse, simply type in the file name directly. When the Item Selector appears, you'll see that the blinking text cursor is already on the selection line. To enter a file name, just start typing. Click OK when you're done. If you type the wrong name, press Backspace to erase the characters, or press Esc to clear the entire line and start over. If you change your mind, click on Cancel. Use the selection line to bypass the mouse, to name a file that does not yet exist, or to create a new name for an existing file.

File filtering

Filtering excludes files that would otherwise clutter up the Item Selector. Look at Figure 2-21. This Item Selector appeared when we loaded text during our tutorial. Notice the extension TXT on the Directory line. Ventura knows that

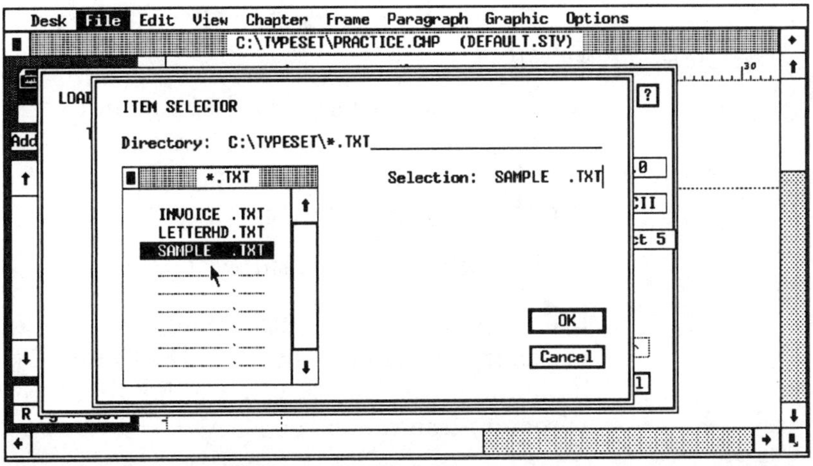

Figure 2-21. The designation *.TXT on the Directory line means that Ventura is filtering out everything except files that end with the TXT extension.

ASCII files should carry this extension. When you tell it to load a TXT file, Ventura shows *only* files with that extension. It automatically filters out all others so they don't show up. These other files are still in the subdirectory. Ventura is simply not showing them so they don't clutter up the list.

Ventura comes with a list of file extensions it prefers to use (Table 2-7). It will use these extensions unless you tell it otherwise. When you tell Ventura that you want to load, for example, a MultiMate text file, it remembers the subdirectory and the file extension you used last time. If you change either of these, Ventura remembers the changes the next time you load MultiMate files.

How do you change the file filter? Simply place the text cursor on the Directory line, type in the new extension and click OK. Ventura immediately filters out all files except those that match the new extension.

Changing directories and disk drives

Ventura Publisher is an intelligent program. When it places an Item Selector on the screen, it remembers where you were the last time and takes you to that subdirectory.

It's easy to change directories and disk drives. One simple method is identical to the way we changed file filters. When the Item Selector appears, place the text cursor on the Directory line and type in the new directory name (and/or the new disk drive). When you click OK, Ventura switches to the new directory.

Another method uses the Backup button (see Figure 2-22). Clicking the Backup button takes you to the directory that is next highest on the tree. Suppose you want to open a chapter and the Directory line now shows:

C:\TYPESET\CHAPTERS*.CHP.

Pressing the Backup button would move you up one level. The Directory line would now read C:\TYPESET*.CHP. Pressing it again would move you to the final, root level, and the Directory line would read C:*.CHP.

Table 2-7. Default file extensions.

Text Files	ASCII	*.TXT
	Generated Text	*.GEN
	Wordstar	*.WS
	MultiMate	*.DOC
	Microsoft Word	*.DOC
	WordPerfect	*.WP
	XyWrite	*.XY
	Xerox Writer	*.XWP
	DCA	*.RFT
	PRN-to-Table (EMS version)	*.PRN
Graphics Files	GEM Line Art	*.GEM
	GEM Image	*.IMG
	AutoCAD	*.SLD
	HPGL	*.HPG
	Mentor Graphics	*.P*
	PostScript	*.EPS
	TIFF	*.TIF
	CGM	*.CGM
	VideoShow	*.PIC
	Macintosh Paint	*.PNT
	Macintosh PICT	*.PCT
	Lotus PIC	*.PIC
	Windows	*.WMF
	PC Paintbrush	*.PCX
Program Files	Chapter	*.CHP
	Style Sheet	*.STY
	Caption File	*.CAP
	Chapter Information File	*.CIF
	Ventura Graphics	*.VGR
	Publication	*.PUB
	Width Table	*.WID

➡ *NOTE: Using the Backup button does not change the file filter.*

When you click the Backup button, the file list changes to show what is available in the new subdirectory. As you browse through the list, you may see names preceded with a diamond

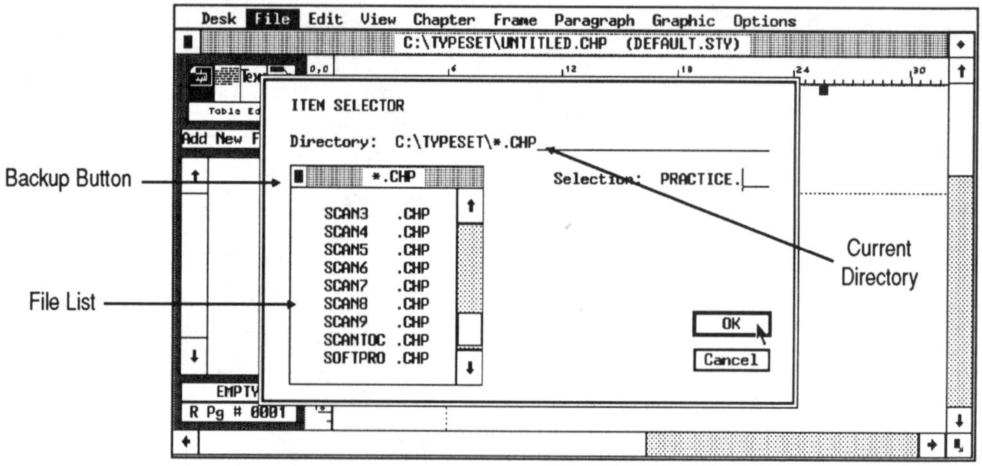

Figure 2-22. The Backup button moves you up to the subdirectory at the next level.

character. These are directories or disk drives. To move to a new subdirectory, click once on the name, as if selecting a file. You will find yourself in the new subdirectory, as confirmed by the Directory line.

If you back up enough times, you eventually see only disk drive letters in the list. To move to a new drive, click on the one you want. You also can type in the letter of the new drive on the Directory line and click OK.

Tips for Using Item Selectors

TIP *You can filter more than just the extension.* For example, when writing this book, we started all our files with the two-letter code VP. To see only our book chapters, we typed in VP*.CHP. Ventura eliminated files that did not start with VP and end with .CHP.

TIP *To see the complete contents of any directory*, go to the Directory line and type "*.*" as the filter. Ventura will show every file. If you just wanted to look to see what was there, click on Cancel to return to the Workspace.

TIP *If you hear a beep* when you enter an Item Selector, it means that Ventura found too many files. It doesn't have room to fit them all onto its list. This is potentially dangerous, since you have no way of knowing how many files have been left off. To cure the problem, enter a different file filter to limit the number of files shown at one time.

TIP *To make files appear at the top* of the Item Selector list for quick reference, precede the file name with a symbol such as !, #, or %. The file list is alphabetical. Symbols appear before the letters of the alphabet.

TIP *If you number your file names sequentially,* use two-digit numbers to ensure that files appear in the proper sequence. For example, use CHAP01, CHAP02 rather than CHAP1, CHAP2. Otherwise, CHAP11 appears before CHAP2.

TIP *You can activate the OK button* by pressing the Enter key. You'll see the OK button turn dark just as if you'd selected it with the mouse. This shortcut works in dialog boxes, too. Anytime you see an OK button, you can select it by pressing Enter.

TIP *You can activate the Cancel button* by pressing Ctrl-X.

TIP *If a disk drive does not appear on Ventura's list,* you can still get to it with the Item Selector. Type the drive letter (and the subdirectory name if you want) on the Directory line and then select OK. For instance, if you add a RAM disk called E: and it doesn't show up, type "E:\" onto the Directory line and click OK.

TIP *To make file selection faster,* move the cursor over the file name and click twice rapidly instead of once. If you press twice in a row without a pause, the second click activates the OK button. This method is faster, but it does have one slight disadvantage. If you've slipped and selected the wrong file by mistake, you won't have any opportunity to check your choice by looking at the selection line.

You can vary the speed of the double-click option using Set Preferences from the Options menu. If you choose fast, you must click very rapidly to invoke the double-click shortcut. If you choose slow you can wait longer between clicks and Ventura still recognizes it as a double-click shortcut.

The Side-Bar

We've learned a good deal about Ventura's user interface already. We've seen how it uses the mouse, the keys, and dialog boxes. These elements were pioneered by the research done at Xerox Palo Alto Research Center. They have become more or less standard in graphic environments. But there's one portion of the Ventura interface that's not like anything else — the Side-Bar. This unique feature gives Ventura much of its power, flexibility, and speed.

The Function Selector

The Function Selector is at the top of the Side-Bar. Its icons control Ventura's modes of operation, as outlined in Table 2-8. Notice that the EMS version has a fifth Table mode not available in the standard version.

You can change modes in three ways. You can select the icon from the Function Selector. You can choose the mode from the View menu. Or you can use the keyboard shortcuts. (By the way, the View menu lists the shortcuts along the right side.)

The Function Selector does not change when you change

Table 2-8. Modes and their functions.

Mode	Purpose	Side-Bar Icon	Keyboard Shortcut
Frame	Create or select a frame for text or pictures.		Ctrl-U
Paragraph	Create, change, or apply a style sheet.		Ctrl-I
Text	Create or modify text.		Ctrl-O
Graphic	Create or modify simple drawings or callouts.		Ctrl-P
Table	Create or modify tables (only in the EMS Version).	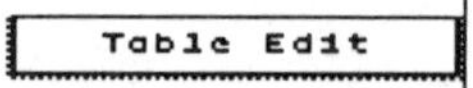	none

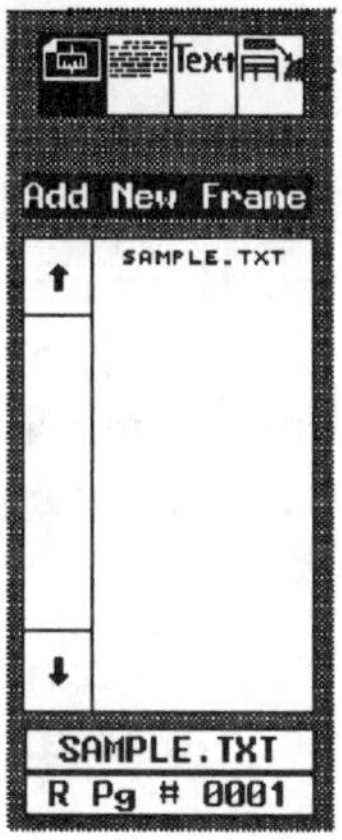

Figure 2-23.

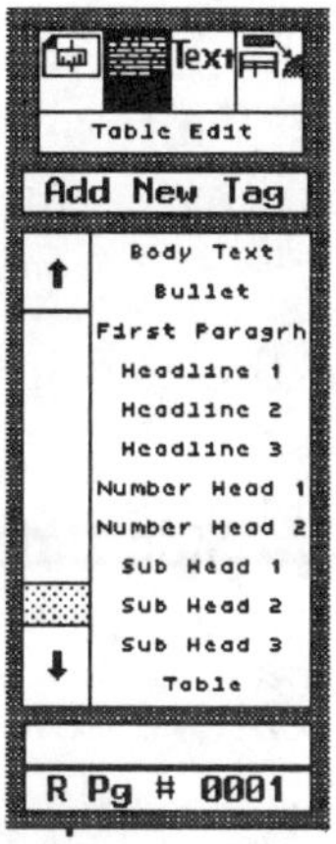

Figure 2-24.

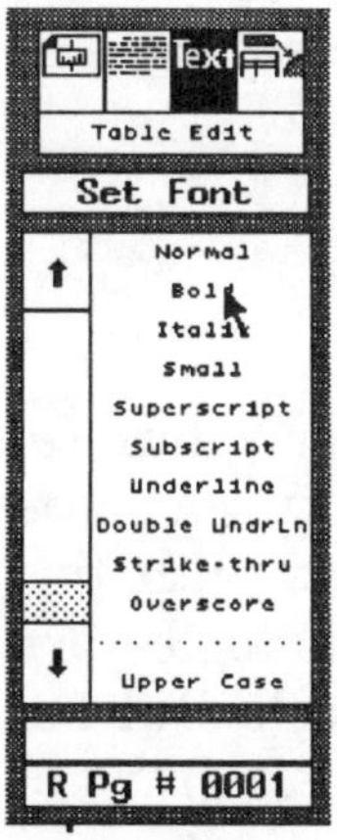

Figure 2-25

modes. Neither does the Page Number Box at the bottom. But the rest of the Side-Bar alters according to the mode you are in. Spend some time familiarizing yourself with the information found in the Side-Bar. Often it's the key to figuring out what's going on in the Workspace.

Frame mode selects and operates on frames, the containers for text and pictures. In this mode you can choose which frame you want, load text and pictures into it, change its size, add a new frame, or change frame attributes such as margins and columns. As shown in Figure 2-23, the Side-Bar exhibits these changes when in Frame mode:

- The Addition button reads "Add New Frame." Select this button to draw a new frame on a page.
- The Assignment List displays the currently available files, whether text or pictures. If you don't see any names in the Assignment List, you have not yet loaded a file.
- The Current Selection Box shows the name of the file in the active frame. If the frame contains no files, it shows the word Empty. If you have not selected a frame, it is blank.

In Paragraph mode you create, modify, and apply tags. The Side-Bar shows these changes (Figure 2-24):

- The Addition button reads "Add New Tag." Select it to create an entirely new tag that is not already listed.
- The Assignment List displays the tags for the current style sheet.
- The Current Selection Box remains blank until you select a paragraph from the document. Then it shows the tag assigned to that paragraph.

In Text mode you create and edit text files. The Side-Bar has these characteristics (Figure 2-25):

- The Addition button shows "Set Font." Use it to change the font attributes of a few words within a paragraph. (To change the entire paragraph, use the Font dialog box while in Paragraph mode.)

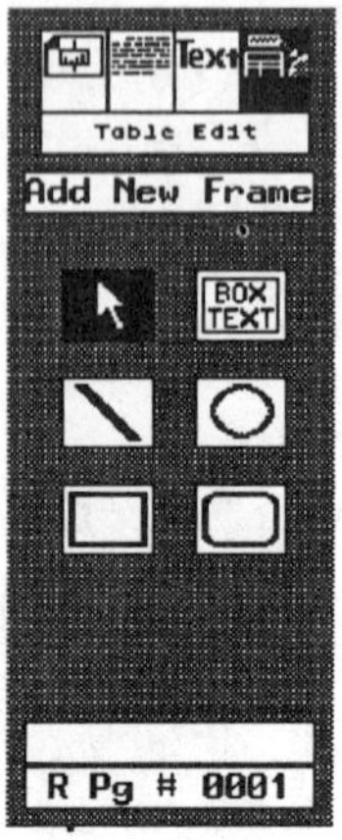

Figure 2-26.

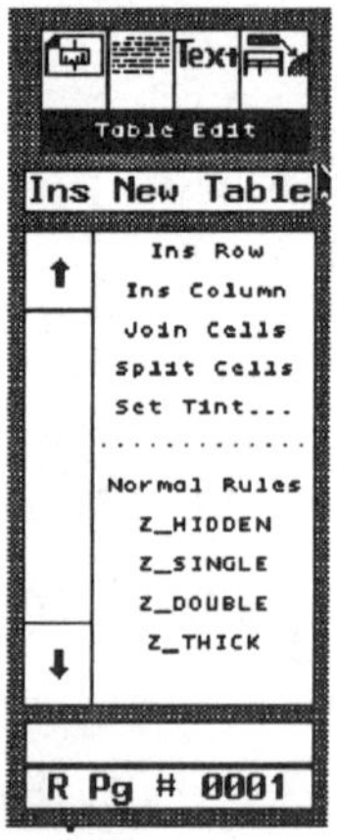

Figure 2-27.

- The Assignment List displays the attributes (normal, bold, italic, etc.) you can apply to the text.
- The Current Selection Box is empty when the cursor is over normal text. But text files also include marks that are usually not visible, such as the signals for italics, for paragraph returns, for index marks, and so on. When you move the cursor over one of these marks, a descriptive term appears in the Current Selection Box.

In Graphic mode you create simple drawings, or enhance drawings imported from outside programs. The Side-Bar shows these characteristics (Figure 2-26):

- The Addition button reads "Add New Frame."
- The Assignment List disappears, to be replaced by buttons. These buttons represent a selection tool and Ventura's drawing tools: the line, the circle/ellipse, the rectangle, the rounded rectangle, and the Box Text tool.
- The Current Selection Box shows the name of the tool in use.

In Table mode you create and modify tables. The Side-Bar shows these characteristics (Figure 2-27):

- The Addition button reads "Ins New Table." It creates a new table immediately in front of the cursor position.
- The Assignment List has two sections. The top half shows commands for creating and modifying rows, columns, and cells. The bottom half has commands for creating and modifying the lines in the table.

Understanding frames and pages

We spent the last few pages describing the user interface. We'd like to present a bit more theory before we turn you loose in the real world. The rest of this section deals with two important ideas: frames and chapter files. Both topics are treated in more depth and detail later in the book. But because they are central to Ventura, you need a basic grasp of them right from the start. Here, then, is the theory behind frames in brief:

Frames are containers for text and graphics. You can give these containers attributes such as margins and columns. The Frame menu lists the various ways you can change a frame's attributes.

Ventura makes things easier by automatically drawing the first frame for you. We call this first frame the Underlying Page or, more simply, the Page. (Whenever we capitalize the word *Page*, we are talking about this special frame.) When Ventura draws the Underlying Page for you, it makes the boundaries equal to edges of the paper. What's more, Ventura will automatically repeat this Page frame as many times as needed to fit a long text file. That's why you don't have to laboriously draw a container on every page of a document (as you must with some other programs).

The Underlying Page, therefore, is a frame with a few special qualities:

- It is created automatically
- It repeats automatically as needed
- It cannot be deleted or copied
- It can have headers and footers
- Text flows automatically from Page to Page (with ordinary frames, text flows to the end and stops)

In many ways, however, the Underlying Page is just like any other frame:

- You can change its size
- You can give it margins and columns
- You can specify its frame typography
- You can put rules above, below, or around

Some documents don't need anything more than the Page. Often, however, you need additional containers. Fortunately, frames can overlap. You can have many frames, one on top of the other, each containing a text file, a picture file, and/or a background pattern. In this fashion, you can create complex documents with almost any format, just by laying frames on top of the Underlying Page.

Chapter Ten, "Special Document Formats," explains frames in more detail. It also explains when to use the Underlying Page by itself, when to combine it with other frames, and how to build chapters where all the text is in frames.

Chapter files

Ventura Publisher is famous for its style sheets. Less well known — but equally important — are its chapter files. The chapter file is the blueprint for the document. It lists all the elements and where they belong:

- Which text files to use and where to put them
- Which picture files to include
- Which style sheet to apply

In short, the chapter file stores a description of the document, the locations of the files on the disk, and the order and manner in which they appear. Ventura doesn't create a separate layout file. Instead, it works with the original text and picture files. This approach saves unnecessary duplication, but it requires some way of keeping things straight.

Ventura does this job with the chapter file. Thus, when we use the word *chapter* in lowercase, we are not talking about a section in a book. We mean a special file, which Ventura uses to store the essential specifications of a document.

The first time you save a document, Ventura automatically builds a chapter file. This file always has the extension CHP. To load an existing document, select Open Chapter from the File menu. Ventura uses the specifications inside the chapter file to reload all the files and rebuild the document in its entirety.

Chapter Five, "Working With Style Sheets," explains the inner workings of chapter files and style sheets.

The Ventura Formula

You need one more fundamental principle before you're ready to tackle the rest of this book: The Ventura Formula:

Text + Pictures + Style = Chapter

As you can see, the formula is a simple one. Yet no matter what kind of document you produce, the Formula always holds true. The next few chapters explain each part of the formula in depth. Here's a preview:

How Ventura works with text

Ventura Publisher works directly with text files from leading word processors (it also can produce text files on its own). These files store text and tags. Tags are the special codes that tell Ventura whether each paragraph is a headline, a subheading, and so on.

How Ventura works with pictures

Most Ventura pictures come from outside files (though you can create simple drawings directly inside Ventura). The files may come from graphics programs, from scanners, or from electronic clip art collections. As with text, Ventura deals with the original file. It uses the chapter file to store a *pointer* to the original picture, with instructions on how to display it.

How Ventura works with style sheets

Ventura places tags into the original text files. These tags are notes that tell Ventura things like "Make these three words a headline" or "make the next five items into a list," and so on.

How does Ventura know how to format those tags? Simple — it stores the format rules in a file known as the *style sheet*. This style sheet contains the specifications for the tags. For example: "Set all headlines in 36-point Helvetica Bold with a one-point rule underneath" or "Indent list items three picas and precede them with a bullet character."

Because it is a separate file, you can reuse a style sheet by applying it to different documents. Or, if you want to vary formats instantly, you can apply different style sheets to the same document.

This chapter has outlined the basic structure of Ventura Publisher. Now it's time to learn how to become productive. We'll start that process in the next chapter, which explores the first part of the Ventura formula: Text.

Chapter Three

Creating Text

The most important element of any document is the text. After all, it is the written word that conveys the message. A desktop publishing program, even one as powerful as Ventura Publisher, cannot produce well-written text. What it *can* do is make text creation as simple as possible. That way, you can concentrate on perfecting your writing rather than on mastering a new tool. Ventura Publisher was created with this philosophy in mind.

Sounds good. I just use my word processor like always — right? Not quite. There are several tricks you should know, simple techniques that smooth the process. This chapter teaches you those techniques. It focuses on creating and editing text. (Chapter Six, "Document Design and Layout," explains loading and arranging that text with Ventura.) This chapter includes two sections appropriate for beginners and a third section for more advanced users:

- creating text with word processors
- creating text with Ventura
- preformatting text files

Ventura's approach to text

Before we get into specifics, it pays to understand Ventura's general approach. The key is the two-way communication between Ventura and text files (Figure 3-1). First Ventura reads in the files and pours them onto the page. When you have finished, Ventura automatically saves your changes back to the same files. At the same time, it inserts formatting codes.

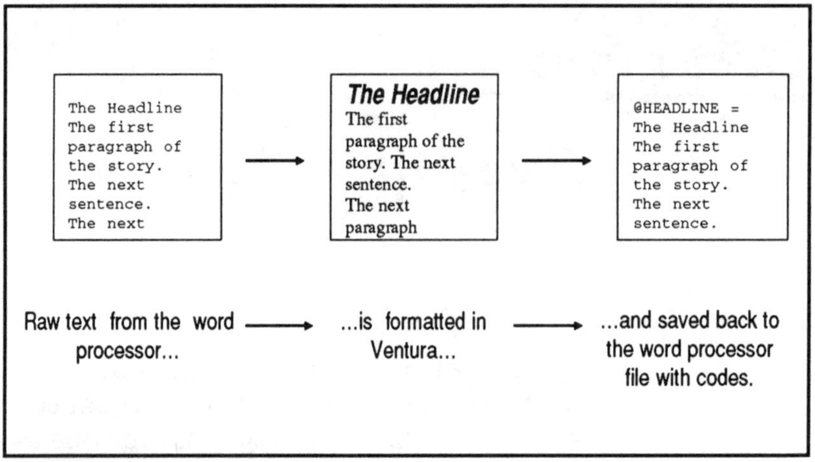

Figure 3-1. Ventura can read and write to the file formats of leading word processors. It stores some of its format codes in the text file.

Some DTP programs lump everything into a single layout file. Ventura, by contrast, continues to use the original files. Pointers in Ventura's *chapter file* tell it which files to use and where to find them. This approach has several advantages:

- Ventura supports numerous word processors, so you can use the one you like best.
- Ventura can also work with database software, spreadsheet software, and programming languages.
- You can combine files from different word processors in the same document.
- You can convert files from one format to another
- You can continue to work with the word processor *after* you bring files into Ventura.

Users find many reasons to continue working with a word processor after initial layout in Ventura. Changes of more than a few sentences are usually faster in the word processor. Word processors have spell checkers, grammar checkers, and search and replace functions absent from Ventura. Since you probably have skilled WP operators in your organization, you may often want to offload editing tasks to WP stations — especially since word processing doesn't require expensive, high-end computer equipment.

If you return to a word processor file after laying it out, you will discover that Ventura has inserted tag names and format codes (Figure 3-2). In the final section of this chapter, you will learn how to insert these codes in advance to preformat files.

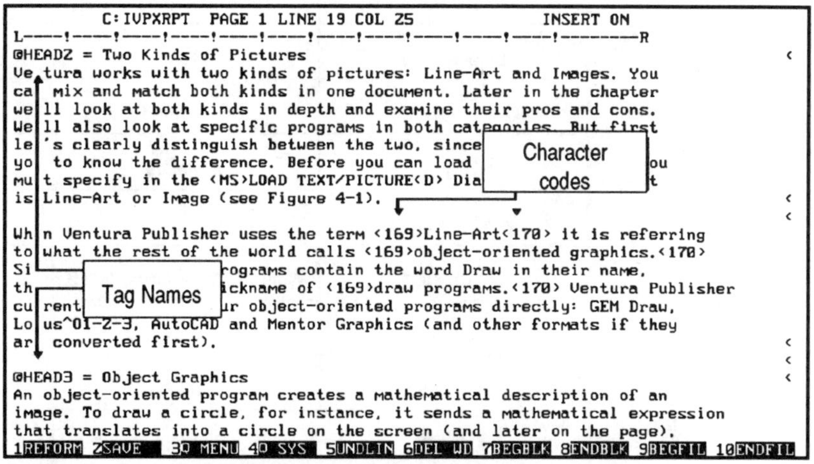

Figure 3-2. Ventura stores tag names and formatting codes in the text file.

Supported word processors

Table 3-1 lists the file formats supported directly by Ventura. Don't give up if your favorite isn't on the list. Later in the chapter we explain several ways to use other programs with Ventura. You will notice from this table that Ventura also supports its own internal format, which has the GEN extension. Ventura creates generated (GEN) files when building indexes and tables of contents.

You bring text files into Ventura with Load Text/Picture from the File menu. Once you make a file part of a chapter, you never have to load it again. Ventura automatically loads all component files when you open a chapter. To remove a file, use Remove Text/File from the Edit menu.

In addition, Ventura supports spreadsheets via the PRN-to-Table option from the Load Text/Picture dialog box. This button converts a spreadsheet's print file (PRN file) to a format Ventura can use in Table mode. Table mode is available only in the Professional Extenssion.

Table 3-1. Word processor formats supported directly by Ventura.

Format	Name in Dialog Box	Preferred Extension
ASCII	ASCII, 8-Bit ASCII	*.TXT
DisplayWrite	DCA	*.RFT
Generated Text	Generated	*.GEN
MultiMate	MultiMate	*.DOC
Microsoft Word	MS-Word	*.DOC
WordPerfect	WordPerfect, WordPerfect 5	*.WP
WordStar	WordStar 3, WS 4.0/5.0	*.WS
Xerox Writer	Writer	*.XWP
XyWrite	XyWrite	*.XY

You also can use Ventura to convert from one format to another. Editors might, for example, collect material from different authors using different word processors. To facilitate copy editing or spell checking, they could convert them to a common format. To convert a file, bring it into Ventura. In Frame mode, choose File Type/Rename from the Edit menu (Figure 3-3). When the dialog box appears, choose the new

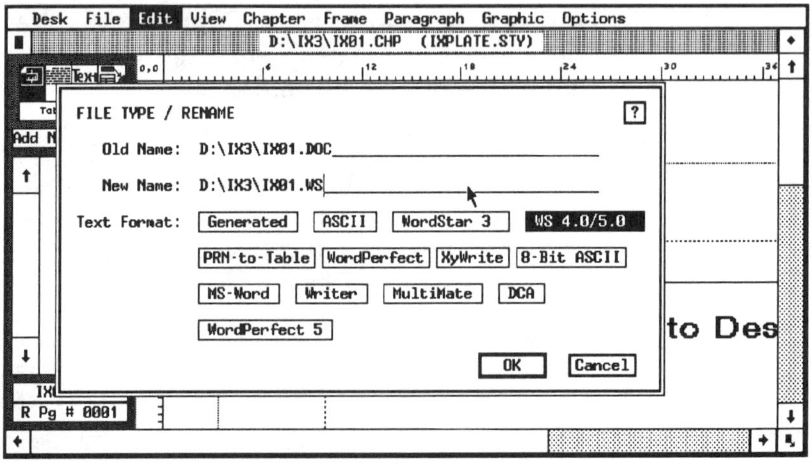

Figure 3-3. With the File Type/Rename dialog box you can convert a file from one format to another.

format. That's all there is to it. The file is saved to the new format the next time you save the chapter.

General rules for creating text

Read this section to learn the ins and outs of creating text before bringing it into Ventura. It begins with general rules for all word processors. It concludes with comments on specific word processing, database, and spreadsheet programs.

As we've already seen, Ventura Publisher views writing, illustration and layout as three separate tasks:

Text + Pictures + Style Sheet = Chapter

Consequently, when using a word processor you should concentrate on writing, not on formatting. Don't worry about fonts, margins, columns, indents, and the rest. You will take care of those factors in Ventura. What's all that mean while writing? Just this: Although your word processor has formatting commands, *don't use them.* At best, Ventura will ignore the commands. At worst, you will have to manually remove the formatting, costing yourself extra effort.

Below we've listed several general rules for text formatting. At the end of the list, we give hints on how to ease the transition to Ventura-style text formatting.

Fortunately, most of the suggestions mean *less* work. If you follow the instructions, you will end up with bare-bones files devoid of any extras. We sometimes call this *raw* text.

Formatting rules for text files

1. *Don't put in formatting commands.* You will do the formatting in Ventura. Just type the text flush left. Margins don't matter — choose anything you like. Do not:

- center
- justify
- create columns

2. *Don't add headers, footers, footnotes, or page numbers.*

3. *Don't indent the first line* of a paragraph, even if you want an indent on the printed page. That means no extra spaces, and no tab characters. You will indent in Ventura.

4. *Don't hyphenate* with the word processor. You're wasting your time, since Ventura has its own hyphenation routine. (You can, however, add discretionary hyphens or suppress hyphenation as discussed later.)

5. *Don't imitate typographic effects.* For instance, don't use asterisks for bullets or three periods for ellipses. To achieve these characters, add them later in Ventura, or put them in with the preformatting techniques explained later in this chapter. *Exceptions*: you can use two dashes (- -) instead of an em dash (—) and inch marks (") instead of open and close quotes (“ ”) because Ventura can filter these automatically.

6. *Don't insert more than one space* after periods and colons. Double-spacing detracts from the appearance of the final document.

7. *Don't insert any spaces after the last sentence* in a paragraph. Even a single extra space can create an unwanted empty line in the document.

8. *Insert only one tab stop* between columns in a table.

9. *Use only true tab characters.* Ventura Publisher recognizes tabs as long as they are real tabs. When you press the tab key, some word processors insert the actual ASCII tab character, Ctrl-I. Others insert a string of spaces instead. Still others — like WordStar 3.3 — let you choose.

Ventura Publisher does not recognize a string of spaces as a tab, even if those spaces were inserted by pressing the tab key. If your word processor cannot insert the true tab character, you must insert Ctrl-I manually into the file. Use the arrow keys to judge if your word processor inserts tabs or spaces. Put the cursor at the left edge of the tab and press the right arrow. If the cursor jumps all the way to the tab stop, you have true tabs. If it moves one space at a time, you have space characters instead.

10. *Use the word processor's native commands sparingly.* Use commands like bold only to change a few words within a paragraph — for instance, to create a bold phrase within an otherwise normal paragraph. To make the entire paragraph bold, type it normally. Add the bold font later with Ventura's Paragraph mode.

Table 3-3. Do's and Don'ts of Ventura text formatting.

DO:	DON'T:
type flush left	center
use attribute commands sparingly	justify
type only one space after periods	insert any spaces at the end of a paragraph
type only one tab between table entries	create columns
use true tab characters	add headers
	add footers
	add footnotes
	add page numbers
	indent the first line of paragraphs
	hyphenate
	insert imitation typographic characters

Trouble spots and how to handle them

The transition from normal word processing to Ventura-specific word processing sometimes takes a bit of effort. For instance, it can be difficult to break the habit of hitting the space bar twice after periods. One solution is to prepare text files as before, then use search and replace to remove unwanted returns, spaces, and so on. Use Table 3-3 as a reminder of the things to search for.

Automatic conversion

Ventura does offer help for three of the most common habits: quote marks, em dashes, and double returns. The standard computer keyboard inserts inch marks (") on both sides of quotations. Typesetting, on the other hand, uses two symbols, open quotes (“) and close quotes (”). Likewise, computer typists typically use two side-by-side hyphens (- -) to represent the em dash (—).

You can instruct Ventura to filter out these symbols and insert true typographic characters instead. Use Set Preferences from the Options menu. Select *“ and — from the Auto Adjustments pop-up menu. (If you select Both*, you will also get the conversion filter.)

You can also filter out double returns between paragraphs. Double returns are desirable in straight ASCII text, but they create problems with normal word processing files. The extra returns cause unnecessary and unwanted blank lines between each paragraph. Unfortunately, single-spacing creates documents that are hard to read on screen. One solution is to strip out the extra returns with search and replace. Another method is to insert Ventura's special PARAFILTR tag at the beginning of the file. The third and final section of this chapter explains how to add PARAFILTR and other tags to text files.

Tab stops

Tabs stops are another potential trouble spot. You must take two steps to make them work successfully with Ventura: (1) insert true tab characters and (2) insert only one tab stop between columns.

We explained above why and how to insert true tab characters. The second problem is inserting too many tabs between columns. Here's what often goes wrong: Many word processors have predefined tab settings. When typing, you may press the tab key several times to jump to the right column (Figure 3-4). But each time you press the key, you insert another tab stop. When you later use Ventura Publisher to format that two-column list, Ventura expects to find only one tab stop between the left column and the right. Instead, the file may contain as many as five or six.

The second rule for tabular material is to insert one and *only* one tab stop between each column. (Certain advanced formatting techniques justify more than one tab character between columns. We cover these techniques in later chapters.)

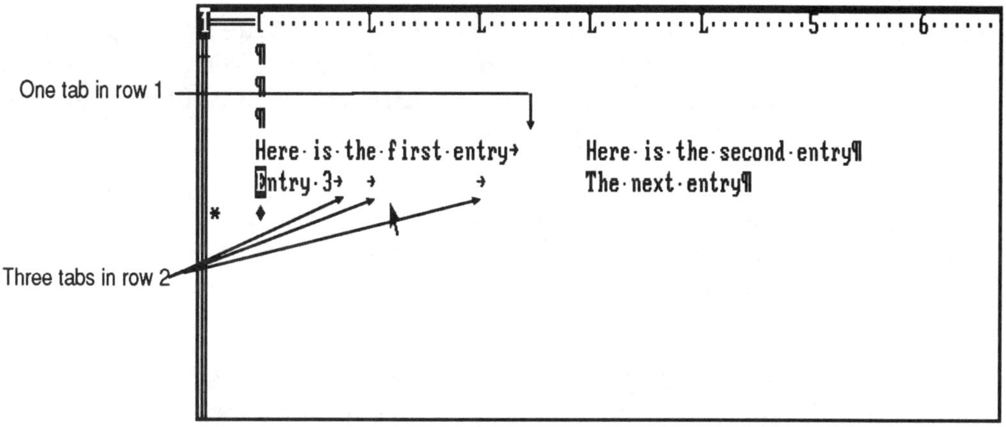

Figure 3-4. Don't use extra tab stops between columns. Put only one tab between columns, regardless of the on-screen appearance.

If you want to go to the trouble, you can set the tabs in the word processor to imitate the appearance on the page. Do so if this makes it easier for you or your typists. But the appearance in the word processor doesn't matter to Ventura Publisher. All that matters is that you (1) insert a true tab character instead of spaces and (2) insert only one tab between columns.

Spell checking text files

We recommend using a spelling checker *before* loading files into Ventura. Ventura inserts special codes to indicate tags, text attributes, fonts and so on. If you check the file after it has been loaded and saved by Ventura, the spell checking software reports these codes as misspelled words.

If you do heavy editing in Ventura, you may feel you need to spell check afterwards. Since Ventura uses the original word processing files, you won't have any compatibility problems with the spell checker. You will, however, need to add the tag names and codes to the user dictionary so the spell checker realizes they are not incorrect. Or, you can use a third-party utility like VP-To-The-Max from Aristocad, Inc.

Naming text files

Ventura Publisher has default file extensions for different word processing programs. Turn back to Table 3-1 to review the extensions assigned to the different file formats. When you load, for instance, a Microsoft Word file, Ventura looks for the extension DOC. You can change this default if you want. Some users, for instance, prefer to use the extension to indicate the type of document — LTR for letters, MEM for memos, etc.

In most cases, however, we suggest staying with Ventura's defaults. Using the standard system makes it easier to assemble documents containing many files. The extension shows which files are in which formats.

We also suggest you adopt a naming system for the rest of the file name. For instance, here's how we named the files that made up this chapter of *Inside Xerox Ventura Publisher*:

- Ventura chapter file: IX03.CHP
- Text file (in WordStar format): IX03.WS
- Picture file: IX03FONT.IMG

As you can see, each file has a two-letter project code (IX) followed by a two-number chapter code (03). It's not necessary to duplicate our system. It is important, however, to develop a procedure and stick to it. A naming system brings many advantages. It makes it possible to share files with a workgroup because users can identify files at a glance. In addition, you can use DOS wildcard functions to archive files. Our system, for instance, lets us copy every file that relates to the book with a single command:

```
COPY IX*.* A:
```

Or we can copy just the WordStar text files:

```
COPY IX*.WS A:
```

Or we can copy only the files for Chapter Three:

```
COPY IX03*.* A:
```

Editing in the word processor after using Ventura

Editing does not end once you create a layout. In all probability, you will continue to revise the text. It is acceptable, indeed often desirable, to edit a text file *after* it has been brought into a Ventura document. Open the file in the word processor just as you would normally. Add text or make corrections to any portion. The next time you call up the Ventura chapter, the changes made in the word processor show up.

When you reopen a text file, you discover codes that were not present when you created it. These are Ventura Publisher's codes for tag names, special characters, text attributes, and other formatting. Be careful not to edit or delete these codes — they control the format and appearance of the Ventura Publisher document.

Attributes in word processor files

Ventura supports a variety of text attributes. You can invoke eight of them directly in most word processors:

1. Bold

2. Underline

3. Superscript

4. Subscript

5. Strikethrough

6. Discretionary hyphens

7. Non-breaking spaces

8. Italic (not available for all word processors)

Ventura supports italic directly in some word processors, though not in all of them. What about small caps and other attributes not on the list? Ventura provides bracket codes for entering these attributes into text files. The final section of this chapter explains how.

For example, if you make a word bold in the word processor, it appears bold in Ventura, too. However, you should use text attributes only for a few words within a paragraph (Figure 3-5). If you want an entire paragraph to be bold, type it normally and make it bold after you bring it into Ventura. When creating a large, bold headline, for example, don't use the bold command from the word processor. Instead, choose a large, bold font in Ventura (Figure 3-6).

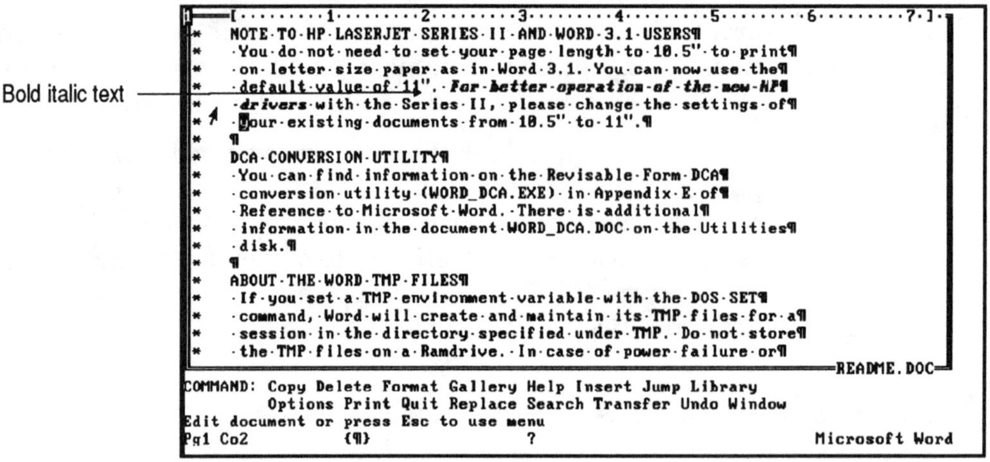

Figure 3-5. You can use a word processor command to make a few words bold within an otherwise normal paragraph.

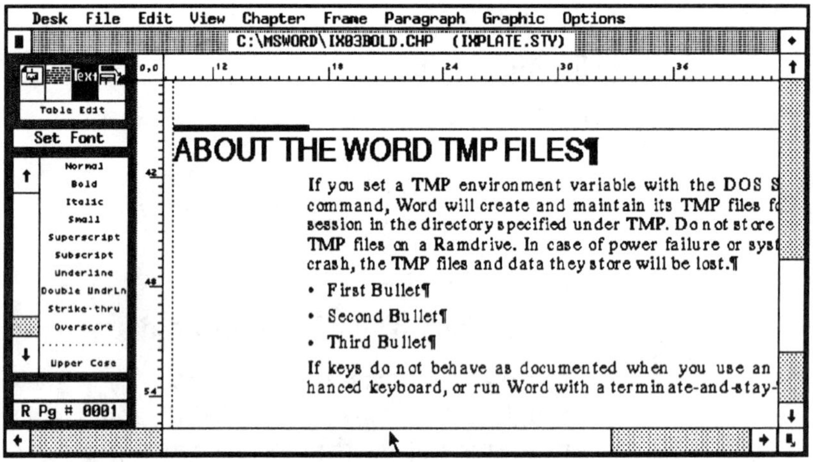

Figure 3-6. To make an entire paragraph bold (as with the headline shown here), type it as normal text in the word processor, then make it bold in Ventura.

Specific word processors

The general rules in the preceding section apply to all word processors. Now we're ready to look at specific programs and file formats. Some of them have special considerations you should know about. At the end of this section, we have suggestions in the event your favorite program is not supported.

Formatting ASCII files

Think of ASCII as a generic brand — the plain vanilla version of text. Most word processors, spreadsheets, and databases can create ASCII in addition to their native file formats. ASCII files differ from word processing formats. For one thing, they contain a paragraph return at the end of every line. (Most word processors use returns only at the end of the paragraph.)

Normally, a return signals a new paragraph. But when Ventura loads an ASCII file, it ignores single returns — otherwise, every single line would be a separate paragraph. How does it know where to end paragraphs? Simple — it interprets *two consecutive* hard returns as the command for a new paragraph. This explanation leads to an important rule: You must always put two returns between paragraphs in an ASCII file.

What if you don't want to put (or can't put) two returns between paragraphs? For instance, some spreadsheet and database programs don't allow this option. In those cases, you can load the file as if it were WordStar 3 format. (Choose WordStar 3 from the Load Text/Picture dialog box). No other conversion is necessary. Ventura will treat single returns as new paragraphs.

How (and why) to create ASCII with other programs

ASCII is a versatile standard. It is the key to working with word processors, database managers and spreadsheet programs that are not directly supported by Ventura. By converting their files to ASCII, you can use them to create text for Ventura.

Some programs have a direct ASCII option (although it may be called "unformatted," "Text-only," "nondocument" or "DOS Text"). Others have a special utility to convert the original file to ASCII. Even if the program doesn't have an ASCII option, you can still create ASCII files. Use the print function, but print to disk instead of to a printer. When a program prints, it strips out special commands and converts to ASCII. Consult the program manual for the commands to print to a disk file.

➥*NOTE: If you print to disk, set margins to zero to prevent unwanted space characters.*

Why use ASCII? Some companies choose ASCII as a common denominator between various word processing programs. In other cases (certain databases, spreadsheets, and programming languages) ASCII is the only text option available — or, at least, the only one compatible with Ventura.

There are other reasons to consider using ASCII. Many typists prefer two returns between paragraphs to make it easier to read text on the screen. But double returns must be removed to bring a file into Ventura (with search and replace or the PARAFILTR tag). If you go back and forth between Ventura and the word processor, you must reinsert and remove the double returns each time. One possible solution is to save in ASCII format. Ventura expects double returns in ASCII, so there is no need to remove them before loading.

➥ *NOTE: Once you save in ASCII format, it is difficult to work with the file again in the word processor. Every line will have a return at the end, making it troublesome to add or delete text.*

Attributes in ASCII files

To create attributes like bold and underline in an ASCII file, use the bracket codes explained at the end of this chapter. This rule applies whether the file comes from a word processor, a database, a spreadsheet, or any other program. Don't use built-in attribute commands if the final output will be in ASCII format.

Two kinds of ASCII

A word to the technically proficient: Ventura supports ASCII in two forms. True ASCII appears in the Load Text/File dialog box as *ASCII*. A variation appears as *8-bit ASCII*. True ASCII uses seven bits of data only. That allows only 128 characters — not enough to convey Ventura's full International Character Set. To allow more characters, Ventura also supports 8-bit ASCII, which uses the eighth bit for data instead of parity. Many word processing and database management programs are capable of producing ASCII files with characters that fall between 128 and 255.

DCA format

Document Content Architecture (DCA) format is supported by a variety of word processors, usually via a conversion utility that translates the native file format. As with ASCII, it often acts as a means of interchange between otherwise incompatible programs. Several popular programs support DCA, including:

- Displaywrite III and IV
- Lotus Manuscript
- Office Writer
- Samna Word
- Volkswriter
- WordStar 2000

Each program has a slightly different procedure for converting. Usually you save the file first in native format. Then you choose the Utilities submenu and select the DCA conversion routine. Sometimes DCA is referred to as Revisable Form Text instead. Refer to the program manuals for more details.

These word processors also allow you to save in ASCII, which is also supported by Ventura. Using DCA instead means that you can enter the text attributes with native commands, and those attributes will be preserved in Ventura. With ASCII format you must enter attributes with bracket codes.

To bring in a DCA file from the Load Text/File dialog box, select Type of File: Text and Text Format: DCA.

MultiMate format

Ventura can read and write MultiMate files. To bring in a MultiMate file from the Load Text/File dialog box, select Type of File: Text and Text Format: MultiMate.

Microsoft Word format

Ventura can read and write files in Word format, including those created by Windows Write and Word for Windows.

Word and Ventura don't always get along. You must use extra caution when applying attributes like bold. Do not select a paragraph return when you are selecting text. If the attribute is applied across a return, it may be lost when Ventura saves the text back to the Word file. Likewise, do not apply any attributes to a tag code, or the tag may not take effect (it may appear as ordinary text instead). These problems are most likely to occur if you use the mouse to select text.

Although Word has style sheets, they are not compatible with Ventura's. Any formatting you do with a Word style sheet will be lost when you bring in the file. Word's style sheets do, however, offer some advantages. You can type only a single return between paragraphs, but set up the style sheet to double the space. This makes it easier to read the text on the screen without bringing on the hassle of stripping out extra returns.

You must also use caution with Word's hidden text. The hidden code will be stripped away when Ventura saves back to Word format.

To bring in a Word or Windows Write file from the Load Text/File dialog box, select Type of File: Text and Text Format: MS-Word.

WordPerfect format

Ventura can read and write WordPerfect files from versions 4.1 and higher.

To bring in a WordPerfect 4.1 or 4.2 file from the Load Text/File dialog box, select Type of File: Text and Text Format: WordPerfect. To bring in a WordPerfect 5 file from the Load Text/File dialog box, select Type of File: Text and Text Format: WordPerfect 5.

WordStar format

Ventura can read and write files from WordStar 3.3, 4.0, and 5.0. Later versions may also be supported. In Version 3.3, you must turn off hyphen-help (Ctrl-OH) and justification (Ctrl-OJ) at the beginning of every editing session. You can also patch or reinstall WordStar so these options are off.

In Version 3.3 you must turn vari-tabs off (Ctrl-OV) if you want WordStar to insert true tab characters instead of spaces. In Version 4.0, you cannot insert tab characters with the tab key. Instead, you must press Ctrl-PI.

You cannot use WordStar's dot command formatting codes. Ventura will treat them as ordinary text. WordStar has a Document mode (D from the main menu) and a Nondocument mode (N from the main menu). WordStar's nondocument text files are straight ASCII files.

➥*NOTE: You cannot convert an existing WordStar document to ASCII simply by opening it in nondocument mode. The exact method of converting to ASCII varies between the different versions of WordStar. The simplest way is usually to print to a disk file.*

To bring in a WordStar 3.3 file from the Load Text/File dialog box, select Type of File: Text and Text Format: WordStar US. Select Text Format: WS 4.0/5.0 for later versions.

Xerox Writer format

Ventura can read and write Xerox Writer 2.0 files. To bring in a Xerox Writer file from the Load Text/File dialog box, select Type of File: Text and Text Format: Writer.

Xywrite

Ventura can read and write Xywrite II and Xywrite III files. Xywrite is a powerful, highly programmable word processor. A skilled Xywrite operator can set up a Ventura front end that allows the user to select and apply tags from a pop-up list. You can also set up a system to make tags and bracket codes visible or invisible with a single command.

To bring in a Xywrite file from the Load Text/File dialog box, select Type of File: Text and Text Format: Xywrite.

Unsupported word processors

What should you do if the word processor you like best is not supported directly by Ventura? You have several options.

First, check with the vendor to see if it has developed a loadable Ventura filter since you purchased the program. If so, all you will need to do is acquire the filter and perform a brief, one-time installation. From that point on, your word processor appears as a choice in the Load Text/File dialog box along with all the others. If you own a modem, check to see if a filter is available from the Xerox forum on CompuServe, or from an on-line bulletin board system.

Second, check the program manual to see if it converts to any other formats. It is almost certain to have ASCII capabilities. It may also be able to convert to DCA or one of the other supported file formats.

Finally, consider a separate conversion program. There are numerous packages on the market that can convert files from one format to another. Usually they have a long list of supported formats, giving you a wide range of options. With a conversion utility, you first save the file, then you run the utility to change the format. You load the converted file into Ventura.

Tips for working with word processors

TIP *Put a single return* between paragraphs. If you prefer two returns, use search and replace or the PARAFILTR technique to strip out the extras before loading into Ventura.

TIP *Use your word processor's spelling checker* on the caption file created within Ventura. This file will have the same name as the chapter and an extension of CAP. Treat the file as an ASCII format. Be careful not to add or delete any extra returns or to change the order of the sentences. Ventura stores all the captions in a single file. It counts returns to determine where to position them, so adding or deleting lines can throw off the captions for the entire chapter.

TIP *Use the word processor to approximate the final document.* If you know in advance the format you will use for the final document, you can imitate that format on screen in the word processor. For instance, you can set your word processing margins to correspond to the line length of the Ventura document. Although only an approximation, this technique helps writers gauge the proper length for sentences and paragraphs. Likewise, you can set up tab stops, spreadsheets, spacing, and other formatting to resemble the final document, making it easier for writers to visualize the results.

Creating text with other programs

Up to this point, we have talked about word processors. You can also create text for Ventura with other programs.

Using a database program

Database management programs are powerful text-generating tools for Ventura Publisher. Database software is more practical than word processing for such things as directories, catalogs, price lists, phone books, and specification sheets. Virtually all database programs, including best-sellers like dBase III, Rbase 5000, and DataFlex, can create ASCII files compatible with Ventura. When you combine the information-handling of a database with the batch processing of Ventura Publisher, you have a powerful team. To coordinate the two packages, program the database to accept and store the data you need. Then print a report to disk. This creates an ASCII file that can be loaded into Ventura and formatted. If you have two returns between every paragraph, load the file as ASCII. If the report has only one return between paragraphs, load it into Ventura as a WordStar file. Be sure to program the database to trim out extra spaces (when entries don't fill all the spaces in the field). And ask it to leave out blank fields entirely.

Tips for generating text with a database

TIP *To reduce the complexity* of the document and speed performance in Ventura, use line breaks in place of carriage returns between two lines that have the same tag. Here's how a listing might look without line breaks:

```
John Doe  ¶

ACME Company  ¶
```

```
123 Main Street  ¶

Anytown, USA  ¶
```

Here's how it would look with line breaks instead (Ventura interprets the <R> bracket code as a line break):

```
John Doe  ¶

ACME Company<R>123 Main Street<R>Anytown, USA  ¶
```

You would read both examples into Ventura as WordStar files. Both look the same on paper, but the line break version consumes less memory in Ventura — a concern when formatting multi-column directories with many entries.

For the ultimate in automated database publishing, read the final section in this chapter. It describes how to insert tags, text attributes, and other formatting information directly into text files *before* they are brought into Ventura. Using this technique, you can produce preformatted database reports. This method cuts days or even weeks from the process of publishing large directories.

TIP *Commercial programs can speed the process of using a database* to create text files for Ventura. You can purchase utility programs from several vendors that simplify and automate the process of pulling information from a database and pretagging it for Ventura.

Spreadsheet programs

Spreadsheet programs like Lotus 1-2-3 and Microsoft Excel can also create text for Ventura Publisher. Spreadsheet software is most useful for financial tables, comparison charts, and other tabular material (see Figure 3-7). For certain applications, you may prefer a spreadsheet. If the balance sheets already exist in Lotus 1-2-3, why bother to retype them for the annual report? And why use a word processor to create a complex financial table when a spreadsheet builds it faster while doing the math?

Disregard formatting options such as right alignment or centering. The spreadsheet is just a temporary format. The final alignment and formatting occur inside Ventura.

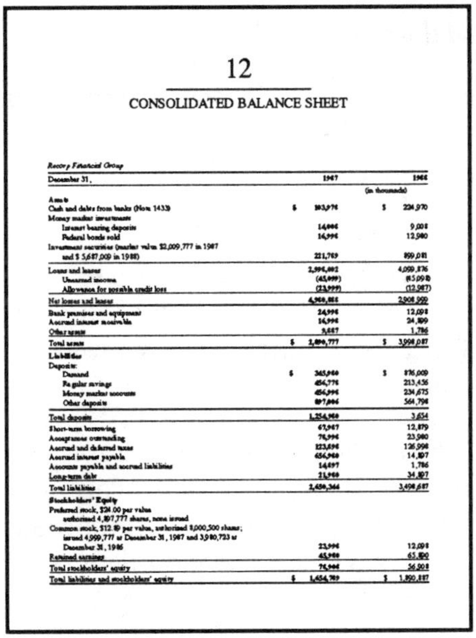
12

CONSOLIDATED BALANCE SHEET

Figure 3-7. You can use a spreadsheet program to generate the letters and numbers for your financial tables.

The steps to convert a spreadsheet file into a usable text file depend on the program. One way is to convert to an ASCII file. Some spreadsheets have a built-in ASCII option. If not, use the technique mentioned above: Print the worksheet, but send it to a disk file instead of the printer. Load the file into Ventura with the ASCII option (if it has two returns between paragraphs) or the WordStar option (if it has one).

Spreadsheet programs use spaces to separate columns. Ventura requires the actual tab character (Ctrl-I), not spaces. The solution is to strip out those spaces and replace them with the tab character. You can do this manually in Ventura (not recommended for anything but the smallest tables), in a word processor, or with special utilities.

Ventura's EMS version includes an external utility that reads ASCII files from spreadsheets and databases directly and converts them into the correct format for Table mode. To use this method, create a PRN file with the spreadsheet. Then use the PRN-to-Table option from the Load Text/Picture dialog box. Ventura will read and convert the PRN file for use as a table.

Tips for working with spreadsheets

TIP *One way to clean up spreadsheet files* is to transfer them into your word processor. Use search and replace to remove multiple spaces and substitute tab characters.

TIP *You can embed a special symbol* within each spreadsheet cell when you first create the table. (Use any symbol not encountered in the text. Possibilities include #, &, or *). Then you search for this symbol with your word processor and replace it with the tab character.

TIP *Lotus 1-2-3 users should consider another option.* Ventura Publisher can directly import Lotus graphic files stored in the PIC format. Consider converting the spreadsheet file into a chart or graph if a visual aid would make your point more effectively than a table.

TIP *To take the use of a spreadsheet program even further*, program the left-most column to contain the tag name along with the labels. Use the spreadsheet's copy or macro function to automate this insertion. Instead of Sales, for example, you might type in:

```
@COLLABEL = Sales
```

TIP *To avoid the need to replace spaces with tabs* use a monospaced font such as Courier after bringing the table into Ventura Publisher. Since all characters — and spaces — in this font have the same width, the columns and rows will align in Ventura Publisher just as they did in the spreadsheet program (which is also monospaced). Use Paragraph Typography from the Paragraph menu to set Normal Space Width to 1.000 so the columns will align perfectly.

Using a programming language

The section at the end of the chapter explains how to insert tags and attributes directly into a file. Once you understand how the process works, you'll realize that programming languages like BASIC and Pascal can insert these tags. There are as many possibilities as there are programmers to create them. One example might be a program that prompts the user for variable information such as the price of gold or the names of the department managers and then outputs a pretagged file for Ventura.

Creating text within Ventura

To this point, we've discussed how to create text files outside Ventura. This section explains how to create and edit text within Ventura. To learn how to arrange text and lay it out on the page, turn to Chapter Six, "Building the Chapter."

Ventura's Text mode was not designed to take the place of a word processor. It doesn't have search and replace, automatic scrolling at the end of the screen, and other features that speed text creation. We don't recommend Ventura for generating more than a page or so, but it's fine for short documents like ads, flyers, letters, and forms.

Typing on the Page

Obviously, you can use Text mode to edit a text file from another program. In addition, you can create separate files from scratch. This saves you from leaving Ventura, calling up a word processor, creating the file, re-entering Ventura, and loading in the file. The easiest way to create a text file is by switching to Text mode and clicking anywhere on a blank Underlying Page. The text cursor appears in the upper left. Now start typing.

You've just created a text file. (To be completely accurate, the file isn't created until you save the chapter; that's when Ventura actually writes it to disk.) To name the file, Ventura uses the same name as the chapter. To decide which format and extension to use, Ventura selects the last format used by the Load Text/File function. To determine where to put the file, Ventura uses the subdirectory containing the chapter file.

Let's say you are working on a chapter called SAMPLE.CHP located in the \TYPESET subdirectory. The last time you used Ventura, you loaded text files in WordStar format with the WS extension. If you start typing on the blank Underlying Page inside SAMPLE.CHP, Ventura automatically creates a text file in WordStar format called \TYPESET\SAMPLE.WS.

To check the name of a file, switch to Frame mode and click on the Page. The file name appears in the Current Selection Box at the lower left of the Side-Bar.

Typing inside a frame

As you will recall, Ventura can put frames on top of the Underlying Page. A slightly different process occurs if you type into a blank frame (as opposed to a blank Underlying Page). In this case, Ventura places the text you type into its caption file. The caption file, which is stored in ASCII format, contains all the captions for all the frames in the document. If you click on this frame in Frame mode, the Current Selection Box will read "Frame Text." That phrase lets you know that Ventura has stored this text in its caption file. If you prefer, you can put this text into a separate file using File Type/Rename from the Edit menu (see below).

Changing a file name, format, or location

You can change the name, format, or path of a text file (or any combination). To change a file:

- Switch to Frame mode and select the Page or frame containing the file.
- Choose File Type/Rename from the File menu.
- When the dialog box appears, enter the new path, name, and format.

When you save the chapter, Ventura saves the text in the new file. The previous file remains unchanged with its old name, format, path, and contents.

You can use the same technique with text typed into frames. When you click on the frame, you see the words "Frame Text" displayed in the Current Selection Box. This signals that the text is currently stored in the caption file. To put this text in a separate file of its own, open File Type/Rename as explained above and type in the name, path, and format you want.

➥*NOTE: The file will not actually be converted until after you save the chapter. Thus, if you abandon the chapter without saving, Ventura will not produce a converted text file.*

Tips for creating files

TIP *Ventura will rename the text file automatically* if it matches the chapter's name and path. When you change the chapter name, Ventura changes the text file name. Thus, if you change \TYPESET\SAMPLE.CHP to \NEW\NEWSAMPL.CHP, Ventura automatically changes \TYPESET\SAMPLE.TXT to \NEW\NEWSAMPL.TXT. The previous file is not deleted.

TIP *You can rename the text in caption frames.* Users generally find it most convenient to leave their captions in Ventura's caption file. However, if you prefer to have a separate file for each caption, use File Type/Rename on each caption frame.

Editing in Ventura

When it comes time to edit, Ventura doesn't care how text was created. Editing commands work identically on all text regardless of its origin.

To edit text, begin by enabling Text mode. Position the mouse cursor at the insertion point and click once. The flashing text cursor appears. To add characters, simply begin typing. The Backspace key erases characters to the left of the cursor. The Del key erases characters to the right of the cursor.

Cutting, copying, and pasting

You can copy, cut, and paste by selecting (highlighting) the text, then selecting the function you want. You can highlight text in two ways. For most applications, place the mouse cursor at the beginning and drag the cursor to the end. This method is the fastest and the easiest. For small edits where placement is difficult, use the Shift-Click method instead. First place the *text* cursor at the beginning of the selection. Now move the *mouse* cursor to the end, and click again *while holding down the Shift key.* The text between the two clicks will be highlighted.

The Shift-Click method allows more accurate positioning. It is best for selecting, for example, a single letter. It is also useful to shorten or lengthen a selection. Let's say you accidentally grab two extra words while making a selection. Place the mouse cursor at the correct end point and click while holding Shift to shorten the selection.

You can only select one continuous range of text at a time. Your selection can cross a column, but not a page boundary, even in Facing Pages View. Once you have selected the text, choose Cut Text, Copy Text, or Paste Text from the Edit menu (Figure 3-8). As you become more familiar with the program, you will find that it saves time to use the keyboard shortcuts:

- To copy, press Shift-Del.
- To cut, press Del.
- To insert, press Ins.

Ventura stores the text in the Text Clipboard (also called temporary memory). It stays there until you cut or copy something else. As a result, you can cut or copy anything from a word to a sentence to a paragraph and repeatedly paste it elsewhere in the document. However, you *cannot* cut several items in a row and then paste them all. Only the last item remains in memory. The others are lost.

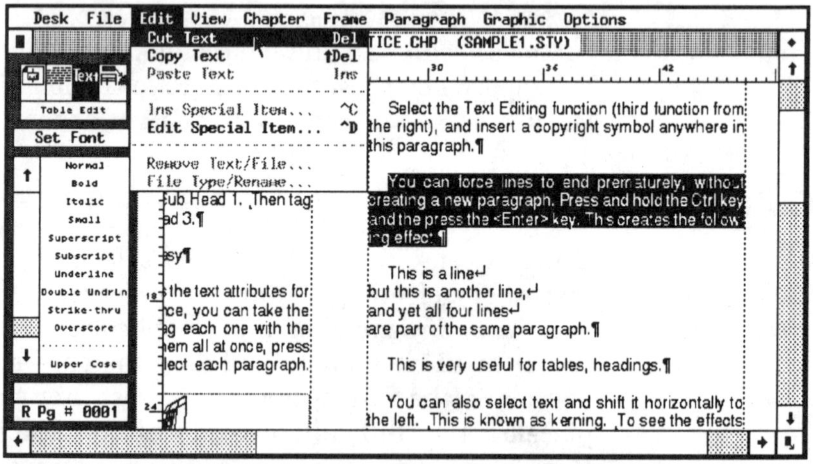

Figure 3-8. To edit, highlight the text, then choose the appropriate command from the Edit menu (or press the keyboard shortcut).

The cut function removes the selection from the page and places it in the Clipboard. The copy function works in exactly the same manner, except that the selection is not removed from the page. To place a selection anywhere in the document, move the mouse cursor to the insertion point and press Ins (or select Paste from the Edit menu).

Ventura maintains three separate Clipboards, one for frames, one for graphics, and one for text. Cutting or copying a frame or a drawing does not affect text. Text remains in the Clipboard when you close a chapter and open a new one. You can, therefore, use the Clipboard to copy or move short text sections from one chapter to another. And there is no need to worry about the original file format of the text. Ventura permits you, for example, to move a section from a WordStar file into the middle of a MultiMate file.

Editing tabs, returns, and other marks

To make editing easier and more accurate, choose Show Tabs & Returns from the Options menu. This choice creates visible marks in the text for tabs, returns, and the other important editing symbols listed in Table 3-3.

Table 3-3. Editing symbols in Text mode.

Name	Description in Current Selection Box
Tab character	Horiz. Tab
Paragraph return	Paragraph End
Line break	Line Break
Discretionary hyphen	Discr. Hyph 1
Fixed spaces (non-breaking, em, en, figure, thin)	NoBreak Space
Index	Index Entry
Anchor	Frame Anchor
Footnote	Footnote
Cross-Reference (EMS version only)	Reference
End of file	End of File
Attributes (bold, italic, etc.)	Attr. Setting

➥ *NOTE: A Return starts a new line and tells Ventura to treat the next item as a separate paragraph. A line break starts a new line, but the line is treated as part of the preceding paragraph, so it retains the same tag formatting.*

You can edit these symbols. Simply highlight the symbol (try using the Shift-Click method) then select an action from the Edit menu. For instance, to move an index reference or a frame anchor, you would cut the degree symbol from the text and paste it into the new location.

Text files also include markers that cannot be made visible. These markers denote the beginning and end of text attributes like bold and italic. Although you can't see these markers, you can edit them as if they were text. They can be cut, copied, and pasted, in conjunction with text or by themselves. At first glance it might seem impossible to edit markers that do not show on the screen. The key to finding attributes and marks is the Current Selection Box at the bottom of the Side-Bar. In Text mode, it remains blank *until you move the text cursor onto an attribute or mark.* Then the box displays the name of the marker.

Try this example. Move to a paragraph of body text and highlight a word. Change it to bold. Move the text cursor to the first letter in that word. The Current Selection Box is blank. Now press the left arrow key once. Result: the Current Selection Box now displays the words "Attr. Setting." In a similar fashion, you can locate other invisible codes within the text, whether they are marks or attributes.

Changing attributes in Text mode

Ventura Publisher retains certain attributes set within the word processor, such as bold and underline. Nevertheless, there will be many cases when you want to add attributes after bringing text in. Ventura makes nine attributes available via the Assignment List in Text mode (Figure 3-9):

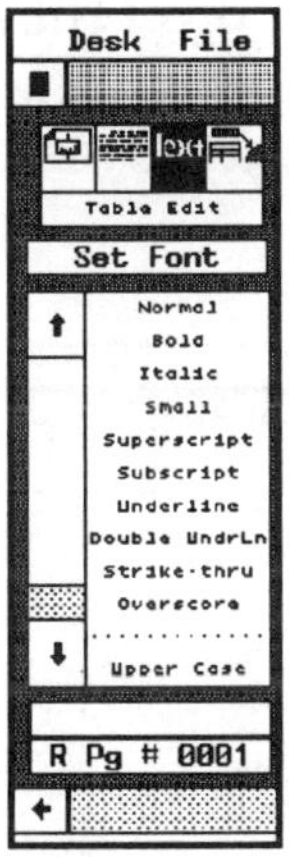

Figure 3-9.

1. Bold
2. Italic
3. Small
4. Superscript
5. Subscript
6. Underline
7. Double Underline
8. Strike-thru
9. Overscore

To add an attribute, highlight the text, then select the attribute from the Assignment List. To combine attributes — Bold and Italic, for instance — highlight the text and select them one at a time. Attributes are not toggle commands — selecting them a second time will not turn them off. To combine attributes, choose them one after another from the Assignment List. To clear attributes, choose Normal from the top of the Assignment List.

➥ *NOTE: Selecting Normal clears all attributes, not just the last one. If you select Bold and Italic, then decide you want only*

Bold, you must clear both attributes by selecting Normal, and then select Bold again.

The fourth item on the assignment list is Small. This stands for small caps, a useful effect not available with standard word processors. The best way to understand small caps is to see them side-by-side with normal caps and lowercase letters:

NORMAL CAPS SMALL CAPS lowercase

Small caps can set a word or phrase apart from the rest of the text. They make a word noticeable without being obtrusive. Small caps also come in handy for logos and headlines, either by themselves or in combination with normal capitals. Before selecting small caps, be sure to capitalize all the letters. When you choose Small from the Assignment List, Ventura is really just changing the letters to a smaller size. You could accomplish the same effect by using Set Font from the top of the Side-Bar. Initially Ventura sets the size of the font for you. You can change this specification, however, with Attribute Overrides from the Paragraph menu (Figure 3-10).

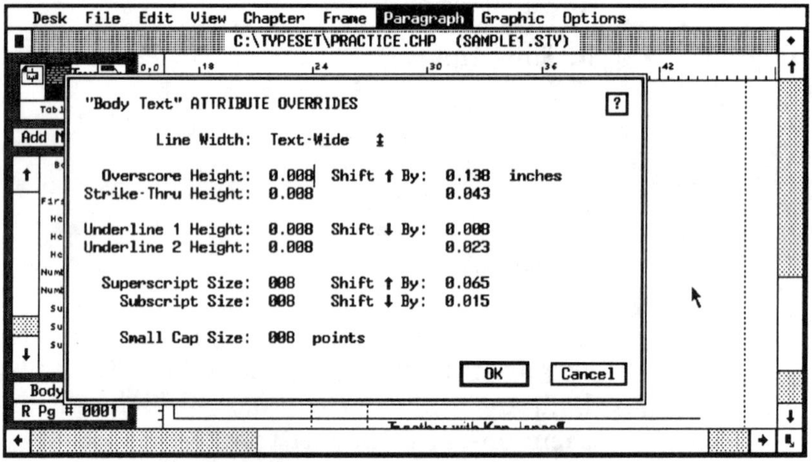

Figure 3-10. The Attribute Overrides dialog box lets you control the size of the font assigned to small caps, as well as the positioning of other attributes.

In addition to the standard attributes, the Assignment List also controls capitalization in Text mode. Scroll to the bottom of the list to see the three options:

1. Upper Case

2. Capitalize

3. Lower Case

Upper Case changes every letter in the selected phrase to capitals. Capitalize changes only the first letter of each word to capitals. Lower Case changes every letter to lowercase.

Ventura users who edit contributions from various authors will appreciate these built-in functions. By selecting one of the three choices, you can quickly make headlines and section titles conform to the capitalization standards you have set forth. It is almost always faster to let Ventura handle the capitalization changes than to correct the letters one-by-one.

Changing fonts in Text mode

Text mode also lets you change the font for any section of text. Use Text mode to change the font when you want a few words to look different from the rest of the paragraph. Use Paragraph mode when you want to change the font of every word in the paragraph.

To change the font, select the text. Then click on the Set Font button at the top of the Side-Bar. The Font dialog box appears. This dialog box is almost identical to the one that appears when you select Font from the Paragraph menu. It works in the same fashion. However, because you access it through Text mode, it affects *only the highlighted words*. When you open the Font dialog box in Paragraph mode, it affects *every word in the paragraph*, and every similar tag in the document.

Font settings made in Text mode override anything done in Paragraph mode. You can choose Bold and Italic from the Font dialog box or the Assignment List. The effect is identical either way. You can also choose Overscore, Strike-thru, Underline, and Double Underline in both places, but the effect differs. If you invoke them in Text mode they apply only to the selected text. If you invoke them in Paragraph mode they apply to the entire paragraph (Figure 3-11).

When you change a font in Text mode, the paragraph retains its original line spacing. If you increase the size, the letters may overlap the lines above and below. To minimize this effect, position the text with the Shift function from the Font

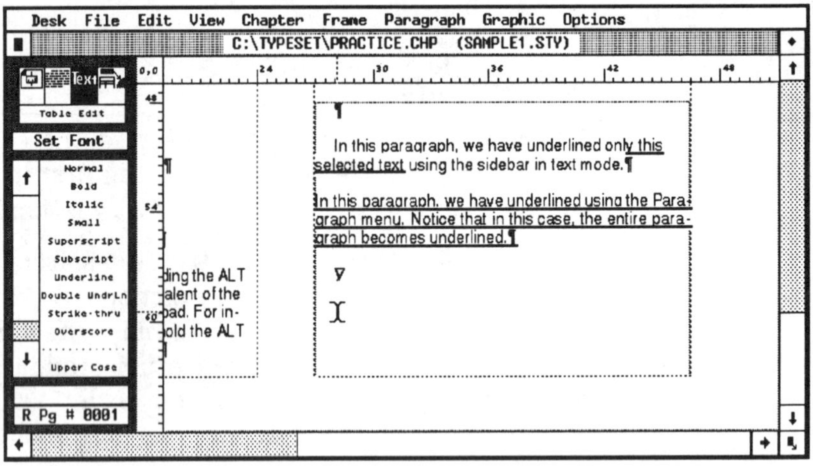

Figure 3-11. Invoking attributes in Paragraph mode applies them to the entire paragraph, not just to selected text.

dialog box. Use Enlarged View for maximum accuracy. Shift the new text up or down a half point at a time until it fits into the space. Shifting affects only the selected words, not the rest of the paragraph.

You can also tell Ventura to automatically add spacing to lines with large type. Use Paragraph Typography from the Paragraph menu. Choose Grow Inter-Line To Fit: On.

Inserting non-keyboard characters in Text mode

Professional-looking pages require characters and symbols not available on the standard keyboard. These *non-keyboard characters* are quite important. For example, the keyboard shows only inch marks ("). True typeset material uses two separate sets of marks, open quotes (“) for the beginning and close quotes (”) for the end. Non-keyboard characters have several important functions:

- typographic symbols
- foreign language characters
- mathematical and scientific notation

In a few cases, Ventura Publisher provides access to these symbols within a dialog box. For example, when creating footnotes or bullets, Ventura lets you choose from a variety of symbols. In addition, Ventura has keyboard shortcuts for the most common symbols, as shown in Table 3-4.

Table 3-4. Keyboard shortcuts and decimal equivalents for selected special characters.

Name	Appearance	Decimal Equivalent	Keyboard Shortcut (If Any)
Copyright mark	©	189	Ctrl-Shift-C
Trademark	™	191	Ctrl-Shift-2
Registered Trademark	®	190	Ctrl-Shift-R
Open Quote	“	169	Ctrl-Shift-[
Close Quote	”	170	Ctrl-Shift-]
Ellipsis	…	193	
Bullet	•	195	
Em Dash	—	197	Ctrl-]
En Dash	–	196	Ctrl-[
Hollow Box	□	none	Ctrl-C-F1
Filled Box	■	none	Ctrl-C-F1

Non-keyboard characters via the keyboard

Most non-keyboard characters are not available through a dialog box or a keyboard shortcut. You can enter non-keyboard characters — whether or not they have a shortcut — by typing their decimal equivalent while holding down the Alt key. Let's backtrack just long enough to understand how the keyboard works. When you press a key, you send a decimal equivalent to the computer. The computer interprets it as a character. For instance, by pressing the lowercase *a* key, you send a 97, which the computer recognizes as an *a*. Press a lowercase *b* and you send a 98, and so on.

Ventura's International Character Set goes up to 218, with each number assigned to a character. The standard keyboard, however, only has codes for about 128 or so. How can you gain access to those extra characters? Simple — hold down the Alt key and enter the decimal equivalent on the numeric keypad.

(Don't use the numbers across the top of the keyboard). Table 3-4 gives the name, symbol, and decimal equivalent of some important non-keyboard characters that have no keyboard shortcut. The Xerox Ventura Publisher Reference Guide lists the entire extended character set in Appendix E.

For example, to place an ellipsis (…) in the text, move the text cursor to the correct spot in the sentence. Hold down the Alt key while typing 193 on the numeric keypad (don't try to use the numbers above the keyboard). The ellipsis will appear on the screen as soon as you release the Alt key.

➡*NOTE: You can use the decimal equivalent to insert characters for bullets and footnotes. The dialog boxes for these options give several choices. If you do not like the symbols shown, choose an alternative and enter its decimal equivalent into the space provided in the dialog box (Figure 3-12).*

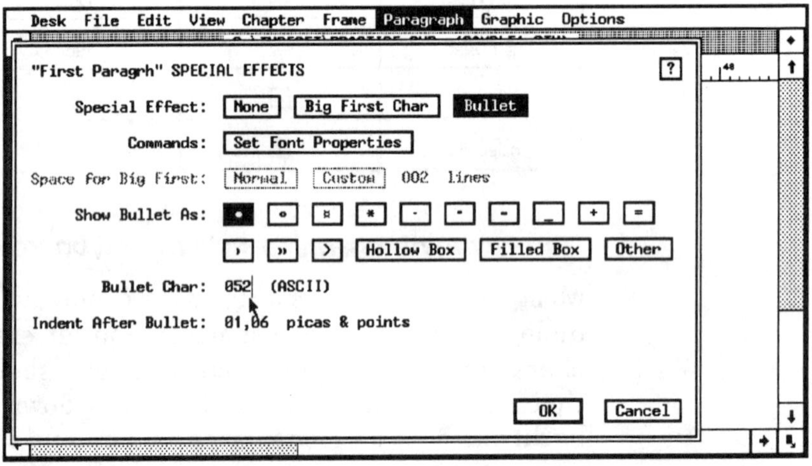

Figure 3-12. You can also use decimal equivalents to create different bullets in the Special Effects dialog box.

Using the Symbol font

Ventura also provides access to an entire alphabet of special characters called the Symbol font. You've already learned how to change fonts. You've also seen how to enter decimal equivalents. By combining these two skills, you can gain access to an entire extra alphabet of symbols appropriate for mathematics and equations.

You switch to the Symbol font the same way you change to any other font. You can access the Font dialog box via the Paragraph menu (if you want an entire paragraph to appear in the Symbol font), or via the Set Font button in Text mode (if you just want to change a few letters).

The Symbol font is different in that *every* character is a symbol. In most fonts, pressing the *a* key gets you some kind of *a*, albeit in a different typestyle. But pressing the *a* key in the Symbol font gets you the Greek symbol *alpha* (α). Here's a more extended example:

Normal font: a b c d e f g h i j k

Symbol font: α β χ δ ε ϕ γ η ι φ κ

The secret to using the Symbol font, then, is to understand that the keyboard has been remapped. To enter a symbol, find it on the chart. Look across to see what it would be in the International Character Set. Then press that key on the keyboard.

What about non-keyboard characters above decimal 128? You access them the same way in the Symbol font as you do in any other: by holding down the Alt key while typing the number on the keypad.

In addition to the symbols explained here, you can also get other fonts with special characters. Most PostScript printers, for instance, contain a Dingbat font. Here's a brief sample:

Normal font: a b c d e f g h i j k

Dingbat font: ❁ ❂ ❃ ❄ ❅ ❆ ❇ ❈ ❉ ❊ ❋

Non-keyboard characters in word processing files

You can also insert the extended character set directly into word processing files before bringing those files into Ventura. In brief, the technique involves enclosing the decimal equivalent inside angle brackets (the same decimal equivalent explained above). Thus, Alt-193 produces the ellipsis in Ventura and <193> produces the ellipsis in a word processing file. See the final section in this chapter for complete details on preformatting word processing files.

Tips for text editing within Ventura

TIP *Don't be alarmed if a sentence disappears* during editing. The sentence has not vanished — it has simply been moved. You'll find it by going to the preceding page (if you're at the top) or the following page (if you're at the bottom). Ventura reformats as you add and delete text. Your changes may invoke automatic widow and orphan control, causing Ventura to push text from one page to another.

TIP *Don't forget about the Shift-Click method* for highlighting text. It's the easiest way to select short sections, or individual characters. You can also use Shift-Click to expand (or shorten) a selection.

TIP *Make use of the Clipboard to speed editing.* Use the copy function to put a commonly used phrase into the Text Clipboard where it can be reused.

TIP *Use small caps as a quick substitute for Set Font.* Normally, Ventura chooses a new font size when you select Small from the Assignment List in Text mode. By using Attribute Overrides from the Paragraph menu, you can change this default setting. You can even use it to make the selected text larger instead of smaller. If you must frequently change the size of a few words within a paragraph, treat them as small caps and use Attribute Overrides to choose which size they should be.

TIP *Use superscript and subscript* for additional quick font changes. As with small caps, Ventura normally chooses a smaller font, but you can change this setting in Attribute Overrides. You can also change the amount that the text is shifted up or down. To use these choices as quick substitutes for Set Font, choose the font size you want and set the shift to zero.

TIP *Learn to tag with the function keys* in Text mode. That way you can type text and tag it at the same time, without switching to Paragraph mode.

Preformatting text files

We wanted this chapter to provide one-stop shopping on the subject of text. For that reason, we added this final, advanced section on preformatting. It gives instructions on all Ventura's preformatting options. Tables and charts provides quick references to key commands.

You don't have to preformat files to use Ventura, so if you're a novice you may want to skim this material and come back later. Eventually, however, most users will want to learn about it. Many professional publishers tell us their greatest productivity gains come from preformatting text files.

Preformatting may seem cumbersome at first, because it means adding codes. In truth, when combined with keyboard macros it is often the fastest way to create documents. Preformatting can save hours of layout time (especially if you use a database or spreadsheet to preformat large documents).

Let's start by quickly reviewing the Ventura approach to text. The process starts with a raw text file. You bring the file into Ventura and apply the style sheet to format the document. When you save the chapter, Ventura saves the original text file as well. If you return to this text file, you find that Ventura has inserted formatting codes.

Given this approach, it is easy to understand preformatting: just type in the codes *before* bringing the file in. You can insert two types of information: (1) tag names and (2) bracket codes. We will explore them both in turn, but remember that the basic concept is the same — you preformat a text file by typing in codes Ventura can understand.

Entering tags in advance

Pretagging is the most obvious and common form of preformatting. If you know (1) the proper format and (2) the exact spelling of the tag names, you can pretag as you type the text file. When you load that file into Ventura Publisher, it is automatically formatted according to the style sheet. Ventura's tagging code is simple to learn: Type the at sign (@)

at the left margin. Then type the name of the tag, followed by a space, an equal sign, and a second space:

```
@TAGNAME =
```

You can use letters, numbers, or symbols in the tag name. Type the tag immediately in front of the paragraph you want to preformat. Put it on the same line. Don't forget the spaces before and after the equal sign. And make sure that the at sign is the first character on the line.

Body text paragraphs do not need a tag name in the text file. Ventura Publisher already assumes anything without a tag is Body Text.

When you insert a tag into a text file, Ventura Publisher treats everything that follows as that tag *until it sees a paragraph return*. Then it reverts to Body Text. It formats the following paragraphs as Body Text *until it sees another tag code*. If you have three paragraphs in a row with the same tag name, you must put the tag code at the beginning of each one. Tag codes do not carry over to another paragraph.

➡*NOTE: If you want to start a new line without ending a paragraph, use a line break instead of a paragraph return.*

When you type a tag into a text file, it's crucial to match the name in the style sheet *letter-for-letter*. You and I might realize that @HEADLINE and @HEADLINES mean the same thing, but to Ventura Publisher they are entirely different. Obviously, then, you can't preformat files until you have settled on the names you plan to use. What happens if you misspell a tag? No harm done — if Ventura Publisher doesn't recognize a tag, it formats the paragraph as Body Text. You can format it correctly later.

Using the PARAFILTR tag

Ventura automatically recognizes one tag name no matter which style sheet is active. It can be used in any text file. This special tag strips out double returns. We explained earlier that word processing files require only one return between paragraphs. But text files are difficult to read without double spacing. This is particularly true since you do *not* want to use any indentation.

But if you put in extra returns, they show up in Ventura as blank lines, throwing off the spacing of the document. Theoretically, you could double space between paragraphs for readability, and then use the search and replace function of the word processor to strip out the extra return. However, you may find it more convenient to use Ventura Publisher's built-in PARAFILTR function.

To activate Ventura's built-in filter, place this special tag name at the top left of a document:

Be sure to make it the first thing in the text file and follow the other rules for tag names. Spell it exactly as shown here. Don't forget the spaces before and after the word "ON" and before and after the equal sign.

➥ *NOTE: When Ventura Publisher saves the text file, the double returns will be gone. You must reinsert them in the word processor if you wish to see double spacing on the screen again, or set up the word processor style sheet to add extra space between paragraphs.*

The PARAFILTR technique is not without drawbacks. Some users put in extra returns to add space in a document — not really the best idea, but in the heat of meeting a deadline it's a quick and easy solution. But if your text file contains the PARAFILTR tag, Ventura will strip out those extra returns. To avoid this problem, put a space on one of the lines, so Ventura no longer sees two returns in a row.

There is no way to turn off or delete PARAFILTR within Ventura. You must return to the word processor to take out the line.

Tips for pretagging

TIP *Make the at sign the first character at the left margin.* If you put it any other column, Ventura does not recognize it as a tag name.

TIP *Don't apply attributes to the tag name.* If you apply a text attribute like bold to the tag, the at sign may not be the first character in the left column. To use text attributes, start them *after* the tag name.

TIP *The tag name must precede* the rest of the paragraph.

TIP *Spell the tag name exactly* as it appears in the style sheet.

TIP *Use a macro processor* to speed pretagging and to avoid incorrect formatting or spelling. Enter macro descriptions for the tags. To pretag, all you have to do is press a key combination. For instance, Alt-1 could stand for ***@HEAD1*** = , while Alt-2 might stand for ***@HEAD2*** =. Many editors prepare macro files in advance and distribute them to their authors. When using multiple tags it's far too easy to forget the correct syntax. Was that supposed to be @HEAD, @HEADING, or @HEADLINE? Does the style sheet use @COLUMN1, @COLUMN ONE, or @COL1? If your authors misspell a tag by even a single letter they nullify the benefits pretagging.

TIP *Capitalization does not matter in the text file.* Ventura makes no distinction between upper and lower case when it sees tags in a text file (although it does make the distinction within the program).

TIP *The tag applies to the entire paragraph.* When Ventura encounters a paragraph return (two returns in an ASCII file) it resets to Body Text. It continues to format as Body Text until it encounters another tag name.

TIP *As an alternative to PARAFILTR,* save the file in ASCII format. Ventura automatically treats double returns as a single return when it loads an ASCII file. After loading, you can later change back to the original word processor format using File Type/Rename from the Edit menu.

TIP *Another alternative to PARAFILTR* may be available via your word processor. Put a single return between paragraphs, but set up the word processor to automatically add space before or after each paragraph.

TIP *You can use Ventura to change tag names* throughout a long file, or series of files. For instance, imagine that you want to change the tag name OLDNAME to the new designation of

NEWNAME, and you need to make the change in 10 different text files. Load all the files into Ventura. Put any one of them on the page (it doesn't matter which one). Click on a paragraph tagged as OLDNAME. Use Update Tag List from the Paragraph menu to change it to NEWNAME. Now save the chapter.

There is no need to load the other nine files onto the page. With that one brief action, you have changed OLDNAME to NEWNAME throughout all 10 files. Although you could also use search and replace in the word processor, it may often be faster to process a batch of files at once in Ventura than to run them one-by-one through a long search and replace routine.

Entering bracket codes in advance

So far we've shown you how easy it is to preformat by adding tag codes to the text file. Now we're ready to tackle bracket codes. The idea is every bit as simple as pretagging. In practice, however, the topic is more complex because bracket codes can carry four different kinds of information:

- text attributes (bold, italics, etc.)
- non-keyboard characters (symbols, etc.)
- formatting codes (font changes, point size changes, etc.)
- special functions (indexes, footnotes, etc.)

Beginning users sometimes struggle with bracket codes. It's not the concept that gives them a bad time. (You type letters or numbers between two brackets; how hard is that?) Rather, many novices don't understand the functions themselves. No wonder — if you don't have training in publishing and the graphic arts, concepts like base line jumps and secondary index references are bound to seem confusing.

So here's our advice to beginners: Try to grasp the theory of bracket codes. Then skim through the explanations of what they can accomplish. Don't worry if you don't understand all the effects yet. You'll catch on as you progress. At that time, you can return to this section for details.

The theory of bracket codes

You've already learned that tag codes use the at sign (@) to signal Ventura. Bracket codes use (you guessed it) angle brackets, one on each side of the code. (On most keyboards, the angle brackets are located above the comma and the period.) For instance, <MI> stands for medium-weight italics and <BI> means bold-italic.

When Ventura Publisher sees brackets in a text file, it does not print them or put them on screen. Instead, it treats the information inside as a formatting code. These formatting codes do not need to appear in the left margin. They can be anywhere in the text, as long as they are enclosed in brackets.

Ventura uses one code to turn on an effect and a second code to turn it off. The "stop" command varies, but the most common one is <D>. The <D> tells Ventura to return to the default (previous) condition. For example, here's how you would turn small caps on and off:

```
An example of <S>SMALL CAPS<D> with bracket
codes.
```

As we step you through the different effects, we will also explain how to turn them off. Incidentally, Ventura automatically reverts to the previous default whenever it sees a paragraph return. It also goes back to normal and starts from scratch if it encounters a new code.

Ventura's use of angle brackets can cause one slight problem. What if you want to put brackets into the text file? If you enter them normally, Ventura assumes they enclose a formatting code. To make angle brackets appear on the page, you must double them up:

- Single brackets (<X>) are treated as a formatting code.
- Double brackets (<<X>>) cause the inside set to print on the page.

The importance of bracket codes

Some of you may wonder why you should bother to learn bracket codes. There are several valid reasons.

Yes, it's true that you can perform all these same tasks in Ventura. In many cases, however, it makes more sense to add the effect in advance. Suppose a computer author wants to use the Courier font in the middle of paragraphs to indicate what readers must type in. It's much better if the author makes the font change with bracket codes. Otherwise the editor must wade through each paragraph and guess which words need special treatment.

There are also occasions to use bracket codes within Ventura. Several important dialog boxes accept bracket codes. For instance, many users want advanced effects in their headers and footers — different fonts on the same line, different sizes on the same line, base line jumps to shift page numbers up or down, and so on (Figures 3-13 and 3-14). You can achieve these effects with bracket codes.

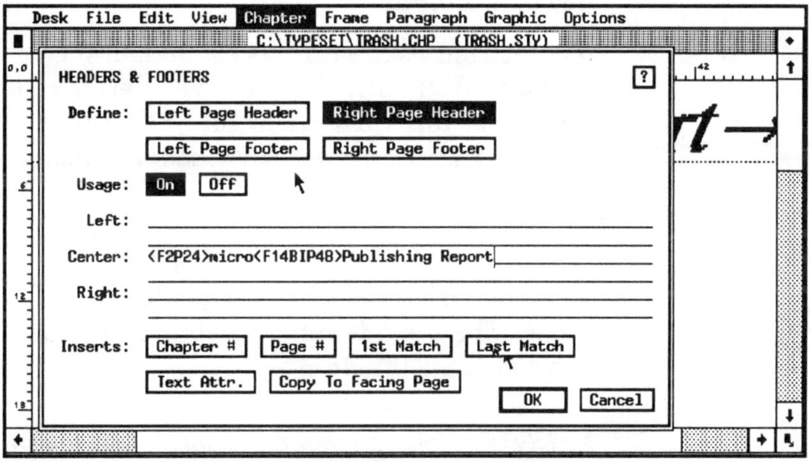

Figure 3-13. By entering bracket codes into the Headers & Footers dialog box, you can create complex formats like the one shown in Figure 3-14.

So much for the theory of bracket codes. Let's turn our attention to the four different effects they can achieve: text attributes, non-keyboard characters, formatting, and special functions.

Figure 3-14. The font change and base line jump shown here in the header were created with bracket codes.

Text attributes

Text attributes are the easiest and most common use of bracket codes. You turn them on with letter codes between angle brackets. You turn them off with the <D> code. Thus, to italicize the phrase *Xerox Ventura Publisher*, you would type:

```
Thus, to italicize the phrase <I>Xerox Ventura
Publisher<D>, you would type:
```

You saw earlier the nine attributes available in Ventura's Text mode. These same nine attributes can also be invoked with bracket codes (Table 3-5).

➥*NOTE: Your printer may not support all the effects. If you specify an effect that is not available, Ventura ignores it.*

Table 3-5. Bracket codes for text attributes.

Text Attribute	Bracket Code
Bold	<B>
Italic	<I>
Small	<S>
Superscript	<^>
Subscript	<V>
Underline	<U>
Double Underline	<=>
Strike-thru	<X>
Overscore	<O>
Medium weight (normal type)	<M>
Restore to default (stop)	<D>

You can combine attributes by putting multiple letters inside one set of brackets. For bold italic, type <BI>. Notice that combining only works if you put codes in one set of brackets. Ventura resets all attributes to default whenever it sees a new code. Thus, if you enter <B><I>, you will get italic only.

No matter how many text attributes you are using together, apply the <D> code once to turn them all off. Even if you do not type in the <D> code, Ventura automatically turns off all text attributes when it encounters a return.

You can also enter most text attributes with the native word processing commands. Why would you use bracket codes then? First, some effects are only available as bracket codes (or within Ventura). Second, bracket codes make it easier to transfer files between formats and systems. Third, you should always use bracket codes if you plan to use ASCII format. Otherwise you will lose attributes when you convert to ASCII.

Entering non-keyboard characters in advance

Earlier in this chapter, we explained non-keyboard characters and their importance. To enter a non-keyboard character into a text file, type its decimal equivalent inside angle brackets.

For instance, <193> denotes an ellipsis (...). To know which numbers to use, read the decimal equivalents listed in Table 3-4 earlier in this chapter. Table 3-4 shows the most commonly used symbols. You can find additional decimal equivalents in the character set appendix of the Ventura documentation. Ventura also supports some characters that do not appear on the character set chart. You can enter these characters with the bracket codes shown in Table 3-6.

Table 3-6. Special bracket codes.

Special Character	Bracket Code
Discretionary hyphen	<->
Filled box	<$B1>
Hollow box	<$B0>
Fraction	<$Enumerator/denominator>
Line break	<R>
Em space	<_>
En space	<~>
Figure space	<+>
Non-breaking space	<N>
Thin space	<|>

Entering formatting codes in advance

In the introduction to this section, we said we would talk about four ways to use bracket codes. So far we've seen how to use them for text attributes and for non-keyboard characters. Bracket codes can also contain formatting codes:

- size changes
- font changes
- color changes
- kerning and tracking changes (space between letters)
- base line jumps (shift text up and down)

Formatting codes consist of a single letter followed by numbers. The letter tells Ventura *what* to do; the numbers tell it *how*. For instance, consider the bracket code <P12>. The letter *P* tells Ventura to change the point size. The number *12* tells it how much — in this case, to 12-point type. Table 3-7 summarizes the bracket codes for all five formatting options. The lowercase *n* stands for the number you enter.

Table 3-7. Formatting options with bracket codes.

Formatting option	Bracket code to start	Bracket code to stop (reset to default)
Change point size	<Pn>	<P255>
Change font	<Fn>	<F255>
Change color	<Cn>	<C255>
Change kerning or tracking	<B%n>	<D%0>
Jump from base line	<Jn>	<J0>

Changing point size with bracket codes

To change the size of type within a paragraph, use the code letter *P*, followed by the point size. To change to 14 point, type <P14>. To return to the previous size, type <P255>. Use this bracket code only to enlarge a few words within a paragraph — like this, for example. To change the entire paragraph, use Font from the Paragraph menu.

Changing fonts with bracket codes

If you are a Ventura newcomer, work with fonts in the program until you gain an understanding of typefaces and point sizes. Once you are familiar with typographical terminology, you can insert font changes in advance with bracket codes.

Often, authors need a certain typographic effect within a line — a special font, for example, or a symbol. It may be easier for them to insert the code while typing the manuscript than to make a note to the editor. You may also need to use bracket codes for font changes within Ventura. For example, many designers like to have the page number larger than the rest of the header or footer. You can accomplish this effect by entering a bracket code in the Headers & Footers dialog box.

To change fonts, use the bracket code *F* followed by the ID number of the font. For example, <F1> tells Ventura to switch to the Courier font and <F128> to switch to the Symbol font. Table 3-8 lists fonts alphabetically with their number codes.

Table 3-8. Font ID numbers. The most popular fonts are shown in uppercase bold

FONT	ID NUMBER	FONT	ID NUMBER
American Typewriter	100	**HELVETICA NARROW**	50
AVANT GARDE	51	Korinna	53
Benguiat	26	Letter Gothic	105
Bodoni	36	Lubalin Graph	24
Bodoni Poster	37	Machine	101
BOOKMAN	23	Melior	31
Century Old Style	38	New Baskerville	33
Cheltenham	39	**NEW CENTURY SCHOOLBOOK**	20
COURIER	1	Orator	104
Courier Oblique	102	Optima	52
Franklin Gothic	56	**PALATINO**	21
Friz Quadrata	28	Park Avenue	35
Galliard	32	Prestige Elite	103
Garamond	22	Souvenir	25
Glypha	27	Sonata	130
Goudy	34	**SYMBOL**	128
HELVETICA (Swiss)	2	**TIMES** (Dutch)	14
Helvetica Black	55	Trump Mediaeval	30
Helvetica Condensed	59	**ZAPF CHANCERY**	29
Helvetica Condensed Black	60	**ZAPF DINGBATS**	129
Helvetica Condensed Light	58	**RESET TO DEFAULT FONT**	255
Helvetica Light	54		

Ventura continues with the new font until it sees another bracket code, a return, or the special code <F255>, which resets to the original font.

As with all bracket codes, font and point changes can be combined. Thus, <F51P24> changes to 24-point Avant Garde. You can also use a font change to switch to Symbol or Dingbat and thereby enter a special symbol in the middle of a text line. Here's how you would enter the alpha character in a text file:

```
The symbol <F128>a<F255> stands for alpha.
```

And here's what it would look like in Ventura:

The symbol α stands for alpha.

Changing colors with bracket codes

Ventura can support colored type for color output devices. Of more practical value, it can create a separate overlay for each spot color, which you can take to a print shop for color printing. Normally, you change colors for an entire paragraph. Nevertheless, if you want to change colors within a paragraph, you can do so with bracket codes in the text file. Use the letter C for the bracket code. Enter a number from zero to seven to specify which color you want (Table 3-9). Enter <C255> to end the change and return to the previous color.

Table 3-9. Bracket codes for color changes.

Color	Bracket Code
White	<C0>
Black	<C1>
Red	<C2>
Green	<C3>
Blue	<C4>
Cyan	<C5>
Yellow	<C6>
Magenta	<C7>
Reset to previous color	<C255>

Changing kerning and tracking with bracket codes

Ventura uses *kerning* and *tracking* to refer to the spacing between letters. You can change these attributes for an entire tag (in Paragraph mode) or for individual groups of letters (in Text mode). You can also enter individual kerning and tracking with bracket codes. Use the two-character code B%, followed by a number that represents the number of ems. Use negative numbers to subtract space. Use positive numbers to add space. Type <D%0> to mark the end of the text to be kerned. If you are not familiar with tracking and kerning as implemented in Ventura, turn to Chapter Eight, "Advanced Functions."

Base line jumps with bracket codes

The base line is the imaginary line on which type rests. A base line jump, therefore, shifts a character up or down from its normal position. A common use of base line jumps is to reposition the page number in headers and footers. Within Ventura, you access this function with the Shift line in the Font dialog box. It is only active if you enter the dialog box in Text mode.

The code letter for a base line jump is J. The numbers that follow tell Ventura how far to jump. For instance, <J231> tells Ventura to shift up six points. To end the effect and return to the previous base line, enter <J0>.

The formula for calculating jumps is a bit complicated, so we have included a chart (Table 3-10) that gives you some common jumps. For jumps not shown here, you can experiment with the Font dialog box, and return to the text file to see what Ventura has entered. Or you can use the following formulas, where N represents the number to use in the bracket code and P represents the amount you want to jump in points. For positive jumps (shifting above the base line):

```
N = 256 - (300/72 x P)
```

For negative jumps (shifting below the base line):

```
N = 300/72 x P
```

Table 3-10. Bracket codes for baseline jumps.

Amount to shift	Bracket Code	Result
Up 1 point	<J252>	Normal Text Shifted Text
Up 2 points	<J248>	Normal Text Shifted Text
Up 3 points	<J244>	Normal Text Shifted Text
Up 4 points	<J239>	Normal Text Shifted Text
Up 5 points	<J235>	Normal Text Shifted Text
Up 6 points	<J231>	Normal Text Shifted Text
Down 1 point	<J4>	Normal Text Shifted Text
Down 2 points	<J8>	Normal Text Shifted Text
Down 3 points	<J12>	Normal Text Shifted Text
Down 4 points	<J17>	Normal Text Shifted Text
Down 5 points	<J21>	Normal Text Shifted Text
Down 6 points	<J25>	Normal Text Shifted Text
Reset to original base line	<J0>	Normal Text Shifted Text

Entering special functions in advance

We are near the end of our section on bracket codes. We have already seen how to insert attributes, non-keyboard characters, and formatting options. Ventura also uses bracket codes for several special functions:

- Footnotes
- Indexing
- Frame anchors

- Hidden text
- Numbering
- Fractions

You can access all these functions within Ventura, and that's our recommendation for beginners. If you are an experienced user who wants to preformat these functions in the text file, the following section will show you how.

Entering footnotes with bracket codes

Chapter Eight, "Advanced Functions," explains how to insert footnotes within Ventura. However, some authors prefer to type in the reference as they create the text. This is generally more convenient than saving the reference information on paper to be typed in later. If you preformat footnotes as explained in this section, Ventura will take care of placing the actual reference on the correct page and in the correct format. Even though the bracket code sits within the main text, the words inside the brackets appear at the bottom of the page.

The bracket code for footnotes is $F, followed by the text you want to appear at the bottom of the page. Place the bracket code in the main text, immediately following the word that is to receive the footnote symbol. For instance, to insert a bibliographic footnote reference to this book, you would type something similar to:

```
<$FCavuoto, James, and Berst, Jesse. 1990. <I>In-
side Xerox Ventura Publisher<D>. Torrance, CA:
Micro Publishing.>
```

The example above uses bracket codes to italicize the book title.

Indexing with bracket codes

If you are not familiar with Ventura's indexing function, review Chapter Eight, "Advanced Functions," before reading the discussion below. As with footnotes, indexing can be accomplished within Ventura, but many users prefer to do it with the word processor. In Ventura, the index entry is invisible. You can see it only by bringing up a dialog box. By contrast, in a word processor, you can see all your index entries side-by-side, making it easier to figure out if you've left anything out.

The bracket code for indexes is similar to that for footnotes, but slightly more complicated. Ventura's indexes can have two levels plus See Also references, as shown below:

Text	
creation	123
editing	115, 125-128
See also Word Processing	

In this example, "Text" is a *primary* entry, "creation" and "editing" are *secondary* entries and "See also Word Processing" is a *See Also* reference.

The bracket code is $I followed by the primary reference and the secondary reference, separated by a semicolon. There are no spaces within the brackets. Thus, in the example above, you'd find the following bracket code at the spot corresponding to page 123 in the final document:

```
<$IText;creation>.
```

The bracket code for See references is $S; for See Also references $A. Thus, the bracket code for the See Also reference in the example above would look like this:

```
<$AText;Word Processing>.
```

Finally, Ventura's indexing function also handles words that must be listed out of normal alphabetic order. You would not, for instance, want to find "The Acme Company" listed under the letter *T*. Instead, it belongs under the letter *A*. Ventura permits you to enter a different sorting criteria. This alphabetizing information is listed inside square brackets. For example, the bracket code <$IThe Acme Company[Acme Company]> creates a primary entry printed as "The Acme Company" but alphabetized as "Acme Company." You can enter alphabetizing information for the primary entry, the secondary entry, or both.

You can put index entries anywhere in the text file *except* in front of a tag name. Tags must always be the first thing in the left column. In practice, however, it is usually best to group index entries together. Otherwise, they interrupt the flow and make it very difficult to read the file in the word processor. Many users group all index entries at the beginning or end of the paragraph.

Anchoring frames with bracket codes

If you are new to Ventura, review the discussion on frame anchoring in Chapter Six, "Building the Chapter," before reading this section. Ventura gives you a way to link pictures to text. Anchoring involves two steps, which can be done in either order. One step is to give the picture an *anchor name*. The other step is to mark where you want it in the text with an *anchor reference*. The anchor reference can be added within Ventura, or within the word processor with bracket codes.

The bracket codes for an anchor reference are the two symbols $&, followed by the anchor name. Thus, to anchor a picture called *barchart*, type <$&barchart>. Here's how it might look within the word processor.

```
As you can see in the nearby chart,<$&barchart>
revenues have increased substantially in the
fourth quarter.
```

You can also append an extra code that tells Ventura where you want the picture to appear. An anchor without an extra code causes the picture to move to the same page as the reference, (in the same relative position it had before it was moved). You can also select above, below, or floating anchors (Table 3-11).

Table 3-11. Bracket codes for anchors.

Type of Anchor	Bracket Code
Same page as reference	<$&anchorname>
Above the reference	<$&anchorname[^]>
Below the reference	<$&anchorname[v]>
Floating	<$&anchorname[-]>

Entering hidden text with bracket codes

Bracket codes can also create nonprinting remarks. These remarks show in the word processor. They do not display or print in Ventura. They are useful for including editorial comments. For example, authors might use hidden text to remind themselves which illustration to use. Editors might make editing comments, or track the revisions with hidden text. Or they might include instructions to authors or data entry operators. Those instructions would appear on the word processing screen, but they would be invisible in the Ventura document. The code symbols for hidden text are $!. Thus, to place the hidden remark "Use the sales chart to illustrate this point" into a word processing file you would type <$!Use the sales chart to illustrate this point>.

Numbering with bracket codes

Ventura lets you place the chapter or page number anywhere on a page. To put this referencing feature directly into a text file, use the code $R, followed by the type of reference in square brackets. To reference a chapter number, type <$R[C#]>. To reference a page number, type <$R[P#]>.

Entering fractions with bracket codes

You can enter fractions with bracket codes. The code symbols are $E. You type these symbols inside the brackets, followed by *n/d*, where *n* is the numerator of the fraction and *d* is the denominator. Thus, to enter the fraction ½, you would type <$E1/2> into the word processing file.

Tips on preformatting files

At first glance, preformatting might seem like a tedious process. In fact, it can be a powerful and workable technique. What's more, there are several techniques that make it faster and simpler.

TIP *A macro facility* is the best answer. You'll find some type of macro program almost essential to effectively enter footnotes and indexes directly into text files. It is cumbersome and time-consuming to repeatedly type brackets and dollar signs. If your word processor doesn't have an adequate macro capability, supplement it with one of the standalone utilities on the market.

TIP *You might also try search and replace.* Ask authors to enter special symbols in place of the codes. At the end of the writing session, they can use the search and replace function to insert bracket codes in place of the symbols. This process can be automated using a keyboard macro program.

TIP *Consider templates for your word processor* for certain structured documents. The first step is to create a raw text file and bring it into Ventura Publisher. Experiment with layout and formatting until it looks perfect. Now save the chapter.

Saving the chapter automatically saves the word processing files. But now the file contains the tag names, text attributes, and formatting codes created by Ventura Publisher. To create a document template, delete the text, but leave the tags and codes intact. The next time you create a similar document, call up the blank file and type in the new text.

To make it easier for users to remember what goes where, replace the deleted text with instructions — "Type name here" or "Place part description here," for example. If you use Ventura's hidden text feature, the instructions will show in the word processor, but not in the Ventura document.

This concept works well for short, fill-in-the-blank type documents like memos and forms. It can also be valuable for applications where authors must follow rigid specifications. Technical and military documentation, for example, often uses a highly structured approach.

When to preformat files

When should you consider preformatting text files? We suggest that you start with the standard method until you've learned Ventura. Create raw text in your word processor, and do the formatting in Ventura Publisher. Stick with the basic approach until you've defined standard formats and tag names. Once you've formed some standards, consider preformatting. It offers several advantages. It saves layout time since the editor doesn't have to tag every single paragraph. Yet it doesn't add significantly to authors' time if they use keyboard macros or templates. There's less room for error when authors insert tags and attributes themselves.

Still, it is not necessary to preformat files. You may prefer to do all your formatting inside Ventura. There's no need to decide immediately. You can switch over at any time.

That's one of the great things about Xerox Ventura Publisher — it gives you choices. In this chapter, we learned about its alternatives for creating text. In the next chapter, we'll discuss Ventura's wide range of choices for creating pictures.

Chapter Four

Creating Pictures

We saw Ventura's versatile approach to text in the previous chapter. You can create files with almost any word processor, then load those files into a document. Ventura's approach to pictures is similar. You can create pictures with your favorite program, then place the resulting files into a Ventura document.

This chapter concerns only the *creation* of pictures. (To learn how to integrate pictures into a document, turn to Chapter Six, "Building the Chapter.") To help you produce outstanding illustrations for Ventura, we will explore four key ideas:

1. the Ventura approach to pictures

2. how to create line-art pictures

3. how to create image pictures

4. how to work with Ventura's Graphic mode

Throughout this chapter, we use *pictures* to refer to any visual. Some of you may be more familiar with expressions such as *images, art*, or *graphics.* We have avoided using those terms generically because Ventura has very specific meanings for them, as you will learn below.

The Ventura approach to pictures

Before you create any pictures for Ventura, you should understand (1) the two kinds of pictures Ventura will accept and (2) how Ventura handles different file formats. With this information, you can choose which program to use, which type of picture to create, and which file format to specify.

As with text, Ventura Publisher deals with the original file from the outside program. But Ventura *does not change or modify picture files*, no matter what you do with the picture after bringing it in. Rather, Ventura uses the chapter file to store a *pointer* to the original file, with instructions on how to display it. This approach allows you to revise a picture *after* using it in a Ventura document. The next time you access or print that document, the new, updated picture will automatically be included, in the correct location and in the correct size.

Consider, for example, corporate editors responsible for a quarterly financial summary. Now they can include bar charts in the first draft, even if based on preliminary data. When the final quarterly results come in, the bar charts will change. The Ventura financial document will automatically be updated, since it merely points to the file containing those charts.

We'd like to emphasize this flexibility in using art from other programs. You can, for example, incorporate graphs from Lotus 1-2-3 or technical drawings from AutoCAD with complete assurance that those important files will not be modified. This holds true even if you use Ventura's Graphic mode to add to the pictures after you bring them into the document.

So far, so good. There is one shortcoming, however. Ventura cannot copy, rename, or change the format of picture files. To accomplish these functions, you must exit Ventura and use DOS. Or you must use an add-in utility program. (By contrast, Rename Text/File from the Edit menu lets you change the name, location, and format of text files.)

Two kinds of pictures

Ventura works with two kinds of pictures: line-art and images. You can mix and match both kinds in one document. Let's clearly distinguish between them, since Ventura requires you to know the difference. Before you can load a picture file, you must specify in the Load Text/Picture dialog box whether it is line-art or image (see Figure 4-1).

When Ventura Publisher uses the term *line-art*, it is referring to what the rest of the world calls *object-oriented graphics* or *vector graphics*. Since many programs that generate object-

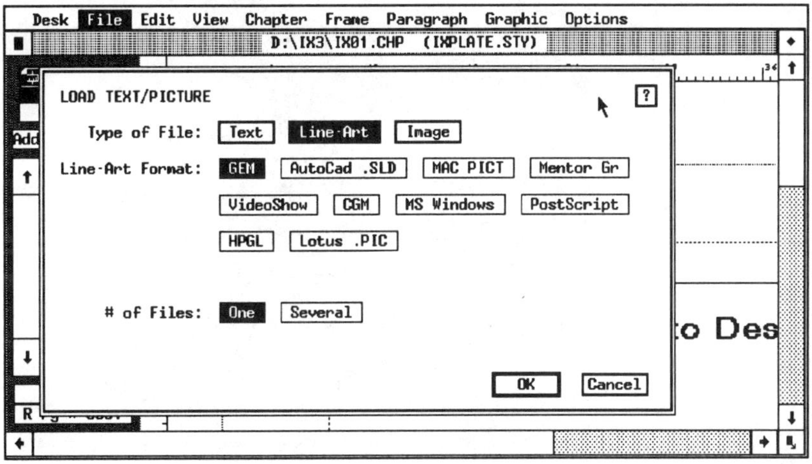

Figure 4-1. The Load Text/Picture dialog box. To load a picture file, you must first tell Ventura whether it is line-art or image.

oriented graphics contain the word "Draw" in their names, they sometimes go by the nickname of *draw programs.*

An object-oriented program creates a mathematical description of a picture. To draw a circle, for instance, it sends a mathematical expression that translates into a circle on the screen. These programs define pictures in geometric terms; each picture is a compilation of lines, circles, squares, and other elementary objects (hence, *object-oriented*).

Contrast this with the second type of picture: *images.* Images come from *bitmap graphics programs,* also known as *pixel-oriented programs.* The words *bit* and *pixel* refer to the individual dots on the computer screen. Since many of the product names contain the word "Paint," they are nicknamed *paint programs.*

To understand bitmapped pictures, consider the card sections that are often part of football halftime shows. Each person in the section holds a card. One side of the card is dark; the other is light. These sections can make patterns to create pictures. Your computer screen is like a miniature card section. To create an image, a bitmap program simply tells some dots to turn on, and others to turn off, just the way the halftime director tells some cardholders to show the light side and others to hold up the dark side (see Figure 4-2). The program creates a *map* showing which bits should be on and which

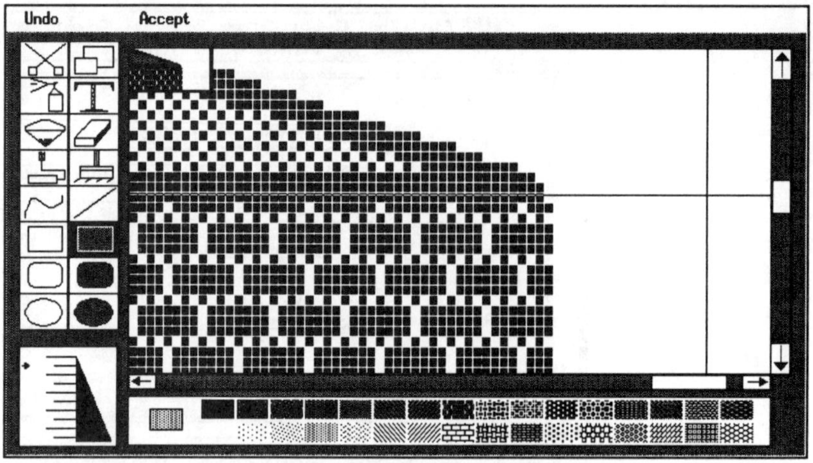

Figure 4-2. As you can see in this sample image from PC Paintbrush, a bit-map program constructs lines and curves by connecting individual pixels.

should be off (hence *bitmap*). To get a hard copy of this image, the program sends the same pattern of dots to the printer.

And therein lies a crucial distinction between line-art and images. When printing, most bitmap programs send *the pattern of dots from the screen*. If the screen image has a resolution of 72 dots per inch (dpi) then the printed image will have an effective resolution of only 72 dpi, even if the printer is capable of better.

At print time we see the vital difference between the two kinds of pictures. When an object-oriented program sends a circle to the printer, it sends the mathematical description. That description translates into the full resolution of the printer. If we send the circle to a typesetter, it prints at 1000 dpi (or higher) and looks even smoother. Object-oriented programs are not limited by the poor resolution of computer screens.

Choosing between line-art and images

Line-art and image art both have their pros and cons. In general, line-art is best for demanding applications such as technical illustrations, and when the picture will be printed at high resolution. Images are suitable for informal applications that do not require the ultimate in accuracy or resolution.

Pros and cons of line-art

Charts, graphs, and other illustrations are an integral part of most corporate publications. Whether you're producing schematics for a technical manual, organizational charts for a departmental brochure, or blueprints for an engineering proposal, the art is often as important as the text. Object-oriented programs such as GEM Draw and AutoCAD are ideal for such illustrations. As noted above, the picture prints at the full resolution of the output device.

And there is a second advantage to line-art: It can be changed in size without any penalty in quality. This advantage allows you to create pictures without regard for the size they'll be on the page. For example, many people produce layouts by allocating text columns and leaving holes for the pictures. Since the size of the hole depends on how much text is on each page, you need the ability to change the picture to fit. The ability to change size — called *scaling* — makes life much easier than if you must worry about drawing the picture to fit the available space.

On the downside, object-oriented programs lack the flexibility of freeform paint programs. Since each image must be constructed from geometric primitives, it is more difficult to touch up a picture by adding or erasing a small portion. Draw programs are usually more expensive and more difficult to use than paint programs.

Appropriate uses for line-art include technical illustrations, diagrams, schematics, charts, and graphs (see Figure 4-3).

Pros and cons of images

Images are created by bitmap programs, which emphasize flexibility and spontaneity. They can create brush strokes, spray paint, air brush, and other effects that simulate hand sketching. One important feature is the ability to edit individual pixels by zooming in on a portion of the image. Such detailed touch-up work is important to many creative designers. In addition, paint programs are often less expensive and easier to learn than line-art programs.

Low resolution is the major disadvantage of the image format.

Figure 4-3. The line-art format is ideal for applications that demand fine detail and accuracy. This illustration was created with GEM Artline.

It is most appropriate to simulate a spontaneous sketch, to import screen captures, or to bring in scanned photographs (see Figure 4-4).

Figure 4-4. The image format is best suited to friendly, informal sketches. This image was created with MacPaint.

File formats

To this point, we've concentrated on the difference between line-art and images. To create pictures, you also should understand how Ventura works with different file formats. There is no point in creating a beautiful drawing if you can't bring it into your document. This section explains why (and how) to choose or convert to a Ventura-compatible format.

Computer users can choose from an astounding variety of graphics programs. Ventura supports many of them directly, as listed in Table 4-1.

Table 4-1. Supported Graphic File Formats

Line-Art	Image
GEM Draw Lotus 1-2-3 AutoCAD Slide Mentor Graphics Macintosh PICT PostScript VideoShow CGM Windows metafiles HPGL	GEM Paint HALO DPE PC Paintbrush Macintosh MacPaint TIFF

Unfortunately, different programs use different formats. Ventura works directly with one line-art format (GEM Draw) and one image format (GEM Paint). When Ventura encounters others, it converts them first. This conversion has several tradeoffs:

- Sometimes Ventura creates a duplicate file in the converted format. File duplication takes up disk space. You must have enough room for both the original and the converted files — a potential problem for long books with many illustrations.
- The conversion may not be complete or accurate. Although Ventura does an amazing job of rendering different formats, it does not always provide 100 percent fidelity.
- Certain formats work only on certain printers (notably PostScript).

Working with unsupported formats

You are not limited to the file formats supported directly by Ventura. You also can use pictures in other formats, provided you convert them first. You have a variety of conversion options:

- use an option from the graphics program to save to a supported format
- print to a disk file
- use a screen capture program
- save to the Windows clipboard
- use a Ventura-supplied conversion utility
- use a commercial conversion program

➡*NOTE: If you have a choice, convert to GEM for line-art and IMG for images. These formats are easiest for Ventura to work with and do not require duplicate files.*

Let's examine each conversion option.

Save to a supported format

Many graphics programs with native file formats also can save or convert to other formats. Examine the documentation of the graphics program. Chances are it can optionally save to one of the formats Ventura understands. Using Table 4-2, see if the program can save or convert to any of the listed formats. When naming files, use the extensions shown on the chart to show what format it is in.

Table 4-2. Recommended extensions for picture files.

Type of File	Format	Extension
Line-Art	GEM	*.GEM
	AutoCAD Slide	*.SLD
	HPGL	*.HPG
	Mentor Graphics	*.P*
	PostScript	*.EPS
	Macintosh PICT	*.PCT
	VideoShow	*.PIC
	Computer Graphics Metafile	*.CGM
	Windows Metafile	*.WMF
	Lotus PIC	*.PIC
Image	PC Paintbrush	*.PCX
	GEM	*.IMG
	TIFF	*.TIF
	Macintosh Paint	*.PNT

➥ *Not only do standard extensions ease working in Ventura, they also make it possible to know the format of a picture just by looking at its extension.*

Ventura looks first for these extensions unless you tell it otherwise. If you do not use them, you may find it difficult to remember which pictures are in which format when you return to a document six months from now. Standard file extensions are essential in work groups, where different people must work with the same files.

Print to disk

You can get a compatible format by printing to a disk file. For instance, if the graphics application supports Hewlett-Packard pen plotters, you can create an HPGL file by specifying the plotter and printing to a file. Then you can bring the file into Ventura.

If the graphics program supports PostScript, you may be able to specify PostScript as the printer, then print to a disk file. You can then convert this file to Encapsulated PostScript (explained in more detail below). You do not have to own a PostScript printer to create a PostScript disk file. You can print to the disk file and send the file to another workstation or a service bureau equipped with a PostScript printer.

Use a screen capture program

If you have a screen capture program you can grab a snapshot of the picture on screen and save it to a file format supported by Ventura. This method has the disadvantage of creating an image at the resolution of the screen, even if the program can normally create line-art files. In addition, if the drawing is larger than the screen, you will get only the portion appearing on the screen. Unfortunately, few capture programs support big-screen monitors.

Save to the Windows clipboard

The DOS/GEM version of Ventura can import line-art from the Windows clipboard. To do so, however, you must first convert the clipboard and save it to a disk file using the program CLIP2VP.EXE provided on the Ventura utilities diskette. Windows users should follow this procedure:

- Copy the file CLIP2VP.EXE from the floppy diskette to the \WINDOWS directory on your hard disk.
- Start Microsoft Windows and run the program CLIP2VP from Windows.
- Shrink the CLIP2VP screen to icon size by clicking on the minimize icon.
- Run the Windows program and create the drawing.

- Select the desired portion of the drawing and copy it to the Windows clipboard.
- Click on the CLIP2VP icon to reopen its screen.
- Select the Save As... option from the Command menu. Type in the file name you wish to use. Ventura automatically adds the extension WMF.

Now close the Windows graphics program and run Ventura Publisher. Once in Ventura, load the graphic image into Ventura specifying MS Windows as the line-art format.

➥ *Note: Ventura Publisher can import only line-art metafiles, not Windows Paint or other Windows image formats.*

Use a Ventura conversion utility

The Ventura Utilities disk (#11) contains two conversion programs. After copying these utilities from the floppy to your hard disk, you invoke them from the DOS prompt.

AutoCAD DXF to GEM. DXF is a standard file format widely used in the computer-aided design field. The DXFTOGEM utility changes .DXF files to GEM Draw format (.GEM). This is not strictly required, since Ventura Publisher also supports AutoCAD via the HPGL, EPS, and SLD formats. We recommend HPGL and EPS as the most accurate ways to bring AutoCAD pictures into Ventura.

However, there may be occasions when you prefer the simplicity and ease of operation of GEM Draw Plus to the power and sophistication of AutoCAD. That's where the conversion utility comes into play. It permits you to bring an existing AutoCAD picture into GEM Draw for modification. At the DOS prompt, type the name of the conversion utility followed by the name of the AutoCAD DXF file you wish to convert. The utility will create a new file with the same name but the GEM extension. Thus, to convert SAMPLE.DXF, type:

```
DXFTOGEM SAMPLE.DXF
```

The utility creates a new file called SAMPLE.GEM.

Text screen to PC Paintbrush. You can capture a text screen of 25 lines or less using a separate utility (such as SideKick), then convert it to PC Paintbrush PCX format using Ventura's TXTTOPCX utility. By converting to PCX, you can capture lines and other screen effects not available if you bring the text in normally.

First capture the screen with a separate utility like SideKick or Hotshot (described below) and save it to a text file. At the DOS prompt, type the name of the utility followed by (1) the name of the file you wish to convert and (2) the type of display you are using. The formula is:

```
TXTTOPCX filename /display code.
```

The four display codes are:

A: AT&T or Xerox 6065

C: Enhanced Monitor (EGA)

M: Monochrome Monitor (EGA)

O: Color Monitor (EGA or CGA)

Thus, a user with a monochrome monitor and an EGA card would convert a text file called EXAMPLE.TXT by typing:

```
TXTTOPCX  EXAMPLE.TXT /M
```

Notice the space before and after the file name. The slash is a *front* slash (found below the question mark on most keyboards). The result is a file with the same name but the PCX extension — for instance, EXAMPLE.PCX in the sample shown above.

➥ *This conversion program does not work with the Hercules, VGA, or higher-resolution video modes. It does not convert reverse video and boldface text.*

Use a file converter

In addition to the conversion methods explained above, you also can buy commercial file converters from outside companies. Many of these programs handle other functions as well. For instance, HotShot Graphics not only converts files, it also edits graphics files, captures screens, and maintains picture libraries. Other popular file conversion programs include HiJaak, Pizaaz, Collage, and Graphics Link Plus. Professionals who use Ventura daily usually find a file conversion program essential. They often have many pictures from different sources in different formats.

Creating line-art

So far you've learned how Ventura distinguishes between line-art and images, and how to select (or convert to) the right file format. Now you're ready to get into more detail.

We will examine several leading packages. Graphics is a fast-growing and fast-moving software category. We can't hope to describe all the available software options here. But we can discuss a few of the favorites to give you a sense of the possibilities.

You bring in line-art files with Load Text/Picture from the File menu. Specify Type of File: Line-Art. Then click on the name of a program to specify the format. Chapter Six, "Building the Chapter" gives complete instructions on bringing pictures into Ventura documents. Ventura can use pictures from other programs provided they are converted to one of these formats.

What should you do if your graphics program can save files in more than one supported format? Experimentation will reveal which is best. As you will read below, most conversions have some limitations. By trying each format out, you can quickly learn which conversion produces the highest quality pictures. Results vary, but Encapsulated PostScript (EPS) is the most popular format for those with PostScript printers.

GEM Draw Plus

GEM Draw Plus is an easy-to-use graphics program for the IBM PC and compatibles. Like Ventura Publisher, it is built around the GEM environment from Digital Research, Inc. Since the interface is similar, most Ventura users will find they can learn GEM Draw quickly and easily (see Figure 4-5).

In addition, Ventura can load GEM Draw files directly, without conversion, saving time and disk space. GEM Draw Plus incorporates a toolbox for selecting boxes, lines, circles,

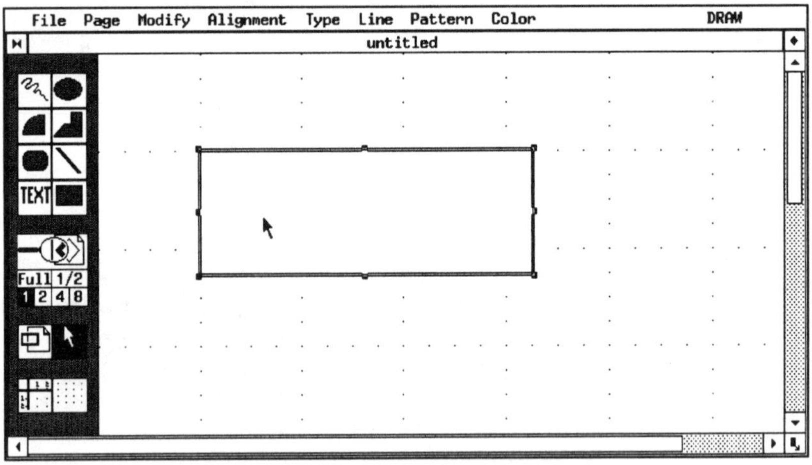

Figure 4-5. The GEM Draw interface will seem familiar to anyone who has used Ventura.

and freehand sketching. You point with the mouse to the desired tool, then position the cursor where you want to begin drawing. You drag the mouse to show the size of the object, such as the length of a line, the corners of a rectangle, or the radius of a circle. When you release the mouse button, the object appears on the page.

The program also features icons for fast and easy zooming to one portion of the page. With the touch of the mouse, you can move between five levels of magnification, plus a sixth view that reduces the full page to fit on screen. Use the panner icon to display different portions of the drawing by selecting the position of the screen window. Other features include on-screen rulers, a grid that can be either shown or hidden, and the ability to have multiple windows, each displaying a different drawing.

GEM Draw Plus can also add several different text fonts to a drawing. This is useful for annotating a diagram or filling boxes in an organizational chart.

GEM Artline

GEM Artline is an easy-to-use program for designer-quality graphics. Like GEM Draw Plus, it uses the same GEM interface as Ventura, giving it a comfortable look and feel. It offers the basic drawing and graphics tools, but it is best known for its ability to run on XT- and AT-class machines. (Many high-end programs suffer poor performance on anything less than a fast 386-based computer.) In addition, the program is rich in text-handling and font manipulation abilities. Artline can save files in GEM or EPS formats.

Corel Draw

Corel Draw is a marketplace favorite in the PC graphics category. It combines ease of use with powerful tools. It is notable for its rich variety of fonts and its text-handling capabilities, including special effects, text along a curve, fills, and rotation. It also includes the full complement of power tools for drawing, including autotracing, Bezier curves, pen shapes, clipping, and so on. It imports and exports the leading graphics file formats. Like other Windows-based products, Corel Draw can cause a few difficulties to users of GEM-based Ventura. In particular, it may be necessary to create two configuration files for your computer (two CONFIG.SYS files), one for Windows and one that has been optimized for Ventura.

Micrografx Designer

Designer is a Windows-based drawing and drafting program noted for its wide range of powerful tools and accurate dimensioning. It also includes autotracing, multiple layers, Bezier curves, text effects, and much more. It can import and export files in many of the leading formats, including EPS.

Lotus 1-2-3

The popular Lotus 1-2-3 spreadsheet program includes a graphics module to convert numbers into graphs and charts. Ventura Publisher adds to these capabilities by allowing you to integrate Lotus 1-2-3 graphs into your documents. This option will be particularly valuable to professionals who produce financial reports and summaries. They can continue to process their financial data in the spreadsheet, and then import a graphic representation for the final report.

To create a graph in Lotus, access the graph menu with the /G command. Select the desired options from the format submenu. Use Graph View to preview the chart and Graph Save to save it to a file with the PIC extension. You will not print the graph, since you can load the PIC file directly into Ventura (see Figure 4-6).

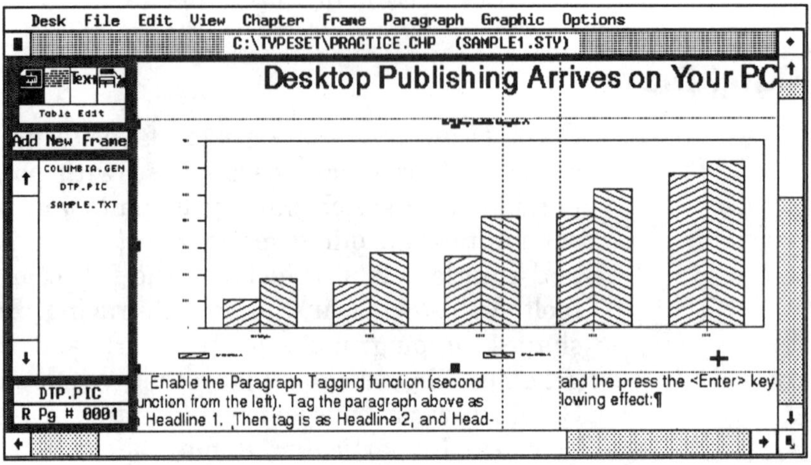

Figure 4-6. A typical Lotus chart after loading into Ventura. If you do not care for the Lotus labels shown here, you can replace them in Ventura.

➥*Notice: The base Version 3 can read PIC files but not WKS worksheet files. You must have the Professional Extension to bring in Lotus WKS worksheet files directly (see Chapter Eleven, "The Professional Extension").*

Tips for working with Lotus graphs

TIP *Touch up Lotus 1-2-3 graphs* with PC Paintbrush's Chart Interpreter module. First create a PIC file in Lotus. Call up PC Paintbrush and select Merge Pic from the page menu. PC Paintbrush will read the Lotus graph onto the screen, where you can edit and enhance it. The advantage to this approach is that Paintbrush offers a wider variety of fonts, patterns, and other effects. The disadvantage is that the resulting picture will be treated as an image rather than line-art. Normally, Lotus graphs are line-art. But once a Lotus graph has been brought into PC Paintbrush it must be loaded into Ventura Publisher as a bitmap PCX file.

TIP *If you change the values in the spreadsheet,* be sure to resave the graph file (PIC file). Otherwise, the old values will remain in the graph.

TIP *You can use Graphics Options (/GOT)* to produce titles and subtitles for your graph. However, these titles are line-art, giving you little control over size and placement. Many users prefer to leave off titles and labels and add them after loading the chart into Ventura. To remove the Y-axis labels, select Graph Options Scale Yscale Format Hidden. To remove X-axis labels, select Graph Reset X.

If you have fill patterns in your Lotus charts and graphs, you may want to preserve the Lotus legend boxes. Select Options Legend A and Options Legend B. You have several options for the labels on the legend boxes. You can insert them in Lotus and use the font that Ventura substitutes when it brings in the file. You can insert them in Lotus and then cover them up with better labels in Ventura. Or you can type in blank spaces in Lotus to create space between the boxes, then create the labels in Ventura.

TIP *If Lotus inserts unwanted labels and percentages* in the final chart, you can hide these labels after loading the chart into Ventura with an opaque white rectangle in Graphic mode. You can replace labels by inserting an opaque white Box Text (formatted the way you want) on top of the Lotus label. With PostScript printers, you must first cover the label with a rectangle, then put the Box Text on top of the rectangle. You may prefer to use this program to produce graphics from your spreadsheets. It can read Lotus WKS files directly.

TIP *Several other programs* can produce charts and graphs using data from Lotus 1-2-3. You can use any program that saves files in a Ventura-compatible format. Table 4-3 lists some of these programs and the file format you must use to bring images into Ventura. In general, modifying a chart and bringing it into Ventura involves the following steps:

- Create the spreadsheet in Lotus.
- Save the desired data range as a WKS, DIF, or SYLK file.
- Import the file into the graphics program.
- Format the graph.

- Save the graph in a Ventura-compatible format.
- Import the graph into Ventura using Load Text/Picture.

Table 4-3. Graphics formats of popular charting programs.

Program	Worksheets Read	Save Graphic As
Microsoft Excel (PC)	WKS	Windows Metafile
Microsoft Excel (Macintosh)	WKS, SYLK, DIF	Mac PICT
GEM Graph	WKS, DIF	GEM
Windows Graph	WKS, SYLK, DIF	Windows
Harvard Graphics	WKS	CGM
Freelance Plus	WKS	VideoShow
Perspective Jr	WKS	IMG

➥ *NOTE: This section has passed on tips for making use of Lotus pictures. For information on Lotus text (spreadsheets), turn to Chapter Three, "Creating Text," and Chapter Six, "Building the Chapter."*

AutoCAD

AutoCAD is the top-selling computer-aided design and drafting program. It can generate sophisticated product diagrams, blueprints, and building designs. Many architects, engineers, and designers use the program in place of manual drafting. AutoCAD images can be brought into Ventura Publisher in SLD format, DXF format, EPS format, or HPGL format.

To create slide files (SLD) in AutoCAD, you must have the ADE-2 Advanced Drafting Extension. Use the MSLIDE command. Give the file the SLD extension.

To use DXF files with Ventura, you must first perform the DXF to GEM conversion from DOS, as described earlier in this chapter. However, this conversion cannot successfully translate many important features, including text mirroring, text expansion, text obliquing, and 3D rendering.

For better results, use the HPGL method (Figure 4-7). After creating and saving the drawing, configure AutoCAD for the Hewlett-Packard 7586. Then plot the drawing to a file with the HPG extension. Load the resulting file into Ventura.

Figure 4-7. This chair was created in AutoCAD and output to an HPGL format file.

Tips for working with AutoCAD.

TIP *Get the orientation right in AutoCAD first,* before bringing line-art into Ventura. Many users will create AutoCAD drawings in landscape mode rather than portrait mode. Landscape offers a larger view of most floorplans and other designs. But unless you want a landscape orientation within the Ventura document, you must rotate the drawing 90 degrees before leaving AutoCAD. Ventura Publisher does not rotate pictures.

TIP *Draw pictures the same size or larger than the frame they will occupy.* After creating a drawing in AutoCAD, you will import it into Ventura and place it inside a frame. Be sure that your drawing is the same size or larger than the frame it will occupy. This prevents Ventura from stretching and distorting the drawing to make it fit the frame.

TIP *If you know the frame size in advance,* try creating drawings at exactly twice the size of the frame. Add borders and annotations (if any). Since the drawing is twice the intended size, make sure that annotations, text, symbols, and dimensions are twice the size you eventually want them to appear.

Mentor Graphics

Mentor Graphics manufactures a sophisticated computer-aided design system for engineering professionals. The company's software runs on Apollo workstations. Ventura Publisher supports the PicED format used by Mentor Graphics. In order to bring a Mentor Graphics image into Ventura Publisher, you must first transfer the PicED format file from the Apollo workstation to an IBM PC. Since PicED has ASCII characters, this is easy to do using telecommunications software.

Windows Metafiles

As a last resort, you can bring art from Windows-based programs into Ventura with the MS Windows option from the Load Text/Picture dialog box. However, if a Windows program supports any of the file formats listed previously in Table 4-1, save to that format instead, and bring the drawing into Ventura directly.

If you have no other option, you can bring in the drawing via the Windows Clipboard. To do so, you place the drawing on the clipboard, then use the Ventura-supplied CLIP2VP.EXE utility. This utility saves the clipboard to a disk file, which you can load into Ventura. This option has several limitations. First, you should use the Windows Metafile option as the Clipboard format if available. Second, Ventura cannot bring in Windows Paint or other image files, only Metafile line-art.

Encapsulated PostScript

Read this next section to learn how to create and work with Encapsulated PostScript pictures. This format will print only on PostScript machines. However, even if you don't have access to a PostScript printer, you may want to understand how to work with PostScript files. You may decide to make use of a

PostScript service bureau to produce high-quality output from Ventura.

Encapsulated PostScript format (EPS) is a standard file structure that permits different applications to share files. A graphics package can create a PostScript image and encapsulate it. You can then import it into a page layout program such as Ventura. Ventura doesn't interpret or modify Encapsulated PostScript files. It merely passes them through to the printer. The printer decodes the files and turns them into pictures.

EPS is a valuable method of incorporating detailed pictures into Ventura Publisher. An EPS file prints at the full resolution of the output device. With Encapsulated PostScript you can take full advantage of PostScript effects, including graded tints (fountains), rotation, text at any size, text along a curved path, and so on. Products such as Adobe Illustrator, Corel Draw, and Micrografx Designer create EPS files (Figure 4-8).

Figure 4-8. Corel Draw is one of the most popular draw programs on the market.

However, EPS has some drawbacks. First, you can print EPS pictures only with a PostScript-compatible printer. In addition, EPS files tend to be large. They hog valuable disk space and take a long time to print. Besides, EPS pictures show on screen only if they contain an embedded screen image, such as a TIFF file or Windows metafile. Otherwise, when you load an EPS picture into Ventura Publisher, a large X is placed on screen where the final image will appear. If there is an embedded screen image, non-PostScript printers can print it, although they cannot print the high-resolution PostScript file itself.

These limitations aside, EPS is a valuable graphics tool. Many graphics programs for the IBM PC and Apple Macintosh support Encapsulated PostScript. Many desktop scanners also can save in EPS format. And many clip art vendors sell high-quality EPS pictures.

Tips for working with Encapsulated PostScript

TIP *You can create PostScript files with Ventura.* Ventura can print to a disk file or to a printer (using the Set Printer Info option from the Options menu). This capability lets you use reduced-size versions of Ventura documents as illustrations. First you select PostScript as the printer type and print the page to a disk file. Then you load the disk file as PostScript format and put it into a frame. We discuss this procedure in greater detail in Chapter Seven, "Producing Output."

➥ *NOTE: PostScript files printed to disk with Ventura are not in true EPS format. Although they will print in Ventura, they must be altered before use in other programs. To alter them, you must insert the correct header information and delete any commands not supported by EPS, as described below.*

TIP *You can shorten the PostScript files created by Ventura* by temporarily renaming the PostScript prologue added by Ventura. This is an advanced technique. You must *not* use it if you plan to send your files to a printer or typesetter on a different system. However, if you plan to print the file with Ventura Publisher, you can eliminate about 20K of redundant information from each PostScript file. The simplest way to handle this chore is to build two batch files, one to remove the prolog and one to restore it. The PostScript prolog is contained in the file PS2.PRE in the \Ventura directory.

TIP *You can create and modify PostScript files* with a word processor. Although PostScript is a sophisticated programming language, you can perform many basic tasks without learning it all. Since PostScript files are pure ASCII text, you can use a word processor to create an EPS picture, provided you follow the PostScript guidelines.

Figure 4-9 shows an example of an EPS file with the required header information at the top of the file. This particular file creates a US Post Office regulation barcode for business reply envelopes (see Figure 4-10). You can duplicate this file by typing it into your word processor and saving it as ASCII format. To change the pattern of tall and short lines, substitute a different sequence of 1s and 0s on the line that begins with the word /code. A *1* creates a tall line. A *0* creates a short line.

```
%!PS-Adobe-1.0
%%Title: Ventura Publisher Document
%%Creator: Ventura Publisher
%%Pages: (atend)
%%BoundingBox: 0 0 324 45
%%EndComments
/inch {72 mul} def
/pitch .0476 inch def
/tall {0 .125 inch rlineto gsave stroke grestore pitch -.125
inch rmoveto} def
/short {0 .05 inch rlineto gsave stroke grestore pitch -.05
inch rmoveto} def
0 setgray
/code [1 1 0 1 0 0 1 1 0 0 0 0 1 0 1 0 1 1 0 0 0 0 0 1 1
0 1 0 1 0 0 1 0 1 0 0 1 1 0 0 0 0 0 1 0 1 0 0 1 1 0 1] def
40 18 moveto
code {
1 eq {tall} {short} ifelse
} forall
```

Figure 4-9. Typing this information as an ASCII file will create an EPSF file that produces a bar code for business reply mail.

Figure 4-10. The bar code printout that results from the EPSF file shown in Figure 4-9.

TIP *Of particular importance* in every EPS file is the header. These lines have nothing to do with the picture itself. They are there to tell Ventura (or another application) how to work with the code and pass it through to the printer.

The most important term is the *%%Bounding Box*. The four numbers that follow give the coordinates of the picture's size. They tell Ventura how much space to allow. By changing these coordinates you can alter the size of the picture, or change which portion of the picture will print.

The coordinates are specified in points. There are 72 points to an inch. When converting from inches to points, you must multiply by 72 *and then subtract one*, since PostScript uses zero as its beginning number (instead of one). Thus, to convert 8.5 in. to points, you would multiply by 72 and subtract one (612 – 1 = 611). PostScript's default mode begins measurements from the lower left corner, which therefore has an X,Y value of 0,0.

The first two numbers following *%%Bounding Box* describe the X,Y coordinates of the lower left corner. The second two numbers describe the X,Y coordinates of the upper right corner. From these two points, PostScript can calculate the size of the rectangle containing the picture. When you load an EPS image into Ventura Publisher, the rectangle with the large X has been specified by these coordinates.

TIP *You can change the size of the bounding box* with your word processor, thereby changing the size of the picture. You can also alter existing drawings, so that only a portion will print. Remember that the origin point (0,0) is the lower left corner. By *adding* numbers to the first two coordinates, you move the left corner up and to the right. By *subtracting* numbers from the second two coordinates you move the right corner down and to the left.

Let's assume for a moment that you have an existing Encapsulated PostScript file. Let's further assume that you don't want to print the outer two-inch margin. You could tell PostScript not to print this portion by *adding* two inches (144 points) to the first two coordinates of the bounding box and *subtracting* two inches from the last two coordinates. The effect, as shown in Figure 4-11, is to move the corners in, creating a two-inch, non-printing "margin."

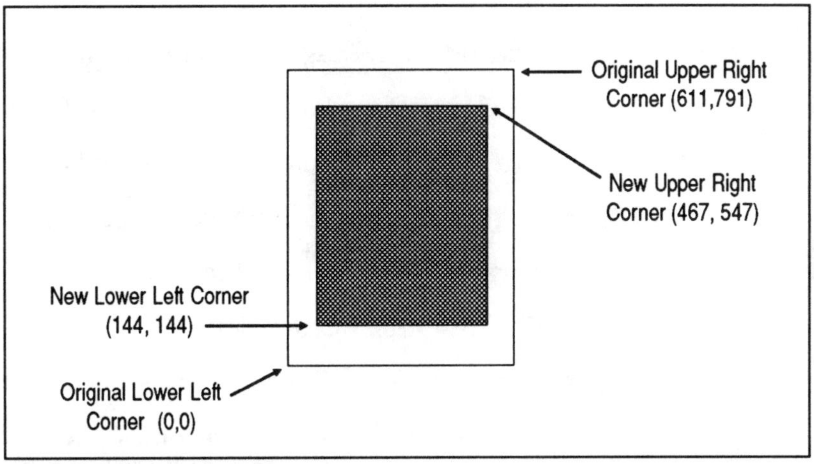

Figure 4-11. By changing the bounding box, you can control how much of an existing EPSF picture will actually print.

TIP *You can turn ordinary PostScript files into Encapsulated PostScript* with a word processor. If your graphics program can print a PostScript file to disk, you may be able to modify it quickly and simply with your word processor so it will be in the Encapsulated PostScript format required by Ventura.

For more information on PostScript programming, Encapsulated PostScript format, and PostScript reference materials, contact Adobe Systems, 1585 Charleston Rd., Mountain View, CA 94039.

VideoShow

VideoShow is a general-purpose graphics program from General Parametrics, Inc., originally developed for producing slide presentations with PC-generated pictures. Many other graphic programs, including Harvard Presentation Graphics and Lotus Freelance Plus, can save files in this format (Table 4-4). Ventura converts VideoShow files with certain limitations. It converts only seven-bit pictures. It does not convert eight-bit pictures, 3D bars, or color (which is turned into

Table 4-4. Partial listing of software packages supporting the VideoShow format.

- Autumn, Zenographics, Inc.
- Chart, Microsoft Corp.
- ChartMaster, DiagramMaster, & SignMaster, Ashton-Tate
- Freelance Plus, Lotus Development Corp.
- GraphWriter, Lotus Development Corp.
- Graphics Decision Support System, Data Business Vision
- Mirage, Zenographics, Inc.
- PC Presents!, Imedia Corp.
- PictureIt, General Parametrics Corp.
- PicturePak, Marketing Graphics, Inc.

shades of gray). It truncates polygons with more than 128 vertices.

HPGL

HPGL refers to Hewlett-Packard's Graphics Language for plotters and other vector-oriented devices. (This is different from the PCL language that resides in the LaserJet and LaserJet Plus.) Most CAD and drawing programs support HPGL as a printing option, including AutoCAD, Microsoft Chart, and VersaCAD. To bring a picture into Ventura via HPGL, first print the picture to a disk file, then load the file into Ventura for conversion.

HPGL is an especially good choice for users of DOS Version 3, since the new version includes an enhanced HPGL conversion routine. This converter gives you lots of control over the final output. For instance, plotters use more than one kind of pen. With Ventura's converter, you can give each pen a different line width and color.

When you select an HPGL file from the Load Text/Picture dialog box, Ventura will present you with an additional dialog box that lets you select among several options. (Figure 4-12).

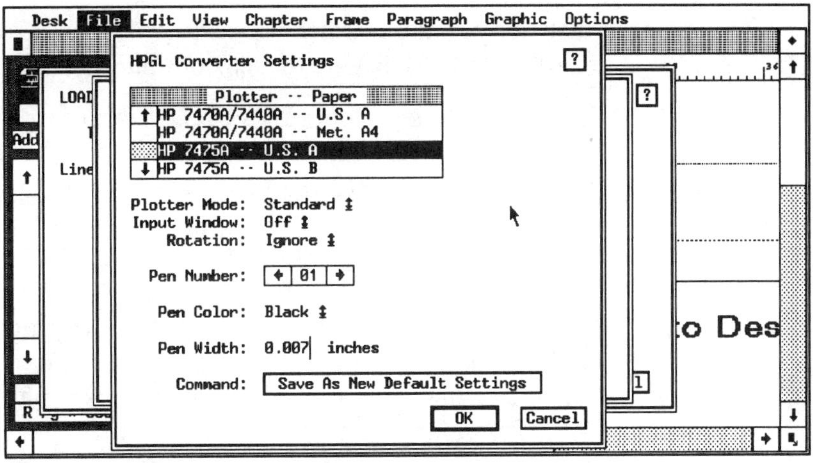

Figure 4-12. Selecting HPGL format gives you access to additional options that let you refine the quality of a line-art image.

However, HPGL has its drawbacks. For one thing, you must go through an extra dialog box to specify your settings when you load an HPGL file. Second, the conversions take longer. Ventura converts all the text in the HPGL file into *stroked fonts*. In other words, it does not substitute standard fonts. Instead, it treats each letter as if it were a tiny drawing.

Macintosh PICT

Macintosh PICT files are line-art created with programs such as MacDraw and MacDraft. DOS Version 3 now also supports the PICT2 format, which enhances the quality of images in several respects, including color. However, some of these applications have their own native file format, so be sure to specify PICT when saving the file.

To use these files with Ventura, you must first transfer them to your PC. Usually the easiest method is to use a telecommunications link between the two computers. You can purchase special programs and cables expressly for transferring files between Macs and PCs, or you can use standard telecommunications programs. If you work in an office with a network that supports both PCs and Macs, you can transfer files over the network. You can also purchase special disk drive units that can read both PC and Mac formats. When transferring files, be sure that the utility transfers only the *data fork*. Some utilities transfer the data fork and the resource fork into a single file, which Ventura cannot successfully convert.

Ventura converts fonts in a PICT file to Times Roman (Dutch) or Helvetica (Swiss). It cannot convert bitmap images embedded within a PICT file.

CGM

CGM format refers to the Computer Graphics Metafile standard devised by Graphic Software Systems and others. This format is used by a long list of software packages (see Table 4-5). It is also used by programs that generate statistics and graphs from mainframe databases. You can also purchase electronic clip art in CGM format. Ventura converts fonts in a CGM file to Helvetica (Swiss). Ventura converts color, but it cannot convert polygons with more than 128 vertices.

Tips for working with line-art programs

TIP *Annotate pictures in Ventura Publisher.* When possible, create callouts, captions, and labels with Ventura, not the graphics program. If you create text in the graphics program, the size may be inappropriate when you bring the picture into Ventura Publisher. For example, 8-point type in your diagram becomes 16-point type if you enlarge the picture by a factor of two. By creating the text in Ventura Publisher, you can enforce a consistent font and point size from picture to picture.

➥ *Note: One exception is rotated text, which can be useful to annotate graphs, vertical boxes, or tight spaces. Since Ventura Publisher has limitations on rotated text, you may prefer to create it in the graphics program, depending on the size and slant you need to achieve.*

TIP *You can convert bitmap images* to line-art using programs such as Streamline, Corel Draw, and others. These programs let you trace a bitmap image to convert it.

TIP *Make the picture as large* as practical in the graphics program so fine detail can be added. Then reduce the image to the correct size when it is brought into Ventura Publisher.

Table 4-5. Partial listing of software supporting CGM.

- Cadwrite, IBM
- DaVinci Business Graphics, Professional Research Consultants
- Display, ISSCO
- Freelance Plus, Lotus Development Corp.
- Graftime, Genigraphics Corp.
- Harvard Presentation Graphics, Software Publishing Corp.
- MathPlan 3.0, WordPerfect Corp.
- MicroCAD, Imagimedia Technologies
- pcExpress, Information Resources
- Personal Engineer, Computervision Corp.
- Redliner, AutoTrol Technology
- R:Base Graphics, Microrim Corp.
- SPD, Tektronix. Inc.
- TextCharts, Hewlett-Packard

Creating images

Ventura Publisher directly supports several image file formats. It can use images from other sources provided they are converted first. You bring in files from bitmap programs with Load Text/Picture from the File menu. Specify Type of File: Image. Then click on the name of a program to specify the image format. Chapter Six, "Building the Chapter," gives complete instructions on loading pictures.

GEM Paint

GEM Paint is a simple-to-use, pixel-oriented graphics program for the IBM PC. Like GEM Draw Plus and GEM Artline, it runs under the GEM environment. But GEM Paint has two important tools not found in GEM Draw Plus and Artline: the eraser and the microscope. The former lets you delete portions of a picture. The microscope magnifies an area of the picture, letting you fine-tune the image by turning individual pixels on or off. Another useful GEM Paint feature is the ability to invert a picture — change white to black like a photographic negative. You can also select a pattern to fill regions of the picture.

Ventura supports GEM Paint files (IMG) directly and does not need to convert them or create duplicate files.

PC Paintbrush

PC Paintbrush, from Z-Soft Inc., is one of the most popular graphics programs for the IBM PC. Unlike many paint programs, it allows editing of images at 300 dpi using a zoom-in mode. It also offers powerful tools and functions for creating detailed paintings. In addition to the ability to draw and fill rectangles, circles, and free-form lines, the program has several powerful tools, including a curve function.

In addition to supporting the original PC Paintbrush, Ventura Publisher can import images created with two enhanced versions, PC Paintbrush IV Plus and Publisher's Paintbrush. All three programs share the same user interface and most of the same commands. PC Paintbrush IV Plus offers the ability to bring in images directly from a scanner. Publisher's Paintbrush allows use of its graphics tools in a zoom-out mode that lets you see the full page as you work.

Ventura converts PCX files, but it does not convert color. You can also convert text to PCX format with the TXTTOPCX conversion utility described earlier in this chapter.

Macintosh Paint Images

Ventura can import images created on the Apple Macintosh computer. These include images created with MacPaint, SuperPaint, and similar programs. You must first convert the Mac file into IBM PC format. Programs such as MacLink and LapLink-Mac can transfer files between a Macintosh and PC using a serial cable. Networks such as TOPS and AppleShare allow PCs and Macintoshes to share files on a network, so that transferring files is as easy as a standard copy command. Finally, several companies manufacture disk drives for the Macintosh that can read and write IBM PC format. Ventura converts Macintosh Paint files. Pictures transfer as 8x10 in. pages, even if you want only a small section.

TIFF

Ventura supports the TIFF format, a popular image format used by many desktop scanners. TIFF is important because it is capable of storing gray-scale information. TIFF is discussed below under the section on scanners.

Tips for image programs

TIP *Produce bitmap pictures larger* than they will appear in the document. You can then reduce the image within Ventura with Sizing & Scaling from the Frame menu (see Chapter Six, "Building the Chapter"). Reducing the size of the image increases its apparent resolution. For example, if the screen has a resolution of 72 dots per inch the original picture will have a resolution of 72 dpi. But if you reduce that image to 50% of its original size, it will print with an effective resolution of 144 dpi. However, you must be careful to enlarge and reduce by an integer amount to avoid unsightly patterns.

TIP *Annotate images in Ventura Publisher* rather than in the paint program. Paint programs have poor font quality. If you must use paint fonts, look for a *stroke* font such as Roman in PC Paintbrush. These fonts scale better than bitmapped fonts. Stroke fonts can be readily identified by examining the name of the file holding the font. Stroke fonts do not contain the word *bit,* which is used to identify bitmapped fonts.

Creating images with scanners

Scanners are devices that examine pictures on paper to create an electronic description for use by a computer. In essence, they look at a picture and create a bitmap image of it. This image can be brought into Ventura Publisher just like the ones created by paint programs — but with certain advantages, as you will see.

To import a picture from a scanner, you must first convert it to one of Ventura's four image formats: GEM Paint (IMG), PC Paintbrush (PCX), Macintosh Paint (PNT), or TIFF (TIF). This conversion is handled by the software that accompanies the scanner. Many scanners on the market produce images in one of the supported formats.

Next you bring the image into Ventura Publisher just as you would bring in any other image file. Select Load Text/Picture from the File menu. Specify Type of File: Image. Then click on the format you are using (GEM Paint, PC Paintbrush, Macintosh Paint, or TIFF). Figure 4-13 shows a scanned image brought into Ventura Publisher from a Canon IX-12 scanner.

Figure 4-13. An image captured with a Canon IX-12 scanner using PC Paintbrush Plus.

Background on scanners

There are two types of scanners: flatbed and sheetfed. Flatbed scanners rest the paper face-down against a glass window, much like an office photocopier. Sheetfed scanners send pages through a slot and past the sensing element. The sensing element creates a bitmap description of the dark and white areas on the page.

Scanning characteristics affect the quality of the image:

- Resolution
- Gray scale
- Brightness
- Contrast

Resolution refers to dots per inch. The higher the resolution, the better the quality. However, high-resolution images take up more space on the disk and require more time to print on a laser printer. In practice, line drawings are less sensitive to resolution than photographs. You can achieve acceptable quality for drawings by scanning with resolutions as low as 100 dpi.

Gray scale is a measure of the different levels of gray (darkness) that make up an image. Line drawings require only two levels of gray — black and white. Each pixel is either on or off. Photographs, however, require at least 256 levels of gray for best quality.

Try examining a newspaper photograph with a magnifying glass. The photo is made up of rows of dots. Although equally spaced within each row, some dots are bigger than others. In dark regions the dots are large; in light regions they're small. The number of different sizes is a measure of the photo's different gray scales.

Interestingly, a typical newspaper or magazine photo is between 85 dpi and 133 dpi. Since both scanners and laser printers are capable of resolving 300 dpi or more, you might think that this is enough to produce magazine-quality photos. Unfortunately, this is not the case. Most laser printers cannot vary the size of the dots they print.

To get around this problem, manufacturers simulate the appearance of gray scale by grouping laser printer pixels into larger halftone *dots* or *cells*. This process, known as *dithering*, allows laser-printed photographs to show different levels of gray. For example, each halftone cell might consist of 16 pixels, four on each side (Figure 4-14). But if you use four pixels in each direction to represent one halftone dot, then you cut the effective resolution by four — from 300 dpi to 75 dpi, for instance.

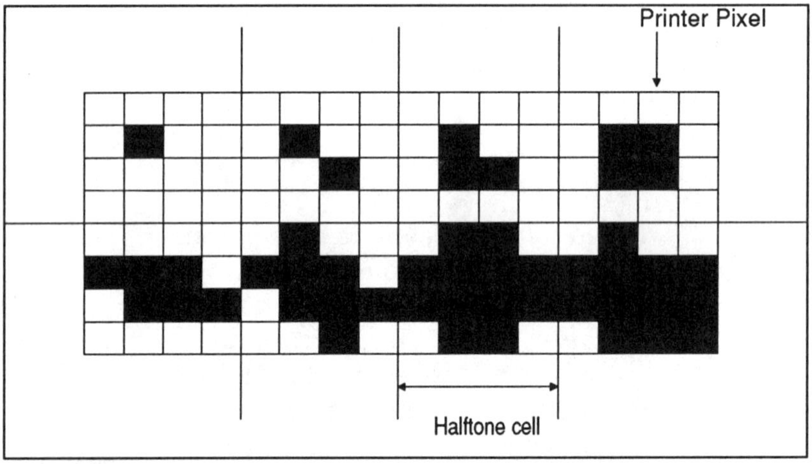

Figure 4-14. Dithering simulates gray levels by constructing halftone cells out of printer pixels. By darkening more or fewer pixels, the printer simulates bigger or smaller halftone dots.

Brightness refers to the overall lightness or darkness of the scanned image. Increasing the scanner's brightness setting is like turning on a brighter light when taking a photograph. If you set the brightness too high, you may wash out some of the detail. If you set it too low, you will get unrecognizable black spots.

Contrast indicates the variation in intensity — the difference between the darkest dark and the lightest light. Increasing or decreasing the scanner's contrast setting has the same effect as decreasing the contrast setting on a television set.

Working with TIFF files

TIFF, which stands for Tagged Image File Format, is a standard format for saving gray-scale photographic images. If given the choice, *always select this file format* when you are scanning photographic images. If you do, Ventura can optimize the image regardless of the output device. If your printer is a 300-dpi laser printer, TIFF files may not look much better than images in IMG or PCX format. But if you later send your document to a high-resolution typesetter, Ventura creates a superior halftone image with excellent quality.

There is another advantage to using TIFF format images with Ventura. When you place a TIFF image in a frame, Ventura enables the Image Settings option from the Frame menu. This option allows you to modify the appearance of the picture.

Tips for scanners

Keep these factors in mind when scanning artwork intended for Ventura Publisher.

TIP *Bringing in photographs* requires experimentation. The only way to arrive at the best parameters is to try different values for brightness, contrast, and gray scale and compare the results.

TIP *To find the best* brightness and contrast settings, start with the contrast at its highest value. Leave it there while you find the appropriate level of brightness. Start at a low brightness level and gradually increase it until the unwanted black areas disappear. Then, maintain this level of brightness and gradually reduce the contrast level until different regions of the image begin to blend in with one another.

TIP *Select only the portion* of the page you absolutely need. Although it is possible to crop an image within Ventura Publisher, you save both scanning time and disk storage space by keeping the image to a minimum.

TIP *To scan a small photograph* into a sheetfed scanner, tape it to a piece of paper. This makes it less likely to jam and allows more precision in selecting the region to be scanned.

TIP *Print scanned images at full size*, if possible. Although both your graphics program and Ventura Publisher can scale an image up or down, the quality may be decreased. If you must go up or down in size, use an integer multiple, such as 200 percent or 50 percent.

TIP *Scan line drawings at 150 dpi.* Since line drawings use only two shades of gray, little is gained by increasing the scan resolution to 300 dpi. A resolution of 150 dpi provides acceptable quality and cuts down on disk space by a factor of four. An exception to this is very fine line drawings, such as you might find on the back of a dollar bill. These fine images frequently need 300-dpi scanning to resolve the detail.

TIP *Consider bringing the scanned image into a graphics program* for touchup prior to importing it into Ventura. Even basic graphics programs allow you to remove backgrounds and lighten shadows by editing pixels. And some programs allow sophisticated retouching.

Screen capture utilities

It is often useful to incorporate a picture from a computer screen into a Ventura document:

- In software documentation, to show the reader a sample screen from the program
- To include a picture from a program not supported directly by Ventura
- To annotate an existing picture with descriptive labels

Many utility programs can help you incorporate screen images into documents. All of them create a bitmap image of the screen that can be loaded into Ventura Publisher like any other image file. A few utilities even let you save the screen in EPS format, for better resolution. And some of the programs include other useful functions, such as graphics editing or file conversion.

Some popular options include:

- Frieze, a support module for the PC Paintbrush graphics program
- HotShot Graphics, which can also edit, merge, and convert graphics files

- HiJaak, which also features powerful editing and conversion functions
- Collage
- Pizazz Plus
- Tiffany, a shareware utility available from many bulletin boards and on-line services, which captures Windows screens and saves them in TIFF format

Clip Art

An electronic clip art collection is a library of pictures on disk. The name comes from the days before graphics software. Companies would assemble catalogs of ready-to-use illustrations, and clients would clip out the ones they wanted. Today, clip art is also available as electronic files you can load into Ventura.

Even if you don't have the time and skill to create your own original art, you can add the power of pictures to your publications via professional clip art. Well-chosen images catch the reader's eye and establish the basic concept of the text. Some people associate clip art with low-quality, cartoon-style pictures. In reality, you can find a wide variety of top-notch business-oriented packages (see Figure 4-15). Some collections have pictures of people and objects; others include symbols, borders, maps, and chart elements.

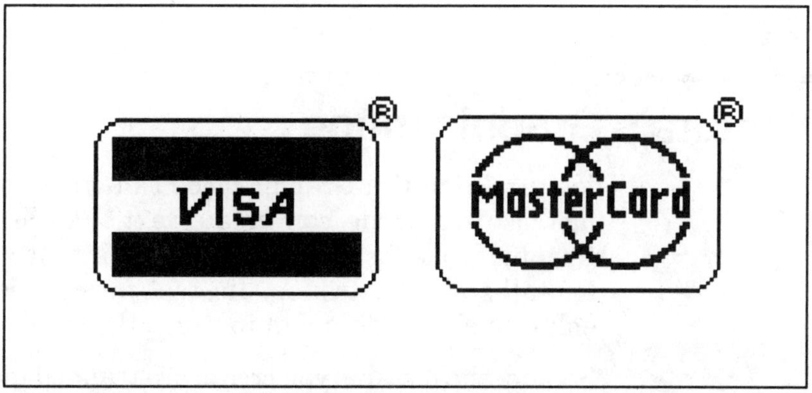

Figure 4-15. Clip art collections can provide useful business symbols and logos.

Tips for clip art

TIP *Try combining two images to produce a third.* Load each one into a frame, then put the frames on top of another.

TIP *To choose a clip art collection*, first consider the subjects you need to cover. You can find theme collections for most major business topics. On the other hand, if you use a wide range of pictures, you may prefer a generalized sampler.

TIP *Make sure the pictures come without copyright restrictions* so you can use and reuse them in your publications as you see fit.

TIP *Try to find collections in a line-art format.* As noted above, line art produces higher resolution and better quality. The exception to this general rule is if you are seeking the informality of paint-type pictures. In addition, several vendors offer paint format pictures that have been scanned at 300 dpi. On a 300 dpi laser printer, their quality rivals that of line art formats.

TIP *Consider how the clip art is presented.* If each picture is in a separate file, you can easily and quickly load the one you want. Some collections — especially paint format collections — put many pictures into one file. You must then crop out the unwanted images with Ventura or a separate graphics package before you can use it.

TIP *Evaluate the documentation.* A large collection is easier to use if every picture is printed and labeled in thumbnail size. That way you can quickly find the one you want. Some collections force you to load each picture in turn to see what it offers.

Ventura's Graphic mode

Ventura's built-in Graphic mode can create simple drawings, just as Text mode can create text. We do not recommend Graphic mode for serious drawing. First, it was not intended for full-scale illustration. Its real purpose is to annotate or enhance pictures brought in from other programs.

Second, the pictures you create are trapped inside the chapter. Ventura does not provide any way to save a picture created in

Graphic mode as a separate file. All the Ventura graphics in a chapter are stored in a single VGR file. You cannot load this file into a different chapter. One of the few options is to enlarge the picture to full-page size and print it to a PostScript file. You can also save the chapter under a new name, thereby creating a copy of the drawing in the new chapter. However, neither of these methods is very satisfactory. If you think you will want to use a picture in a different document, create it as a separate file with an outside graphics program.

Still, many people use Ventura's built-in drawing tools for simple illustrations. This section, therefore, explains the basic techniques for creating pictures with Graphic mode.

Graphic mode basics

Despite the limitations of Graphic mode, a skilled user can create complex technical illustrations by combining the basic shapes available in Ventura. Drawing inside Ventura is much easier if you understand the basics of Graphics mode, which lets you add three types of drawing elements:

- lines
- shapes
- Box Text

These elements are line-art, not images. They print at the full resolution of your printer. When you use Graphic mode, Ventura stores the resulting drawings in a separate file with the VGR extension. The file name is the same name as the chapter. Thus, Ventura stores drawings for a chapter called SAMPLE.CHP in a file called SAMPLE.VGR.

To do any drawing, you must first enter Graphic mode by clicking the right-most icon on the Function Selector (or by using the keyboard shortcut Ctrl-P). The Side-Bar changes to show icons representing the drawing tools. While in this mode, you can also create, select, resize, or move frames. However, you must enter Frame mode to cut, copy, or paste frames or load files into frames. To use a tool, first select the icon. The mouse cursor changes shape when you return to the workspace. The shape depends on the tool you select. Figure 4-16 shows the different shapes and their meanings.

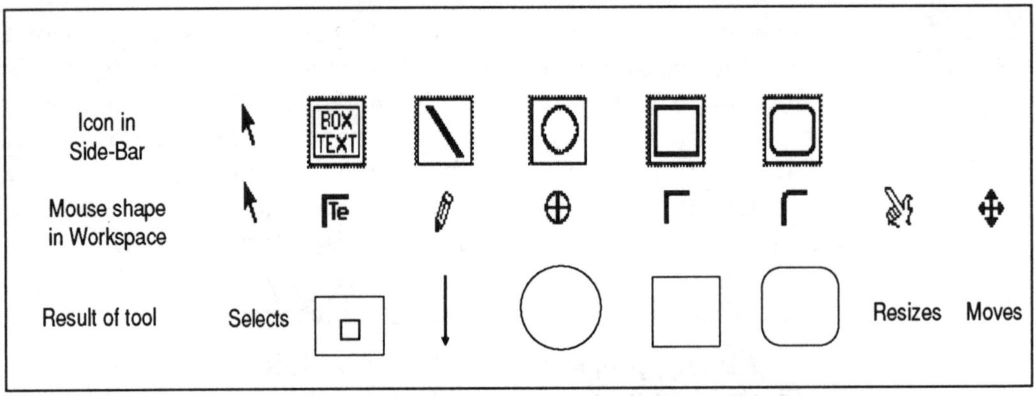

Figure 4-16. Side-Bar icons, cursor shapes, and their results in Graphic mode.

To draw, move the mouse to the beginning point. Press and hold the mouse button. While holding it down, drag the cursor to the end point. Release the mouse (Figure 4-17).

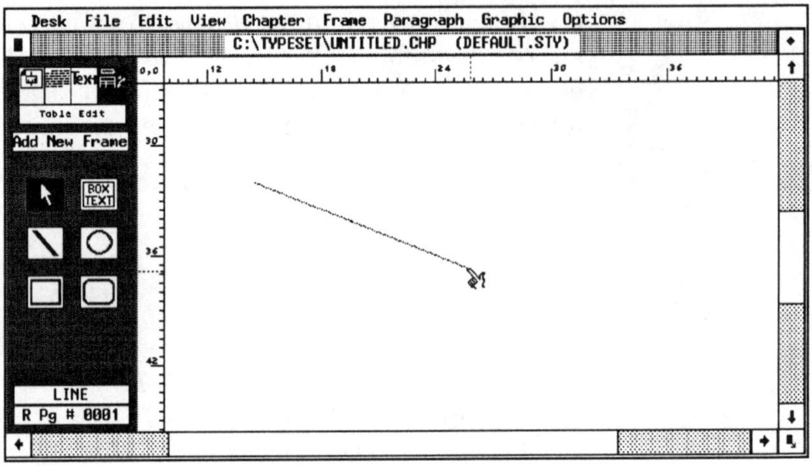

Figure 4-17. To draw a line, press and hold the mouse button at the beginning point. Then drag the mouse to the end point and release.

You will have an easier time in Graphics mode if you follow these three steps:

1. Select the parent frame.

2. Set up the grid.

3. Create and modify the graphic.

Selecting the parent frame

Every Ventura graphic is attached to a "parent," which can be a frame or a page. You have three choices:

1. You can attach a graphic to the current page, in which case it appears only on that page.

2. You can attach a graphic to all pages, in which case it appears on every page of the document.

3. You can attach a graphic to a separate frame that resides on top of the Underlying Page, in which case it appears wherever the frame appears. If you move the frame, the graphic moves with it. If you delete the frame, the graphic disappears. If you make the frame into a repeating frame, the graphic repeats with it.

It makes no difference if the parent frame is empty, contains text, or contains a picture. The parent is whatever frame was active just before you drew the graphic. To attach a graphic to the current page:

- Enable Graphic mode.
- Select the Underlying Page (click anywhere on the workspace). Gray handles appear around the edge of the page.
- Select the tool you want and draw. The graphic is now attached to the current page.

To attach a graphic to a frame:

- Enable Graphic mode.
- Select the frame (click anywhere on the workspace). Gray handles around the outside confirm your selection.
- Select the tool you want and draw. The graphic is now attached to the frame.

To attach a graphic to all pages:

- Enable Graphic mode.
- Select the Underlying Page.
- Draw the graphic.

- With the graphic still selected, choose Show On All Pages from the Graphic menu.

If you change your mind and want the graphic on one page only:

- Select the graphic.
- Choose Show On This Page from the Graphic menu.

If you accidentally attach a graphic to the wrong frame:

- Select the graphic and cut it (using Cut Graphic from the Edit menu or the Del key). This deletes the graphic and places a copy in temporary memory.
- Select the correct frame.
- Choose Paste Graphic from the Edit menu (or press the Ins key). This reinserts the copy from temporary memory, which is now attached to the correct frame.

Different graphics can have different parents, even if they are on the same page. Moreover, a graphic does not have to be within the boundaries of its parent frame. As you can see in Figure 4-18, a graphic and its parent can be separated by a wide distance, as long as they are on the same page.

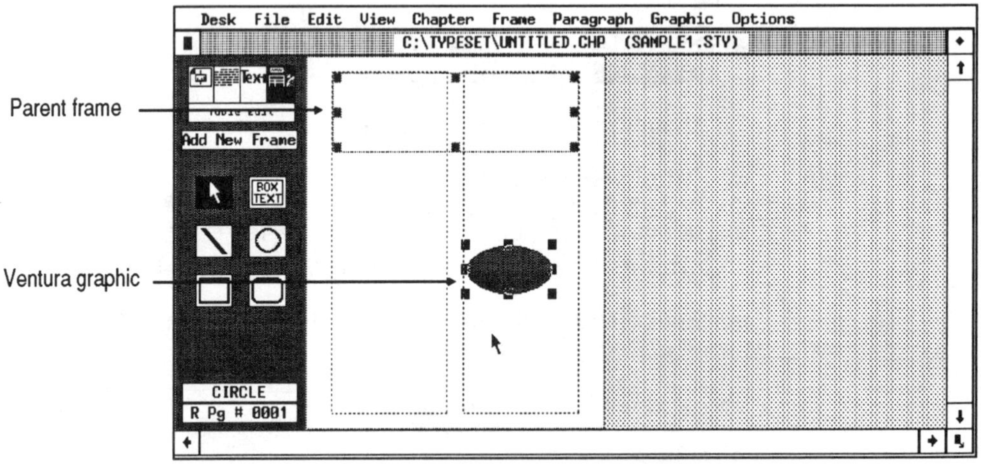

Figure 4-18. A Ventura graphic does not have to reside within the boundaries of its parent frame. It can be separated by a wide distance, as long as it is on the same page.

It is crucial to choose the correct parent. Usually it's best to attach the graphic to a frame. That way you can move the frame and automatically move all the graphics with it. Obviously, if you are creating callouts (labels), you want them attached to the frame for that picture.

TIP If you are creating graphics that must be positioned with precision, attach them to a frame. Then move the frame using Sizing & Scaling from the Frame menu. The graphics will move by a corresponding amount.

TIP If there is no obvious choice as the parent frame, create a small, "invisible" frame. Place it outside the margins so it won't interfere with the text flow. Make sure it does not have a fill pattern or ruling lines. Even though it is invisible when the page prints, you can see this frame on the screen in Frame mode. You can copy, move, or delete the frame to copy, move, or delete its associated graphics.

Setting up the grid

Beginners sometimes have trouble tapping the full power of Graphic mode. If there is a single secret to fast, efficient drawing, it is the use of a grid. You probably don't need a grid if you are producing a single label or a single line. But if you want to create two or more graphics at the same time, you should usually create a grid before you start. If you set up a grid, Ventura does the hard work for you. It makes sure that everything you draw is the right size and in the right position.

To turn on the snap-to grid:

- Enable Graphic mode.
- Select the frame or page.
- Choose Grid Settings from the Graphic menu. The Grid Settings dialog box appears (see Figure 4-19).
- Choose Grid Snap: On, then type in the units you want for both horizontal and vertical units.

The grid applies to the frame selected when you opened the dialog box. If you apply the grid to the current page, it will

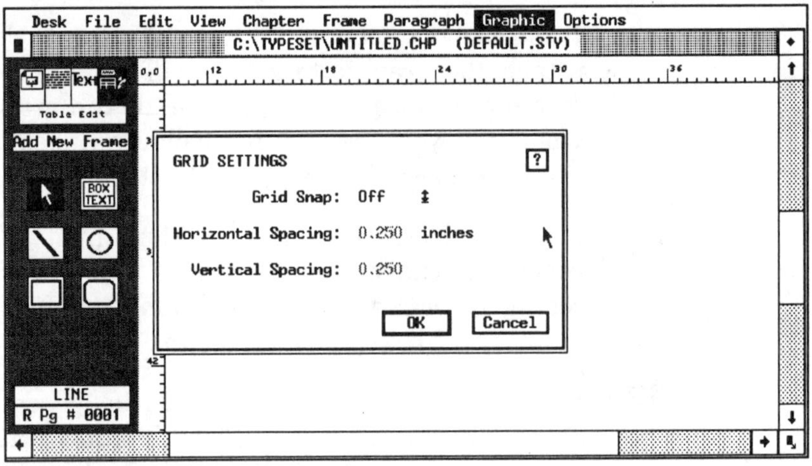

Figure 4-19. Use the Grid Settings dialog box to choose the units of the invisible snap-to grid.

stay the same for every page in the document (until you change it). If you apply the grid to a frame, it stays in effect whenever you return to that frame, even if the grid settings for the Underlying Page are different.

The invisible grid starts from the upper left corner of the frame or page *no matter what the margins are.* This grid acts like a magnetic field. Any graphic you place on the page automatically snaps to the nearest grid line. You cannot misalign a shape; Ventura won't let you. With a four-pica grid, for example, you can draw a shape that is four picas wide; or eight picas wide; or any multiple of four. But you cannot draw a shape six picas wide unless you change the grid.

As you may have guessed, the key to working with Grid Snap is to choose the right units. If you know the sizes you want in advance, you can plan the grid for easy drawing. First consider the margin setting. Let's say your document has six-pica margins. Let's further assume that you want to draw shapes that are four picas square, and some of these shapes must line up with the left margin.

If you set the grid to four picas vertically and horizontally, the shapes will be the right size, but they will not snap to the six-pica margin. Since the invisible grid begins at the left edge of the page, it has snap-to lines at four, eight, twelve and so on.

One strategy is to set the grid to the common denominator. In the example above, a grid setting of two picas will let us draw four-pica shapes and align them to the six-pica left margin. Alternatively, you could start with a four-pica grid to draw the shapes, then switch to a six-pica grid to position them on the margin.

Remember — Column Snap does not operate with graphics, so you must use the grid to automatically align shapes with the margin.

The snap-to grid is the solution for painlessly producing tables, forms, calendars, and other documents that require lines and shapes to align (Figure 4-20). Many beginners try to construct such applications by painstakingly positioning boxes with the eye. Inevitably they have misalignments. The secret is to set up a grid so the shapes align automatically and perfectly.

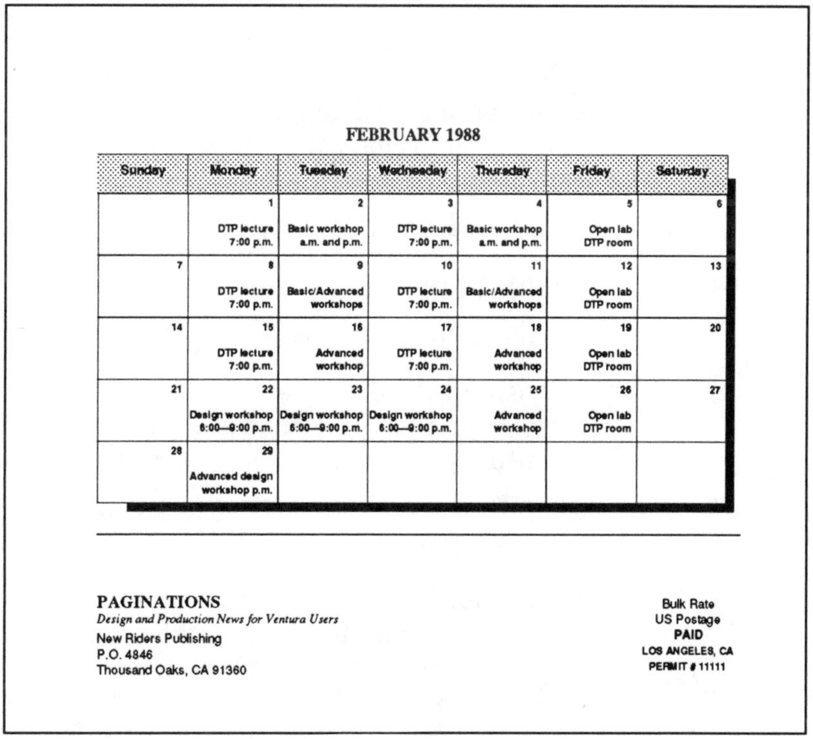
FEBRUARY 1988

Sunday	Monday	Tuesday	Wednesday	Thursday	Friday	Saturday
	1 DTP lecture 7:00 p.m.	2 Basic workshop a.m. and p.m.	3 DTP lecture 7:00 p.m.	4 Basic workshop a.m. and p.m.	5 Open lab DTP room	6
7	8 DTP lecture 7:00 p.m.	9 Basic/Advanced workshops	10 DTP lecture 7:00 p.m.	11 Basic/Advanced workshops	12 Open lab DTP room	13
14	15 DTP lecture 7:00 p.m.	16 Advanced workshop	17 DTP lecture 7:00 p.m.	18 Advanced workshop	19 Open lab DTP room	20
21	22 Design workshop 6:00—9:00 p.m.	23 Design workshop 6:00—9:00 p.m.	24 Design workshop 6:00—9:00 p.m.	25 Advanced workshop	26 Open lab DTP room	27
28	29 Advanced design workshop p.m.					

PAGINATIONS
Design and Production News for Ventura Users
New Riders Publishing
P.O. 4846
Thousand Oaks, CA 91360

Bulk Rate
US Postage
PAID
LOS ANGELES, CA
PERMIT # 11111

Figure 4-20. Calendars and similar applications are simple and fast to produce with Box Text if you use a snap-to grid to align the shapes automatically.

So far we've shown you how to select the parent frame and how to set up the grid. Now you are ready to create the drawing. As you will recall, Ventura has three types of tools: lines, shapes, and Box Text.

Drawing a line

We assume that you have enabled Graphic mode, selected the parent frame and (if necessary) set up a grid. To draw a line, follow the same three basic steps that operate all the graphic tools:

- Select the line tool from the Side-Bar.
- Position the cursor at the beginning point. Press and hold the mouse button.
- Drag the mouse to stretch the line to the end point. Release the mouse button.

TIP To draw a straight line, hold down the Alt key while you draw. When the Alt key is down, Ventura forces the line to conform to either the vertical, the horizontal, or the 45 degree slant (whichever is closest).

Resizing and moving lines

To change the size of a line:

- Select the line. Handles appear along its length.
- Position the cursor exactly over the handle at the end you wish to change. Press and hold the mouse button. Wait until a pointing hand cursor shape appears.
- Move the end of the line to its new position. Release the mouse button.

If the pointing hand does not appear, you have not placed the cursor exactly on top of a handle. Release the mouse button. Reposition the cursor so it is on top of a handle, then follow the steps above.

To move a line:

- Select the line. Handles appear along its length.

- Position the cursor on top of the line anywhere *except* over one of the handles. Press and hold the mouse button. Wait until a four-way arrow cursor appears.
- Move the line to its new position. Release the mouse button.

If the four-way arrow does not appear, release the button immediately without moving the mouse. Now reposition the cursor so it is not over an end handle. Then follow the steps above.

Cutting, copying, and pasting a line

To delete a line:

- Select the line.
- Delete it by selecting Cut Graphic from the Edit menu or by pressing the Del key on the numeric keypad.

The line is now in temporary memory where it will remain until you replace it with something else. If you have suffered from the *agony of delete* — in other words, if you have accidentally cut something you wanted to keep — you can restore it immediately by pasting it back from temporary memory.

To copy a line into temporary memory without deleting it:

- Select the line.
- Copy it by choosing Copy Graphic from the Edit menu or by pressing Shift-Del. (Use the Del key on the numeric keypad.)

To paste a line, place it on the clipboard by deleting it or copying it. Then choose Paste Graphic from the Edit menu, or press the Ins key. Ventura inserts the line at its previous location. If you press the Ins key five times, Ventura inserts five copies, one on top of the other. These copies will not be visible until you move them from the stack.

You can select, cut, copy, and paste multiple lines at the same time, as long as they have the same parent frame.

Changing line attributes

Ventura permits different line colors, widths, and end styles (Figure 4-21). To change line attributes:

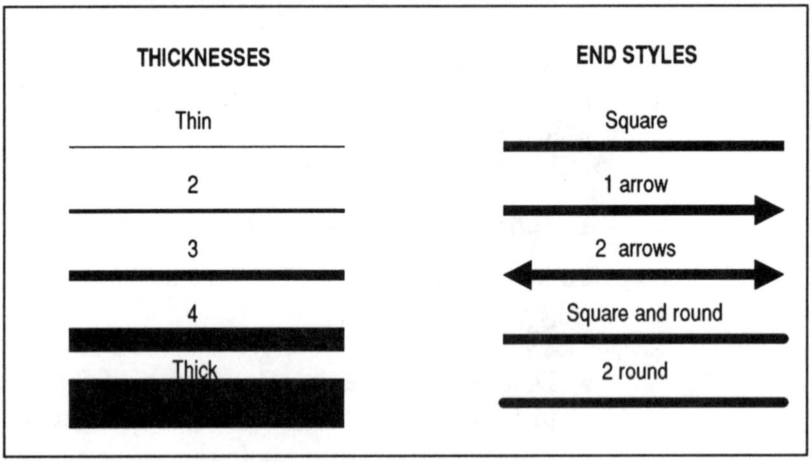

Figure 4-21. Line attribute options.

- Enable Graphic mode.
- Select the line.
- Select Line Attributes (by choosing from the Frame menu or by typing Ctrl-L).
- Choose the attributes you wish and click OK.

Ventura has five preset thicknesses. It also allows you to set a line of any thickness with the Custom option. Choose Thickness: Custom, then type in the thickness you want. You can use any units to specify the thickness, but most professionals prefer to measure rules in fractional pts. Since type sizes and line spacing are specified in fractional pts., it makes sense to use the same units for rules.

When you choose end styles, a check mark indicates the current choice. You can make a line the same at each end or different at each end. When selecting an end style, be aware that the left-most choice in the dialog box does not necessarily represent the left end of the line. The left-most choice stands for the beginning of the line — the first point you draw. If you draw a line from right to left, then the beginning — in Ventura's eyes — is on the right.

If you have a color printer, you also can choose the color of lines with this dialog box. A more common application is to use the line color to put a white arrow on a black background.

Storing line attributes

If you have many similar lines to draw, you do not want to reset the line attributes for each one in turn. Get the first line looking the way you want, then store its attributes. Once you store attributes, all future lines you draw will automatically take on those identical attributes. To store line attributes:

- Create the line and change its attributes until it looks the way you want.
- With the line still highlighted, select Line Attributes.
- Choose Defaults: Save To. Click OK to close the dialog box.

The attributes you just created are now the default choices. They will automatically apply to all future lines until you change them.

Copying attributes

You can also copy attributes from one line to another:

- Select the line from which you wish to copy.
- Select Line Attributes.
- Choose Defaults: Save To and click OK to close the dialog box.

You have just made those attributes the default settings. Now you can copy those settings to another line:

- Select the line you wish to change.
- Select Line Attributes.
- Choose Defaults: Load From and click OK to close the dialog box.

Drawing a shape

You draw shapes in much the same way you create lines. Assuming that you have enabled Graphic mode and (if necessary) set the grid, you then:

- Select one of the shape tools from the Side-Bar.
- Position the cursor at the beginning point. Press and hold the mouse button.
- Drag the mouse to stretch the shape until it is the size you want. Release the mouse button.

You draw shapes by dragging diagonally. After you release the button, the shape appears on the page.

Drawing a perfect circle or square

To draw a perfect circle or square (as opposed to an ellipse or rectangle), hold down the Alt key while you draw:

- Select the tool from the Side-Bar.
- Position the cursor at the beginning point.
- Press and hold the Alt key. Without releasing the Alt key, press and hold the mouse button.
- Drag the shape to the size you want. Release the mouse button and the Alt key.

Resizing and moving shapes

To resize a shape:

- Select the shape. Handles appear around the outside.
- Position the cursor exactly over a handle. Press and hold the mouse button. Wait until a pointing hand cursor appears.
- Move the end of the shape to its new size. Release the mouse button.

If the pointing hand does not appear, you have not placed the cursor exactly over a handle. If you grab a handle at a corner you can change both dimensions at once. If you grab a handle in the middle, you can change only one dimension at a time. For instance, if you want to change the width of a rectangle without changing its height, be sure to grab a handle in the middle. That way you can be sure that the height will not change accidentally.

To move a shape:

- Select the shape. Handles appear around the outside.
- Position the cursor anywhere *inside* the shape. Do *not* put the cursor over one of the handles. Press and hold the mouse button. Wait until a four-way arrow cursor appears.
- Move the shape to its new position. Release the mouse button.

If the four-way arrow doesn't appear, release the button immediately without moving the mouse. Now reposition the cursor so it is not over a handle and follow the steps above.

Cutting, copying, and pasting a shape

You cut, copy, and paste shapes exactly as explained above for lines.

Changing and storing line attributes

You can change and store line attributes for shapes just as described above for lines. All aspects of the dialog box work the same. In the case of shapes, the Line Attributes dialog box controls the line around the outside. If you do not want a line around the outside, choose Thickness: None.

Changing, storing, and copying fill attributes

Fill attributes refer to the color or pattern inside a graphic shape. You can have a fill pattern whether or not you have a line around the outside. To fill a shape:

- Select the shape.
- Select Fill Attributes (by choosing from the Graphic menu or by typing Ctrl-F). The dialog box shown in Figure 4-22 appears.

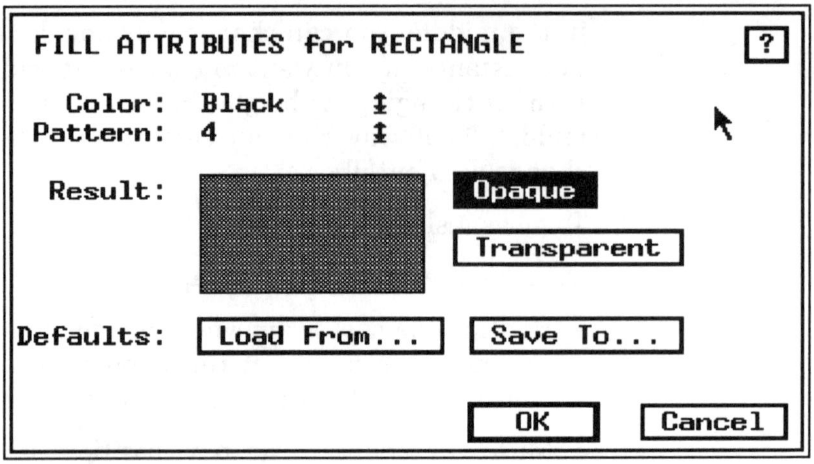

Figure 4-22. The Fill Attributes dialog box controls the patterns in the interior of a shape. Default values can be set or recalled using the Load From and Save To buttons.

- Choose the attributes you want and click OK to close the dialog box.

Ventura has nine fill variations, ranging from Hollow (no pattern) to Solid (black), as shown in Figure 4-23. These options are preset and cannot be changed. If you have PostScript programming know-how, you can print to a disk file and use a word processor to modify the fill patterns. Or you can use Define Color from the Paragraph menu to create new gray shades (PostScript printers only).

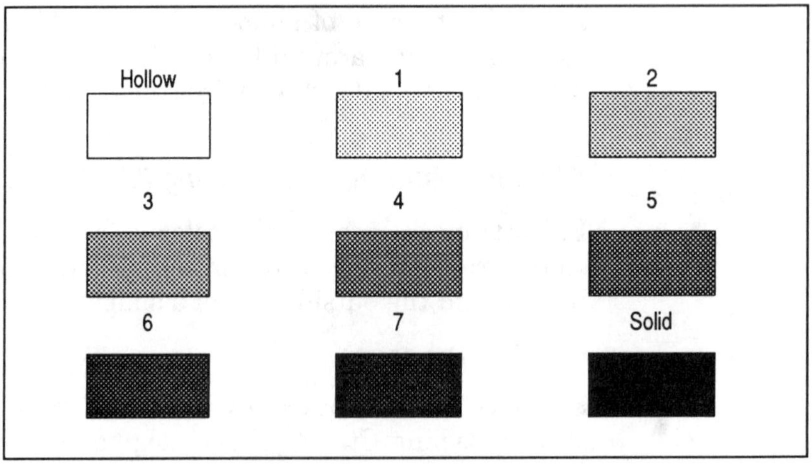

Figure 4-23. The nine fill options available in Ventura.

Opaque versus transparent

The Fill Attributes dialog box also lets you choose between opaque and transparent fill patterns. An opaque pattern hides anything beneath it. For instance, you can hide text by putting an opaque white rectangle on top of it — the electronic equivalent of white-out fluid. A transparent graphic lets anything below show through (provided your printer can handle transparent graphics; PostScript printers cannot).

➥ *NOTE: Some printers, including PostScript and LaserJet-compatible printers, cannot handle transparent graphics. No matter what you choose in the Fill Attributes dialog box, the graphic will print with an opaque background.*

If your printer cannot handle transparent graphics, you can still combine different graphics into bigger pictures. You must understand, however, that one graphic cannot show through another. Any time you put one graphic on top of another, the top graphic will obscure everything underneath.

Drawing Box Text

Box Text is a special type of graphic. It behaves like a cross between a graphics rectangle and a frame. Like a rectangle, it is created and modified in Graphic mode. Like a frame, it can contain text.

You draw Box Text exactly as you create a shape. Assuming that you have enabled Graphic mode and (if necessary) set the grid, you then:

- Select the Box Text tool from the Side-Bar.
- Position the cursor at the beginning point. Press and hold the mouse button.
- Drag the mouse to stretch the box to the size you want. Release the mouse button.

In other respects, Box Text performs like any other shape. You can constrain it, resize it, move it, cut it, copy it, paste it, fill it, or change its line attributes as described above for other shapes. The difference lies in the ability to place text inside the box.

Putting text inside Box Text

When you draw a Box Text rectangle, you will see a small end-of-file square inside. This is your signal that you can place text inside. To place text inside a Box Text rectangle:

- Enable Text mode.
- Place the cursor immediately in front of the end-of-file symbol. Click once to activate the text cursor.
- Type in the words you want to appear.

If the text you type is too long for the box, it disappears from view. Nevertheless, it has not been deleted. If you switch back to Graphic mode and enlarge the box, you will see the text.

Formatting text inside Box Text

When you type text inside the box, Ventura automatically tags it as Z_BoxText. You can change the format of this tag in Paragraph mode, or you can retag the text with a different name. If there is no Z_BoxText tag in the current style sheet, Ventura copies the attributes of Body Text. You can change these attributes just as you change any other tag:

- Enable Paragraph mode.
- Select the paragraph.
- Use the options from the Paragraph menu to change the formatting.

But there is nothing that says you have to leave the text inside a box tagged as Z_BoxText. You can retag it as anything else, exactly as you would retag any other paragraph.

- Enable Paragraph mode.
- Select the paragraph.
- Select the new tag from the Assignment List.

➥ *NOTE: Like all of Ventura's self-generated Z_Tags, Z_BoxText does not appear on the Assignment List unless you choose Generated Tags: Shown from the Set Preferences dialog box.*

Differences between Box Text and frames

Since you can place text in frames and in Box Text, some users become confused between the two. Here are a few of the key differences:

- The text you type into a Box Text is stored in the caption file for that chapter. You cannot save it as a separate file. By contrast, frame text is also stored in the caption file, but it can be saved to a separate file with File Type/Rename from the Edit menu.
- You cannot load a text file into a Box Text rectangle. You must type in the material while in Ventura.
- You cannot load a picture file into a Box Text rectangle.
- You cannot set margins or columns inside a Box Text rectangle, nor can you use padding. Frames, on the other hand, can have margins, columns, and padding.
- Text flows around a frame (unless you turn Text Flow to Off). By contrast, text flows under a Box Text rectangle.

Box Text effects

Box Text is the method of choice for placing text anywhere on a page, without regard to margins and columns. It is ideal for forms, brochures, and advertisements. Although Ventura is known for its long document capabilities, Box Text provides design flexibility that rivals any other page layout program on the market.

By combining text with different borders and backgrounds, you can create a wide variety of useful effects. We show a small sampling in Figure 4-24.

Working with multiple graphics

Often the answer to creating useful drawings with Ventura is to combine multiple graphics. The techniques below will help you with this process.

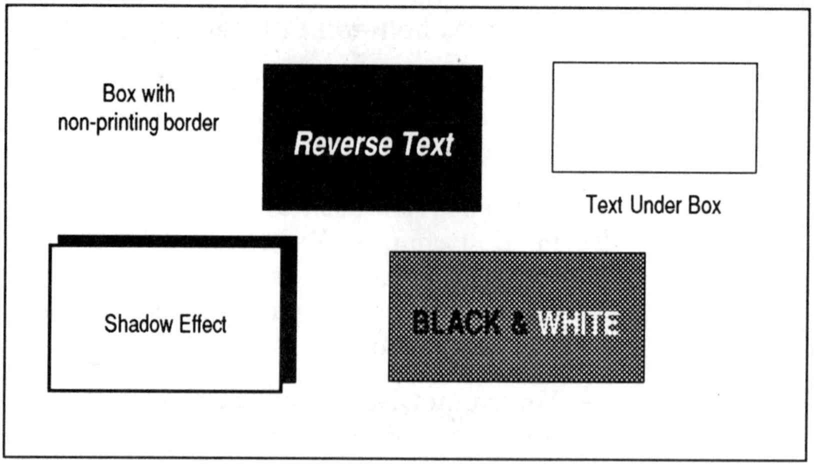

Figure 4-24. A small sample of the effects possible with Box Text.

Creating multiple graphics

To create several graphics one after another, hold down the Shift key while you are drawing. When you release the mouse button to end the first graphic, the cursor remains in drawing mode. You can then draw another graphic without returning to the Side-Bar to choose the tool again. For instance, if you want to draw four different rectangles, one after another, hold down the Shift key as you draw the first one. Continue to hold it down as you draw the second and third rectangles. Release it before you draw the fourth one so the mouse cursor will return to the normal selection arrow when you have finished.

On the other hand, if you want to create four identical rectangles, the fastest method is to draw the first one, then copy it to temporary memory. Then paste copies onto the page and move them into location.

Selecting multiple graphics

You can select more than one graphic if they all have the same parent frame. To select several graphics, click on them one after another while holding down the Shift key.

Once you have selected the graphics, you can perform operations as a group. For instance, you can copy them all to temporary memory. Or you can move them all at once. To move several graphics at a time, carefully position the mouse over the center of one graphic. Press and hold the mouse button until the four-way arrow appears. While holding the button down, move the shapes to the new location.

You must take extra care not to let the mouse button up, and not to click on a handle. If you do, you will select the graphic underneath the cursor and deselect all the others. Often a better way to move multiple graphics is to move the parent frame, which automatically moves the graphics with it.

Working with multiple graphics is one key to faster drawings. Imagine, for instance, that you want to draw a calendar. Rather than drawing 31 rectangles one at a time, you might draw just the first row individually (using the snap-to grid for exact size and positioning). Next you could copy the entire row into memory. Then you could paste three copies of the row back onto the page and move the rows into position to complete the calendar.

Drawing in layers

Ventura allows you to put one graphic on top of another. Drawing in layers is the secret to using simple elements to construct complex drawings (see Figure 4-25).

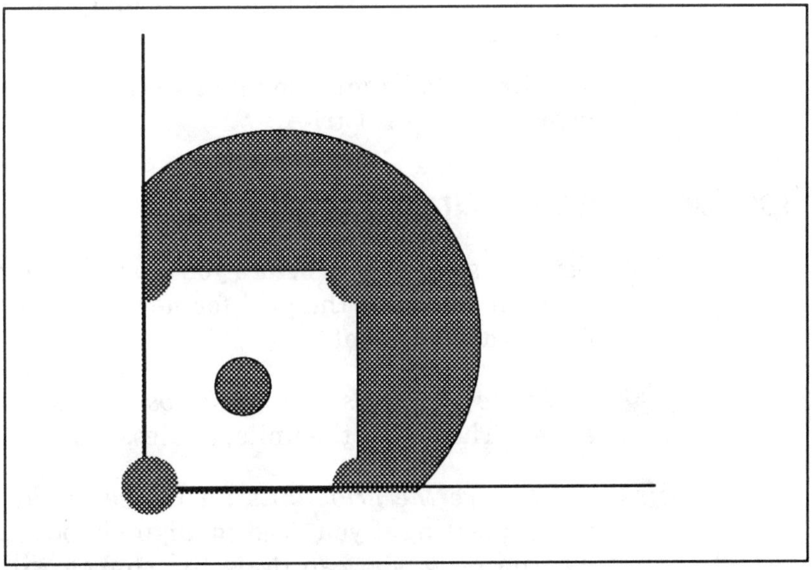

Figure 4-25. This sketch of a baseball diamond is a simple example of building a more complex shape from simple elements in Graphic mode.

You can use a stack analogy to understand how Ventura handles layers. The first graphic you draw is on the bottom. The second is on the top of the first. The third is on top of both of the first two, and so on. When graphics appear one on top of another, it can be difficult to select the shapes underneath. Ventura solves this problem with the Ctrl-Click technique. Place the cursor on top of the stack of graphics. If you hold down the Ctrl key while clicking, Ventura cycles through the stack. The first mouse click selects the graphic on top. The second click selects the next layer down, and so forth. This same technique works for frames.

Changing the layers

What happens if you want to change the order of the graphics in a stack? One way to bring a graphic to the top of the stack is to delete it, then immediately reinsert it. When you reinsert it, Ventura considers it to be the last graphic drawn and therefore puts it on top. Ventura also has commands for sending graphics to the top or bottom of the stack. To send a graphic to the bottom of the stack:

- Select the graphic.
- Select Send to Back from the Graphic menu (or press Ctrl-Z).

The Bring to Front command works the same way. Its keyboard shortcut is Ctrl-A.

Tips for working in Graphic mode

TIP *Set up a snap-to grid* before you start drawing. It takes only a moment to adjust the grid for new sizes or to turn it off for free-form placement.

TIP *Make the grid units as large as possible* (all other things being equal). The bigger the units, the less chance for error.

TIP *Try to give the grid units* an integer relationship with the margin setting if you need to align shapes along the margin. Alternatively, you can draw the shapes with one grid, then change the settings to align them.

TIP *To move a very small graphic*, attach it to a larger frame. The frame can be invisible if you don't want it to print. Then move the frame, and the graphic moves with it.

TIP *Consider tying graphics to a repeating frame* if you want them to appear on every page of the document. Although you can accomplish the same effect with Show On All Pages from the Graphic menu, that option does not give you the same control. When graphics are tied to a repeating frame, you can move the graphics by moving the frame. This gives you the ability to fine-tune position using Sizing & Scaling from the Frame menu.

TIP *Use a white rectangle or circle* to block out unwanted portions of a picture.

TIP *If fill patterns from superimposed graphics* bleed through to the layer above, separate each layer with a white, opaque shape.

TIP *Although you can put only one rule around a shape* in Graphic mode, you can add additional lines in Paragraph mode.

TIP *To select a graphic underneath another*, press the Ctrl key while clicking the mouse. Each time you click, Ventura selects the next layer down in the stack.

TIP *It may be easier to create complex graphics* if you create a blank page for a "sketchboard." When assembling multiple graphics, you can work on each individual element by itself on the blank area. Then you can copy it to temporary memory and paste it onto the page where it belongs. Be sure to select the correct parent when you paste the graphic back in.

TIP *To draw several graphics in a row*, hold down the Shift key as you draw. The mouse cursor stays in drawing mode and you can draw another graphic immediately without choosing the tool again from the Side-Bar.

TIP *When drawing similar graphics*, take the time to get the first one just right. Then you can use Defaults: Save To in Line Attributes and Fill Attributes to make these settings the defaults. All subsequent graphics will now match these settings.

TIP *Use Box Text in place of rectangles* for forms and other applications where you might want to fill in information. Even if you originally leave the box blank, Box Text gives you the option to fill in the form on screen in Ventura.

This chapter has examined several approaches to creating pictures for Ventura Publisher. Still to come are a variety of techniques for integrating those pictures into a document, which we explore in Chapter Six, "Building the Chapter."

We have now examined text and pictures, two of the three critical building blocks that form a Ventura Publisher document. The third piece of the puzzle, style sheets, is discussed in the chapter that follows.

Chapter Five

Working with Style Sheets

This chapter talks about style sheets, the third part of the Formula and the key to Ventura's sophistication and flexibility. Accordingly, it is one of the most important parts of this book. It covers both theory and practice. You can skip the theory and go straight to the hands-on section if you're the impatient type — but we don't recommend it. Understanding style sheets is the key to unleashing the full power of Ventura.

When you finish this chapter, you'll understand how Ventura works with style sheets and chapter files to control the format of a document. You'll also know how to load, apply, and change a style sheet. Along the way, you'll become acquainted with three key menus: the Chapter menu, the Frame menu and the Paragraph menu.

Style sheet basics

You'll be surprised how much easier it is to work with Ventura once you understand a few basic principles. Most beginners quickly learn their way around Ventura's menus. Even so, they aren't sure what's going on and how things work together. The truth is, most users don't figure out the big picture until they reach intermediate level.

This section will give you a boost up the learning curve. It begins with an explanation of two key points: how Ventura builds documents; and the differences between style sheets and chapter files.

Understanding Ventura documents

Ventura can combine different files into a single finished document. The first step to becoming a Ventura wizard is to understand how those files work together, and what role style sheets play. Let's quickly review what we've covered in earlier chapters before we plunge into new territory. You've already encountered the Ventura Formula:

Text + Style + Pictures = Chapter

As the Formula implies, the chapter file is the key to integrating the other three. It contains *pointers* to the other files, plus instructions on how to assemble them on the page. Think of the chapter file as the supervisor on a construction job. Supervisors may not hammer many nails, but they know what everybody else should be doing.

How Ventura combines files

Besides the chapter file and the style sheet, Ventura Publisher creates other files as needed. You will be ahead of the game if you learn to recognize these files, which fall into three main groups: document files, multi-chapter files, and program files. Figure 5-1 diagrams them.

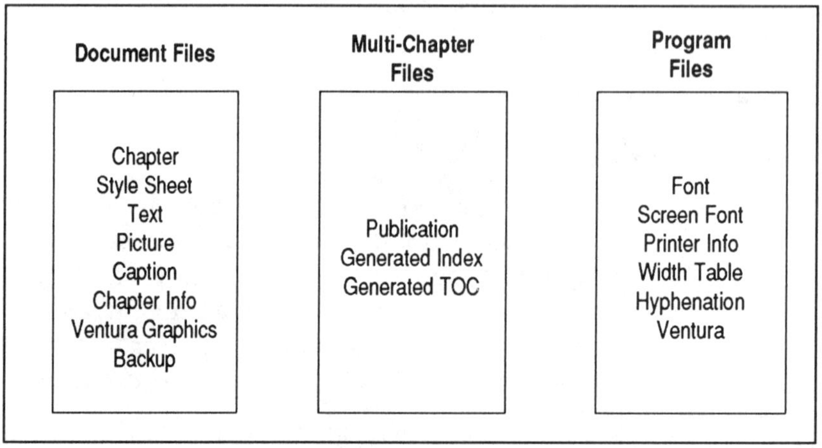

Figure 5-1. The types of files used in Ventura Publisher.

Document files

As Ventura builds a document, it uses different files to hold information. Some of these document files are named by the user (text files, for example). Others are named by Ventura (caption files, for instance). They all have two things in common: (1) they contain information about one specific document and (2) if you use Ventura's Multi-Chapter function to move a chapter, these files automatically move with the chapter.

In a sense, then, we can define document files as those that are linked to a specific document. There are eight document files in all, four of which users can name:

Chapter file. The chapter file contains pointers to the other files needed to construct the document. In addition, it includes certain formatting information. Ventura creates the chapter file, but the user names it. It must always ends with the CHP extension, as in SAMPLE1.CHP.

Style sheet file. The style sheet contains formatting information — fonts, alignment, spacing, and much more. The user can choose any name for a style sheet as long as it has the STY extension — for instance, SAMPLE1.STY.

Text files. Text files are usually created with a word processor and loaded into Ventura (they also can be created within Ventura). You can have more than one text file in a document. Text files can have any name or extension, although most people choose an extension that indicates the file format: WP for WordPerfect files, WS for WordStar files, DOC for Microsoft Word files, and so on. SAMPLE1.WS would be a typical text file name.

Picture files. Picture files contain graphics created with outside graphics programs. They can have any name or extension, although most people choose an extension that indicates the file format: .PCX for Publisher's Paintbrush files, .SLD for AutoCAD slide files, and so on.

So much for the four document files that can be named by the user. By contrast, when Ventura creates and names the files described below, it uses the same name as the chapter. To tell them apart, it uses a different extension:

Caption file. The caption file contains the text you type into caption frames or empty frames. No matter how many captions you type, Ventura stores them all in a single file. Ventura creates it automatically (if needed) and gives it the same name as the chapter, with an extension of CAP — for instance, SAMPLE1.CAP.

Ventura graphics file. This file contains any graphics you make with Ventura's built-in drawing tools. Ventura gives it the same name as the chapter, plus the extension VGR — SAMPLE1.VGR, for instance.

Chapter information file. Ventura's programmers developed the chapter information file to describe a chapter's contents. Third-party add-on products such as VP Manager use the CIP file to store information and create useful management reports. Created automatically by Ventura, its name matches the chapter name, except that it ends with the extension CIF, as in SAMPLE1.CIF.

Backup files. If you tell Ventura to keep backups in the Set Preferences dialog box, it creates copies of every document file *except picture files.* It uses the same name, but changes the first letter of the extension to $. The backup of SAMPLE1.CHP is SAMPLE1.$HP, SAMPLE1.WS becomes SAMPLE1.$S, and so on.

Multi-Chapter files

We call this next category *multi-chapter files* because you create them with Multi-Chapter from the Options menu. Three types fall into this group.

Publication file. To tie more than one chapter together, Ventura builds a *publication*. This file links chapters so you can, for example, print six chapters with one command. You can give a publication any name as long as it has the PUB extension. For instance, if you had four chapters called SAMPLE1.CHP, SAMPLE2.CHP, SAMPLE3.CHP, and SAMPLE4.CHP, you might combine them all into a publication called SAMPLE.PUB.

Generated index file. Ventura permits you to mark index entries in chapters. Ventura searches chapters to find each entry and generates a file to hold the page numbers. To name the file, Ventura uses the first five letters of the publication. Then it adds the three letters IDX (for index) and the extension GEN (for generated file). Thus, the index file for SAMPLE.PUB would be SAMPLIDX.GEN. (You can change this file name if you want.)

Generated TOC file. You build a table of contents (TOC) like an index, by searching through the chapters to find page numbers. Ventura names the resulting file with the first five letters of the publication, plus the letters TOC, plus the extension GEN. Thus the TOC file for SAMPLE.PUB is SAMPLTOC.GEN. (You can change the file name if you want.)

Let's review document and multi-chapter files with an example. Suppose you want to produce a book called SAMPLE. You decide to name the individual chapters SAMPLE1, SAMPLE2, etc. They will all use the same style sheet, SAMPLE.STY. Your word processor is WordStar and your graphics program is GEM Draw Plus. Given those assumptions, Table 5-1 summarizes what your file names might look like:

Table 5-1. Typical file names.

File Name	File Type
SAMPLE1.CHP	Chapter file
SAMPLE1.STY	Style sheet
SAMPLE1.WS	WordStar text file
SAMFIG1.GEM	Picture file
SAMPLE1.CAP	Caption file
SAMPLE1.VGR	Ventura graphics file
SAMPLE1.CIF	Chapter information file
SAMPLE.PUB	Publication file
SAMPLIDX.GEN	Generated index file
SAMPLTOC.GEN	Generated TOC file

Program files

To this point, we have discussed document files and multi-chapter files. We call the third and final category *program files*. You won't encounter these files as often, but it pays to know what they do. Program files are not associated with any particular document. They usually reside in the \VENTURA subdirectory. We don't have the space to list every type, but here are a few of the most important:

Font files. Printer fonts. They use extensions such as FNT, SFP, SFL, PFA, and PFB.

Screen font files. Generic fonts for screen display. They carry extensions like EGA, CGA, or VGA.

Hyphenation dictionaries. These files include the hyphenation algorithms (HY1 and HY2 extension), the exception dictionary (HYPHEXPT.DIC), and the user dictionary (HYPHUSR.DIC).

Printer information files. Configuration details about the printers you install, such as where to find fonts. They carry the CNF extension, as in HPLJPLUS.CNF.

Width table files. Different printers and different fonts use different spacing for each character. Ventura stores these character widths in width files, which use the WID extension. Ventura calls the default width table OUTPUT.WID, the PostScript width table POSTSCPT.WID, and so on.

Ventura files. The program itself is contained in a half dozen or so files that start with the letters VP and use a variety of extensions. One of them, with the INF extension, is the initialization file. It remembers how you left things the last time you worked with Ventura.

As you may have noticed, recognizing file types is generally a matter of recognizing their extensions, as summarized in Table 5-2.

Table 5-2. File extensions and their meanings

Category	Extension	File Type
Document Files	CAP	Caption file
	CHP	Chapter file
	CIF	Chapter information file
	GEM, PCX, etc.	Picture files
	STY	Style sheet
	TXT, WP, etc.	Text files
	VGR	Ventura graphics file
Multi-chapter Files	GEN	Generated TOC and index files
	PUB	Publication file
Program Files	CNF	Printer information files
	INF	Initialization file
	EGA, VGA, CGA	Screen fonts
	FNT	Font files
	DIC	Hyphenation exception dictionary and user dictionary
	HY1 and HY2	Hyphenation algorithms
	SFP and SFL	Fonts
	WID	Width table

Understanding style sheets and chapter files

Now that you have some insight into Ventura's files, you are ready to examine style sheets and chapter files, and the differences between them. Understanding these differences is crucial to the advanced techniques we cover later in the book.

Contents of a style sheet

A style sheet contains formatting rules. Every chapter has one (and only one) style sheet. (You can, however, use the same style sheet for more than one chapter.) So far we haven't told you much that is new. Most people get the general idea behind style sheets. But not everyone understands specifically what a style sheet does — and *doesn't* — contain.

A style sheet holds formatting rules. These rules fall into two categories: (1) rules for the document as a whole and (2) rules for individual elements. Document-wide formatting relates to the Underlying Page — its margins and columns, for instance. The individual formatting applies to *tags*. Tags control such things as the font, alignment, and spacing for page elements such as headlines, body text, subheads, and so on. Table 5-3 shows the contents of a style sheet, divided into these two categories.

Table 5-3. Formatting controlled by the style sheet.

Document-Wide Formatting	Tag Formatting
Page Layout (paper size, etc.)	Font
Widows & Orphans	Alignment
Auto-Numbering	Spacing
Footnote Settings	Breaks
Margins & Columns of Underlying Page	Tab Settings
Sizing & Scaling of Underlying Page	Special Effects
Vertical Rules on Underlying Page	Paragraph Typography
Ruling Lines on Underlying Page	Ruling Lines Associated with Paragraphs
Background of Underlying Page	Paragraph Backgrounds
Printer Info	Color Definitions

Contents of a chapter file

Style sheets get most of the attention, but chapter files also contain important formatting information.

- file information
- frame information
- header and footer information
- graphics information
- numbering information

Some of this information is in the chapter file itself. The rest is in the caption file (CAP) and Ventura graphics file (VGR) associated with that chapter. Table 5-4 lists some of the formatting information contained in a chapter file and its associated CAP and VGR files.

How chapters work with style sheets

Now that you've seen the contents of chapters and style sheets, let's consider what this means when creating documents. Many users fail to understand a vital concept: *To get a complete picture of a document's format, you need both a style sheet and a chapter file.* You cannot capture all your design decisions in a style sheet alone.

Perhaps the best way to make this point is to review some key page elements. Table 5-5 lists a few elements encountered frequently in business documents. You will notice that the chapter file controls most of them.

Because the chapter file controls part of the formatting, the best way to harness the power of Ventura is to work with *chapter templates*. Templates combine three important elements — a chapter, a style sheet, and sample frames — into a single, ready-to-run blank document. Chapter Ten, "Special Document Formats," explains templates in detail.

Table 5-4. Formatting controlled by the chapter file.

Type of Information	What It Contains or Controls
File information	Pointers to the component files
Frame information	Position on the Underlying Page Size Margins Columns Ruling lines Anchor name Fill attributes Caption frame Caption text (in CAP file) Frame text (in CAP file)
Header and footer information	Position of header and footer frames Size of header and footer frames Margins of header and footer frames Header and footer text
Graphics information	Position Parent frame Box text (in caption file) Size of graphics (in VGR file) Line attributes (in VGR file) Fill attributes (in VGR file)
Numbering information	Starting page number Starting chapter number Starting figure and table numbers Numbering format

Table 5-5. How style sheets and chapter files work together.

Page element	What the style sheet controls	What the chapter file controls
Text	Font, alignment, spacing, breaks, ruling lines, etc.	Which text files go where
Frames	Underlying Page only.	Position, size, ruling lines, contents
Captions	Font, alignment, spacing, breaks, ruling lines, etc.	Which picture files go in which frames, position of caption frame, figure and table numbering, starting numbers, numbering format, caption labels, caption text (via .CAP file)
Headers and footers	Spacing, ruling lines, overall font	Margins of frame, header text, page numbers, starting number, numbering format, tag matches within header, font changes within header, baseline jumps within header
Section numbering	Which tags will be numbered, plus font, alignment, spacing, etc.	Starting number, numbering format
Graphics	Text attributes of Box Text	Position, size, attributes, parent frame, text of Box Text

Loading and saving a style sheet

The previous section explained the theory behind style sheets. If you grasp these fundamentals, you are already ahead of the game. It often takes months of trial and error before beginners decipher the relationship between style sheets and chapter files. Now you are ready to learn how theory translates into practice. The next few sections explain how to work with style sheets:

- loading and saving style sheets
- applying style sheets
- changing style sheets and building new ones

The discussions that follow are not step-by-step tutorials.

Nonetheless, many of you may want to read this material while next to the computer, so you can experiment as you learn new ideas. To work with a new chapter, select New from the File menu. You will see UNTITLED.CHP in the Title Bar, followed by the name of the last style sheet you used (Figure 5-2). Ventura keeps the old style sheet active until you specifically request a new one.

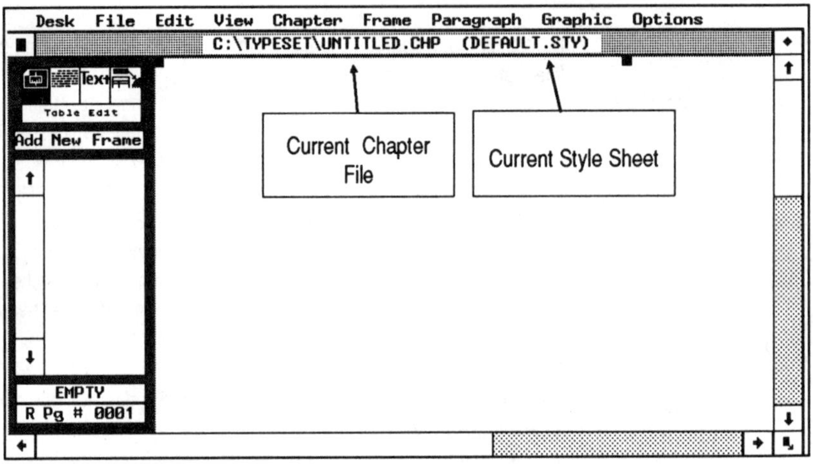

Figure 5-2. The Title Bar displays the chapter and style sheet that are currently active.

To load an existing chapter, choose Open from the File menu. Ventura automatically loads a style sheet when it opens a chapter. The name of the style sheet shows in the Title Bar after the name of the chapter. You will replace that style sheet when you load a new one.

Loading a style sheet

Obviously, you can only load style sheets that already exist. In the beginning, therefore, you must work with the style sheets distributed with the program. Once you know your way around, you can build your own style sheets, or buy them from outside companies.

Most of the style sheets distributed with Ventura begin with the ampersand character (&), as in &BOOK-P1.STY. If you request the example files during installation, they are installed automatically in the \TYPESET subdirectory.

➥*NOTE: If you didn't install the style sheets but you want them now, run the VPPREP installation program again from the floppy disk. When asked if this is your first installation, reply "No." Then answer the questions. When asked at the end if you want the example files, answer "Yes."*

Appendix L of the Ventura Reference Guide describes the starter style sheets. You will learn later how to use pre-existing style sheets to build new style sheets of your own.

To load a new style sheet:

- Select Load Diff. Style from the File menu.
- Use the Item Selector to move to the subdirectory containing the style sheet you want.
- Select the style sheet from the list (Figure 5-3). Click once on the style sheet name and once on the OK button, or double-click on the name.

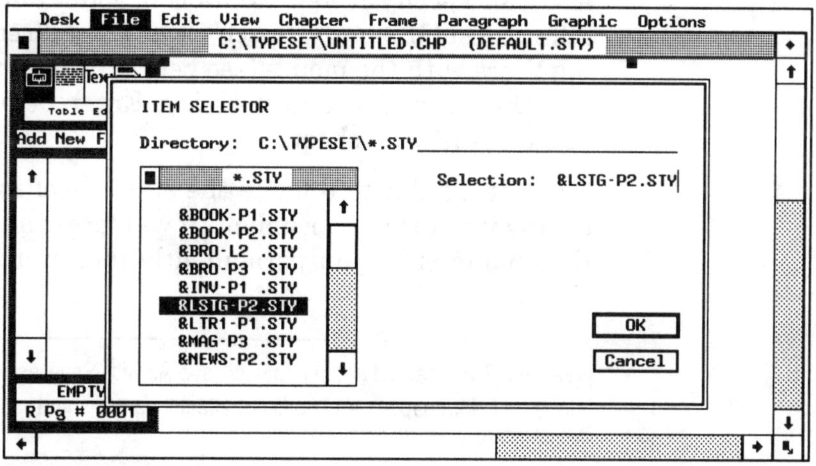

Figure 5-3. Use the Item Selector to navigate to the proper subdirectory and choose a style sheet.

Saving a style sheet

As soon as you load the style sheet, save it under a new name — unless, that is, you want to save all your changes under the old name. Here's how:

- Select Save As New Style from the File menu.

- Type the new name into the Item Selector (Figure 5-4) and click OK.

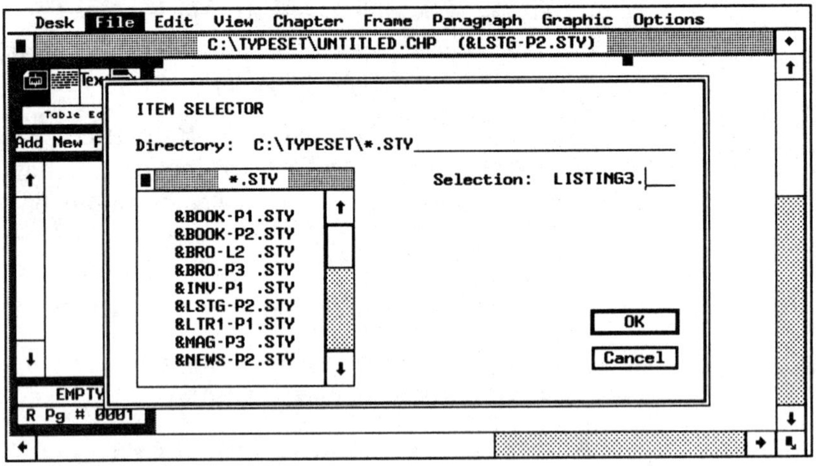

Figure 5-4. Renaming a style sheet.

Ventura automatically adds the STY extension for you. You also can specify a new location if you want to store it in a different subdirectory. Specify a new subdirectory by navigating there with the mouse (see below) or by typing its name on the Directory line and pressing Enter *before* you type the name of the style sheet.

Make it a habit to rename the style sheet immediately after calling it in to your document. If you forget and then later save the chapter file, you permanently modify the previous style sheet.

WARNING: Be careful not to confuse Save As with Save As New Style (Figure 5-5). Save As is for chapters and does not affect the style sheet.

Remember: Whenever you save the chapter, Ventura automatically saves all the associated files — including the style sheet. It saves under the old name *unless* you used Save As New Style first. You must rename the style sheet *before* saving or renaming the chapter.

Almost everyone who uses Ventura learns this lesson the hard way. At one time or another, we have all destroyed an existing style sheet (or chapter) because we absent-mindedly hit Ctrl-S

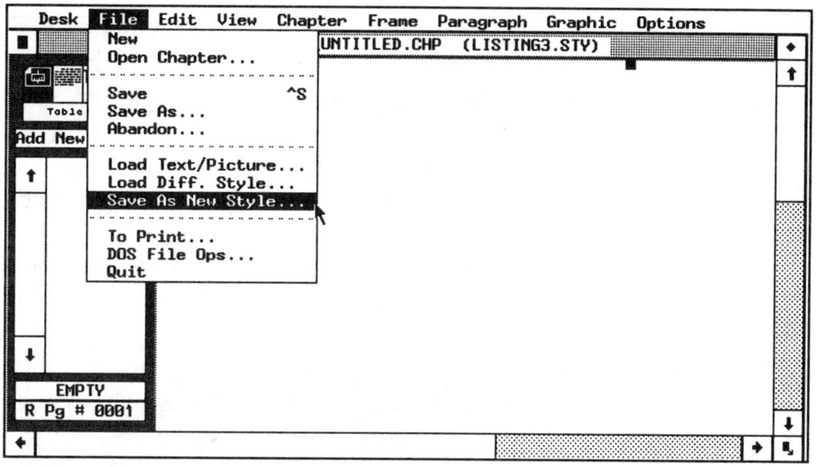

Figure 5-5. To rename the style sheet, you must choose Save As New Style. Do not use Save As, which renames the chapter and does not affect the style sheet.

before renaming. It is sometimes possible — but not always — to recover in DOS by using the backup files.

Tips for loading and saving style sheets

TIP *If the Item Selector becomes too crowded* with style sheet names, use the Selection line to filter some of them out. Better yet, move the style sheets you don't use very often to a separate subdirectory.

TIP *Treat style sheets as you would any computer file* — that is, *be sure to back them up*. Every time you create a new one, make a copy on floppy diskette for safekeeping.

TIP *One way to back up a style sheet without leaving Ventura* is to use Save As New Style. Use the same name, but change the location to the A: drive. Be careful, however, to use Load Diff. Style immediately afterward to load the style sheet from its location on the hard disk. Otherwise, Ventura will look for the style sheet on the A: drive the next time you open the chapter.

TIP *You can recover the previous version of a style sheet* or a chapter if you have chosen Keep Backup Files: Yes from the Set Preferences dialog box. Quit Ventura *without* saving the chapter again. Obviously, if you have made other changes, you must decide which is more important: recovering the style sheet or preserving the changes. Once out of Ventura use DOS to move to the subdirectory containing the style sheet. You should see the backup file — an identically named file with the extension $TY. Rename this file to a new name with the STY extension. Return to Ventura and use Load Diff. Style from the File menu to bring in the restored style sheet.

TIP *To move a style sheet*, you must rename it to a new location, then delete the old style sheet. Many people find it more convenient to delete files in DOS. You also can move and copy style sheets in DOS. Remember, however, that if you move or copy with DOS, you do not change the pointers in the chapter file. The chapter still looks for the style sheet in the old location. If you want the chapter to use the style sheet at the new location, you must use Save As New Style or Load Diff. Style. (If you use a utility program such as VP Manager, you can use the mouse to move, rename, delete, and copy files, style sheets, and chapters within Ventura without returning to DOS.)

Applying a style sheet

Loading a style sheet attaches it to the current chapter. As you recall, style sheets contain two kinds of formatting: document-wide and tag. Document-wide formatting takes effect immediately. Tag formatting takes effect only if you already have text on the screen *and* that text contains the same tag names as the new style sheet. Otherwise, you must *apply* the style sheet.

To apply a style sheet, you tell Ventura which paragraphs are which — which paragraphs you wish to treat as headlines, which as subheads, which as bullet lists, and so on. We call the procedure *tagging*. You must assign a tag to every paragraph except Body Text. (Ventura automatically treats anything without a tag as Body Text.)

Obviously, you must have paragraphs of text on the page before you can apply a style sheet. Let's quickly review Ventura's definition of a paragraph before we go any further. Back in junior high school, we all learned a definition that had to do with *topic sentences* and *units of thought*. Wrong kind of paragraph. In Ventura parlance, a paragraph is anything that ends with a return. It can be many lines, a single line, a single word, a single letter, or an empty paragraph with nothing but a return.

The idea of an *empty paragraph* deserves further discussion. You can apply a tag to an empty line. All you need is a paragraph return (see Figure 5-6). You can tag this return and assign attributes to it just as you tag text. Some people use empty paragraphs for such effects as page breaks, spacing, and ruling lines with no text.

Now that you've got the definition of *paragraph* straight, you're ready to learn about tagging. You can tag text in three ways: with the mouse, with the function keys, or with the word processor.

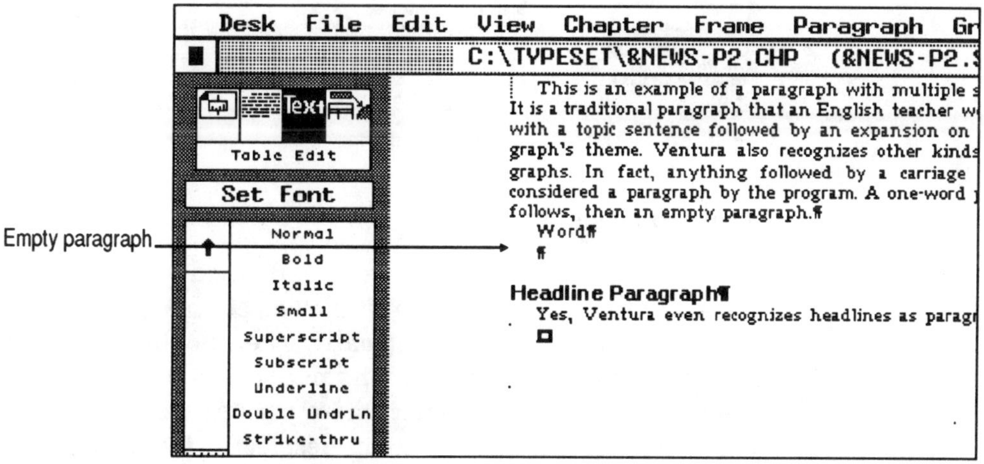

Figure 5-6. A Ventura paragraph is anything that ends with a return: several sentences, a single sentence, a single word, a single character, or even a paragraph return with no text.

Tagging with the mouse

The mouse provides the simplest method of tagging. Here's how it works:

- Enable Paragraph mode (click on the icon at the top of the Side-Bar or press Ctrl-I).

- Click once anywhere on a paragraph to select it. Ventura highlights the entire paragraph.
- Select a tag name from the Assignment List (Figure 5-7). As soon as you click on the tag name, Ventura applies its format.

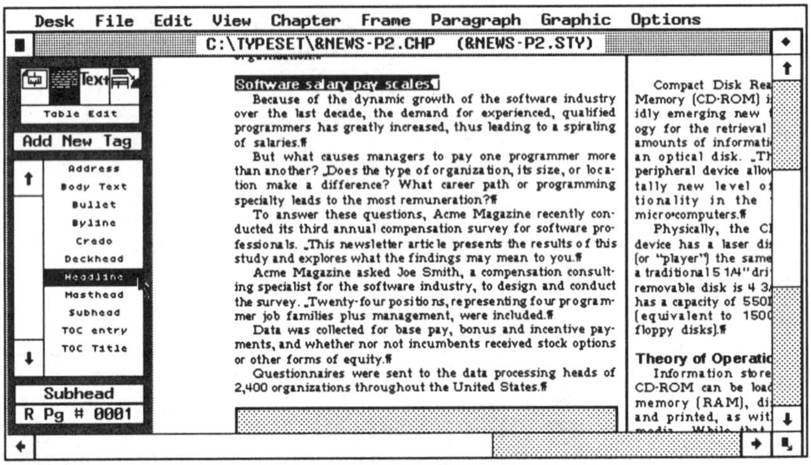

Figure 5-7. Applying the Headline tag to a paragraph.

Tagging multiple paragraphs

You can tag single paragraphs as explained above, or you can tag several at a time. For multiple selection, click on the first paragraph as you would normally. Then hold down the Shift key while clicking on the second paragraph. Continue to hold the Shift key while you select more paragraphs. If you select a paragraph by mistake, you can deselect it by clicking on it a second time while still pressing the Shift key. You can select as many paragraphs as you want on a single page. You cannot, however, tag multiple paragraphs across page boundaries, even in Facing Pages View.

Once you have selected multiple paragraphs, choose the tag from the Assignment List as before. Ventura immediately applies it to all the highlighted paragraphs. Figure 5-8 shows how you might use this function to tag all the items in a list at once.

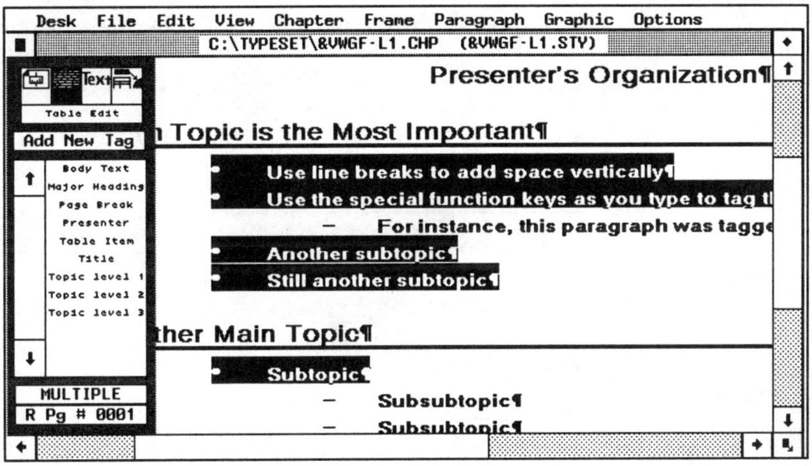

Figure 5-8. By holding the Shift key while you click with the mouse, you can highlight and tag several paragraphs at once.

Tagging with the function keys

Ventura permits you to assign tags to the 10 function keys. You only need to assign the keys once — from then on, they are available whenever you use that style sheet. Once assigned, you can select a tag by pressing a function key (instead of clicking on the tag name in the Assignment List). More importantly, with the function keys you can tag items while in Text mode as well as in Paragraph mode.

Tagging with the function keys presents several possible advantages. First, it eliminates the back and forth motion of the mouse, from text to Assignment List and back. Second, it permits you to edit and tag simultaneously (in Text mode). Third, it lets you compose documents directly in Ventura and tag them as you go along, without switching back and forth between Text and Paragraph modes. Fourth, it allows you to work with the Side-Bar hidden, since you don't need to access the Assignment List. This lets you see more of the page on screen.

Assigning function keys

It's up to you which tags to assign to which function keys. Here's how it works:

- Open the Paragraph menu.

- Select Update Tag List. A dialog box appears (Figure 5-9).
- Select the Assign Func. Keys button.
- Type the names of the tags into the blank spaces and click OK.

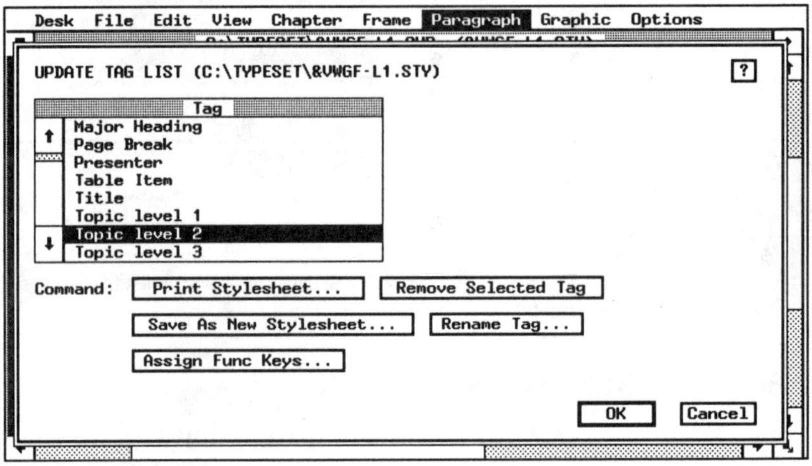

Figure 5-9. The Update Tag List dialog box.

Figure 5-10 shows one way to assign the function keys. We suggest you choose a standard way of assigning function keys and stick with it for all your style sheets. An alphabetic system is probably the most practical, especially since the Assignment List is alphabetic, too. But you may find certain style sheets lend themselves to different mnemonic devices. When tagging this book, for example, we used the tag names Head1, Head2, etc. It was an obvious and easy-to-remember choice to assign Head1 to F1, Head2 to F2 and so on.

We suggest that you always use F10 for Body Text. The style sheets distributed with Ventura follow this convention. If you follow it, too, you will always know where to find the Body Text tag at the press of a key. As you become more proficient, you may find yourself experimenting with tags. It's not hard to do something so bizarre that all the text disappears from the page. Often, the easiest way to recover is to press F10, thereby reassigning the paragraph as Body Text.

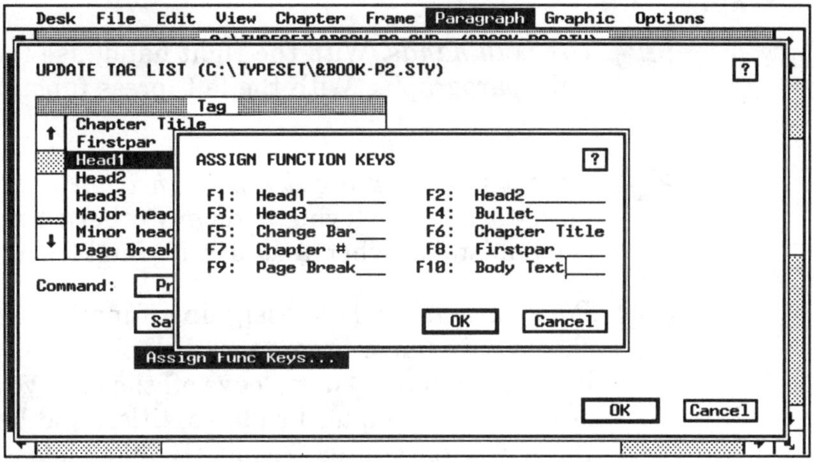

Figure 5-10. Assigning tag names to function keys.

Using the function keys

Once you've assigned the function keys, you can use them in Paragraph mode or in Text mode. In Paragraph mode, select a paragraph as before. Instead of using the mouse to select a tag, simply press the appropriate function key.

In Text mode, *you do not need to highlight the entire paragraph*. Simply make sure the cursor is anywhere in the paragraph, then press the function key. To tag more than one paragraph in Text mode, highlight everything with the mouse, then press the function key.

Tagging paragraphs in the word processor

When you tag with the first two methods explained above, Ventura inserts the tag names into the text files. If you prefer, you can insert the names in advance. Refer to the end of Chapter Three, "Creating Text," for detailed instructions on how to preformat word processing files.

Tips for tagging

These techniques can speed up the tagging process:

TIP *Use shift-click* to highlight as many similar paragraphs at once as possible, then apply the tag to all of them at once.

TIP *Use both hands.* With the right hand, use the mouse to highlight paragraphs. With the left, press function keys to assign tags.

TIP *Consider making a quick pass through the document* just to place tags before trying to do any other editing. It is easier to catch mistakes when text is in its final format.

TIP *Plan carefully* when assigning function keys. Some style sheets have ten or fewer tags; they present no problems. If you have more than 10 tags, leave off the ones you'll only use once or twice, like chapter headings, titles, and headlines. Include those you encounter frequently, like lists, tables, and subheads.

Changing or building a style sheet

Now we come to the crux of the matter, the techniques that enable you to tailor Ventura to your requirements. This section gives you a game plan for changing an existing style sheet or building a new one.

When you work in Ventura, you always start with an existing style sheet. Consequently, changing an existing style sheet and creating a new one are the same process. If you save under the same name, you change the existing style sheet. If you save under a new name, you create a new one.

A plan of attack

Style sheets are versatile, powerful tools. If you approach them haphazardly, you are almost certain to get confused by the multitude of options. You need a plan of attack. We're not pretending that our method is the only way. But if you are starting out, our system provides a proven, tested method that saves time and prevents you from overlooking important steps.

Here are the eight steps we recommend for changing or building a style sheet:

1. Create a thumbnail sketch.
2. Load an existing style sheet.
3. Put text on the page.
4. Change the document-wide formatting.
5. Change the existing tag formatting.
6. Add new tags (if necessary).
7. Remove and rename tags (if necessary).
8. Save the style sheet.

Step one: make a thumbnail sketch

Before you start working with Ventura, make a simple drawing of the format you want (or of the changes you want to make to an existing design). Figure 5-11 shows an example. A thumbnail helps you make as many decisions as possible before you start. Figure out the page size, margins, columns, gutters, spacing, and so forth in advance. Write these numbers down on the sketch. Otherwise you doom yourself to endless fiddling as you try option after option.

Step two: load an existing style sheet

Obviously, if you are changing an existing style sheet, you must load it (or open a chapter using the style sheet). But even if you are creating a new style sheet, you must start by loading an existing one.

Which style sheet should you load? If an existing style sheet is close to what you want, it's the obvious choice. The sample style sheets included with Ventura Publisher are one place to start. You also can buy additional style sheets from third-party vendors.

Often, however, starting with an existing style sheet is more work. You can end up doing so much changing, renaming, and deleting that you would have been better off to start from scratch. Many users prefer to start with DEFAULT.STY, which does not contain any tags except Body Text. Beginners tend to start from existing style sheets, since it's the easiest

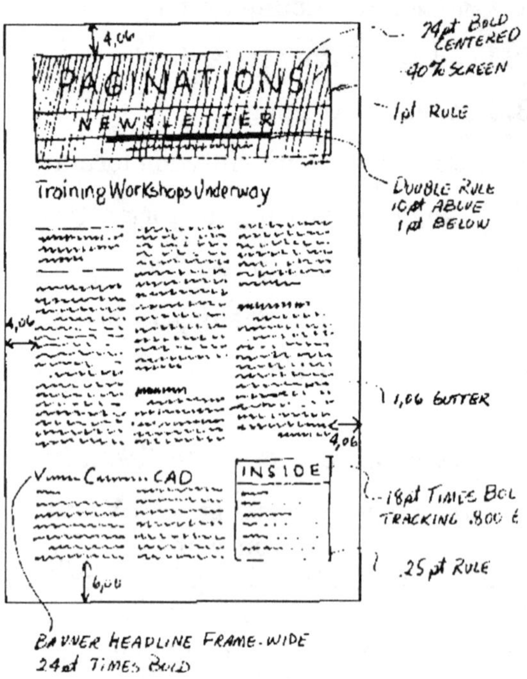

Figure 5-11. Put your ideas on paper before you start to work with Ventura.

way to create a document in a hurry. Power users tend to start from a blank slate so they can have complete control over every aspect of the style sheet.

> WARNING: Whichever style sheet you use as the starting point, be sure to rename it immediately to avoid corrupting the original.

Step three: put text on the page

Load a text file and place it on the page to see the results of changes as you make them. Ideally, you should use the same text that will be in the final document. But the main thing is to have something to work with. You can't change a tag without assigning it to a paragraph — and that means you have to have some text on the page.

Step four: change the document-wide formatting

Start by altering the attributes that concern the document as a whole. Until you set up the basics like margins, columns, headers, and footers, you cannot accurately judge the effects of your other changes.

To change the document-wide formatting, use the dialog boxes listed in Table 5-6. These dialog boxes affect the chapter as a whole and many of them are found, appropriately, in the Chapter menu. You do not need to select a paragraph before changing document-wide formatting, nor do you need to be in Paragraph mode.

Table 5-6. Document-wide formatting.

Menu	Dialog Box	What It Controls
Chapter	Page Size & Layout	The orientation and size of the paper, single or double-sided printing, and which side to start on
	Chapter Typography	Widows and orphans, column balancing, kerning, and other typographic decisions that apply to the entire chapter
	Update Counters	Numbering style and format
	Headers & Footers	Content and position of headers and footers
	Footnote Settings	Format of footnotes
Frame	Margins & Columns	Number and format of margins, columns, and gutters
	Vertical Rules	Rules between columns and their format
Options	Set Printer Info	The printer and width table to use with this style sheet

Step five: change existing tags

Once you have changed the overall, document-wide formatting you can move to the existing tags. To change an existing tag, assign it to a paragraph. Now you can change the tag's attributes with dialog boxes from the Paragraph menu (Figure 5-12). (The Paragraph menu is discussed in detail later in the chapter.) Your changes show up immediately, not just in the highlighted paragraph, but in all the paragraphs with the same tag name throughout the document.

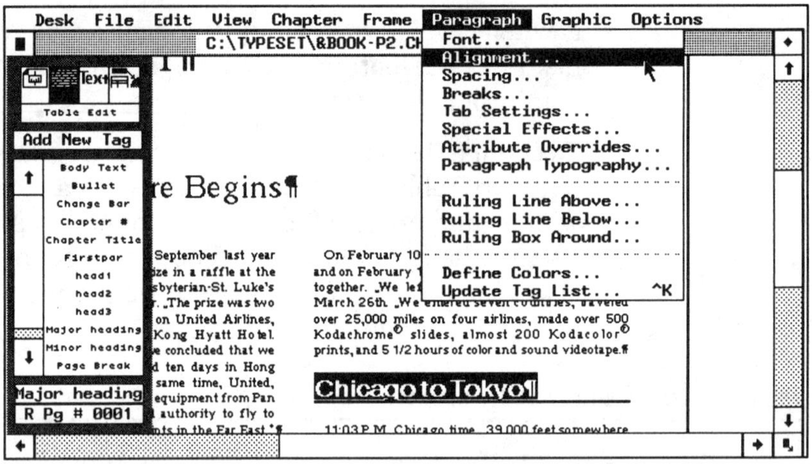

Figure 5-12. To change an existing tag, assign it to a paragraph, then select options from the Paragraph menu.

We recommend changing Body Text first. Body Text is usually the foundation for the entire design. For instance, Ventura uses the line spacing of Body Text for the Line Snap function. In addition, Body Text is often the basis for other tags, so it pays to get it in shape right away.

Once you have formatted Body Text, you can start from the top of the document and work your way down, changing each tag as you come to it. Alternatively, you can start at the top of the Assignment List and work down. The key is to establish a systematic plan that prevents you from accidentally overlooking any tags.

We also recommend a systematic plan for working with the menus. To avoid overlooking key points, we suggest you go step-by-step through the three menus that contain most of the options stored in style sheets: the Chapter menu, the Frame menu, and the Paragraph menu.

We suggest you start with the Chapter menu, which you should normally need to go through only once. Next, go to the Frame menu, which you must use once for the Underlying Page and once for each additional frame in the document. Finally, move on to the Paragraph menu, which you must use once for each tag you add or change. At first, you may have to look at each menu choice to discover which ones you need to change. As you improve, you'll quickly learn which ones to skip and when.

Step six: add new tags

If you can't get the look you want by changing the document-wide attributes and the existing tags, you must add new tags. You create a new tag by copying an existing one. From there, you make changes until the new tag fits your specs. The previous tag is not changed.

You can copy attributes from any existing tag. Naturally, it makes sense to select the one that most closely resembles what you want. Here's how it works:

- Enable Paragraph mode
- Click on the Add New Tag button at the top of the Side-Bar. The dialog box shown in Figure 5-13 appears.
- Type the new name on the top line. On the bottom line, type the tag name to copy from and click OK.

A faster way to tell Ventura where to copy from is to select a paragraph with that tag *before* you select Add New Tag. Ventura then places the old tag name on the bottom line, saving you the trouble of typing. If you have not selected a paragraph, Ventura assumes that you want to start with Body Text.

When you click OK to close the Add New Tag dialog box, Ventura creates the new tag and puts its name on the Assign-

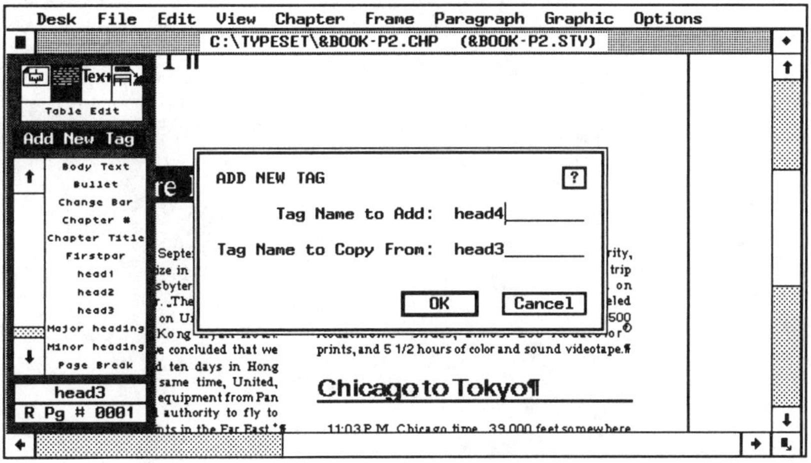

Figure 5-13. The Add New Tag dialog box names the new tag and tells Ventura which tag to copy from.

ment List. If a paragraph was highlighted when you selected Add New Tag, Ventura assigns the new tag to that paragraph. At this point, the new tag is identical to the old one. You will use the Paragraph menu to change its format (see below).

How Ventura adds tags

Ventura sometimes add tags to a document on its own. In about a dozen instances, Ventura automatically generates both a paragraph and a tag to go with it. For instance, when you build a header with the Headers & Footers dialog box, Ventura creates paragraphs at the top of every page and tags those paragraphs as Z_Header. Tables 5-7 and 5-8 summarize the other instances where Ventura generates paragraphs and tags.

As you can see from the tables, Ventura begins the names of generated tags with the prefix Z_ (the letter *Z* followed by an underline character). Because the Assignment List is alphabetic, generated tags show up together at the end of the list. Generated tags do not show on the Assignment List, however, unless you select Generated Tags: Shown from the Set Preferences dialog box.

If the style sheet does not have a format for a generated tag, Ventura copies the attributes of Body Text. You can change this format the same way you change any other tag.

Table 5-7. Generated tags and where they are created.

Tag	Where Created
Z_Boxtext	Box text created in graphics drawing mode
Z_Caption	Captions typed into frames created with Anchors & Captions
Z_Fnot Entry	Footnote entries created with Insert Footnote
Z_Footer	Footers created with Headers & Footers
Z_Header	Headers created with Headers & Footers
Z_Index Main	Paragraphs in index files created with Multi-Chapter
Z_Index Ltr	Letters of the alphabet used as separators in index file
Z_Index Title	Title of Index
Z_Label Cap	Caption labels without automatic numbering
Z_Label Tbl	Caption labels with automatic table numbering
Z_Label Fig	Caption labels with automatic figure numbering
Z_SecN	Numbers (or letters) created with Auto-Numbering. The *N* stands for a sequential number, as in Z_SEC1, Z_SEC2, etc.
Z_TOC Lvl1	Paragraphs in TOC files created with Multi-Chapter
Z_TOC Title	Title of TOC

Table 5-8. Additional generated tags in EMS version only.

Tag	Where Created
Z_HIDDEN	Lines in tables
Z_SINGLE	Lines in tables
Z_DOUBLE	Lines in tables
Z_THICK	Lines in tables

Tag	Where Created
Z_TBL_BEG	Begins a table
Z_TBL_BODY	Defines the tags to be used for each column in a table
Z_TBL_END	Ends a table
Z_TBL_HEAD	Defines the tags to be used for column headers in a table

Just because Ventura tags a paragraph as Z_Boxtext or Z_Caption doesn't mean it has to stay that way. With certain exceptions, you can retag generated paragraphs. For instance, you can have as many different caption tags as you want. To group them together on the Assignment List you might choose to name them Z_Caption1, Z_Caption2, etc. If you prefer, you can give them entirely different names.

The following generated paragraphs cannot be retagged. In these cases, Ventura must have the names intact to accomplish certain special functions:

- Z_Header
- Z_Footer
- ZFnot Entry
- Z_Sec
- All table tags from the EMS version

All other generated tags can be retagged. Generated tags are covered in more detail under their respective sections in later chapters. Thus, Z_Header tags are discussed under headers, Z_Index tags under indexing, and so on.

Step seven: remove or rename tags

Our discussion of how to change style sheets would not be complete if we didn't talk about removing and renaming tags. Since you start from an existing style sheet, you often need to remove extraneous tags that do not apply to the new document. Also, you will often want to rename tags so they conform to a consistent in-house system.

We urge you to be stringent about cleaning out unused tags each time you create a new style sheet or change an old one. Otherwise, unused tags proliferate. Soon the Assignment List becomes overrun with mysterious tags that no longer have any function. The style sheet becomes unusable for anyone but the original authors — and even they will have trouble. To a beginner, Ventura's limit of 128 tags seems very large. Yet we have seen style sheets that bumped into this ceiling — largely because the operator was not strict about keeping the style sheet clean.

Both removing and renaming tags occur with Update Tag List from the Paragraph menu. When you select this option, Ventura first asks if you want to save the changes to your chapter. Then it takes you to the dialog box. The dialog box shows the Assignment List at the left. To remove a tag:

- Scroll down the list until you see the tag name and highlight it with the mouse.
- Click on Remove Selected Tag. Ventura displays a secondary dialog box (Figure 5-14). The top line shows the tag to be deleted (if you accidentally selected the wrong one, type in the correct name).
- On the bottom line, type in the tag name to convert to. Click OK.

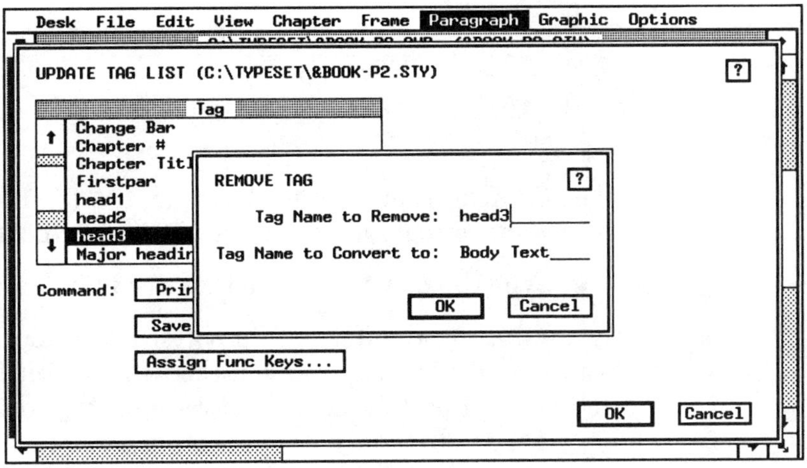

Figure 5-14. The Remove Selected Tag dialog box.

Why convert? There may be paragraphs with this tag name somewhere in the document. Ventura wants to know what to tag them instead. Ventura assumes that you want to convert them to Body Text, so it enters that tag name on the bottom line. To convert to something else, delete "Body Text" and type in the other tag name.

Once you close the secondary dialog box, you return to the Update Tag List dialog box. The old tag disappears from the Assignment List.

Renaming also occurs in the Update Tag List dialog box:

- Select the tag to be renamed from the list.
- Click on the Rename Tag button. A secondary dialog box appears (Figure 5-15).

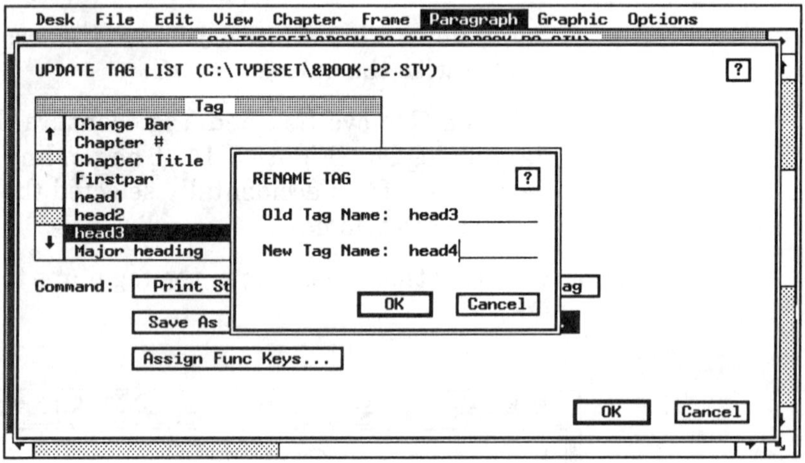

Figure 5-15. The Rename Tag dialog box.

- Confirm that the tag shown on the top line is the one you want to rename (if not, type in the correct name).
- Type the new name into the bottom line and click OK.

Anything you enter on the bottom line, including capitalization and spaces, appears on the Assignment List. You can use this function to rename and regroup tags on the Assignment List to make them easier to find and remember.

Step Eight: Save the style sheet

Save the chapter one last time to capture your changes. When you save a chapter, Ventura saves the style sheet as well. We are going to assume that you followed our advice to rename the style sheet immediately. Once you have renamed the style sheet (and the chapter if necessary), you can hit the Ctrl-S shortcut at intervals to save your work.

Tips for changing and building style sheets

TIP *Make changes to tags in the first few pages* if possible. When you change a tag, Ventura reformats all the preceding pages. The closer you are to the front of the document, the less time it takes.

TIP *Build a better DEFAULT.STY.* The idea behind Ventura's DEFAULT.STY was to provide a clean slate. Unfortunately, it has some unnecessary settings. In particular, it has Vertical Rules On (rules between columns), and eight unwanted tab settings associated with the Body Text. Since you must build tags by copying from Body Text, those settings are duplicated throughout the style sheet in every new tag you create. It's not the end of the world, but these settings eat up memory and cause problems when they crop up unexpectedly. We recommend creating a new version of DEFAULT.STY called BLANK.STY. BLANK.STY has Vertical Rules Off, and the tab settings removed from Body Text. You can make these changes yourself.

TIP *Use Remove Tag to retag paragraphs.* Assume that you have tagged many subheads as Head4. Now you decide that you want them all to be Head3 instead. You could go through the entire chapter and retag each one with the mouse. Or you could remove Head4 and convert to Head3. Now you have correctly tagged all the paragraphs with one command.

TIP *Use at least one lowercase letter* in the tags you create with Add New Tag. You may sometimes bring in a text file that contains tag names that are not in the style sheet. When Ventura encounters such tags, it gives them the attributes of Body Text. It displays their names in upper case in the Assignment List. If your normal tag names use lower case, you can quickly spot these troublesome tags by their capitalization.

TIP *You can view the function key assignments* quickly by hitting Ctrl-K while in any mode except Paragraph mode. This bypasses the Update Tag List dialog box.

Working with the menus

Now that you have a game plan for style sheets, you can turn your attention to the specifics. This section provides an introduction to the three menus you use to build style sheets:

- the Chapter menu
- the Frame menu
- the Paragraph menu

We have deliberately avoided describing every option in every dialog box in every menu. Instead, we have covered the basics below — the fundamental skills you need to build the style sheet for an average business document. Those who want to go further will find the more complex functions covered in later chapters.

In the previous section, we suggested establishing a routine. One idea was to start with document-wide formatting before proceeding to individual tags. Another was to systematically proceed down three menus in order: the Chapter menu, the Frame menu, and the Paragraph menu.

As it happens, these two suggestions work hand-in-hand. Most document-wide functions are found in the Chapter and Frame menus. Most individual tag functions reside in the Paragraph menu. Thus, if you work from left to right (from Chapter to Frame to Paragraph), you automatically do document-wide formatting first and the tag formatting second.

We will follow our own advice and proceed down each of the three menus in turn. We have skipped the menu options that don't apply to building style sheets (we cover them in later chapters). We have made no attempt to duplicate the Reference Guide. Instead, we have spotlighted key features, with special attention to trouble spots and difficult functions.

The Chapter menu

The Chapter menu contains formatting options that apply to the entire document. You might think that it would also include all the options for the Underlying Page, since the Underlying Page repeats throughout the document. But the Underlying Page is actually a special kind of frame. Many of its options are controlled, therefore, by the Frame menu.

Page Size & Layout

This menu choice controls the size of pages and the way they print (Figure 5-16).

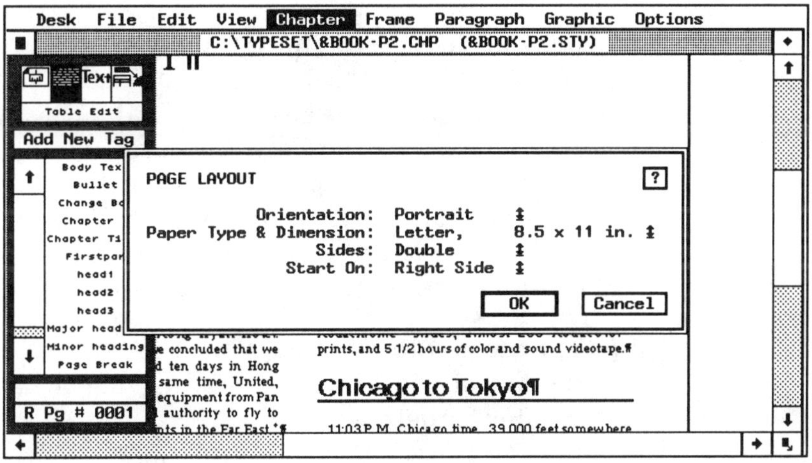

Figure 5-16. The Page Size & Layout dialog box.

Orientation refers to whether the text appears vertically (Portrait) or horizontally (Landscape).

Paper Type & Dimension refers to the size of the paper:

- *Half* sets up an Underlying Page that is 5.5x8.5 in. (half a standard letter-size sheet). Since laser printers don't have a paper tray for half-size sheets, Ventura positions this smaller page in the middle of an 8.5x11 in. sheet of paper.

- *Letter* is a standard 8.5x11 in. page. Warning: Most laser printers can only print to within a quarter inch of the paper's edge. Consequently, you have a quarter-inch dead zone on all four sizes.

- *Legal* is the 8.5x14 in. size standard in American courts and law offices. Most laser printers can optionally use a legal-size paper tray.

- *Double* is an 11x17 in. sheet.

- *B5* and *A4* refer to paper sizes popular in Europe.

- *Broad Sheet* is the 18x24 in. size used for newspaper and tabloid layouts.

If you select Double or Broad Sheet, Ventura presents you with several options, depending on the capabilities of your printer. These options let you print a larger format on a small format printer.

If you have a PostScript printer, you can shrink the page to fit on an 8.5x11 in. sheet. This option makes proofing possible on a laser printer before sending final output to a large-format typesetter. Alternatively, Ventura overlaps several output sheets that can be pieced together to form a large page for camera-ready output. The option "3 strips" (Broad Sheet only) applies only to certain typesetting machines that can produce eight-inch strips that are 24 inches long.

TIP You can create other page sizes not shown here. See the discussion of the Sizing & Scaling dialog box further in this chapter for details.

Sides determines whether the document is single-sided, like most business letters and memos, or double-sided like books and magazines. This is an important option, since it controls other Ventura features.

For instance, if you choose Single, you cannot choose Facing Pages View (there are no facing pages in a single-sided document). Also, you cannot create different headers and footers for left and right pages.

If you choose Double, Ventura automatically makes mirror copies of headers, footers, repeating frames, and margins —

that is, identical but reversed. Suppose you place the page number on the upper left of the left-hand page and then copy this to the facing page. Ventura automatically mirrors the command. It places the page number on the upper *right* of the right-hand page.

It is important to understand that the Sides option refers to the *finished* form of the document. When assembling camera-ready pages for the printer, you print on only one side of the paper. The one-sided pages are assembled into a double-sided document at the print shop.

Start On sets the first page of the document. It is traditional in publishing to make page one a right-hand page. We suggest you stick with this convention — it is convenient to know that right-hand pages always have odd numbers. Choose Start On: Right Side to make page one a right-hand page. Choose Start On: Left Side to make page one a left-hand page.

Chapter Typography

This dialog box controls important typographic settings for the chapter as a whole (Figure 5-17). You can override these settings by putting text inside a frame and using Frame Typography from the Frame menu.

Widows & Orphans control the number of isolated lines allowed to appear at the top and bottom of a page or column (Figure 5-18). The number you enter into the dialog box represents the minimum number of lines that must appear together. The default setting is 2. If two lines appear together, Ventura allows them to remain on the page. If one line appears alone at the top or bottom, Ventura moves the line to another page or column so it remains with the rest of the paragraph. If you increase the setting to 5, Ventura moves text any time it encounters four or fewer lines by themselves.

Eliminating isolated lines makes text easier to read. However, it also creates a problem by leaving a blank space where the lines would otherwise have appeared. Some users prefer to set Widows & Orphans to 1. Then they page through the document and manually correct widows and orphans by editing text or by changing the size of frames. For most purposes, you should select the smallest number that makes the text easy to

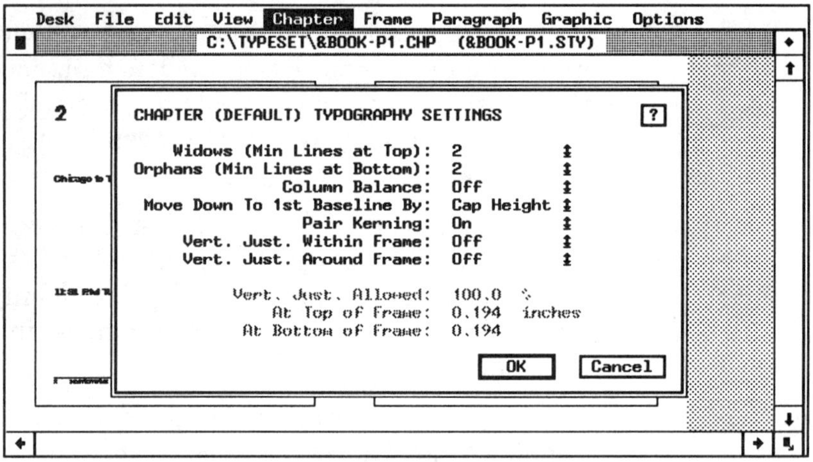

Figure 5-17. The Chapter Typography dialog box.

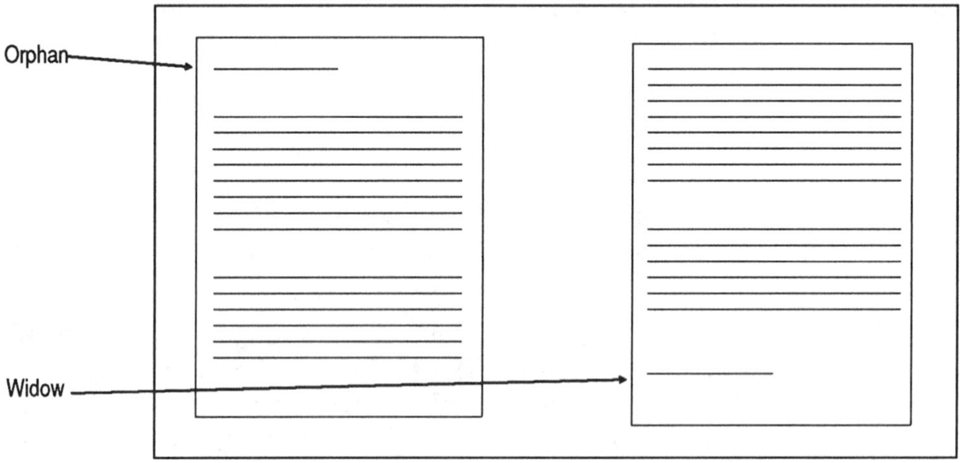

Figure 5-18. Widows are isolated lines at the bottom of a page (right). Orphans are isolated lines at the top (left).

follow (usually 2). But for books, manuals, and similar documents with only one column and long paragraphs, you might want to increase the setting to 3.

Column Balance determines whether Ventura fills up one column before it moves to the next. The left example shown in Figure 5-19 has Column Balance: Off. Notice how Ventura filled up all of column one before putting any text into column two. Conversely, the right example has Column Balance: On. Ventura made all three columns as even as possible.

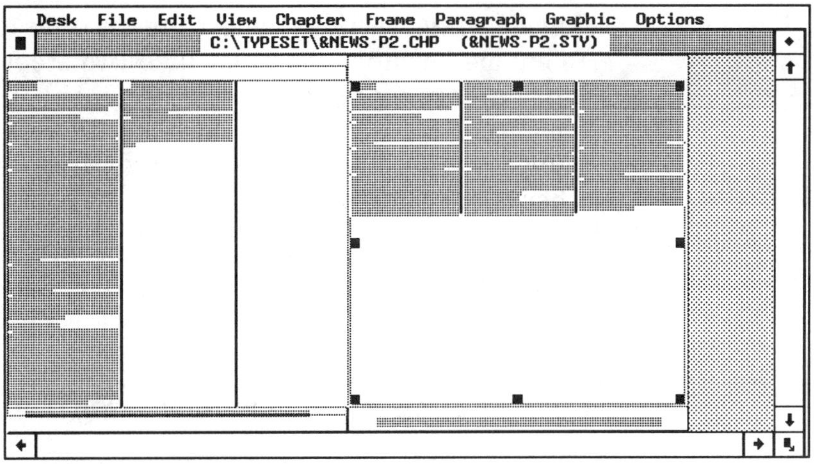

Figure 5-19. Ventura has attempted to equal out the column lengths in the right example because it has Column Balance: On.

For most applications, choose Column Balance: Off. For newspaper-style layouts, you can combine Column Balance: On with frame-wide alignment to create banner headlines. See Chapter Ten, "Building the Chapter."

Move Down To 1st Baseline By determines where Ventura starts the first line of text. In either case, it measures down from the top of the column. If you choose Cap Height, Ventura counts down the height of the tallest capital letter. If you choose Inter-Line, Ventura counts down by the Inter-Line spacing.

Suppose, by way of example, that you have 10-point capital letters and your Inter-Line spacing is 12 points. If you choose Cap Height, the first baseline starts 10 points from the top of the column. If you choose Inter-Line, it starts 12 points down.

Most people would never notice the effect of this setting in single-column documents. In multi-column documents, however, it can affect whether text aligns across columns. With careful planning, you can set up the line spacing of your tags so text in adjacent columns will align. You do this by making all spacing an integer of the Body Text spacing (see Chapter Six, "Building the Chapter," for details). But this scheme is thwarted if Ventura uses the cap height. The more columns, the more the discrepancy multiplies. For this reason, we suggest selecting Inter-Line for most applications.

Pair Kerning overrides the kerning settings of individual tags. To enable kerning, you must take two steps. First you must turn on kerning for the entire document in this dialog box. Then you must turn it on for each tag. (Not as hard as it sounds; you simply turn it on for Body Text, then clone all your other tags from that.)

Users of the Professional Extension will also find vertical justification features in this dialog box. See Chapter Eleven, "The Professional Extension."

Update Counters and Auto-Numbering

These two menu options affect document-wide formatting and the style sheet. However, because of their complexity, we decided to discuss them separately in Chapter Eight, "Advanced Functions."

Headers & Footers

The Headers & Footers option is not recorded in the style sheet. The settings in this dialog box apply only to the current chapter. However, this function creates two generated tags, Z_Header and Z_Footer. The attributes that you apply to those tags *are* recorded in your style sheet, though the contents are not. Think of it this way: The Headers & Footers dialog box determines the contents of a header (what it says). This information is stored in the chapter file. The style sheet controls the header's format (how it looks).

Footnote Settings

Footnote settings are stored in the style sheet. This menu option has been treated separately in Chapter Eight, "Advanced Functions."

The Frame menu

The Frame menu comes mostly into play during document layout (covered in Chapter Six). That is when you place frames on the page and decide how you want them to look. However, three of the options affect document-wide formatting. That's because the Underlying Page — which affects the entire document — is also a frame.

➥ *NOTE: Only the attributes of the Underlying Page are recorded in a style sheet. Attributes of separate frames are stored in the chapter file.*

Margins & Columns

This dialog box specifies the number and size of margins, columns, and gutters (Figure 5-20).

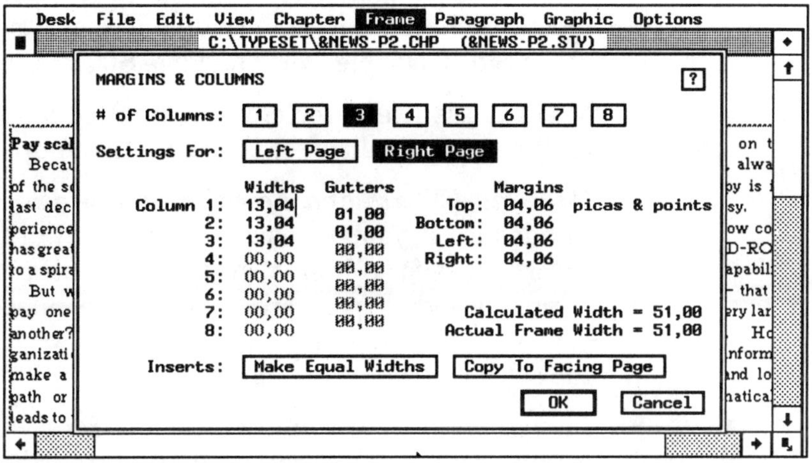

Figure 5-20. The Margins & Columns dialog box.

# of columns is self-explanatory. Click on the desired number.

Settings For tells Ventura which page is being described, in case you wish to have different left and right pages.

Widths / Gutters sets the widths of the columns and the spaces between them (the gutters). The columns are numbered from the left. When you enter values for Column 1, you are describing the left-most column on the page. For columns of equal width, enter only the measurements for the first column and the first gutter. Then click on Make Equal Widths.

Margins sets margins on the inside of the frame or the Underlying Page. To set the margins of the Underlying Page, enable

Frame mode, then select the Underlying Page before opening the dialog box.

In the case of the Underlying Page, the margins usually represent where you want the text to appear. Ventura also lets you create supplementary text margins with the Spacing dialog box.

To set equal margins on both pages, enter the settings for either the left or the right page, then click OK. Ventura automatically copies them to the other page. To create mirrored margins (identical but reversed), set one side, then click on Copy to Facing Page. To have different left and right pages, set each one separately *before* you click OK. Ventura won't let you create different left and right pages unless you previously chose Sides: Double from the Page Size & Layout dialog box.

Mirroring is useful for creating binding margins (extra room on the inside to allow for the space taken up during binding).

Calculated Width and Actual Frame Width enable you to see in advance if your measurements fit into the frame. As you enter values for columns, gutters, and margins, Ventura adds them up and displays the results. Calculated Width shows your settings. Actual Frame Width shows the overall size of the selected frame for comparison.

Inserts contains two important functions. To make columns equal, enter the first column and gutter, then click on Make Equal Widths. To mirror all your values to the opposite page, click on Copy to Facing Page.

Sizing & Scaling

We'll have more to say about the Sizing & Scaling dialog box in Chapter Six, "Building the Chapter." It permits some sophisticated techniques with frames and pictures.

But Sizing & Scaling also can affect document-wide formatting, because you can use it to change the size of the Underlying Page. We have already mentioned that the Underlying Page is similar to an ordinary frame. As with any other frame, you can change its dimensions with the Sizing & Scaling dialog box.

Most people are satisfied with the page sizes available in the Page Size & Layout dialog boxes. When you select one of these sizes (Half, Letter, Legal, etc.), Ventura changes the dimensions of the Underlying Page for you.

If you want an unusual size not available from Page Size & Layout, you can create a different Underlying Page:

- Enable Frame mode and select the Underlying Page.
- Select Sizing & Scaling (Figure 5-21).

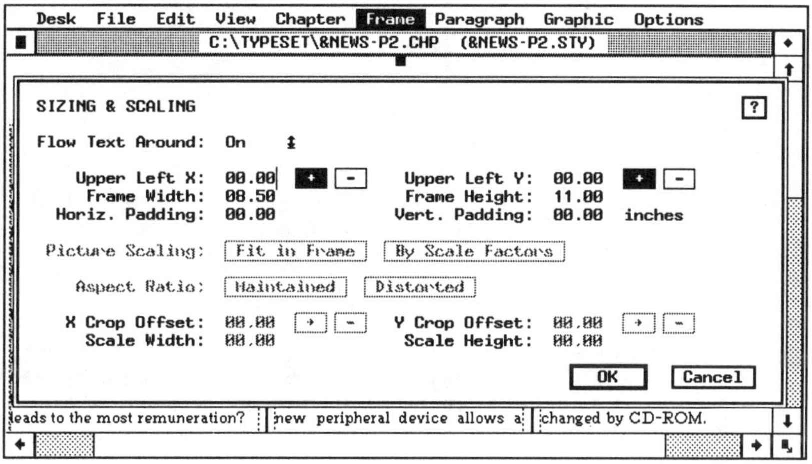

Figure 5-21. The Sizing & Scaling dialog box

- Enter the new width of the Underlying Page on the Frame Width line. Enter the new height on the Frame Height line.

When printed on an 8.5x11 in. sheet of paper, this new, smaller Underlying Page appears in the upper left (Figure 5-22).

To center the smaller Underlying Page on the larger sheet of paper, use Upper Left X and Upper Left Y from Sizing & Scaling. Upper Left X controls the position from the top to bottom. Upper Left Y controls the position from left to right.

To center a page horizontally, subtract the new width from the old width and divide by two. Enter this number into the Upper Left X line. For instance, suppose you create a new Underlying Page that is 6x8 in. To center the new page horizontally:

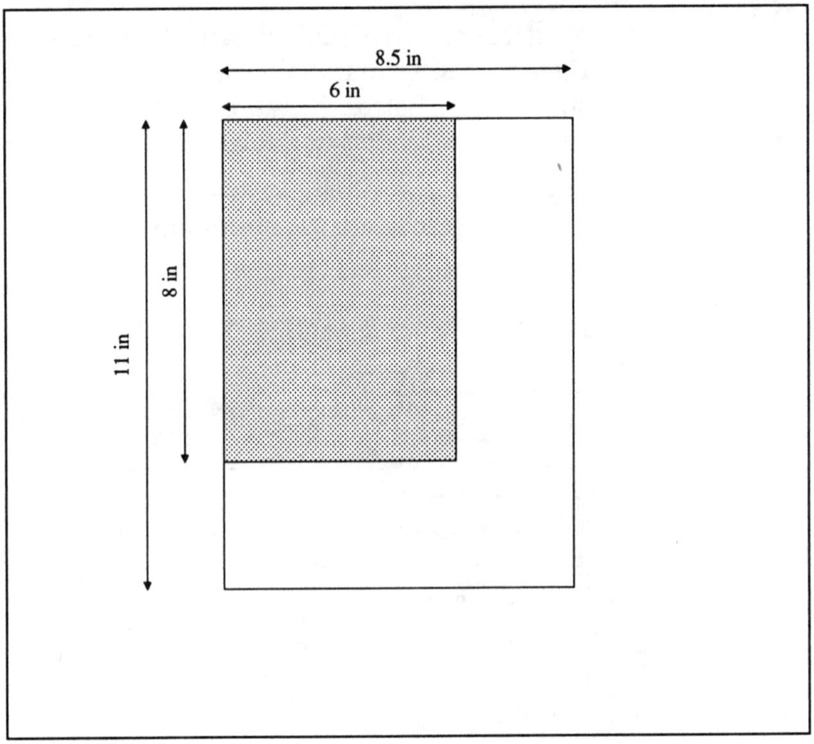

Figure 5-22. If you create a smaller Underlying Page with Sizing & Scaling, it initially appears in the upper left corner of the larger sheet of paper.

```
8.5 (old width) - 6 (new width) = 2.5

2.5/2 = 1.25
```

You would enter Upper Left X: 01.25 inches.

To center the page vertically, subtract the new from the old and divide by two:

```
11 (old height) - 8 (new height) = 3

3/2 = 1.5
```

You would enter Upper Left Y: 01.50 inches.

Figure 5-23 illustrates the results of these example settings.

Vertical Rules

This menu option lets you put rules between columns, or anywhere on the page (Figure 5-24).

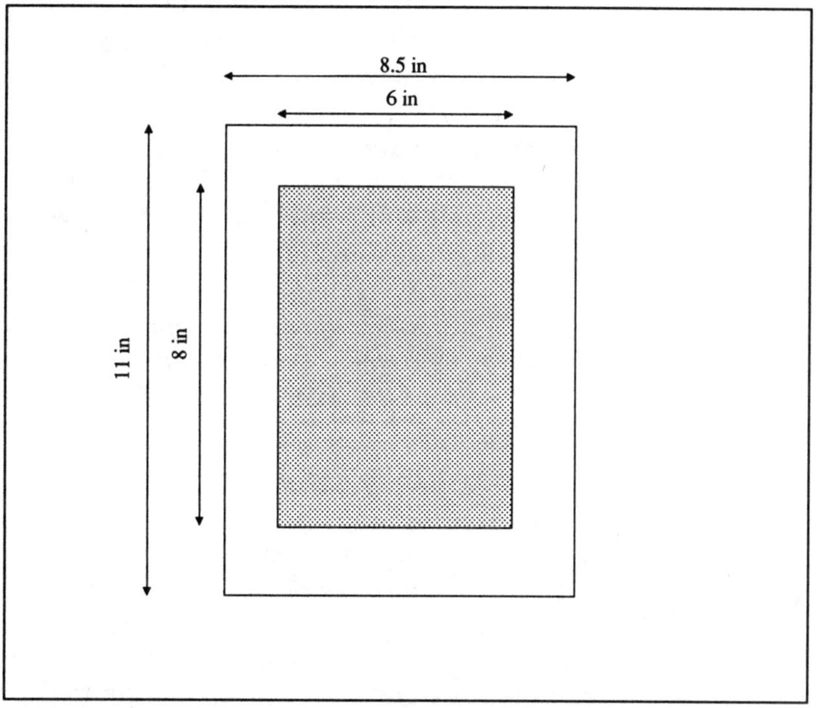

Figure 5-23. Use X and Y Offset to center a smaller page on a larger sheet of paper.

Rule 1 units of measurement

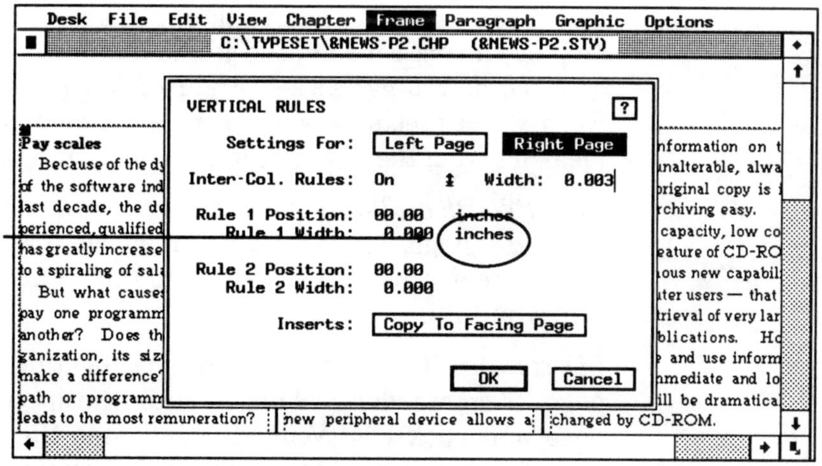

Figure 5-24. The Vertical Rules dialog box.

Settings For tells Ventura which page you are working on.

Inter-Col. Rules creates vertical rules between columns. To put a rule between every column, choose On and specify the width. Ventura automatically makes the rule the length of the column and centers it in the gutter. Ventura can create rules as small as a fraction of a point and as large as 36 points. Usually, you will want a thin rule between columns (00.25 fractional pts. or smaller).

➡ *NOTE: All measurements are controlled by the units shown for Rule 1. If the Rule 1 Width is in inches, the number you type for the width of the Inter-Col. Rules also will be interpreted as inches.*

Rule 1 Position and Rule 2 Position lets you place one or two vertical rules anywhere on the page (not just between columns). One possible application would be to place vertical rules on the *outsides* of columns. However, Ventura provides no way to automatically control the length of these rules. This feature, therefore, should be used only if you want vertical rules that extend from the top margin to the bottom margin.

Rules created in this dialog box appear throughout the document. You cannot turn them on or off for selected pages. Although Ventura does not allow control of the length of the vertical rules, it does permit their placement from left to right. To place a vertical rule, specify its distance *from the left edge of the Underlying Page* (see Figure 5-25), not from the margin. Even when placing a vertical rule inside a frame, you must measure from the left edge of the Page containing that frame.

Rule 1 Width and Rule 2 Width apply to rules placed separately on the page. They have no effect on Inter-Column rules, which are specified in the space to the right of the Inter-Col. Rules line.

Inserts permits you to copy your specifications to the opposite page. To create identical pages, enter the specifications for one page and click OK. Ventura duplicates the settings on the second page. To create mirrored pages, enter the specs for one page, then click on Copy to Facing Page. To create different pages, enter each page separately *before* you click OK.

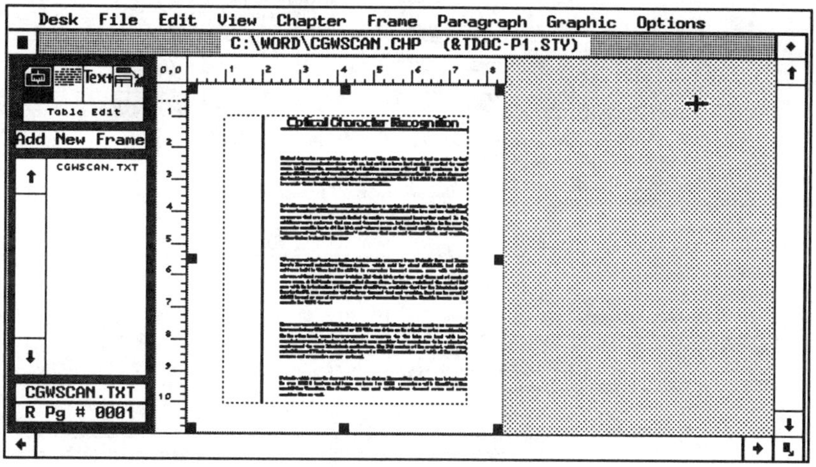

Figure 5-25. To place a vertical rule, specify the distance from the left edge of the Underlying Page, which is 2 inches in this example.

Paragraph menu

The Paragraph menu controls the typographic attributes of tags. Using this menu, you can create an amazing assortment of formats and effects. You can have up to 128 separate tags in a single style sheet.

A tremendous amount of typographic sophistication lurks in the Paragraph menu. Plan to spend some time mastering its options. It is time well spent. Ventura Publisher is so powerful that many tasks can be accomplished in several ways. Generally, *it is best to do the job with a tag* even if you have other options. Once you create a tag, you can effortlessly duplicate the format.

Font

First a word about type terminology. A type*face* is a particular design — Times, for instance. A type *font* is a specific variety — for example, Times 14-point Bold Italic.

When you select Font, a dialog box appears with four scrollable lists. The contents of these lists vary according to the printer you use. Figure 5-26 shows the Font dialog box for a PostScript printer. Figure 5-27 shows the same dialog box as it appears for a Hewlett-Packard LaserJet Plus.

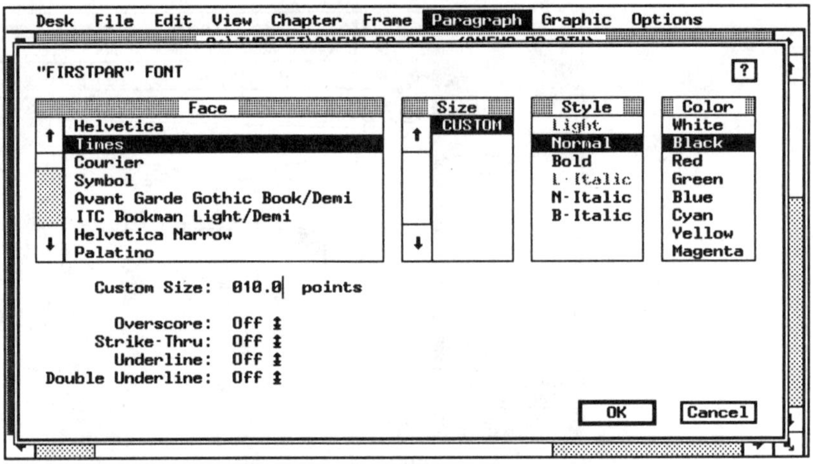

Figure 5-26. The Font dialog box for PostScript printers.

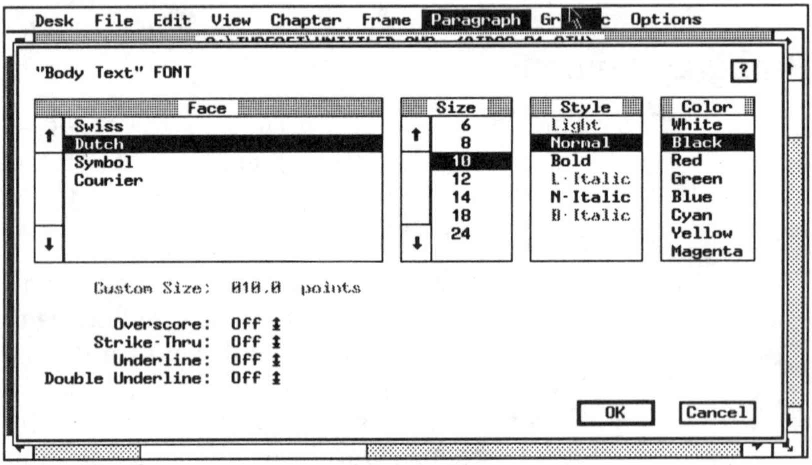

Figure 5-27. The Font dialog box for Hewlett-Packard LaserJet printers.

Face specifies the typeface for this tag. To choose a new typeface, scroll down the list. Highlight the one you want with the mouse. If you install a PostScript printer, you will see a long list of fonts. Not all of these are necessarily active for your particular printer. (See Chapter Seven, "Producing Output," for tips on how to add fonts.)

Size controls the point size of the type. The numbers vary according to the capabilities of your printer. If you are using a printer with scaleable fonts, the word Custom appears. You then type in the desired point size (in half-point increments).

For other printers, the list shows the available point sizes. Highlight the size you want with the mouse.

Style enables you to control the weight (light, medium, bold) and the slope (normal or italic) of the typeface. If a style shows in gray, it is not available for your printer. You choose a style by clicking on it with the mouse.

Overscore, Strike-Thru, Underline, and Double Underline apply attributes to the entire paragraph and to every paragraph with the same tag name. You also can change the Font and apply attributes in Text mode. However, changes in Text mode affect only the highlighted text at that one point in the document.

Alignment

This option governs the way text lines up (Figure 5-28).

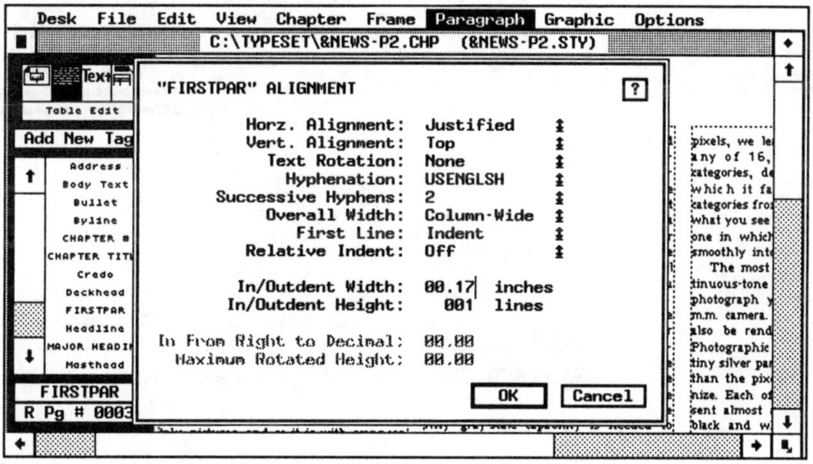

Figure 5-28. The Alignment dialog box.

Horz. Alignment controls the five basic methods of setting type horizontally. Figure 5-29 shows the effects of the five choices.

Vert. Alignment governs vertical alignment with reference to the margins of the frame or Page containing the text. Figure 5-30 shows the effects of the three choices.

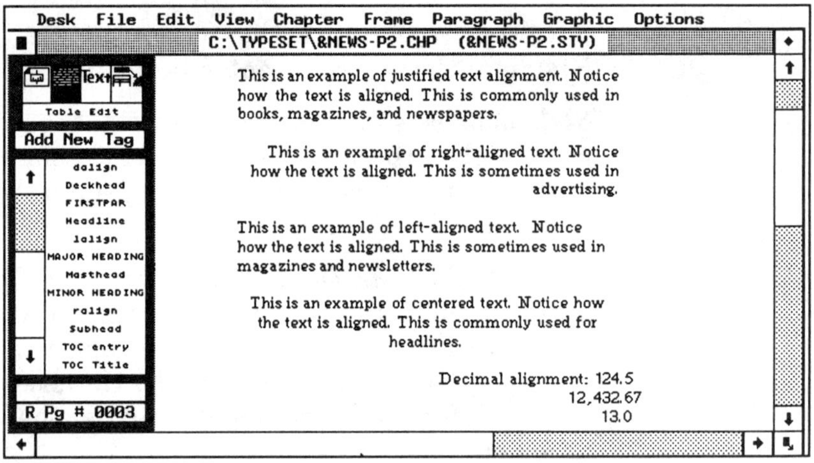

Figure 5-29. The five horizontal alignment options.

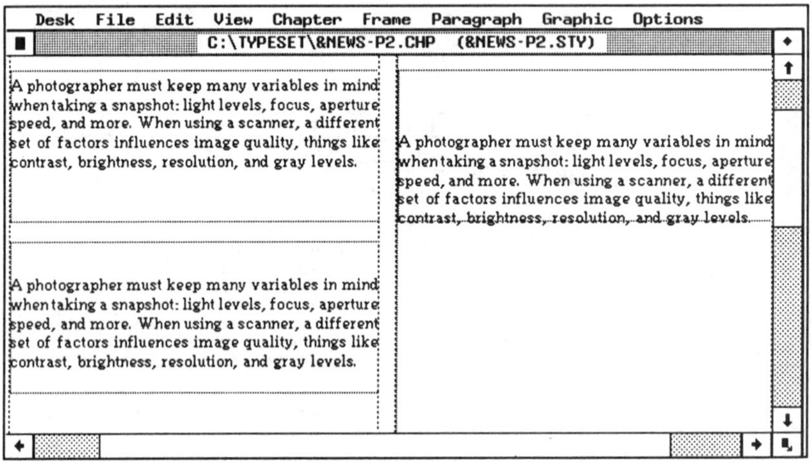

Figure 5-30. The three vertical alignment options.

Text Rotation permits you to revolve text from its normal position along the baseline. Figure 5-31 shows the results of the four choices. Rotated text is particularly useful for tables, labels, forms, and callouts.

If you rotate text, other effects rotate with it, such as ruling lines and boxes around. You can limit how much vertical space the rotation takes up with the Maximum Rotated Height line at the bottom of the dialog box. Be sure to allow enough space here. If in doubt, enter a large number. Otherwise, your rotated text will bump up against a ceiling.

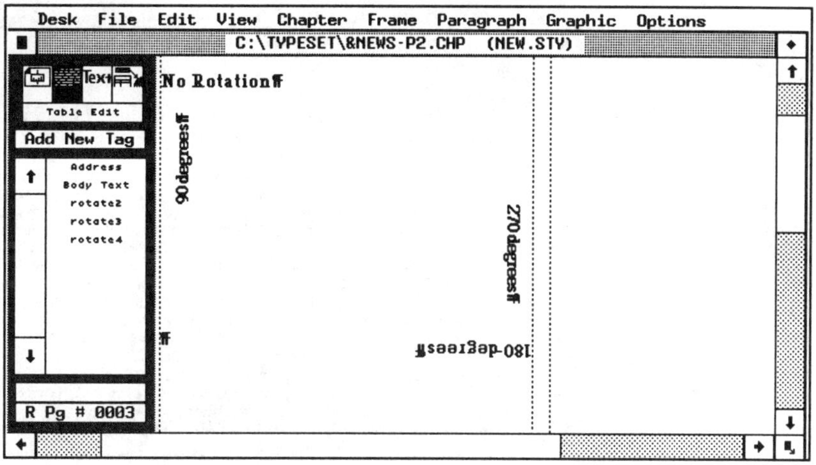

Figure 5-31. The four options for rotated text.

Hyphenation governs whether text for this tag is hyphenated, and if so, with which dictionary. By choosing the name of a hyphenation dictionary (such as USENGLSH), you tell Ventura to use that dictionary to place discretionary hyphens into the text file as it is loaded into Ventura. Ventura then uses these hyphens if needed to justify lines. By choosing Off, you force Ventura to keep words undivided.

In general, you want text hyphenated. There are, however, exceptions, including headlines and other display type. See Chapter Eight, "Advanced Functions," for a further discussion of Ventura's hyphenation alternatives.

Successive Hyphens controls the number of lines in a row that can be hyphenated. This problem comes into play in narrow, justified columns where Ventura has to hyphenate frequently. Without a hyphenation limit, you can end up with a so-called *ladder* of hyphens in the right column. Most designers suggest a limit of two or three successive hyphens.

Overall Width determines whether the tagged text is confined to the column or spaced across the entire frame. Choosing frame-wide causes a headline to be spread across the entire page, though the rest of the text is restricted to narrow columns (Figure 5-32). Frame-wide, in other words, overrides the normal column boundaries. It causes a paragraph to stretch the full width of the frame even if the rest of the text is restricted to columns. However, if you put a frame-wide head-

Figure 5-32. A frame-wide banner headline.

line in the middle of a page, it will overlap the text in the left column *unless* you set Column Balance On.

You turn on Column Balance for the Underlying Page with the Chapter Typography dialog box. Even if Column Balance is off for the Underlying Page, you can place a frame on top of the Page and override the chapter defaults with the Frame Typography dialog box.

First Line is misleading because it can affect more than the first line of a paragraph. You also may notice that there is a space between Relative Indent and the In/Outdent settings immediately below. In fact, these four choices — First Line, Relative Indent, In/Outdent Width, and In/Outdent Height — function together to control how (and whether) text lines is indented and outdented from the rest of the paragraph.

Thanks to the First Line option, there is no need to insert tabs or spaces to indent the first line of a paragraph. Type the paragraph flush left in your word processor, then use this option to tell Ventura to indent the line. If you choose Indent, the line is pushed to the right. If you choose Outdent, the line is pushed left, overriding the margin settings. Outdent is useful for so-called *hanging indents*. And by entering a high number like 99 into the In/Outdent Height line, you can effectively cause an entire paragraph to shift to the left of the normal margins.

Neither Indent nor Outdent takes effect unless you enter an amount in In/Outdent Width. *In / Outdent Width* controls the amount of fixed space you add. This amount applies to both Indent or Outdent (whichever you chose above). The standard indent is one em (equivalent to the point size of the type). Long text lines and other special circumstances demand larger indents. If you do not want an indent, make this amount zero. The In/Outdent Width is measured from the left margin. If you have created temporary margins with In From Left in the Spacing dialog box, then it is measured from this temporary margin.

In / Outdent Height specifies the number of lines for which the indent or outdent takes effect. Under most circumstances, this is one. However, you may want an indent (or outdent) of two or more lines to produce a special effect.

Relative Indent is covered in more detail in Chapter Eight, "Advanced Functions." For most purposes it should be turned off by choosing None. If you choose On, each line will automatically start where the previous line ended (Figure 5-33). This effect is useful when you want to put two separate tags on the same line, and you don't know where the first one will end.

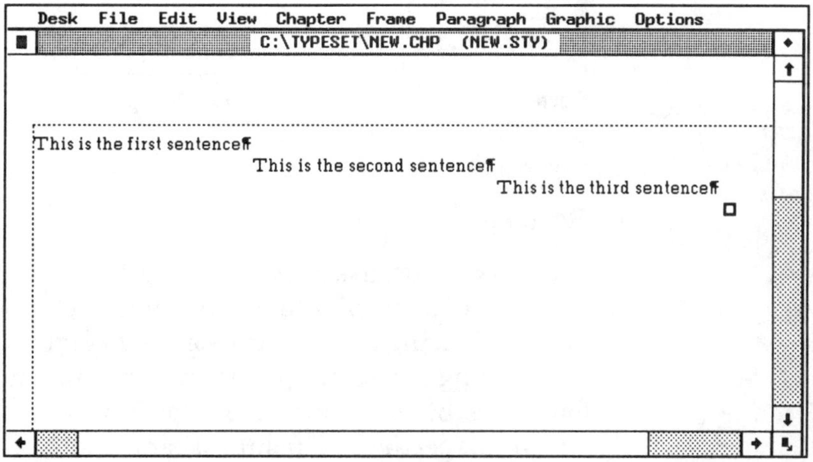

Figure 5-33. A relative indent starts each new paragraph where the previous one left off.

In From Right to Decimal is grayed out and inactive unless you choose Decimal alignment from the Horz. Alignment pop-up menu. When active, it specifies the distance from the right margin to the decimal point. Ventura then lines up all the decimal points at this spot.

Maximum Rotated Height is grayed out and inactive unless you rotate the text. If you do not set a maximum rotated height, Ventura pushes the text below out of the way to make room for the rotated text, no matter how much space it requires. If you set a maximum height, Ventura sticks to that limit. If it cannot fit the rotated line into the maximum, it wraps it and creates additional rotated lines (Figure 5-34).

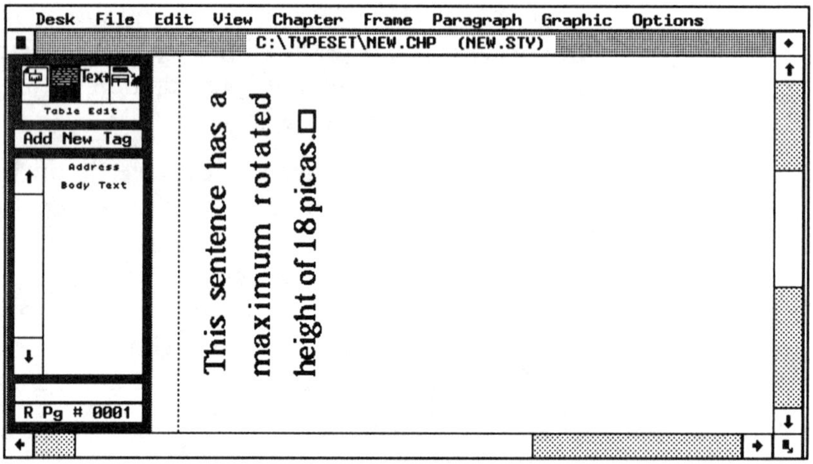

Figure 5-34. You can limit the vertical space taken up by rotated text.

Spacing

It is easy to confuse Spacing with Alignment, the menu choice that precedes it. Alignment controls the *way* in which text is placed. Spacing controls the *amount* (Figure 5-35). We recommend using fractional pts. to measure the spacing in the first four lines of this dialog box. Spacing is related to type size, which is specified in points. Using the same units makes it easier to create consistent, pleasing designs.

Above and *Below* refer to extra space above or below *the entire paragraph*. They do not affect the space between the lines. They should, however, have a relationship with Inter-Line spacing. If, for example, Inter-Line is 12.00 fractional pts.,

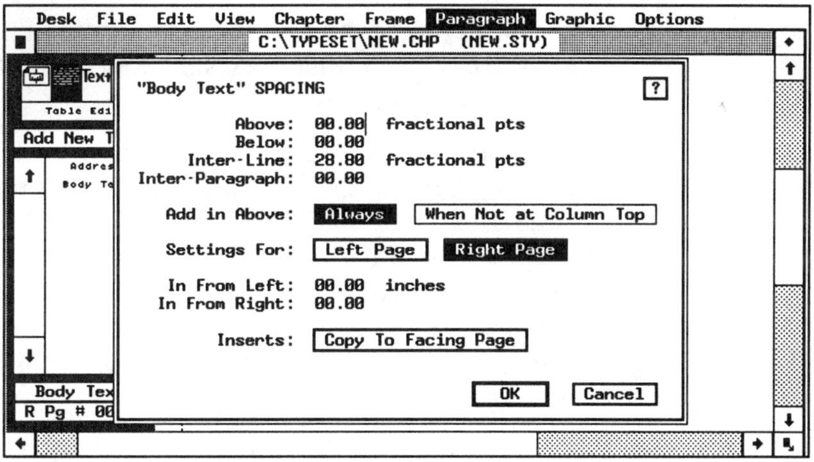

Figure 5-35. The Spacing dialog box.

then 06.00, 12.00, 18.00, and 24.00 would be appropriate choices for above and below space.

In some ways, you can think of Above and Below space as minimum settings. If Ventura encounters two tags in a row with conflicting amounts of Above and Below space, it uses the larger of the two. It does not add them. Thus, you do not have to worry that spacing effects will accumulate and give undependable results.

A good rule for beginning desktop publishers is to use only Above space (if you need extra space at all; often Inter-Line spacing is all that is required). Spacing effects are more predictable if all the tags use Above space rather than a mixture of Above, Below, and Inter-Paragraph. In addition, Above spacing can be partially controlled with the Add in Above line (see below). If you cannot get the effect you want with Above space alone, then use Below space.

Inter-Line refers to the spacing between lines of a paragraph. Typographers call this *leading* (pronounced *ledd-ing).* As a rule, type of 14 points or below should have an extra point or two of space between lines for easy readability. Thus, 10-point type should have Inter-Line spacing of 11 or 12 points (written in the dialog box as 11.00 fractional pts. or 12.00 fractional pts).

Larger type sizes can usually be *set solid* — the typographic term which means to use the same Inter-Line spacing as the point size — for instance, 30-point type with 30 points of Inter-Line spacing.

Ventura automatically adjusts the Inter-Line spacing each time you change the Font size *unless* you use the Set Preferences dialog box to disable this feature. Once you disable it, Ventura remembers your preference in the future. If you pick Auto-Adjustments: Both or Auto-Adjustments: Style, Ventura will change the spacing. Since this can have unpredictable results, we recommend working with Auto-Adjustments set to *None* or " and - -.

Inter-Paragraph adds space between identical paragraphs. Most users get best results by setting Inter-Paragraph to zero for all tags. They use Above and Inter-Line to control the spacing of most tags, and Below for occasional special purposes.

The *Add in Above* line lets Ventura do some of the thinking for you. The program will look at a page and decide if Above spacing is appropriate. Text elements like subheads need extra space above them when they are in the middle of the page. This space helps set them apart from the body text (Figure 5-36). But these same subheads don't need the space when they are the first line at the top of a column. In that case

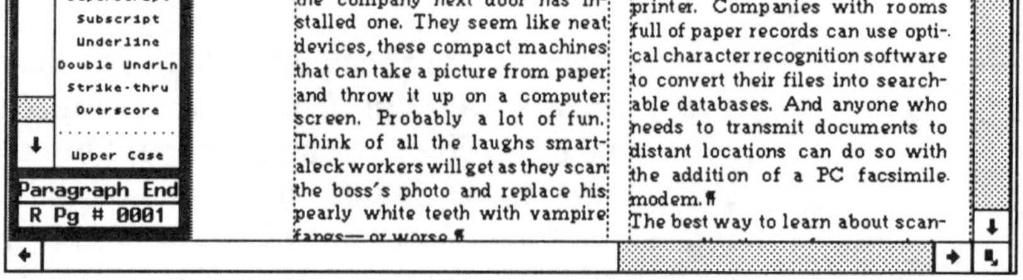

Figure 5-36. The example at right has the above spacing set to take effect only when it is not at the top of a column.

the additional white area would throw off the balance of the page. To control this problem, select When Not At Column Top. If you want extra space at all times, select Always.

In From Left and In From Right are supplementary margin settings that can be used in addition to the original margins of the frame. They have several applications. The most common is for temporary indents. Long quotations, for instance, are often set apart from the rest of the text by temporary indents on the left and the right (see Figure 5-37).

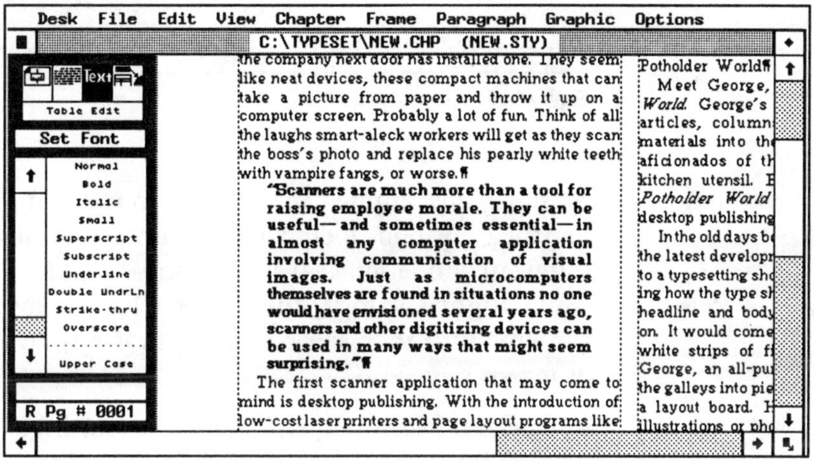

Figure 5-37. Temporary margins created with In From settings in the Spacing dialog box.

There are other cases when you want supplementary margins different from those of the frame or column. Mirrored (or *complementary*) left and right pages are one example. In that case, the frame margin is identical for each page, but the text is spaced in from left on one page and in from right on the other.

It is important to distinguish the In From option from the In/Outdent in the Alignment dialog box. Use *In/Outdent* to affect the first line (or first few lines). Use *In From* to affect every line in the tag.

The two options can be used together. Figure 5-38 shows one idea. In this example, In From Left pushes the entire paragraph to the left. Then In/Outdent pushes the first line back to the right again. The result is a hanging indent.

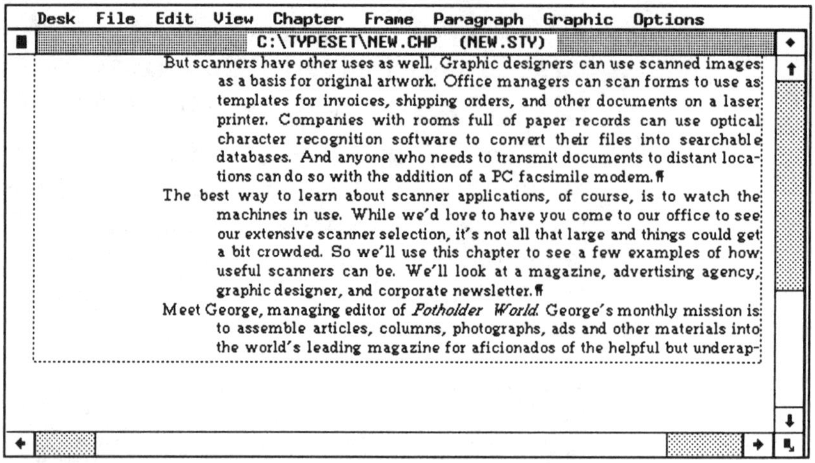

Figure 5-38. A hanging indent.

Settings For applies to the *In From* settings. As with other Ventura options, facing pages can be identical, mirrored, or different. For identical pages, enter the In From Left and In From Right settings, then click OK. For mirrored pages, set the amounts then click on Inserts: Copy to Facing Page. For different pages:

- Click on Right page and enter its settings.
- Click on Left page and enter its settings.
- Click OK.

Breaks

Breaks is a versatile option with advanced applications. It provides a high degree of control over the text placement. We cover special uses such as tables and auto-numbered section headings in Chapter Eight, "Advanced Functions."

The Breaks dialog box determines what happens before and after a paragraph. It controls whether a paragraph should jump (break) to the next page, the next column, or the next line (Figure 5-39).

Page Break sends tags to a new page. Selecting Before creates a page break before the tag. In other words, the paragraph always starts on a new page. Selecting Before/Until Left means that Ventura will keep breaking pages until it finds a

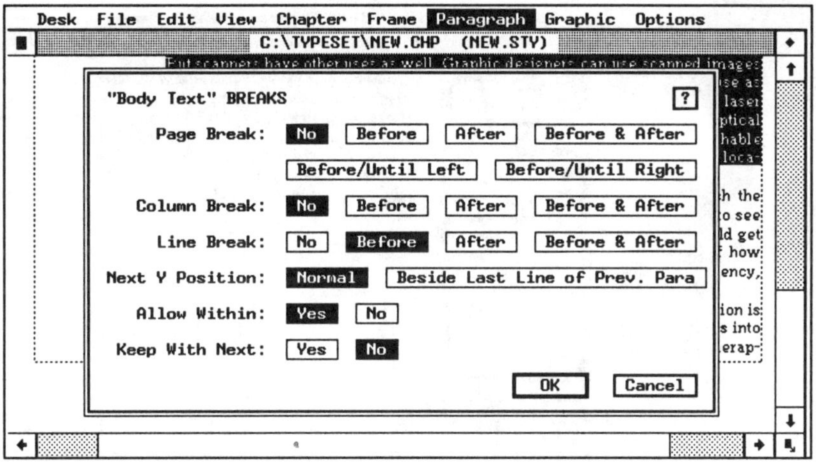

Figure 5-39. The Breaks dialog box.

left page. Then it will start the paragraph. This is useful for technical manuals, for instance, where you want each section to start on the left to create a double page spread.

Before / Until Right means that Ventura will skip pages until it can place the paragraph on a right page. This might be appropriate, for example, for chapter titles in a book. The traditional rule is to start a chapter on a right-hand page. If you give the first tag in the chapter (the title, for instance) a Before/Until Right, Ventura will automatically create blank pages if necessary to force the title paragraph to start on a right-hand page.

Selecting *After* puts a page break after the paragraph. In other words, the next paragraph is forced onto the next page. Page Break: After is valuable for creating a special page break tag that can be applied to an empty paragraph. If you set the Alignment to Right, and the Line Break to None, the page break paragraph resides out of the way in the right margin on the same line as the previous paragraph (Figure 5-40).

Selecting *Before & After* isolates the tag on a page by itself, because Ventura puts page breaks before and after.

Column Break operates in the same fashion as Page Break. Most tags use the No option here, which lets Ventura decide where to end columns. Selecting Before forces a column break before the paragraph, causing it to start at the top of the next column. Selecting After puts a break after, sending the follow-

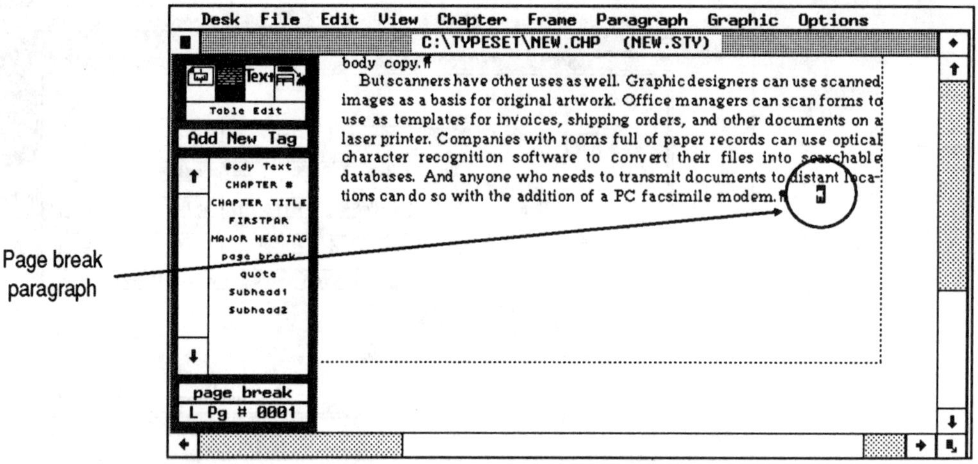

Figure 5-40. Page Break: After gives this empty paragraph the power to force the following text onto the next page.

ing text to the top of a new column (no matter how much space is left below). Selecting Before & After causes the tag to stand alone in a column.

Line Break works in the same fashion as the previous two options. Most tags include some kind of line break. Before puts a line break ahead of the paragraph, causing it to start on a new line, no matter what precedes it. Choosing After puts the line break after the paragraph, forcing the next paragraph to a new line. This choice is useful for the last entry in a table. Choosing Before & After means that the tag is always separated by line breaks above and below. Choosing No means that the tag can reside on the same line with other tags. This option is useful for newsletter layouts (Figure 5-41).

The line break option does not affect lines *within* a paragraph. It concerns itself with breaks *between* paragraphs. If you choose Line Break: No, words within the paragraph still wrap to the next line when they reach the right margin. Ventura will not, however, put a line break before or after that paragraph.

The line break choice of one paragraph can override that of another. For example, assume that you want a paragraph to reside on the same line as the preceding paragraph. You choose, therefore, Line Break: No. If the paragraph still

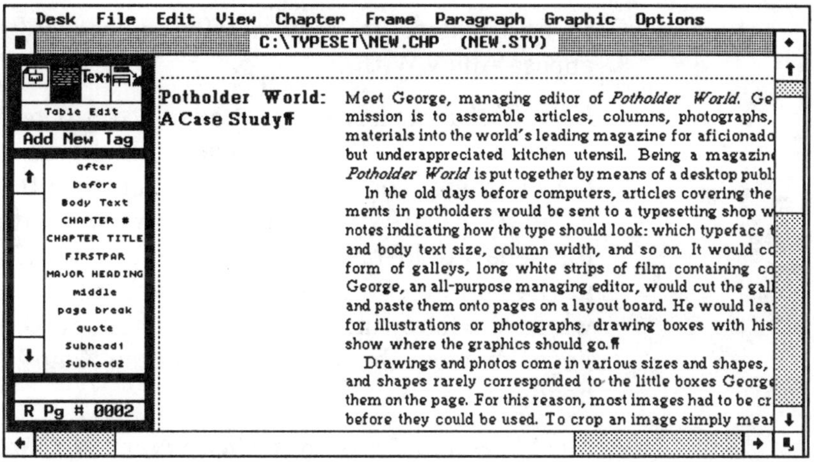

Figure 5-41. The second column of this newsletter has no line break before and thus can reside on the same line as the headline.

resides on a separate line, check the paragraph that precedes it. It probably contains an After or a Before & After line break.

Next Y Position refers to the vertical position of the tag. It applies only if you have *not* specified a line break before. If you choose Line Break: Before, Ventura is going to start the paragraph on a new line anyway. If you do *not* specify a line break before, you have two options. Normal places the beginning of the tag at the same spot vertically as the *first* line of the previous tag. Beside Last Line of Prev. Paragraph places it next to the *last* line.

Allow Within controls whether to allow line breaks within a paragraph. Choosing Yes allows line breaks. If there isn't room for an entire paragraph at the bottom of a page (or column), Ventura will break it in two and send part of it to the next page (or column).

Choosing No does not permit line breaks within the paragraph. It has the effect of forcing the entire paragraph to stay on the same page. If there is not enough room at the bottom, it is sent to the next page (or column).

Allow Within is another feature that automates formatting by letting Ventura make some of the page layout decisions. It is useful when you have special paragraphs that should not be separated. For instance, many people like to put warnings inside special boxes. Normally, you don't want these warnings to be divided. To prevent such paragraphs from splitting, choose Allow Within: No.

Keep With Next forces a paragraph to stay on the same page or column as the following paragraph. If there is not room for both of them, Ventura moves both of them to the next page (or column). Keep With Next can prevent headings from becoming separated from the text they refer to. If a heading occurs at the bottom of a page, it is possible that it could be isolated, while the following paragraph is sent to the next column or page. To avoid this possibility, choose Keep With Next: Yes for headings.

Most tags should use Keep With Next: No, since forcing tags to stay on the same page reduces Ventura's ability to produce balanced pages. It is possible to choose Keep With Next: Yes and return to the Workspace to find that all your text has disappeared. You have created an impossible situation, where Ventura cannot keep all the paragraphs together, so it endlessly creates new pages looking for one where everything will fit. To repair this situation, open the Breaks dialog box again and choose Keep With Next: No.

Advanced Paragraph attributes

The Tab Settings, Special Effects, Attribute Overrides, and Paragraph Typography menu options are covered in Chapter Eight, "Advanced Functions."

Ruling Line Above, Ruling Line Below, Ruling Box Around

These three menu options are almost identical in function except for the position of the line — whether it is above, below, or around the paragraph. Figure 5-42 shows a few of the possible permutations.

It is important to distinguish between the lines created in these dialog boxes and those created with Graphic mode. Graphic lines are drawn with the mouse. They are linked to frames — move the frame and the lines move with it. Move the text within the frame, however, and the lines stay in their original position. By contrast, ruling lines from the Paragraph menu are drawn automatically by Ventura and linked to a

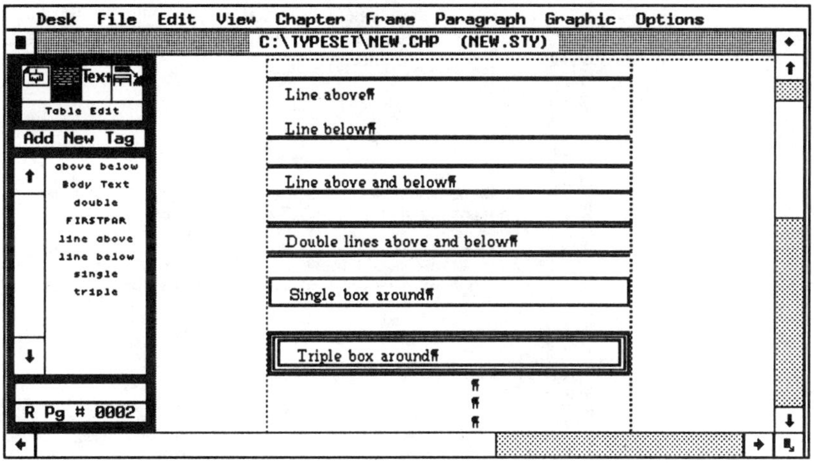

Figure 5-42. A few of the many lines possible with Ventura.

paragraph. If you move the paragraph, the lines move with it. Throughout the document, every paragraph with the same name has the identical lines.

There are limitations to the use of these ruling lines. Lines above and below can appear either separately or together. You cannot, however, combine a box around with lines above or below. You can have up to three lines of varying widths, up to a total of 36 points. Although you can vary the widths, all the rules from one dialog box must be the same pattern and color. Boxes around will not extend past column and page boundaries. If the paragraph continues onto the next page (or column), the box does not show up for the second portion.

Figure 5-43 shows the dialog box for Ruling Line Above.

Width determines the line's width in relation to the paragraph and the margins. Choose None to turn off a ruling line. Choose Text to create a line that is only as wide as the text. Choose Margin to create a line the width of the margin (no matter how short or long the text). Choose Column to make lines that extend to the column boundaries. Choosing Frame to draw a line the full width of the frame margin. Choose Custom to create a line with a fixed length and position that you specify. Figure 5-44 illustrates the options.

Color controls the color of the line. The same color is assigned to all lines you create in this dialog box. Black is the normal

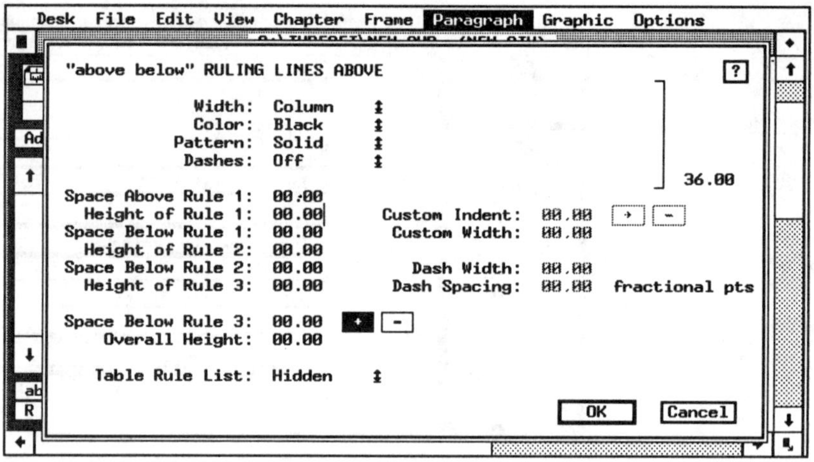

Figure 5-43. The Ruling Line Above dialog box.

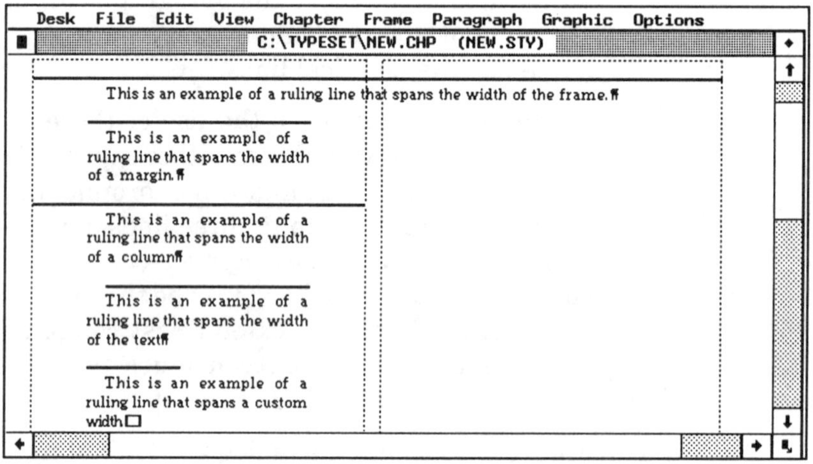

Figure 5-44. Ventura provides five options for line widths. The Custom option can be any length and any position.

choice for rules. The other colors refer to printing options covered in Chapter Seven, "Producing Output," or special gray tints, as covered in Chapter Eight, "Advanced Functions." White creates an invisible line under normal circumstances. However, white lines are visible against gray or black backgrounds.

Pattern varies the shading of the lines. The same pattern is assigned to all the lines created by this dialog box.

Dashes Off turns dashed lines on or off. *Dash Width and Dash Spacing* control the size of the dashes and the space between them (Figure 5-45).

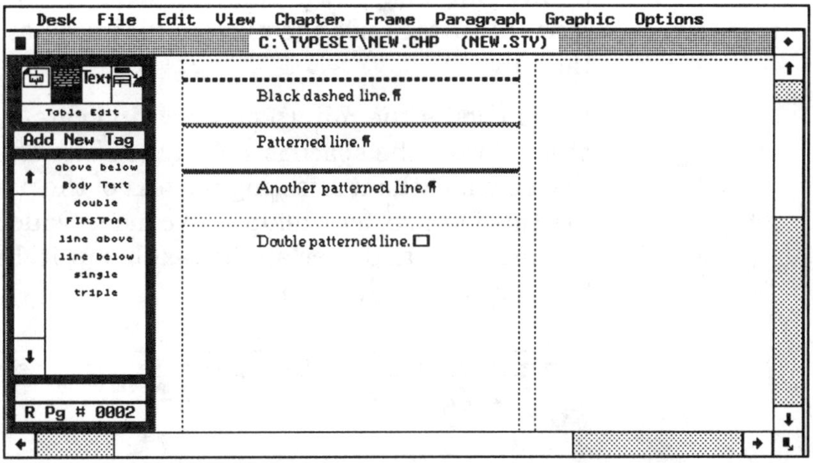

Figure 5-45. Examples of the effects possible with dashed and patterned ruling lines.

Custom Indent and Custom Width specify the position of a Custom rule. Indent specifies how far from the left margin the rule should start. By choosing a negative indent you can force the rule to the left of the margin.

Space Above Rule 1 allows you to allot extra space between the rule and the top edge of the frame. If you put space above rule 1 for a ruling box around, you create space around the entire outside of the box.

Height of Rule 1 specifies the thickness of the rule. Although you can use any units, we recommend the fractional pts.

When you change the units to fractional pts, you see the number 36.00 displayed in the upper right of the dialog box. This is your reminder that you can preview any combination of rules and spaces up to a maximum of 36 points. You can create ruling lines larger than 36 points, but you cannot preview them in the dialog box.

Space Below Rule 1 affects the white space allotted between rules.

Height of Rule 2, Space Below Rule 2, and *Height of Rule 3* work the same as their counterparts for Rule 1.

Space Below Rule 3 can be misleading. The number you enter here can indeed apply to the space below the third rule. But it might better be called "Space Below *Last* Rule." The plus and minus Buttons shown here can lead to some interesting effects. Most tags use the plus, to indicate positive space below the rule.

If you choose the minus sign, you indicate negative space. In other words, the space is *subtracted*. The effect is to shift the line down, without affecting the text of the paragraph. You can use this feature, for example, to cause a wide ruling line above to shift down and overlap the text below it. Figure 5-46 shows two possible applications.

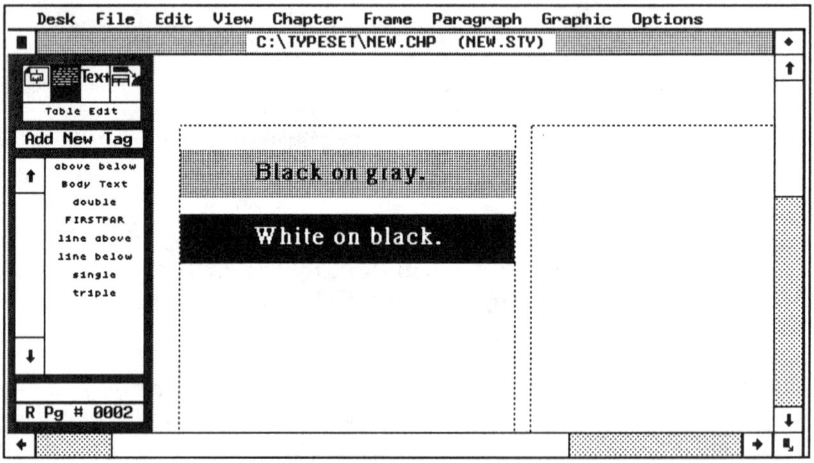

Figure 5-46. Use Space Below Rule 3 to shift a ruling line down on top of the text underneath.

Overall Height shows the total of all ruling lines and spaces. The space taken up by ruling lines is *added* to any above or below space specified for the paragraph. Thus, if you request 12 points of space above the paragraph and add a 3-point ruling line above, you will have a total of 15 points above the paragraph.

Tips for working with menus

TIP *Ctrl-X* brings up the previous dialog box when you're in the Workspace. When creating a new effect, you often need to experiment: try a setting, return to the page to see the results, try something else, return to the page. Hitting Ctrl-X brings up the last dialog box without the need to reach for the mouse. If you are *inside* a dialog box, Ctrl-X is the equivalent of clicking on the Cancel button.

TIP *If you make a change and text disappears*, don't click the mouse. Though the paragraph has disappeared, it is still active. You can return to the Paragraph menu and undo your last change to recover. If you click the mouse, you deactivate the paragraph, and you may have a hard time recovering. If you always assign the F10 function key as Body Text, you also can recover by pressing F10 before clicking the mouse.

TIP *If you make an irretrievable mistake*, try using the Abandon option from the File menu. Abandon takes you back to the previous version of the document. If you save every five minutes or so, it may be faster just to revert to the previous version than to fix a troublesome mistake.

Managing style sheets

The bulk of this chapter has been devoted to skills for building style sheets. Once you master this stage, you will find that your problems are related to administration, not to the software. You won't have trouble remembering how to change options. But you may have other problems:

- What did I call that brochure style sheet?
- Where did I store the chapter template for repair manuals?
- What was the name of the tag that created a special caption effect?
- Is this the most recent version of the style sheet? Or did I load the old one by mistake?

This section provides tips that will help you overcome these hurdles and create an efficient production environment. Even if you work by yourself, these ideas will save you time and money. If you share files with others, they are virtually mandatory. You don't have to adopt the specific strategies we recommend below. But you *do* need to establish and maintain some kind of logical system. Without one, you won't get the productivity benefits promised by desktop publishing. Instead of control and cost savings, you'll get chaos and confusion.

Naming tags

You can make your life easier with a systematic plan for naming tags.

Agree in advance on a core group of tag names, and use these names in every style sheet. With standard tag names, you can completely change the look of a document just by loading a new sheet. If the tag names are identical, the tag attributes from the new style sheet are instantly applied throughout the document. If the names are different, you must page through the document to retag the paragraphs.

More importantly, standard tag names make it easy and simple for authors to pretag their text files. Most users report that pretagging and preformatting result in dramatic productivity gains.

What should the tag names be? As you choose your standard system, keep several things in mind. First, remember that the Assignment List shows tags in alphabetical order. Use this fact to group similar tags together. Names like Subhead1, Subhead2, and Subhead3 are listed together where they are easy to find. Names like Firstsub, Secondsub, and Thirdsub are scattered.

Try to decide which tags you will use together, and group them alphabetically. Tables, for instance, are easier to build if the style sheet lists the columns as Table1, Table2, and Table3, and the title as TableTitle.

Technical documentation groups and other sophisticated users may already have a standard list of page elements. In such cases, the best idea is to use this list in Ventura. Make Ventura conform to your way of doing things, not the other way around. It's simple to rename tags, and Ventura gives you enough space to use the words people are already familiar with.

Management tips

TIP *Large departments report less confusion* when one individual is designated as the Ventura lead. This person is generally responsible for designing, coding, and distributing style sheets to the rest of the workgroup.

TIP *Try to reach agreement* on when and how style sheets can be changed. The style sheet approach lets you create a unified, high-quality look for all your company documents. If people change style sheets without guidance, this consistency may be lost. Even worse, an important style sheet can be lost if someone copies over it with a corrupted sheet that has the same name.

TIP *Some companies use the DOS ATTRIB command* to change the style sheet to read only status. That lets users read and apply the style sheet. They can make temporary changes if necessary to solve a one-time formatting problem. And they can save the style sheet under a new name. They cannot, however, save their changes back to the original style sheet.

TIP *To prevent people from using an old, outdated version,* put a date tag on the Assignment List. This tag does not format any text. Its only function is to contain the date, so users can confirm they have the most recent one.

TIP *Document your style sheets* with Ventura's Print Stylesheet function from the Update Tag List dialog box. This function creates a generated text file. You then create a chapter and load the report into the chapter. Ventura provides a style sheet on the \TYPESET directory called STYLOG.STY to format the report, or you can build one of your own. Print the report as a hard copy backup and a reference tool. You can use it to record the tag names, and to reproduce complex tags in other style sheets. You also can buy third-party utilities that produce style sheet reports and add other functions.

With the conclusion of this chapter, we have shown how to build all three elements of the Ventura Formula. Now it's time to bring them together. In the following chapter we outline an efficient way to lay out documents with Ventura Publisher.

Chapter Six

Building the Chapter

Once you've created text, pictures, and a style sheet, you're ready to assemble them into a document. This chapter explains document layout techniques. When you finish reading, you'll know how to create the underlying structure and how to add text and pictures. You also will know the different layout strategies for the three types of Ventura documents. This chapter concerns itself with overall strategies and basic skills. For advice on specialized applications, turn to Chapter Ten, "Special Document Formats."

Three document categories

Ventura documents fall into three categories: page, frame, and free-form. These categories refer to text and the way it is handled. It is important to understand the distinctions so you know which methods to use when building documents of your own.

In page-style documents:

- The main text is in a single file.
- The main text resides on the Underlying Page.
- The basic format is the same from page to page.

In frame-style documents:

- The text is in multiple files.
- The text resides in separate frames.
- The format has an overall structure, but changes a lot from page to page.

In free-form documents:

- The text is in Ventura's caption file, or in multiple short files.
- The text resides in Box Text, or in separate frames.
- The format differs from page to page.

These three types are the key to Ventura's versatility. They give you the efficiency of page style for long documents *and* the adaptability of frame style for multiple-article publications *plus* the flexibility of free-form for design-intensive pages. Table 6-1 shows the differences in more detail.

Table 6-1. Ventura's three document categories.

Document Type	Location of Main Text	Format	Typical Examples
Page	Single file On the Underlying Page	Consistent from page to page	Books Directories Reports Manuals
Frame	Multiple files Multiple frames on top of the Underlying Page	Varies from page to page within confines of a grid structure	Newsletters Magazines Newspapers Marketing materials
Free-form	Caption file or multiple small files Box Text or multiple frames	Varies widely from page to page with few restrictions	Advertisements Forms

How category determines layout strategy

Different document types demand different layout strategies, as summarized in Table 6-2. In this chapter, you will learn the procedures for page-style documents. Page-style documents are the most common and have the widest applications. In addition, the basic skills for building page-style documents apply to the other types as well. Chapter Ten, "Special Document Formats," discusses the special requirements of frame-style and free-form chapters.

Table 6-2. Layout strategies for different document types.

Page	Frame	Free-Form
Create the underlying structure	Create the underlying structure	Create the underlying structure
Load, place, tag, and edit text	Create frames for the text	Create Box Text or frames for text
Create frames for pictures	Load, place, tag, and edit text	Type in, tag, and edit the text
Load, place, and edit pictures	Create frames for pictures	Create frames for pictures
Save the chapter	Load, place, and edit pictures	Load, place, and edit pictures
	Save the chapter	Save the chapter

A game plan for building a chapter

Throughout the first few chapters, we've referred to the Ventura formula: Text + Pictures + Style = Chapter. The formula illustrates how a Ventura chapter is constructed from three essential components. In that sense, the formula describes what happens *before* you build a chapter. If we rearrange the formula, it also becomes a good model for what goes on *while* you build a chapter:

Style + Text + Pictures = Chapter

Table 6-3 lists layout strategies for page-style documents, showing the best order for working on things:

Table 6-3. How the revised formula guides chapter layout.

Style	Create the underlying structure
Text	Load, place, tag, and edit the text file
Pictures	Create frames for pictures Load, place, and edit pictures
Chapter	Save the chapter Create a chapter template

The new version of the formula suggests an efficient way of working. We think a game plan is crucial for beginning Ventura users. First-timers often complain that Ventura is too much of a good thing. It has so much power and so many options that people don't know where to start and what to do next. For maximum efficiency, resist the temptation to strike out randomly. Instead, take a systematic, step-by-step approach. If you become uncertain about the next step, try using the revised formula as a guide:

- Have you finished the underlying structure (style)? If so, it's time to move on to text.
- Have you loaded, placed, and edited the text? You're ready for pictures.
- Done with the pictures? Now move on to the chapter phase.
- Have you saved the chapter and turned it into a reusable template? Time to pat yourself on the back.

Once you become proficient, you'll invent your own work strategies and formulas. Until then, the formula offers a starting point.

Building page-style chapters

This section steps you through the techniques for building a page-style document. You will learn essential skills that apply to all kinds of documents:

- completing the underlying structure
- working with text
- working with frames and pictures
- creating a chapter template

A page-style document puts the main text file onto the Underlying Page. You can still have other small files associated with the chapter. You may, for example, want to keep tables and spreadsheets in separate files inside frames. And the format may vary slightly. You are likely to have illustrations, charts, diagrams, tables, and pictures in different combinations.

Nevertheless, the *main* text is in a single file, the structure of the Underlying Page does not change, and the document uses the same basic typography throughout. If you tend to think of the document as a single unit, you probably have a page-style document. If you think of it as separate articles lumped together, you probably have a frame-style document.

Building an underlying structure

It makes sense to complete the underlying structure — the document-wide formatting — before you start adding text and pictures. You lose the advantage of the WYSIWYG screen if you don't have the page design in place.

In the previous chapter, "Working with Style Sheets," you began the process of building a structure. (If you haven't built a style sheet yet, review Chapter Five before going on.) Many of the properties you assigned — the page size, the margins and columns, the chapter typography — apply to the Underlying Page and, therefore, to the document as a whole.

Now you're going to complete the basic structure by adding elements that are stored with the chapter file: headers, footers, and page numbers. To do so, you will start a chapter, load a style sheet, and create the headers and footers.

One quick tip before you start: You may find it easier if you use the option and preference settings listed in Table 6-4. They help you visualize the page more accurately.

Starting a chapter

To start a new chapter from scratch:

- Select New from the File menu.
- Select Save As from the File menu. An Item Selector appears.
- Enter the chapter's new name (and, optionally, its new location) in the Item Selector. Click OK.

Table 6-4. Recommended option settings for building a chapter.

Feature	Setting	What It Does
Set Preferences	Generated Tags: Shown	Displays automatically generated tags at bottom of Assignment List
	Text to Greek: 6	Shows unreadable small text as blocks to speed screen redraw
	On-Screen Kerning: None	Eliminates screen kerning to speed redraw
	Auto-Adjust " and - -	Converts symbols to typographic equivalents
Set Ruler	Horizontal & Vertical Units: Picas	Conforms to standard typographic measurement
Rulers	Shown	Displays rulers on top and left side of page
Column Guides	Shown	Displays lines to show column boundaries
Tabs & Returns	Shown	Shows visible marks in text indicating tabs, returns, line breaks, end-of-file markers, etc.
Column Snap	On	Aligns frames with column edges
Line Snap	On	Aligns frames vertically with line spacing of body text

Your new chapter has been opened. If you are continuing work on a chapter you started earlier, you take a different approach to reopen that document:

- Choose Open from the File menu. An Item Selector appears.
- Navigate to the correct subdirectory with the mouse (or by typing the path name on the Directory line).
- Scroll down the Item Selector until you see the name of the chapter.
- Select the chapter and click OK.

Ventura loads the chapter and its associated files.

Loading the style sheet

In theory, it is best to have the style sheet complete before building the chapter. In practice, you probably will change it the first few times you use it (usually to add a tag for an unexpected contingency).

If you make changes, consider whether you want them to be reflected in the original style sheet, or if you want to create a new one. To alter the previous style sheet, do nothing. Ventura will save your changes under the original name when you save the chapter. To preserve the original intact, use Save As New Style *as soon as you bring in the original style sheet.*

To load a style sheet:

- Select Load Diff. Style from the File menu.
- Use the Item Selector to navigate to the proper subdirectory.
- Select the style sheet from the list, and click OK.

Creating headers and footers

A header is a line or two of text that repeats at the top of every page. Traditional typesetters often call them *running heads.* A footer repeats at the bottom of the page.

In the following section, we explain how to create and format a header. The explanations apply equally to footers. We'll get into the mechanics in a moment. First, though, let's take a moment to understand the theory.

When you ask for a header, Ventura responds by adding a frame at the top of the page. It matches the side margins of that frame to the Underlying Page. Then it centers the header text between the top of the page and the top of the column (Figure 6-1). If you don't like these settings, you can change them. It pays to set page margins *before* creating the header. That way, Ventura does the work of matching the header frame to the rest of the page.

Unless you say otherwise, the header appears on every page. It can have one or two lines of text. Each line can have text at the left, in the middle, at the right, or any combination (Figure 6-2).

Creating headers is a two-step process. First, you use the

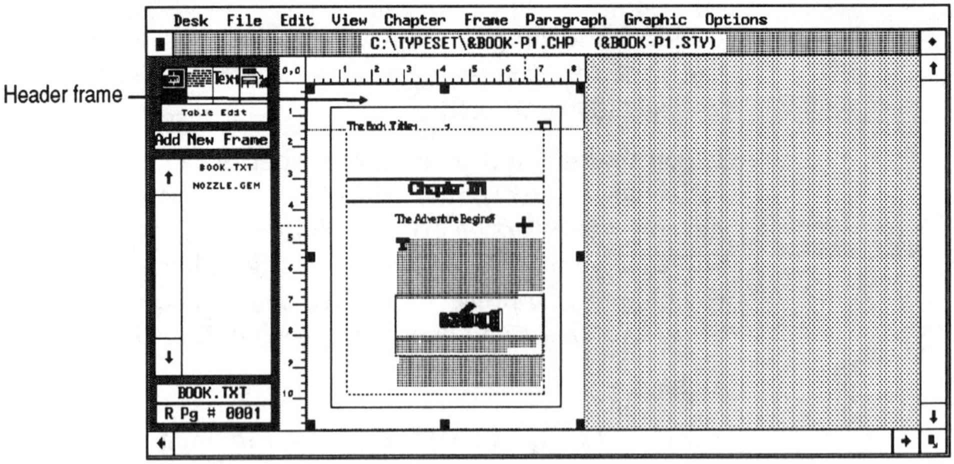

Figure 6-1. When Ventura creates a header frame, it matches the side margins to the Underlying Page and fills up the space between the top of page and the top of column.

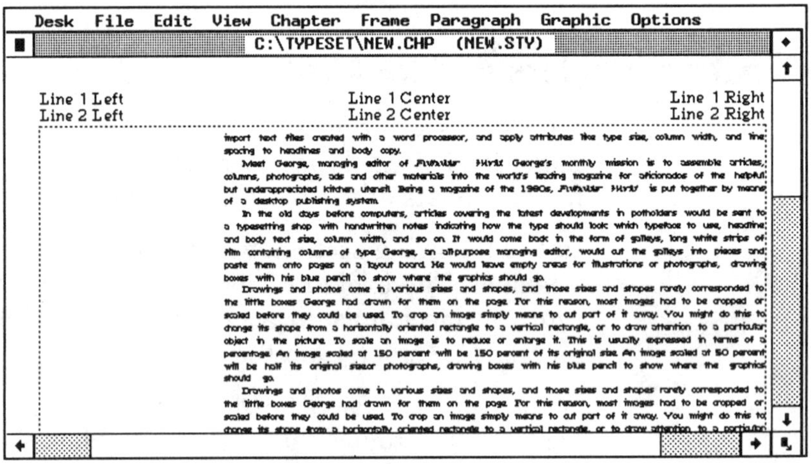

Figure 6-2. You can have up to two lines of header text on the left, center, or right, in any combination.

Headers & Footers dialog box to create the header frame and put something in it. Second, you format the resulting text.

Creating the header frame and contents

The first step to generating a header is to specify what goes where. Select Headers & Footers from the Chapter menu. Ventura responds with a dialog box that has space to type in what you want (Figure 6-3).

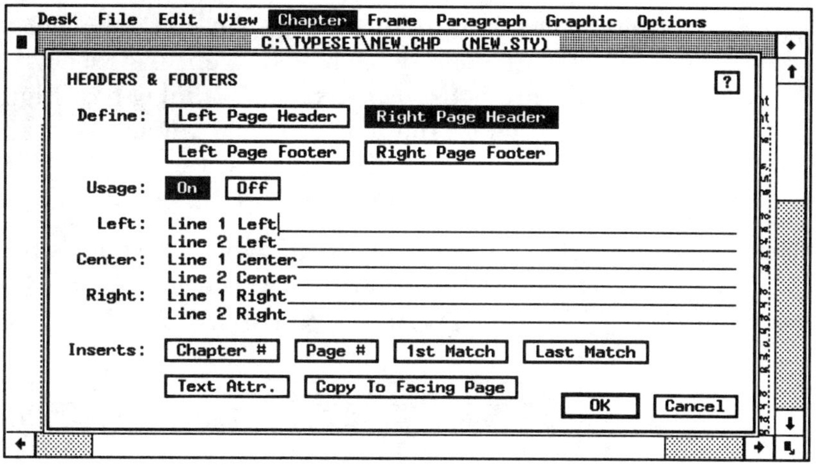

Figure 6-3. The Headers & Footers dialog box.

Define tells Ventura what you want and what page to put it on. To create mirrored (identical but reversed) headers:

- Click on Left Page Header.
- Type in what you want.
- Click on Copy to Facing Page.

To create different headers, one for the left page and one for the right page:

- Click on Left Page Header.
- Type in what you want to appear on the left page.
- *Without closing the dialog box*, click on Right Page Header.
- Type in what you want for the right page and click OK.

➥*NOTE: You cannot have different headers on left and right pages unless you've previously selected Sides: Double from the Page Size & Layout dialog box.*

Usage turns on a header or footer for the entire document. (Later you will see how to turn off headers for a single page while leaving them elsewhere.) You must click on Usage: On for each header on each page. If you select Copy to Facing Page, Ventura turns Usage to On for that facing page.

Left, Center, and Right tell Ventura what to put in the header.

You can type in text, or you can ask Ventura to insert it for you. If you type in text, Ventura inserts it on every page. Figure 6-4 shows text in the dialog box. Figure 6-5 shows how it looks on the page. As you can see, text entered on the Left line is left-justified. Text on the Center line is centered. Text on the Right line is right-justified.

You are not limited to typing text directly onto the header lines. By entering codes, you can instruct Ventura to insert text. For instance, you can ask for the page number. Ventura

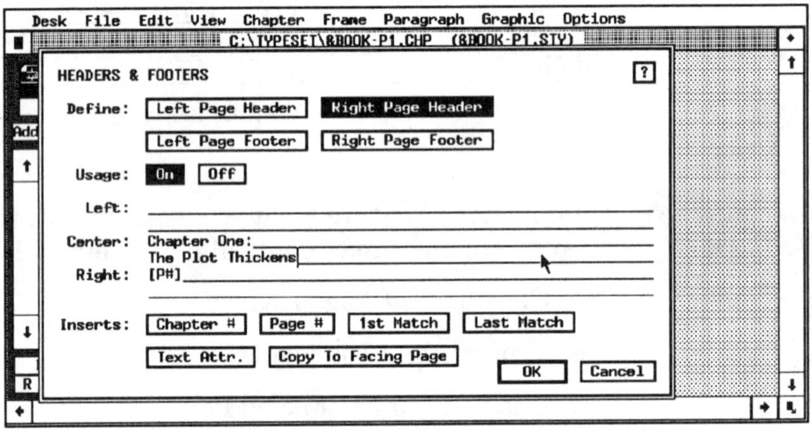

Figure 6-4. The entries in this dialog box create the header shown in Figure 6-5.

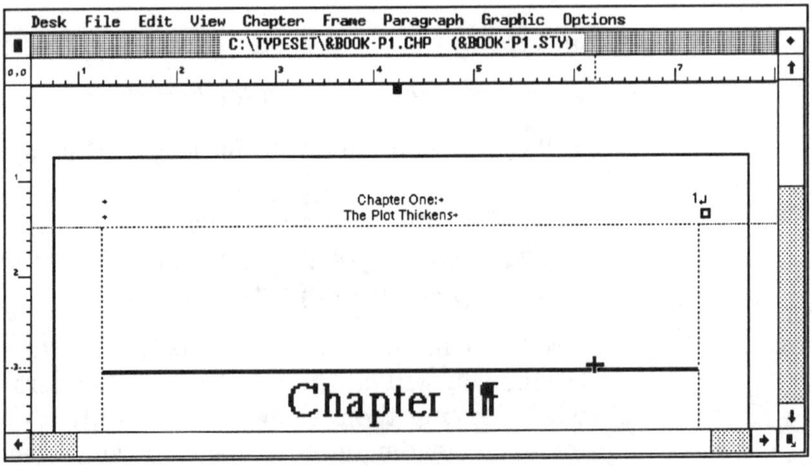

Figure 6-5. This header was created with the dialog box shown in Figure 6-4.

will take care of the counting and insert a different number on each page.

The buttons next to *Inserts* provide shortcuts for entering codes. First you put the cursor on the line where you want the code (Left, Center, or Right). Then you click on a button, and Ventura puts the code onto the line. If you prefer, you can type in codes directly.

The first two buttons, *Chapter #* and *Page #*, insert codes for numbers. If you click on Chapter #, Ventura inserts the code [C#]. This tells Ventura to put the current chapter number into the header. The Page # button inserts the code [P#]. This code instructs Ventura to find and insert the current page number. You can combine these codes with each other, and with other text on the same line. For instance, here's what you might type to create the chapter-by-chapter numbering favored in technical documentation:

```
Page [C#]-[P#]
```

Here's what this code would create on page five of the third chapter:

Page 3-5

Chapter Eight, "Advanced Functions," elaborates on Ventura's counting and numbering functions.

The *1st Match* and *Last Match* buttons are the key to creating powerful and versatile *live headers*. Live headers change for each page, depending on the contents of that page. Pick up any phone book for an example. You'll see something like "Smith-Snider" on the top of one page and "Snider-Socha" on the next. Figure 6-6 shows another example.

You've previously seen how to place chapter and page numbers into the header. Live headers are created in a similar fashion. Let's recreate the phone book example used above. Suppose we want a live header at the center of each page. Let's further assume that we tagged surnames as LastName. We will tell Ventura to (1) look on each page and find the first and last instances of the LastName tag and (2) put those paragraphs on the center line of the header.

Here's the procedure:

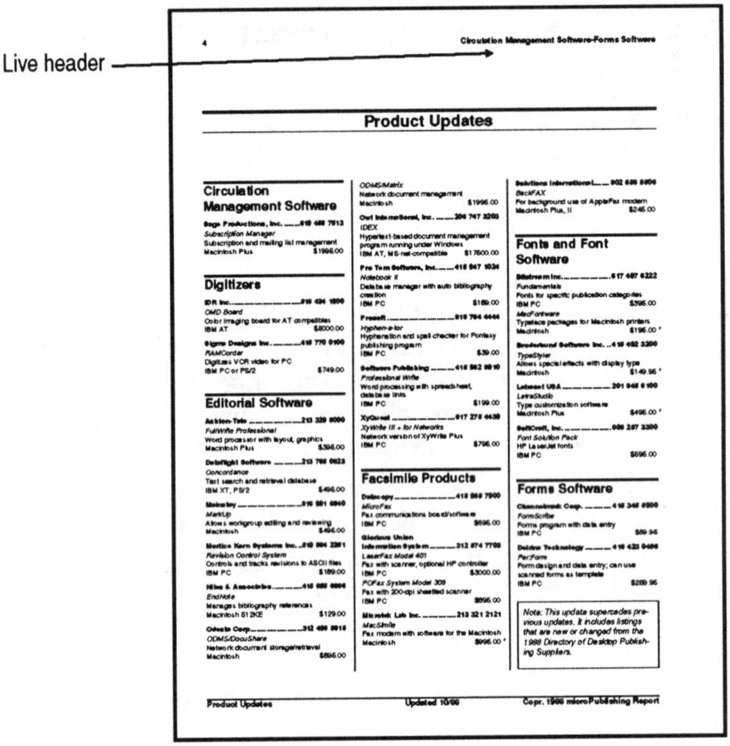

Figure 6-6. Live headers make it easier to find information in directories, listings, and catalogs.

- Open the dialog box and activate the header by selecting Define: Right Page and Usage: On.
- Put the cursor on the center line. Click on 1st Match.

Ventura places this code on the line:

```
[<tag name]
```

- Erase the words "tag name" *without erasing any of the brackets*. In its place, type LastName. Now the code reads:

```
[<LastName]
```

So far you've instructed Ventura to examine each page, find the first paragraph tagged as LastName, and place that text on the center line of the header. To finish building the header:

- Type a hyphen, then click on Last Match. Ventura inserts a similar code. This code, however, tells Ventura to find the *last* paragraph on the page.

- Replace "tag name" with LastName again. Figure 6-7 shows the result.

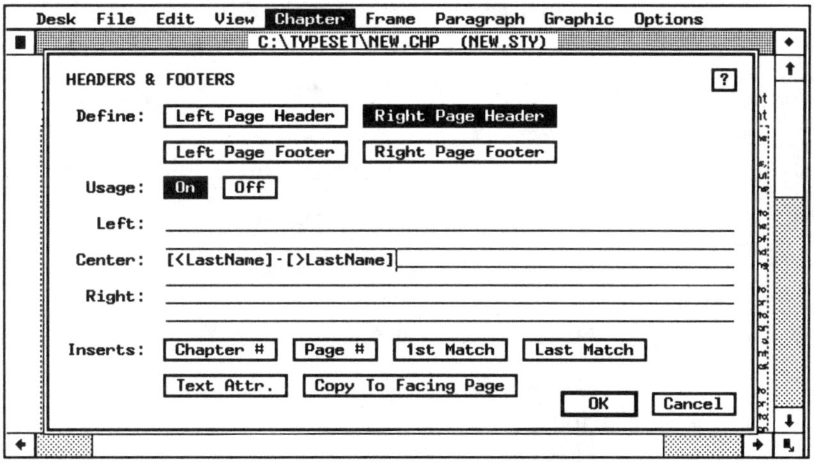

Figure 6-7. These codes tell Ventura to find the first and last paragraphs tagged as LastName and put the text into the header.

This formula creates a different live header for each page containing the first and last surnames. The first header of your directory might look something like this:

Aames-Anderson

The second header might read something like this:

Andrews-Bryant

And so on, with Ventura doing the work of searching each page and finding the appropriate text.

In real life, we would have added page numbers to the header. Although we used LastName in the example, we could have easily used any other tag name, like Section Head, Head1, Product, Category, or whatever. Live headers make it easier for readers to find their way around. They have wide applications for directories, price lists, catalogs, proposals, reports, technical manuals — any medium-to-long reference document. For instance, if you look at the pages in this book, you will see that we insert headings at the top of pages to make it easier for you to find the passage you want.

Formatting headers

So far we've shown you how to create a header frame and tell Ventura what to put inside. Now we'll look at the ways to format the header — to change its appearance and position. You have four alternatives, which you can apply alone or in combination:

- bracket codes inside the header dialog box
- tag formatting in Paragraph mode
- changing the header frame
- turning headers on and off

As with our previous discussion, the concepts apply equally to footers.

Formatting with bracket codes

Look back at any picture showing the Headers & Footers dialog box. Previously, we examined every button in the Inserts section except *Text Attr.* This button lets you add attributes like bold and italics. The technique is identical to entering bracket codes in text files, as explained in Chapter Three. When you click on Text Attr., Ventura inserts the code <D> on the line. This bracket code is the signal to turn *off* an effect. You erase the *D* and type in the bracket code for the attribute you want to apply. For instance, to turn on bold you would use the bracket code <B>. To turn on italics, you would enter <I>. For bold-italics, you would use <BI>, and so on.

Use this technique sparingly. To make the *entire* header bold, make the change in Paragraph mode instead. Use text attributes *only to make a word or short phrase different from the rest of the header.* Don't forget to turn off the effect. Ventura applies the attribute until it encounters a paragraph return or the ending code (<D>).

Here's how you'd make the page number bold while leaving the rest of the header in normal text:

```
Left: Chapter [C#]

Center:
```

```
Right: Page <B>[P#]<D>
```

As you can see, the code for the page number is surrounded by the bracket codes to turn bold on and off. We've been using bold as an example, but you can apply any of the bracket codes explained in Chapter Three, including:

- attributes
- font changes
- point size changes
- baseline jumps (shifting text up or down)

Changing the tag attributes

Formatting headers in Paragraph mode is easier to understand once you realize that Ventura generates its own header tag. When it creates the text, Ventura gives it a tag called Z_Header. (Footers are Z_Footer). If there are no specifications for Z_Header in the current style sheet, Ventura uses those of Body Text. If you don't want your headers to look like the main text — and you probably don't — you can change the tag specifications.

You cannot change the pre-assigned tag name or give header text a different tag. With this limitation, header tags can be formatted like any others. The tag name appears in the Assignment List provided you choose Generated Tags: Shown from the Set Preferences dialog box.

To change a header's font, for instance:

- Enable Paragraph mode.
- Click anywhere on the header to select it.
- Select Font from the Paragraph menu.
- Make the changes you want and click OK.

The changes apply to all the text in the header, and to every header throughout the document. Not every dialog box applies to header text. You cannot, for example, change the alignment. The Spacing dialog box, however, is one key to changing the header's vertical position. When Ventura first creates the header, it centers the text between the top of the page and the top of the column. You can use Spacing from the Paragraph menu to add space above, pushing the header down toward the rest of the text. Or you can subtract space above to push the header up (Figure 6-8).

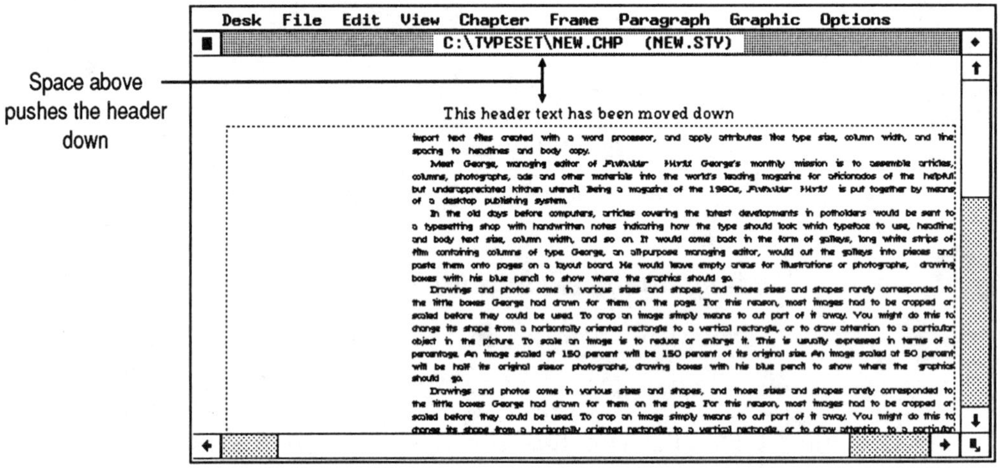

Figure 6-8. The Spacing dialog box provides one way to change the position of the header.

Changing the header frame

It's not always possible to get the look you want with bracket codes and paragraph attributes. Sometimes, you may need to alter the header frame. To do so:

- Enable Frame mode.
- Select the header frame.
- Select Margins & Columns from the Frame menu.
- Make the changes you want and click OK.

When Ventura creates a header frame, it uses the side margins of the Underlying Page. By altering these margins, you can create hanging headers, or indented headers (Figure 6-9). By changing the top and bottom margins, you move the text up or down.

➥*NOTE: To change the vertical position of a header, try to use the Spacing dialog box before trying frame margins.*

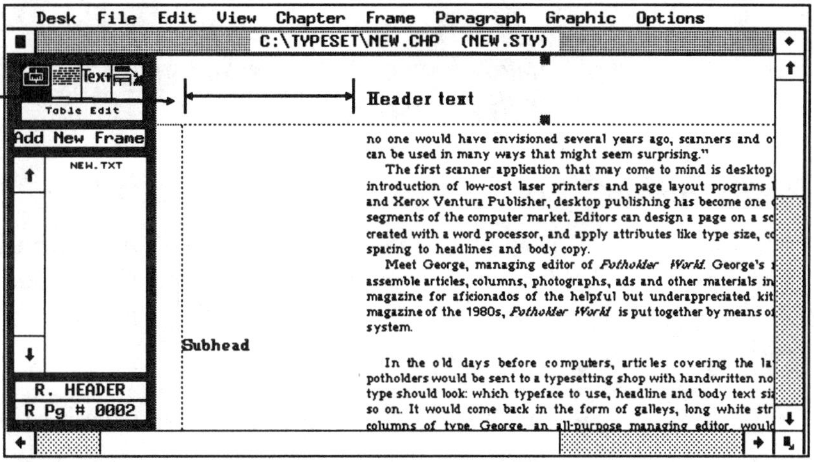

Figure 6-9. Certain header formats require you to change the margins of the header frame.

The settings of the Spacing dialog box are stored with the style sheet. You can have the identical spacing in another document just by loading the same style sheet. The margins of the header frame, by contrast, are stored with the chapter file. To recreate this effect, you must use a chapter template, or you must build it again from scratch. Although you can change the margins of a header frame, you cannot resize or reposition it. You also can apply a frame background.

Turning headers off

You may want to turn off the header on a page, though you want headers in the rest of the document:

- to keep page numbers and other header text off the title page or chapter opening
- to create extra space for a full-page illustration
- to create a completely blank page

To turn off the header for an individual page:

- Go to the page.
- Select Turn Header Off from the Chapter menu.

If you change your mind, return to the Chapter menu and select Turn Header On.

➥*NOTE: Don't turn off headers until you finish the layout. If you make changes too early, you may find the headers turned off on the wrong pages.*

Page numbering

You've already seen how to create a page number in a header or footer. Ventura also lets you put page numbers anywhere on the page. To insert a page number (or a chapter number):

- Enable Text mode.
- Place the text cursor where you want the page number to appear.
- Select Ins Special Item from the Edit menu.
- Press F6 to bring up the secondary dialog box (Figure 6-10).
- Choose Page #.

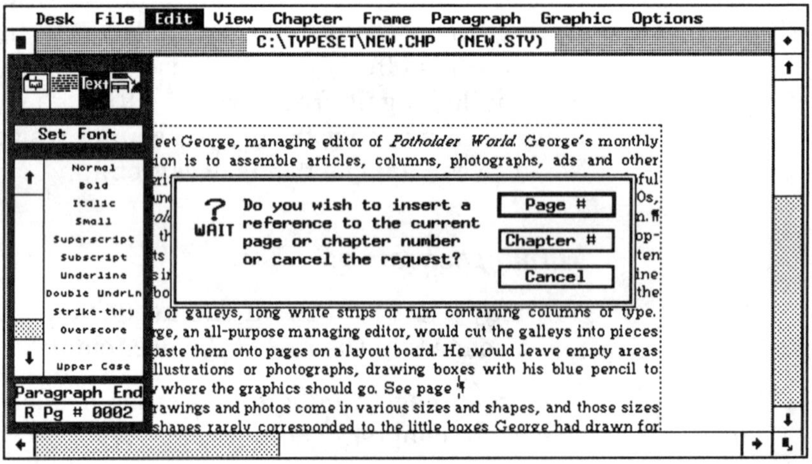

Figure 6-10. Insert Cross Reference Dialog Box.

The current page number appears. You can use this feature to put page numbers anywhere, including inside repeating frames, captions, or box text.

Working with text

Earlier we suggested a revised version of the Ventura Formula as a model for building a chapter: Style (Format) + Text + Pictures = Chapter. So far you've learned to load a style sheet and create headers and page numbers. Now you are ready to work with text — to load, place, tag, and edit it.

Loading text

To load a single text file:

- Select Load Text/Picture from the File menu.
- Select Type of File: Text. Then choose the file format you want to load.
- Select # of Files: One and Destination: List of Files. When you click OK, an Item Selector appears with which you can select the text file you want.
- Use the Item Selector to navigate to the subdirectory containing the file. Select the file name from the list and click OK (or double-click on the file name).

There is a brief pause while Ventura brings the file into memory and inserts discretionary hyphens. Once hyphenated, the file name shows up on the Assignment List in Frame mode.

To load more than one file at a time:

- Follow the procedures above, but select # of Files: Several. The Item Selector appears.
- Select the first file name. Ventura loads and hyphenates that file, then redisplays the Item Selector so you can select another one.
- When you are through selecting files, click Cancel to return to the workspace.

➥*NOTE: To load multiple files in different formats, you must open Load Text/File once for each format.*

When you return to the workspace, the file names appear

alphabetically in the Assignment List in Frame mode. They are available to be placed on the page.

Placing text files

Now you're ready to place the text file(s). The process differs depending on the type of document. Ventura Publisher has three modes for placing text: page, frame, and free-form. The key points to remember:

- When you place text on the Underlying Page, Ventura automatically creates new pages to accommodate the entire file.
- When you place text in frames, Ventura fills the frame to the bottom. Then it stops and waits for you to tell it where to put the rest of the file.
- When you type text into Box Text, Ventura stores it in the caption file. Each Box Text can be positioned independently of the others.

When you load a file, Ventura puts the name on the Assignment List (visible in Frame mode). If you are in Frame mode and you select the Page *before* loading a single text file, Ventura places it on the Page. If you did not select the Page or you were not in Frame mode, you must tell Ventura where to put the file:

- Enable Frame mode.
- Click once on the workspace to select the Underlying Page.
- Click on the file name in the Assignment List.

Ventura pours the file onto the page (Figure 6-11). Although you can't see it, Ventura also creates as many additional pages as necessary for the rest of the file.

Placing more than one file on the Underlying Page

Page-style documents usually have a single text file on the Underlying Page. Still, there may be occasions when you want to place more than one file.

For short sidebars, spreadsheets, and tables, place a frame on top of the Underlying Page, and pour the file into the frame.

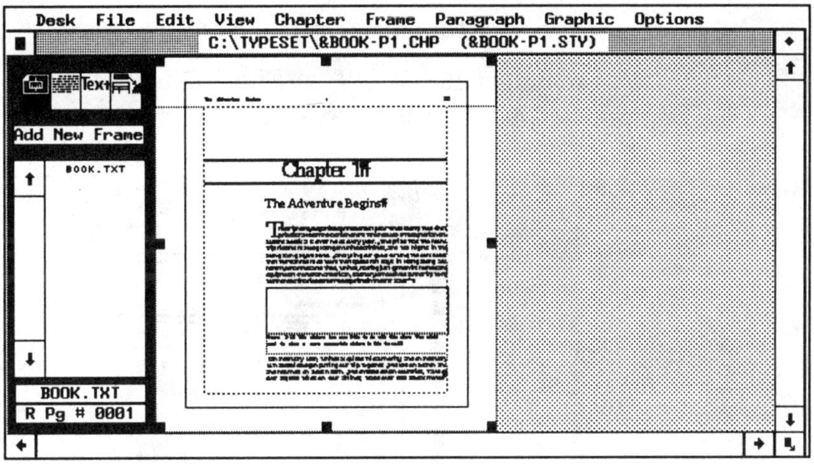

Figure 6-11. To place text on the Underlying Page, select the Page, then select the file name from the Assignment List.

This is especially useful if you want to separate the new text with a ruling box around, or give it a different graphic treatment, such as a different type style or a gray screen.

But what if you want to place two text files one after the other on the same Underlying Page? The easiest way is to pour in the first file, then enter Text mode. Position the cursor where you want to insert the second file, and select Load Text/Picture from the File menu. Select Destination: Text Cursor to make the new text file appear at the text cursor. The new text will then be poured into the desired location and merged with the previous text.

Removing a Page

You cannot remove an Underlying Page if it contains a text file. You can, however, delete a Page if the text is in frames. When you remove a page, you delete the frames as well.

Removing text files

To remove a text file from the Page (or from a frame on top of the Page):

- Enable Frame mode.

- Select the Page (or the frame).
- Select Remove Text/File from the Edit menu. A dialog box appears (Figure 6-12).

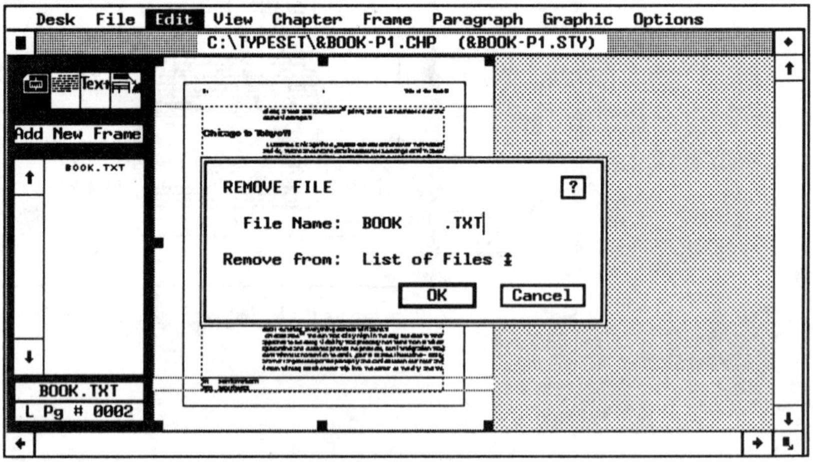

Figure 6-12. The Remove Text/File dialog box.

- Confirm that the file you want to remove shows on the top line. If not, clear the line and type in the correct name.
- Choose Remove from: List of Files to delete the file from memory and from the Assignment List. Choose Remove from: Frame to delete it from the current Page (or frame) while still leaving it on the Assignment List, where it will be available to be placed somewhere else.

If you select the Underlying Page and then click on a second file name in the Assignment List, Ventura assumes that you want to replace the first file. This is a shortcut method of removing a file from a frame. Ventura removes the old file and replaces it with the new one. The old file remains on the Assignment List.

Renaming and relocating text files

To give a text file a new name or to specify a new location (to put it on a different disk or subdirectory):

- Enable Frame mode.
- Select the Page or frame containing the file.

- Select File Type/Rename from the Edit menu (Figure 6-13).

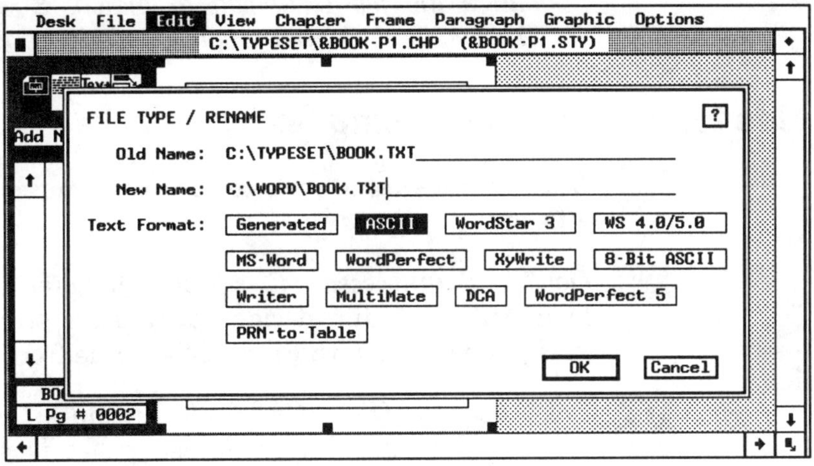

Figure 6-13. The File Type/Rename dialog box.

- You see the old name and location (path) on the top line. Type in the new name and/or the new location on the New Name line and click OK.

➥*NOTE: If the text file has the same name and path as the chapter, Ventura automatically changes the text file name when you change the chapter name.*

You can rename and relocate any text file on the Page or in a frame, including text you typed directly into Ventura. You cannot rename or relocate picture files inside Ventura (unless you are using an add-on utility such as VP Manager). The changes do not take place until you save the chapter.

Converting to a different file format

To convert to a different file format, follow the procedure for renaming and relocating a file. When the dialog box appears, you will see one button darkened to indicate the current format. Click on the new format, then click OK to close the dialog box. The change takes effect the next time you save the file. If you abandon the chapter without saving, the change is not recorded. You can rename, relocate, or change the format of files with this dialog box.

➥*NOTE: If you change the file format, we suggest that you change the file extension to match. See Chapter Three, "Creating Text," for our recommended extensions.*

Tips for loading and placing text

TIP *Load all the files at once* to save time and make layout more efficient.

TIP *Don't load unnecessary files.* Each file takes up memory. If you load a file and later decide not to use it, remove it from the Assignment List with Remove Text/File from the Edit menu.

TIP *Don't use the USENGL2.HY2* alternate hyphenation algorithm unless absolutely necessary. It is slower than the default algorithm. See Chapter Eight, "Advanced Functions," for more about Ventura's hyphenation options.

TIP *If you want to keep the original text file* unchanged, use File Type/Rename from the Edit menu to assign a new name before you make any edits. This tip may be useful for technical documentation where editors must keep an unchanged copy of the original manuscript. If you write over the original file by mistake, you can retrieve the backup copy made by Ventura. This file has the same file name as the original, except that the first letter of the extension has been changed to a dollar sign ($).

TIP *End-of-file markers* are useful for confirming that you have placed all of the file. End-of-file markers are small squares that appear immediately after the last character in a file. They appear only if you select Show Tabs & Returns from the Options menu.

Tagging text

The next step in building a chapter is to tag the text:

- Enable Paragraph mode.
- Click anywhere on the paragraph you wish to tag.
- Select the tag name from the Assignment List.

For faster tagging, use Shift-Click to select all the similar paragraphs on the page, and apply the tag name to them all at once. If you prefer to edit and tag in separate steps, we recommend tagging first. It is easier to spot mistakes when text is in its proper format. Tagging is covered in more detail in Chapter Five, "Working with Style Sheets." If you prefer to pretag the word processing file, you will find complete instructions in Chapter Three, "Creating Text."

Editing text

Once you have created the underlying structure and tagged the document, you are ready to edit the text. At this point, your pages should look very close to their final form. Many users like to make a final edit at this time, before they add the illustrations. We do not recommend the editing tools in Ventura for wholesale changes and large block moves. For large-scale editing, return to the word processor. However, the editing functions in Ventura's Text mode are fine for last-minute changes and corrections.

Working with pictures

This section explains Ventura's many options for putting pictures into documents. It also explains how to create time-saving frame templates. Once you have the text loaded, placed, tagged, and edited, you're ready to add pictures. The most efficient method involves three steps:

1. Load the picture file(s).

2. Add a frame for the first picture.

3. Place the picture.

Repeat these essential three steps for each additional picture. You also may want to consider the following three options:

4. Edit and enhance the picture.

5. Caption the picture.

6. Anchor the picture.

We recommend that you tackle pictures *after* finishing the format (style) and the text. The underlying structure needs to be in place before you position and size frames. For instance, there is no point in snapping frames to column guides if the column guides are in the wrong place. What's more, you can't tell where pictures belong until the text is in its final format. Yes, Ventura gives you the power to move the pictures if you decide to change the text. But you don't want to spend all your time moving frames back and forth because you added pictures too early in the process.

Loading pictures

Loading picture files is a straightforward process. You use the same dialog box as you did for text files. You can remove picture files with Remove Text/File from the Edit menu. You cannot, however, rename a picture file or change its format.

To load a single picture file:

- Select Load Text/Picture from the File menu.
- Select Type of File: Line-Art or Type of File: Image. (See Chapter Four, "Creating Pictures," for a full discussion of the differences between line-art and image pictures.)
- Choose the file format you want to load from the line labeled Line-Art Format or Image Format.
- Select # of Files: One. An Item Selector appears.
- Use the Item Selector to navigate to the subdirectory containing the file. Select the file name from the list and click OK (or double-click on the file name).

Ventura loads the file and converts it (if necessary). Once loaded, the file name appears on the Assignment List in Frame mode.

To load more than one file at a time:

- Follow the procedures above, but select # of Files: Several. The Item Selector appears.
- Select the first file name. Ventura loads that file, then redisplays the Item Selector so you can select another one.

- When you are through selecting files, click Cancel to return to the workspace.

➥*NOTE: To load multiple files in different formats, you must open Load Text/File separately for each format.*

When you return to the workspace, the file names appear alphabetically in the Assignment List (if you are in Frame mode). They are ready to be placed on the page. Before you can place a picture file, however, you must create a frame to contain it. Whatever type of illustration you want — drawings, photos, diagrams, charts — you will need a frame to contain it. To add frames efficiently and correctly, you need to understand how they work.

Understanding frames

This section provides a quick course in frames and how to use them. To work efficiently, you need six basic frame skills:

1. drawing
2. cutting, copying, and pasting
3. fine-tuning size and position
4. putting margins inside

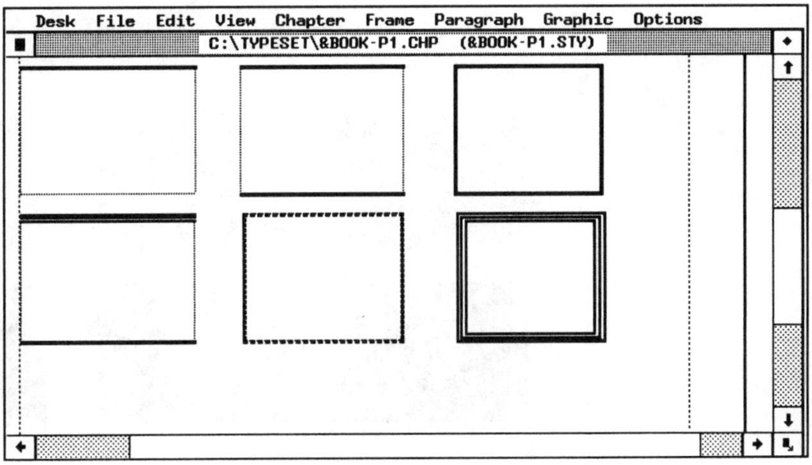

Figure 6-14. Ventura lets you put ruling lines and boxes around frames.

5. putting padding outside

6. creating borders and backgrounds

Frames are containers for text or picture files. They have an invisible boundary. In Frame mode, Ventura defines the boundary with on-screen borders that do not show on the printed page. To make the border visible, you must add ruling lines or a box to the frame (Figure 6-14).

Frames can have margins and columns inside their boundaries. These margins override the margins of the Underlying Page. Thus, it is possible to have a one-column frame on top of a three-column Underlying Page.

You can draw frames anywhere on the page and you can overlap them. You can also add backgrounds (Figure 6-15).

Text flows automatically around a frame unless you specifically tell Ventura otherwise (Figure 6-16).

You can attach a caption frame to any frame (Figure 6-17). When you move, copy, resize, or delete the original frame, the caption frame changes too.

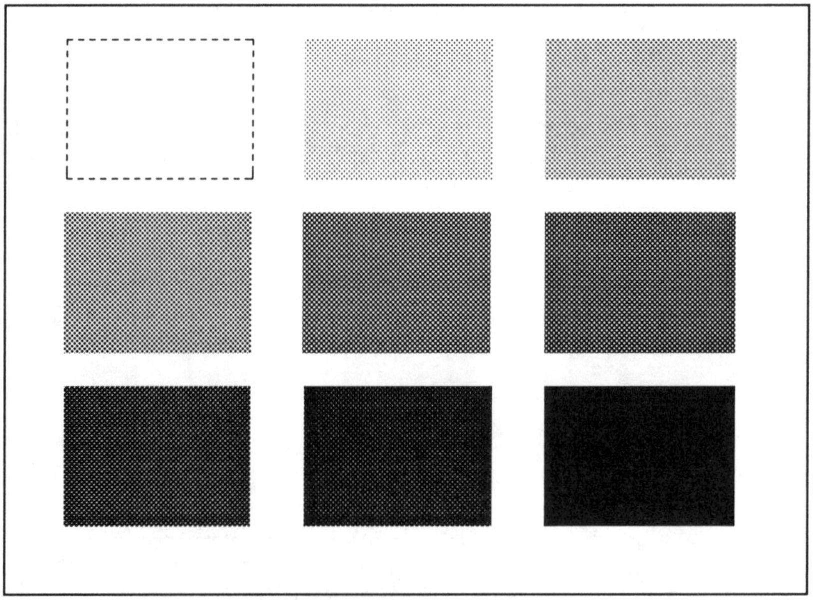

Figure 6-15. The nine standard backgrounds available through the Frame Background dialog box.

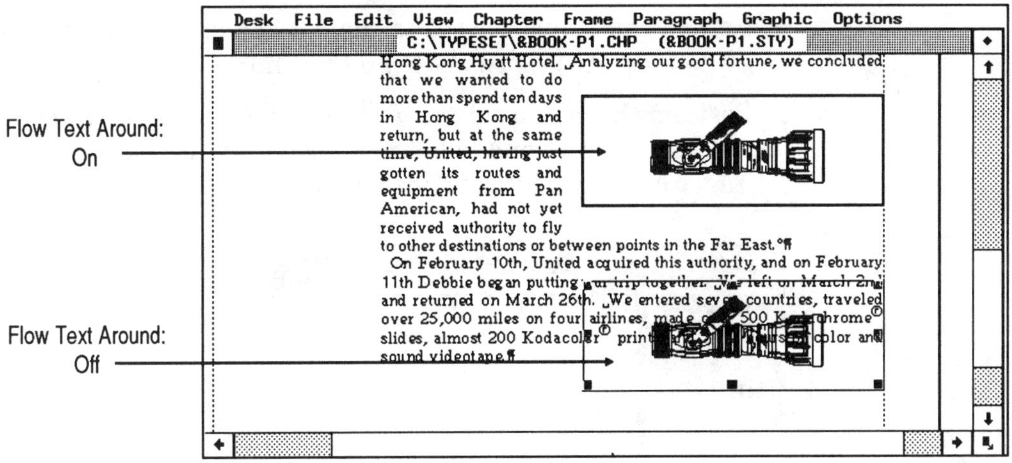

Figure 6-16. Text flows automatically around frames unless you use the Sizing & Scaling dialog box to tell Ventura otherwise.

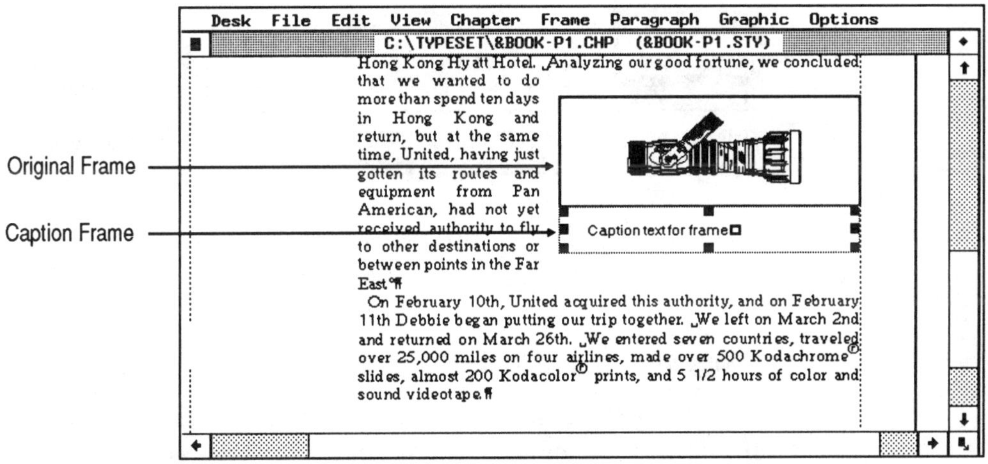

Figure 6-17. Caption frames are attached to the original frame and move along with it.

Drawing frames

With some frame theory under our belts, let's move on to the practical steps to using them for pictures. Before you can place a picture on the page, you need a container. To draw a frame:

- Enable Frame mode.
- Select the Add New Frame button from the Side-Bar (or press the keyboard shortcut Ctrl-2).

- Return the mouse cursor to the workspace. It changes to a FR to indicate it is ready to add a frame.
- Position the cursor where you want the upper left corner of the frame. Press and hold the mouse button until a pointing finger cursor appears (Figure 6-18).

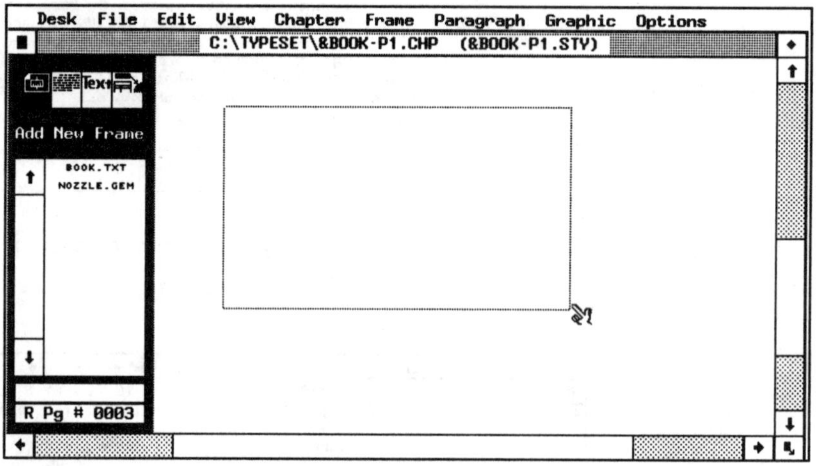

Figure 6-18. To draw a frame, press and hold the mouse button until the pointing finger appears, then stretch the frame to its full size.

- Drag the cursor to the lower right corner of the frame and release the mouse button. The new frame appears.

Snapping frames to columns and lines

Ventura provides two snap-to functions that make frame placement easier and more accurate. Snap-to functions are similar to magnets. If you get a frame close to a snap-to element, it automatically locks into position.

To enable the snap-to functions, select Turn Column Snap On or Turn Line Snap On from the Options menu (these are toggle selections, so use the same menu choices to turn them off again). Column snap forces the sides of the frame to align with the sides of the columns, provided they are close enough to bring the "magnet" into play (Figure 6-19). The column guides don't have to be showing, but they make it easier to see what you're doing. Select Show Column Guides from the Options menu to make them appear.

Line snap forces the top and bottom of the frame to align with the line spacing of Body Text. If Body Text has line spacing of one pica (12 fractional pts.), then the vertical frame will be in increments of one pica. Your frames could be one pica tall, or five picas, or fifty picas, but they could never be one and a half picas, or five and a quarter picas (Figure 6-19).

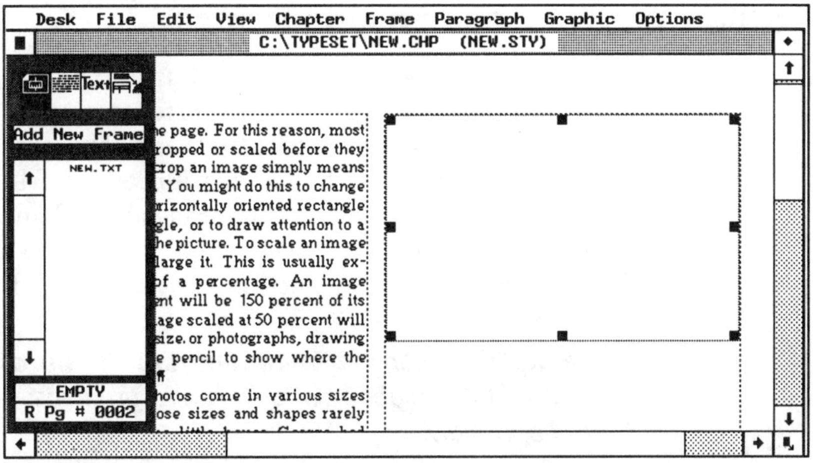

Figure 6-19. Column snap forces frames to align with the left and right edges of the columns. Line snap is like having a grid of invisible magnetic lines across the page. Frames align automatically to one of the lines.

The column and line snap functions are valuable allies. You can draw frames free-hand knowing that they are properly sized and positioned to work with the rest of the page design. For this reason, it is important to set the format of the Underlying Page and the Body Text before you add frames. Otherwise you will be snapping frames to incorrect positions.

Drawing multiple frames

To draw several frames in a row, hold down the Shift key as you draw. The cursor stays in its add shape, showing that you can draw another frame immediately without clicking Add New Frame again. Continue to hold down the Shift key until you are ready to draw the last frame. Release the Shift key before drawing the last frame.

Drawing a perfect square

To draw a perfect square, hold down the Alt key while you draw. Ventura lets you control the size of the frame, but it won't let the frame become a rectangle. To create a perfect square from an existing rectangle, press and hold the Alt key as you resize the frame.

Cutting, copying, and pasting frames

Frames can be cut, copied, and pasted just like text, using the Edit menu or the keyboard shortcuts. Copying or cutting puts the selected frame *and all its attributes and text* into temporary memory. If there was already a frame in temporary memory, copying or cutting erases it and substitutes the new frame instead. The new frame stays in temporary memory until you erase it by putting another frame there.

➥*NOTE: Putting a frame into the Frame clipboard does not affect the clipboards for text and graphics, which are retained separately.*

To cut a frame:

- Enable Frame mode.
- Select the frame.
- Select Cut Frame from the Edit menu or press the Del key.

The frame is deleted from the page and placed in memory. To replace a frame cut by mistake, press Ins immediately.

To copy a frame:

- Enable Frame mode.
- Select the frame.
- Select Copy Frame from the Edit menu or press Shift-Del.

The frame remains on the page, but Ventura places a copy on the clipboard. If you watch closely, you will see the disk drive light go on as Ventura stores the information.

To paste a frame:

- Enable Frame mode.

- Cut or copy the frame to put it on the clipboard.
- Move to the page where you want the frame to appear.
- Select Paste Frame from the Edit menu or press Ins.

The frame appears on the page at the same position it occupied when you put it on the clipboard.

Pasting multiple copies

Each time you press the Ins key (or select Paste Frame) you place another copy of the frame on the page. You will see Ventura redraw the screen each time. Each copy appears exactly on top of the previous one. What looks like a single frame can actually be multiple frames stacked one on top of the other. To see the other copies, select the top frame and move it out of the way.

Selecting overlapping frames

When frames overlap, it can be difficult to select the ones underneath. To grab a frame at the bottom of a stack, place the mouse cursor on the top frame. Hold the Ctrl key while clicking with the mouse. Each time you Ctrl-Click, Ventura selects the next frame down in the stack. When you reach the bottom, Ventura starts at the top again.

Putting multiple frames onto the clipboard

You can put multiple frames onto the clipboard, but you must cut or copy them simultaneously:

- Enable Frame mode.
- Move all the frames to the same page. It doesn't matter whether they overlap.
- Use Shift-Click to select all the frames at once.
- Cut or copy all the frames to the clipboard.

Moving or copying to another page

Use the clipboard to move or copy a frame (or several frames) to another page. First, cut or copy the frame(s) to the clipboard. Then move to the new page and paste in the frame(s).

Moving or copying to another chapter

You can use the clipboard to move or copy frames from one chapter to another. First, open the chapter containing the frame (or frames) you want to copy. Put the frame(s) onto the clipboard. Open the second chapter. Move to the correct page and paste the frame(s). Be sure to paste the frames before you cut or copy anything else to avoid erasing them from the clipboard.

Fine-tuning size and position

Ventura provides several aids to refine the size and position of frames:

- rulers and cross hairs for easier positioning
- the ability to move with the mouse
- handles for resizing with the mouse
- a dialog box for mathematical precision

Using the rulers and cross hairs

Rulers are optional measuring guidelines at the top and left side of the workspace. You can choose the units of measurement. You also can use them with the cross hairs (Figure 6-20) for measuring frames and other page elements.

To turn the rulers on, select Show Rulers from the Options menu. To change the units of measurement, select Set Ruler from the Options menu. When the dialog box appears (Figure 6-21), use the pop-up menus to select the units you want for the horizontal (top) and vertical (left side) rulers. You can have different units for each if you prefer.

By default, the ruler measures from the edge of the page, but you can change the zero point in this dialog box. Suppose that your page had one-inch margins on all sides. Setting the zero point at one inch (so the rulers would begin at the margins)

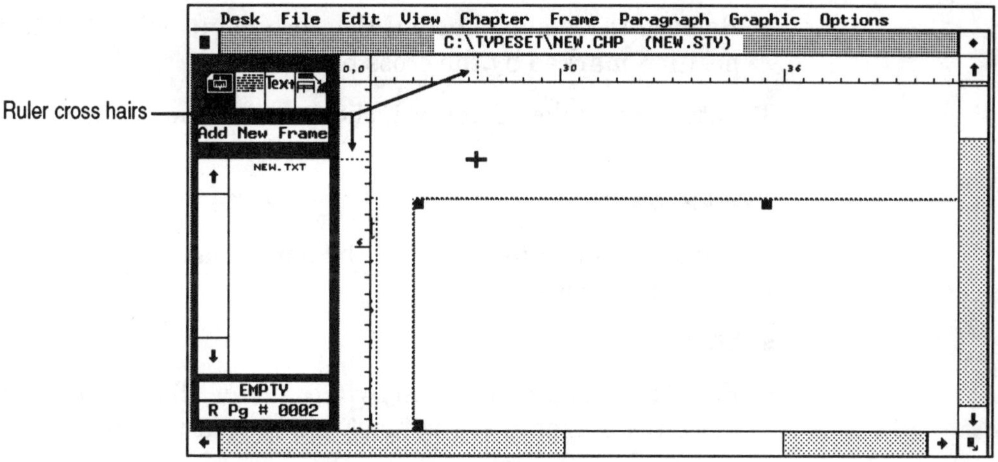

Figure 6-20. The cross hairs move along with the cursor to show its current position. Use them to measure page elements.

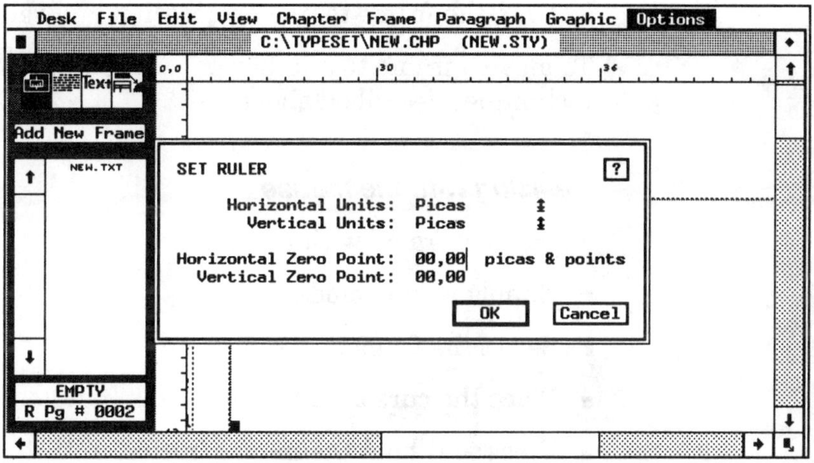

Figure 6-21. The Set Rulers dialog box.

would make it easier to gauge spacing, indents, and tab settings.

Ventura also provides a freehand way to set the zero point:

- Move the cursor to the 0,0 box at the upper left of the rulers.
- Press and hold the button until a four-way arrow appears.
- Drag the cursor to the new starting point. When the cursor moves over the page, it becomes cross hairs. Place it at the upper left corner of the item to be measured.

- Release the mouse button; the zero point will reset to the position marked by the cross hairs.

To return the ruler to normal, click once in the 0,0 box.

Moving frames

To move a frame anywhere on the same page without changing its dimensions:

- Select the frame.
- Place the mouse cursor anywhere *inside* the frame. Do not place the cursor onto the black handles at the edge.
- Press and hold the mouse button until a four-way cursor appears.
- Drag the frame to its new location and release the button.

To move a frame to another page, use the cutting and pasting techniques described above.

Resizing with the mouse

To resize a frame with the mouse:

- Enable Frame mode.
- Select the frame.
- Place the cursor on top of a black handle.
- Press and hold the mouse button until the cursor changes to a pointing finger. (If it does not change to a finger, you were not on top of the handle. Try again.)
- Drag the edge of the frame to its new position.

Selecting a corner handle lets you change both the horizontal and the vertical dimensions (as you did when drawing the frame). Selecting a middle handle moves only one dimension at a time (Figure 6-22).

Resizing and repositioning with a dialog box

For precise sizing and positioning, use Sizing & Scaling from the Frame menu (Figure 6-23). The two "Upper Left" lines

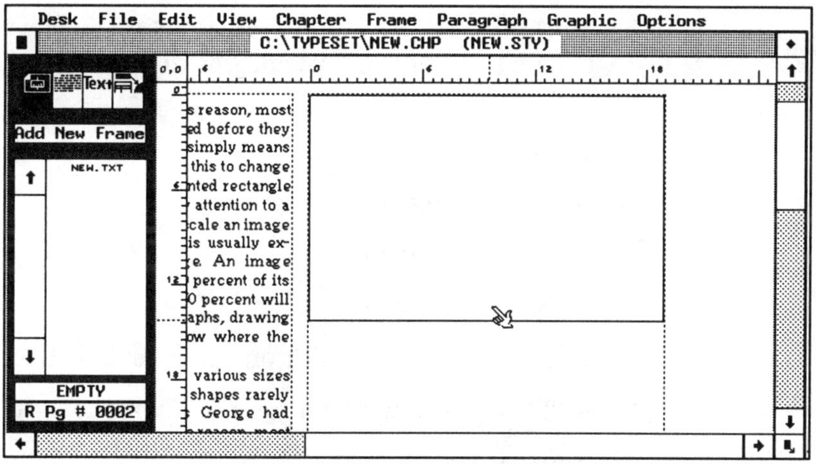

Figure 6-22. To prevent both dimensions from changing, grab a middle handle when resizing a frame.

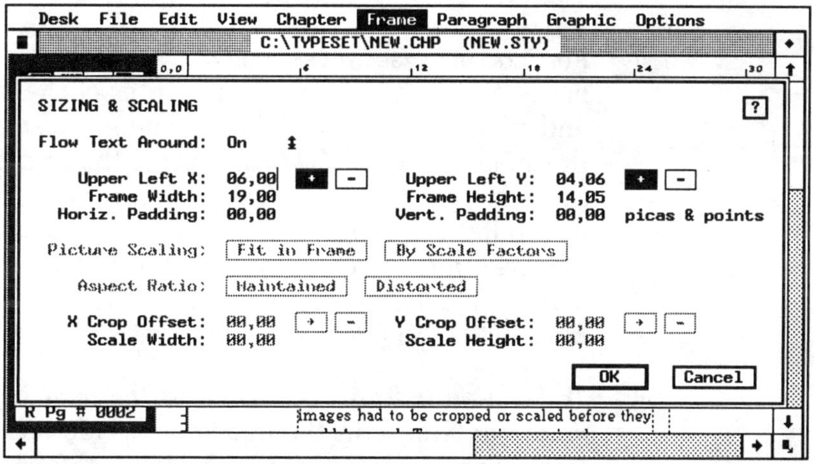

Figure 6-23. The Sizing & Scaling dialog box.

specify the position of the frame's top left corner; the following two lines specify its size.

To reposition a frame with the dialog box:

- Select the frame.
- Select Sizing & Scaling.
- On the Upper Left X line, type in the distance you want the frame from the left margin.

- On the Upper Left Y line, type in the distance you want the frame from the top margin. Click OK.

When you return to the workspace, the screen redraws and the frame moves to its new position.

To resize a frame:

- Select the frame.
- Select Sizing & Scaling.
- Enter the new width on the Frame Width line.
- Type the new height on the Frame Height line. Click OK.

You will learn more about the Sizing & Scaling dialog box when we discuss how to crop and scale pictures.

Tips for adding and positioning frames

TIP *For more precise movement on-screen,* use Ventura's keyboard mode. Place the cursor in the center of the frame, then press and release Ctrl-RightShift. The numeric keypad now controls the mouse. To drag the frame, press the End key. The four-way arrow cursor appears. Use the arrow keys to move the frame in small increments. When it's in the right spot, press Home. For even more precision, press the Shift key while using the arrows. The frame will move in smaller increments. Press and release Ctrl-RightShift again to return to mouse mode.

TIP *To position a frame partially off the page,* specify a negative value for X or Y in the dialog box. This has limited value on laser printers unless the Underlying Page is smaller than 8.5x11. Most laser printers cannot print close to the edge of the page. It does have application with some phototypesetters for producing bleed pictures.

TIP *Be careful about which handle you grab* when fine-tuning frame position. If you've got the vertical dimensions correct, don't grab a corner. Select a middle handle from either side. When you select a middle handle, Ventura changes only one dimension, leaving the other one intact.

TIP *Creating identical frames* is faster and easier by copying than by drawing. Add the first frame, then copy and paste it repeatedly to create the others.

TIP *For more accurate measurements,* change to Enlarged View and use hairline marks on the rulers. These hairlines move as the cursor moves. Use them to set the beginning and end of the frame.

Adjusting frame margins

You've already learned how to add and change frames. You also need to know how to create margins and padding for frames — white space buffers on the inside and outside, respectively.

If you place pictures or text inside a frame with no margins, they extend the full width and height. Often, however, you want extra white space inside, especially if you have a ruling box around the frame (Figure 6-24).

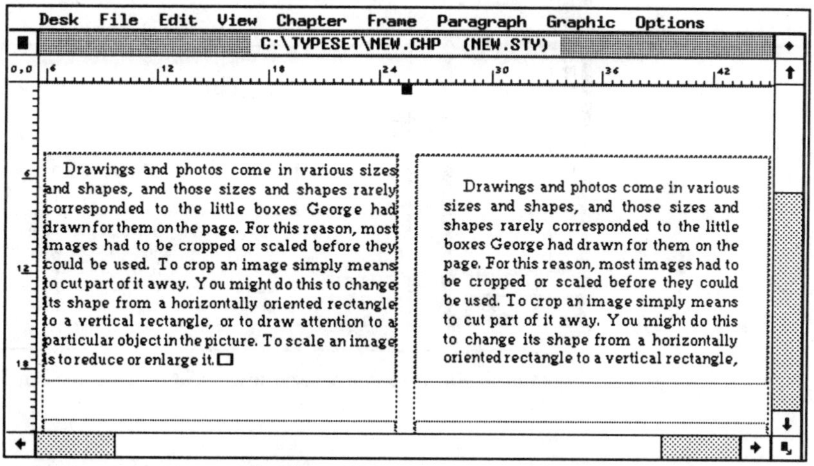

Figure 6-24. Without a margin, pictures and text extend the full height and width of a frame (left side). With a margin, frames have a white space buffer inside (right side).

You add a margin to a frame the same way you do to a page:

- Enable Frame mode.
- Select the frame.
- Select Margins & Columns from the Frame menu.

- Enter the amounts you want for Top, Bottom, Left, and Right, and click OK.

Sometimes you want only a point or two — just enough to keep the picture inside from overlapping and obscuring a ruling box around. In other cases, however, you want a more generous margin. As a rule of thumb, use the line spacing of Body Text for interior frame margins, especially if you will be putting text inside the frame.

Adding frame padding

When you add a frame, text flows *around* it (unless you use the Sizing & Scaling dialog box to specify otherwise). But even though the text doesn't penetrate inside the frame, it butts flush against the edge (Figure 6-25).

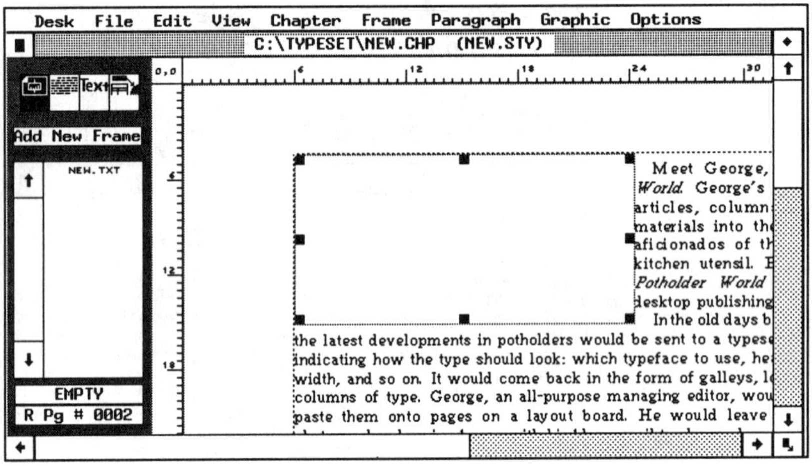

Figure 6-25. Without frame padding, text sits flush against the frame boundary.

To get some breathing room, use the Sizing & Scaling dialog box. By entering a value on the line labeled Horiz. Padding, you put buffer space along the left and right side of the frame. Vert. Padding puts space along the top and bottom.

Vertical padding can keep lines of text from resting flush upon a frame. How much to add depends on the layout of your pages. Generally, use vertical padding that has an integer relationship with the line spacing of body text. For instance, if

Body Text has 12-point inter-line spacing, consider adding 6, 12, or 24 points of frame padding.

Together, horizontal and vertical padding can provide a white space buffer on all sides for frames that must be placed in the middle of text blocks. Figure 6-26 shows how a page from this book might look without horizontal padding.

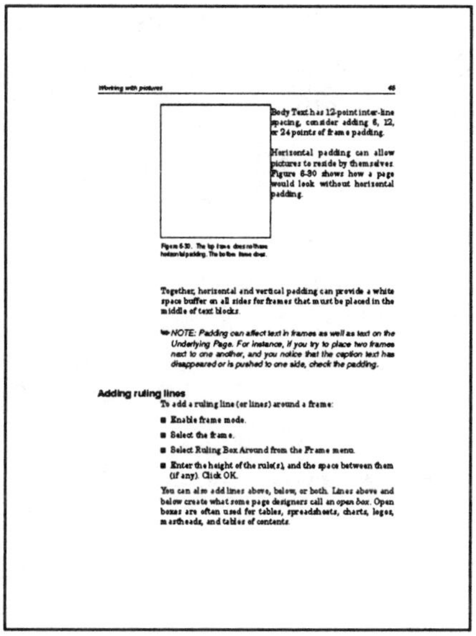

Working with pictures

Body Text has 12-point inter-line spacing, consider adding 6, 12, or 24 points of frame padding.

Horizontal padding can allow pictures to reside by themselves. Figure 6-30 shows how a page would look without horizontal padding.

Figure 6-30. The top frame does not have horizontal padding. The bottom frame does.

Together, horizontal and vertical padding can provide a white space buffer on all sides for frames that must be placed in the middle of text blocks.

➥*NOTE: Padding can affect text in frames as well as text on the Underlying Page. For instance, if you try to place two frames next to one another, and you notice that the caption text has disappeared or is pushed to one side, check the padding.*

Adding ruling lines

To add a ruling line (or lines) around a frame:

- Enable frame mode.
- Select the frame.
- Select Ruling Box Around from the Frame menu.
- Enter the height of the rule(s), and the space between them (if any). Click OK.

You can also add lines above, below, or both. Lines above and below create what some page designers call an *open box*. Open boxes are often used for tables, spreadsheets, charts, logos, mastheads, and tables of contents.

Figure 6-26. How a page from this book might look if we did not use horizontal padding to keep text from intruding next to frames.

➥*NOTE: Padding can affect text in frames as well as text on the Underlying Page. For instance, if you try to place two frames next to one another, and you notice that the caption text has disappeared or is pushed to one side, padding may be at fault.*

Adding ruling lines

To add a ruling line (or lines) around a frame:

- Enable frame mode.
- Select the frame.
- Select Ruling Box Around from the Frame menu.

- Enter the height of the rule(s), and the space between them (if any). Click OK.

You also can add lines above, below, or both. Lines above and below create what some page designers call an *open box*. Open boxes are useful for tables, spreadsheets, charts, logos, mastheads, and tables of contents.

Whether to add a ruling line around depends on the type of picture. In general, use ruling lines when there is a lot of open space in the picture. Certain pictures, such as graphs and charts, already have rules or borders. Photographs can usually do without a box around.

Choose a single thin rule for most applications. Thick rules and multiple lines draw attention to themselves and away from the picture. However, some applications demand multiple rules. For instance, you may want to put several rules around a caution note in a technical manual. (You also can put a ruling box around the text in Paragraph mode if you don't want it to reside in a frame by itself.) Or you may need multiple rules to imitate computer screens. If you glance through this book, you will see that our sample dialog boxes have two rules around them, closely approximating the appearance of dialog boxes on screen.

Some users like to use boxes with rounded corners to imitate the shape of the standard monitor. Ventura does not have a rounded box around, but you can get the same result by attaching a rounded rectangle in Graphic mode.

Adding a round rectangle

To add a rounded rectangle (*round rec*) to a frame:

- Enable Graphic mode.
- Select the frame.
- Choose the round rec tool from the Side-Bar. Draw the round rec to match the frame's dimensions (Figure 6- 27).

Obviously, the frame should not have a ruling box or it will conflict with the round rec. If you make the round rec slightly larger than the frame you need not worry about adding a margin. The frame boundary will keep the picture from touch-

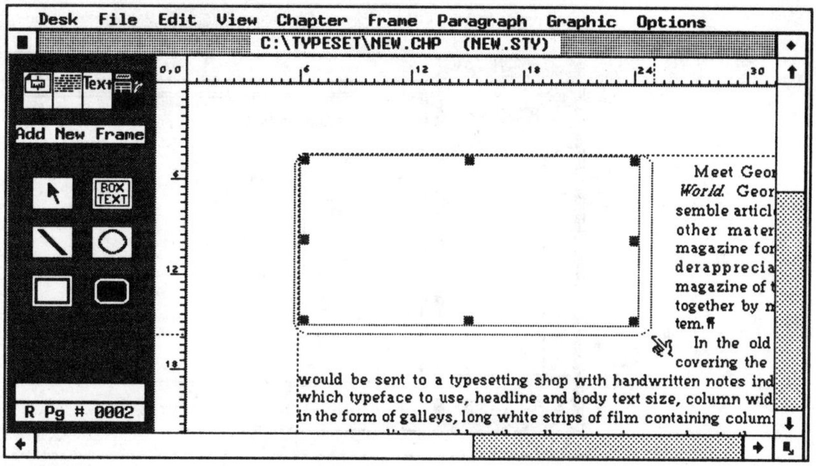

Figure 6-27. To imitate a computer screen, attach a rounded rectangle to the frame in Graphic mode.

ing the rectangle. The rectangle is attached to the frame and moves with it.

Adding a circular border

The same method described above for adding a round rectangle also allows you to put a circle around a frame (and, therefore, a circle around the text or picture inside that frame).

Adding frame backgrounds

Frame backgrounds are useful for a variety of effects, including reverse text and tint blocks for sidebars. To add a background pattern to a frame:

- Select the frame.
- Select Frame Background from the Frame menu (Figure 6-28).
- Select the color and pattern you want. You will see a preview of your choice in the Result box. Click OK.

In addition to the standard patterns available in this dialog box, you can define other shades of gray by assigning them to a color, as described in Chapter Eight, "Advanced Functions."

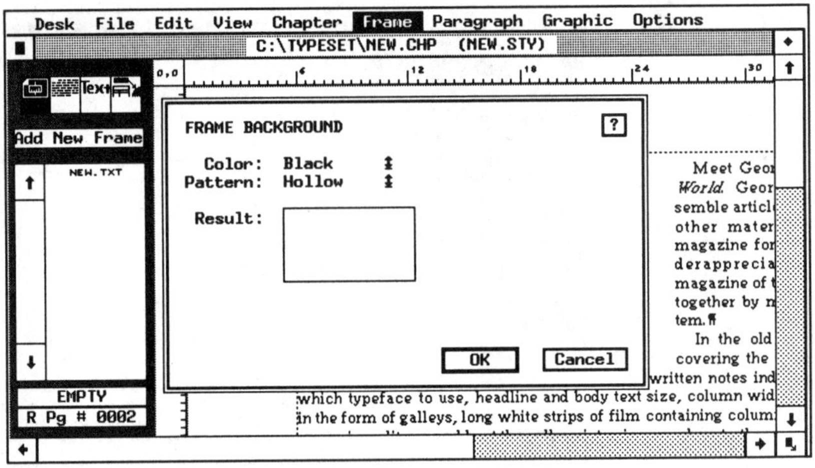

Figure 6-28. The Frame Background dialog box.

Layered frames

You can put frames on top of one another to create special effects. One application is to create a shadow effect (Figure 6-29). Another use is to combine two (or more) pictures into one by loading the pictures into frames, then putting the frames on top of one another.

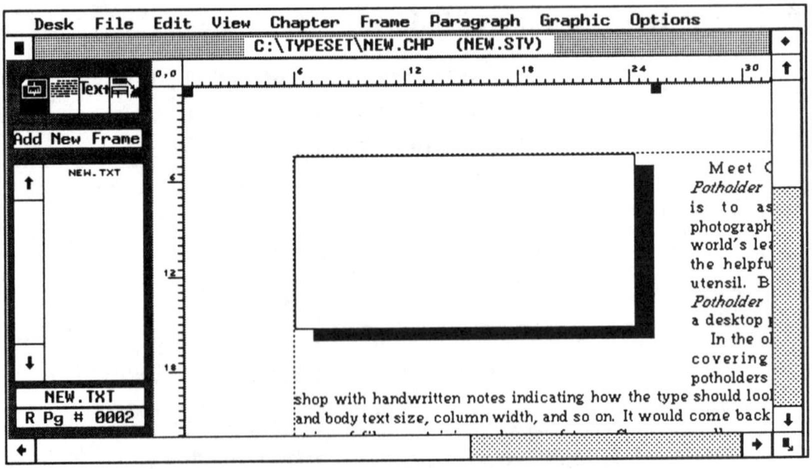

Figure 6-29. By putting a white frame on top of a black one, you create a shadow effect.

Placing pictures

Let's pause for a quick recap. The process of putting pictures into a chapter has three essential steps: load the picture file; add a frame; place the picture. And it has three optional steps: edit and enhance the picture; caption the picture; anchor the picture. So far we've covered loading files and adding frames.

As you learned earlier, you can place text files on the Underlying Page *or* in a frame. Picture files, by contrast, must always be in a frame. To place a picture file:

- Enable Frame mode.
- Select the frame.
- Select the file name from the Assignment List.

If you place the wrong picture into the frame, remove it with Remove Text/File from the Edit menu.

Editing pictures

We use the word *editing* to cover anything that affects the way pictures look. You can edit pictures in four ways:

- scaling
- cropping
- adding graphics
- changing the image settings

These editing tools affect the way pictures look on the screen and on the printed page. They do not affect the original graphics file, which remains untouched.

Scaling pictures

Scaling a picture means to enlarge or reduce it. Look again at the previous illustration of the Sizing & Scaling dialog box. The top half controls the frame. The bottom half controls the picture *inside* the frame.

Your first decision is how to scale the picture. If you want Ventura to do the work, choose Fit in Frame. If you want to control the size manually, choose By Scale Factors.

If you choose Fit in Frame, you can enlarge or reduce the picture by enlarging or reducing the frame. Whatever size you make the frame, Ventura will change the picture to fit.

Both line-art and images can use the Fit in Frame option. Ventura enlarges the image until it fills the frame margins (or the entire frame if you did not set any margins). If you pick Aspect Ratio: Distorted, Ventura stretches the picture as much as necessary to completely fill the frame (Figure 6-30). Use this option when accurate dimensions don't matter (as with cartoons) or when the shape of the picture matches the shape of the frame (as with a square picture and a square frame).

But often — as with technical drawings, for example — you cannot afford to distort the picture. In such cases, use Aspect Ratio: Maintained. Ventura still tries to fit the picture into the frame. But it stretches it only as much as it can *without* changing the existing ratio between horizontal and vertical. Although this option guarantees that the aspect ratio remains the same, it may leave extra white space around the picture.

Suppose, for instance, that the original picture is 4x5 in. Ventura would permit enlargements to 6x7.5 in., or 8x10 in., or any other measurement that preserved the same ratio.

If you prefer, you can control the scaling yourself. Select Picture Scaling: By Scale Factors. Ventura then displays the

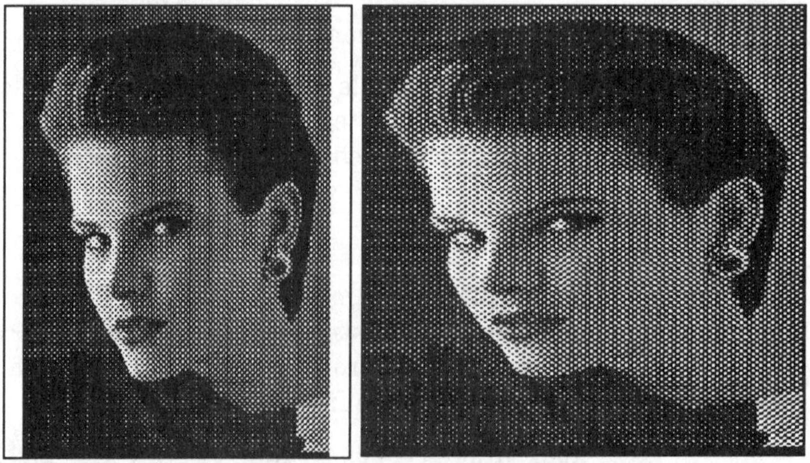

Figure 6-30. If you choose Aspect Ratio: Distorted (right), Ventura stretches the picture as much as necessary to fill the entire frame.

current dimensions at the bottom of the dialog box (Scale Width and Scale Height). The current dimensions are the actual size of the picture before it was brought into Ventura.

To change a picture's size, type in the new dimensions. When using By Scale Factors, you enlarge or reduce the picture independently of the frame size. For instance, you can make the picture larger than the frame. If so, Ventura shows as much as it can, starting at the upper left corner. To show the portion you want, use the cropping feature explained below.

If you select Aspect Ratio: Maintained, Ventura lets you change only the width. (Scale Height appears in gray to show it is not available.) After you enter the new width, Ventura calculates the height necessary to maintain the aspect ratio. For instance, to double a 2x3 in. picture, enter a new width of four inches. Ventura calculates the height necessary to maintain the same aspect ratio (in this case, six).

If you choose Aspect Ratio: Distorted, Ventura lets you change either the Scale Width or the Scale Height. For instance, you could enlarge a 4x5 in. original to 6x9 in. by entering Scale Width: 06.00 in. and Scale Height: 09.00 in. Be careful — you have the power to stretch and distort the picture, so choose the settings with care. Table 6-5 shows the effect of the four possible combinations.

Table 6-5. Effect of picture scaling options.

	Apect Ratio: Maintained	Aspect Ratio: Distorted
Fit in Frame		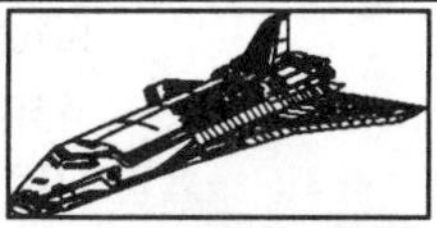
By Scale Factors		

Tips for scaling pictures

TIP *When scaling bit-mapped images* keep an integer (whole number) relationship between the original and the final size. This produces the cleanest image and reduces the possibility of moiré patterns. For example, note the original scale dimensions and enter new ones that are 2.0 times as big, not 1.73 times. Choose Aspect Ratio: Maintained to help you preserve the integer relationship.

TIP *Scanned images* should be printed at the original size if possible (or at least at an integer multiple of the original size). To make an image the same size as the original, select Aspect Ratio: Maintained. Then select By Scale Factors. Switching to By Scale Factors while the aspect ratio is maintained gives you an image the same size as the original.

Cropping pictures with Sizing & Scaling

Scaling is one way to edit a picture. Cropping is a second method. Scaling changes the size of a picture. Cropping changes which part of the picture shows inside the frame.

Think of the frame as a window onto the picture. You can change the position of that window to display any portion of the picture. Originally, Ventura places the window at the upper left (Figure 6-31). You can use the mouse or the Sizing & Scaling dialog box to alter the position of the window. You can only crop pictures that are larger than the frame. Otherwise, there's nowhere to move the window — it already shows the entire picture. Thus, if you select Fit in Frame, you cannot crop a picture, because it will never be larger than the frame.

One way to crop a picture is with the Sizing & Scaling dialog box. If a picture is larger than the frame, Ventura starts by showing the upper left corner. Use X Crop Offset to move the window left or right (Figure 6-32). Positive X values move it to the right. Negative X values move it to the left. Positive Y values move the window down. Negative Y values move it up.

You also can crop interactively with the mouse. As with the dialog box method, this technique only comes into play if the picture is larger than the frame. To crop with the mouse:

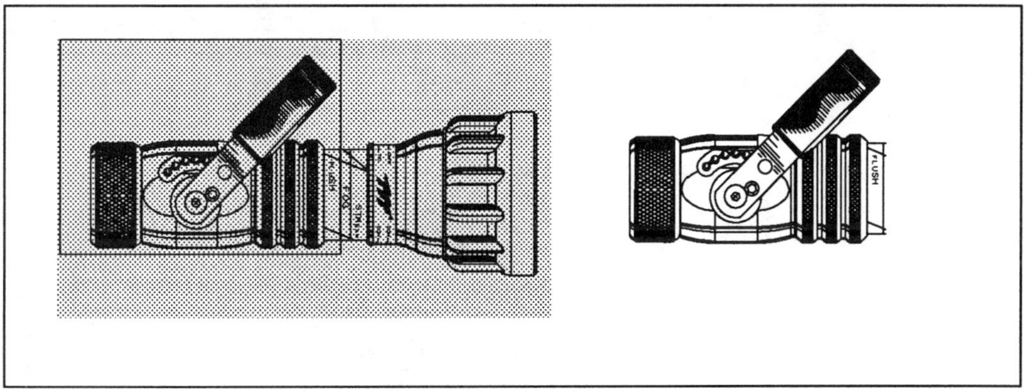

Figure 6-31. If the picture (gray region) is larger than the frame , the frame acts as a window onto the picture. The image at right shows the result that would be displayed on screen.

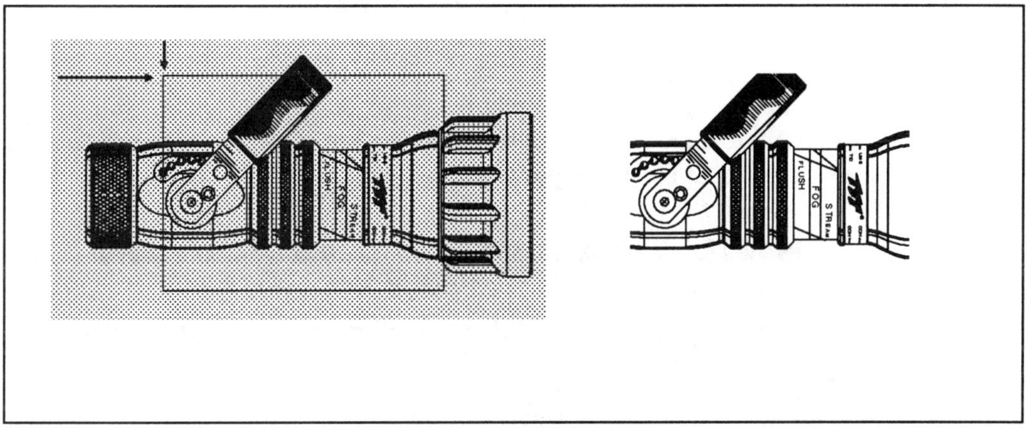

Figure 6-32. The result when a crop offset distance is specified (arrows indicate distance of X and Y crop offsets).

- Select the frame.
- Place the cursor in the middle of the picture.
- Press and hold the Alt key. Press and hold the mouse button until a small hand appears (Figure 6-33).
- Move the mouse in the direction you want the picture to move. When the image is repositioned, release the Alt key and the mouse button.

Changing the image settings

Ventura can alter TIFF and PostScript gray-scale images. When you place a TIFF image into a frame, Ventura enables

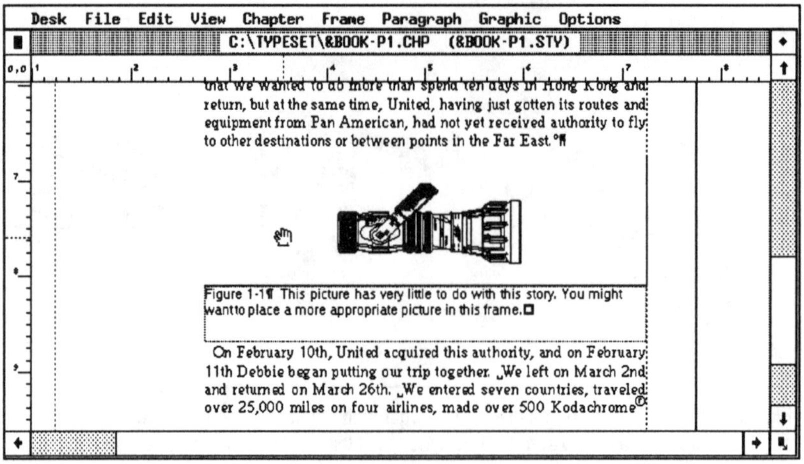

Figure 6-33. To crop with the mouse, hold down the Alt key while pressing down the mouse button.

the Image Settings option at the bottom of the Frame menu (until then it stays gray). This option allows you to modify the appearance of the picture.

➥ *NOTE: The Image Settings function is available only if (1) the image is in TIFF or PostScript format and (2) the image contains gray-scale information, and (3) the image is sent to a PostScript output device.*

You are not required to modify the image settings. Ventura automatically chooses the most appropriate ones for your printer. The following section applies only to those who wish to experiment with the appearance of halftone images.

As shown in Figure 6-34, the dialog box lets you modify three parameters: the screen type, the screen angle, and the screen frequency (lines per inch). The screen type refers to the shape of the halftone cells in the image. You have five choices: Default, Dot, Line, Ellipse, and Custom.

Normally you will select Dot, which creates a circular halftone cell. However, you can obtain some interesting effects by using Line or Ellipse. If you select Default, Ventura chooses the screen type for you.

Screen angle refers to the rows of halftone dots. Generally, the rows are rotated 45 degrees. This minimizes conflicts between halftone rows and vertical or horizontal lines within the pic-

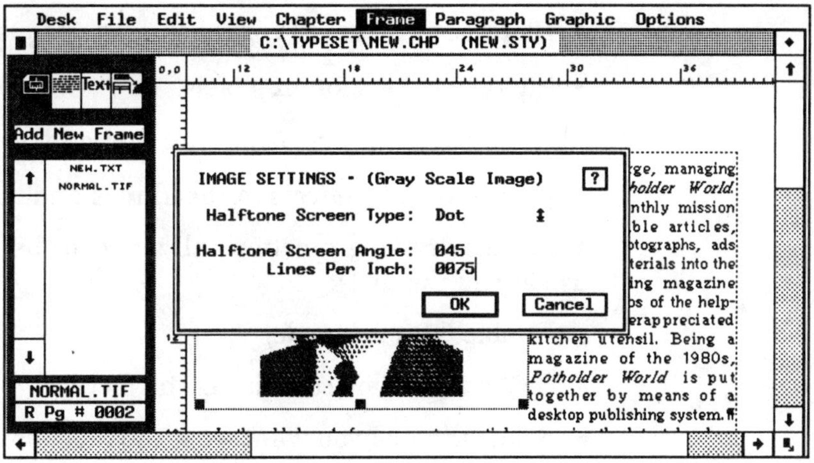

Figure 6-34. The Image Settings dialog box.

ture. Screen frequency (lines per inch) refers to spacing between dots. The more lines, the higher the resolution (the more dots per square inch).

The greater the lines per inch, the better the resolution. Unfortunately, the greater the resolution, the fewer gray scales. There is always a trade-off between screen frequency and gray scale. For 300-dpi laser printers, the optimal screen frequency is about 60 lines per inch, which allows for 25 levels of gray. If you are sending your output to a 2540-dpi laser imagesetter, you can produce a 150-line screen, while still allowing for 256 levels of gray.

Normally, you will want to leave these settings at the default. Each printer manufacturer optimizes screen type, angle, and frequency. This information is available to Ventura when it prints.

Using Graphic mode to enhance pictures

This section explains how to change pictures after bringing them into a chapter. Review Chapter Four, "Creating Pictures," for more on the basics of Graphic mode. This section concentrates on how to use Graphic mode to dress up pictures. And Graphic mode does indeed provide an excellent way to enhance and modify pictures:

- Add simple lines to complete a drawing.

- Block out unwanted portions using opaque white shapes.
- Shade portions for emphasis.
- Annotate drawings using Box Text and arrows.
- Create shadow effects for headlines and banners.

Ventura's drawing functions all work in the same fashion. To use any of the tools:

- Enable Graphic mode.
- Select the frame containing the picture.
- Select the tool you want from the Side-Bar.
- Position the cursor where you want the graphic to start. Press and hold the mouse button.
- Stretch the graphic to the correct size. Release the mouse button.

> WARNING: Be sure to select the correct frame before you start drawing. Otherwise the graphics may be attached to a different frame or to the Underlying Page by mistake.

The lines, arrows, shapes, and patterns you draw *do not have to be within the boundaries of the parent frame.* As you can see in Figure 6-35, box text and arrows (or any other graphic) can extend outside the frame. Second, you can link graphics to a frame. If you move the frame, the graphics move with it, whether or not they are inside the frame.

Box Text for annotations

Ventura's Box Text tool provides a way to annotate pictures. It does, however, have certain limitations. To use it most efficiently, follow this procedure: First, decide in advance what to say for each annotation to gauge the approximate size of the box. Then create a box text big enough for the largest annotation. Now get the box just the way you want it. Adjust the line attributes, fill attributes, and size until they are just right. Do not type in the words yet.

Once you have the look you want, use the first Box Text as a

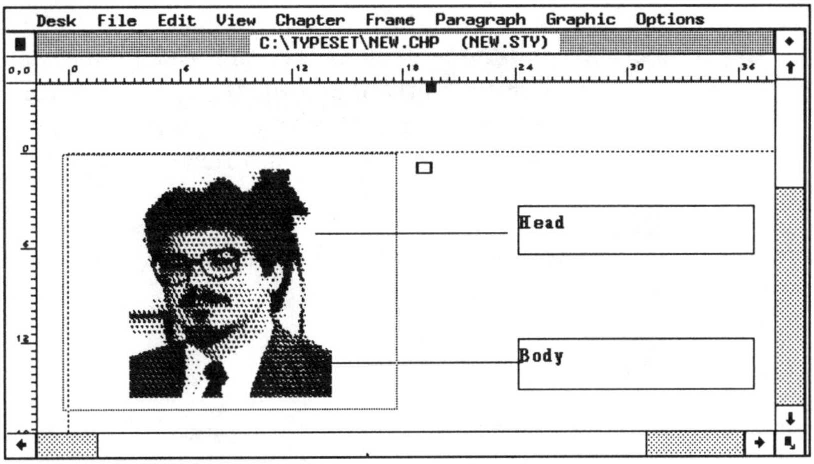

Figure 6-35. Even though you can attach Box Text and lines to a frame, they do not have to stay within the boundaries of that frame.

template. Copy it repeatedly until you have Box Text for every annotation. Move the boxes into position around the drawing.

➥ *NOTE: If you change your mind about attributes after placing all the Box Text rectangles, use Select All from the Graphic menu (or Ctrl-Q) to select and change them all at once.*

Now you can switch to Text mode and type in the annotations. Then switch to Paragraph mode and change the font (if necessary). Finally, switch back to Graphic mode, choose the line tool and draw arrows from text to picture.

Tips for annotations

TIP *Put in arrows after typing text.* Until then, you don't know exactly where to position the arrow.

TIP *Keep annotations as short as possible* to avoid clutter.

TIP *Use the Shift-Click method* to select more than one graphic at a time, just as you use it to select multiple paragraphs in Paragraph mode. Likewise, you can deselect a graphic (and leave all the others selected) by Shift-Clicking a second time.

TIP *To select all the graphics* associated with a frame, use Select All from the Graphic menu, (the keyboard shortcut is Ctrl-Q).

TIP *If you have trouble* getting Box Text to print, set the fill attributes to transparent. If you must cover up what is underneath, cover it first with a rectangle that has a solid white fill pattern. Then put the Box Text on top of the rectangle.

TIP *For more accurate placement* of Box Text and other graphics, use Grid Settings from the Graphic menu. This option creates an invisible snap-to grid.

Adding captions

After you load the picture, place it in a frame, and edit it, you can add captions. It's probably easiest to think of captioning as a three-step process:

1. Attaching the caption frame and label.
2. Typing the caption text.
3. Formatting the caption.

Attaching the caption frame

Attaching the caption occurs with the Anchors & Captions dialog box from the Frame menu (Figure 6-36). This dialog box performs four functions. First, it determines the position of the caption. Second, it can optionally add a brief caption label. Third, it can record the anchor name for a frame. Fourth, it

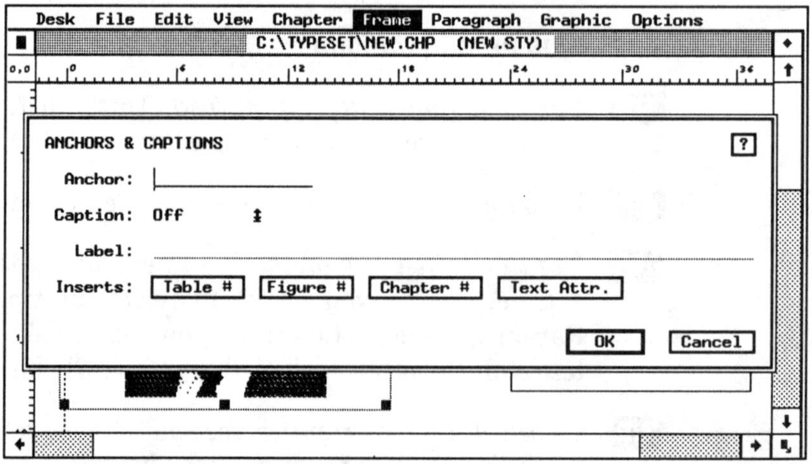

Figure 6-36. The Anchors & Captions dialog box.

can turn on automatic numbering functions. Let's begin first with the most straightforward application: determining the position of the caption frame.

To create captions in Ventura, you attach a caption frame to the frame containing the picture. You can have only one caption frame per picture. The caption frame is linked to the picture frame. It moves when you move the frame.

The caption frame butts up flush against one side of the picture. In addition, one dimension of the caption frame is linked to the frame and must be identical. For instance, a caption frame beneath a picture can be as deep as you want, but it can never be wider than the picture (Figure 6-37). If you make the caption frame wider, the picture frame becomes wider, too.

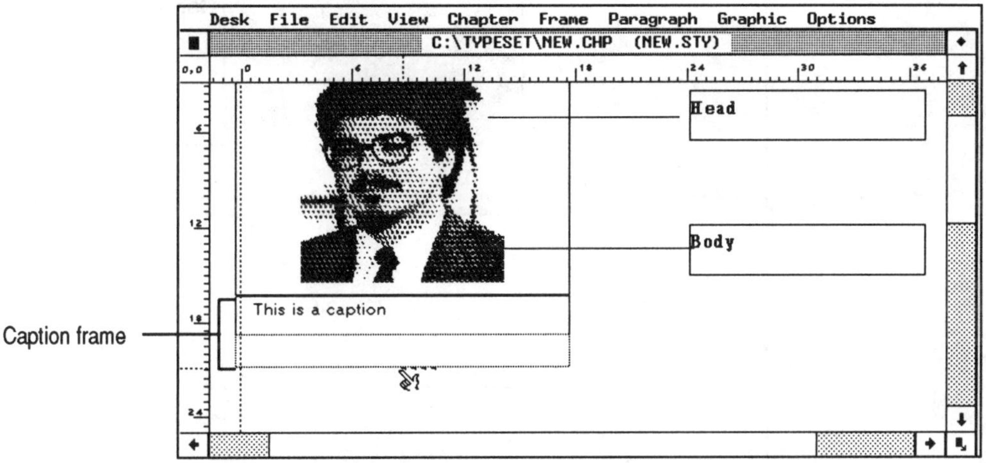

Figure 6-37. The caption frame shares one dimension with the picture frame.

To create a caption frame with no label inside:

- Enable Frame mode.
- Select Anchors & Captions from the Frame menu.
- Select the position of the frame from the pop-up menu next to the line labeled Caption and click OK.

When you return to the workspace, Ventura has drawn a caption frame. Figure 6-38 shows the five options.

To change the size of a caption frame, use the mouse to resize

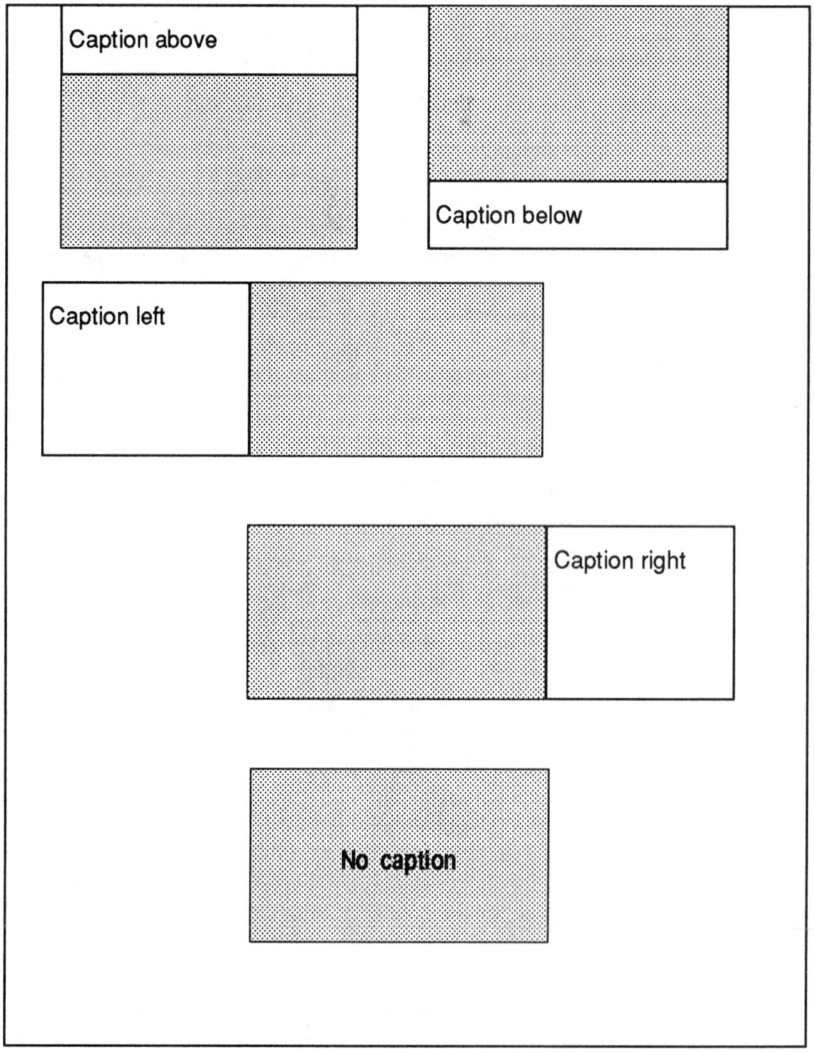

Figure 6-38. Ventura lets you choose the position of the caption frame, but you can have only one per picture.

it the same way you would resize any other frame. To avoid accidentally changing the dimensions of the picture frame, always grab caption frames by a middle handle.

Adding a caption label

You also can use Anchors & Captions to create a brief label. The most common use for this label is to number figures and tables. This short label may be only a small portion of the entire caption. Later, you can add more text by typing directly into the caption frame.

To add a label, use the Anchors & Captions dialog box as described above to choose the position of the caption frame. Then, with the dialog box still open:

- Move to the Label line. Type in the label you want to appear. This label can be up to 60 characters long. It is generally best to keep the label as short as possible.
- Click OK. When you return to the workspace you will see the label in the caption frame.

➥ *NOTE: Anything you type here can be edited only by returning to this dialog box. By contrast, text added to the caption frame can be edited in Text mode.*

Adding figure or table numbering

While you are adding a label, you can enable automatic figure or table numbering. With automatic figure numbering, you can let Ventura worry about the sequence of pictures. It will scan the pages, count the figures, and enter the correct sequential number into the caption label.

Ventura lets you have both table and figure numbering in the same chapter, so tables and figures can have a separate numbering sequence. In the discussion below, we refer to figure numbering, but the techniques we discuss apply equally to table numbering.

To invoke figure numbering, enter codes on the Label line. You can type them in yourself, or you can enter them by clicking on the Inserts buttons at the bottom of the dialog box.

Look at any caption from this book. The label portion is the phrase "Figure C-F," where *C* represents the chapter number and *F* the figure number. For instance, the seventh figure in Chapter Four is labeled "Figure 4-7."

You create such a label in the Anchors & Captions dialog box. First you type the word *Figure* followed by a space on the Label line. Then you click on the Chapter # button to insert the code [C#]. Next you type a hyphen, then click on the

Figure # button to insert the code [F#]. If you wanted punctuation (a period, for instance), you would type it into the dialog box. The resulting code would read:

```
Figure [C#]-[F#].
```

You could type "Figure 1-1," but you would have to edit the label whenever you changed the order of the pictures. With automatic numbering, Ventura keeps track of the sequence.

Incidentally, you don't have to label your pictures as "Figure" and your tables as "Table." You can just as easily use "illustrations," "charts," or nothing at all. Some people use the label line to contain a number with no words.

Changing the numbering style

Unless you tell it otherwise, Ventura starts with the number one and uses Arabic numerals. To change the starting number for figure numbers:

- Select Update Counters from the Chapter menu (Figure 6-39).
- Click on Initial Figure.
- Choose the Update Method you want.

To ask Ventura to number across chapter boundaries, select

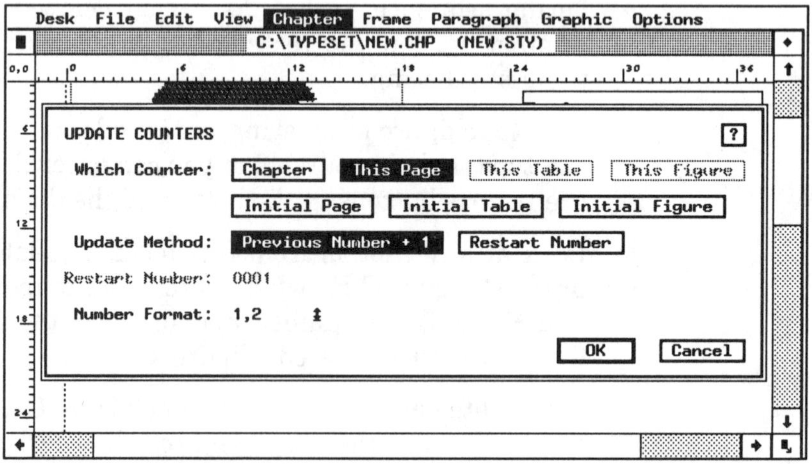

Figure 6-39. The Update Counters dialog box.

Previous Number + 1. If you print multiple chapters at one time, Ventura remembers the last number from the previous chapter. It adds one to that number to start the first figure in the next chapter.

To start with a different number, select the Restart Number button. Move the cursor to the Restart Number line. Type in the starting number you want to use.

To change the numbering format:

- Select Update Counters from the Chapter menu.
- Click on Initial Figure.
- Use the Number Format pop-up menu to choose the style you prefer.

You can choose Arabic or Roman numerals or you can have Ventura spell out the numbers. You also can choose letters instead of numbers to sequence figures or tables, with full control over capitalization.

See Chapter Eight, "Advanced Functions," for other tips on Ventura's numbering functions.

Creating the caption text

So far we have shown you how to create a brief caption label with the Anchors & Captions dialog box. But what if you want a longer caption? Simply go to the caption frame and type in the caption with Text mode. We call words typed into the caption frame *caption text* (as opposed to the caption label). You can combine labels with text (as we do in the captions for this book), or you can use either one separately. Here's how it works:

- Enable Frame mode and attach a caption frame as explained above.
- Select the caption frame and stretch it until it is at least twice as large.
- Enable Text mode. If you haven't done so already, select Show Tabs & Returns from the Options menu. An end-of-file marker appears in the caption frame.

- Position the text cursor in front of the end of file marker. Start typing. If you run out of room, stretch the caption frame further.

The text you type in this way is stored in the caption file, with the caption label (if any).

Changing the format of captions

When you create caption labels and caption text, Ventura automatically assigns tags to them. Initially, it assigns these tags the same attributes as Body Text. You can change tag formats, thus changing the appearance of caption labels and text. The generated tag names vary:

Labels without numbering: Z_LABEL CAP

Labels with figure numbering: Z_LABEL FIG

Labels with table numbering: Z_LABEL TBL

Caption text: Z_CAPTION

You can change the format of these tags, or you can retag the paragraphs. For instance, to change the format of a caption label with figure numbering:

- Enable Paragraph mode.
- Select the caption label. You will see the assigned tag name Z_LABEL FIG in the Current Selection Box.
- Use the Paragraph menu to change its format.

Changes apply to every Z_LABEL FIG paragraph in the document. Alternatively, you could select a different tag from the Assignment List.

Caption labels and caption text on the same line

When Ventura generates tags for caption labels and text, it uses the same attributes as Body Text. Since Body Text usually has a line break before or after, the paragraphs first reside on different lines. To place both paragraphs on the same line, remove the line break for caption text:

- Enable Paragraph mode.

- Select the caption text paragraph.
- Select Breaks from the Paragraph menu. Choose Line Break: No.

At this point, both tags are on the same line, but they probably overlap, making it impossible to read either one. One solution is to align the label flush left and the text flush right, using Alignment from the Paragraph menu. However, this solution works only if both the label and the text are short enough that they don't meet in the middle. Another solution is to leave the caption text flush left, but to give it a relative alignment:

- In Paragraph mode, select the caption text.
- Select Alignment from the Paragraph menu. Choose Relative Indent: On.

Now the text is aligned relative to the previous paragraph, which means it begins where the label leaves off. This still leaves us with a small problem: the caption text begins *exactly* where the label stops. To create some space between the two you can type a space after the last letter of the label in the Anchors & Captions dialog box. Or you can use the Alignment dialog box to create a small first-line indent — just enough to keep the text from touching the label.

Tips for captions

TIP *Check the caption file* separately with a spelling and/or grammar checker, just as you would check any other file. Don't forget to use ASCII format.

➥ *NOTE: Be careful not to delete any paragraph returns in the CAP file. Ventura keeps track of its captions by counting them. If you delete a return, you'll throw off the numbering, and captions will appear in the wrong frames.*

TIP *You can put padding around a caption frame.* Be careful, however, because the padding can affect text in the picture frame, or in adjacent frames and captions.

TIP *To get the effect of padding* on one side of a caption, add an extra blank line to the caption frame. This preserves extra space without the problem of padding encroaching into the picture frame. This method is not appropriate if you put a ruling box around your captions, since it would leave too much white space at the bottom of the caption frame.

TIP *You cannot edit the label* in Text mode as you can the rest of the caption. To change the label, use Anchors & Captions from the Frame menu to return to the original dialog box.

TIP *Don't get frustrated* by the process of getting captions to look right. You are creating tags that can be reused.

Anchoring frames

Ventura provides a method for ensuring that frames appear on the same page as the text that refers to it. This feature does not have perfect judgment; it doesn't do away with the need to check each page. But it can speed the layout process.

Most editors wait until all text changes have been made to place pictures. If they do it too early, the text may move to another page, while the picture stays behind. By inserting a frame anchor, you ensure that frames can be returned to the same page as the text reference. Ventura will move them for you. When a frame moves, everything attached to the frame moves with it — text, pictures, captions, or graphics.

Anchoring links a frame to a particular spot in the text. It involves two steps: (1) giving an anchor name to the frame and (2) putting an anchor marker in the text. Anchor names provide a means for Ventura to tell which frames are which. The anchor markers show Ventura where to place those frames.

Assigning an anchor name

To attach an anchor name to a frame:

- Enable Frame mode.
- Select the frame.
- Select Anchors & Captions from the Frame menu.
- Type the anchor name on the line labeled Anchor.

What should you use as the anchor name? Ventura permits up

to 16 characters. The shorter the name the easier it is to work with. The key to naming anchors is to choose something that is (1) unique, so Ventura can tell frames apart and (2) easy to remember, because you must use the identical name for the text marker.

If you have small chapters with few pictures, you can use any descriptive name, as long as you write it down for later reference. For longer documents, it is essential to come up with a naming system, especially if different people work on the same document. If the frame contains a picture file, we recommend using the file name as the anchor name. This suggestion is especially appropriate for technical documentation.

You should *avoid* the temptation to use sequential numbers as anchor names. Typing in Fig-1, Fig-2, etc., may seem logical at the time. However, there is nothing in these anchor names that would let someone else decipher the contents of the frame. More importantly, the order of pictures often changes — if not in this first version, then in some future revision. If frames are added, deleted, or rearranged, you could end up with a frame that reads Figure 4 on the page, but whose anchor name is Fig-7. The potential for confusion is enormous.

Where should you place the marker? The most obvious answer is immediately after the text reference. Thus, if you use references such as "see Figure 4-7," consider placing the anchor marker immediately after this phrase. If you do not use text references, choose the spot next to which you'd like the frame to appear.

Some users prefer to put the marker at the end of the paragraph containing the text reference, rather than in the middle of a sentence. Ventura signals frame anchors (and other special items) in the text with a degree symbol (°). This small mark is visible only if you select Show Tabs & Returns. Even then, it is hard to spot. Placing it at the end of the paragraph makes it easier to find, especially if you are consistent throughout the document.

Inserting the anchor marker

Once a frame has an anchor name, you can mark its anchor spot in the text. To insert an anchor marker:

- Enable Text mode.
- Place the cursor at the spot in the text where the marker should appear.
- Select Ins Special Item from the Edit menu (or press Ctrl-C). A secondary menu appears.
- Highlight Frame Anchor and click once (or press F5). The Insert/Edit Anchor dialog box appears (Figure 6-40).

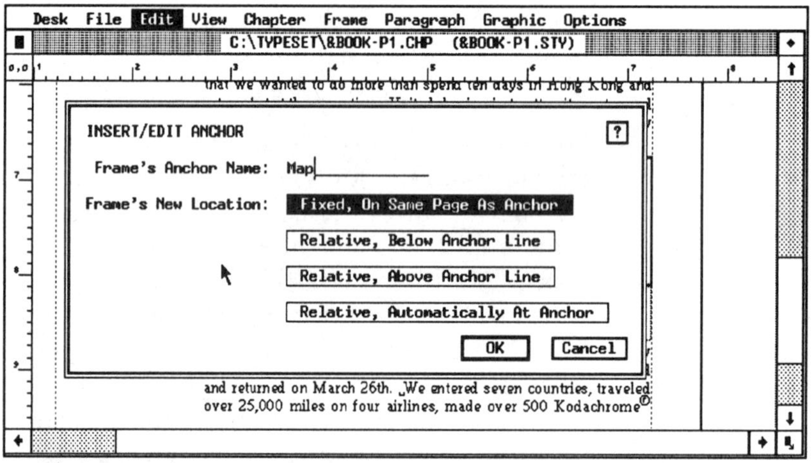

Figure 6-40. The Insert/Edit Anchor dialog box.

- Type in the anchor name of the frame on the top line. Be sure to match the spelling you used in the Anchors & Captions dialog box.
- Choose the location you want and click OK.

Ventura provides four anchoring options. The first three leave the frame in its old location until you issue a re-anchor command. Then the frame is moved to the same page as the text marker. The fourth option moves frames automatically with the text.

Fixed, On Same Page As Anchor moves the frame to the new page when you issue the re-anchor command. It places the frame at the same spot it had on the old page. You can reposition it after reanchoring.

Relative, Below Anchor Line puts the frame on the new page when you issue the re-anchor command. It places the frame below the line containing the text marker. This option may cause the frame to be pushed below the margins. You can reposition the frame after re-anchoring. This is probably the most common choice, since most editors want pictures to appear after the text reference.

Relative, Above Anchor Line is the same as the previous command, except that the frame appears immediately above the text marker.

Relative, Automatically At Anchor causes frames to move with the text. You do not need to use the re-anchor command. One application is to associate logos, symbols, key caps, or other small drawings with a paragraph of text. These drawings can reside within the paragraph, or they can sit in the margins as marginal icons. Ventura treats the frame as if it were a character.

To use the automatic anchor with a small frame, choose Grow Inter-Line to Fit: On from the Paragraph Typography dialog box. This allows Ventura to adjust the line spacing as necessary within the paragraph to fit the frame.

To use the automatic anchor with a large frame, you must meet several conditions. You must insert a line break (Ctrl-Enter) at the end of the paragraph. The anchor marker must follow this line break immediately. The frame should be snapped to both sides of the column guides and column snap should be on (Options menu).

➥*NOTE: Use of automatic anchoring may override frame padding and other frame settings.*

Issuing the re-anchor command

Automatic frame anchors move the frame every time you add or delete text. The other three options do not move the frame until you issue the command:

- Select Re-Anchor Frames from the Chapter menu or press the keyboard shortcut Ctrl-B. A brief dialog box appears (Figure 6-41).
- Choose whether you want to move the frames that appear on the current page, or all the frames in the document.

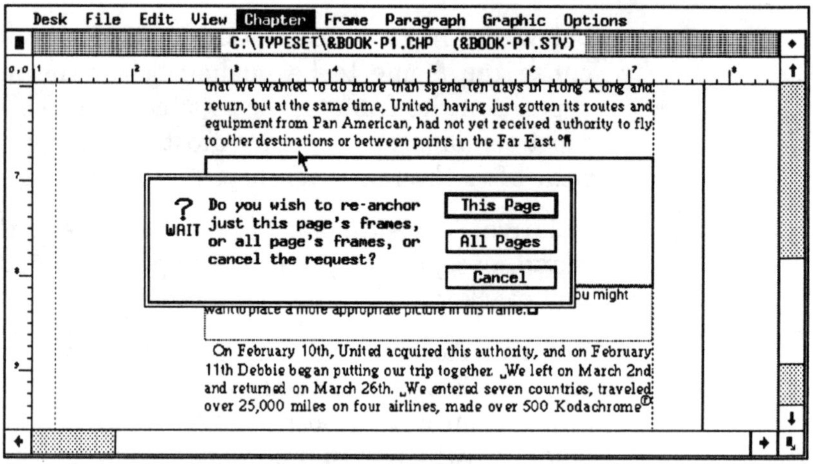

Figure 6-41. The Re-Anchor Frames dialog box.

Ventura moves the frame(s) to the same page as the anchor marker(s). This feature is merely a starting point. It may cause frames to extend past the margins or to overlap each other. It also fails to move frames if the user forgets to insert a text marker or to match the anchor names exactly. After anchoring frames, you should check each page and manually adjust those frames that are improperly positioned. Do not select Re-anchor Frames again or you will undo the repositioning.

Creating a frame template

As you have seen in this section, Ventura offers many options to control the appearance of frames. To name just a few:

- margins
- captions
- padding
- ruling lines
- backgrounds

You can spend lots of time reinventing the wheel if you must redo every setting for every frame. The alternative is to create reusable frame templates.

A frame template is a simple concept. First, get the frame to look just right. Then make sure that it is empty (that it doesn't have any text or picture inside). Now copy it to the clipboard. To place a copy of this template anywhere in the document, move to the page, enable Frame mode, and press Ins. Your frame template appears, complete with all specifications including (if you want) caption frames and figure numbering.

Don't delete the template after putting it onto the clipboard. If you cut, copy, or paste another frame, you will erase the template from memory. Put it out of the way at the end of the document in case you need it again.

A single frame template is all that's required if you only have one size and type of picture per document. Most publications have several standard sizes. One solution is to create all the templates and put them on a page (or pages) at the end of the chapter. When you need a specific frame type, jump to the end, copy the template to the clipboard, and jump back to the page where it's needed.

Be sure to erase the templates and any unnecessary blank pages at the end of the document if you want Ventura to do automatic numbering across chapter boundaries. Extra pages throw off the counting function.

Marking pictures in the text file

You can save time by asking authors to mark the spot in the text file where they want a picture to appear. This can be as simple as a separate line saying "Put the picture of the space shuttle here." If you want to get a little fancier, you can ask authors to insert captions or frame anchors too. You can even set up special tags that leave space for frames, or do away with frames altogether.

By using the preformatting techniques in Chapter Three, "Creating Text," you can set up macros that automatically insert the correct codes and phrases. While they are at it, authors can insert the caption, figure number, description, or anchor name, if they know this information in advance.

You also can ask authors to insert a special tag that creates extra room in the document. You can use this spacer tag for a quick preview of the chapter's ultimate length. Depending on the way you work, you may be able to do away with frames altogether.

Some publications strip in photos and illustrations manually. They use frames only to create a blank space of the correct size. You may be able to save time by using tags to create the space. This will save you from the trouble of creating frames on a page-by-page basis. It also will allow authors to specify illustrations *and their locations* as they create the text. You can even create captions with tags, and have Ventura number the captions consecutively.

Let's begin with a simple example: a single-column format that has one standard illustration size. You could create a tag called Picture. Use the Spacing dialog box to add enough space above to create a blank area of the correct size. Choose Add In Above: Always so Ventura does not remove the white space if it happens to fall at the top of a column. Next go to Breaks and choose Allow Within: No. This means no line breaks are allowed within the paragraph, forcing it to remain together on one page. (It wouldn't be much help to have half of the picture space on one page and half on another).

That's all there is to the basic technique — a tag that adds the correct amount of space for an illustration. In this form, you might ask authors to insert the tag into documents. When you bring them into Ventura, you have immediate feedback on the approximate length of the chapter, since the spacer tag creates space where the illustrations will go.

Now let's consider some variations on the theme:

- Apply the tag to a return for a blank space with nothing inside.

- Apply the tag to text to create a message inside the space. The message could be a standard phrase such as "Place illustration here." It also could be a special phrase typed in by the author, such as "Place third quarter sales chart here." To center the message vertically, add equal amounts of space above and below. To center it horizontally, choose Horz. Alignment: Center from the Alignment dialog box.

- Use a margin-wide ruling box around to create a keyline.

Add space above rule 1 to create a white space buffer. Make the space equal to body text line spacing.

- To caption the illustration, give the tag the font, spacing, alignment, ruling lines, and other desired attributes for captions. You can have a single tag that creates space and formats the caption at the same time. Or you can have one tag to create space and describe the illustration, and a separate tag for the caption. If you choose two tags, use Keep With Next from the Breaks dialog box to keep both on the same page.
- To automatically number the captions, use the Auto-Numbering feature explained in Chapter Eight. With auto-numbered captions, you can move illustrations around and Ventura will keep track of the correct sequence.

Set up as many different sizes as you need. Simply give each size a different tag name. You can have different widths as well as different heights by varying the tags between column-wide or frame-wide.

You may encounter spacing problems because Allow Within is set to No. The larger the illustration, the greater the chance of a white space gap if Ventura has to move the tag to another page. The solution is very simple. Move the spacer paragraph just as you would move any other. Place it slightly higher or lower on the page until the blank space fills with text.

Tips for frames

TIP *Add several frames in quick succession* by holding down the Shift key as you draw. Ventura lets you continue to add frames until you release the Shift key.

TIP *Move frames as a group* by Shift-Clicking to select them all. Carefully place the cursor in the center of one frame. When you drag it to a new location, the others will move along.

TIP *Hide pictures for faster layout.* Pictures take a long time to redraw on the screen. Select Hide All Pictures from the Options menu.

TIP *Hide pictures for faster proof printouts.* If you hide the pictures on screen, Ventura will ask if you want to leave them hidden when you print. When printing copies simply to proof the text, leave the pictures hidden to greatly speed the printing, especially for bit-map images on PostScript printers.

TIP *To overlap two pictures* put them into separate frames, and overlap the frames. You cannot load two picture files into the same frame.

TIP *Create a library* of complex frames in a special library chapter. They can be empty frame templates in different sizes and styles. Or they can contain pictures you want to reuse. If the frame size is important (as with a frame template), leave them at their original size. If the contents and effects are important (as with a logo), reduce them to thumbnail size so you can fit multiple frames on one page. To use the library, open the library chapter, gather all the frames you want on one page, select them all, and copy them to the clipboard. Now open the chapter you want to work on and paste in the frames. Move and resize them as necessary.

Controlling page and column breaks

You may occasionally find a page or column that ends awkwardly. Several options are available to correct this. First, you can add a bit of white space by creating a very small frame. Second, you can adjust the size of pictures on the page. Third, you can edit the text. This is often a good choice, since you can sometimes gain or lose a line just by adding or deleting a few words from a paragraph.

In cases where you want to force a page or column to end, you can create a special tag called Page Break, as we mentioned in Chapter Five. You also can use the same idea for column breaks. Don't worry about the tag's font or other appearance, since you will apply it to empty paragraphs.

Completing the chapter

To get a handle on Ventura's enormous power, we've suggested taking a structured, step-by-step approach to building a chapter. We recommended the Ventura Formula as a guideline: Style + Text + Pictures = Chapter. You've covered style, text, and pictures already. Now you are ready to finish with chapter techniques.

Saving the chapter

Your document is finished. You've loaded the style sheet, and worked with the text and pictures. You've paged through the document one last time to make sure everything looks right. Your final step, then, is to save the work you've done.

We've discussed this step last. In reality, we advise renaming and saving style sheets, text files, and chapters *immediately*, at the start of the work session. That's your best guarantee that you won't forget. It also means you can hit Ctrl-S periodically without worrying that you will accidentally overwrite a file you wanted to save. Ctrl-S is the keyboard shortcut for Save. You should use it several times during layout. As with any computer application, it's smart to periodically back up in case of a power outage, head crash, or other disaster.

To save the chapter, simply choose Save from the file menu. The first time you do this, Ventura asks for the name you want to use. We recommend a file naming system for every file that goes into a chapter. One easy method is to start every file with the same brief code.

These codes are more than a convenience. Used carefully, they provide a way to filter out unnecessary files. For example, because we always used the IX code for this book, examining a subdirectory for IX*.* files would reveal every file created for the book. Filtering with IX06*.* lets us restrict things to Chapter Six only.

To save a chapter, choose Save or Save As from the File menu. Both choices save not only the chapter file, but all component files as well. Changes made to the chapter, including renaming style sheets and text files, do not take effect until you save.

Choose Save to store under the original name (if you haven't chosen a name, Ventura will prompt you). Choose Save As to save under a new name. When you rename a chapter file, Ventura automatically renames the caption file (CAP extension), chapter information file (CIF), and Ventura graphics file

(VGR) to match. If the text file has the same name and path as the chapter, Ventura renames it as well.

With those exceptions, all files retain their previous names and locations. This has several important consequences. First, you must rename style sheet and text files *before* you save the chapter. Otherwise they are written to the original file names. You must rename each text file separately.

To work on this document from now on, choose Open from the File menu. Ventura opens and loads not only the chapter file, but all other files needed to construct the document.

See Chapter Nine, "Advanced Tips and Techniques," for more tips on file and chapter management.

Abandoning your work

To abandon your last changes and return to the previous version of the chapter, select Abandon from the File menu. Ventura reloads the previous version — the chapter as it existed the last time you saved. If you press Ctrl-S often enough, Abandon can act as a primitive Undo function. It will take you back to the point where you were the last time you pressed Ctrl-S.

Creating chapter templates

As we've seen, building a chapter can be hard work the first time around. Fortunately, there is a simple way to save most of that work in a reusable form. A *chapter template* is a collection of elements that work together to give a complete picture of the document's format. Its purpose is to store everything that can be reused, so you don't have to build it again. A template typically includes:

- a chapter file
- a style sheet
- frame templates
- elements that don't change from version to version, such as logos, standing heads, mastheads, mailing labels, headers, footers, page numbering, and so on.

If you rely solely on style sheets, you must redo work for each new chapter: retype header text, redraw frames, etc. You also risk discrepancies. If you are building a long technical manual, for instance, every chapter must have the identical format. And if you are sending your pages out for offset printing, it is essential that crop marks, headers, and other repeating elements are in the same position for every chapter.

Let's discuss footers in more detail as an example. Imagine that you are doing a technical manual with 10 chapters. You want a sophisticated footer. You make these choices:

- 10-point Helvetica normal italic
- Hairline ruling line above
- Page numbers in the footer
- Header frame has wider margin than text, so page numbers project beyond text margin
- Live header, with different match on left and right page
- Font change in header, so page number is larger than text
- Baseline jump in header, so text aligns with top of page number instead of bottom
- Turn off the footer on the first page of every chapter

Of these choices, *only the first two are stored in the style sheet.* To duplicate this footer in the other 10 chapters, you would have to turn on all the other effects one at a time, for each of the 10 chapters. If you make a mistake, you risk having an inconsistent chapter. Obviously, it makes sense to do the footer formatting only once, then reuse it.

Also, a style sheet does not specify frame formatting. Yet frames must be very carefully sized, positioned, and captioned to create a pleasing page. For instance, frame padding — the white space buffer outside the frame — should have a relationship with the line spacing of the body text. If the body text has 12 points of line spacing, the frame padding should be 12 or 24 points. There are several other frame-related attributes that you can store in a document template, such as caption, numbering, and anchors.

The first template

You can't build the first template until you've completed the chapter. There's no sense storing the format until you have everything looking the way you want. Then you can take the chapter and turn it into a template, following these steps:

- Save the chapter under a new name. You can choose TEMPLATE.CHP or any other name that reminds you that this is a reusable format. The template for this book is called IXPLATE.CHP.
- Remove all text files *except* those associated with reusable elements like logos and so on (Remove Text/File from the Edit menu).
- Remove all picture files *except* those associated with reusable elements.
- Keep one example of each frame style in the chapter. Put these empty sample frames together on one or two pages. Delete all other frames.
- Save the chapter.

Notice that we did not rename the style sheet. We want the template to call up the style sheet we plan to use for our documents. Usually a chapter template only needs to be a few pages long.

Templates for frame-style documents

The template process is slightly different for frame-style documents (which are discussed in detail below). Frame-style documents such as newsletters contain all their text files inside frames. To create a useful template, you remove the text files, but you leave all the frames in place (Figure 6-42). Then you can create a new issue just by pouring new text files into those frames.

Templates for free-form documents

Free-form documents have most of their text in Box Text or frames. Since most free-form documents are only a page or two long, it is usually easiest to leave the Box Text in place in the

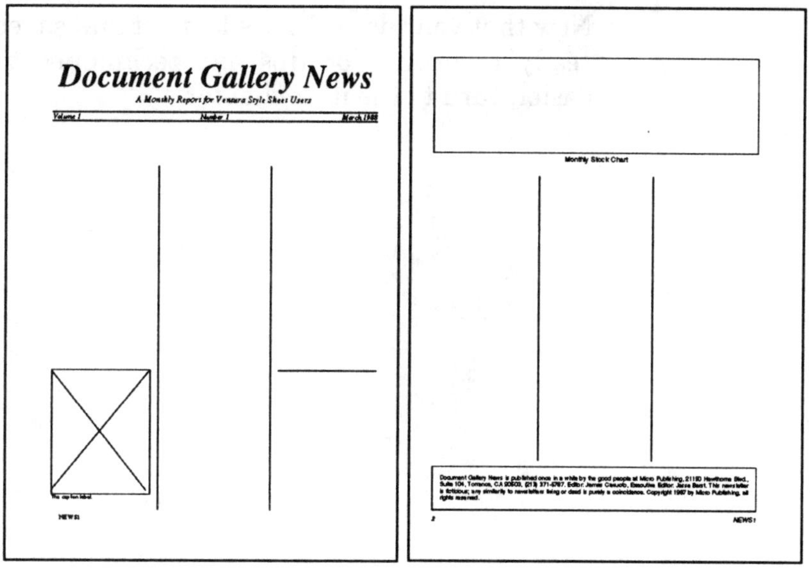

Figure 6-42. A chapter template for a newsletter.

template. Simply save a chapter under a template name. To create a new document from this template, save it under a new name and type in any new text you need.

Keeping templates up to date

In real life, you sometimes have to redo the template. Document formats typically evolve and change. If changes are made to the style sheet only, you need not redo the template. But if the changes involve formatting stored in the chapter file, you must either make the same changes to the template chapter, or go through the template creation process again.

Using a template

To use a template chapter:

- Open the template.
- Rename it immediately. Always rename before doing anything else to preserve the template intact.
- Format the document as you would normally.

Now that your document is laid out and saved to disk, you are ready to print. For tips and techniques to make printing easier, turn to the next chapter.

Chapter Seven

Producing Output

The work described in previous chapters — text editing, picture creation, style sheet design, and page layout — has been done on screen. In this chapter we get to the bottom line of desktop publishing: the printed page. No matter how nice a document appears on screen, it is the paper output that readers receive and react to.

Ventura Publisher can print anything from one page to thousands of pages. It can use any of dozens of output devices. This chapter will help you get a handle on all this power and show you how to produce better printed pages. It explores several important topics, including:

- understanding your printing options
- getting ready to print
- using more than one printer
- printing single and multiple chapters
- binding pages after they are printed
- preparing laser-printed pages for offset printing

Throughout this chapter, we use the term *printing* to mean sending a document from Ventura Publisher to an output device. We use the term *lithography* to refer to the process of duplicating original pages on an offset press. Thus, when we speak of a printer, we are referring to hardware that outputs pages from Ventura Publisher. When we mention a lithographer, we mean the person who supervises offset printing.

Understanding your printing options

Read this section if you meet any of the following conditions:

- you have not yet selected a printer
- you plan to buy a second printer or replace an existing one
- you would like to improve or upgrade an existing printer
- you want to know more about printer technology

Ventura Publisher has a wide range of printing options. It supports dot-matrix printers, ink-jet printers, laser printers, and phototypesetters. As you'll see below, you can easily configure Ventura Publisher to work with more than one printer. That way you can use the one that's most appropriate for the task at hand. Even if you own only one output device, you can use your own (inexpensive) printer for proofing, and send the final output to a (high-end) phototypesetter.

Which output device is best for you? The best way to tackle that question is to examine the issues that set them apart: resolution, engines, page description languages, and speed. These issues apply equally to existing machines, since you can often find upgrade options that add new capabilities.

The resolution issue

The most obvious distinction between printers is the resolution of the type. Resolution is typically measured in dots per inch (dpi). Resolution affects the smoothness of the letter forms and the quality of fine lines and diagonals. At low resolutions, the eye can distinguish the individual dots that form letters and lines. At higher resolutions, the dots merge so they cannot be seen by the naked eye. Resolution has an even more dramatic affect on image quality (see Figure 7-1).

Most professionals consider 1200 dpi to be the threshold for true typeset quality. The resolutions of dot-matrix printers (usually less than 250 dpi) are clearly inferior. The 300-dpi resolution of most desktop printers falls somewhere in between — good enough for some applications, but too coarse for others. You can also find printers that bridge the gap between typeset and desktop, with resolutions of 400 dpi to 1000 dpi.

Figure 7-1. The top image was printed on a 300-dpi laser printer; the bottom image was produced on a 2540-dpi Linotronic imagesetter. The images were scanned with a 256-gray-level Microtek scanner.

The higher the resolution, the higher the price. Choosing the right resolution means determining your uses. If you are producing slick brochures or advertisements for glossy magazines, typeset quality is essential. If your budget cannot afford the outright purchase of a high-resolution output device, you can use a low-resolution unit for sample pages. Then you can send the final document to a service bureau that charges on a per-page basis for high-resolution output.

The engine issue

Even when the resolution is the same, output quality can vary according to the engine. Different printers use different *engines* — the internal components that put marks on paper. To produce a complete output device, an engine is combined with a *controller* — hardware and software that tells the engine where those marks should go.

In the widest sense of the word, you could consider a dot-matrix printer to be a marking engine. Likewise, a laser printer is an engine. You can also interface Ventura with laser imagesetters (in essence, high-resolution laser printers) and with phototypesetters. Each different engine gives different results.

But even within one class, there are wide differences in approach, price, and quality. Many consumers, for instance, do not realize the distinctions in the category of 300-dot-per-inch (dpi) printers. Most 300-dpi devices share technology with office copiers. Usually, a laser marks where toner should go — hence, the popular nickname *laser printers*. In other cases, a liquid-crystal shutter does the marking. One way or another, the controller signals where to put the dots. Once that is done, heat fuses the toner to the paper, creating recognizable letters, numbers, and symbols.

Today's inexpensive desktop printers produce type at 300 dots per inch (dpi). Despite this common resolution, there is a quality difference between different engines. Which engine is best depends on how you intend to use the printer.

Write-black engines mark only the spots that get toner (the spots that will be black). This method often does a better job of producing fine lines and serifs. On the other hand, it is sometimes accused of producing washed-out blacks. This type of engine is often preferred by people who use laser-printed pages as masters for offset lithography. Offset tends to fill in and darken the original page, so it is important that the master is not too dark to begin with.

Write-white engines mark the spots that do *not* get toner. They often produce blacker blacks, but they sometimes fall down in the area of fine lines and serifs. These engines are sometimes preferred for applications where the laser printed page will be the distribution copy. In such cases, the thicker lines and blacker blacks may make a better impression.

Resolution enhancement refers to a technology that makes low-resolution type look better. Pioneered by the Hewlett-Packard LaserJet Series III, this technique varies the size of the dots. Normally the Series III prints at the 300 dpi typical of most laser printers. But when forming diagonals and curved lines, the Series III creates smaller dots, thereby giving the impression of 600-dpi resolution.

All other things being equal, the smaller the dot, the better the results. Although there is no way for the ordinary consumer to test dot size, you can gain a rough idea by comparing output (see below for one suggested procedure).

Most printer manufacturers do not make the engine itself. Rather, they buy an engine from one of several leading manufacturers. Consequently, you can buy two different printers from two different companies that have the identical engine. In such cases, other considerations such as speed, fonts, and page description language may determine which one is best for you.

Incidentally, the engine usually includes the entire chassis, so it also affects paper handling, durability, supply costs, service costs, and replacement costs.

The page description language issue

A page description language (PDL) is a software program that controls where to put text and graphics on a page. These languages endow an output device with more power and flexibility. In addition, page description languages are *device independent.* A page description driver can send pages to any compatible printer. Without a page description language, each separate printer requires a separate driver.

Ventura Publisher supports PostScript, which qualifies as an industry standard, bringing a certain margin of safety to users. PostScript, which was developed by Adobe Systems, is not only supported by numerous laser printers, but also by phototypesetters.

When choosing a printer, you should give careful consideration to whether or not you need a PDL. At first glance, it would seem that a PDL printer is more expensive. In the long run, however, a non-PDL printer can be just as costly. If you need typographic sophistication, you may have to buy additional fonts, add-on boards, or hard disk storage to bring a non-PDL printer up to the same level of performance.

A PDL printer uses outline fonts. The system stores one set of outlines for any given typeface (see Figure 7-2). From those outlines it generates bit-maps on the fly. Whenever it needs a certain type in a certain size it generates a bit-map and sends it to the printer. In other words, it tells the printer which dots to turn on and off to produce each character.

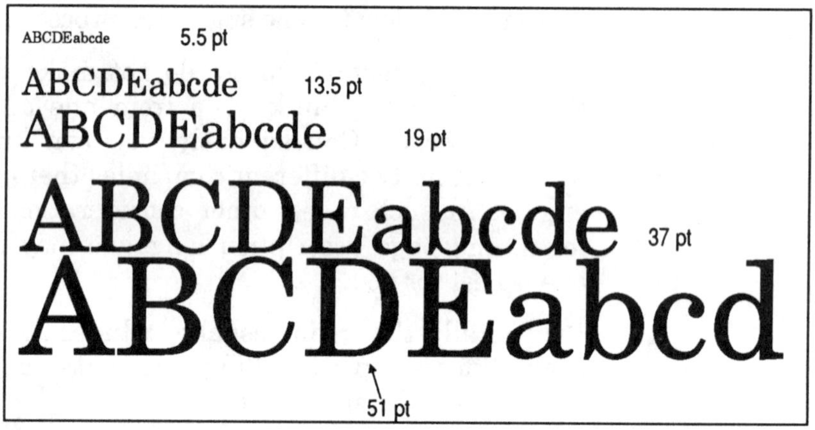

Figure 7-2. Printers with a page description language like PostScript can scale any size font from a single set of outlines.

By contrast, many non-PDL machines must generate a bit-map *in advance* for each and every size and style. Since there are literally thousands of variations, a non-PDL printer must either (1) store many megabytes of font information or (2) make do with a partial set of fonts. Non-PDL printers may also have size limitations. They may not, for instance, be able to produce type larger than 30 points. These size restrictions can severely hamper your efforts to produce truly professional-looking pages.

In addition, many PostScript printers come with a wide variety of typefaces built in. By contrast, you must usually purchase fonts separately for non-PDL printers. When you add up the cost of the fonts, the time to install them, and the expense of the hard disk space, a non-PDL printer can end up costing more in the long run.

PDL printers do have shortcomings. First, the initial price is higher — you must pay for the printer plus the PDL software and hardware. Second, they are often slower than other devices. In high-pressure environments, slow printing times can produce a production bottleneck. Fortunately, you can often solve this bottleneck via print buffers (see below).

If your budget permits, we recommend a laser printer with a page description language. On the other hand, if you are sure you will be producing only simple documents that do not require a wide variety of typefaces or sizes, then a non-PDL printer will be adequate. If you already own a non-PDL printer, there are several upgrade options that permit LaserJet printers to add PostScript compatibility.

What about PostScript clones?

The popularity of PostScript has led to the development of PostScript compatible languages, popularly called PostScript clones. In theory, these alternate languages can interpret all PostScript commands. Unfortunately, not all of them are entirely successful.

PostScript clones advertise themselves as being cheaper, or faster, or both. It is difficult to judge the validity of these claims. Before considering a clone, be aware of the risks. Perhaps the greatest potential danger comes in the area of fonts. If the clone fonts do not match standard Adobe spacing, you sacrifice device independence. One advantage to PostScript is the ability to print a sample page on a laser printer, then send that page to a typesetter. If your PostScript clone cannot match the standard fonts used by PostScript typesetters, you lose this capability.

A second danger is in quality. Be sure that a clone language produces high-quality type, especially at the 300-dpi resolution of a laser printer. Most clones produce fine type on high-resolution typesetters. At lower resolutions, however, some cannot match the quality of Adobe's fonts, which contain built-in *scaling hints*.

What about PCL?

Printer Command Language (PCL) designates the internal command set that operates the Hewlett-Packard LaserJet printers and compatibles. Although not a full-scale page description language, it does provide some of the same functions, including scaleable fonts. In addition, it has achieved the status of an industry standard.

If you cannot afford a PDL printer, you should at the least insist on LaserJet compatibility. Most of today's important software programs support LaserJet PCL. However, some LaserJet clones do not provide perfect emulations. Problems tend to show up in the printing of pictures, shades of gray, or landscape orientations.

The speed issue

Once you have looked at the other factors, you should also consider the speed of a printer. Speed depends on several factors, including the coprocessor (if any), the controller version, the interface, and the memory.

A *coprocessor* is an auxiliary chip that offloads printing tasks from your personal computer. All PostScript printers have some type of processor, because PostScript printers must scale fonts and turn them into bit-maps before printing. More recent models sometimes have special processors optimized just for PostScript. Some non-PostScript printers also use coprocessors to speed operation.

The *controller version* is important because manufacturers continue to improve their systems. In addition, Adobe Systems periodically revises PostScript. Always question vendors to verify that you are receiving the latest controller. Otherwise you may receive an older model that has been languishing on a warehouse shelf.

The *interface* is the way the controller connects to the printer. The controller tells the printer which marks to put where on the page. After the controller makes these decisions, however, it must send the information to the printer. Today's printers generally use one of three options: serial, parallel, or high-speed (sometimes called *video* or *direct* interfaces).

A serial interface sends information one bit at a time. It is the same method used to send data over phone lines via modem. It is also the slowest of the three options. Because of their association with telecommunications, serial ports go by the name of *COM* ports (for communications). Ventura designates them as COM1 and COM2 (see Figure 7-3).

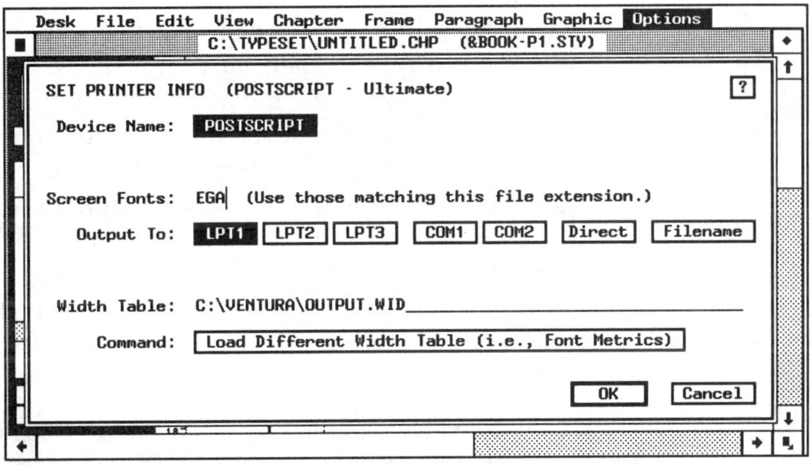

Figure 7-3. The Set Printer Info dialog box. The words LPT, COM, Direct, and Filename designate the output port or destination.

A port is an output connector that lets a computer send information to another device. These ports usually appear as connectors on the back of the machine. In addition to COM ports, most computers also have parallel ports. These interfaces send information eight bits at a time. Consequently, they are faster than serial ports. Because of their widespread use to send information to printers, parallel interfaces are often designated as *LPT* ports (for line printer). Ventura designates them as LPT1, LPT2, and LPT3.

A high-speed interface sets up a direct link between computer and printer. Usually, the printer controller resides within a card inside the computer (rather than inside the printer). This controller card has its own cable to the printer. This direct connection is many times faster than a parallel port. Because they bypass the output ports, Ventura designates high-speed interfaces as *Direct*.

Putting the controller card inside the computer does have drawbacks. It ties the printer closely to that particular computer — you can't just unplug a cable and plug the printer back into a different machine. Sharing printers over a network is also more difficult when the controller is in the computer instead of the printer. In addition, printers that use the Direct setting cannot print to a file because of the large file sizes that result.

The *memory* in a printer also affects speed. Some printers use memory as a scratch pad for composing bit-maps of the page. Without sufficient memory, you are limited in the size of graphics you can produce. In addition, some printers cache fonts — they store font bit-maps for reuse. Storing the font in high-speed RAM memory saves the time to generate it from an outline and/or to send it to the printer. Obviously, the more RAM, the more room to cache fonts. In general, 2 MB or more can speed printing. Although font caching doesn't affect the first page printed, it does help subsequent pages, provided they use fonts already in memory.

Depending on the model, you may be able to add a coprocessor, controller, interface, or memory to an existing printer to improve its performance.

Testing a printer

As you can see from the previous discussion, printer performance depends on a variety of interlocking factors. The best way to judge printers is to test them head to head. We suggest using a *loupe*. This small device, available at art supply stores, magnifies type for easy inspection.

Ventura provides a convenient test page. Ventura's install program automatically copies a chapter called CAPABILI.CHP to the \TYPESET subdirectory. By loading

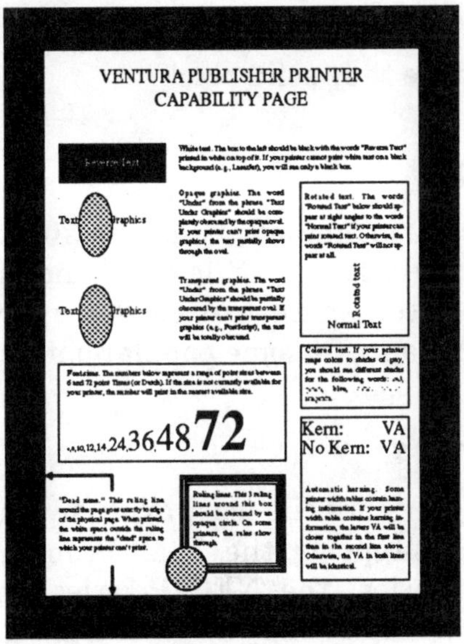

Figure 7-4. Print CAPABILI.CHP from the \TYPESET subdirectory to test a printer's capabilities, including the range of type sizes, the ability to handle reverse text, and the size of the imaging area.

and printing this single-page chapter for each printer, you can gauge its strengths and weaknesses (see Figure 7-4). If you are new to Ventura and don't know how to print yet, follow the procedure outlined later in this chapter.

Even if you have already purchased a printer, it is wise to print this page to find out exactly what it can (and *can't*) do. If you haven't yet bought a printer, ask your dealer to perform the test for several printers. If you time each printout, you can also get a rough measure of speed. Once you have identical samples, examine these areas with special care:

- Type of 10 points or less. Small type presents the toughest challenge, especially for 300-dpi devices. Check with the loupe to see if letters are too coarse and bulky. Look to see if loops and serifs have filled in.
- The edges of large type. Do you see a noticeable waviness or stair-step effect?
- Fine lines. Does the printer produce them with precision?
- Diagonals. Check for a jagged, stair-step effect.

- Solid dark areas. Do they have a gray, washed-out appearance, or are they solid black?

A look at specific printers

Now that we have examined the issues affecting printer performance, we can look at specific types and brands. Although we do not have the space to consider every brand on the market, we can glance at some popular options.

Dot matrix printers

Dot matrix printers are the least expensive alternative. Ventura Publisher supports the IBM Proprinter, the Epson MX/FX/RX/LQ series, the NEC P-series, and the Toshiba P351SX (plus any brand capable of emulating one of these).

➥ *NOTE: Some inexpensive laser printers advertise Epson compatibility. Ventura Publisher can drive these machines in Epson emulation mode, but the output will be at dot-matrix resolution (120 x 140), not at the 300-dpi maximum resolution of the laser printer.*

Frankly, we can't recommend dot-matrix printers for most business applications. Although it is surprising how far Ventura Publisher can push the limits of these inexpensive devices, the final output simply is not up to professional standards. The whole point of desktop publishing, after all, is to create top-notch pages.

Nor is a dot-matrix printer a good option as a proofing device. Theoretically you might produce dot-matrix pages for proofreading, then transmit them (via phone or disk) to a phototypesetter for final output. But printing a page on a dot-matrix printer is so slow that it creates a production bottleneck.

If you *must* use a dot-matrix printer with Ventura Publisher, we recommend a print spooler to permit you to continue using the computer for other tasks during the many minutes it will take to print each page. Print buffers and spoolers are covered later in this chapter.

Xerox 4020 color ink jet

This printer produces text and graphics in up to eight colors at up to 240 dpi. This resolution makes it unacceptable as camera-ready art for professional-quality publishing. However, the 4020 can produce color originals for in-house documents, including business charts, maps, and presentation materials. It can also be useful as a proofing device for documents produced via color offset lithography.

➡ *NOTE: Color overlays for offset printing should be produced on a higher-resolution printer using the technique explained later in the chapter, not with a color printer.*

The Hewlett-Packard LaserJet family

This product family now includes the LaserJet III, the low-cost LaserJet IIP, and the heavy-duty LaserJet IID. The LaserJet has both pros and cons. On the plus side, it is supported by many software packages — an important consideration if you plan to use it for other tasks. The LaserJet prints graphics at 150 dpi or 300 dpi. However, it comes up short in the area of graphics and typesizes when compared with printers equipped with a page description language. However, its low cost and wide availablity make it an excellent choice as a starter machine. If you later find that you need PostScript capability, you can add it via a plug-in cartridge and extra printer memory. Since DOS Version 3 of Ventura Publisher now supports duplex (double-sided) printing on the LaserJet IID, users who produce distribution copies directly from Ventura Publisher may want to consider this printer.

The Xerox 4045

This laser printer is roughly equivalent to the HP LaserJet Plus in typestyles, point sizes, and capabilities. It does, however, offer a unique advantage: a built-in convenience photocopier suitable for light-duty applications. The 4045 Model 50 features 1.5 megabytes of memory, which allows graphics to be printed at a full 300 dpi.

The Apple LaserWriter family

The Apple LaserWriter, which now includes the LaserWriter II NT, NTX, and Personal LaserWriter models, is the most widely used PostScript printer. It shares the pros and cons of all PostScript devices: more typographic flexibility versus slower performance and a higher price.

The LaserWriter II uses the same Canon LBP-SX engine found in the LaserJet Series II. This engine has blacker blacks than the Canon LBP-CX engines used in the original LaserWriter and the original LaserJet. It also has improved paper handling. On the down side, the print tends to be slightly too dark for producing offset masters. However, if the machine is turned to its lightest setting, it produces acceptable quality for offset reproduction.

QMS Printers

This PostScript machine also uses the Canon LBP-SX engine. Its controller uses a faster processor, thereby achieving better print times that some other PostScript machines. It can be configured with additional RAM for even faster printing. The QMS 820 is a heavier-duty version of the 810. It features dual paper trays and a hard disk for font storage. The QMS ColorScript 100 (Figure 7-6) is a popular color PostScript printer. It is useful for producing color "comps," or mock-ups of color publications that will be output on a PostScript imagesetter.

The Varityper VT600

With high-resolution output devices often costing $50,000 and up, it's no wonder that so many people have convinced themselves that 300-dpi output is perfectly adequate, thank you very much. The Varityper VT600 represents a middle ground in both price and performance. Prices vary with different models, but all of them are under $20,000.

The PostScript-compatible VT600 prints at 600 dpi. The VT600 could be an excellent choice for book publishers who need something better than 300 dpi but don't require full-scale typesetting. Likewise, it might be a good compromise for technical documentation. Such documents require fine lines to

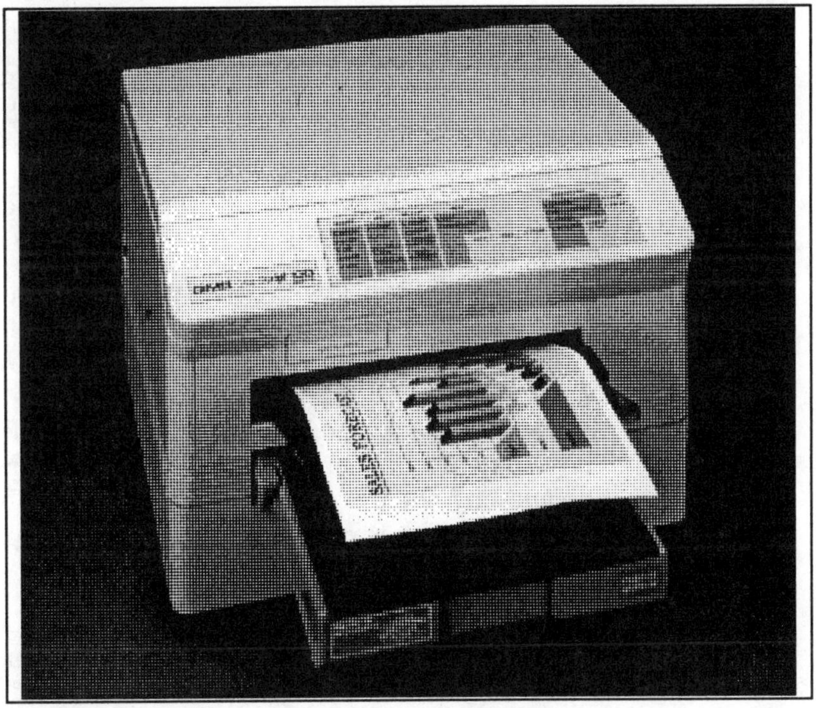

Figure 7-5. The QMS ColorScript 100 is a popular color PostScript device.

reproduce the subtleties of technical documentation, blueprints, diagrams, and so on.

Although not as razor sharp as a typesetter, VT600 print is an improvement over 300 dpi that is easily visible with the naked eye. Small type is crisper, display type is smoother, and fine lines are finer. It is suitable for all but the most demanding applications. On top of all that, it is faster than most desktop laser printers.

The JLaser board

The JLaser board from Tall Tree Systems is not a printer, but a special add-in board that works with many different brands of printers. You buy a JLaser board to speed and improve the performance of an existing printer. The board plugs into your computer. It is not, strictly speaking, a controller. Rather, it provides a large amount of memory where your computer can build a bit-map of the page. Then it sends this bit-map over a high-speed interface directly to the printer.

This direct-connect device offers several advantages. It can drive several different laser printers, including some models that are not otherwise compatible with Ventura Publisher. Because the JLaser board contains 2 megabytes of RAM, printing is faster than with many other laser printers. The RAM can also be used as extended memory for other programs, or as an image buffer for a scanner.

In the area of typestyles and sizes, the JLaser does not match the flexibility of a PostScript printer. For instance, it is limited to fonts of 48 points and smaller. It can, however, use third-party fonts for the Hewlett-Packard LaserJet Plus, and third-party font packages, such as Bitstream's Fontware. It also bogs down when printing in landscape format. Since most people buy the JLaser for speed, they will be in for a disappointment if they produce lots of landscape pages.

Because it is a memory card, the JLaser maps memory into the PC's address space. This can cause compatibility problems with clone computers, fast computers, or other memory cards. The company offers versions for slow and fast computers. Check for compatibility before you buy.

The LaserMaster CAPcard

The LaserMaster CAPcard is a controller board that resides inside the computer. As with the JLaser, it provides memory for page construction and a high-speed direct interface. But the CAPcard is a complete controller. It has a high-speed coprocessor and separate font memory. The company has developed special printer drivers for leading applications, including Ventura Publisher, AutoCAD, GEM, and Windows.

Like a PostScript controller, the CAPcard can generate fonts on the fly from outlines stored in memory. The CAPcard also offers performance advantages. It is one of the few output devices that can print everything on the Ventura capabilities page. In addition, it offers enhancements such as rotated, outline, and filled type — effects you cannot achieve in Ventura even with a PostScript printer unless you buy a separate utility. Depending on the model you buy, the LaserMaster card delivers resolutions up to 1000 x 400 dpi — a significant improvement over a standard laser printer. On top of all that, the card comes with more than 100 typefaces for no extra charge.

It is important to note, however, that the CAPcard is not a PostScript machine. It does offer fonts with the same widths as standard PostScript fonts. But if you want to print true PostScript pages, you must first use a software utility to convert the page, thereby losing the speed advantage. For emulation of the HP LaserJet, you must run a memory resident program. These utilities provide a means to print through the CAPcard even with applications that do not support it directly.

The CAPcard also comes with other utilities for fast font downloading, for adding fonts to Ventura, and other useful tasks.

Phototypesetters

Most people associate desktop publishing with laser printers. But Ventura Publisher users can also send their documents to phototypesetters. Typesetting service bureaus around the country can accept documents via disk or modem. The resulting high-quality pages are shipped or delivered to the client. This option is particularly useful since Ventura lets you use inexpensive laser printers to create test copies for proofreading. When everything is perfect, the document is sent to the typesetter for the final version.

Many of the typesetters use PostScript, with the most well-known being the Linotronic 200SQ and 300. This is an appealing option, since you can use the PostScript printer to create a laser-printed page, then send the identical document to a Linotronic.

Alternatively, third-party manufacturers have developed typesetter drivers for non-PostScript typesetters. For example, Edco Services Inc. offers a Ventura driver for the Linotype 202. This model can't print graphics, but it can produce type and rules. There are many other typesetter options.

Getting ready to print

Read this section to learn about the steps you must take *before* you can start printing. It covers how to install more than one printer, how to switch between printers, and how to choose the paper stock.

Installing a second printer

One of Ventura's most valuable features is its ability to change the output device. Ventura permits you to have many printer drivers installed at one time. (To conserve disk space, install only printers you plan to use.) You can choose among dot matrix printers, laser printers, phototypesetters, or disk files. There are several situations where this proves useful:

Using a typesetting service. High-quality documents such as magazines, advertisements, and brochures require the superior resolution of typesetters. You might, therefore, print the document on a laser printer for proofreading, then send it to a typesetting service bureau for final output.

Speeding production. If you have more than one brand of printer in your office, you might use the fastest one to produce working copies, and another to produce final copies of higher quality. For example, a LaserMaster board can produce extremely fast copies of a lengthy report, but it lacks the graphic capabilities of a PostScript printer. Since the LaserMaster hooks up to existing printers, you can actually use the same printer in two modes. Use LaserMaster mode for speed and convenience; use PostScript mode for the ultimate in graphic quality.

Color proofs. You might want to use a color inkjet printer to get a rough idea of color combinations on the final page. Because inexpensive ink-jet printers don't have high resolution, you would use a different device to print the actual overlays.

Electronic distribution and disk files. You may decide to distribute copies of Ventura Publisher documents on diskette or via a data communications network, rather than on paper. In this case, recipients might have access to different output devices than the one you used to create the document. For instance, you might want to print PostScript files to disk, even though you don't have a PostScript printer yourself.

There are two steps to using a second printer: (1) installing its driver and (2) selecting it while in Ventura.

To use a second printer, you must first install its driver. The easiest way to specify the second printer is during the original installation. When Ventura asks if you would like to install another printer, answer "Yes" and choose the second device from the list of options.

The Ventura installation program also asks you to specify the communications port for each printer. Thus, it is possible to have more than one printer connected at a time. You might, for instance, install the first printer to a parallel port and the second to a serial port. Conversely, you can use only one port and switch cables when you switch printers. Don't worry if you are not sure which port to use when installing a printer. You can switch ports at the click of a mouse within Ventura.

If you've already installed Ventura and you want to add a second printer, the process is almost as easy. Get out the floppy disks again, and proceed as if you were going to reinstall Ventura. However, when the install program asks if you are installing for the first time, answer "No." That way, the install program will only copy over the new printer files. It will not take you through the entire installation process again. You will, however, need to tell Ventura again which graphics board and which mouse type you are using.

Installing serial printers

If you are using a serial printer, you may have to take additional steps to configure the port. For the Apple LaserWriter, the Hewlett-Packard LaserJet, and many other popular printers, the typical command is:

```
MODE COM1:96,n,8,1,p
```

The first word ("MODE") invokes the DOS mode command, which must be on the root directory. If it is not, copy it from a DOS floppy disk or subdirectory. The second word ("COM1") assumes that you are using the COM1 port. If you were using

COM2, you would substitute that port instead. The remaining letters and numbers tell DOS how to set up the port:

- 96 = 9600 baud
- n = no parity
- 8 = eight data bits
- 1 = one stop bit
- p = configuring for a printer

If you are using more than one serial printer with different settings, you will need to set up batch files to reconfigure the port each time you switch. If you are using only one serial printer, you may want to automate the procedure by adding the mode command line to your AUTOEXEC.BAT file so it is automatically invoked when you turn on the computer. You could also add it to the batch file that starts Ventura (typically called VP.BAT or VPPROF.BAT). Review your DOS manual for more information on the MODE and batch file commands, and your printer manual to verify the settings.

Switching printers

The first printer you install becomes the default printer. If you do not tell Ventura otherwise, it uses this printer automatically. To change to a new printer driver, use Set Printer Info from the Options menu (see Figure 7-6). You must take two steps. First, tell Ventura which printer you want. Second, load the width table for that printer.

Selecting the printer driver

The first line of the dialog box shows the printer drivers currently available. The default driver is darkened. To choose another driver, simply select it with the mouse.

➥ *NOTE: If you are using a PostScript printer and want to use a different PostScript machine, there is no need to switch printer drivers. All PostScript devices use the same driver.*

When you install a printer driver, you also tell Ventura which communications port to use. The program remembers this

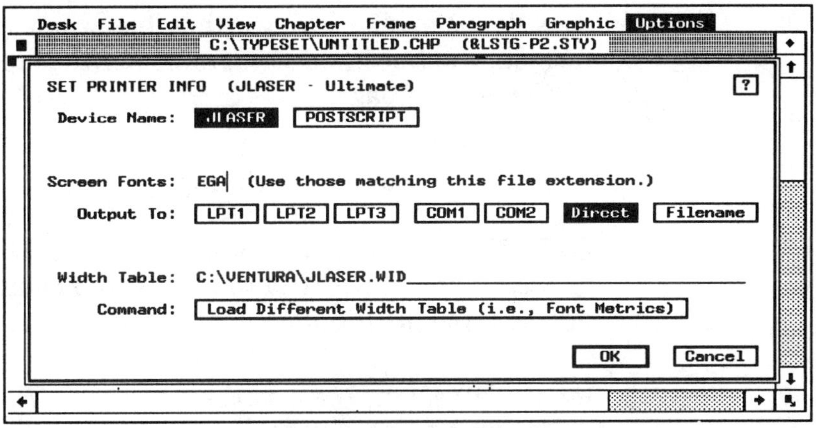

Figure 7-6. With the Set Printer Info dialog box, you can switch between the output devices shown next to Device Name. You must also select the width table you want.

information. When you switch printer drivers, Ventura switches to the correct port, as shown on the Output To line. If you've changed the setup, click on the new port and Ventura will remember from now on.

➡*NOTE: The option Direct applies only to devices such as the LaserMaster CAPcard, which uses a direct connection rather than a serial or parallel port.*

If you select Filename, Ventura will direct the output to a disk file, as explained below.

So far switching printers has been a simple point-and-click process. But there is one more step you must take to guarantee high quality output: use the correct width table.

Understanding width tables

One of Ventura's most important features is its WYSIWYG display. What you see on the screen is an accurate representation of the printed page. Yet Ventura Publisher sometimes uses the same screen fonts for different printers. To make sure those screen fonts match the printed fonts, Ventura uses *width tables* (also called *WID files* or *font metrics*).

These tables store the space taken up by each character. When Ventura displays a character on screen, it first consults the width table. This tells it how much space to allot. It also consults the identical width table when printing. In this fashion, the lines and paragraphs on the screen match those on the printed page.

As long as you are using only one printer, the width table is handled automatically. During installation, Ventura copies the width table for the first printer to a default file called OUTPUT.WID. Ventura uses this default width table *unless you tell it otherwise*. And that's just the point — *if you switch printers, you must switch width tables.*

➡ *IMPORTANT: The contents of OUTPUT.WID changes depending on the printer you install first. If you install a Xerox 4045 first, it contains the width table for that printer. If you install a PostScript printer first, it contains PostScript widths.*

Changing width tables

The Width Table: line shows which width table is currently in use. To change width tables, select Load Different Width Table. An Item Selector appears (see Figure 7-7). Choose the width table that matches the new printer. The names of the WID files clearly identify which printer they support.

There's an easy way to make sure that the width table matches the printer. Simply check the last line of the dialog box, labeled Quality. If it reads "Ultimate," then the table

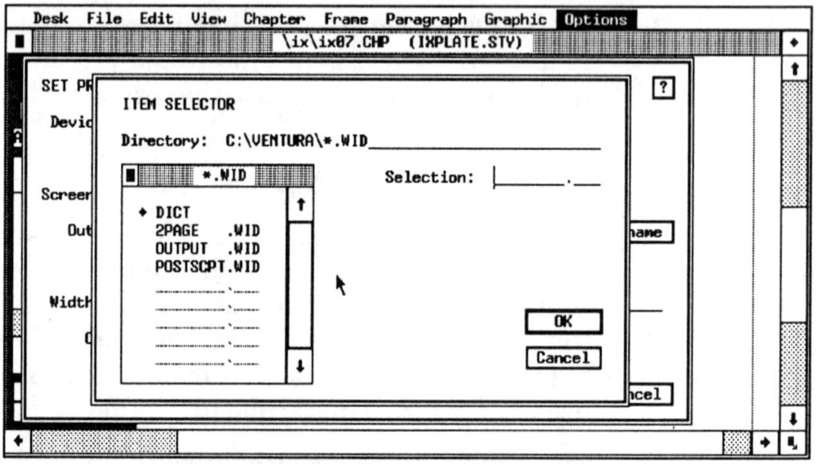

Figure 7-7. The names of the width files identify the printer they support. OUTPUT.WID is the default width table. It is a duplicate of the width file for the first printer you installed .

matches the printer. If it reads "Draft," then you have loaded a width table that does not match the printer.

➥*NOTE: Sometimes you may want to deliberately load the wrong width table, so one printer can imitate another.*

Imitating another printer

On occasion, you may want to imitate another output device. For example, you may want a laser printer to imitate the final output from a phototypesetter. You can proofread the laser printed pages, then send the document to the phototypesetter when everything is perfect.

Consider the case of a magazine publisher who wants to create proof pages on his Xerox 4045, then send to a PostScript typesetter to create camera-ready art. If she does this without making any modifications, she'll be in for an unpleasant surprise. The pages may look perfect when they come out of the 4045, but they will have flaws when returned from the typesetter.

The reason for the problem goes back to width tables. Every printer uses slightly different character widths, even for the same typestyle in the same size. The differences aren't great, but they add up. It only takes a difference of a character or two to push a word down to another line. It only takes an extra line or two to throw off the formatting of an entire page, and, therefore, the formatting of the entire document.

Fortunately, Ventura Publisher provides a simple solution. To make one printer imitate another, simply load a different width table. To make the Xerox 4045 imitate a PostScript device, load the PostScript width table. It's that simple. True, the resulting 4045 output won't look terrific since the printer will be using the wrong spacings. But the important thing is that lines will end where they are supposed to end and pages will break where they are supposed to break.

If you don't imitate other printers very often, simply load the different width table whenever you need it. Those who do it routinely can take a shortcut. Reinstall Ventura Publisher as if for the first time. This time install the final output device first, thereby making it the default OUTPUT.WID file. For example, the magazine publisher could install PostScript as the first printer. Then the PostScript tables would be stored in the default OUTPUT.WID file. The publisher can choose the Xerox 4045 as the device and know that Ventura will still use the PostScript widths stored in OUTPUT.WID. (As you will recall, Ventura uses OUTPUT.WID unless you tell it otherwise.) She can confirm this by checking the Quality line to verify that it shows "Draft." To print a document with the proper 4045 character widths, she need only use the Set Printer Info dialog box to load the 4045 width tables.

➥*NOTE: The width table is recorded in the style sheet for that document. If you change width tables to something other than the default OUTPUT.WID, the style sheet looks for that new width table whenever it is loaded. You do not have to change tables again unless you use a new style sheet.*

Choosing paper stock

So far in this section on getting ready to print, we have discussed how to install and switch between different printers. The paper you choose can also affect the quality of the output. Several companies now make special paper stocks for 300 dpi. These special papers do not curl from the heat that occurs when toner is fused to the page. In addition, many brands are coated to provide a smooth, bright surface that shows off laser printing at its best. As an added bonus, these coated papers create less paper dust inside the printer.

In addition, you can find specialty papers. For instance, several brands feature a wax holdout on one side. This makes it easier to use the paper for traditional paste-up. You can print type or graphics and then wax the paper without worrying that the wax will bleed through. You can also find special transparency materials that will stand up to the heat of a laser printer. By loading the transparencies instead of paper, you can create instant slides for overhead projectors. Likewise, some companies make sheets of adhesive-backed labels that can be printed with a laser printer. And you can buy colored stock, including paper that is colored on two-thirds of the sheet. When you print on this paper then fold it in thirds you have a brochure that is colored on the outside and white on the inside.

For everyday, in-house reports, you can make do with ordinary 20 lb. bond. If you are using laser-printed pages as masters for offset reproduction, consider spending the extra money for special coated papers. Although the results are not dramatically different, these papers do produce a slightly cleaner, crisper type.

Some printers have more than one print tray, so you can keep several kinds on hand. See below for instructions on how to tell Ventura which print tray to use.

Selecting size and orientation

This section has covered the steps you must take to get ready to print. Certain decisions that affect the printout are made in advance. Choices such as paper size, orientation, and single versus double-sided must be made before you design and lay out the document. Chapter Six, "Building the Chapter," discusses these options and how to select the right ones.

Printing a single chapter

The following section explains how to print a single chapter. It assumes that you are ready to print — that you have installed and selected the correct printer, as described above. Printing multiple chapters is described separately below. Remember: always select the printer you want *before* using the To Print dialog box.

To print a single chapter, load the chapter using Open Chapter from the File menu. Then choose To Print from the File menu (see Figure 7-8). You can be on any page when you choose To Print; you need not move to the beginning or end.

The dialog box presents you with a variety of options, which we will discuss in turn. Several lines, however, are there for information only. The top line, for instance, displays the name of the printer in parentheses. If you have the correct width table for that printer, you will see the word "Ultimate" follow-

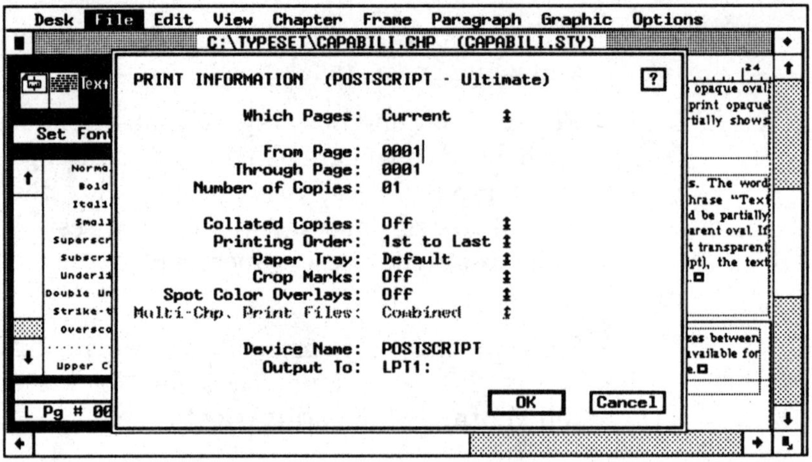

Figure 7-8. The To Print dialog box.

ing the printer name. If not, you will see "Draft." Checking the top line is a good way to verify that you have the matching width table. At the bottom of the dialog box, the printer name is repeated again on the Device Name line. The output port is also shown. Once again, this is a good way to check that things are set up properly before you start printing.

You cannot change these informational settings within the To Print dialog box. If you discover an error when checking these lines, use the Cancel button to close the To Print dialog box. Then use Set Printer Info to change the settings, as described above. In addition, one of the pop-up menus does not operate when printing a single chapter. The Multi-Chp. Print Files line is grayed out for single chapters. It operates only if you access this dialog box via Multi-Chapter from the Options menu.

Choosing which pages to print

Your first choice is which pages to print. Ventura allows you to print all the pages in the chapter, selected pages, or only the *current* page — the page you were on when you entered the dialog box. You can also elect to print only the left-hand or right-hand pages to create double-sided printing by sending the paper through twice.

Printing a single page

The default setting is Current. This allows a quick shortcut for a single copy of the current page. Select To Print and immediately press Enter. Ventura will print a single copy of the page you were on when you opened the dialog box.

Printing all pages

To print every page in the chapter, open the Which Pages pop-up menu and choose All. Ventura will print every page in the document. You can control whether it starts from the first page or the last (see below).

Printing selected pages

To print a range of pages within the chapter, move to the Which Pages pop-up menu and choose Selected. Now move to From Page: and type in the starting page. Move the text cursor to Through Page: and type in the ending page (see Figure 7-9). When you click OK, Ventura will print only the pages you have specified.

Printing left and right pages for double-sided printing

By printing first the left and then the right pages, you can do double-sided printing on an ordinary laser printer. If the chap-

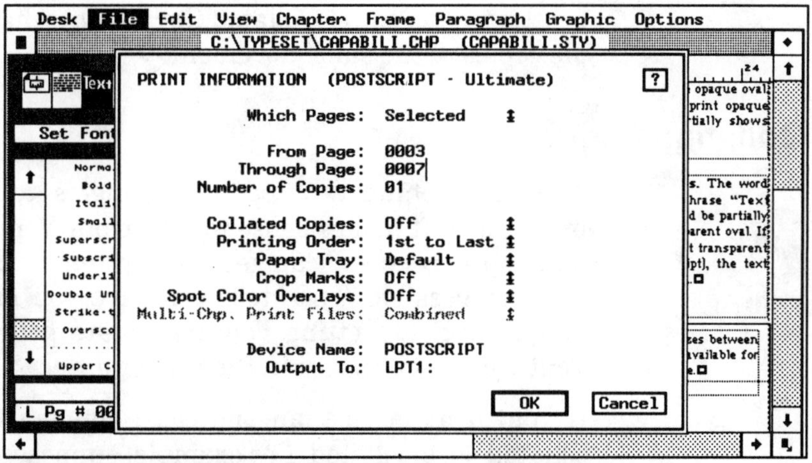

Figure 7-9. To print selected pages, type in where you want Ventura to begin and end.

ter begins on a right page, start by printing all the left pages. Then turn the stack of paper over and print the right pages on the opposite side. Here it is step-by-step:

- Select the Which Pages pop-up menu.
- Select Left.
- Press Enter (or click OK) to print only the left pages.
- Turn the stack of pages over and re-insert them in the paper tray. Be sure they are inserted so they will print on the blank side. With some printers this means putting them face down in the paper tray. With others it means putting them face up.
- Repeat the printing process, this time selecting Right from the Which Pages pop-up menu.

➡*NOTE: Use this technique only to produce a few final copies in-house. For offset printing, your lithographer will require single-sided original pages.*

Printing more than one copy

To print more than one copy, move the cursor to the Number of Copies line. Type in the number you want. To avoid excessive wear on the printer, and excessive print times, we don't recommend printing more than five copies. For larger quantities, take a master to a photocopy shop or offset printer. To reduce printing time, select Collated Copies: Off when printing multiple copies of the same document.

Collating pages

The idea behind desktop publishing is to make you more productive. It makes sense to figure out Ventura's paper handling options so you can get your system to do as much of the work as possible. Two steps can save you needless shuffling and sorting: (1) letting Ventura collate pages and (2) letting Ventura put the pages in the proper order.

If you print more than one copy, you may choose between collated or uncollated. For example, suppose you want to print five copies of a 20-page chapter. If you choose Collated Copies:

Off, Ventura will print five copies of page 1, five copies of page 2, and so on. If you choose Collated Copies: On, Ventura will print pages 1 to 20, then start over and print 1 to 20 again, and so on until it has produced five copies of the chapter, each in sequential order.

There's a drawback to letting Ventura collate the pages: it takes much longer to print. Therefore, we recommend Collated Copies: Off if you want the fastest possible print time. You will have to do the sorting yourself. Collated Copies has no effect if you are printing a single copy. Ventura always prints single copies in collated order.

Choosing the printing order

By choosing the right printing order, you make it unnecessary to shuffle through pages to rearrange them. If your printer stacks pages face down in the output tray, choose 1st to Last from the printing order pop-up. When you turn the stack over, you will find the first page on top, where it belongs. If your printer stacks pages face up, choose Last to 1st. This choice avoids the need to reshuffle the pages after printing to put them in proper reading sequence.

Choosing the paper tray

Some desktop publishers use alternate paper trays to hold different types of paper — letterhead in one tray, for instance, and plain paper in another; or legal size in one, letter in another. If your printer has multiple paper trays, you can select among them using the Paper Tray pop-up menu. Set it to Default if you have only one tray. To choose a different tray, select Alt #1 or Alt #2. Choose Manual to print single pages one at a time with the manual feed slot.

Printing crop marks

The Crop Marks pop-up menu turns Ventura's automatic crop marks feature on or off. With Crop Marks: On, Ventura prints crop marks at the four corners of the Underlying Page. These marks appear on every page, but only on the printout; they do not show up on screen. They show which portions of the paper to trim off after printing. They help the lithographer maintain consistent positioning.

Obviously, there is no point in putting crop marks on an 8.5x11 in. page if the paper size is already 8.5x11 in. The crop marks option is only meaningful if the Underlying Page is at least an inch smaller than the paper. Otherwise, the crop marks fall into the printer's dead zone — the area near the edge where the printer cannot produce any marks.

You don't have to tell Ventura where to put the marks — it automatically uses the corners of the Underlying Page. To change the position of Ventura's crop marks, change the size of the Underlying Page with Sizing & Scaling from the Frame menu, as described in Chapter Six, "Building the Chapter."

If you previously selected the Half option as your page size (using Page Size & Layout from the Chapter menu), Ventura changes the size of the Underlying Page to 5.5x8.5 in. In addition, Ventura centers this smaller page on the 8.5x11 in. sheet of paper.

If you change the size of the Underlying Page yourself, you must also center it yourself. Unless you tell it otherwise, Ventura starts the page from the upper left corner of the sheet of paper. That would make some of the crop marks fall outside the printing area. To center the Underlying Page, use Sizing & Scaling from the Frame menu. Change the Upper Left X and Upper Left Y to move the upper left corner down and to the right.

If you don't want automatic crop marks, you can draw them yourself on the Underlying Page. Create the crop marks in Graphic mode. Then select all the crop marks, and choose Show On All Pages from the Graphic menu to make them appear on every page of the document. This is also the way to produce registration marks (see Figure 7-10).

Printing color overlays

Spot Color Overlays option is useful for reproducing multi-color documents on an offset press. In order to produce a multi-color document, the lithographer requires several originals for each page of your document; one for each ink color. For example, if you are producing a brochure with blue

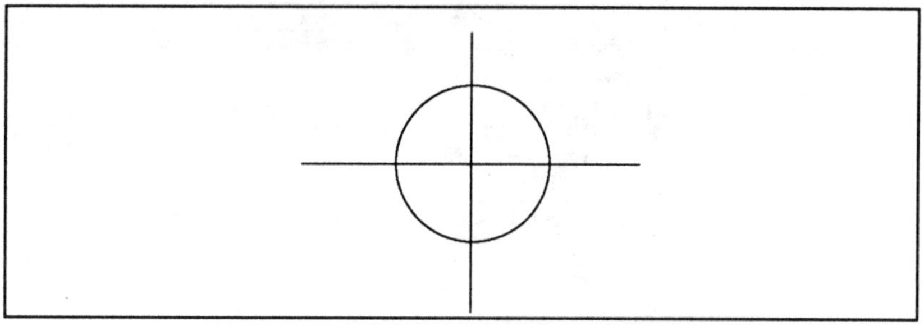

Figure 7-10. A registration mark can be created with Ventura's graphic mode.

headings and black text, the lithographer needs two sheets. One sheet has only headings; the other has only the text. The lithographer produces two printing plates, using black ink with one and blue ink with the second.

Lithographers can make these plates on their own, if you tell them which portions of the page are supposed to be in which color. Most people do this via see-through tissue overlays on top of the printed pages. They circle the colored text on the tissue and write in instructions to the lithographer.

You may be able to save money and time by creating the two versions in advance. Ventura's Spot Color function will automatically print a separate page for each color (including black). The lithographer uses these pages to make separate printing plates. In the example mentioned above, Ventura would print two pages, one for black and one for blue (plus a composite page). Each page is labeled at the top so you don't get the colors mixed up.

To enable the printing of separate overlays, choose Spot Color Overlays: On. You should be aware, however, that this choice has no effect unless you take two previous steps: (1) choose colors for text and/or graphics and (2) enable the colors using Define Colors from the Paragraph menu.

To choose colors for text, use the Font dialog box in Paragraph mode (see Figure 7-11). For instance, in the example above, you would click on a heading and change its color to blue. You can also assign colors to ruling lines, boxes, graphics, backgrounds, and fill patterns with their respective dialog boxes.

After you have chosen colors for each individual element, you must also enable the colors using the Define Colors dialog box (see Figure 7-12). Choose Color Setting: Enabled one by one

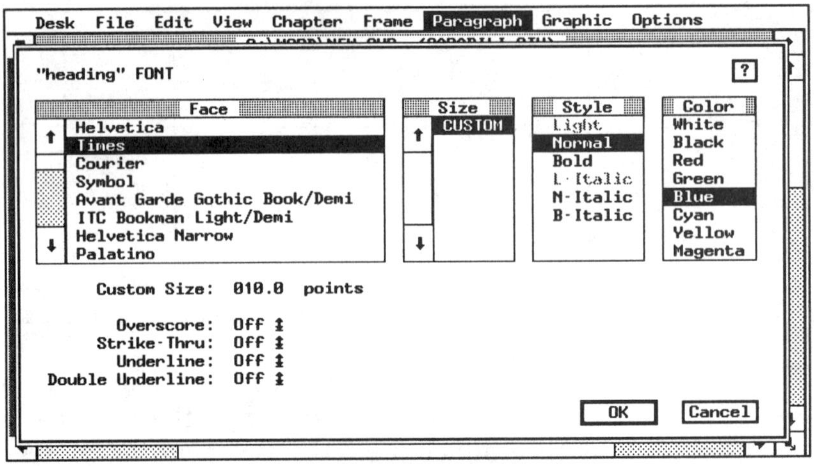

Figure 7-11. Use the Font dialog box to select colors for text. You can also assign colors to ruling lines, boxes, graphics, backgrounds, and fill patterns.

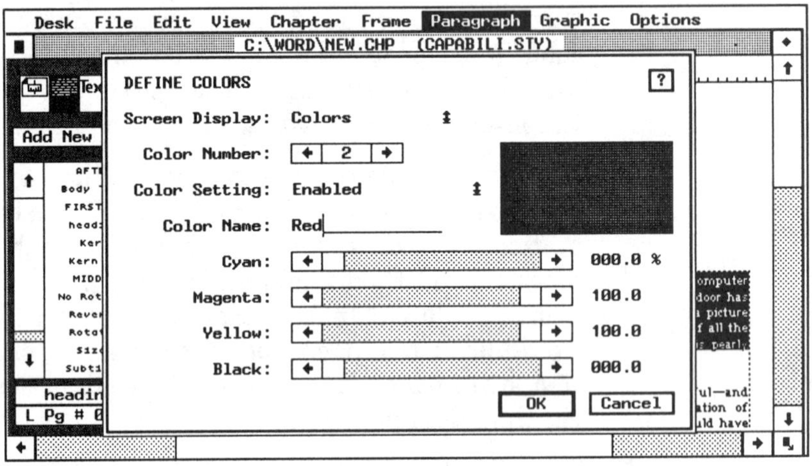

Figure 7-12. Use the Define Color dialog box to enable each color you wish to use for spot color overlays.

for each color you plan to use. Each color you enable in this dialog box will then print out on a separate page when you select Spot Color Overlays: On.

For more on the Define Colors dialog box and its other functions, turn to Chapter Eight, "Advanced Functions."

➥*NOTE: You do not need a color monitor or a color printer for overlays.*

Color is not added until paper reaches the printing press. It is perfectly acceptable for your laser printer to use black toner to create the original for each color. In fact, lithographers don't want spot color overlays in color. They want them in black, clearly labeled with which pages are for which colors. However, if you have a color monitor or a color printer, you can use them to preview the color combinations and get a rough idea how they will appear together.

Printing large pages

If you have selected Double (11x17 in.) from Page Size & Layout in the Chapter menu, you do not need to do anything differently in the To Print dialog box. After you click OK, however, you will see a second dialog box. Choose Overlap to create four 8.5x11 in. pages. You can paste those four pages together to create a single 11x17 in. sheet. Choose Nothing if you are sending the file to a typesetter that is capable of printing an 11x17 in. page. If you have a PostScript printer, you can choose Shrink to reduce the large page to fit an 8.5x11 in. sheet of paper. If you have selected Broadsheet (18x24 in.), the secondary dialog box gives you a Print in Strips option. This option applies only to typesetting machines that can produce strips 24 inches long.

Stopping a print job

To stop a print job in progress, press the Esc key. Don't be alarmed if it takes a while for the command to take effect. When you press Esc, Ventura finishes the page it is working on before it stops. Complex pages can take several minutes to process on certain printers. If you press Esc by mistake, Ventura gives you the chance to continue (see Figure 7-13).

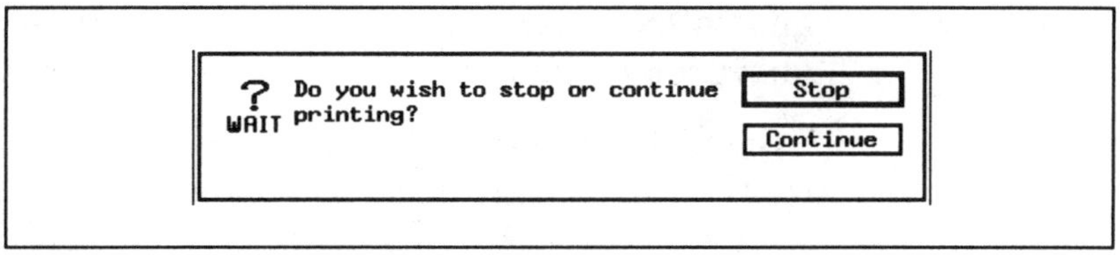

Figure 7-13. Press Esc to cancel a print job in the middle. Ventura gives you a chance to continue printing, or to confirm the cancellation.

Printing to a disk file

Ventura includes a handy print to disk option. You may want to use it for any of several reasons:

- To send the resulting file (via modem, network, or floppy disk) to another location for printing.
- To speed operations (printing to disk is faster than printing to an output device).
- To spool the file so printing can go on in the background, freeing the computer for other activities.
- To produce a PostScript file that you can load into Ventura and use as an illustration.

Printing to disk involves two steps. First, use Set Printer Info to specify that the output is supposed to go to a file. Second, use the To Print dialog box to start printing.

Refer back to the picture of the Set Printer Info dialog box shown earlier in this chapter. Use this dialog box to send the output to a file instead of to a port. Thus, instead of selecting LPT1 or COM2, choose Filename. If you plan to send the disk file to someone else, be sure to specify the device (printer) and width file that match the printer setup at the other location.

➥ *NOTE: You don't have to actually own or use a printer to create a compatible disk file. For instance, you can create PostScript print files even if you don't have a PostScript printer. Simply install PostScript as one of your secondary printer choices. Then specify the PostScript device and width table before you print to a filename.*

After selecting the correct printer, open To Print as you would normally. Select the printing options you want (Which Pages, and so on). After you click OK, an Item Selector appears to allow you to name the file and specify its location.

Type in the name and location of the file. Ventura automatically adds the extension C00 to print files, but you can choose a different extension if you prefer. If you are printing multiple chapters, Ventura also lets you specify if you want each chapter in a separate file or all the chapters in one big file. Ventura then proceeds to print to the file name you have selected. Printing to a disk file almost always takes less time than printing to an output device.

➥ *NOTE: Disk files can become very large. All the downloaded fonts are sent to the file. This creates huge files with the LaserJet Plus. PostScript files can also become unwieldy.*

See below for tips on how to reduce the size of print files. Direct devices such as the LaserMaster CAPcard do not have a print to file option. These devices gain their speed by creating a one-megabyte bit-map of each page and sending it directly to the printer. This expedites printing, but it creates disk files that are too large to be practical.

Printing Encapsulated PostScript files

Using the PostScript printer driver, you can print single pages to disk. Then you can load those single-page PostScript files into a Ventura chapter as if they were Encapsulated PostScript (EPSF) pictures. You load an EPSF print file using the Load Text/Picture command and specify PostScript as the line art format. You can then crop or scale this figure as you would any other graphic. The PostScript page does not appear on the screen (an X shows the spot) but it does appear on the printed page. The sample pages that appear throughout this book were created in this fashion.

Although the disk file prints in Ventura, it is not in true EPSF format. You cannot export it to other software programs without modification. See Chapter Four, "Creating Pictures," for more on how to create and modify Encapsulated PostScript files.

Printing multiple chapters to a file

Printing multiple chapters is covered in detail below. If you print multiple chapters to a file, Ventura gives you the choice of putting them all in one file, or each chapter in a separate file. To put them all into one large file, choose Multi-Chp. Print Files: Combined from the To Print dialog box. Unless you specify otherwise, Ventura uses the extension C00 for the single file. To put them into separate files, choose Multi-Chp.

Print Files: Separate. For separate files, Ventura uses the sequential extensions C00, C01, C02, etc.

Copying a print file to the printer

You can get a hard copy of a print file by copying it to the printer. Use the standard DOS copy command. For example, to send a print file called SAMPLE.C00 to a non-PostScript printer attached to LPT1: type the following command at the DOS prompt:

```
COPY/B SAMPLE.C00 LPT1:
```

Press enter to begin copying. The /B parameter alerts DOS that the file contains binary information. The /B switch is not necessary for PostScript printers, since PostScript files are pure ASCII text.

If the file is located elsewhere than the current directory, include the path in front of the file name:

```
COPY/B C:\CHAPTERS\SAMPLE.C00 LPT1:
```

To copy a print file to a serial printer, you must (1) configure the serial port, (2) reroute the output to the serial port, then (3) execute the copy command. For most serial printers, the correct series of commands is:

```
MODE COM1:96,N,8,1
MODE LPT1:=COM1:
COPY/B SAMPLE.C00 LPT1:
```

Press Enter after each line.

If you are using a PostScript printer, you must copy a handshaking utility to the printer in advance. Once you send this short file, it remains in the printer, even when power is off. You will not need to send it again. You can find the file, called DTR.TXT, on the \POSTSCPT subdirectory of the Utilities disk that came with Ventura. Place the floppy disk in the A: drive. Now copy the file to the printer. For instance, if your printer uses the LPT1 port:

```
COPY A:\POSTSCPT\DTR.TXT LPT1:
```

Press Enter to copy the file. You do not need to copy this file if you are printing normally from Ventura, only if you plan to copy files directly to the printer.

Tips for printing to a disk file

Reducing file size

You can reduce the size of print files by making Ventura think the fonts are resident in the printer. If Ventura thinks the fonts need to be downloaded, it will include the space-consuming bit-maps in the print file. If it thinks the fonts are already resident in the printer, it will leave them out. The print file will be much smaller and the print time much faster.

Before printing to disk, use Add/Remove Fonts from the Options menu to tell Ventura the fonts are resident. (If you don't know how to use the Add/Remove Fonts dialog box, the subject is covered later in this chapter). First select the face. Then click on the word Download at the bottom of the Style list. The word will change to Resident to show that Ventura now thinks they are already in the printer. You must repeat this process for each typeface in the document.

➡ *NOTE: To print a shortened file, you must download the fonts in advance, because they were omitted from the print file. Load the fonts before starting Ventura with the utilities supplied by the printer manufacturer or the font vendor. If you turn off the printer, you must reload the fonts.*

Shortening PostScript print files

This is an advanced technique not recommended for beginning or intermediate Ventura users.

In this chapter and in Chapter Three we talked about creating PostScript files by printing to disk. These files are not in true EPS format. They will print in Ventura, but they may not work correctly in other applications. In Chapter Four, "Creating Pictures," we mentioned how to modify these files with a word processor.

Advanced users may also want to know that Ventura's PostScript files contain almost 20K of redundant information. This extra information does not do any harm, but it does take up space and slow printing. You can do away with it if you prefer more compact files.

At the beginning of every PostScript print job, Ventura sends a prolog to the printer. If you are printing to disk files, it sends the same prolog to each file. You can avoid this unnecessary duplication by temporarily renaming the prolog file before printing to disk. By renaming the file, you "hide" it from Ventura.

When you are ready to print to an output device (instead of to a disk file), *you must restore the prolog.* Likewise, if you are creating files to be sent to another program or output device (such as a typesetter), you must leave the prolog in place. This method is valid only if you plan to print the files with Ventura itself. Since Ventura will send the prolog when it starts the print job, you don't need to duplicate it in each file.

Here's how to eliminate the prolog. You must perform this brief procedure in DOS before loading Ventura. The prolog file, called PS2.PRE, resides in the \VENTURA subdirectory. Go to the \VENTURA subdirectory and use DOS to give it a new file name. For instance, from the DOS prompt, type the following line and press Enter:

```
RENAME PS2.PRE PS2.BAK
```

Now load Ventura and print to disk as you would normally. When you are ready to print to an output device, return to DOS. Go back to the \VENTURA subdirectory and restore the prolog:

```
RENAME PS2.BAK PS2.PRE
```

If you do a lot of printing to disk, set up the renaming/restoring process in batch files. Then you can rename and load Ventura with one command. The trick is to merge the renaming commands with a batch file that loads Ventura.

The easiest way to create the batch file is to type it with a word processor that saves in ASCII format. You might call one batch file VPNOPRO.BAT to indicate that it does away with the prolog. Start by typing in these lines:

```
CD\VENTURA
RENAME PS2.PRE PS2.BAK
```

Now read in the VP.BAT command to merge it with this file (use VPPROF.BAT if you have the Professional Extension). VP.BAT is a batch file created by Ventura during installation. It varies depending on the configuration of your system. For instance, if you have a mouse, you may have included a command to load the mouse driver before loading Ventura. It probably looks something like this:

```
MOUSE
CD\VENTURA
DRVRMRGR VP 1% /S=SD_xxxxx.xxx/M=xx
```

(The *x*'s represent specific information about your graphics card and mouse.)

Now go to the end of the batch file and enter commands to restore the prolog so Ventura will be ready for normal printing the next time you need it:

```
CD\VENTURA
RENAME PS2.BAK PS2.PRE
CD\
```

Assuming you are using the C: drive, the end result should look similar to this:

```
C:
CD\
ECHO OFF
MOUSE
CD\VENTURA
RENAME PS2.PRE PS2.BAK
DRVRMRGR VP 1% /S=SD_xxxxx.xxx/M=xx
RENAME PS2.BAK PS2.PRE
CD\
```

Now you've got a batch file that renames the prolog, loads Ventura, and returns and restores the prolog when you've finished.

Printing multiple chapters

Printing more than one chapter at a time is a two-step process. First, you create a *publication*. A publication is a list of the chapters to be printed, in the correct order. Once you have a publication, you can use it to (1) print all the chapters at once, (2) create a table of contents, (3) create an index, or (4) archive the publication (make a backup copy).

Chapter Eight, "Advanced Functions," covers the creation of a publication. It also explains indexing, creating tables of contents, and archiving.

Printing multiple chapters is very similar to printing a single chapter. You use the same To Print dialog box. The main difference is that you access the dialog box in a different way — via Multi-Chapter from the Options menu. Multi-Chapter is the dialog box where you combine separate chapters into publications. Before it can print multiple chapters, Ventura needs to know which chapters you want, and in which order you want to print them. That is the function of the Multi-Chapter dialog box.

Creating the publication

The first step in printing multiple chapters is to combine the chapters into a publication. Although we don't have space to duplicate the material on building publications in Chapter Eight, the following list summarizes the steps:

- Select Multi-Chapter from the Options menu. The Multi-Chapter dialog box appears (see Figure 7-15).
- If an existing publication is already active, select New from the secondary menu to the right of the dialog box. Selecting New clears the screen.
- Select Add Chapter. An Item Selector appears. Use it to choose the first chapter you want in the publication.
- Continue adding chapters until the publication is complete.
- Click on Save or Save As to save the publication.

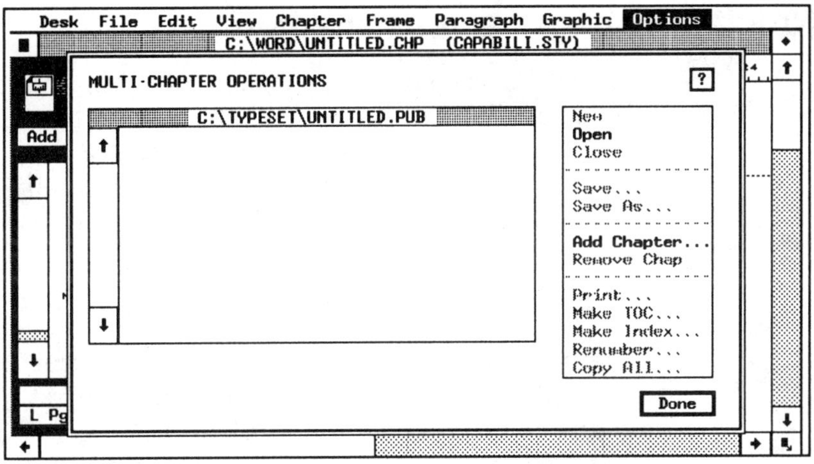

Figure 7-14. The Multi-Chapter dialog box is the first step to printing multiple chapters.

Printing the publication

Once you've built the publication, you're ready to renumber it (if necessary). Renumbering is discussed in the section that follows this one.

After renumbering the publication, you are ready to print. If it is not already open, use Multi-Chapter to open it again. Make sure the list shows all the chapters in the correct order. If you have chapters for a table of contents and an index, be sure to put them in their proper sequence.

Now select Print from the secondary menu. The familiar To Print dialog box appears. Use the dialog box to select the print options you wish, just as you do to print a single chapter. For instance, you can use the Which Pages pop-up menu if you want Ventura to print only the first four pages of each chapter.

➥*NOTE: The Multi-Chp. Print Files line in the dialog box does not operate unless you are printing multiple chapters to a disk file, as described earlier.*

When you click OK, Ventura Publisher prints each of the chapters in order. It's as if you have created a large *macro* file. This macro file opens each chapter in turn, prints it, and then gets the next one.

Numbering pages across chapters

Most users split long documents into chapters of 15 to 50 pages. Ventura permits you to number these pages sequentially. You can ask Ventura to number across chapters automatically as it prints. Or you can do it manually by changing the starting page number for each chapter yourself.

Automatic numbering

Automatic numbering occurs with Ventura's Multi-Chapter printing *provided you take two steps.* First, you must set up the chapters correctly in advance. Then you must remember to renumber the chapters before you print.

The first chapter does not need any changes. Each succeeding chapter, however, must have the counters set so they will use the previous chapter's numbers as the starting point:

- Open the chapter.
- Select Update Counters from the Chapter menu (Figure 7-15).

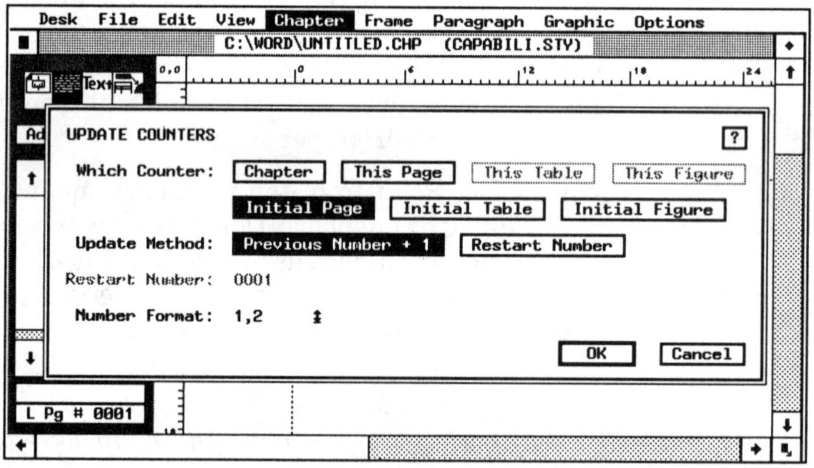

Figure 7-15. For automatic numbering across chapters, use the Update Counters dialog box to start the initial page with the previous chapter's last number plus one.

- Click on Which Counter: Initial Page to specify the starting page number.
- Choose Update Method: Previous Number + 1.

Previous Number + 1 tells Ventura Publisher to use the last number of the previous chapter to figure out where to start numbering. For instance, if Chapter One ends on page 24, Ventura will start Chapter Two with page 25 (24 + 1 = 25).

If your document uses chapter numbers in any of its numbering functions, you must also make the same change to the chapter counter. For instance, many users reference the chapter number in their captions, as in "Figure 8-3," or "Table 5-1." Ventura will automatically change the chapter counter for you as well, if you set up the chapter properly. Assuming you have loaded the chapter and opened the Update Counters dialog box:

- Choose Which Counter: Chapter.
- Choose Update Method: Previous Number + 1.

You must perform these steps *for each chapter except the first.* Once you have done it, you need not worry about manually updating the first page number in each chapter.

The work you did to set up the chapters won't take effect unless you also renumber the chapters *before you start printing.* This step updates all the counters used by Ventura Publisher for pages, figures, numbers, and other sequenced items. To renumber:

- Use the Multi-Chapter dialog box to open the publication containing the chapters.
- Select Renumber from the secondary menu.

Manual numbering

Some users may prefer manual numbering for several reasons:

- You want to print chapters separately as you finish them, without waiting to print them all together as a publication.
- You want to create a gap in the numbering to insert illustrations or other materials.
- Your chapters contain extraneous material at the end that would throw off the numbering.

Some users store things at the end of their chapters. For instance, they may have several pages devoted to frame templates — blank frames in standard sizes that can be reused. Frame templates save the time of drawing the same sizes over and over again and adding margins, padding, captions, and so on. Likewise, some desktop publishers use the end of the chapter to store an edit history, or editing comments from reviewers. These extra pages will throw off the numbering if Ventura does it automatically.

In any case, you should know how to manually number pages for other reasons. In many cases, you do not want to start a chapter as page one. For instance, many books start the page numbering with the front matter. Chapter One may actually start with a number like 17.

You use the Update Counters dialog box for manual numbering. Open the chapter and the dialog box. To start page numbering at something other than one (or one plus the previous chapter's last number):

- Choose Which Counter: Initial Page.
- Choose Update Method: Restart Number.
- Move to the Restart Number: line and type in the new starting number.

Tips for manual renumbering

TIP *Plan on which number to start with.* For instance, you may need to carefully count the pages for the TOC, preface, and other front matter. Likewise, problems can arise if you want each chapter to start on a right-hand page with a blank left-hand page facing it. In our experience, it is best to add blank page(s) at the end of the previous chapter. You can use Insert/Remove Page from the Chapter menu. Alternatively, you can tag an empty paragraph at the bottom of the page with a page break, thereby forcing a new page.

If the previous chapter ends on a right page, you must add a blank left page to the end. If you want headers and/or footers to appear on the blank page(s), do nothing. If you do *not* want them to appear, use Turn Header (Footer) Off from the Chapter menu.

These steps are only necessary if you want blank left pages for each chapter opening.

Troubleshooting tips for printing

The suggestions below may help you pinpoint problems with Ventura and your printer.

Won't print anything

TIP *Printer malfunction.* Press the self-test button. If the printer doesn't have one, try turning it on and off again. Some printers put out a test page upon start-up. If you can't get a test page, the problem probably lies with the printer.

TIP *Printer switch settings.* The printer's configuration settings may be incorrect. For instance, some printers let you choose between serial and parallel cables. If you switch from one to another and forget to change the switch, the printer will not operate.

TIP *Cables.* Are they attached correctly and securely? Cables can look like they are connected when one side is loose. If the problem occurs the first time you use Ventura, you may have the wrong cable. Most printers have a flashing light or LED indicator that tells you when the printer is receiving data. Try printing while watching this light. If it shows the printer is receiving data, you know that the cables are properly attached (although it is still possible you have a cable that is incorrectly wired).

TIP *Serial cables* present a special problem. Many laser printers don't use a standard serial cable. Instead, they use a wiring scheme similar to a null modem cable. The diagrams in Appendix F of the Ventura Reference Guide give serial cable specifications. Check with your dealer or the printer manufacturer for other guidelines.

TIP *Serial port.* If you are using a serial port, make sure it is configured properly with the DOS MODE command. If you have more than one COM port, verify that they do not conflict. Set one to COM1 and the other to COM2.

TIP *Wrong port.* You may have installed Ventura with the wrong port. It is very easy to type LPT2: by mistake when you meant LPT1:. If the printer operates normally from other programs, but won't work with Ventura, check the Set Printer Info dialog box to verify that you have selected the right port.

TIP *Driver conflicts.* Certain device drivers such as GEMPRINT.SYS may keep Ventura from printing properly. If you have previously installed GEM applications with this driver, remove it from the CONFIG.SYS file.

TIP *Copying files to the printer.* Some users print to disk files, then copy the files to the printer. Several things can go wrong.

If you are printing through a serial port, you must have it correctly configured, as explained earlier in this chapter.

If you are using a PostScript printer, you must copy the handshaking utility DTR.TXT to the printer in advance, as explained earlier in this chapter under "Printing to a disk file." When you copy a print file to a non-PostScript printer, you must also use the /B switch to alert DOS that the file contains binary data. For instance, to copy the print file SAMPLE.C00 to LPT1, enter:

```
COPY/B SAMPLE.C00 LPT1:
```

Won't print over network

TIP *To print a PostScript file* on an Apple network, you must modify the POSTSCPT.CNF configuration file in the \VENTURA subdirectory. Change the line that reads "eoftype(PC)" to "eoftype(MAC)". This suppresses the printing of Ctrl-D characters, which the Apple network may read as end of file markers. You must make this change prior to printing PostScript files to disk.

Boxes and borders won't print

TIP *Non-printing borders.* You may be confusing a non-printing screen border with ruling box around. Frames and graphics show borders on screen *even if you have not specified any boxes around.* These borders help you position the page elements and see where they are. They do not show in Paragraph mode. To verify that you have a printing border, change to Paragraph mode. Hit the Esc key to redraw the screen. If the lines disappear, they were non-printing screen borders. Use the Ruling Lines and Ruling Box Around dialog boxes from the Frame menu to add rules that will print. Use Line Attributes from the Graphic menu to add ruling lines to graphics.

TIP *Overlapping graphics in PostScript.* If you have a PostScript printer, the picture inside the frame may be overlapping and therefore obscuring the ruling line. PostScript cannot print transparent overlapping graphics. When one graphic overlies another, the one on top blocks out anything underneath, *even though it looks correct on screen.* The solution is to put a small margin inside the frame. This margin prevents the picture from overlapping the ruling line.

TIP *Ruling boxes that cross boundaries.* If you created the ruling box in Paragraph mode, you should be aware that such borders will not cross column or page boundaries. The box will print on the first page (or first column). But if the text continues, the text will print, but the box disappears. Put the text inside frames or Box Texts if you want boxes to appear one after another following page or column boundaries.

Dashed lines won't print

TIP Ventura cannot display or print thick dashed rules. If the rule does not show on the screen, it will not print. Reduce the thickness until it displays properly. To achieve a thick, dashed effect, try combining two or more dashed rules. You can also use a dashed ruling box around. Use negative space below rule three to delete the space in the middle of the box until the top and bottom rules touch. The effect is to create a large dashed line.

Edges blank or header/footer won't print

TIP You have probably put text or graphics into the dead zone of the printer. Different printers vary in their ability to print close to the edge of the paper, but almost all of them have a thin strip around the outside that cannot print. If you put text in this area, it will show on the screen, but it will not print out. To test your device, print CAPABILI.CHP from the \TYPESET directory as described earlier in this chapter. Then move the text until it is inside the live area.

Wrong spacing between lines

TIP You may have set Auto-Adjustments to Styles (found in Set Preferences in the Options menu). With this function enabled, Ventura automatically changes the line spacing every time you change the font size. You can override this by opening the Spacing dialog box and resetting the spacing *after* changing the font size. Or you can turn off the Styles adjustment so that Ventura will not make any adjustments on its own.

Wrong spacing between letters

TIP You may have the wrong width table for the printer. To change printers, you must use Set Printer Info to change both the device name *and* the width table. To verify that you have the right width table, check to see that the To Print dialog box shows the word "Ultimate" at the top and the bottom.

Working with a service bureau

Throughout this chapter we have mentioned that you can use service bureaus for high-resolution output. In this section, we give you more details.

Around the country, shops have sprung up to provide desktop publishing services. They go by names like *image-setting services, remote printing services,* or *desktop publishing service centers.* Many of them are copy shops and print shops that have added desktop services to their product mix.

These centers usually offer consulting, training, plus rental time on personal computers with DTP software. In addition, most offer access to a high-resolution printer. Some have typesetters on the premises. Others, especially the franchise chains, have access via a telecommunications link.

High-resolution means different things to different service bureaus. Some centers offer 600-dpi output. Others use 1000-

dpi output from plain-paper laser imagesetters. Others use Linotronic machines that produce type on phototypesetting paper at resolutions of 1270 dpi or 2540 dpi. And some centers can give you a choice.

Some service centers require a disk file — usually a PostScript file. Follow the instructions elsewhere in this chapter for printing to a PostScript file. If the service bureau charges by the hour (as opposed to the page), you can save time (and therefore money), by printing a disk file that has the fonts set to Resident. Other service bureaus have Ventura up and running on their own machines. In those cases, you can simply take a Ventura chapter to the center on a floppy disk. Be sure to use Multi-Chapter to copy the chapter to the floppy.

Check closely for compatibility before you head to a service center. For instance, chapters created on Ventura 3 may not open and print on a machine equipped with Ventura 2. In addition, the fonts used in your document must match the fonts available in the typesetter. This is most likely to be a problem if you are using downloaded fonts.

Expect some discrepancies. Patterns and backgrounds look different on a laser printer than they do on a typesetter. To avoid return trips, don't go to the typesetter until the pages are perfect. By carefully proofreading in advance, you avoid costly reprinting charges. To learn how to use a laser printer as a typesetter proofing device, read the section in this chapter titled "Using one printer to imitate another."

Where do you find service bureaus? The *TypeWorld Directory of PostScript Printout Services* is a good source. Another is the local computer paper, such as *Micro Publishing News* in Southern California. If you don't have access to such a publication, try the yellow pages under Printing or Copying Services. Be sure to comparison shop. Rates can vary by 100 percent, even within the same city. When evaluating potential service bureaus, ask these questions:

1. Can it print Ventura chapters directly, or must you first create a disk file? If so, what type of disk file? (Usually the answer is a PostScript file.)

2. What resolutions does it offer? What are the charges for each level of resolution?

3. Does it charge by the page, or by time, or both? (By the page is the safest for you.)

4. Does it guarantee turnaround time?

5. Does it offer volume discounts?

Some bureaus can accept files by modem, but sending anything more than a few pages over the phone can tie up your lines for many minutes (even hours), and rack up long distance charges if they are outside the local area.

Fonts

The question of fonts confuses most beginning Ventura users. Part of the confusion arises because there are several interrelated issues. This section explores all five aspects:

- understanding fonts
- buying fonts
- installing fonts
- downloading fonts
- screen fonts

Understanding fonts

Before it can produce characters, a laser printer needs a bit-map for each one — a blueprint, if you will, describing just where to put the dots to form each letter, number, or symbol. PostScript printers generate bit-maps as needed. They store an outline of each typeface. When you, for instance, request the letter *a* in 10-point Times, the PostScript printer uses the outline to generate a bit-map. This process is known as *scaling* the font.

Most non-PostScript printers, by contrast, need to have the bit maps created in advance. Those bit maps are stored on the hard disk. When you request the letter *a,* the bit map is sent from the hard disk to the printer. Whereas a PostScript printer stores only one outline — from which it can make virtually any size — many non-PostScript printers need a separate bit-map for each size and style of each typeface. Thus, they must have a bit-map for 10-point Times, and a separate one for 12-point Times. If you want 11-point Times, most non-PostScript machines cannot produce it unless there is already an 11-point bit-map.

➡ *NOTE: There are exceptions to these general rules. For instance, non-PostScript printers from Hewlett-Packard, Canon and LaserMaster can scale fonts.*

Ventura comes with font information for both PostScript and non-PostScript printers. For PostScript printers, it contains the information necessary to access the font outlines that reside with the printer controller. For non-PostScript machines, Ventura has a set of bit-maps for three typefaces in a range of sizes.

For users of non-PostScript printers, Ventura provides a good, basic starter set: Swiss, Dutch, Courier, and Symbol. Advanced desktop publishers, however, will soon find they need a much broader range of sizes and styles. Fortunately, you can supplement this starter set by buying additional fonts, as we describe below.

Width tables

We mentioned width tables earlier in this chapter. As the name implies, these tables tells Ventura how much space to allot for each character. When Ventura installs a printer driver and font information, it also installs a matching width table. When you buy new fonts (see below), you should look for vendors who supply a Ventura-compatible width table. Otherwise, you must generate the width table on your own. You must merge the new width table with the old one, so Ventura has width information for all the fonts it may have to use.

Buying fonts

You can find a wealth of additional output fonts compatible with Ventura Publisher. They may be provided by the printer manufacturer or by outside companies. Ventura Publisher provides a core set of basic fonts, so you need not purchase standard fonts such as Dutch or Swiss. You may, however, want to buy supplemental Dutch and Swiss fonts that fill in the missing sizes and styles from Ventura's basic set for non-PostScript printers. When choosing new fonts, you should obviously consider style. Each typeface has a slightly different "flavor." In addition to aesthetics, however, you should also verify that the fonts conform to the Ventura Font Guideline. This system assigns different numbers to different fonts, so Ventura can tell them apart. And they should include a Ventura-compatible width table. It is preferable if they also include matching screen fonts.

➥ *NOTE: Bit-map fonts can take up many megabytes of disk space. Two MB or more per font family is not unusual. (Outline fonts for PostScript take up much less room.) Before purchasing fonts, verify that you have enough space to store them.*

Installing fonts

Some font vendors include a special Ventura program that automates font installation. If not, you can do it yourself with a four-step process:

- Copy the new font files.
- Copy the new width table.
- Merge the new width table with the old one.
- Tell Ventura the status of each new font.

Copying font files

For PostScript printers, copy font files to a subdirectory called \PSFONTS.

For non-PostScript printers, copy font files to the \VENTURA subdirectory.

PostScript and LaserJet users can also choose to put fonts in different subdirectories, as long as they tell Ventura where to find them. PostScript users must edit the first line of the ASCII file POSTSCPT.CNF, which is found in the \VENTURA subdirectory. This line currently reads:

```
PSFONTS(C:\PSFONTS)
```

Note that there are no spaces in this line. If you have decided to put your PostScript fonts in, for example, C:\POSTFONT instead, change this first line to read:

```
PSFONTS(C:\POSTFONT)
```

If you use a different subdirectory, substitute its name in place of C:\POSTFONT.

LaserJet users can also set up a separate font subdirectory. You must type the location into a LaserJet configuration file stored in the \VENTURA subdirectory. Let's assume that you have created a subdirectory called C:\LJFONTS to contain LaserJet font files. Now create an ASCII text file called HPLJPLUS.CNF. On the first line of the file, type:

```
HPFONTS(C:\LJFONTS)
```

If you use a different subdirectory, substitute its name in place of C:\LJFONTS. Now save the file. That's all that the configuration file needs to contain to tell Ventura where to find fonts. (Advanced users: you can also use this configuration file together with the HPDOWN utility to download fonts in advance. See below under "Downloading fonts.")

Copying width tables

The first step in installing fonts was to copy the font files to the correct subdirectory. The second step is to copy the width table for those fonts. You can put the width table in the same subdirectory where you put the fonts, or in the \VENTURA subdirectory. Width tables have an extension of WID. Use DOS to copy the file.

Merging width tables

The third step in font installation is to merge the width tables. Ventura's current width table contains the spacing information for the fonts it uses already. Now you must merge in the new information, so Ventura can use the new fonts, too. If you were planning to use *only* the new fonts, you could simply switch to the new width table. In practice, however, it makes more sense to merge width tables. That way, Ventura has the spacing information it needs no matter which fonts you use.

The merging takes place in Ventura, but you may want to use DOS first to take a safety precaution. Go to the \VENTURA subdirectory and make a backup copy of the current width table. If something goes wrong, you can revert to the backup. For instance, if you currently use XRX4045.WID, you might make a copy called XRX4045.OLD.

Now load Ventura. First make sure that you have the correct width table:

- Select Set Printer Info from the Options menu (see Figure 7-16).

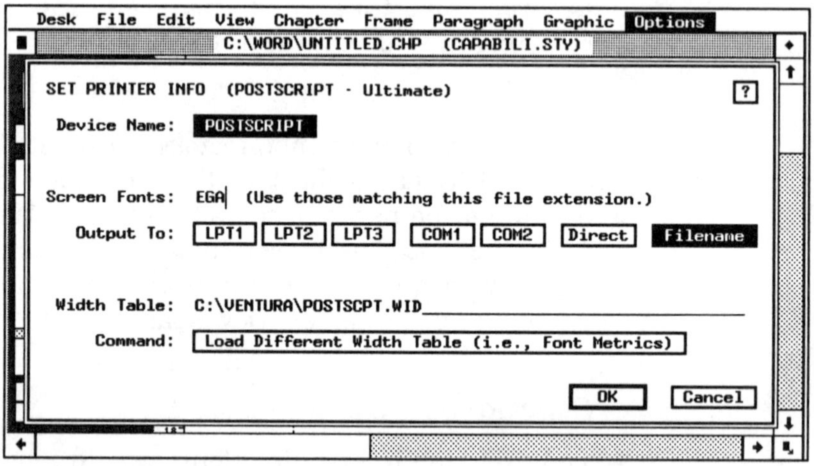

Figure 7-16. Before merging width tables, check Set Printer Info to make sure the old width table is loaded already.

- Check the Width Table line to confirm that the right width table is currently active.
- If the wrong width table is shown, click on Load Different Width Table. An Item Selector appears. Choose the correct width table and click OK.

➥ *NOTE: Do not load the new width table. You must load the old width table before you can merge in the new one.*

Now that you have confirmed that the old width table is active, you can merge in the new one:

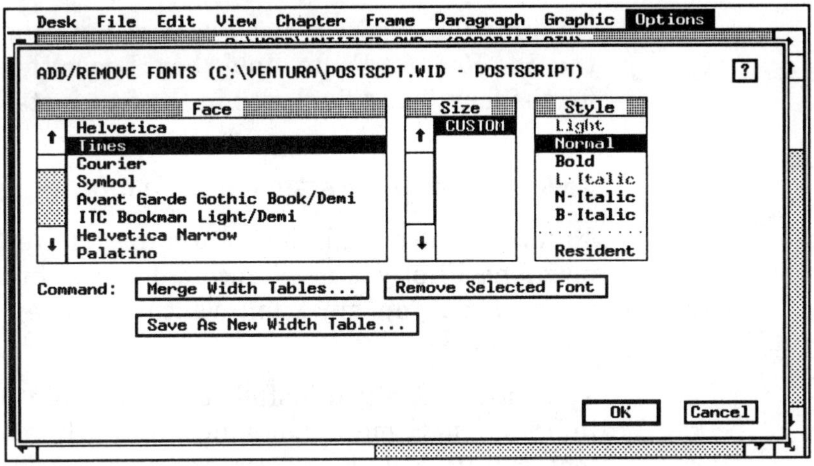

Figure 7-17. Use the Add/Remove Fonts dialog box to merge the new width table with the old one.

- Select Add/Remove Fonts from the Options menu (see Figure 7-17).
- Select Merge Width Tables. An Item Selector appears. Select the *new* width table and click OK. You return to the Add/Remove Fonts dialog box.

You have merged the two width tables. You must now decide what name to give it. If you use the same name as the old width file, you will overwrite it. The only way to restore the old width file would be to copy it over from the Ventura distribution disks, or to rename a backup copy. For safety's sake, therefore, some people rename the merged width file with a new name. Be sure to give it the WID extension.

Unfortunately, there is a drawback to using a new name. Ventura stores the name of the width file with the style sheet. If you want to have the new fonts available for these existing style sheets, you will have to use Set Printer Info to load the new width table for every single style sheet. For that reason, many people prefer to use the previous name, thereby making the new fonts immediately available to previous style sheets.

To save under a new name, select Save As New Width Table. To save under the old name, do nothing. Ventura will automatically save the merged width file under the old name.

After merging width tables, the new fonts appear on the list in the Add/Remove Fonts dialog box. Leave this dialog box open for the fourth and final step in the font installation process.

Telling Ventura the status of each font

To finish font installation, you must tell Ventura about each new font. First you must decide if you want to remove any of them. Then you must tell Ventura if they are resident or downloaded.

The width table you installed may contain unnecessary font information. Some vendors include width tables for the entire font family, including sizes and styles you don't even own, much less plan to use. Leaving these extra fonts in the width file won't hurt anything. However, it can be confusing to see a size or style in the Font dialog box that you don't really have available on disk. For this reason, you may want to remove fonts from the width table. Simply click on the font, the size, and the style you wish to delete. (PostScript users do not need to select a size.) Then choose Remove Selected Font.

Do not remove Times (Dutch) or Helvetica (Swiss) fonts. Ventura uses them as a reference point for certain operations.

The only remaining task is to tell Ventura whether to treat each font as downloaded or resident. Downloaded means that you are asking Ventura to take charge of the downloading. Each time you print, Ventura looks to see which fonts are needed, then downloads them to the printer.

Resident means that the fonts are already in the printer. When Ventura encounters the resident designation, it knows that it doesn't have to bother with downloading. Some fonts are resident because they are built into the printer. But you can also make fonts resident by downloading them yourself *before* running Ventura.

We recommend specifying fonts as resident, even if that means you must download them first before running Ventura. In everyday work situations, you often find yourself printing test pages and samples. If the fonts are not resident, Ventura must download them, even to print a single page. If you make a few changes and want to print the same page again, Ventura must download the fonts all over again. See below for more on downloading fonts in advance.

To tell Ventura the status of a font, first click on the face, size, and style (PostScript users don't have to choose a size). Then check the word that appears at the bottom of the Style section in the Add/Remove Fonts dialog box. This is a toggle button that switches back and forth between "Resident" and "Download." If you want Ventura to treat the fonts as resident, be sure "Resident" is showing. If you want Ventura to download the fonts each time, be sure "Download" is showing.

Font-building utilities

Some vendors sell fonts in discrete sizes — in other words, you buy a separate font file for every size and style you want (PostScript users need only one font file for each style). Other vendors sell font-building utilities. These utilities let you decide which sizes and styles you want. Once you have chosen, the program then generates the font files. In most cases, these programs also build screen fonts that match the fonts and fit the resolution of your screen. We believe font-building utilities can be an excellent value, since they allow you to tailor a collection of fonts to your specific needs.

Downloading fonts

Before you can use a downloaded font, you must first install it and merge its width table as described above.

Ventura Publisher can automatically download fonts to a laser printer whenever it needs them. *Download* simply means to copy the font files from the hard disk to the laser printer. Although this process is automatic, you may want to fool Ventura Publisher into thinking that all your fonts are resident (see above). You can dramatically improve print speed by downloading once at the beginning of each day, instead of at the beginning of each and every print job. Once you've downloaded the fonts, you cannot turn off the printer; if you do, you will erase the fonts, and you will have to download them again.

Many font vendors and printer manufacturers supply downloading utilities. Follow the directions in their manuals to send the fonts to the printer before loading Ventura Publisher. Owners of LaserJet-compatible printers can also download fonts with the HPDOWN utility supplied with Xerox Ventura Publisher. First you list the fonts in a configuration file (a one-time process). Then you run the HPDOWN program.

Begin by using DOS to copy HPDOWN.EXE from the Utilities disk to the \VENTURA subdirectory. Next, create the configuration file. This is the same ASCII text file described above in the section on installing fonts. The first line of the file contains the name of the subdirectory where you store the fonts. The following lines list which fonts to download. The example below shows a configuration file that will download four fonts from the C:\LJFONT subdirectory.

```
HPFONTS(C:\LJFONTS)
PERMFONT(1 TMSN3010.SFP)
PERMFONT(2 TMSN3012.SFP)
PERMFONT(3 TMSB3010.SFP)
PERMFONT(4 TMSB3012.SFP)
```

To download more fonts, you would simply continue the listing. Obviously, you should strive to conserve time and printer memory by downloading only fonts you will really use. Once you've built the configuration file, you can reuse it over and over again with HPDOWN. To use this utility, use DOS to move to the \VENTURA subdirectory. Be sure the printer is on and ready to receive commands. At the DOS prompt, type:

```
HPDOWN
```

Once you press Enter, the fonts will be sent to the printer. They will remain in memory until you turn it off. Be patient. Depending on the printer, it can take up to 30 seconds for each font file.

For speed and convenience, put HPDOWN into a batch file that also loads Ventura. You might call it VPDOWN.BAT to signal that it downloads fonts as well as loading Ventura. Here is a sample batch file you can modify to match your particular system setup:

```
C:
MOUSE
CD\VENTURA
HPDOWN
DRVRMRGR VP 1% /S=SD_xxxxx.xxx/M=xx
```

(The *x*'s represent specific information about your graphics card and mouse.)

This downloading explanation assumes that you have already tricked Ventura into thinking the fonts are resident. If not, use Add/Remove Fonts from the Options menu to do so, following the instructions above in the section titled "Telling Ventura the status of each font."

> WARNING: Downloading fonts to a laser printer can use up memory that would otherwise have been available for printing graphics. Downloading can therefore cause out of memory errors for complex pages with large graphics.

Screen fonts

Just as you were starting to think you understood this whole font thing, we're going to ask you to sit still for one more topic. So far, we've only discussed *printer* fonts (or *output* fonts). Ventura also uses a second type of fonts: *screen* fonts. Screen fonts are nothing more than a way to imitate printer fonts on a monitor. In general, a computer display has lower resolution than an output device. Accordingly, screen fonts rarely match precisely the bit-for-bit pattern produced in a printer. Fortunately, they don't need to — it is the printed page, not the computer display that your readers receive.

During the installation program, Ventura copies over screen fonts. Their resolution is matched to your screen. These are *generic* screen fonts; that is, they represent a wide range of different typefaces. If you select any serif typeface — whether Times, Bookman, or Schoolbook — Ventura uses its generic serif screen fonts. Thus, Times and Bookman look the same on screen, even though they appear very different on paper. If you select a sans-serif face — Helvetica or Avant Garde, for instance — you see the generic sans-serif screen font. And if you use a monospaced font like Courier, Ventura displays its generic monospaced screen font.

How can Ventura get away with using the same screen font for different printer fonts? The answer is by adjusting the space on screen to match the spacing of the printer font. By consulting the width table, Ventura knows how much space to allot. Even though the character shapes are the same on screen for Times and Bookman, the line endings are different. Ventura Publisher adjusts the space between words on screen as necessary to assure that each line ends at the correct location — namely, the same place they will end on paper.

This generic font approach is adequate for most applications. Nevertheless, there are several reasons to consider adding others:

- so the monitor will more closely match the printed page.
- so you can see symbols and dingbats on screen.
- to add higher-quality fonts.
- to speed the display.

The more closely the monitor matches the page, the less need for test prints. With a true imitation of the font on screen, you can more accurately judge the subtle distinctions between different typefaces.

In addition, Ventura's screen fonts only contain characters for its own *international* character set. If you use symbols or dingbats, they may not appear on screen. This is one reason, for example, many people with PostScript printers choose to buy and use the PostScript screen fonts.

You may also want to add higher-resolution fonts if you upgrade to a big-screen monitor. Some monitor vendors provide screen fonts with their units. Others use Ventura's EGA fonts. However, many people will prefer the superior appearance of the higher-resolution VGA fonts provided with Ventura 3.

In some cases, however, you may want to add screen fonts with a *lower* resolution. The lower the resolution, the fewer pixels to move around. The fewer the pixels, the faster the display. If you have a large display that is hampered by slow redrawing time, try using lower-resolution VGA or EGA fonts.

Although Ventura's CGA fonts would be even faster, they are so coarse as to be nearly unreadable at smaller point sizes.

Where to obtain screen fonts

Most font vendors provide matching screen fonts. (If a font vendor does not, you can still use the printer fonts. Ventura will substitute its generic screen fonts.) Adobe Systems, for instance, sells screen fonts in Ventura Publisher form. And many font-generating utilities can generate screen fonts, too. This is a particularly appealing option, since you can specify the resolution of your monitor. If you later switch to a different monitor with a different resolution, you can generate new screen fonts to match.

In addition, Ventura has three sets of its own. By necessity, its CGA fonts are low-resolution, to match the 640x200 resolution of the CGA display. EGA fonts are middle of the road in resolution. They are matched to the 640x350 resolution of a standard EGA monitor. VGA fonts are the best. They match the VGA resolution of 640x480.

Installing screen fonts

If you obtain screen fonts from an outside source, installation is usually as simple as copying the files to the \VENTURA subdirectory.

Things are not quite so simple if you are trying to get different fonts from the Ventura distribution disks. Ventura's fonts come in compressed form, so adding fonts is not just a simple matter of copying the files to the \VENTURA subdirectory. To get the new files off the disk, you must reinstall Ventura. During the installation process, Ventura will expand the font files from their compressed format. At that point they will be available for use. Be careful, however. The reinstall process creates a new batch file. Rename your old batch file (usually called VP.BAT or VPPROF.BAT) to avoid copying over it.

Switching screen fonts

Switching to a new set of screen fonts is simple once you have installed them in the \VENTURA subdirectory. All screen fonts of a given type have the same extension. To switch screen fonts, use Set Printer Info to tell Ventura the new extension to look for. For instance, here is how you would switch to the PostScript fonts with the extension PSF:

- Select Set Printer Info from the Options menu.
- Move the text cursor to Screen Fonts.
- Erase the existing three character extension and type `PSF` in its place.
- Click OK.

After you click OK, Ventura reads the hard disk and builds a list of the available screen fonts. Don't be alarmed — if the list is a long one, it can take a minute or two. When it has finished building the list, Ventura returns you to the document.

Disadvantages and problems with screen fonts

You may experience problems if you install screen fonts in large sizes, or if you install many different sizes. You may see a message at startup indicating that Ventura did not have room to load all the screen fonts.

You may also experience a significant slowdown. Although Ventura can theoretically handle hundreds of screen fonts, keeping track of them all places a burden on DOS. Ventura must read from disk when a new font is loaded to the screen. These disk accesses slow the system. A set of PostScript screen fonts, for instance, can take 2 MB on your hard disk.

Solutions include deleting unneeded screen fonts, adding memory (if you have less than 1 MB), adding a disk cache, or upgrading to Professional Extension, which can use EMS memory for increased capacity.

You may also encounter certain scaling problems, especially if you use fonts that are not precisely matched to those of your monitor. For instance, many early users obtained PostScript screen fonts originally designed for the Macintosh computer. Although converted to PC format, they have a different aspect ratio than fonts for a typical PC screen. The problem arises because Ventura uses the 10-point Times (or Dutch) as the basis to scale the rest of the page. When it uses a Macintosh font to do this, it ends up with a measurement that is not quite tall enough. As a result, the entire page appears smaller than normal on certain monitors.

Other problems can crop up when buying screen fonts from outside vendors. These screen fonts may not match the resolution of your screen. For instance, you may have a VGA monitor. Yet some screen fonts only come in EGA resolutions. This can present you with the need to sacrifice your high-quality VGA fonts to use the EGA versions. See below for a tip on how to get around this difficulty.

Tips for working with screen fonts

TIP *You can combine screen fonts of different resolutions* by giving them all the same extension. If you use VGA fonts, but you want to add some additional EGA screen fonts, rename the EGA files to the VGA extension. Be careful when renaming files not to overwrite high-resolution fonts with low-resolution versions.

TIP *Rename screen fonts you don't use.* For instance, if you install the complete set of PostScript screen fonts, you may want to rename the ones you don't use very often. Ventura expects PostScript screen fonts to have an extension of PSF. Change the extension to anything else and those files will be invisible to Ventura. You can always rename them back if you later start using a different font.

TIP *To improve screen redraw time*, increase the buffers in the computer's CONFIG.SYS file. Buffers set aside areas in RAM where DOS can temporarily store information. More buffers means more room to store screen fonts and other screen information. Your CONFIG.SYS file probably contains a line reading "BUFFERS=15" or "BUFFERS=20." Change this line to "BUFFERS=30." If this still doesn't help, try "BUFFERS=50." Warning: two buffers consume about 1K of RAM, so BUFFERS=50 uses up 25K that cannot, therefore, be used for a document.

Do not increase the buffers if you are using only Ventura's standard screen fonts. The extra memory is not needed. Adding buffers would only serve to reduce the RAM available for creating documents.

TIP *To make things even easier on Ventura,* study the documents you produce, then create screen font groupings that match those documents. Each different screen font grouping will contain only screen fonts in the sizes and styles you use, and nothing more. By giving each group a different extension, you could use different groupings for different documents. Of course, you would preserve the original, all-in-one grouping for those cases where you are building a new document and you don't know in advance what you will need.

TIP *To speed up a large screen display,* switch from high-resolution screen fonts to low-resolution EGA fonts. Although they do not look as good, they draw in about half the time. If you need better resolution for a particular job, you can always switch back to the high-res screen fonts.

TIP *For even faster* screen redraws (and a boost in overall Ventura performance), install a disk cache. See Chapter Nine, "Special Tips and Techniques," for specific suggestions.

Speedup tips for printing

Download the PostScript prolog

TIP You can shave 10 seconds or so from every PostScript print job by downloading the PostScript prolog in advance. The prolog is a set of subroutines Ventura uses to set up PostScript for its way of doing things. Normally, Ventura sends the prolog at the front of every print job. If you prefer, you can download a permanent version of the prolog to your printer before running Ventura.

You must download the permanent prolog every time you start your printer, so most users will want to make it part of a batch file. First copy the file PERMVP.PS from the \POSTSCPT subdirectory of the Ventura Utility disk, so you will have it available whenever you need it. Then use DOS COPY to download the file to disk, as described earlier in this chapter. For instance, to copy it to a printer attached to LPT1:

```
COPY/B C:\VENTURA\PERMVP.PS LPT1:
```

Once you have downloaded PERMVP.PS, you must rename PS2.PRE, which is the temporary prolog Ventura normally uses. Refer to the previous section in this chapter on how to rename PS2.PRE and how to make the renaming part of a batch file.

➥*NOTE: Be sure you've configured the serial port correctly (if you have a serial printer), and that you have sent the one time file DTR.TXT to the printer before you try to copy PERMVP.PS to the printer.*

Download fonts

TIP For faster printing with downloadable fonts, do the downloading once before running Ventura. Otherwise, Ventura will download the fonts each time you print, greatly increasing print times. See the previous section in this chapter for how to download fonts.

Hide pictures

TIP Ventura Version 3 can hide pictures not only on screen, but also at print time. For draft printouts, choose Hide Pictures from the Options menu before you print. You can save many minutes this way, especially if you use a PostScript printer.

Use a print spooler/buffer

TIP Earlier in this chapter we told you how to print to a disk file, then copy this file to the printer. Print buffers are programs that automate this process. Some of them can be set up so they are transparent to the user. You print normally, but the buffer program intercepts the output and puts it on hard disk. (If you set up the buffer to print and copy from a RAM disk, you will achieve even greater speed improvements.) Then it sends this disk file to the printer.

The beauty of a print buffer is that it works in the background. While it doles out information to the printer, you get your keyboard back and can continue to work. Although a print buffer won't make your printer any faster, it will remove the need for you to stop working until the printer is finished.

One of our favorite buffers is PrintCache, from LaserTools Corp. (see Appendix B). Print buffers do use some memory, so they reduce the space available for your document.

Add a direct printer interface

TIP Consider adding a direct-interface controller card like the LaserMaster to your existing printer. You can still use it in its previous mode if certain applications demand it. But for everyday printing and draft printouts, you will appreciate the speed of the direct interface.

Binding pages

Many Ventura Publisher documents are used as camera-ready art for offset printing. (We offer guidelines for offset printing below.) In this case, the lithographer handles the issue of binding the output. But some Ventura users will distribute laser-printed originals or photocopies of Ventura Publisher pages. In that instance, it's up to the user to take care of binding. We feel many desktop publishers undermine their efforts by using amateurish bindings to hold together their documents.

The binding solutions suggested below range in price from a few dollars (three-hole punching) to fifty dollars (a bare-bones saddle stapler) to hundreds of dollars (spiral, Velobind, and glue-binding units).

Three-hole punching is the simplest, easiest way to bind pages. It is appropriate for certain manuals and reports, particularly if they are subject to frequent revision. It's simple to snap out just one section and replace it with a new one. Pay special attention to the inside margin to allow enough room for the holes. We recommend leaving an extra 3 picas (half inch). In other words, if you normally leave 3 picas, leave 6 instead. Although a three-hole punch is adequate for small jobs, those who do more than a few dozen pages should consider buying prepunched paper. It is available from most suppliers at prices only slightly higher than ordinary paper. One disadvantage: Three-ring bindings have a distinct schoolbook connotation. Although practical, they do not convey a slick, professional image.

Saddle-stitching is an option, especially for small booklets of less than 50 pages. Swingline sells a tabletop, manual saddle stitcher, the model 615, for less than $75. Electric models cost several hundred dollars.

Comb or spiral binding is appropriate for short manuals and other applications where the user will want to lay the book flat. The Ibico binding system, for example, consists of a paper punch and an insertion tool for the plastic combs that hold the pages together. Spiral bindings of more than about 100 pages are often inconvenient to use. As with three-hole punching, leave an extra 3 picas (half inch) on the inside margin. Disadvantage: Spiral binding has the same inexpensive connotations associated with three-ring binders.

Velobinding does not steal as much space as spiral and three-ring binding. It is more secure than either, with less chance of losing pages. And, Velobind offers a more professional look. Disadvantage: Velobound documents cannot easily lie flat when opened.

Guidelines for offset printing

Some users will distribute laser-printed pages of their Ventura Publisher documents. But many others will use those pages as camera-ready art. The pages will be taken to a lithographer, where they will be used to create printing plates. The tips and techniques outlined below will help you improve the quality of pages intended for offset printing.

Creating windows for photos

As we saw in Chapter Four, Ventura Publisher allows you to bring pictures directly into the document. But you may sometimes prefer to leave windows (spaces) in the document where photographs can be inserted using traditional methods. There are several reasons to consider this approach:

- To incorporate high-quality halftones.
- To incorporate color artwork.
- To allow space for artwork that will be photographically enhanced.
- To allow space for artwork that is not yet completed or that will be supplied by another party.
- To allow space for an oversize picture such as a poster or blueprint that will be reduced in your document.

In general, laser printers are not capable of reproducing high-quality photographs, as explained in Chapter Four. The quality may be acceptable for in-house publications or certain tabloid newspapers. But for professional books, magazines, brochures, and advertisements, you may want to handle photographs in the traditional manner.

Here's how to prepare the Ventura pages to receive those photos: First, decide which photographs you plan to use, and where they belong in the text (approximately). Next, create an empty frame to accommodate the photograph. When choosing the size and shape of the frame, keep the subject of the photo in mind. If you are using a shot of Wilt Chamberlin, for example, do not make the frame wider than it is tall. If you are using a photo of a dachshund, do not make the frame taller than it is wide. Add a caption to the frame, as you would with any other pictures.

Remember that you don't need to use the entire contents of the photo; you may crop it by selecting new top, left, right, and bottom edges. In this case, make sure that the shape (aspect ratio) of the frame matches that of the cropped image area.

You may want to add a ruling box around the empty frame. This gives positioning information to the lithographer. Alternatively, consider setting the frame background to black, so the frame will print as a solid black rectangle. Depending on the prepress process used by your lithographer, black windows may make it easier to insert photographs. (Consult your lithographer to see if this is required.)

Next, draw lines on the border of the photo to indicate the cropping region (the portion you want to save). Finally, compute the percentage of enlargement or reduction necessary to make the cropped photo fit the empty frame. Write this number on the back of the photo with a felt pen so the lithographer will know how much to enlarge or reduce the picture.

Proof photos

You may want to consider a second approach for photographs. You can use a scanner to digitize the photos, then place them into the Ventura document. These low-quality digitized images serve only as proofing copies; the actual photos will be reshot by the lithographer as explained above. The advantage is that you see a complete mockup of every page before sending it off. What's more, it's easier for lithographers to avoid mixing up photos when they can refer to low-resolution sample pages.

You should scan the photographs as discussed in Chapter Four, "Creating Pictures." Use the scanner's software to crop the photo. Create frames just as if you were going to make blank windows for the photos. But now you will fill those frames with the digitized photos using the Load Text/Picture dialog box. After loading the photo, select Sizing & Scaling from the Page menu and select Fit in Frame. If the shape of the frame corresponds to the shape of the cropped photo, the photo will fill the frame without significant distortion. Note: We don't recommend using Fit in Frame or fractional scale factors when you are dealing with scanned images that will actually be used as final camera-ready artwork. Use the technique described here only for proofing purposes.

➥*NOTE: Use this technique only for scanned images used for proofing purposes. Scanned images used for final camera-ready copy should be original size if possible.*

Tips for photos

TIP *When sizing photos,* pay attention to the relative sizes of objects in nearby pictures. If you have a picture of a building next to a picture of a thumbtack, for instance, do not enlarge the thumbtack so that it looks bigger than the building.

TIP *If you routinely used standard-sized windows* for photos, consider using the advanced tag technique described in Chapter Nine. This technique is faster than placing frames for creating blank spaces.

Working with your lithographer

Check with your lithographer before you take in laser-printed pages for reproduction. She may be able to suggest steps you can take to improve the quality of the finished product. The exact recommendations will depend on the equipment and the way she prefers to work. Some of the possibilities include:

- Using special paper in the laser printer.
- Over- or underexposing the negatives to fill in the dots and make letters appear more dense.
- Photo-reducing the final pages to make the low resolution less apparent.

With the conclusion of this chapter, we have now covered the basics required to produce a Ventura Publisher document. These essentials are all you need to know to build straightforward, everyday applications. For those of you who want to go further, who want to achieve true high-performance desktop publishing, we offer more. Our final four chapters explore the advanced functions and special techniques that turn Ventura Publisher into a desktop publishing powerhouse.

Chapter Eight

Advanced Functions

Previous chapters discussed Ventura's basic features. In this chapter, we move on to advanced functions. Novice desktop publishers may not use these features in the beginning. But nearly everyone will eventually encounter publications that can benefit from added power and functionality. We grouped the advanced functions into eight categories:

- File management
- Indexing
- Table of Contents
- Footnotes
- Numbering
- Tab Settings
- Typography
- Hyphenation

File management techniques

We made file management the first topic for two reasons. First, it's an important issue that everyone should understand. Second, it involves the Multi-Chapter dialog box, which you will meet again when you learn to create indexes and tables of contents.

This section recaps and amplifies file-handling material mentioned in previous chapters. In addition, it introduces some new techniques and concepts. It covers four topics:

- individual file functions
- multi-chapter file functions
- DOS file functions
- file utilities

Individual file functions

Ventura has several functions for working with the individual files that make up a chapter: text files, picture files, style sheet files, and chapter files.

Working with text files

To load a text file into a chapter, use Load Text/File from the Edit menu. You must know and specify the file format and the destination — whether you want to send it to the Assignment List, to the Text Clipboard, or to a spot marked by the cursor where it will be merged with an existing file. When you have made your choices, Ventura brings up an Item Selector, with which you can locate and choose the file.

To rename a text file, use File Type/Rename from the Edit menu. First enable Frame mode, then select the Page or frame containing the text file. Choose File Type/Rename and type in the new name. You can also specify a new location and a new format at the same time. The previous file remains on the disk under its old name and location.

To copy a text file to a new disk or subdirectory, use File Type/Rename. Specify the new location. The previous version remains on the disk under its old name and location. The change does not take place until you save the file.

To convert to a different file format, use File Type/Rename. Click on the button that represents the new format. If you choose a different file name, extension, or location at the same time, the old version remains on the disk. If you choose the identical name and path, you will overwrite the old version. Ventura warns you before the overwriting takes place. File format changes do not take place until you save the file.

To remove a text file from the chapter, enable Frame mode and click on the frame or Page containing the file. Select Remove Text/File from the Edit menu. You can remove the file from the chapter, in which case it is no longer available for use. Or you can remove it from the current frame or Page, in which case it remains on the Assignment List for use elsewhere in the chapter.

To move a text file to a new disk or subdirectory, you must use File Type/Rename to copy it to another location, then delete the old version in a separate step.

To delete a text file from the disk, use DOS File Ops from the File menu. You can also delete it with DOS before or after loading Ventura. (Both methods are explained later in this section.)

Working with picture files

To load a picture file into a chapter, use Load Text/File from the Edit menu. You must know and specify the file format. When you have made your choices, Ventura brings up an Item Selector, with which you can locate and choose the file.

You cannot rename a picture file, copy it to a new location, move it to a new location, or convert it to another format within Ventura. To rename or move a picture file, you must exit Ventura. Use DOS to rename or move the file. Then return to Ventura and reload the picture file into the chapter under its new name or location.

To remove a picture file from a chapter, enable Frame mode and click on the frame or Page containing the file. Select Remove Text/File from the Edit menu. You can remove the file from the chapter, in which case it is no longer available for use. Or you can remove it from the current frame or Page, in which case it remains on the Assignment List for use elsewhere in the chapter.

To delete a picture file from the disk, use DOS File Ops from the File menu. You can also delete it with DOS before or after loading Ventura. (Both methods are explained later in this section.)

Working with style sheets

To load a style sheet file into Ventura, use Load Diff. Style from the File menu.

To remove a style sheet from a chapter, load a new one in its place.

To rename a style sheet file, leaving the original intact, use Save As New Style. Do *not* use Save As, which applies only to the chapter file. Be sure to use the extension STY. If you do not type in an extension, Ventura automatically adds STY for you.

➡*NOTE: If you have two versions of a style sheet with the same name, it is possible to accidentally overwrite the new version with the old one. It is good policy to use a different name or extension for backups.*

To move a style sheet, rename it to a new location with Save As New Style, then delete the old version from the old location.

To delete a style sheet file, use DOS File Ops from the File menu. You can also delete it with DOS before or after loading Ventura. (Both methods are explained later in this section.)

To bring in a new version of a style sheet file from a floppy disk without exiting Ventura, use Load Diff. Style from the File menu. Navigate to the floppy disk with the Item Selector, and load the style sheet. Rename it immediately to its proper name and location on the hard disk with Save As New Style.

Working with chapter files

To create a new chapter, select New from the File menu. You will get a blank, untitled chapter without any picture or text files. This chapter uses the style sheet that was active when you selected New. To attach a different style sheet, select Load Diff. Style.

To open an existing chapter, select Open from the File menu. Use the Item Selector to find and choose the chapter you want. Ventura loads the chapter file, along with all other files necessary to build the document.

To revert to the previous version of a chapter, select Abandon from the File menu. Ventura discards the changes you have made and reloads the previous version of the chapter.

To rename a chapter, use Save As from the File menu. If you also want the text files and style sheet to have new names, you must rename them separately *before* you use Save As. Exception: if the text file has the same name and same path as the chapter, Ventura renames it automatically when it renames the chapter. The previous chapter remains on the disk under its old name.

To copy a chapter to a new location, use the Multi-Chapter technique described later in this section. Use Multi-Chapter even if you only want to copy a single chapter. To move a chapter, use Multi-Chapter, then separately delete the chapter file *and all its component files* from the old location.

To archive a chapter to a new disk or subdirectory, use the Multi-Chapter function described later in this section.

To move a chapter and its component files, you must first move the text files, picture files, and style sheet individually. Then you can use Save As to save the chapter to the new location. The old chapter will remain in its previous location and must be deleted manually. (Don't forget to delete the CAP, VGR, and CIF files as well.)

➡ *NOTE: If the text file has the same name as the chapter and is located in the same subdirectory, Ventura will automatically rename and/or relocate the text file when you rename or relocate the chapter.*

To delete a chapter from the disk, use DOS File Ops from the File menu to delete the chapter file *and all of its component files*. Do not delete the style sheet if it is used by other chapters. You can also use DOS to delete the chapter.

Ventura's built-in DOS functions

You will find Ventura's built-in DOS functions under DOS File Ops in the File menu (Figure 8-1). The first step in using this dialog box is to specify the correct file. You can do this by typing the path and name directly onto the File Spec line and clicking OK. Or you can choose Operation: Select Different

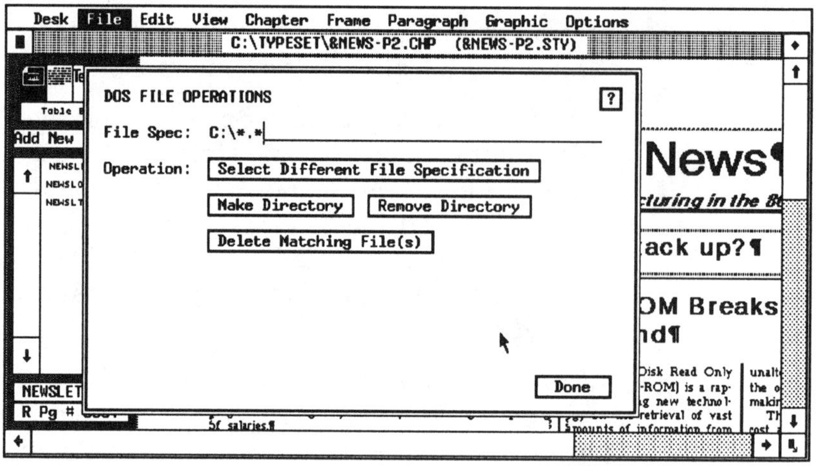

Figure 8-1. The DOS File Operations dialog box.

File Specification. In that case, Ventura brings up an Item Selector so you can use the mouse to select the file name you want.

Once you have entered the new specification you can create or delete a subdirectory, or you can delete files. To make a directory, type its full path designation on the File Spec line. Click once on the Make Directory button. Then click Done to close the dialog box.

You can delete any type of file, including chapter files and style sheets. DOS wild card functions work as normal. Thus, if you enter C:\BOOK\TEST.* on the File Spec line, and then select Delete Matching Files, you will delete every file in the \BOOK subdirectory with the name TEST, regardless of extension. For instance, this command would delete TEST.CHP, TEST.STY, TEST.CAP, and TEST.TXT among others.

➥ *NOTE: Deleting a chapter file by itself does not automatically delete all the component files, nor does it delete any backup files created by Ventura.*

It can be virtually impossible to remember all the component files that make up a large chapter. For this reason, it is essential to establish a file-naming system. Such a system should establish unique code letters or numbers for every file in a chapter. That way, you can use wild card functions to speed file management.

Multi-Chapter file functions

Normal DOS commands work on Ventura files, but they can cause problems, as we will explain in a moment. To avoid these problems, use the Multi-Chapter dialog box when moving, copying, and archiving chapters.

➥*NOTE: Don't be fooled by the name of the dialog box. You should use Multi-Chapter for single chapters as well as for multiple chapters that are combined in a publication.*

Why the need for a special copy function? The answer lies in the way Ventura constructs documents. Ventura uses the original text and picture files. Ventura's chapter file merely "points" to these component files. If you move these files, Ventura can't find them (Figure 8-2). It opens the chapter, but displays a message that it cannot locate the component files.

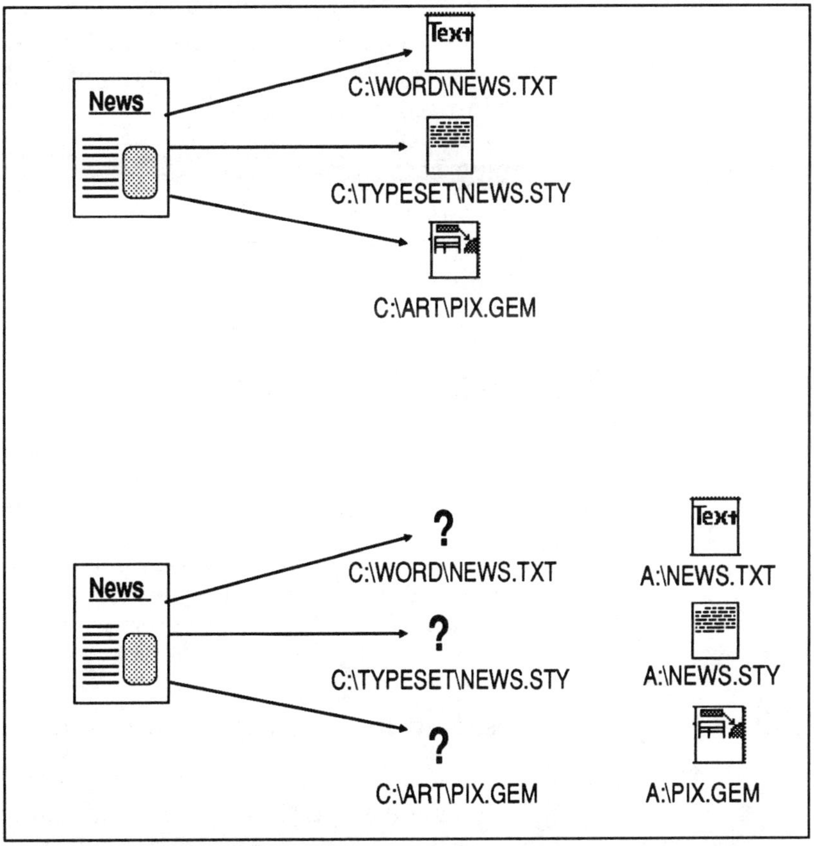

Figure 8-2. Ventura's chapters point to the component files (top). If you move the files with DOS, Ventura doesn't know where to find them (bottom).

➥*NOTE: If you accidentally move files, you can rebuild the chapter by reloading the component files from their new locations.*

You can use the Multi-Chapter dialog box to copy a single chapter, or to copy multiple chapters that have been combined into a publication.

Copying a single chapter with Multi-Chapter

Let's assume that you are working on a chapter called SAMPLE.CHP. You've finished formatting and printing and you want to back up the chapter by copying it to the A: drive.

- Select Multi-Chapter from the Options menu. Ventura will give you an opportunity to save your work if you haven't already done so. The Multi-Chapter dialog box appears (Figure 8-3). Ventura automatically opens the last publication used. If you haven't used the Multi-Chapter function since loading Ventura, it shows a new, untitled publication containing the current chapter.

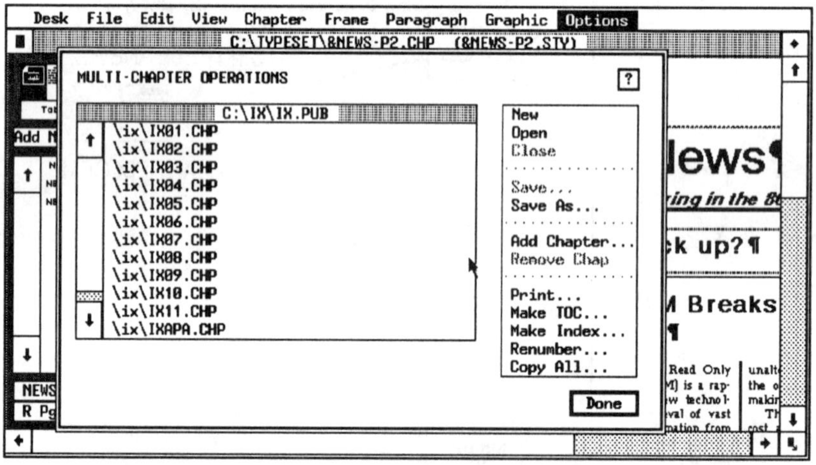

Figure 8-3. The Multi-Chapter dialog box has a secondary menu. You use it to move chapters and publications. You also use it to create indexes and tables of contents.

- Choose New from the secondary menu. The list clears.
- Choose Add Chapter from the secondary menu. An Item Selector appears. Use it to select the chapter you want to copy.

- After adding a chapter, you see its name highlighted on the list (Figure 8-4). If the chapter name is not highlighted, click once on the name with the mouse.

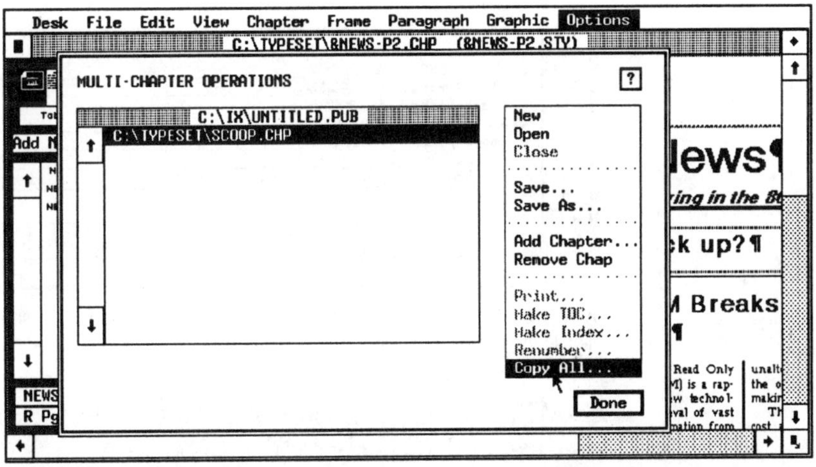

Figure 8-4. To copy a single chapter, highlight the chapter name before choosing Copy All.

- Once the chapter name is highlighted, select Copy All from the secondary menu. The Copy All dialog box appears. Ventura lists the chapter to be copied at the top of the dialog box, under the section called SOURCE.
- Move to the first line of the Destination section, which is labeled "PUB & CHPs." Type in the full path and name of the new location.

If you want all the component files to go to the same location as the publication and chapter files, click on Make All Directories the Same As the First. Ventura copies the destination from the first line onto all the other lines (Figure 8-5).

If you want different types of component files to go to different locations, type these locations on the different lines.

- When you have entered all the destinations, click OK to start the copying process.

Ventura copies the entire chapter and all its component files to the locations you specified. It also changes the pointers. Suppose, for instance, you copy SAMPLE.CHP and all its component files to the A: drive. If you now open the version of

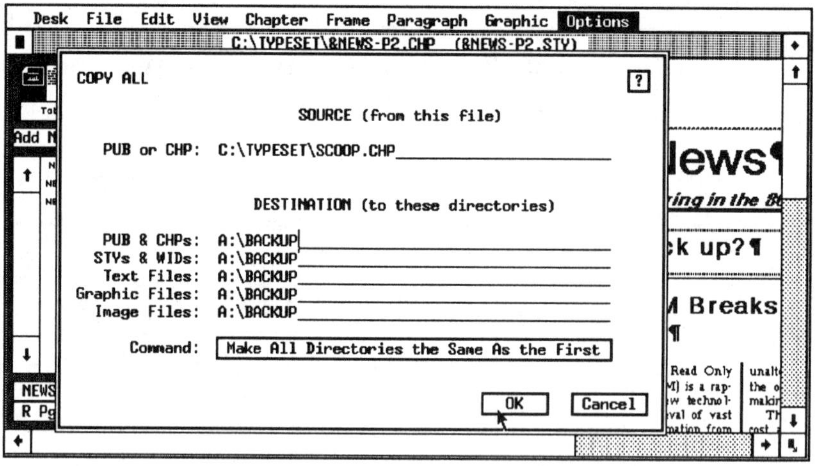

Figure 8-5. Click on Make All Directories the Same As the First to send all the component files to the same destination.

SAMPLE.CHP that is on A:, Ventura will expect all the text, picture, and style sheet files to be on A:.

Ventura does not provide a choice for leaving files behind. You cannot, therefore, copy some of the files without copying all of them. You can, however, accomplish much the same thing by copying a file to the subdirectory on which it already resides — in essence, copying it to itself.

The most troublesome file is the width table. This file contains spacing information for different printers. There are very few occasions when you would want to copy this file. Unfortunately, Ventura insists on copying it whenever it copies the rest of the chapter. Width files often take up more than 100K. If you have a medium-to-large chapter, the size of the width file will often prevent you from fitting the entire chapter onto a 360K floppy disk. This is particularly frustrating since the width table is rarely (if ever) of any value.

One solution is to set the Copy All dialog box so the width file is copied back to its original subdirectory. Unfortunately, the dialog box groups width files with style sheets, so it must go in the same subdirectory with the width file.

➥*NOTE: You do not have to create new subdirectories when using the Copy All function. If you specify a new subdirectory, Ventura automatically creates it for you before copying files.*

Copying multiple chapters

To copy multiple chapters with Ventura, you must first group them into a *publication*. Then you copy the entire publication. Later in this chapter we will show you how to use a publication to build indexes and tables of contents.

Creating a publication

To create a publication:

- Select Multi-Chapter from the Options menu.
- Select Open from the secondary menu.

Now you are ready to add chapters one by one until you have a complete list.

- Select Add Chapter from the secondary menu. An Item Selector appears.
- Use the Item Selector to locate and select the chapter you wish to add.
- Repeat the process until all the chapters show on the list.
- When the listing is complete, select Save from the secondary menu to name and save the publication. Ventura automatically assigns the extension PUB to publications.

To change the order of a chapter in the listing, move the mouse cursor on top of the chapter name. Press and hold the mouse until a hand appears. Drag the chapter to its new location in the list and release the mouse button.

To display a list of the component files in a chapter, highlight a chapter on the Multi-Chapter listing. Now select Open from the secondary menu. Ventura displays a list of the files. To return to the normal Multi-Chapter display, select Close from the secondary menu.

Loading an existing publication

To access a publication created earlier:

- Select Multi-Chapter from the Options menu.
- Select Open from the secondary menu.

- Use the Item Selector to find and select the publication you want. Click OK to open the publication and display a list of the chapters in the publication.

Copying a publication

To copy an entire publication:

- Create or open a publication as explained above.
- Make sure you have *not* highlighted any individual chapter on the list. If you have, you will copy just the chapter, not the entire publication.
- Select Copy All from the secondary menu.
- Enter the destination as you would for a single chapter (see above).

Multi-Chapter copies every chapter on the list. It copies not just the chapter files, but every component file as well.

Copying a single chapter that is part of a publication

To copy a chapter that appears in a publication, highlight the chapter name with the mouse. Then select Copy All. Ventura will copy only that chapter and ignore the rest of the publication.

Backing up a chapter or publication with Multi-Chapter

You will often use Multi-Chapter to place a backup copy of a chapter onto a floppy disk. If you have occasion to use the backup, remember that it now points to the floppy disk. To put a chapter (or a publication) from a floppy disk onto the hard disk, use Multi-Chapter again. Specify the appropriate subdirectories on your hard disk where you normally keep text, chapter, pictures, and style sheet files.

You cannot change the name of a chapter during Multi-Chapter. You cannot, therefore, create special names for backup versions. You will have two versions of the chapter under the same name, one with pointers to the floppy disk and one in the original location. Be careful not to copy an old version on top of a new one.

Backing up a chapter or publication with DOS

Many users find it more convenient to back up their work with DOS. You can safely do this as long as you remember that the pointers do not change when you use DOS. Let's assume that the chapter currently resides on the C:\SAMPLE subdirectory.

If you copy the chapter to the A: drive with DOS, you cannot open it from A: (since the pointers are still looking for C:\SAMPLE). Nor could you copy it to D:\SAMPLE, or to any other location except C:\SAMPLE.

You can also use DOS to copy chapters from one computer to another, as long as you put all the files in the same location on the second computer. In other words, if the chapter and all its files reside on C:\TYPESET, you can use DOS to move them to another computer as long as you copy them to C:\TYPESET on that computer.

➡ *NOTE: Be careful when using DOS Copy to move chapters. It is very easy to overlook one or more of the component files in a Ventura Chapter.*

The most efficient way to use DOS with Ventura is to place all the files for one project — and *only* the files for that project — into a single subdirectory. Then you can move the entire chapter with the DOS *.* wildcard.

File management utilities

You can purchase third-party utilities for Ventura, some of which include file management functions. VP Toolbox from SNA is a product you can use before or after working with Ventura. It adds a variety of useful functions, including the ability to copy or delete chapters. A single command moves the chapter and all its files.

VP Manager from AristoCad is a utility that works "inside" Ventura. It adds numerous file management functions, along with document management, style sheet management, and timed backup. Its dialog boxes are available in Ventura at the press of a key combination (Figure 8-6).

With VP Manager, you can copy, move, rename, or delete any

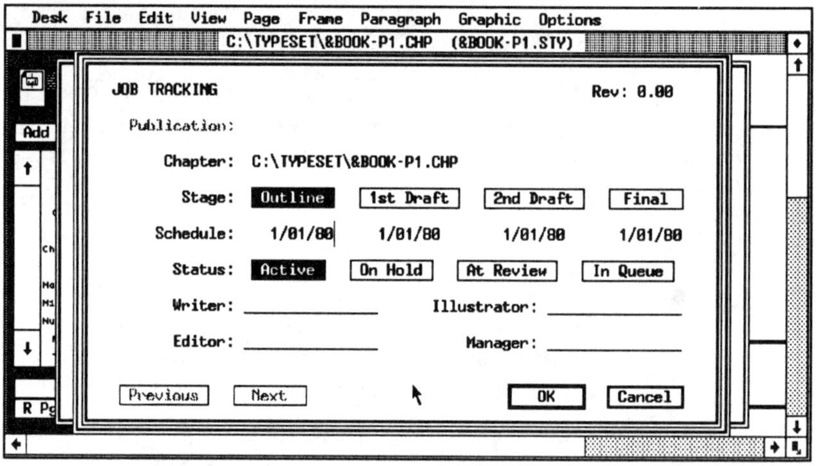

Figure 8-6. VP Manager is a file and document management utility that runs "inside" Ventura.

file, style sheet, chapter, or publication with a single command. In addition, VP Manager provides full control over which files move and which files stay behind.

File management tips

TIP *To copy just one chapter* from a publication, select Multi-Chapter, then select Copy All. You do not need to create a publication for one chapter.

TIP *Floppy disks can contain subdirectories, too.* If you can't locate a file on a floppy disk, it may be inside a subdirectory. Use the Item Selector to find the subdirectory and view its contents.

TIP *To see a list of all the files* associated with one chapter while in the Multi-Chapter dialog box, click on the chapter name and then select Open. A list is displayed.

TIP *Quick start-up technique.* Ventura loads a chapter automatically if you specify its name and path at the DOS prompt. To open TEST.CHP on the \TYPESET subdirectory, enter

```
VP \TYPESET\TEST.CHP
```

TIP *We highly recommend a standard naming system* for chapters and their component files. For instance, we suggest that every file belonging to the chapter start with a unique two-letter code. The jobs of moving, renaming, archiving, and deleting are much easier if you can use wild card functions and if you can identify files at a glance by their names.

Indexing

This section explains how to produce and format indexes with Ventura. The process involves three steps:

1. Insert index entries into the text.
2. Generate the index.
3. Format the index.

Inserting index entries

Your first step is to tell Ventura what to index by inserting marks into the text file. When you later generate the index, Ventura searches for these marks, called *index entries*. It lists them in alphabetical order, along with the page number on which they appear. The eventual result is an index.

Index entries do not appear on screen or on the printed page. Ventura stores them in the text file. Figure 8-7 shows a listing as it appears in the Ventura dialog box, the word processor, and the final version.

Although entries are invisible on screen, Ventura marks their spot with the degree symbol (°). This special item symbol is visible in Text mode if you select Show Tabs & Returns from the Options menu.

Inserting index entries in Ventura

You can insert entries in Text mode or directly in the word processor. To insert an entry while in Ventura:

- Enable Text mode.
- Place the text cursor at the spot you wish to mark.
- Select Ins Special Item from the Edit menu (or press the

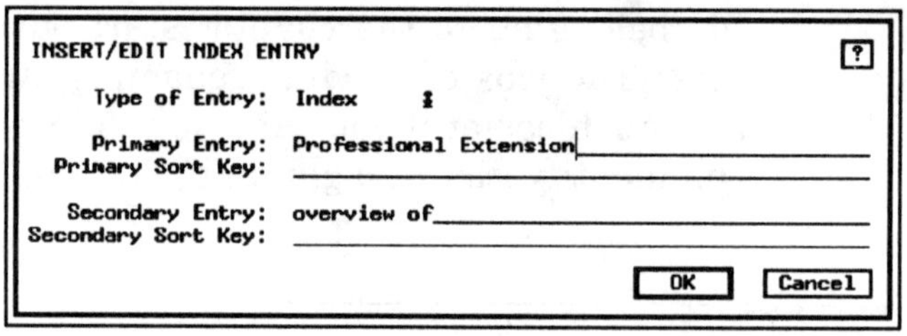

<$IProfessional Extension;overview of>

Professional Extension
overview of 255

Figure 8-7. A typical index entry as it appears in the dialog box (top), the word processor (center), and the final index (bottom).

keyboard shortcut Ctrl-C). A secondary dialog box appears (Figure 8-8).

Figure 8-8. The secondary menu for Ins Special Item.

- Select Index Entry from the list (or press the Keyboard shortcut F3). The Insert/Edit Index Entry dialog box appears.
- Define the entry (explained below) and click OK.

When you click OK, Ventura inserts the degree symbol onto the screen to show the spot (assuming you have chosen Show Tabs & Returns). When you save the chapter, Ventura stores the information you just typed inside brackets.

Defining the entry

You use the Insert/Edit Index Entry dialog box to define the entry — that is, to type in the words you want to appear in the index. It may be helpful to start by reviewing a typical two-level index so you are sure you know the terminology. A two-level index contains *primary entries*, representing broad categories, and optional *secondary entries*, representing specific topics. For example, here is a primary entry with four secondary entries, as they would appear in an index:

Frames
    Adding 135, 137
    Deleting 138
    Loading pictures 14, 147-153
    Loading text 13, 141-144

To create the first two lines in this example, you would go to page 135. There you would type "Frames" and "Adding" into the dialog box:

```
Type of Entry: Index

Primary Entry: Frames

Secondary Entry: Adding
```

You would place an identical entry on page 137. On page 138, you would insert this information

```
Type of Entry: Index

Primary Entry: Frames

Secondary Entry: Deleting
```

You do not have to include a secondary entry. If you do not insert a secondary entry, the page number appears next to the primary entry in the finished index.

You can put more than one index entry at the same spot. In this fashion, you can index the same topic several different ways. For instance, in addition to "Frames; Loading pictures," you might also want other entries, such as "Pictures; Loading into frames," "Containers; See Frames" and so on. The entries can go one after another in the file.

Page numbers in the index

You must put a separate entry on any and every page you want to appear in the final index. For instance:

Frames
    Adding 135, 137

You create this listing by inserting the same entry twice, once on page 135 and once on page 137. As you can see, Ventura creates only one listing for the words, but includes the page numbers one after another separated by a comma.

If you put identical entries on the *same* page, Ventura ignores the duplicate and lists the page number only once. If you put identical entries on *consecutive* pages, Ventura lists the beginning and ending pages. For instance, Ventura does *not* create listings like this:

Frames
    Loading pictures 147, 148, 149, 150, 151, 152, 153

Instead, it shows:

Frames
    Loading pictures 147-153

You must enter identical entries on seven consecutive pages to create the listing "147-153" in the example above. If your document has live headers, you can use a shortcut to create page ranges. You could have created the same listing with a single entry, provided the phrase "Loading pictures" appeared in a header or footer on page 147 through 153.

Look at the headers in this book. We include headings and subheadings to make it easier for you to find your way around. We use Ventura's matching feature to look on the page for paragraphs tagged as Headchap and Head1. When it finds such paragraphs, it displays them in the header. It continues to list them on following pages until it encounters a different Headchap or Head1 paragraph.

If you put an index entry into a paragraph that shows in a header, Ventura puts the entry into the header along with the text. In other words, it lists all the pages where the header appears, not just the page with the entry. For instance, suppose we had a second-level subheading "Loading pictures." Imagine further that we added an index entry for "Frames;loading pictures" on the same line. If we made second-level subheadings appear in the headers, it would have the effect of duplicating the entry on every page on which the header appears. If the subheading "loading pictures" appeared on pages 147 through 153, then the listing shown above would result — even though we only typed the entry once.

You can have more than one index entry associated with the current word. The entry, or entries, must appear in the same paragraph. Otherwise, Ventura will not carry them over into the header or footer.

Adding See and See Also entries

To create a standard index listing, choose Type of Entry: Index. You can also choose Type of Entry: See or Type of Entry: See Also to generate two other kinds of listings. When you choose See (or See Also), the words you type on the Primary Entry line still become a listing in the final index. But the words you type on the Secondary Entry line are not shown with a page number. Instead, the words See (or See Also) are placed in front of the subheading.

See listings redirect readers. They tell readers to look for information under a different topic instead:

Containers
    See Frames

See Also listings tell readers where to look for additional information:

Paragraph mode
    Cursor shapes in 124
    Enabling 122
    Functions 122-127
    See Also Tags

When creating these references, you do not type the words *See* or *See Also* into the dialog box. Ventura inserts these words (or any other words you choose to substitute) automatically when it generates the index. To create the See listing described above, you enter:

```
Type of Entry: See

Primary Entry: Containers

Secondary Entry: Frames
```

To create the See Also listing, you enter:

```
Type of Entry: See Also

Primary Entry: Paragraph mode

Secondary Entry: Tags
```

Because Ventura generates the phrases *See* and *See Also* itself, you must take a special step to add parentheses. Some editors believe See Also references belong inside parentheses:

Paragraph mode
  Cursor shapes in 124
  Enabling 122
  Functions 122-127
  (*See Also* Tags)

To accomplish this, you must type the *closing* parenthesis into the dialog box. You add the opening parenthesis when you generate the index, as explained later in this section. For instance:

```
Type of Entry: See Also

Primary Entry: Paragraph mode

Secondary Entry: Tags)
```

Changing the sort key

In most cases, you can ignore the lines labeled Primary Sort Key and Secondary Sort Key. When alphabetizing the index, Ventura uses the words on the entry lines *unless you put something different on the sort key lines.*

One use for the sort key is to force correct alphabetization. For instance, the rules of grammar say that you should ignore prepositions and conjunctions when alphabetizing. You might, for example, have an index entry for The Wilcox Company. You want this entry to be listed under *W* (for Wilcox), not under *T* (for The). In such cases:

- Type how you want the listing to *appear* on the Entry line.
- Type how you want the listing to be *alphabetized* on the Sort line.

There are several other applications for Ventura's Sort Key feature. The rules of grammar say that numbers should be alphabetized as though they were spelled out. To accomplish this, enter the numerals on the Entry line(s) while spelling them out on the Sort line(s). For instance:

```
Primary Entry: 20th Century Fox

Primary Sort Key: Twentieth Century Fox
```

You can also enter *artificial* alphabetization to force an entry to appear at the very top or very bottom of a listing. For instance, some experts believe See Also references should appear at the top of the sub-listings, so readers can see the other alternatives immediately:

Multi-Chapter
    See Also Publication
    Archiving
    Indexing
    Printing
    Table of Contents

To force a See Also reference to the top of the list, enter *AAA* as the sort key:

```
Type of Entry: See Also

Primary Entry: Multi-Chapter

Primary Sort Key:

Secondary Entry: Publication

Secondary Sort Key: AAA
```

Other people believe See Also references should come at the end of the listing, under the theory that they are of secondary importance. To force it to the bottom of the list, enter *ZZZ* as the sort key.

Editing an index entry

To change an existing entry:

- Enable Text mode. Choose Show Tabs & Returns from the Options menu.
- Return to the page where you originally placed the index entry. Locate the degree symbol that marks its spot. Place the cursor next to the degree symbol.
- Use the arrow keys to move the text cursor back and forth over the degree symbol until the Current Selection Box reads "Index Entry," "Index—See," or "Index—See Also."
- Select Edit Special Item from the Edit menu (or press the keyboard shortcut Ctrl-D). The Insert/Edit Index Entry dialog box appears, showing the previous entry.
- Move to the line(s) you want to alter and make your changes. Click OK.

Because there is no way to make entries visible in Ventura, it can be difficult to find the right page and the right entry, especially if there are multiple entries on the page. Many users find it easier to edit index entries in the word processor (see below).

Deleting an index entry

To delete an index entry, simply delete the degree symbol that marks its spot:

- Enable Text mode.
- Place the text cursor on top of the degree symbol. Confirm that the Current Selection Box reads "Index Entry," "Index—See," or "Index—See Also."
- Press Del (or select Cut Text from the Edit menu).

You can also delete by backspacing over the degree symbol. Either method places the index entry onto the clipboard.

Moving an index entry

To move an index entry, move the degree symbol that marks its spot:

- Delete the entry as described above. This places it in temporary memory.
- Move the text cursor to the new location. Press Ins (or select Paste Text from the Edit menu).

Copying an index entry

To copy an index entry, first place it onto the clipboard. Copy the degree symbol as you would copy any other text. It can be hard to select the degree symbol without accidentally grabbing nearby text as well. Try using the Shift-Click method. Or use the Del or Backspace keys. Delete, then immediately replace the entry at its original location, thereby placing it onto the clipboard where it can be repasted.

Where to place index entries

Where should you insert the entry? For the ultimate in page numbering accuracy, place the entry immediately preceding the word or phrase. This ensures that the listing will show the page where the phrase starts, even if it breaks across a page boundary and continues onto the next page.

If you don't need this level of precision, you can make things easier by grouping entries. Many people feel that an index is equally helpful if it lists the page where the general topic starts, even if the actual phrase occurs later in the paragraph. If you agree, you can streamline indexing by standardizing the location of entries. We suggest grouping them at the *end* of headings and subheadings, and/or at the *beginning* of paragraphs.

As mentioned, index entries show on screen as a degree symbol (°). You will have trouble finding these marks later if they are scattered throughout the text. With a standard location, you always know where to look. If your document has headings and subheadings, put index entries at the end of these lines (Figure 8-9). Group all the index entries for that subsec-

Multiple index entries at the end of the heading

Figure 8-9. If your document has headings and subheadings, consider grouping all your index entries at the end of those lines.

tion in one spot; Ventura doesn't care how many entries you put in a row.

This is an easy location for editors and authors to find when revising. In addition, by putting index marks at the end of each heading, you keep them out of the way in the text file. If you ever decide to edit a Ventura chapter with the word processor, you'll find that numerous index entries can be quite distracting if they are scattered about. The same file is simpler to read and edit if entries are grouped at the end of each heading.

By putting entries at the end of headings, you can also create page ranges with a single entry, by placing the heading into a live header or footer (as described earlier).

Still, you cannot always put index entries after headings. Some documents don't have any headings. Others have them so infrequently that it would be unfair to readers to use them as a catchall for every topic in the section. Remember — wherever you put the entry is the page number that Ventura lists in the index. If entries are too far from the actual phrase, the index is useless.

If the document doesn't average one subhead per page, you probably shouldn't group entries after headings. In that case, put them all together at the beginning of each paragraph. The end of the paragraph would actually be a more convenient spot, but that runs the risk of inaccurate page numbers in the index.

What to choose for index entries

So far our discussion has centered on *how* to insert index entries. You should also consider *what* to enter.

We don't have the space for an in-depth discussion. *The Chicago Manual of Style,* for instance, devotes almost 50 pages to the topic. We have, however, listed a few of the most important principles below.

- In most books, you can safely index every heading and subheading. Since headings usually indicate the main areas of interest, spend extra time to consider the other terms people might use to describe those same topics. Include entries for those other terms as well.
- Index proper names when they apply to the subject of the book, except when they are used in a passing or trivial reference.
- Determine your target audience, and structure the index for them. In a technical book for a lay audience, therefore, the indexer must index subjects by their common names as well as their technical titles. In a technical book for scientists, the indexer can eliminate lay terminology.
- Index every major subject. This is much harder than it sounds, and may require the services of a professional indexer.
- If the primary entry is listed on three or more pages, add secondary entries so readers know which aspects are discussed on which pages.
- Primary entries should usually be nouns or noun phrases.
- Secondary entries can be nouns, adjectives, verbs, or phrases that describe some aspect of the primary entry.
- Do not index trivial passing references.
- Do not employ cross references unless they actually lead to new information.

- Use a *See* reference when you want the reader to look somewhere else instead.
- Use a *See Also* reference when you want the reader to look somewhere else in addition.
- Entries must be spelled identically or Ventura will index them separately. For instance, the words "Frame" and "Frames" create two different entries.

When to Index

Most people agree that indexing should be done at the end of the writing or editing process. The indexer needs to concentrate only on indexing until it is finished. If you do the indexing as one task, it's easier to stay consistent. When manually indexing with pencil and paper, it's not hard to realize that "Frame" and "Frames" mean the same thing. To Ventura, however, those are two separate listings. If you enter one spelling on one page, and another spelling somewhere else, you'll have to go to extra work to correct the error. You must correct the generated index file, or you must return to one of the entries, edit it, and regenerate the index.

Inserting index entries in the word processor

If you prefer, you can insert index entries directly into the word processor, either before or after the initial layout in Ventura. You *cannot*, however, use the word processor's indexing function. Whether or not the word processor has its own indexing feature, you must use bracket codes to put Ventura-compatible index entries into the file.

Chapter Three, "Creating Text," explains in detail how to add bracket codes, including the codes for index entries. Here is a brief recap. Use the bracket code <$Ip;s> for normal index entries, where *p* equals the primary entry and *s* represents the secondary entry.

There are no spaces before or after the semicolon. If you want a primary reference without a secondary reference, enter it by itself inside the brackets, without a semicolon:

```
<$IFrames>
```

See references use the code <$Sp;s>. Don't type the word See; Ventura inserts it automatically when it generates the index:

```
<$SContainers;Frames>
```

See Also references use the code <$Ap;s>. Do not type the words See Also. Here is a typical word processor entry for a See Also reference:

```
<$AFrames;Pictures>
```

Here is the resulting index listing:

Frames
See Also Pictures

For all three kinds of entries, place sort keys in square brackets immediately following the entry. Thus, to sort 20th Century Fox as if the number were spelled out, you would type:

```
<$I20th Century Fox[Twentieth Century Fox]>
```

Generating the index

At the beginning of this section, we said that indexing is a three-step process:

1. Insert entries.

2. Generate the index.

3. Format the index.

To this point, you've learned how to insert entries. These entries, which are stored in the text files, have no effect until you generate the index. This function extracts the entries and their page numbers, puts them in alphabetical order, and lists them in a separate file.

You generate an index with the Multi-Chapter dialog box. First you open the publication you want to index. If you have not yet created a publication, turn back to the explanation earlier in this chapter. It shows you how to add chapters, change their order, and save them as a publication.

Incidentally, you should use Multi-Chapter even if you only want to index a single chapter. In that case, you simply create a publication that contains only one chapter.

- Open the publication.
- Make sure all the chapters show on the list and that they are in the right order. (The sequence can affect the page numbering.)
- Select Renumber from the secondary menu.

If you have set Ventura to perform automatic numbering across chapter boundaries, you must renumber *before* you index. Otherwise the numbers won't be correct. If you have set the starting page numbers manually, you can skip this step. For more on numbering, see the section later in this chapter.

- Select Make Index from the secondary menu. The Generate Index dialog box appears (Figure 8-10).

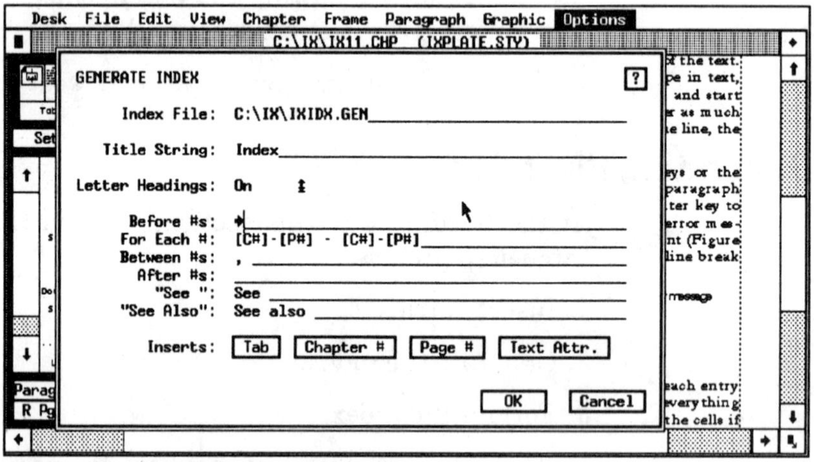

Figure 8-10. The Generate Index dialog box.

This dialog box appears with certain default parameters. If you don't like what Ventura has selected, you can change things. We will step through each line of the dialog box, so you understand what your options are.

Index File names and locates the file containing the index. Ventura initially places the file in the same subdirectory as the chapter. It names this file by starting with the name of the publication. It then substitutes the three letters IDX for the last three letters of the name. It also adds the extension GEN. Thus, if the publication is C:\TYPESET\SAMPLE.PUB, Ventura will call the index file SAMPLIDX.GEN. If you don't like

Ventura's choice, you can change the name and/or the location by typing something different on this line.

Title String simply means the title. Ventura places whatever you type here at the top of the index file. It tags this word (or words) as Z_INDEX TITLE.

Letter Headings controls whether or not Ventura places letters between each alphabetic group — an *A* before the listings that begin with *A*, a *B* before the *B* listings, and so on. Ventura inserts these letters as separate paragraphs on their own line, tagged as Z_INDEX LTR. If your index does not have any listings for a certain letter, Ventura does not create a letter heading. Thus, if you have no *Q* listings in the index, Ventura will not create a *Q* letter heading. All listings that do not begin with a letter of the alphabet are grouped together at the top of the index with an exclamation mark (!) serving as the letter heading.

Before #s defines what Ventura inserts between the listing and the page number. The default is a tab character, represented by a small arrow. The tab character is useful if you want the page numbers to be right-aligned across from the listing, as shown in Figure 8-11.

Some editors prefer an index where the page number follows immediately after the listing (Figure 8-12). To produce this effect, delete the tab character and insert a space.

For each # controls the appearance of the page numbers. If you use chapter-by-chapter numbering, leave the default codes [C#]-[P#]. The code [C#] stands for chapter numbers. The code [P#] stands for page numbers. As shown here, the index will generate listings like this:

Frames 1-4

In the example immediately above, the index entry for "Frames" appears on the fourth page of the first chapter.

Consecutive pages will show like this:

Frames 1-4 – 1-7

In this example, index entries for "Frames" appear consecutively on the fourth, fifth, sixth, and seventh pages of the first chapter.

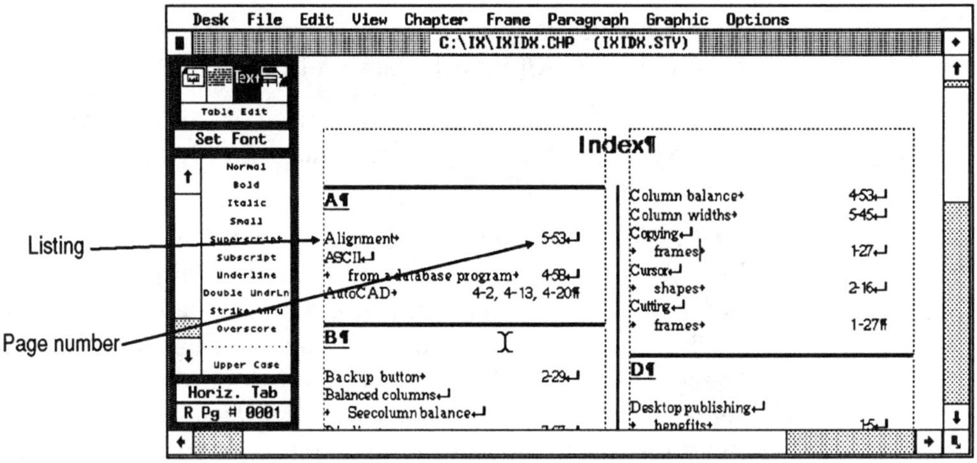

Figure 8-11. In this example, a tab character produces the space between listing and page number, and aligns the numbers flush right.

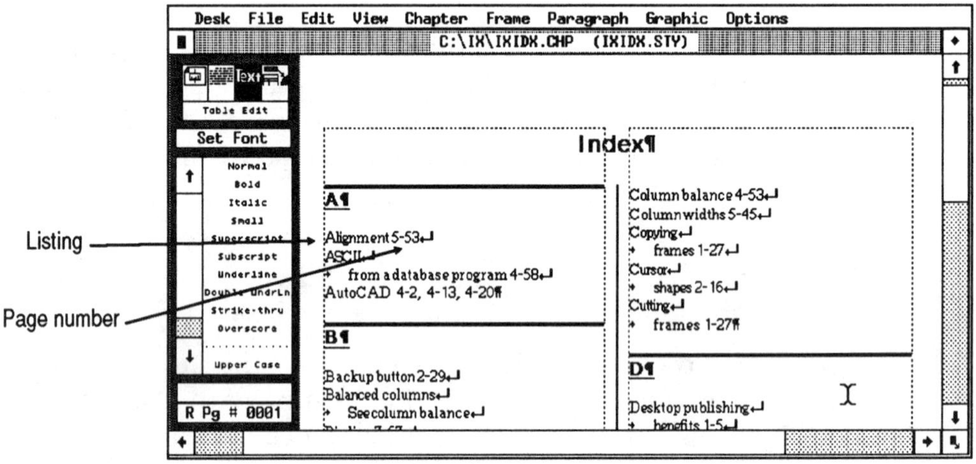

Figure 8-12. In this example, a space separates the listing from the page number.

If you do not use chapter-by-chapter numbering, be sure to delete both instances of the [C#] code and the hyphen. The line will then look like this:

```
For Each #: [P#] - [P#]
```

Listings will look like this:

Frames 4

Consecutive pages will show like this:

Frames 4 - 7

Between #s defines the punctuation and spacing between page numbers, when a listing appears on more than one page. In most cases, you will want to use the default of a comma and a space. However, if you prefer a semicolon or other punctuation instead, type it onto this line. The default parameters produce listings like this:

Frames 4, 7, 18

After #s controls the punctuation that appears after the final page number (if any). The default is no punctuation. If you want punctuation, type it on this line. For instance, if you type a period on this line, index listings will look like this:

Frames 4, 7, 18.

Punctuation after numbers is most useful for indexes where the secondary entries follow one another in a paragraph format. For instance, here is how such a listing might look by adding semicolons after each secondary listing:

Paragraph mode
    Cursor shapes in 124; Enabling 122; Functions 122-127, 134, 138; Keyboard shortcut 122; *See Also* Tags

"See" defines the text that appears in front of See listings. The default is the word *See,* which produces listings like this:

Containers
    See Frames

You can substitute another word or phrase. For instance, if you type "Look under" on this line, you will create listings like this one:

Containers
    Look under Frames

See Also controls the text that appears in front of See Also listings. The default is the phrase *See also,* which produces listings like this:

Paragraph mode
    See also Tags

You can substitute a different phrase, or different capitalization if you do not like the default.

Inserts provides a convenient way to enter codes into the dialog box. Clicking on Tab inserts a tab character. Clicking on Chapter # and Page # inserts the codes [C#] and [P#], respectively. Clicking on Text Attr. inserts the code <D>. Since <D> is the code for turning off a text attribute, you would replace <D> with the attribute you wanted to add. Use text attributes only for making a word or phrase different from the rest of the text in the index. For instance, to make page numbers bold, while leaving the rest of the paragraph in normal text, you would enter the code <B> in front of the page number code. If you use a code to turn on a text attribute, be sure to insert the ending code to turn it off again. Chapter Three, "Creating Text," gives details on bracket codes. Any text attribute that can be added to a text file can also be added to a dialog box.

When the Generate Index dialog box specifies the format you want, click OK to start the indexing process. Ventura loads each chapter in turn, in the order you specified in the publication. It searches the file for index entries and records their page number. When finished, it alphabetizes them and records them in a file. You can load and format this file as you would any other text file.

After generating the index file, Ventura returns to the Multi-Chapter dialog box. If you save the publication at this time (using Save from the secondary menu), the index settings will be saved along with it. You will not have to change them the next time you generate an index from this publication.

➡ *NOTE: If you use Multi-Chapter to copy a publication to a new location, the path for the generated index file is not changed. You must open the Generate Index dialog box and regenerate the index to make this change.*

Formatting the index

So far you have learned to insert index entries and generate an index file. Formatting the index is the third and final step.

To format an index, you create a chapter and load in the generated index file created in the previous step. Most indexes resemble the page format of the main document, but with several differences. Most indexes, for instance, use a two-column format, even if the main document is in a single column. And most indexes use a smaller type size to fit more information onto the page.

For this reason, it is often best to create a separate style sheet for the index. By starting with the style sheet for the main document, you minimize the time to build the new one.

Here are the steps you might take to build an index chapter:

- Select New from the File menu to start a new chapter. Use Save As to give it a name.
- Load the style sheet from the main document. Rename it immediately using Save As New Style.
- Select Load Text/File from the File menu.
- Select Type of File: Text, Text Format: Generated, # of Files: One, and Destination: List of Files. When the Item Selector appears, use it to find and load the index file generated previously.
- Place the file on the page and format it as you would any other document.

Ventura assigns three tags to the text it generates for the index file:

- Z_INDEX TITLE is assigned to the title word or phrase at the top of the page.
- Z_INDEX LTR is assigned to the letter headings between alphabetic categories (if any).
- Z_INDEX MAIN is assigned to the listings.

Initially, Ventura gives these tags the same attributes as Body Text. You can change the format of these tags with the Paragraph menu. You can also assign a different tag to any or all of the text. Figure 8-13 shows a typical index. Notice that Ventura does not use paragraph returns to separate listings within a letter category. For instance, everything between *B* and *C* is a single paragraph. New lines are created with line breaks.

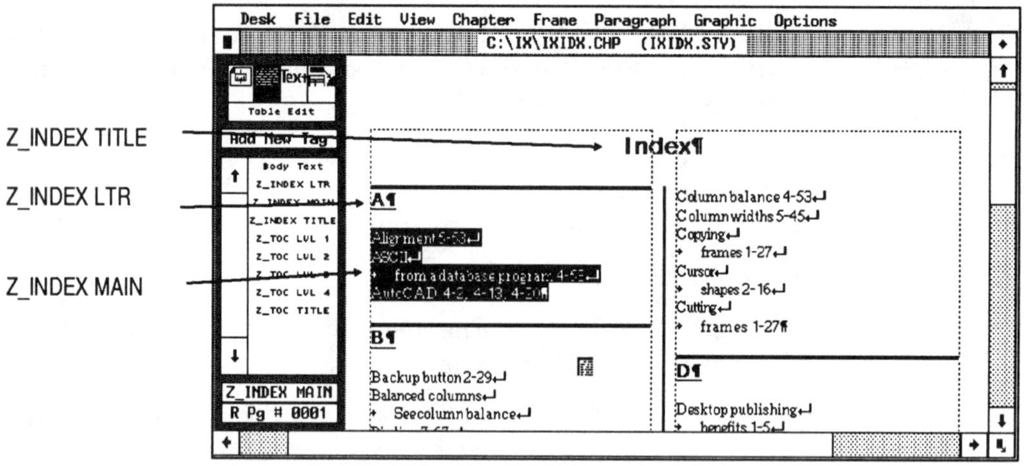

Figure 8-13. Ventura tags the index file when it generates it.

Tips on Indexing

TIP *To index an item under several different names,* insert as many index entries as you need. Ventura permits you to create multiple entries at the same spot in the text.

TIP *Try to place the index mark in front* of the item you are indexing. Proper indexing procedures call for the index to list the page on which the material begins. If you insert the mark after a long phrase or section you could end up with improper page numbering.

TIP *Try placing index marks in a separate pass* through the document. We feel indexing is too complex to do simultaneously with layout and editing. Instead, we suggest saving it until the end, and moving through the entire document at one time. You are likely to be more consistent in your categorization if you do it all at once.

TIP *To avoid inconsistent indexing in a long document* generate and print out the index for each chapter as you go along. Begin with the first chapter. After inserting the index entries, generate the index file, and format an index chapter. Print it out for reference. Now you have an alphabetized reminder of the topics, categories, and spellings you used for the first chapter. Now insert the index entries for the second chapter, and repeat the process. With each chapter you will have a longer and more comprehensive partial index as your guide. You will find automated indexing much easier, faster, and more accurate if you have a printed reminder.

TIP *To edit an existing index* consider using a word processor rather than Ventura. Within the word processor, all the index entries are visible as bracket codes. This visibility makes it easy to locate, compare, and alter entries. In Ventura, by contrast, you must open the dialog box for each entry one by one — a time-consuming process.

Creating a table of contents

Ventura's built-in table of contents (TOC) function is similar in many ways to its index facility. In both cases, you use the Multi-Chapter dialog box to extract information from the chapter(s) and put it in a separate file. Then you load this text file into a chapter to format its appearance.

To create an index, however, you must go through the document to mark the entries. To create a TOC, you simply tell Ventura which tags to use. Ventura searches the document, pulls out every paragraph with those tags, and lists them along with their page number in its special TOC file.

For instance, to make Ventura create a one-level TOC, we would instruct it to look for Head1 tags and extract the text and page number. To create a two-level TOC, we'd tell Ventura to look for Head1 and Head2. In real life, we would also extract the chapter title and chapter number and include them in our TOC.

Let's run through the process in detail. To begin:

- Select Multi-Chapter from the Options menu. Use the Multi-Chapter dialog box to open the publication you want to work with. Confirm that the chapters are in the correct order.

➥*NOTE: To build a TOC for a single chapter, put it into a publication by itself.*

- Select Renumber from the secondary menu.

If you have set Ventura to perform automatic numbering across chapter boundaries, you must renumber *before* you generate the table of contents. If you have set the numbers manually, or if you only have one chapter, you can skip this step.

- Select Make TOC from the secondary menu. The Generate Table Of Contents dialog box appears (Figure 8-14).

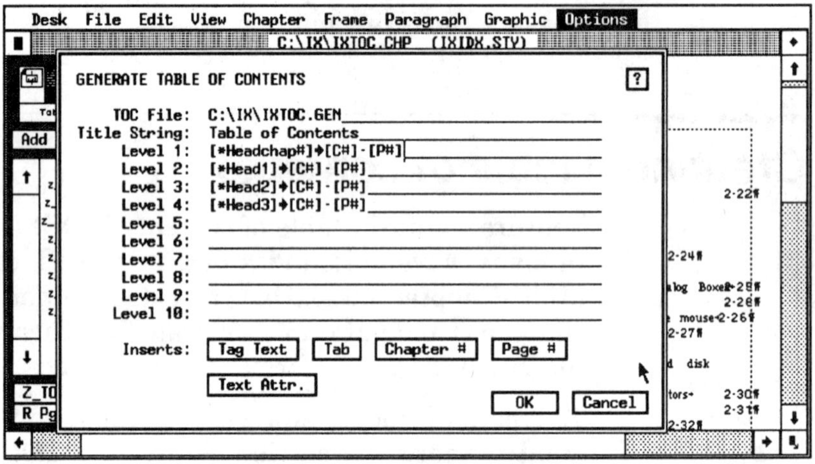

Figure 8-14. The Generate Table Of Contents dialog box.

With this dialog box, you control the name and path of the TOC file, plus its contents.

TOC File specifies the name and location of the file. Ventura makes a suggestion on this line, but you have the option to change it. Ventura starts with the name of the publication and substitutes "TOC" for the last three letters. Thus, if the publication is SAMPLE.PUB, Ventura suggests SAMPLTOC as the file name. Since this is a file generated by Ventura, it appends the extension GEN. It puts the file in the same subdirectory as the chapter file. If you don't like any of these choices, you can change them by typing something else onto the line.

Title String specifies the title that will appear at the top of the file. Ventura suggests "Table of Contents." Most editors prefer to use just the word "Contents." You can make this substitution, or any other change, by typing it onto the line. When it generates the TOC file, Ventura puts this phrase at the top of the file and tags it as Z_TOC TITLE.

Level 1 specifies the first tag to extract. In our example, we told Ventura to find and list the tag containing the number of the chapter, called HeadChap#. To do this, we used the Tag Text insert button at the bottom of the dialog box:

- Place the text cursor on the Level 1 line. Click on Tag Text.
- Ventura inserts a code onto the line:

```
[*tag name]
```

- Erase the words "tag name" without erasing the rest of the code. In place of "tag name," type in the name of the tag you want Ventura to extract for the TOC. In our example, we typed in:

```
[*HeadChap#]
```

Ventura will now extract every paragraph in the publication tagged as HeadChap# and put it into the generated TOC file. It will be tagged as Z_TOC1.

On the *Level 2* line, repeat the process to tell Ventura the second tag to extract. In this case, we typed in the tag name Head1, which is our tag name for section heads.

- Click on Tag Text. Erase "tag name" and replace it with "Head1."

Since we also wanted page numbers with this text, we added additional codes to the line. To force the page numbers to align with the right margin, we inserted a tab character:

- Move the text cursor immediately after the rightmost bracket in the code [*HeadChap]. Click on the Tab button. Ventura inserts an arrow character to mark the tab location.

➥*NOTE: You must click on the Tab button to insert the tab character. You cannot insert it by pressing the Tab key on the keyboard.*

Next we added the chapter and page numbers:

- With the text cursor immediately following the tab character, click on the Chapter # button. Now type a hyphen to separate the chapter and page numbers.

- Click on the Page # button.

At this stage, we are ready to format our TOC. However, we could have continued to add levels. For instance, we could have asked Ventura to extract second- and third-level headings as well as first-level heads. In addition, we could have used the Text Attr. command to help us enter bracket codes, as described in the indexing section of this chapter.

When you have entered all the tag names and codes:

- Click OK. Ventura loads each chapter in the publication and extracts the requested text and page numbers. It stores this information in the file name and location you specified.
- When Ventura finishes generating the TOC, it returns you to the Multi-Chapter dialog box. Use Save to save the publication. The settings you created for the TOC are now saved for future reuse.

Formatting the TOC

As with an index, generating a TOC with Multi-Chapter gives you a pretagged text file. You load this file into a chapter and format as you would any other document. You may want to use the style sheet from the main document, and simply add formats for the TOC tags. Or you may want to create a separate style sheet for the TOC, starting with the style sheet for the main document.

Here are the steps you might take to build a TOC chapter.

- Select New from the File menu to start a new chapter. Use Save As to give it a name.
- Load the style sheet from the main document.
- Rename it immediately using Save As New Style if you want a separate style sheet for the TOC. Otherwise, you can skip this step.
- Select Load Text/File from the File menu.
- Select Type of File: Text, Text Format: Generated, # of Files:

One, and Destination: List of Files. When the Item Selector appears, use it to find and load the TOC file generated previously.

- Place the file on the page and format it as you would any other document.

Ventura assigns tags to the text it generates for the index file:

- Z_TOC TITLE is assigned to the title word or phrase at the top of the page.
- Z_TOC1 is assigned to text you extracted with the Level 1 line in the Generate Table of Contents dialog box.
- Z_TOC2 is assigned to text from Level 2, and so on for the maximum of 10 levels.

Initially, Ventura gives these tags the same attributes as Body Text. You can change the format of these tags with the Paragraph menu. You can also assign a different tag to any or all of the text.

Tips for TOCs

TIP *You can use Ventura's TOC feature* several times on the same document for different purposes. You might do it once to create a TOC. You might do it a second time to create a list of illustrations. Just be sure to give the generated file a different name each time you use the feature for a different purpose. Otherwise, you will overwrite the first file.

TIP *You need not reconstruct the chapter* containing the generated TOC file each time you regenerate the TOC. Ventura will automatically update the chapter for you. This allows you to place a frame containing the TOC file within a chapter holding all the front matter of a book.

Inserting footnotes

Ventura Publisher permits you to create footnotes. A symbol or number appears in the main text next to the item you wish to comment on. The same symbol or number appears at the bottom of the page, where you can type in the reference (Figure 8-15). Ventura creates a special frame to hold footnotes, and permits you to put a line between the footnotes and the main text.

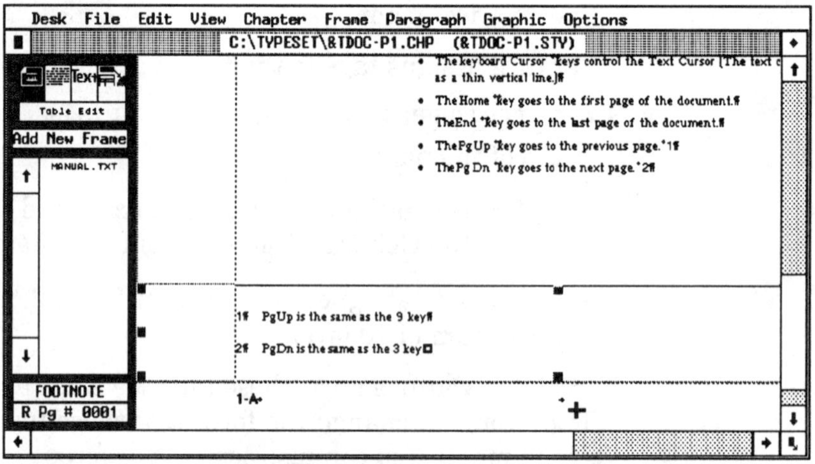

Figure 8-15. Footnotes are signalled by a number or symbol in the main text. The reference appears at the bottom of the page inside a special footnote frame.

To create footnotes, you must first enable the feature with Footnote Settings from the Chapter menu. In this dialog box you also determine the format. Once you have turned on footnoting, you can then insert references in Text mode.

Enabling footnotes

Begin by enabling footnotes and determining their format:

- Select Footnote Settings from the Chapter menu. The dialog box appears (Figure 8-16).

The Footnote Settings dialog box may seem a bit intimidating the first time you encounter it. Most of the functions are straightforward, if you have the patience to work through the dialog box from top to bottom. You only need to determine the settings once. From then on they stay with the style sheet.

The main purpose of this dialog box is to control the symbol or number that appears in the main text. To enable footnotes, choose one of the buttons from Usage & Format. Two of them insert numbers into the main text to signal a footnote. The third one inserts symbols, such as asterisks.

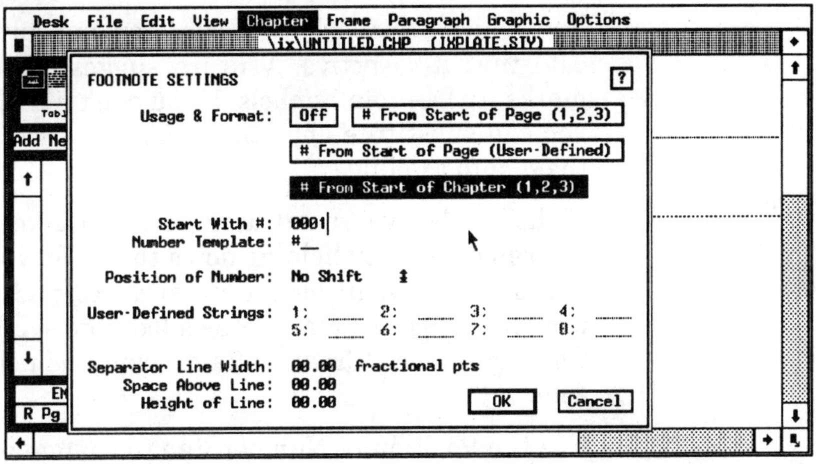

Figure 8-16. Use the Footnote Settings dialog box to enable footnotes and determine their format.

To insert numbers, choose # From Start of Page (1,2,3) if you want Ventura to start the numbers over again with each page. Under this system, if you had three footnotes on page one and two footnotes on page two, the page one symbols would read 1, 2, and 3, while the page two symbols would read 1 and 2.

If you want Ventura to number consecutively throughout the chapter, choose # From Start of Chapter (1,2,3). Under this system, page one symbols would be 1, 2, and 3. Page two symbols would read 4 and 5.

To start with a number other than one, move to the Start With # line and type in the new number.

To put parentheses or brackets around the number, use the Number Template line. For instance, to put parentheses around every number or symbol, type:

```
Number Template: (#)
```

To add square brackets, type:

```
Number Template: [#]
```

To put a hyphen in front of every number, type:

```
Number Template: -#
```

To mark footnotes with symbols instead of numbers, choose # From Start of Page (User-Defined). The User-Defined Strings line, which previously was gray, now appears in black to indicate that it is active. Ventura suggests asterisks and plus marks for footnote symbols. If you don't like these suggestions, you can substitute any other characters you prefer by typing them onto the line.

If the symbol you want is not a normal keyboard character, you can enter it by holding down the Alt key while you type its decimal equivalent on the numeric keypad. For instance, to use the cross character (†) as a footnote symbol, type Alt-187. Chapter Three, "Creating Text," explains non-keyboard characters.

Use the Position of Number line to change where the symbol appears. If you select No Shift, they appear on the same baseline as the normal text, in the same type size. If you select Superscript, Ventura shifts them above the baseline and puts them in a smaller type size. If you select Subscript, Ventura shifts them below and puts them in a smaller type size.

➡*NOTE: You can control the point size and the amount of the shift with Attribute Overrides from the Paragraph menu.*

The final few lines in the Footnote Settings dialog box control the width and height of the separator line. If you do not want a separator line, leave these lines blank.

To create a separator line, first determine the width you want. Six to twelve picas is a typical width, but if your footnotes are long and involved, you may want the line to run the full width of the column.

Unfortunately, you cannot create a six-pica separator line by typing 06,00 picas onto the Separator Line Width line. Ventura measures the line from the left edge of the page, not the left edge of the margin. Thus, if you have a four-pica left margin, you must enter 10,00 picas onto the line (4 + 6 = 10) to achieve a six-pica line.

Even though Ventura measures the separator line from the left edge of the page, it only prints the portion within the column guides.

To set the thickness of the separator line, type in the correct measurement into Height of Line.

Normally Ventura places the separator line at the top of the footnote frame. To move the line down from the top (closer to the footnote text), place space above the line. The amount you type on the Space Above Line is the amount the line is pushed down. This amount does not affect the position of the footnote text. If you place enough space above the line, you can push it completely below the footnote text, or even into the bottom margin (Figure 8-17).

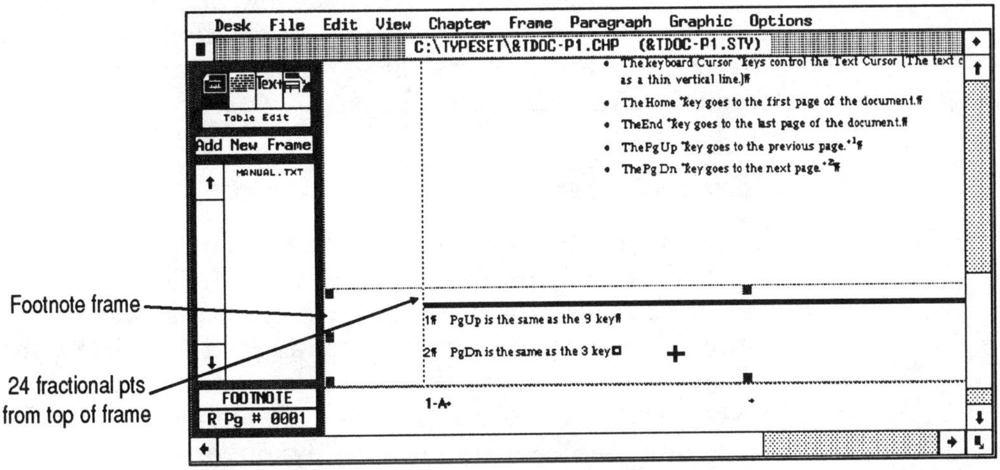

Figure 8-17. Use Space Above Line to push the separator line down from the top of the footnote frame.

Adding footnotes to the text

Once you have enabled footnoting and set its parameters, you can insert footnotes anywhere in the text. To create a footnote:

- Enable Text mode.
- Move the cursor immediately after the word you wish to reference.
- Select Ins Special Item from the Edit menu (keyboard shortcut: Ctrl-C).
- Select Footnote from the secondary menu (keyboard shortcut: F2).

A number or symbol appears in the text next to the word, in the format you chose in the Footnote Settings dialog box. At the same time, Ventura creates a footnote frame at the bottom of the page. This frame contains two separate paragraphs.

One paragraph repeats the footnote number or symbol from the main text. The second paragraph is for the text of the footnote. You will type your own text into this second paragraph as follows:

- Move the text cursor to the bottom of the page. Erase the phrase "Text of Footnote" and type in the correct phrase.

Each time you insert another footnote on the same page, Ventura enlarges the footnote frame and inserts another line. The footnote frame cannot be any larger than half the size of the page. If the footnotes are longer, Ventura will create a frame for them on the next page.

Formatting footnotes in Paragraph mode

Ventura initially tags the footnote number or symbol as Z_FNOT # and the footnote text as Z_FNOT ENTRY. You cannot change these names or retag the paragraphs. You can, however, change the format of the tags in Paragraph mode. When Ventura creates the tags it assigns the attributes of Body Text. You can change these attributes by selecting a paragraph and changing it with the options from the Paragraph menu.

Inserting footnotes into word processing files

Authors can insert footnote references directly into word processing files with bracket codes. Chapter Three, "Creating Text," explains how to use bracket codes for footnoting and other functions. Footnotes inserted in advance do not appear in Ventura until you enable the footnoting function. They are not lost — they are simply invisible until you use Footnote Settings from the Chapter menu to turn them on.

Tips for footnoting

TIP *To put the footnote symbol or number on the same line* with the footnote text, use the Breaks dialog box to make sure there is no line break between the two. The most common method is to give the number a line break before and the text a line break after. Use In From Left in the Spacing dialog box to keep the footnote text from overlapping the number.

TIP *To make the number or symbol at the bottom of the page* into a superscript (or subscript), put Z_FNOT # and Z_FNOT ENTRY on separate lines, but give Z_FNOT # a very small line spacing. First make sure there is a line break between Z_FNOT # and Z_FNOT ENTRY. Now give Z_FNOT # a smaller font and a smaller inter-line spacing. For instance, if Z_FNOT ENTRY has a line spacing of 10 points, try five points for Z_FNOT #.

Numbering functions

Ventura's numbering capabilities set it distinctly apart from ordinary desktop publishing software. Although Ventura's numbering options are powerful, they require some study. This section provides details on how to make best use of them. We have divided the information into two categories: (1) document numbering and (2) auto-numbering.

Document numbering options

Ventura's document numbering functions can automatically keep track of chapters, pages, figures, and tables. In Chapter Six, "Building the Chapter," we explained how to insert chapter numbers, page numbers, figure numbers, and table numbers into your documents by placing one of the following codes into a header, footer, caption, heading, or other location:

- [C#] (chapter number code)
- [P#] (page number code)
- [F#] (figure number code)
- [T#] (table number code)

Placing the code tells Ventura to display the number at that location. In this section, we will show you how to change and customize those numbers. To control the format and other parameters, you use the Update Counters dialog box.

- Select Update Counters from the Chapter menu (Figure 8-18).

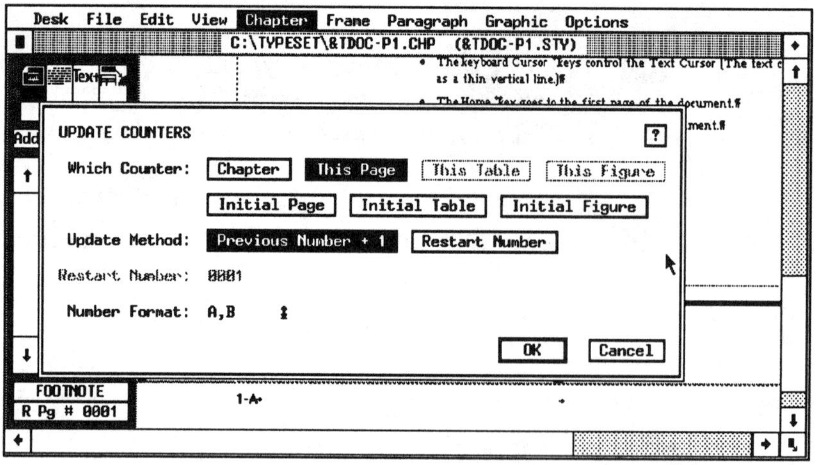

Figure 8-18. The Update Counters dialog box.

If you want the counters to start with the Arabic numeral *1*, you don't need to make any changes. If you want it to start with anything else, you should use the dialog box:

- Select the type of counter you wish to modify from the line labeled Which Counter.

To change the chapter numbering, select the Chapter button. You can manually change the number, or you can ask Ventura to number chapters in order automatically. To manually adjust the chapter number:

- Select Which Counter: Chapter.
- Select Update Method: Restart Number.
- Move the text cursor to the Restart Number line and type in the new number. For instance, to set the chapter number to five, type "0005."

To automatically continue the numbering from the previous chapter:

- Select Which Counter: Chapter.
- Select Update Method: Previous Number + 1.

This causes Ventura to look at the number of the previous chapter and number the current one consecutively. You will not be able to see this choice on screen while working on the document. It does not take effect until print time. For automatic numbering across chapter boundaries you must (1) print the chapters with the Multi-Chapter dialog box and (2) select Renumber from the Multi-Chapter dialog box *before* you print.

To change the appearance of the chapter number:

- Select Chapter
- Select the format you want from the Number Format: pop-up menu (Figure 8-19). For instance, to display chapter numbers as uppercase Roman numerals, choose *I, II.*

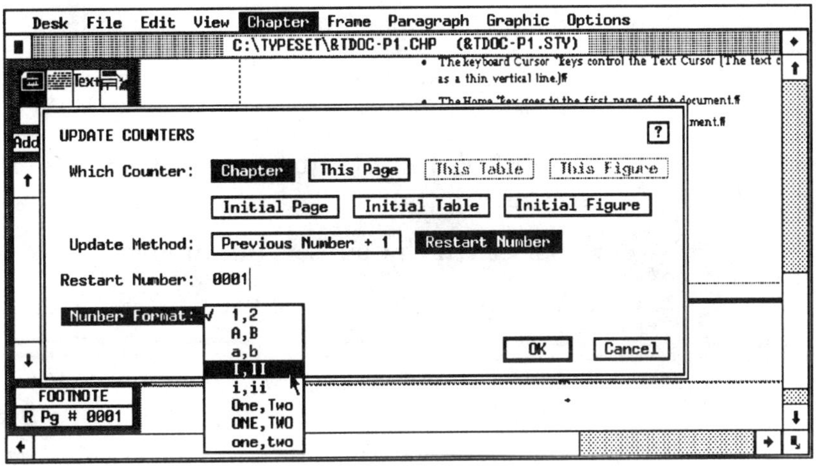

Figure 8-19. Select the numbering format you prefer from the pop-up menu.

To change the page numbering on the current page, select This Page. Use Update Method: Restart Number to change the current page by typing a new number on the Restart Number line.

You can restart the page numbering as many times as you want within a single chapter. If you wanted, for some reason, to have seven *Page 3*'s in a row, you could restart the number at *0003* for each of those seven pages. If you wanted the rest of the chapter to number itself consecutively, you would choose Previous Number + 1 for those pages.

Any page numbering choices you make to the Underlying

Page apply to every page *after* that until (and unless) you make another change.

To change the appearance of the page numbers, use the pop-up menu from Number Format. You can mix and match numbering styles in the same document. Any change you make affects the current page and every page after that until (and unless) you make another change.

To change the page numbering on the first page of the document:

- Select Which Counter: Initial Page.
- Select Update Method: Restart Number.
- Type in the new starting number on the Restart Number line.

To cause Ventura to number consecutively from the previous chapter:

- Select Which Counter: Initial Page.
- Select Update Method: Previous Number + 1.

➥*NOTE: If you restart page numbering, the new numbers will not show in the Page Number box at the bottom of the Side-Bar. That box always displays the true consecutive page count of the current chapter. To use the Go To Page function, or to print selected pages, you must refer to the on-screen page numbers, not the artificial numbering you have created with the Update Counters dialog box.*

You can also change the starting number and the numbering style of figures and tables, provided you have inserted figure or table numbering into the Anchors & Captions dialog box. To change the numbering style for one picture only:

- Enable Frame mode.
- Select the frame containing the picture.
- Select Update Counters.
- Select Which Counter: This Table or Which Counter: This Figure.
- Change the numbering and click OK.

The changes affect that frame only. If you move the frame, the new numbering moves with it.

Auto-Numbering

Ventura's auto-numbering is a versatile, powerful function. You can use it to keep track of simple lists. Or you can use it for military style section numbering. Or you can use it to create traditional outlines:

I. First level
  A. Second level
    1. Third level

You can also use it to generate text automatically. For instance, you can automatically insert the word "WARNING" or "CAUTION" at the beginning of every cautionary note in your product manual. We used this technique to generate the TIP labels in this book (see page 431).

Or you can use Auto-Numbering for formatting. In the section heads in this book, the thick rule above the heading is created with the heading tag, but the second, thin rule that accompanies it is created with Auto-Numbering.

In all these cases, if you rearrange, delete, or add to the list, Ventura automatically renumbers for you. In this section, we will step you through the creation of a variety of auto-numbering effects.

Auto-Numbering basics

All auto-numbering functions work in the same basic manner. You open the Auto-Numbering dialog box and turn the function on. Then you tell Ventura which tag name(s) to watch for. Ventura scans the document and numbers those paragraphs. It generates a separate paragraph to contain the number.

Seems simple enough. The first-time user, however, is apt to be confused by Ventura's ability to number multiple levels. Bear with us for a moment while we explain the multi-level concept before getting back to Ventura's implementation. Anybody who went to grade school is familiar with one type of multi-level numbering:

I.
A.
1.
2.
3.
B.
1.
2.

True, parts of this traditional outline use letters instead of numbers, but Ventura can handle alphabetic as well as numeric sequencing. If you have been in the military, you are familiar with another multi-level numbering style:

1.
1.1
1.1.1
1.1.2
1.2
1.2.1
1.2.2
1.2.3

This second example is a good place to introduce Ventura's nomenclature. It is obviously a three-level numbering scheme and it is easy to see which level is which. Level 1 has one number, Level 2 has two numbers, and Level 3 has three numbers. But our traditional outline was also an example of three-level numbering. However, the traditional outline showed only one level of numbering at a time. Here's how it would look if all the levels were shown simultaneously:

I.
I.A
I.A.1
I.A.2
I.B
I.B.1
I.B.2
I.B.3

Whether or not all three levels are shown, Ventura would still refer to the Roman numeral (I) as Level 1, to the uppercase letters (A and B) as Level 2, and to the Arabic numbers (1, 2, and 3) as Level 3.

Auto-Numbering for simple lists

Let's start with a simple example. Suppose you want to include an occasional list in your documents, and you want Ventura to do the numbering for you. First you would create a special tag. You'd probably call it List or something equally obvious. Next, you would assign this tag to each paragraph in the list. Finally, you would open the Auto-Numbering dialog box and tell it to number every paragraph with that tag:

- Select Auto-Numbering from the Chapter menu (Figure 8-20).

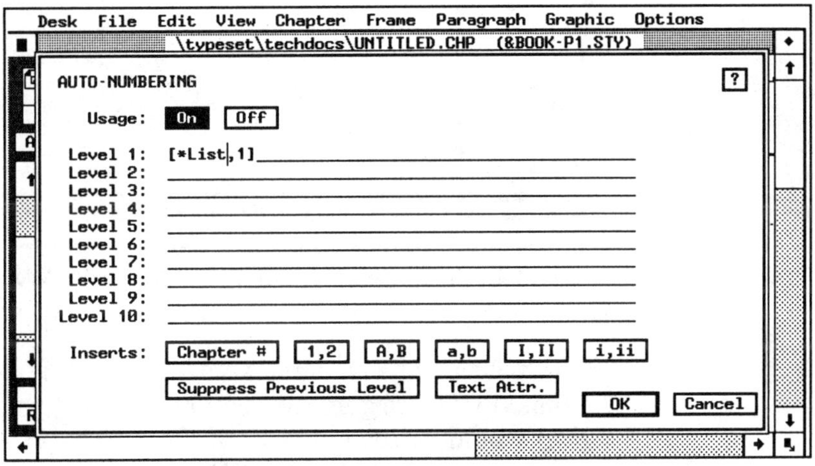

Figure 8-20. The Auto-Numbering dialog box.

- Select Usage: On.
- Move the text cursor to the Level 1 line. Click on the *1,2* button. Ventura inserts the code:

```
[*tag name, 1]
```

This button specifies arabic numerals, starting with the number one. If you wanted a different numbering style, you would click on a different button —*A,B* for uppercase letters, *a,b* for lowercase letters, and *I,II* or *i,ii* for uppercase or lowercase roman numerals.

- Erase the words "tag name" and insert the tag you want Ventura to number — in this case, List. The code now reads:

```
[*List,1]
```

- Click OK to close the dialog box.

When you return to the workspace, Ventura has generated a paragraph and a number for every paragraph tagged as List (Figure 8-21).

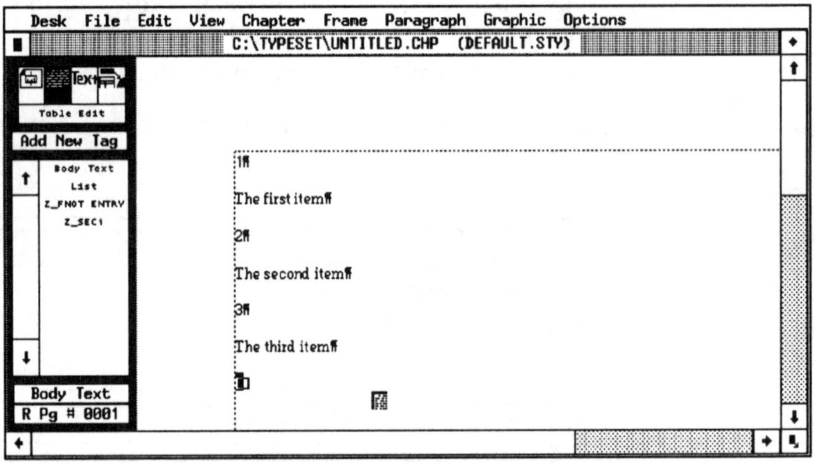

Figure 8-21. The numbers in this example were generated by Auto-Numbering.

The paragraphs in our example are tagged as Z_SEC1, because they were generated on Level 1. If you had used Level 2, they would be tagged as Z_SEC2, and so on. Initially, Z_SEC1 has the same attributes as Body Text, but you can change its format in Paragraph mode. (You cannot, however, change the name of the tag or assign a different tag name to the number.)

Since Body Text normally has a line break before or after, Z_SEC1 will initially reside on a line by itself. If you prefer, however, you can change the formatting so it resides on the same line with the list paragraphs.

Numbers and paragraphs on the same line

To put the number on the same line with the list paragraph, you must change both the Z_SEC1 tag and the List tag. Table 8-1 provides a summary of the changes you must make:

Table 8-1. Tag attributes used for Auto-Numbering.

Tag	Dialog box	Change	Reason
Z_SEC1	Breaks	Line Break: Before (or None)	Allows it to appear on same line with following tag
LIST	Breaks	Line Break: After	Allows it to appear on same line with preceding tag
LIST	Alignment	Relative Indent: Length of Previous Line	Positions heading immediately to the right of the number
LIST	Alignment	Fixed Indent: one en space (equal to half the point size of Font)	Puts a space between the number and the heading

These are the changes you *must* make to the tags. You can also make other changes. For instance, you can make the numbers bold. Or you can use the Spacing dialog box to indent listed items from the normal margins. Or you can add space above or below Z_SEC1 to create extra space between each item in the list.

Multi-level numbering with punctuation

Now that you've seen how to build a simple list with Auto-Numbering, let's try a multi-level example, with punctuation added to the numbers. Your first step is to decide which tags you want to number. To illustrate, let's assume we want two-level, military-style numbering for the tags Heading and Sub-heading, like this:

1. First Heading
   1.1 First subheading
   1.2 Second subheading
2. Second Heading
   2.1 First subheading
   2.2 Second subheading
   2.3 Third subheading

As before, select Auto-Numbering from the Chapter menu. Then take these three steps. First, put the text cursor on the level you want. Next click on the *numbering style* you want to use. Finally, type in the name of the tag to number, followed by a period for punctuation. The dialog box will have the following entries for the two levels:

```
Level 1: [*HEADING,1].

Level 2: [*SUBHEADING,1].
```

Since you want Arabic numbers, you would put the cursor on Level 1 and click on the *1,2* Button. Ventura inserts [*tag name,1] onto the line. You delete "tag name" and replace it with HEADING. To separate the numbers, type a period on the same line immediately after the code. Without a period, a number such as *1.1* would read as *11*. The final code reads:

```
[*HEADING,1].
```

To number the Subheading paragraphs, repeat the process on the Level 2 line so it reads:

```
[*SUBHEADING,1].
```

This example used a period for punctuation, but you can add any punctuation — or, as we'll see below, any text at all.

Traditional outline style

With slight modifications, you can use the techniques explained above to create a traditional outline style. The first change is simply to click on different number styles when in the Auto-Numbering dialog box. For Level 1, click on the *I,II* Button to get Roman numerals. For Level 2, use *A,B* for uppercase letters, and so on.

The second change hides the numbers from the previous level so they are not printed. Type the tag name into Level 2 as previously, but before leaving the line, click on the Suppress Previous Level Button. This inserts the code [-], which tells Ventura not to print the previous number. This code can appear at the very beginning or very end of the line. Without the code, the outline looks like this:

I. First Heading

I.A. first subheading
I.B. second subheading

With the suppress code inserted, it looks like this:

I. First Heading
  A. first subheading
  B. second subheading

➥ *NOTE: Clicking on the buttons at the bottom of the dialog box is merely a convenient way to enter codes. If you prefer, you can type them in directly.*

Figure 8-22 shows how the dialog box would look for a three-level traditional style outline. Note the periods at the end of the lines, which provide the punctuation after the numbers.

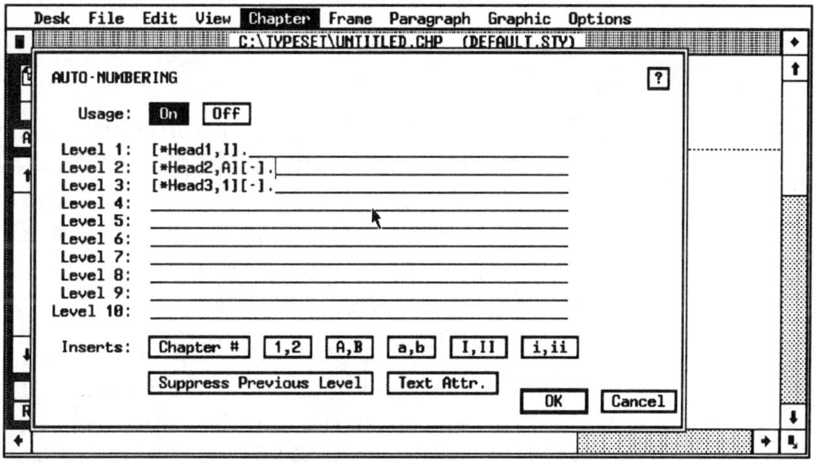

Figure 8-22. The Auto-Numbering dialog box to establish a three-level outline. The indents would be created by formatting in Paragraph mode.

Restarting the numbering

The techniques explained so far create a numbering system that is sequential throughout the chapter. We've been showing examples with the list items grouped one after another:

1. First item
2. Second item
3. Third item

But you can also use Auto-Numbering with paragraphs scattered throughout the chapter. You could place the first paragraph on page one, and the second on page eight. Ventura will still number them correctly and in sequence.

In some cases, you may want to start from one again within the same chapter. For example, perhaps you are compiling parts lists for a repair manual, and you have several lists in the chapter. You want each of those lists to start over again at one.

A simple technique enables you to reset to one. Basically, it tricks Ventura into resetting the numbering. To understand how it works, glance over this numbering scheme:

```
1.
   1.1.
   1.2.
   1.3
2.
   2.1.
   2.2.
```

Notice how the Level 2 numbering started at one and proceeded sequentially (1.1, 1.2, etc.) *until it encountered a Level 1 number.* At that point, it reset and started over (2.1, 2.2, etc.) To reset numbering, then, all you have to do is use Level 1 to contain a tag that resets the numbering to one. When Ventura sees the Level 1 tag, it resets all the lower levels to one.

For instance, you could put Body Text on Level 1. That way, Ventura will reset the numbering to one every time it sees a Body Text paragraph. However, we don't want a number next to every paragraph of Body Text. Fortunately, Ventura provides a way to count the paragraphs (thereby resetting the lower levels to one) without actually printing the numbers. To keep Ventura from inserting the numbers, move the text cursor to the code line and erase the comma and number. To insert numbers for Body Text, the code reads like this:

```
Level 1: [*BODY TEXT, 1]
```

To count Body Text without inserting numbers, it reads like this:

```
Level 1: [*BODY TEXT]
```

Now that you've used Body Text at Level 1 to reset lists, you can construct a numbering scheme using Levels 2 through 10.

If you prefer, you can use another tag name to reset numbering. For instance, you could create a tag with formatting identical to Body Text. Call it Reset. Now you have the ability to reset the numbering at will by tagging the previous paragraph as Reset.

Starting with a number other than one

To start the list with something other than one, erase the *1* in the code and type in the new number. For instance, to start the list with the number five, the code would read:

```
[*List,5]
```

Renumbering the chapter

When you close the Auto-Numbering dialog box you immediately see the numbers Ventura has generated. However, if you later make changes to the text, Ventura has to be told about it. To do this, you select Renumber Chapter from the Chapter menu. You can also use the keyboard shortcut Ctrl-B.

By giving the Renumber Chapter command, you instruct Ventura to start from page one and count everything over again. A simple example: You have a chapter with four numbered sections:

1 2 3 4

Later you decide to delete #3 and put #2 last. At this point, the section numbers look like this:

1 4 2

By selecting Renumber Chapter, you force Ventura to recount from the beginning:

1 2 3

Adding chapter numbers

Chapter numbers can be added to any or all levels of a numbering scheme. Simply place the text cursor where you want the number, and click on the Chapter # Button. Ventura inserts the chapter numbering code ([C#]) at that spot. For instance, here's how to include chapter numbers in our previous section numbering example:

```
Level 1: [C#].[*Heading,1].

Level 2: [C#].[*Subheading,1].
```

Notice that we put a period after the chapter number, as well as after the section number. The result would look something like this in the first chapter:

1.1 First Heading
  1.1.1. First subheading
  1.1.2. Second subheading

And something like this by the seventh chapter:

7.1. First Heading
  7.1.1. First subheading
  7.1.2. Second subheading

Numbers in the margin

Some documents require that section numbers appear on the same line as the text, but in the left margin. You can achieve this format automatically in Ventura by making a few slight changes to the tags.

First change the Z_SEC tags. Use the Alignment dialog box to create an outdent for the first line. On the Fixed Indent line, enter the amount you want to push the section numbers left. Be careful not to push them so far left that they disappear into the gutter. Then make sure the tags for the text paragraphs themselves do not have any indent in the Alignment dialog box. If they do, remove this indent so the first line of the text is flush with the left margin.

Generating text with Auto-Numbering

Earlier in this section we showed you how to add punctuation by typing it into the Auto-Numbering dialog box. In the same fashion, you can ask Ventura to automatically insert text during auto-numbering. You can insert text along with numbers, or you can do away with the numbers entirely and use Ventura strictly for text.

The example below shows how to ask Ventura to automatically generate the word "CAUTION!" every time it sees the Warning tag in the document. Notice that we erased the comma and the number inside the square code brackets. Because of this, Ventura will not print any numbers, only the text. We've shown it on Level 1, but you can produce the exact same effect using any of the 10 levels:

```
Level 1: [*Warning]CAUTION!
```

Section symbols and text attributes with Auto-Numbering

You saw above how to use Auto-Numbering to generate text. You can also generate symbols. For instance, some legal documents require section symbols " § ." You can enter a section symbol, or any other non-keyboard symbol, directly into the Auto-Numbering dialog box with bracket codes. Put the text cursor on the line where you want the symbol to appear. Type in the bracket code. If you prefer, you can click on the Text Attr. button, which inserts the code <D> for you. Erase the D and type the correct code between the brackets. For instance, the decimal code for section symbols (§) is <185>.

You can also insert bracket codes for different attributes, fonts, point sizes, or colors, as described in Chapter Three, "Creating Text."

Auto-Numbering for ruling lines

You can also use the Auto-Numbering dialog box to attach a ruling line to a paragraph. This is most useful when you want to add a second line in a different format. For instance, if you turn to any first level heading in this book, you will notice a double rule above — a short, thick rule combined with a long, thin rule. The thick rule is attached to the heading tag. The thin rule, however, is generated automatically by Auto-Numbering:

```
Level 3: [*Head1]<|>
```

This code creates a paragraph containing nothing but a thin

space (the <|> bracket code stands for a thin space). We then used Paragraph mode to attach the thin ruling line to this paragraph.

We eliminated the numbers because we don't want numbers associated with our headings. We added the thin space because you cannot generate an empty paragraph. You have at least two ways to get around this. First, you can allow numbering, but set the font to white. The numbers, therefore, will be invisible — white text on a white background. Alternatively, you can eliminate the numbering, but generate a space character. For instance, by entering the bracket code <|> on a line, you generate a thin space. The code <~> generates an en space.

Combining numbering

In this section, we have hinted at the vast array of effects possible with Auto-Numbering. One key to effective use of this function is to understand that you can combine multiple effects within the dialog box. There is absolutely nothing to say you cannot use Level 2 for something else just because you've already used Level 1 for numbering. For instance, here's just one possible way you might load up the Auto-Numbering dialog box with useful functions:

Level 1: Reset tag to reset lists to 1.

Level 2: Make simple lists.

Levels 3, 4, 5: Format three-level traditional outline.

Level 6: Generate the word *NOTE:* to accompany special notations in the text.

Level 7: Generate the word *WARNING:* to accompany cautionary paragraphs.

Level 8: Generate the word *Chapter* to accompany chapter numbers.

Levels 9 and 10: Generate ruling lines for special formatting effects.

Tab settings

Ventura Publisher permits you to apply up to 16 tab settings. A tab is a means of *jumping* text to a new location. When Ventura encounters a tab stop, it jumps to the spot you have specified (Figure 8-23). Ventura can fill the space with dots, underlines, blank spaces, or other characters.

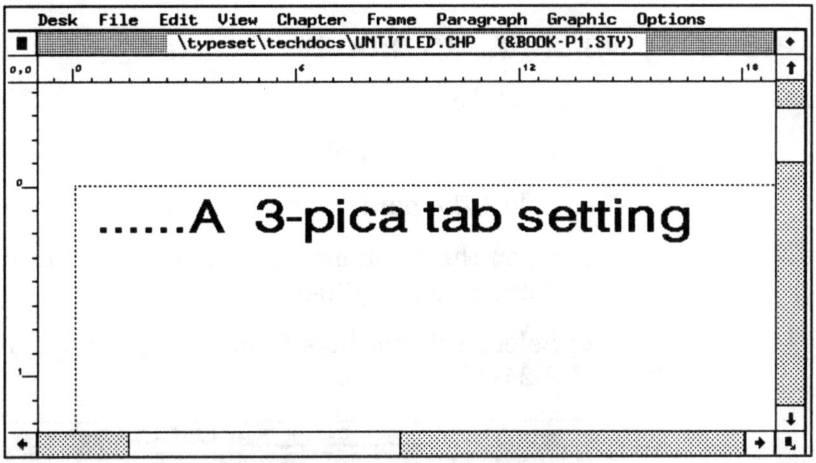

Figure 8-23. As you can see from the ruler, Ventura was instructed to jump to a position three picas from the left margin. In addition, it has filled the space with dots.

Setting a tab stop has four steps:

- choosing which tab stop to set
- choosing the type of tab (the alignment)
- choosing the location of the tab
- choosing the leader character (if any)

Before we get into specifics, we should make a few comments about *when* to use tab stops and about their limitations. Tabs are used most frequently for tables. They are appropriate if the table has one line per entry.

However, if you produce tables with more than one line per entry, you should not use tab stops. You can use the side-by-side paragraphs method explained in Chapter Ten, or you can use Table mode.

Tab settings have several limitations. First, as implied above, they cannot wrap words. If you have a long entry that belongs on more than one line, you must manually enter line breaks to force new lines. Otherwise, the tab may force it outside the right margin. Second, you cannot have tab stops in justified text. To be more accurate, you can set tabs, but they will not take effect until you use the Alignment dialog box to choose a different alignment option.

Choosing which tab to modify

To set tabs:

- Enable Paragraph mode.
- Select the paragraph to which you wish to assign tabs.
- Open the Alignment dialog box and confirm that the alignment is not justified.
- Select Tab Settings from the Paragraph menu (see Figure 8-24).

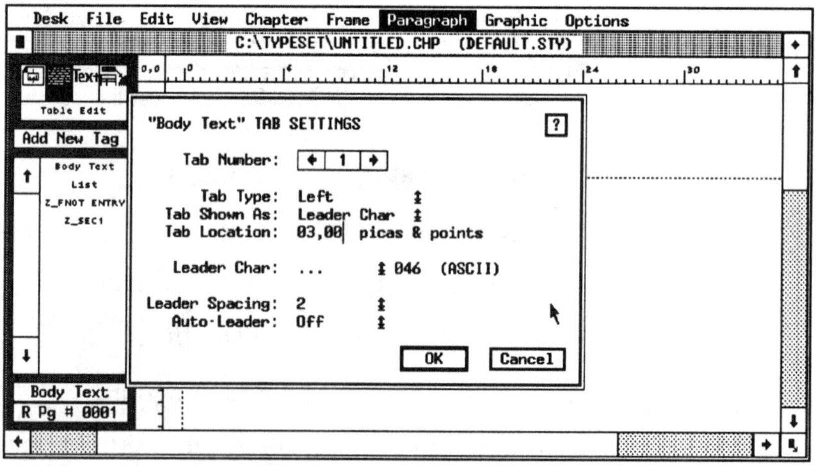

Figure 8-24. The Tab Settings dialog box.

- Move the mouse cursor to the Tab Number line. Click on the arrows to select the tab you want to modify.

Tabs are identified by number. These numbers are a simple sequence, and have nothing to do with the position of the tab on the page. However, each tab has to be to the right of the previous one — you cannot jump backwards with a tab setting. Likewise, tabs do not take effect if the text cursor is already to the right of the tab stop. For instance, suppose you set tabs at one, two, and three inches. You type in some text that, let's say, reaches to 2.5 inches. If you press the tab key now, the cursor will jump to tab stop number three, at three inches. It will not jump backwards to the first stop at one inch.

Incidentally, you can set more than one tab at a time. Once you've set one, just click the Tab Number line to get to the next one. Click OK when you've finished with them all.

Choosing the tab type

To enable the tab stop, select a tab type: Left, Right, Center, or Decimal. Figure 8-25 illustrates the differences.

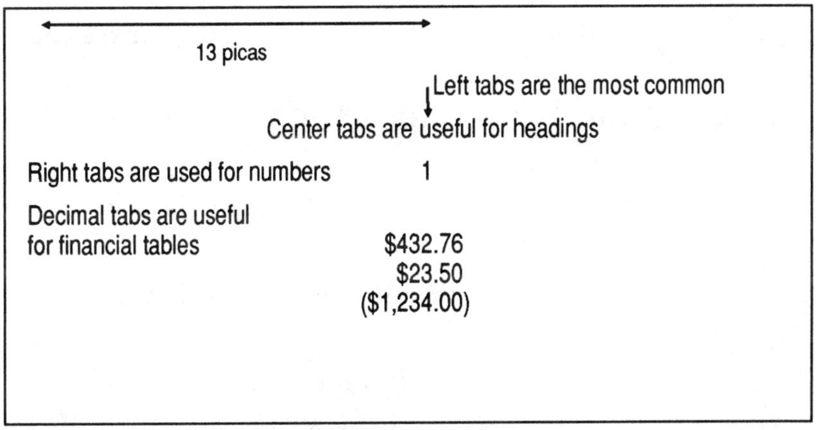

Figure 8-25. The four lines shown here all have the tab stop set at 13 picas, but all four are different tab types.

Choosing the tab location

There are two keys to accurately setting tab locations. The first is to realize that tabs are measured from the left margin, not from the left edge of the page. If you are using the rulers to gauge the position, reset the zero point to the edge of the margin. That way, the ruler will show the correct measurements. Otherwise, you must subtract the left margin setting to get the correct tab setting.

The second key is to forget whatever you may have learned about tabs in high school typing class. Typewriters, and some word processors, have tabs set at fixed intervals (often one inch). To jump to a position four inches from the margin, you would press the tab key four times. When working in Ventura, however, you should abandon this approach. To jump four inches, set a single tab stop at (you guessed it) four inches.

Always set as few tab stops as possible. First, tab settings take up memory. Second, using multiple tab stops makes it impossible to know how many times to press the tab key to create the spacing you want. Third, with multiple tab stops you cannot change the spacing with a single change of the tab settings. You have to change all (or most) of them. Instead, use one and only one tab stop for each jump you want to make.

Unfortunately, Ventura's default style sheet has tabs set in the fashion of a typewriter. This is poor typographic practice. In Chapter Five, we explain how to create a new default style sheet that corrects this and other mistakes.

Choosing the leader character

When the tab character jumps to a new location, it creates a gap. You can fill this gap with blank spaces, or with any other character.

Ventura's default is for open (blank) spaces. To create leader characters:

- Select Tab Shown As: Leader Char.
- Move to the Leader Char line and use the pop-up menu to choose the type of character you want.

Ventura provides four options. *Spaces* places blank spaces as leader characters. It accomplishes the same thing as choosing Tab Shown As Open Space. The option ... creates leader dots. The option _ creates an underline. The *Custom* option lets you specify any character you want to fill the gap.

To create a custom leader character, choose Custom, then type in the decimal (ASCII) equivalent of the character you want. For instance, to use an asterisk as a leader character, you would type in 042.

You can also vary the spacing between the characters.

- Use the pop-up menu from Leader Spacing to choose the number of extra spaces you want between each leader character.

For instance, an underline with no spacing (Leader Spacing: 0) creates a solid line. An underline with spacing creates a dashed line effect. Figure 8-26 shows some common leader effects.

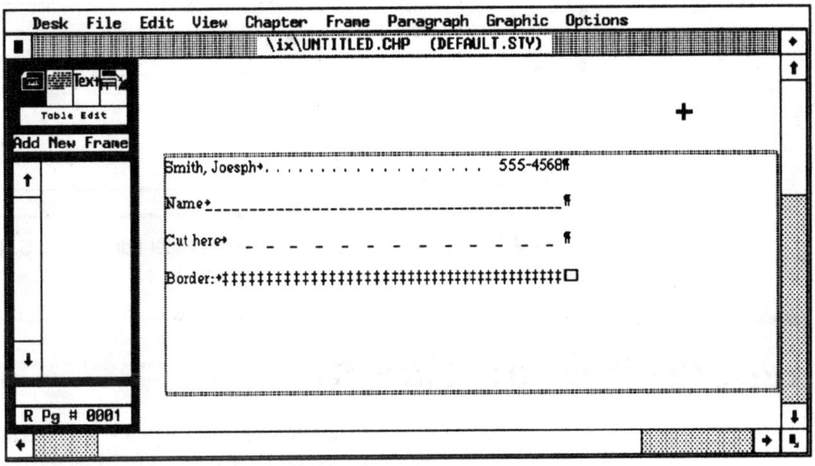

Figure 8-26. A few of the many leader characters you can create with tab settings.

➥ *NOTE: Leader dots in directories and listings are more attractive if you set them up with two tab stops. The first tab stop creates the dots between the listing and the number. The second tab stop creates a small amount of open space between the dots and the number. This makes the numbers easier to read. It also makes the page more attractive, because all the leader dots end at the same spot, even if the numbers vary in size.*

Leader dots without tabs

Choose Auto-Leader: On to create leader dots without the need to insert a tab character. Ventura will automatically place dots between the end of the paragraph and the right column (Figure 8-27). You can vary their spacing with the Leader Spacing line.

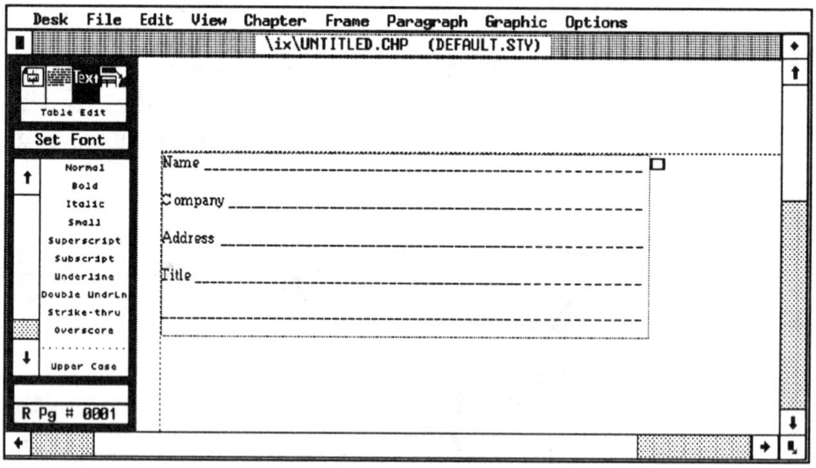

Figure 8-27. Leader dots created with Auto-Leader from the Tab Settings dialog box are useful for creating forms.

Typographic functions

Power users will discover an array of built-in typographic features for fine-tuning the look of pages. This section covers four important dialog boxes from the Paragraph menu:

- Define Colors, for setting font color or shading
- Special Effects, for adding true typographic bullets, drop caps and other effects
- Attribute Overrides, for changing the look of underscores, superscripts, and other effects
- Paragraph Typography, for kerning, letter spacing, and space band control.

As we go along, we will mention other dialog boxes that affect typography.

Defining colors

Ventura lets you assign colors to text, ruling lines, frame backgrounds, and graphics patterns. Despite its name, most people will not use the Define Colors dialog box for changing colors. Instead, they will find it more useful for defining and modifying shades of gray for background patterns.

Changing colors

Changing colors may be useful in two situations. First, if you own a color printer, you can create exactly the color you want for the output device. You can choose from millions of possible color combinations, but you can only define seven colors at a time.

Second, if you have a color monitor, you can use this option to change the on-screen colors so they more closely match what you want on the page. Even though the actual colors will be created in the printing process with ink, you can use the screen as a preview.

To modify colors, select Define Colors from the Paragraph menu (Figure 8-28).

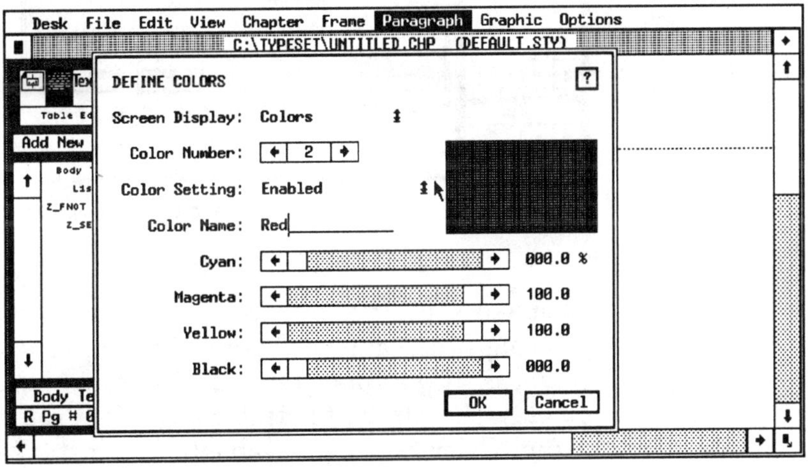

Figure 8-28. The Define Colors dialog box.

Select Screen Display: Colors if you have a color monitor and want to use it to preview the colors. Choose Screen Display: Shades of Gray if you have a black and white monitor, or if you prefer to see colors represented by different patterns of gray.

Now use the Color Number line to choose the number of the color you wish to modify. Ventura has nine colors, but you cannot modify white (0) and black (1). That leaves numbers two through seven available. Click on the arrows to change the number.

As you click, you will see the names that are currently assigned. These are the same names that appear in dialog boxes such as Font, Frame Background, Ruling Lines, and so on. To give a color a new name, simply type it onto the Color Name line. The changes you make to the names appear immediately in the other dialog boxes, where they are available for selection (Figure 8-29).

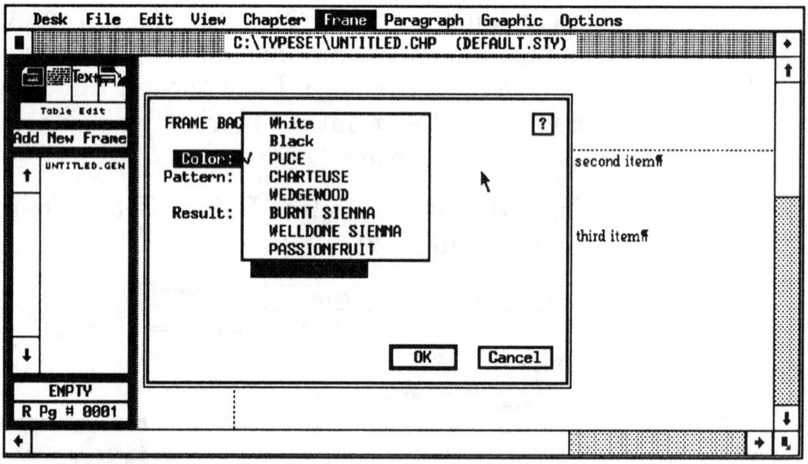

Figure 8-29. After you redefine and rename colors, the new names appear in other dialog boxes.

To make a color active during Ventura's spot color overlay printing function (see Chapter Seven), choose Color Setting: Enabled. If you plan to print separate sheets for spot color overlays, be careful to disable any colors you won't actually be using (Color Setting: Disabled). For instance, if you wanted red headlines and black text, you should disable all the colors except red. Otherwise, Ventura will print a separate page for each of the other colors even though you are not using them.

The four slider bars at the bottom of the dialog box control the colors. You can add or subtract amounts of cyan, magenta, or yellow. By mixing these colors in different percentages, you can create millions of combinations. You can slide the bars with the mouse. Or you can click on the arrows to increase by two tenths of a percent with each click. If you have a color monitor, the results show in the preview box.

Changing shades of gray

To change any color to a shade of gray, slide the top three color bars all the way to the left. This turns off all the color. Then use the bottom slider bar to add as much gray as you want. We recommend following the industry practice of naming these shades according to the percentage of gray, as shown on the right side of the Black slider bar. For instance, Gray 5%, Gray 10%, Gray 15%, and so on. Enter these names on the Color Name line.

If you are using a laser printer, be aware that patterns with small percentages of gray print darker on a laser than on a typesetter. You might, therefore, want to compensate. Conversely, patterns with a high percentage of gray look darker on a laser printer.

For instance, even the lightest of Ventura's standard patterns is too dark for use behind text of less than 14 points (when printed on a laser printer). By using the Define Colors dialog box you can easily create lighter patterns that are more appropriate for sidebars and tint blocks. Rather than assign a standard pattern to a frame background, you would assign a color instead — except that the color has been redefined as a shade of gray.

You can put these shades into frames, graphics, or hollow boxes. With a PostScript printer, you can also have gray text. In addition to the standard patterns offered in many of these dialog boxes, you can have different, alternative gray patterns by assigning colors instead of patterns. Do not mix patterns with colors that have been redefined as shades of gray.

Special Effects

The Special Effects option from the Paragraph menu provides two useful features: big first characters and bullets. To use either of these:

- Enable Paragraph mode.

- Select the paragraph you want to change.
- Select Special Effects from the Paragraph menu.

You can have a big first character, or a bullet character, but not both. *Big first characters* are useful for setting off the first paragraph in a chapter (as done in this book), article, or section. Once you click on the Big First Char button, you can then specify its size and position.

To set the size of the big first character, click on Set Font Properties within the Special Effects dialog box. The Font dialog box will appear, where you can choose the size and style you want. The choices you make here will affect only the first character, not the rest of the paragraph. Most people choose a bold font two or three times as large as the rest of the paragraph. Thus, if the paragraph is 12-point Times normal, the big first character would typically be Times Bold in the 24- to 36-point range.

The most common choice is to use the same face as the rest of the paragraph. Quite often, however, designers will vary the first character for contrast (Figure 8-30).

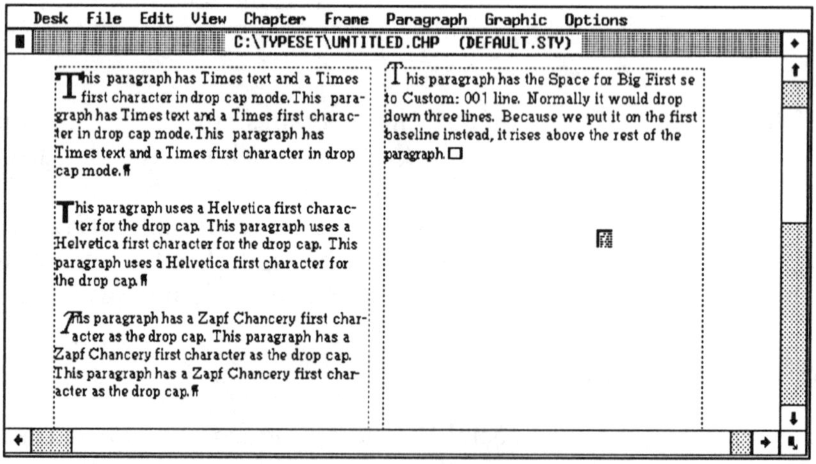

Figure 8-30. A few of the effects possible with a big first character.

Changing the position of the big first character

When you create a big first character, Ventura positions it for you. You can change this position.

When you select the font size, Ventura creates space for the new, enlarged character. It treats the character as a *drop cap* — a larger character that extends down into the text paragraph. First it decides how many lines to indent. It does this by aligning the top of the big first character with the top of the paragraph. Then it indents these lines as far as necessary.

You have two options for changing the position of the big first character. First, you can change the number of lines it drops down. Space for Big First is usually set to Normal. The number of lines shows in gray text. To change this setting, click on Custom, and type in the number of lines you want instead. As you can see in Figure 8-30, this can force the big first character to rise above the rest of the paragraph. Conversely, you might want to drop it further into the text, to leave room to put a black or shaded box around the big first character.

If this function does not accomplish what you're after, you can make even finer adjustments in the Font dialog box. Click on Set Font Properties again to bring up the dialog box (Figure 8-31). Then use the Shift function to move the big first character up or down.

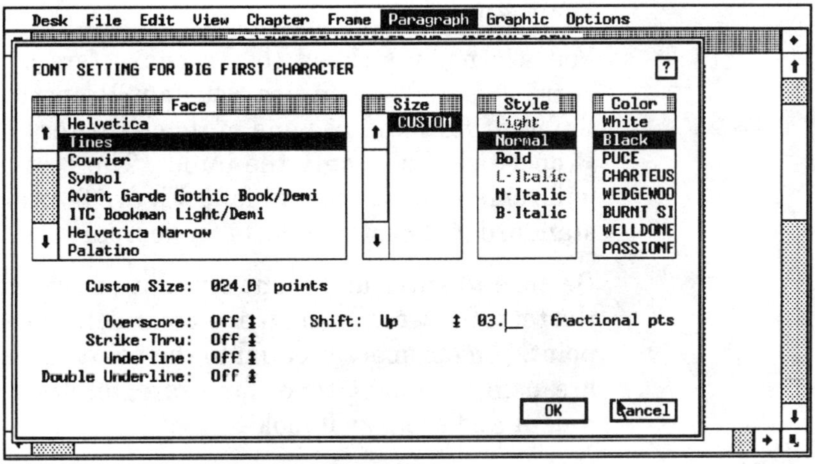

Figure 8-31. Use the shift function from the Font dialog box to adjust the Big First Character up or down.

➥*NOTE: Ventura's on-screen preview is only an approximation. You may have to produce a test print to accurately judge very fine spacing adjustments.*

Bullets

The Special Effects dialog box also controls bullet characters at the beginning of a paragraph. Bullets are an excellent way to set off lists, warnings, notes, and so on. To create a bullet:

- Select Special Effect: Bullet.
- Select the bullet you want by clicking on one of the options next to the Show Bullet As: line.
- Move to the Indent After Bullet line and type in the amount of space you wish to leave between the bullet and the rest of the paragraph.
- Use Set Font Properties to change the size of the bullet, and/or make it bold, and/or switch to a different font (if necessary).

If you do not use Set Font Properties, the bullet is the same type size as the rest of the paragraph.

If you do not like any of the bullet styles shown, you can create others by clicking Other. Then move the cursor to the Bullet Char line and type in the decimal equivalent of the character you want.

You are not restricted to the characters available with the current font. You can use Set Font Properties to switch to a different font and use one of its characters instead. Set Font Properties affects only the bullet. The rest of the paragraph will remain in its original font. Figure 8-32 shows a few of the standard and custom effects for comparison.

Be sure to enter an indent amount or the bullet will overlap the text. We recommend a one-em indention as a good starting point. (An em space is equal to the point size of the type. If you are using 10-point type, for example, start with a 10-point indent and see how it looks.)

➥*NOTE: You can also enter bullet characters at the beginning of a paragraph (or anywhere within a paragraph) by holding down*

- A paragraph with a solid bullet.

□ A paragraph with a hollow box bullet.

■ A paragraph with a filled box bullet.

☞ A paragraph with a pointing hand bullet.

➥ A paragraph with a curved arrow bullet.

✔ A paragraph with a check mark bullet.

Figure 8-32. A few of the bullets you can create with the Special Effects dialog box.

the Alt key and typing the decimal equivalent. However, if you want the rest of the paragraph to be indented automatically, you should use the Special Effects dialog box.

Hanging bullets

You can create bullets that hang in the left margin. First create a bullet as explained above. Note the amount of the Indent After Bullet. Now go to the Alignment dialog box. Choose First Line: Outdent. For the In/Outdent Width, enter the same amount as the Indent After Bullet. The Indent After Bullet pushes the paragraph right. The First Line: Outdent pushes it left again. The end result is that the paragraph lines up at the original margin, but the bullet hangs out to the left.

Attribute Overrides

The Attribute Overrides dialog box (Figure 8-33) lets you adjust the positioning and size of several text attributes:

- Underline
- Overscore
- Superscript
- Subscript
- Small Caps

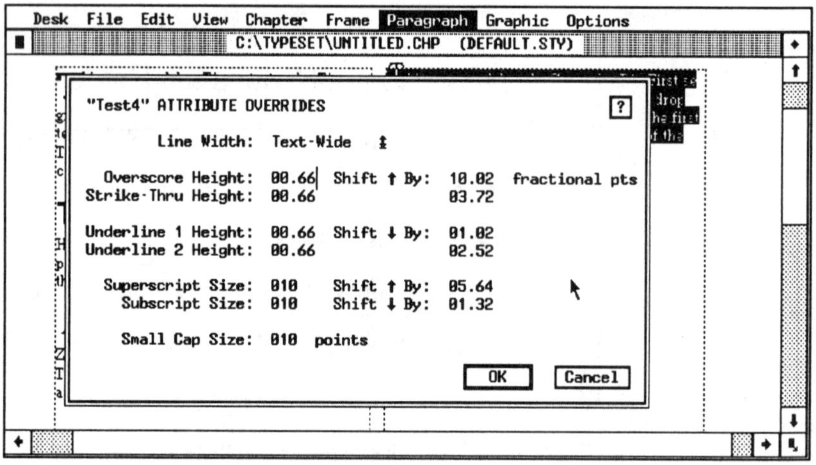

Figure 8-33. The Attribute Overrides dialog box.

These attributes are available from the Assignment List in Text mode. Normally, Ventura makes these choices for you. For instance, it positions the underline for you when you make this choice. When you choose superscripts, it automatically chooses a font size two points smaller than the rest of the paragraph.

To overrule these default choices, enter new values in this dialog box. In addition, you can choose whether underlines and overscores will be the width of the words or the entire width of the margin. Margin-wide lines are useful for creating table effects and special graphic designs.

Incidentally, you can use Superscript, Subscript, and Small Cap as shortcuts for font changes. You can specify any font size in the Attribute Overrides dialog box (including fonts larger than the paragraph). In addition, you can choose not to have super- and subscripts shift from the baseline. By selecting three different font sizes and assigning them to these attributes, you can select them at any time from the Assignment List in Text mode.

Paragraph Typography

Ventura Publisher has a wide range of typographical spacing controls. To apply these controls to a tag:

- Enable Paragraph mode.

- Select a paragraph with the correct tag.
- Make the changes and click OK.

The choices made in the Paragraph Typography dialog box (Figure 8-34) apply only to the selected paragraph. Let's examine it from top to bottom to learn how it can help achieve professional-looking results.

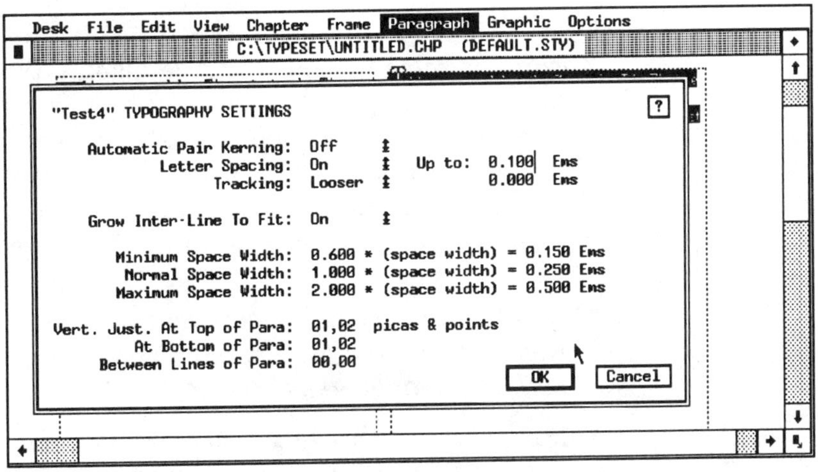

Figure 8-34. The Paragraph Typography dialog box.

Automatic Pair Kerning is the first option. Kerning reduces the spaces between selected pairs of letters to make them look better. The letters *A* and *V* provide an example:

AV

AV

The top example shows normal spacing. The bottom example has been kerned. Notice how the shapes of the two letters permit them to be pulled together slightly for a more attractive appearance.

Automatic kerning is accomplished by building a kerning table for each font. These lists contain different pairs of letters that need special spacing, with the amounts the spacing should be changed. By selecting Automatic Pair Kerning: On, you are telling Ventura to consult this table, and make minute adjustments in spacing if necessary.

Kerning tables must be supplied with the font. Ventura does not create them on its own. All of the fonts supplied with Ventura Publisher have kerning information. Most third-party font vendors also include kerning information with their products.

Kerning is most obvious in large display type. It also subtly improves the appearance of body text. We recommend that kerning be used throughout most documents, for every tag. However, kerning the body text will increase formatting time. If you have an old, slow computer and response time is a problem, consider turning kerning off to speed it up.

➡ *NOTE: Kerning takes effect only if you previously selected Pair Kerning: On from the Chapter Typography dialog box to turn kerning off for the entire document.*

Ventura lets you choose whether or not to show kerning on the screen. Set Preferences from the Options menu includes a line specifying which type sizes should be kerned on screen. On-screen kerning slows down the display and has little value. Screen fonts are only an approximation of the printed version. Their on-screen kerning, therefore, is only an approximation as well. In most cases, it makes sense not to show kerning on the screen. At most, select kerning only for large type sizes (24 points and larger).

Letter Spacing is the next option. To understand its effect, you should grasp how Ventura justifies lines. It tries to fit as many words on each line as possible by adjusting the spaces between words. If the space between words falls below the preset minimum (shown in this same dialog box), then Ventura moves the last word to the next line. Likewise, it adds space between words if necessary to stretch out the type to fit between the margins.

Occasionally, this leads to *rivers,* large gaps between words. Letter spacing cures this defect by adding space between letters as well as between words. It does not affect most lines. But *loose lines* — lines with an unacceptable amount of space between words — usually look better if a tiny amount of space is added between all the letters.

When should you use letter spacing? It is only required for tags that are justified. Generally you can do without it if you have only one fairly long column. Narrow columns, however, often need letter spacing. If you are unsure if it's needed, select Show Loose Lines from the Options menu. This highlights all loose lines. The more loose lines, the more value to letter spacing.

To use letter spacing:

- Choose Letter Spacing: On.
- Enter the maximum amount of space to allow between letters. A typical value is 0.100 ems. Anything higher than 0.150 ems may cause problems if the space between letters approaches the size of the space between words.
- Set Minimum Space Width less than 1.000, for instance 0.600.
- Set Normal Space Width to 1.000.
- Set Maximum Space Width to greater than 1.000, for instance 2.000.

These width settings give Ventura the latitude it needs to compress or expand word spacing first, before it resorts to letter spacing.

Ventura's letter-spacing feature increases the room between letters, but only if necessary to improve the appearance of a particular line. The *Tracking* command, by contrast, forces Ventura to add or subtract space between each and every letter on each and every line.

Tracking Off
TrackingTighter
T r a c k i n g   L o o s e r

The most common application for tracking is to improve the appearance of display type. We have already explained kerning, which decreases the spacing between certain pairs of letters. Tracking applies to all the letters. The larger the type, the greater the need to reduce the space between letters. As type is enlarged, the proportional amount of space needed decreases. When 36-point type is spaced the same as 10-point type, it looks too loose, even though the proportional amounts are the same.

You specify tracking in ems. One em is equivalent to the point size of the type. Thus, for 12-point type one em equals 12 points; for 24-point type, one em equals 24 points. The amount varies widely according to the printer, the type size, and your personal taste. We cannot give you any hard and fast rules. We do think, however, that display type larger than 16 points should be tracked tighter. Many designers feel type should be spaced so the letters almost (but not quite) touch. Experiment to find the right amounts. Create a series of tags, and tighten each one a different amount. It's best to experiment with tracking in units of 0.05 ems or so.

You can even use tracking on body text. Be careful, however, not to sacrifice legibility.

Grow Inter-Line To Fit causes Ventura to automatically add more space between lines if you put big letters into the middle of a paragraph. One most common application is in scientific and technical papers where you occasionally want to insert a formula or equation within a paragraph. Unless the line spacing is enlarged, the larger font will overlap the lines above and below.

When the line spacing is expanded, however, it creates an unsightly gap in the middle of the paragraph. For this reason, we do not recommend it except for special applications.

The *Minimum, Normal* and *Maximum Space Widths* control the space between words. The smaller the amount of the Normal Space Width, the closer words are together. The smaller the amount you set as the Minimum Space Width, the closer Ventura spaces words when trying to squeeze as many words as possible onto a line. The larger the Maximum Space Width, the wider the space Ventura will allow when trying to stretch a line out, before it resorts to letter spacing.

The numbers shown are a percentage of the normal width. For a tighter look, enter a lower percentage for the normal space width. Anything less than 75% (0.750) for Body Text usually results in lines that are so crowded that they are difficult to read.

Chapter Eleven covers the vertical justification options in the Paragraph Typography dialog box.

Manual kerning

We saw above how Ventura implements automatic pair kerning. There may be other times when you want to manually change the spacing between letters. For these situations, Ventura Publisher provides a manual kerning feature. Tracking adds or subtracts space between every letter in the paragraph. Manual kerning adds or subtracts space only for the letters you select.

Manual kerning takes place in Text mode, since that is the only mode in which you can select individual letters.

- Enable Text mode.
- Highlight the letters to be kerned.
- Hold down the Shift key. Press the left arrow to move the letters closer together. Press the right arrow to move them farther apart.

If you prefer, you can accomplish the same function by highlighting the text and choosing Set Font. Choose Kern: Looser to add space between the letters. Choose Kern: Tighter to subtract space. Enter the amount in ems. It is usually best to experiment with kerning in units of 0.05 ems.

Manual kerning is appropriate for headlines and logos. Don't use it to reduce the space between letters of an entire logo or headline. In that case, the tracking feature is a better way to accomplish the effect.

Table 8-2 summarizes the typographic effects possible with Ventura Publisher, and offers some application information on each.

Table 8-2. Summary chart for typography.

Function	Effect	Dialog Box	Typical Uses
Pair Kerning	Adjust spacing between certain loose letter pairs throughout document	Chapter Typography Frame Typography Paragraph Typography	Headlines and display type; professional publications
Manual Kerning	Adjust space between two letters at one point in the document	Set Font (Also keyboard control)	Headlines and display type; special effects
Tracking	Adjust letter spacing equally within a line	Paragraph Typography	Aiding readability of lengthy text blocks; copyfitting
Grow Inter-Line	Adjust line spacing automatically when font size changes	Paragraph Typography	Equations; free-form text
Letter Spacing	Resolve "river" problem in loose lines of text	Paragraph Typography	Extremely narrow columns; unhyphenated text
Space Widths	Control spacing between words	Paragraph Typography	Reduce overall "whiteness" of text; alleviate rivers problem
Attribute Overrides	Change size and position of underlines, overscores, sub- and superscripts, and small caps	Attribute Overrides	Redlining; forms; mathematical expressions
Big First Character	Create dropped or raised initial capital letter	Big First Character	Book chapters; magazine articles
Bullets	Automatically generate "flag "character and outdent from text	Special Effects	Lists; instruction booklets; directories; forms; questionnaires

Hyphenation options

Beginning users rarely give thought to Ventura's hyphenation. They are quite happy with the default settings. However, more advanced users will discover that the program has several hyphenation options and controls:

- Change hyphenation algorithms
- Hyphenate foreign languages
- Customize the hyphenation
- Suppress hyphenation

Ventura's hyphenation feature comes into play when text files are loaded. It looks at each word and adds discretionary hyphens according to preprogrammed rules. These discretionary hyphens tell Ventura where it can safely break a word if necessary to justify a line. This method is sometimes called logic-based hyphenation. Because English is not a very logical language, Ventura also contains an exception dictionary. The exception dictionary overrides decisions made by the hyphenation algorithm.

Hyphenation can be turned on or off for any paragraph. The control is located in the Alignment dialog box (Figure 8-35). In general, hyphenation should be off for headlines and other display type. It should be on for most other paragraphs.

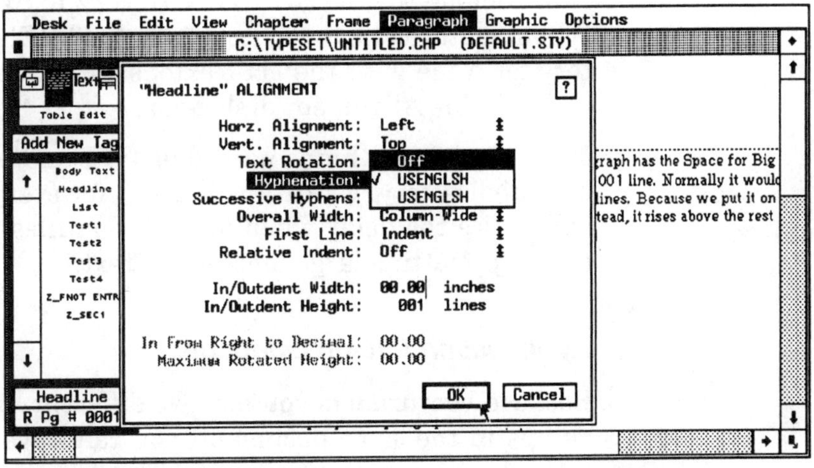

Figure 8-35. Select Hyphenation: Off for headlines and other paragraphs that should never be hyphenated.

Changing hyphenation dictionaries

Ventura's standard hyphenation algorithm shows in the Alignment dialog box as USENGLSH. It rarely adds an incorrect hyphen, but it sometimes misses hyphenation opportunities. This is most noticeable in publications with narrow, justified columns. Such formats demand frequent hyphenation to avoid rivers and white space gaps.

If you create multi-column documents, or you want improved hyphenation, you can choose a more efficient algorithm in place of the default version:

- Use DOS to copy the hyphenation file USENGLS2.HY1 to the \VENTURA subdirectory on your hard disk. Rename the file to SLOWENGL.HY2.
- Run Ventura. Open a chapter and enable Paragraph mode.
- Open the Alignment dialog box for every tag you wish to hyphenate with the slower, more accurate dictionary. Select Hyphenation: SLOWENGL.

You can use two algorithms in the same document, so it is not necessary to use the slow algorithm for every tag. However, if you want Ventura to automatically use the slow algorithm for every tag in every document, remove the original USENGLSH.HY1 file from the \VENTURA subdirectory. Now rename the file SLOWENGL.HY2 to SLOWENGL.HY1. When Ventura starts up, it looks in the \VENTURA subdirectory for a file with the HY1 extension and makes it the first choice in the Alignment dialog box.

If the slow algorithm is named as HY1 and is the only one in the subdirectory, Ventura will use it for every document. You will notice the delay when loading text files, or when adding and reformatting large amounts of text.

Hyphenating foreign languages

Because Ventura lets you use two different hyphenation algorithms in the same document, you can have one for English and one for another language. This capability is useful for dual-language publications, such as government documents that must show two official languages. You can have one set of tags for English and another set for the foreign language. Use the Alignment dialog box to specify the correct algorithm for each tag.

To add hyphenation for French, Spanish, Italian, German, or British English, use DOS to copy the appropriate algorithm from the Utilities that came with Ventura. Copy it to the \VENTURA subdirectory on the hard disk. All the algorithms have the extension HY2. USENGLISH will show as the first hyphenation option and the foreign language as the second. Do not copy more than one extra algorithm to the subdirectory. (Or if you do, don't allow it to duplicate the HY1 and HY2 extensions.)

Customizing hyphenation

Ventura Publisher provides a dictionary for your personal use. You can use it to add hyphenation points for words, or to suppress hyphenation (for instance, to make sure a product name or company name is not hyphenated). Add too many words and you will slow down hyphenation. But, within reason, you can add words if you find Ventura's logic does not hyphenate them as you like.

To add words, use your word processor to insert them into the ASCII file HYPHUSER.DIC on the \VENTURA subdirectory. The file already has a few words in it to get you started. Remember that the hyphens you enter here will only appear in the document if the word happens to fall at the end of a line. Be sure to save in ASCII mode. Follow these rules:

- Enter words in lowercase only.
- Alphabetic order
- One word per line
- Type in hyphens where you want them to appear in the word.
- Type an asterisk between each letter after the eighth letter.

This last rule needs further explanation. The hyphenation algorithm looks in the user dictionary, but it only reads the first seven letters of each word. To force it to read further, you must place an asterisk in front of each extra letter. Thus, to enter plural into the user dictionary, you would type:

```
plu-ral
```

Plural has only six letters. But to add indefatigable, you would type:

```
in-de-fat-*i*g*a-*b*l*e
```

If you want, you can do away with asterisks after the final hyphen. For instance, if you enter `con-sid-e*r-*a*b*l*e`, Ventura will correctly hyphenate that word, even though it contains more than seven letters. If you enter `con-sid-e*r-*able`, it will also hyphenate consideration and considerate, because the algorithm will only read to the *a*.

You can also enter words you do *not* want hyphenated. For example, you might want a multi-syllable company name to remain intact, so it is never divided at the end of a line. To make it unavailable for hyphenation, enter it as described above *without any hyphens*. For instance:

```
micropublishing
```

You can even create separate hyphenation dictionaries for separate applications. For example, you might have one dictionary HYPHUSER.MED for medical terms, another HYPHUSER.LAW for legal terms, etc. In order to activate one of these application dictionaries, first make a backup copy of the original exception dictionary. Now put the new dictionary in the Ventura subdirectory and name it HYPHUSER.DIC.

Suppressing hyphenation

You can suppress hyphenation in several ways, some of which we have already mentioned in passing. To tell Ventura *never* to hyphenate a word, enter it into the user hyphenation dictionary without any hyphens.

To suppress hyphenation for certain tags (while leaving it on for the rest of the document), select a paragraph with that tag, then choose Hyphenation: Off from the Alignment dialog box.

To suppress hyphenation for a single word at one spot only, enter a discretionary hyphen (Ctrl-hyphen) immediately in front of the word.

Tips for hyphenation

TIP *By adding the renaming process* to batch files that also load Ventura, you can create different batch files that automatically rename different language algorithms and/or different user dictionaries for different document types. You could have one for French and English documents, another for French and German translations, another for legal documents (with a special legal user dictionary), one for technical documents, and so on.

TIP *If your word processor lets you create a user dictionary* for spell-checking, you can merge proper names from this dictionary into the HYPHUSER.DIC file.

We have explored many of Ventura's advanced functions in this chapter. These functions demonstrate the superiority of this software for producing sophisticated documents in a short amount of time. But this is not the whole story. You can extend Ventura's capabilities even further — *if* you know the tricks, tips, and inside secrets. In the next chapter of this book, we present special techniques for power users.

Chapter Nine

Advanced Tips & Techniques

This chapter presents a series of tips, tricks, and shortcuts that make Ventura faster and easier to use. We suggest you skim through this chapter to locate the techniques that can help with your particular job. We made the explanations as to-the-point as possible. We assume that you understand the basic skills from earlier chapters. Our goal is to point you toward power techniques you might miss on your own.

This chapter is devoted to techniques that apply to any type of document. (If you are looking for help on specific document types or formatting effects, turn to Chapter Ten, "Special Document Formats.") You will find two sections. The first explains how to create an efficient systems environment. The second passes on performance techniques.

Creating a systems environment

"Systems environment" is a phrase we borrowed from the mainframe world. It refers to the process of setting things up — the computer, the software, the work process — for maximum productivity.

Once you've mastered the basics of Ventura, your attention turns to making it as efficient and comfortable as possible — in other words, to make it fit the way you like to work. This section covers a variety of ways to customize Ventura:

- Establishing and saving preferences
- Setting up the hard disk
- Using batch files

Establishing and saving preferences

Ventura has a variety of controls that affect how it operates and how it appears on screen. We have described these controls below. We have also included charts that show which settings to choose for speed, for accuracy, and for WYSIWYG preview. At the end of the section, we explain how to save these settings for reuse. As you will see, you can store and reuse different preferences on the same computer.

Most preference settings are found in the Options menu (Figure 9-1). Let's step through some of the key functions.

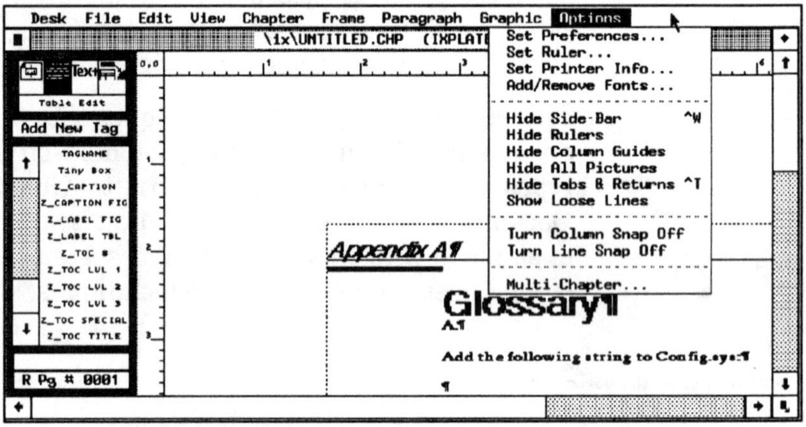

Figure 9-1. The Options menu controls most of Ventura's customization alternatives.

Set Preferences

The Set Preferences dialog box (Figure 9-2) controls more options than any other.

Generated Tags governs the tags Ventura creates on its own for such things as headers, footers, captions, and so on. Generated Tags: Hidden means they will not appear on the Assignment List. Generated Tags: Shown means they will be

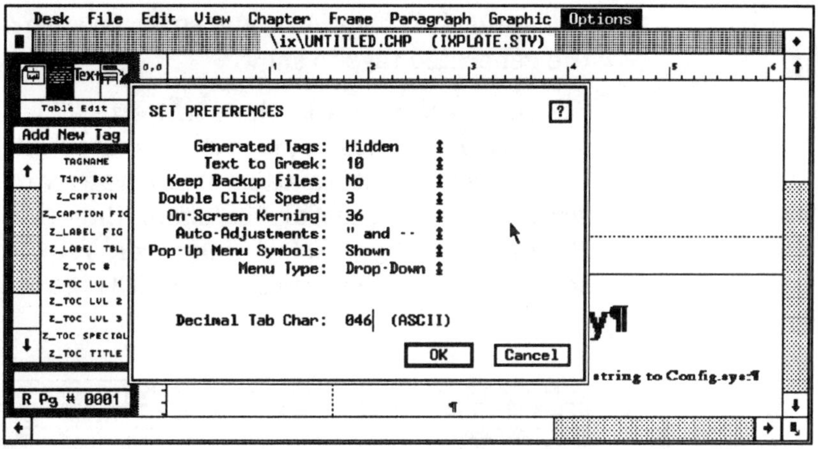

Figure 9-2. The Set Preferences dialog box.

visible. Since generated tags always begin with *Z_*, they show up at the bottom of the list (Figure 9-3).

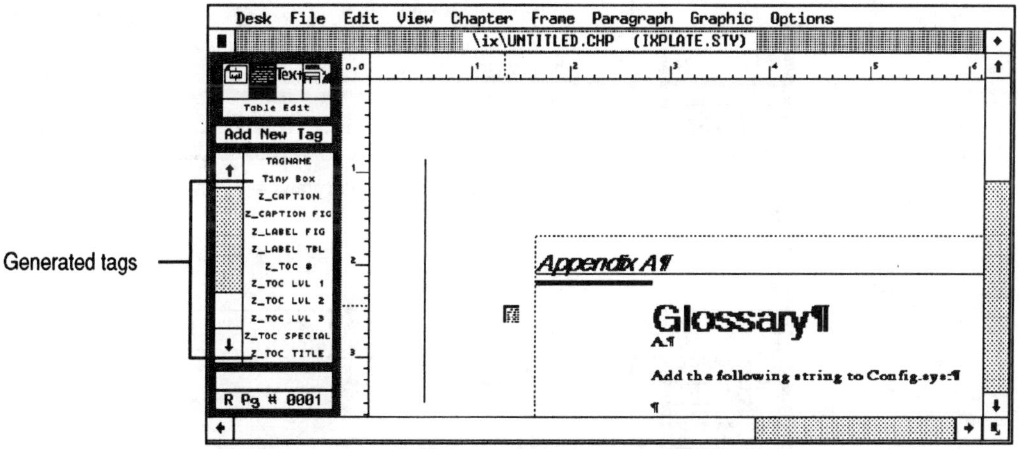

Figure 9-3. Ventura's generated tags begin with the letter *Z*. They do not show up on the Assignment List unless you select Generated Tags: Shown.

The theory behind leaving them hidden is that Ventura does the assigning, so you don't need to have them available. In practice, however, it is not unusual to mistag a paragraph, and need to retag it correctly. Since the Z-tags are all at the end of the list, they don't get in the way. In addition, many users need to have more than one caption format, for instance. In such cases, it makes sense to name the additional formats

Z_Caption1, Z_Caption2, and so on. In such a case, you'll want the generated tags to show.

Text to Greek refers to the point size at which Ventura substitutes gray bands in place of actual text. If you select Text to Greek: None, Ventura attempts to draw every character on the screen, even if they are so small that they cannot be read (Figure 9-4). If you select a number, Ventura turns anything that size or smaller into gray bands (Figure 9-5).

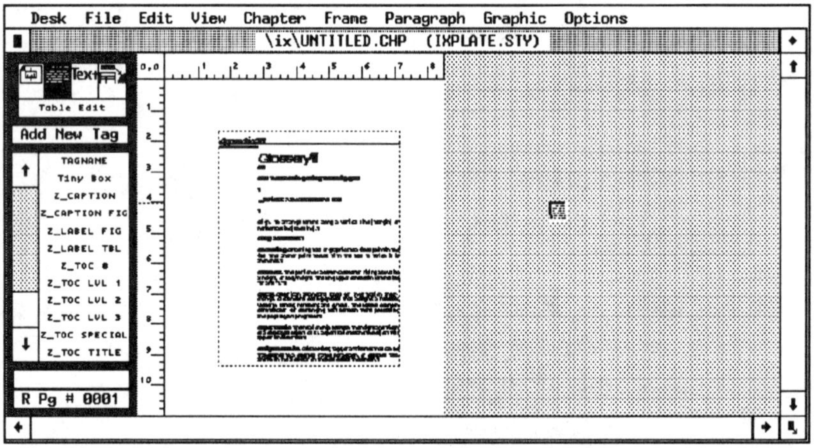

Figure 9-4. If you select Text to Greek: None, Ventura draws every character, even those that are too small to read.

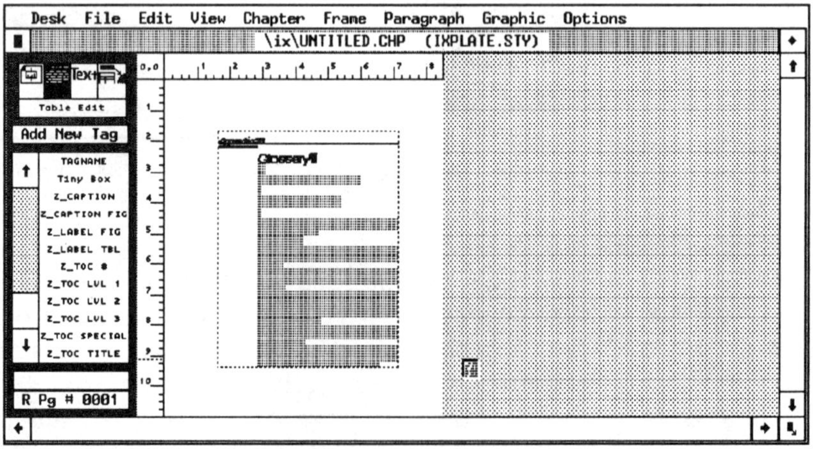

Figure 9-5. Because this example has Text to Greek: 6, Ventura has substituted gray bands for the smaller type.

The numbers refer to the height of the characters in pixels on the screen. Why bother to greek the text? Greeking greatly decreases the screen redraw time. For maximum speed, therefore, ask Ventura to greek smaller sizes. Generally speaking, anything less than *6* is unreadable, so *6* is a good starting point. However, for visualizing layouts, sometimes it helps to see the shape of the characters, even if you can't read them correctly. In those cases, choose Text to Greek: None.

Keep Backup Files refers to the chapter file, style sheet, and text file. If you select Yes, Ventura creates new files, with the same name and the first letter of the extension changed to $. Thus, SAMPLE.CHP becomes SAMPLE.$HP, SAMPLE.STY becomes SAMPLE.$TY, and so on. Ventura leaves these files behind when you close a chapter. If you select No, Ventura creates these backup files for its own use, but then it erases them when you close the chapter.

Yes is the safer choice. If you have a system crash, you can use DOS to rename the backup files to the original extensions, and load the old version. That way, you lose only the work you did since the last time you saved the chapter. However, this system has the disadvantage of strewing lots of backup files around your hard disk. You will need to periodically clean them off to free up space for current applications.

Because Ventura creates backup files anyway, you can often recover with DOS even if you've chosen Keep Backup Files: No. If the system crashes during a work session, look for files with the $ extension. Ventura doesn't erase them until you close the chapter (that is, until you open a new one or quit Ventura).

Double-Click Speed controls how long Ventura waits for a double click before starting an action. Double-clicking is a shortcut for selecting and then clicking OK. Every time you click, Ventura waits a specific amount of time to see if you will click again, thereby turning the original action into a double click. The lower the number, the longer Ventura waits (and, therefore, the slower its response time). The higher the number, the less Ventura waits. If you don't use the double-click method, choose Fast — there's no sense having Ventura waiting around if you won't be using the double click anyway. If you do use double click, the number you select depends on the speed of your index finger. The faster you are able to double-click, the higher the number you can pick.

On-Screen Kerning governs whether or not Ventura attempts to imitate the printed kerning on screen. It only applies if you have (1) set Pair Kerning: On with Chapter Typography *and* (2) selected Automatic Pair Kerning: On with Paragraph Typography. Since screen fonts are only rough approximations of the printed fonts, on-screen kerning can never be precise. In general, it serves only to slow down the screen display without adding any real benefits. We recommend On-Screen Kerning: None for most applications. If you are doing demanding applications where kerning is a consideration, you may want to select On-Screen Kerning: 24, which shows it for type size of 24 points or above. Kerning is difficult to detect on screen for smaller sizes. The choice you make here has no effect one way or another on the kerning for the printed page.

Auto-Adjustments refers to two separate and very different options. Auto-Adjustments: Style means that Ventura automatically changes the inter-line spacing every time you change the font size. Ventura changes spacing the same amount you change the font. Assume you have 12-point type with inter-line spacing of 14.00 fractional pts. You increase the font to 14 points — an increase of roughly 16.66%. Ventura then increases the inter-line spacing the same 16.66% — in this case, to about 16.34 fractional pts. You can override this choice with the Spacing dialog box.

Such odd spacing sizes are poor typographic practice. We recommend that you avoid choosing Auto-Adjustments: Styles. This same pop-up menu, however, provides access to a useful conversion feature. The selection Auto-Adjustments: " and -- automatically converts inch marks (") to true open and close quotes (“ and ”) and double hyphens (- -) to em dashes (—). The conversion takes place when Ventura brings in the text file. It is set up to allow you to continue to use inch marks with numerals as an abbreviation for inches. Most users should choose this option. If you don’t want either one, select Auto-Adjustments: None.

Pop-Up Menu Symbols refers to the up/down arrows in dialog boxes that signal the existence of a pop-up menu. Whether or not you have the symbols hidden or shown, the menus work in the same way. The menu appears if you hold down the mouse button anywhere to the left of the symbol (or where the symbol would have been if it is hidden). The symbols aren't necessary for the operation of the menus, or to remember where to press, but they are a good reminder of which selections have pop-up menus available and which ones don't. We recommend choosing Pop-Up Menu Symbols: Shown.

Menu Type controls the way in which you access the menus. If you choose Drop-Down, the menus descend the moment you touch them with the mouse cursor. To activate a choice, you highlight it and click the button. If you choose Pull-Down, menus do not appear until you click and hold the mouse button. To activate a choice, you drag the mouse to highlight the selection, then release the button. If you are converting from a different computer system or operating environment with pull-down menus, you may want to select that style to make the transition easier.

Decimal Tab Char governs the character used for decimal alignment. In the United States, this character is the period (ASCII 046), as in 12.44. Many European countries, however, use the comma (ASCII 044) instead, as in 12,44. To tell Ventura to align numbers around the comma instead of the period, enter 044 on this line. Otherwise, leave the default setting of 046 for the period.

Set Ruler

This dialog box controls the units and zero point of the onscreen rulers (Figure 9-6). You can use inches, centimeters, or picas for the horizontal and/or the vertical ruler. If you wish to match the traditional newspaper system, you can select picas for the horizontal and inches for the vertical.

You can also change the zero point. Many people prefer to do this interactively with the mouse. If you prefer, you can set it here. For instance, if you know that your left margin is six picas (one inch), you might want to set the horizontal zero point to one inch. That way you can more easily gauge such things as In From Left spacing, Tab Settings, and indents, all of which measure from the left margin, not the left edge of the page.

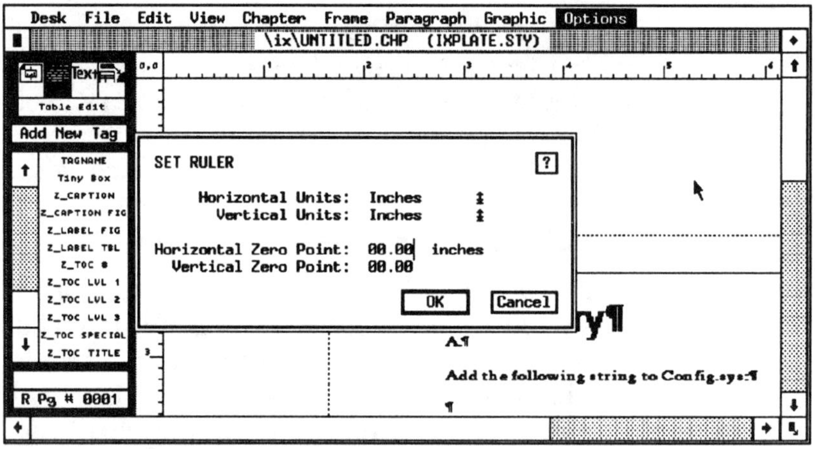

Figure 9-6. The Set Ruler dialog box.

Screen display options

Six of the selections from the Options menu affect the screen display. We will briefly describe them and their uses.

Show/Hide Side-Bar

This option toggles the Side-Bar on and off. With the Side-Bar gone, you can see and work on more of your document at one time (Figure 9-7).

Many users initially shy away from hiding the Side-Bar, since

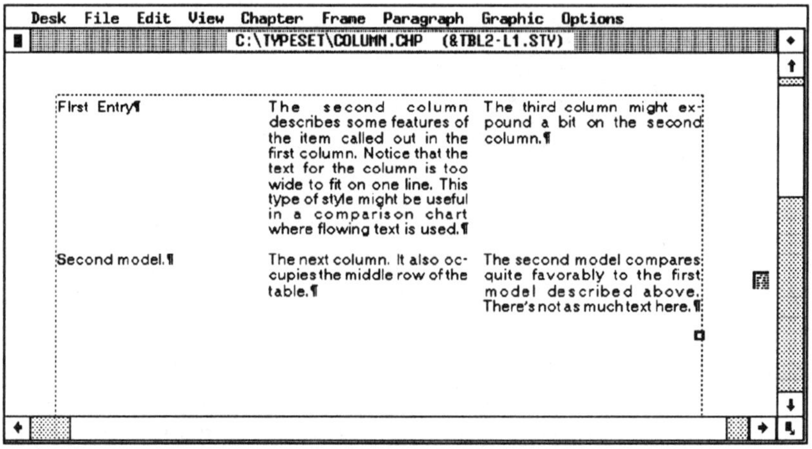

Figure 9-7. By hiding the Side-Bar, you can see more of the document at one time.

it controls so many important functions. However, if you take the time to learn Ventura's keyboard shortcuts, you will discover that you can perform most actions with the Side-Bar hidden. For instance, Ctrl-2 activates the Addition Button. Likewise, you can change modes with the keyboard, and tag paragraphs with the function keys. If you can't afford a big-screen monitor, hiding the Side-Bar is one way to improve the efficiency of your current display. You can also use the keyboard shortcut Ctrl-W to toggle the Side-Bar on or off.

Show/Hide Rulers

This choice toggles the ruler display on or off. Working with the rulers on makes it easier to measure and specify settings. Working with them off speeds the screen redraw and fits slightly more of the page into the workspace. You must show both rulers; you cannot select just one. To change the units or the zero point, use Set Ruler from the Options menu.

Show/Hide Column Guides

This toggle turns on (or off) a non-printing border around the columns. Working with the column guides visible makes it easier to position frames, to create balanced layouts, and to visualize the live area. Working with them off gives you a better preview of what readers will see on the printed page.

Show/Hide Picture

This choice can hide all the pictures in the document, or any picture individually. To hide an individual picture, enable Frame mode and select the frame containing the picture. When you pull down the Options menu you will see the selection Show (or Hide) This Picture. To hide all the pictures in the document, select the Underlying Page in Frame mode, then pull down the Options menu and select Show (or Hide) All Pictures. If you pull down the Options menu in any mode other than Frame mode, it controls all pictures.

Hiding pictures greatly improves the speed of the screen display. We recommend hiding pictures all the time except when you are specifically working with a given frame. If you are working on a page with several pictures, hide all the pictures in the document, then show only the the one you are working on right now.

When you print a document with hidden pictures, Ventura lets you choose whether or not to hide them during printing, too.

Show/Hide Tabs & Returns

This selection should have been named *Show/Hide Editing Marks* because it applies to more than just tabs and returns. It toggles the screen display of several other important symbols as well, including end-of-file symbols, line breaks, and special spacing characters.

Working with these marks shown makes editing easier, faster, and more accurate. Working with them hidden gives you a screen preview more like the printed page.

Show Loose Lines

This option toggles the display of lines where Ventura has had to space words too far apart. You can view and control the maximum space between words in the Paragraph Typography dialog box. Ventura tries not to exceed these maximums, but sometimes it must to justify a line. Loose lines are highlighted (shown in reverse video) when you select this option.

Basically, this option is for those who feel they must have the utmost in typographic sophistication. It permits them to spotlight problem lines so they can attempt to correct them (by editing, by inserting hyphens, by using Letter Spacing, and so on).

Turn Column Snap On/Off

This option forces new frames to align with the columns. If you move or stretch a frame close to a column guide, it automatically snaps to the position of the guide, as if magnetically attracted. In most cases, it is wise to work with Column Snap On. Ventura is more accurate at aligning elements than you can be. However, in some cases you will need to turn it off to position frames at other locations.

Turn Line Snap On/Off

This function forces new frames to align with the inter-line spacing of Body Text. It is helpful in creating pleasing layouts where all the page elements relate to one another. If Body Text has an inter-line spacing of one pica (12 fractional pts), then all frames will snap vertically to units of one pica.

You can also use Line Snap to create a bigger grid. Temporarily set Body Text to a large line spacing — for instance, six picas. Line Snap will then force all frames to become increments of six picas. When you've finished drawing the frames, return Body Text to its normal setting.

You can override column and Line Snap with the Sizing & Scaling dialog box. However, the next time you move or resize the frame, it will again snap to the guides (unless you have turned the snap-to features off).

Different settings for different purposes

In everyday working situations, you will often find yourself switching back and forth between different preferences for different purposes. Table 9-1 shows three possible combinations. The settings for "speed" refer to Ventura. They reduce the overhead so Ventura can reformat and redraw the screen as fast as possible. This combination of settings will be most appreciated by those who work on slower XT-class computers.

The settings for *efficiency* help you do a better, faster job of positioning and editing page elements. In general, they turn on a variety of layout marks and aids. The settings for *WYSIWYG preview* turn off marks that will not appear in the final printout. Most of these WYSIWYG settings, however, slow Ventura down. Taken together, they can make quite a difference, so you may want to reserve these settings until the end, for a final, on-screen proof. You will also notice that we recommend Paragraph mode for accurate previews, since that mode turns off the non-printing borders around frames and graphics.

Table 9-1. Preference settings for different purposes.

	SPEED	EFFICIENCY	WYSIWYG PREVIEW
Generated Tags	Hidden	Shown	Hidden
Text to Greek	8	6	None
Double Click Speed	Fast	4	NA
On-Screen Kerning	None	24	All
Set Ruler	NA	orizontal zero point to left margin	NA
Show/Hide Side-Bar	Shown	Shown	Hidden
Show/Hide Rulers	Hidden	Shown	Hidden
Show/Hide Column Guides	Hidden	Shown	Hidden
Show/Hide Pictures	Hidden	Hidden (except when working on a specific picture)	Shown
Column Snap	On	On	NA
Line Snap	On	On	NA
Mode	NA	NA	aragraph

Saving preferences for reuse

When you exit the program, Ventura saves the current settings in a file called VP.INF. For instance, if you have the rulers showing when you quit, Ventura remembers and turns them on again when you start up the next session.

You can save different *versions* of Ventura — that is, you can save different combinations of options. You could, for instance, have a speed version, an efficiency version, and a preview version, as explained above. A more likely application, however, is to permit different people to use Ventura on the same machine. Each person can have his or her own customized version, without the need to reset the options each time.

The key is to modify the batch file that loads Ventura, which is called VP.BAT. You simply specify a different subdirectory for each user's personalized INF file. Thus, Bill's INF file might be stored as C:\BILL\VP.INF, while Susan's is stored as C:\SUSAN\VP.INF. Bill would load Ventura with a batch file that specified his INF. Susan would load it with a slightly different batch file that specified the location of her INF file.

Later in this chapter we explain how to use batch files for this purpose and for other enhancements.

Setting up the hard disk

This section is about establishing a productive systems environment. One key is organizing the hard disk properly. Ventura can work with files that are scattered anywhere on the hard disk. Unfortunately, this opens the door to deficient organization. As your library of Ventura documents grows, you will find it harder and harder to locate the files you want; to archive and back up documents; and to update old documents when it is time for revision.

In its default state, Ventura stores everything in the \TYPESET directory. Soon, however, that directory becomes overcrowded with chapter, style, text, and graphics files. Just scrolling through the Item Selector becomes a pain. The solution is to set up an electronic filing system.

Paper filing systems usually work best when each project is stored in its own folder. The same holds true for electronic filing. You will find Ventura easier to work with if all the files for each project are in a separate subdirectory. That way you can back up a project in DOS just by copying the contents of the subdirectory. Likewise, you can delete an unwanted document with a single command.

Use File Type/Rename to move a text file to a new subdirectory. Use Save As New Style to move a style sheet. Use Save As to move a chapter to a new location. You must go back to the old location and delete the previous versions if you don't want them anymore. (Alternatively, you can use a third-party utility programs to move chapters with a single command.)

Tips for hard-disk management

Here are a few of the things to keep in mind as you create and name subdirectories. *Some of these tips conflict with one another.* You must mix and match between conflicting alternatives to pick the best solution for the way you like to work.

TIP *DOS permits only 112 subdirectories* in the root directory. Although this initially sounds like a large number, it is not unusual to use several dozen for programs and utilities. Depending on the nature of your work, you may find yourself with more projects (documents) than you can store in the root directory. To avoid this problem, put document subdirectories under another subdirectory, where the limitation does not apply. For instance, some people store all documents in subdirectories underneath \TYPESET. Remember, however, that the longer the path, the more trouble it is to remember and type.

TIP *The shorter the subdirectory name*, the easier and faster it is to type. We like to use two-letter codes for document subdirectories — for instance, we stored this book in C:\IX. We often use the same two code letters for file names, too, making it easy to find and manipulate documents.

TIP *The shorter the subdirectory name*, the easier it is for people to forget what it means. If different people must use the same computer, you may want to forsake the convenience of short names for the safety and ease of use of longer names.

TIP *For complex documents,* use subdirectories under the subdirectories. For instance, you could have a separate sub-subdirectory for each chapter. Or a separate sub-subdirectory for pictures, to keep them from overcrowding and confusing the main subdirectory. Sub-subdirectories are not necessary for shorter, simpler projects.

TIP *Identical subdirectories on different computers* make it simple to share documents across computers. When we have more than one person working on a project, we set up the same document subdirectories on each machine. That way we can use DOS to copy chapters, and we know that the pointers in the chapter file will match from computer to computer.

TIP *Consider one subdirectory for drafts and a second for final copy.* Documents like newsletters can benefit from using the same file names issue after issue. That way, you can use the same template chapter. Ventura automatically loads in the same file names for each issue. It doesn't care that you changed the contents of the file in the meantime. Thus, you could have one subdirectory for the final edition of a newsletter, and a separate subdirectory for the text files of each monthly issue.

Using batch files

Advanced users can use batch files in a variety of ways to enhance Ventura. The first aspect is to understand the batch file that loads Ventura, called VP.BAT. Then you can combine VP.BAT with other batch files to customize Ventura.

The VP.BAT file

A batch file gets special treatment from DOS. When DOS sees the BAT extension, it treats each line in the file as a separate instruction. When you type VP at the DOS prompt, you are actually invoking a batch file called VP.BAT. Ventura creates this file during installation, but you can modify it to change and customize the program.

Here's a typical VP.BAT program:

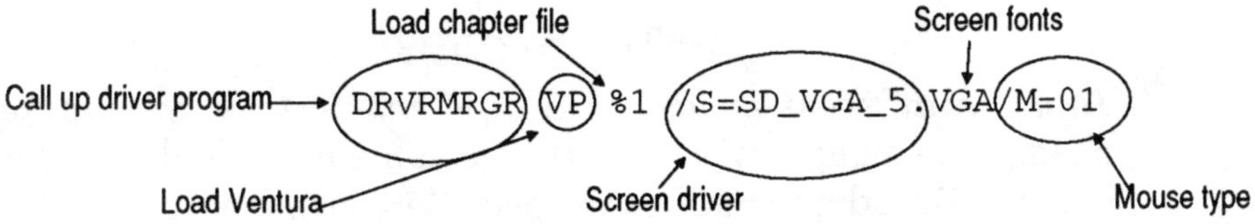

The heart of the batch file is *DRVRMRGR VP*, which loads the operating environment and Ventura. All the commands that follow are options. If you reinstall Ventura, the installation program may modify some of these options for you. Advanced users, however, can change the batch file on their own to customize Ventura without reinstalling. In addition, certain options are available only by adding to the batch file.

To edit this (or any) batch file, use a word processor or text editor capable of saving in ASCII format. Let's step through the available options so you can learn how to change them.

To open a chapter at the same time you load Ventura, simply type the name and path of the chapter after you type VP. Thus, to open C:\TEST\SAMPLE.CHP, type:
VP C:\TEST\SAMPLE at the DOS prompt and press Enter. You do not need to change the batch file to use this feature. The *%1* in the batch is a variable for the purpose of receiving the name you type in and passing it along to Ventura.

The rest of Ventura's options are controlled by *switches*. These switches are signaled by a forward slash. You use a letter to show what kind of switch it is, followed by an equals sign. For instance, the switch to specify a mouse is *M=*. After the equals sign, you type in the value you want. For instance, M=01 signifies the COM1 serial port (the zero) and the Mouse Systems mouse (the one).

You must have a screen driver switch and a mouse switch (except in the unlikely event you plan to work without a mouse). The other switches are optional. You can use them alone or in combination. To combine switches, list them one after another with no punctuation or spaces in between.

To use a different screen driver, change the value of the screen driver switch (/S=). You must first copy over the correct driver from the installation disk and place it in the \VENTURA subdirectory. Then you must enter its name in the batch file after the screen driver switch. For instance:

```
DRVRMRGR VP %1 /S=SD_CGA_5.CGA/M=01
```

To use a different mouse, or a different port for the mouse, change the mouse switch (/M=). The value is a two-digit number. The first digit signifies the port. Zero represents COM1, *1* represents COM2, and *2* or *3* both signify any other connection (such as a bus mouse). The second digit signifies the mouse type. The number *1* represents the Mouse Systems mouse, the *2* represents any MOUSE.COM or MOUSE.SYS mouse, the *3* represents the Microsoft serial mouse, and the *4* represents the IBM PS/2 mouse. For instance, to install the Microsoft serial mouse in COM2:

```
DRVRMRGR VP %1 /S=SD_VGA_5.VGA/M=13
```

So far we have discussed options that are automatically inserted by Ventura whenever you reinstall the program. There are also several options that can be entered only by editing the batch file.

To show additional drives in the Item Selector, use the /X= switch. You can access any valid drives on your system by typing their names into the Selection Line. But if you add their names with the additional drives switch, you can see them in the Item Selector (Figure 9-8).

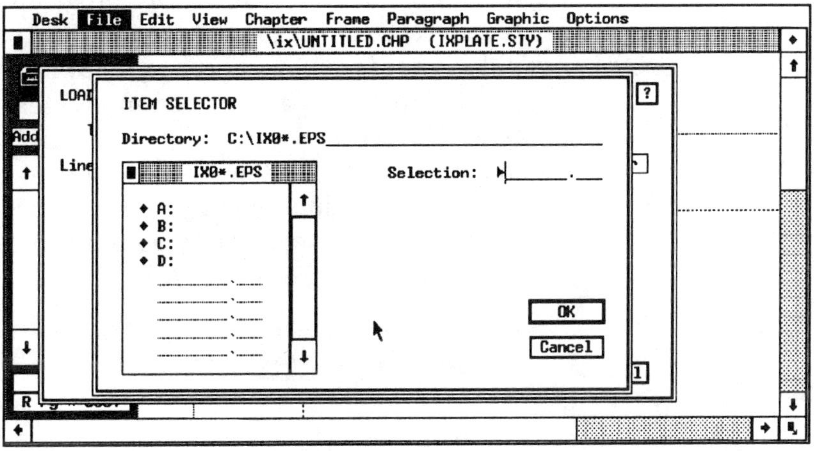

Figure 9-8. The D: drive shows on this Item Selector because the switch /X=D: was added to the VP.BAT batch file.

You can add more than one drive, one right after another. For instance:

```
DRVRMRGR VP %1 /S=SD_VGA_5.VGA/M=01/X=D:/X=E:
```

To set up a different subdirectory for the VP.INF file, use the /I= switch, followed by the full path name of the subdirectory. For instance:

```
DRVRMRGR VP %1 /S=SD_VGA_5.VGA/M=01/I=C:\BILL
```

VP.INF is the initialization file that stores the preferences and options you have specified for Ventura. If you do not use the /I= switch, it is automatically stored in the \VENTURA subdirectory. See the section titled "Saving preferences for reuse" earlier in this chapter to learn how and why to use different subdirectories to store different INF files.

To change the drive for overflow files, use the /O= switch. Normally, Ventura stores temporary files on the hard disk. To speed up operation, you can reroute the files to a RAM disk. Enter the letter designation of the drive after the switch. For instance:

```
DRVRMRGR VP %1 /S=SD_VGA_5.VGA/M=01/O=F:
```

To take memory from the screen buffer and add it to the text area, use the /A switch. When a document exceeds memory, Ventura spools portions to disk. This slows down operation and, in earlier versions, made the program less reliable. By transferring screen (graphics) memory to text, you can build longer documents before spooling becomes necessary. However, you pay a penalty, since you must steal memory used to display and convert pictures. In fact, some printers and conversions won't work without the full screen buffer. We do not recommend this option unless you do not use pictures in your documents. You can specify any amount in 1K increments up to a maximum of 32. For instance:

```
DRVRMRGR VP %1 /S=SD_VGA_5.VGA/M=01/A=16
```

Other batch files

Once you understand how to modify the VP.BAT file, you can use it together with other batch files to create different versions of the program:

- Different INF files
- Different hyphenation routines
- Different screen drivers
- With or without the PostScript preamble
- With or without a RAM disk
- With or without memory-resident utilities

In addition, you may want combinations of these options. Or you may want to set up the batch file so it automatically invokes a menu or a DOS shell when you exit. The variations are almost endless. We can't give them all to you here. What we can do is make a few general comments about how to write batch files for Ventura, followed by a few examples.

Quick course in batch files for Ventura

Since we don't have the space for a full-scale run-down on batch file programming, we will start by telling you where to get more information. Your DOS manual has the basic information, but you may not find it easy to use. You may want to consider a book instead. One of our favorites is *Staying with DOS* (Ventana Press).

Most people recommend putting batch files in their own special subdirectory, usually called C:\BATCH or something similar. Then you can put a path command in the AUTOEXEC.BAT file. AUTOEXEC.BAT is a special batch file that runs automatically when you start up the computer. A path command tells the operating system where to search for things it can't find in the current location. To tell DOS to always look in the C:\BATCH subdirectory, you would enter the following line into AUTOEXEC.BAT:

```
PATH C:\BATCH
```

You can specify multiple paths by separating them with a semicolon:

```
PATH C:\BATCH;C:\DOS;C:\UTILITY
```

If you store all the batch files in a subdirectory, and specify that subdirectory path in AUTOEXEC.BAT, you can invoke any batch file from any location. Just type the name of the batch file. DOS will automatically search in the batch file subdirectory if it can't find it in the current location.

The examples we provide are for a representative system. To use these batch files, you must type in the actual names and paths for your computer. If you are new to batch files, we recommend that you comment your efforts heavily. Not only does this make it easier for someone else to use the file, it also makes it easier for you to remember what you had in mind when you come back to revise a batch file weeks or months from now. To add a comment, begin the line with a semicolon.

The idea behind the examples below is to use batch files along with the VP.BAT file we have already explained. The basic trick is to have each batch file call up the VP.BAT file at the end. In other words, the batch file can first accomplish some function (such as renaming hyphenation dictionaries), then it can load Ventura by invoking VP.BAT. Invoking VP.BAT is as simple as typing in the letters VP on a line by itself.

If you really want to get fancy, you can add additional commands that will take place after you quit Ventura. These commands must appear in the batch file after the VP line. DOS will wait until you quit from Ventura before it executes these commands. For instance, you could set up the batch file to rename the hyphenation dictionaries back to their old names after you finish each Ventura session. Or you could instruct it to load a menuing program or DOS shell when it's through. Some of the examples below illustrate this technique.

You may also want to search the bulletin boards and user groups for special utilities to improve your batch files. If you have a modem, you can find these utilities on most Ventura bulletin boards. If not, perhaps a friend who does can download them for you. Or perhaps you can get them on a floppy disk at a users group meeting. One useful example is the shareware utility COLDBOOT.COM. This utility resets the computer (as if you had pressed Ctrl-Alt-Del), thereby clearing all the memory. It is useful when you want to remove resident programs to free up memory for Ventura.

With the general comments out of the way, you are ready to examine some examples. Remember that most of them can be combined. In addition, you can set them up as individual choices from a master menu.

Multiple INF batch files

This batch file lets different people share Ventura on the same computer. Each person can preserve his or her favorite preferences in an INF file on their own subdirectory. This batch file loads a version of Ventura with the I= switch set to load and store VP.INF from a different subdirectory.

BILL.BAT

```
DRVRMRGR VP %1 /S=SD_VGA_5.VGA/M=01/I=C:\BILL
```

You can use the same technique to create different INF settings for different versions for your own use. For instance, you could have a speed version, an efficiency version, and a preview version, as explained above. You can also set this up in a menu, so that different people access their own versions by pressing a letter or number corresponding to their names.

Different hyphenation dictionaries

You can set up different hyphenation options by first copying all of Ventura's hyphenation options to the hard disk. Then you can set up batch files that rename these hyphenation algorithms so Ventura can find them. (Ventura won't access hyphenation algorithms unless they have a specific file name.) Before returning to DOS, these batch files rename the algorithms back to their original names.

This batch file makes the slower, more accurate hyphenation algorithm the first, default choice, then changes back after the Ventura work session is over:

HYPSLOW.BAT

```
CD \VENTURA
COPY USENGLISH.HY1 USENGLISH.FAS
COPY USENGLISH.HY2 USENGLISH.SLO
COPY USENGLISH.SLO USENGLISH.HY1
COPY USENGLISH.FAS USENGLISH.HY2
DRVRMRGR VP %1 /S=SD_VGA_5.VGA/M=01
CD\VENTURA
COPY USENGLISH.FAS USENGLISH.HY1
COPY USENGLISH.SLO USENGLISH.HY2
```

Memory-resident programs

Depending on your system, the amount of memory, and other variables, you may be able to safely use certain memory-resident utilities with Ventura Publisher. However, resident utilities do rob memory that Ventura could otherwise use for building the document. For that reason, you may want to set up batch files that automatically load the resident utilities. That way, if you have a particularly long document to format, you can load a maximum memory version of Ventura (see below), eliminating the overhead of the utilities.

There are many ways to manage memory. You may prefer to use one of the many available programs that can load and unload programs. Our batch files use a very simple technique

— they put a message on screen reminding you to hit Ctrl-Alt-Del to reboot the computer if you want to clear the memory. For a more elegant solution, substitute the shareware utility COLDBOOT.COM in place of this manual technique. Or type in the correct commands for the memory manager you use.

This batch file loads the HotShot screen grabber program, then loads Ventura. Use it if you need to capture Ventura screens to print later in another document.

HOTVENT.BAT

```
CD\HSG
GRAB
DRVRMRGR VP %1 /S=SD_VGA_5.VGA/M=01
ECHO: REBOOT TO CLEAR MEMORY-RESIDENT PROGRAMS
```

The next example loads the popular Lightning disk-caching program, for faster operation. There are other good cache programs on the market. You could also clear memory by using Lightning's own unload command.

CACHE.BAT

```
L A OFF 412
DRVRMRGR VP %1 /S=SD_VGA_5.VGA/M=01
```

Document batch files

You can set up different batch files that will not only load Ventura, but automatically open the correct chapter. For instance, if you use a template chapter, the batch file could open the template. Then all you would have to do is save it under a new name to start work.

For an even more automated approach, use the same text and picture file names for each issue. For instance, you might name the lead story in a newsletter NLLEAD.TXT. The news department might go by the name of NLNEWS.TXT, and so on. Each month you would write different stories. When they were perfect, you would copy them to the old file names (NLLEAD.TXT, etc.). Since this will copy over the old versions, you should be sure to make a backup copy first.

Now set up a newsletter chapter that always looks for these file names. Your batch file can specify the same chapter name each time — for instance, NEWSLET.CHP. This chapter will also load in the same files. It won't know (or care) that you have changed those files in the meantime. With all the files in their proper frames, all you have to do is fine-tune the new articles to fit the space.

This batch file will automatically copy the constituent text files to the file names the template is expecting each month. To use this, supply the batch file with the three-letter file extension for the appropriate month; for example, type NEWSLET JAN to move all of the January files into the template.

NEWSLET.BAT

```
COPY \WORDSTAR\*.%1 \ISSUE\*.TXT
CD \VENTURA
DRVRMRGR VP \ISSUE\NEWSLET /S=SD_VGA_5.VGA /M=32
```

Performance techniques

The tips in this section will help you get more performance from Ventura. Most of them are advanced techniques that require some understanding of DOS, as well as a basic grounding in Ventura.

Adding buffers

The disk operating system provides a special area where it stores frequently used information. These buffers speed operation. A program like Ventura can find what it needs in the buffer — which uses high-speed RAM memory — rather than by searching the (relatively) slow disk.

You may be able to speed Ventura's operation slightly by increasing the number of buffers. You can control these buffers with the CONFIG.SYS file. DOS looks for this special file every time it starts up, and uses it to configure the system the way you want it. To edit this file, use the ASCII mode of a word processor or text editor.

Adding additional buffers is as simple as adding a line to the file. For instance, to increase the buffers to 30, type:

```
BUFFERS=30
```

Ventura requires a minimum of 15 buffers for proper operation. Every buffer eats about .5K of RAM, so 30 buffers will use up about 15K. This RAM is no longer available for use by Ventura in building long documents. The game, therefore, is to experiment to use the fewest possible buffers while still speeding up performance.

You are most likely to need the extra speed if you have installed additional screen fonts. If so, you may find that adding more buffers still won't do the trick. In that case, try a commercial disk-caching utility (see below), or try restricting the number of screen fonts (see Chapter Seven).

Adding a disk cache

A disk cache sets up a large buffer area for information from the hard disk. Every time you get something from the disk, the cache stores it in case you need it again. When you ask for information, the program looks first in the RAM memory of the cache. Only if it can't find it there does it resort to the slower hard disk.

There are numerous utilities on the market. Not all utilities work with all types of computers and all types of memory. Shop around to find the one that matches up best with your system. Look for a cache utility that uses as little core memory as possible. Instead, find one that uses extended or expanded memory, so you can reserve the core memory below 640K for Ventura's use. A disk cache of 512K is probably the minimum for seeing true performance improvements with Ventura. A cache of one to two megabytes is even better.

Adding a RAM disk

We have previously explained how to modify the VP.BAT program so that Ventura will store overflow files on a RAM disk. You may also want to consider loading the Ventura program files onto the RAM disk at the beginning of every work session. Then you can load and unload Ventura much more quickly if you need to use other programs in the middle of a publishing session. You must reinstall Ventura with the RAM disk operational to configure the program to look to the correct disk drive for its program files. Then you must copy over all the necessary files from the \VENTURA subdirectory to the RAM disk every day before beginning the work session.

Usually a disk cache is superior to a RAM disk, offering the same speed benefits with fewer drawbacks and much less setup. You must specifically copy information to and from a RAM disk. A disk cache, however, automatically intercepts information and stores it for reuse. If, however, you cannot use a cache for one reason or another, consider a RAM disk as an alternative.

Memory management techniques

Most users will never experience memory problems. When Ventura can't fit all of a document into RAM, it swaps out portions to the hard disk. Operation slows down, but otherwise everything works fine. However, large, complex documents may encounter memory problems.

If you have encountered memory problems or error messages, read this section for some possible solutions. Because memory is a confusing and (let's be honest) tedious subject for most users, we are going to start with solutions. At the end we will include some theory for those of you who want to know more about the inner workings.

➥*NOTE: The easiest and fastest way to overcome memory problems is to add EMS memory to your computer as explained later in this chapter.*

If your budget won't permit a memory upgrade, three strategies will help you solve memory shortcomings. First, learn to free up as much memory as possible. Second, learn which document elements are memory-hungry, so you can avoid them. Third, review our list of tricks and tips for overcoming memory shortages.

Spotting memory problems

You know that you have run into a memory-related limitation if you see one of these error messages:

```
Not enough memory to run the program. Either add
```

memory to your system or check your CONFIG.SYS and AUTOEXEC.BAT files for any drivers or resident applications that can be removed.

Fatal Error! The VP.RSC file couldn't be found or would not fit in memory.

Fatal Error! The GEM VDI screen driver couldn't be loaded.

Fatal Error! There wasn't enough memory for the screen graphics buffer.

You're out of memory. Save your document and quit the program as soon as possible.

You're trying to load a file containing a paragraph that is larger than 8000 characters. This has corrupted memory, so quit as soon as possible.

This frame is too complex to completely format. Try splitting it into two frames or reducing the number of columns, tabs, leaders, and lines of text.

There wasn't enough memory to load and hyphenate all of the text file you requested. You may have to split this chapter & file into two parts and try again.

There wasn't enough space for all the requested font files. Some fonts may not display or print correctly.

There was not enough memory to begin the archive process.

Freeing up memory

If you are running into memory problems, the first step is to free up as much RAM as possible. Here are some alternatives:

- Do not use any memory-resident applications whatsoever.
- Eliminate device drivers from the CONFIG.SYS file unless they are absolutely necessary.

- Reduce the buffers to 20 (Substitute "BUFFERS=20" for the current buffers command in the CONFIG.SYS file).
- Use only one hyphenation algorithm.
- Reduce the size of the user hyphenation dictionary if it has more than a few words in it.
- As a last resort, consider switching to an older version of DOS, which uses less RAM that your current version. For instance, DOS 3.0 uses about 15K more than DOS 2.0. Likewise, an EGA board consumes slightly more system memory than a Hercules card.
- If you have Microsoft Windows on an AT or 386 computer, you can use the file HIMEM.SYS to add 64K of DOS RAM to your system. Add the line DEVICE=HIMEM.SYS to your CONFIG.SYS file, and make sure that at least 64K of extended memory is available for it.
- You may be able to increase memory to 704K if you have an extended memory board such as the JLaser Plus AT board. The JLaser board can allocate an additional 64K of memory to DOS. Ventura Publisher will recognize this additional memory. Insert this command into the CONFIG.SYS file:

  ```
  DEVICE=JBOOT.BIN 704K
  ```

➥*NOTE: Ventura generally recognizes memory on the JLaser board as EMS memory. Unfortunately, you must have at least one megabyte of memory not allotted to EMS in order to use the JLaser for output. If you wish to disable EMS memory, you must put the switch /E=0 in your VP.BAT file.*

Avoiding memory-hungry page elements

Certain page elements eat into available memory. In particular, tabs, tags, and leader dots are memory hungry.

Eliminate unneeded tags from your style sheet since they consume memory whether used or not.

Use the Body Text tag for the most common page element. Ventura Publisher always has a body text tag. You cannot eliminate it, so make good use of it. Each time you add a tag you consume another amount of memory. You can minimize the use of additional tags by making sure the pre-existing body text is assigned to the page element that appears most often.

Use line breaks instead of paragraphs, particularly for large documents such as directories with many paragraphs per page. Wherever possible, start new lines with a line break instead of a carriage return to preserve memory.

Link chapters at print time. This suggestion is not a memory management technique *per se* but a reminder that Ventura can link multiple chapters into a publication. This publication can be printed at one time. Since Ventura prints a publication by sequentially opening and printing each individual chapter, this approach requires no more memory than does the largest chapter in the publication. Perhaps the simplest way to overcome memory problems in a long chapter is to split it into two parts and then link them when you print. It is also much easier to work on short documents.

Understanding memory requirements

Three different factors can limit available memory. You need to know about all three, since any one of them can create problems. Each of these limitations acts independently of the others; the ones that you encounter will depend on the type of system you have and the kind of documents you create. We'll describe all three.

System memory refers to the RAM memory available when Ventura Publisher loads a document. In general, you want as much as possible. The amount of system memory is determined by the total RAM (640K) minus the amounts consumed by:

- DOS
- Any device drivers present in your CONFIG.SYS file
- Any RAM-resident utilities
- The hyphenation algorithm and exception dictionary
- The first eight font descriptions in the width table

- The screen driver
- Ventura Publisher itself

Anything left is available to Ventura Publisher documents. Ventura requires that there be at least 100K of leftover memory in order for it to run, or 40K if you have EMS memory.

Frame memory. Ventura Publisher places a limit on the amount of memory that can be consumed by one frame. You will seldom encounter this limitation. If you do, you can often overcome it by dividing your page into two or more frames, using the frame-by-frame layout approach discussed in Chapter Six. For example, in a three-column document, you could create three one-column frames. If the problem is chronic throughout a long document, create repeating frames on top of the Underlying Page. We wish to emphasize that steps like these are necessary only if you run out of frame memory and you see this error message:

```
This frame is too complex to completely format.
Try splitting it into two frames or reducing the
number of columns, tabs, leaders, and lines of
text.
```

Line elements memory. Ventura Publisher places a limit on the number of lines on a page, regardless of how many frames are on that page. You may run into this memory limitation if you use a very small font, such as 6-point type, and more than three full-length columns per page. If you run out of page memory, an entire column of text may disappear from the screen. The text has not been lost. Ventura is simply not able to deal with it on this page.

Diagnosing memory problems

A little-known dialog box may help you diagnose memory problems. Select Publisher Info from the desk menu. You will see an informational dialog box (Figure 9-9).

Click on the word "Ventura" in the "Ventura Software, Inc." box. Doing this will bring up a second dialog box, as shown in Figure 9-10.

Some of the information in this dialog box is highly technical

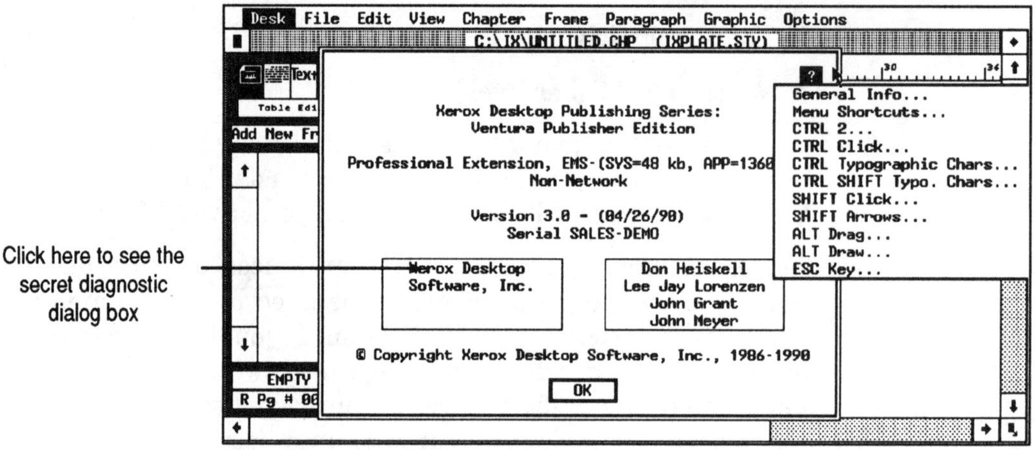

Figure 9-9. The Publisher Info dialog box.

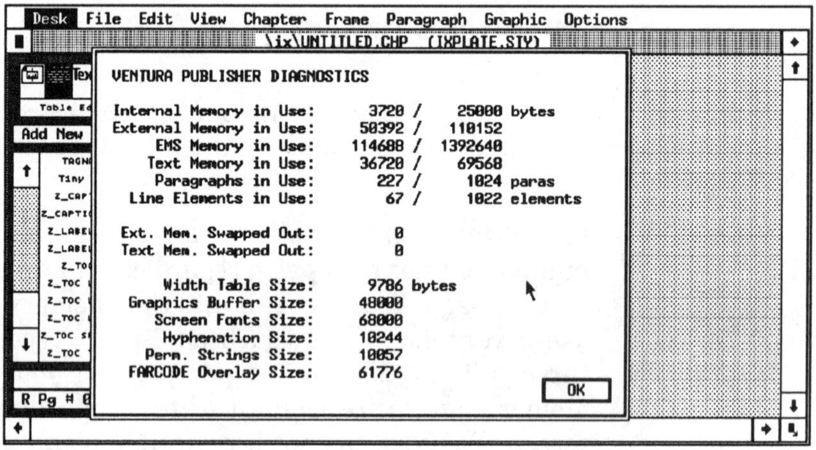

Figure 9-10. This diagnostic dialog box can help you spot memory problems.

in nature and beyond the scope of this book; however, you may be able to get some insight into your memory problems by observing the data presented here. At the top of the box is a list of memory factors. The left number shows the actual memory in use. The right number shows the total possible. If you think of the slash as standing for the phrase "in use out of a possible..." you will understand the numbers. Thus, the top line 3720 / 25000 bytes means "3720 in use out of a possible 25000."

The actual numbers you see on your screen will vary depending on your computer, your operating system, your version, your monitor, and other factors.

Internal Memory in Use is the amount of RAM for internal program functions. The number on the right is the total amount reserved. The number on the left is the amount actually used at the moment. You cannot affect these numbers.

External Memory in Use is the most important number in the dialog box. On the right it shows the total amount of RAM you have available for the document. To the left of the slash it shows how much you have used so far. When the document size exceeds the RAM available, Ventura swaps the overflow to the hard disk, slowing operations.

EMS Memory in Use refers to the amount of EMS memory available and actually used by Ventura. The number to the right shows how much EMS memory is available. The number to the left shows how much you are using so far.

Text Memory in Use displays the amount of external memory devoted to your text files. This is roughly equal to the size of the text file(s) in the Side-Bar.

Paragraphs in Use refers to the maximum number of paragraphs per chapter. In Version 3, this is 1024.

Line Elements in Use is another important number, one that will affect people who produce directories and similar documents. These documents have small type and many lines per page. Line elements are not the same as lines of text. Every line of text counts as *two* line elements. Other effects can also eat up line elements. For instance, font changes, tab settings, and leader tabs all use additional line elements. You can have 725 line elements per page (1022 if you have EMS memory). Subtract the number on the left from the number on the right to see how many line elements you have left for the current page or frame. If the result is below 100, you will soon need to break to a new page or frame.

Ext. Mem. Swapped Out shows how much of the document Ventura has had to store on disk. If the value is greater than 0, this indicates that Ventura Publisher has made use of its disk-swapping capability because the size of the document exceeded the External Memory available.

Text Memory Swapped Out shows how much text memory has been swapped to the disk.

Width Table Size displays the memory taken up by the current width table. In general, it does not pay to remove fonts from the width table to reduce its size, since Ventura puts only the first few fonts into RAM and gets the others from disk as needed.

Graphics Buffer Size is the amount of RAM reserved to convert and display pictures on the screen. If you do not have pictures in your document, you can transfer some of this buffer for use by the document. To do so, use the /A= switch in the VP.BAT file as explained earlier in the chapter.

Screen Fonts Size is the amount of RAM used by the screen fonts. You can reduce this amount by deleting screen font sizes that you do not use in your documents. Or you can make up different groups of screen fonts for different documents, so you always use the minimum amount of RAM for screen fonts. See Chapter Seven.

Hyphenation Size shows the RAM taken by the hyphenation algorithm and exception dictionary. Ventura must have at least one hyphenation algorithm and one exception dictionary. If you have a second algorithm, and/or a very large user dictionary, you can delete them to free up some RAM.

Perm. Strings Size shows the RAM used for program functions such as error messages. You cannot reduce this amount.

FARCODE Overlay Size refers to the program segments outside the limits of the C compiler used to develop Ventura. Ventura maintains this information in RAM for quick access. You cannot reduce this amount.

Adding EMS memory

EMS, the Expanded Memory Specification, is a standard method of addressing more memory than allowed by MS-DOS (640K). If you have installed additional memory that conforms to the EMS standard, Ventura can make use of it. With EMS memory, Ventura can (1) run more quickly, (2) create longer and more complex documents, and (3) use the advanced Edco hyphenation dictionary.

One limitation of MS-DOS computers is the 640K memory barrier. When Ventura loads a long document on a conventional DOS computer, it keeps part of the document on disk, swapping sections in and out to the hard disk as needed. Swapping slows the program, since disk operations are sluggish compared to operations performed in memory. Limited memory also restricts maximum document size and prevents creation of complex chapters with many frames and tags.

A number of companies have developed a way to go beyond the 640K barrier. It's called EMS, for Expanded Memory Specification. To use expanded memory, you must install a memory board that conforms to the EMS standard. You also need software — a Lotus/Intel/Microsoft EMS driver (version 3.0 or later). If you own a computer based on the Intel 80386 chip that comes with *extended* memory, you use it as expanded memory by running an expanded memory emulator. Contact your computer manufacturer to find an EMS driver or emulator compatible with your machine.

As long as EMS is properly installed, Ventura recognizes it automatically. It uses EMS to, among other things, swap long documents, thereby avoiding slower disk swapping. It also loads program overlays into EMS, for faster operation. In addition, the EMS memory permits Ventura to format complex documents that would otherwise cause out-of-memory error messages.

To use EMS, you may need to add a command line to your computer's CONFIG.SYS file. The manual that comes with your memory board will tell you how. By looking at the statistics in the Desk menu, you can see how much EMS memory is installed and how much is available to the program, as explained earlier in this chapter.

Configuring your computer system to run Ventura most productively can be a time-consuming and frustrating process, particularly if you have other hardware and software that is equally demanding of system resources. But once you have arrived at the optimal configuration, you should find that

Ventura Publisher performs quite well, considering the complex tasks it must perform.

Now that you are proficient in using Ventura's tools properly, we would like to give you some practical advice on using the program for a variety of document applications. We explore these in the next chapter.

Chapter Ten

Special Document Formats

Previous chapters have delved into Ventura's functions and options. This chapter concentrates on applying those options to different kinds of documents and formats. We have divided it into four sections:

- *Special formats and effects* — an assortment of formatting tricks and ideas.
- *Building frame-style documents* — how to create newsletters, magazines, and similar frame-intensive publications.
- *Building free-form documents* — the best strategies for creating forms, ads, and similar documents.
- *Document notes and suggestions* — a final section with advice and tips on the major document types.

Special formats and effects

Think of this section as a menu of tricks, tips, techniques, and ideas. We have assumed that you already understand Ventura's commands and functions. If not, you should review the previous chapters. Those chapters explain the *how* of Ventura's functions. This section explains the *why*, *where*, and *when*. It suggests ways to apply Ventura creatively to produce a wide range of formats and effects.

Ventura is so powerful that there is virtually no end to the things you can do with it. The effects shown below, however, should give you a starting point for your own experiments.

- Ballot boxes
- Bullets
- Chapter openings
- Coupons
- Fill-in lines
- Fractions
- Frames and pictures
- Headers
- Headings
- Indents
- Jump text
- Kickers
- Labels
- Logos and nameplates
- Page numbers
- Pull quotes
- Ruling lines
- Tables
- Thumb tabs
- Title pages
- Type effects

Browse through them and find the effects or page elements you need for your document. For each one, you will find a few brief pointers, tips, or examples. Where necessary, we have mentioned other chapters of this book that give further details.

Ballot boxes

Ballot boxes are hollow squares. Most people use them as check-off boxes in questionnaires and similar documents (Figure 10-1). You may also find these hollow boxes useful as bullet characters (in place of the typical round bullet) or as end-of-article symbols in magazines and newsletters.

Ventura provides several ways to create a ballot box. By far the most convenient is the hollow box character. To insert a hollow box anywhere in a line of text, position the text cursor, then select Ins Special Item from the Edit menu (keyboard shortcut: Ctrl-C). Choose Box Char from the secondary menu (keyboard shortcut: F1). Ventura lets you choose a hollow or filled box. The hollow version creates the ballot box effect.

You can edit this hollow box like any other text character. For instance, you can use Set Font in Text mode to make it bigger or smaller (while leaving the rest of the paragraph un-

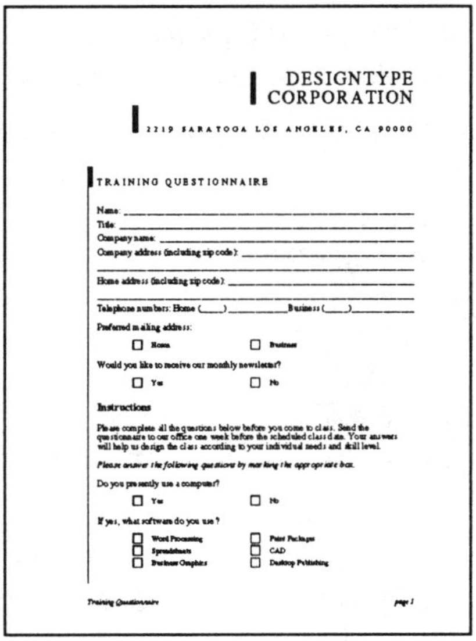

DESIGNTYPE
CORPORATION

2219 SARATOGA LOS ANGELES, CA 90000

TRAINING QUESTIONNAIRE

Name: ______________________
Title: ______________________
Company name: ______________________
Company address (including zip code): ______________________
____
Home address (including zip code): ______________________
____
Telephone numbers: Home (____) ____________ Business (____) ____________

Preferred mailing address:

☐ Home ☐ Business

Would you like to receive our monthly newsletter?

☐ Yes ☐ No

Instructions

Please complete all the questions below before you come to class. Send the questionnaire to our office one week before the scheduled class date. Your answers will help us design the class according to your individual needs and skill level.

Please answer the following questions by marking the appropriate box.

Do you presently use a computer?

☐ Yes ☐ No

If yes, what software do you use?

☐ Word Processing ☐ Paint Packages
☐ Spreadsheets ☐ CAD
☐ Business Graphics ☐ Desktop Publishing

Training Questionnaire *page 1*

Figure 10-1. Ballot boxes for a questionnaire.

changed). To enter a hollow box character directly into a text file, enter the bracket code <$B0>. (The bracket code <$B1> creates a filled box.)

To position a ballot box at the front of the first line of a paragraph, use Special Effects from the Paragraph menu. Choose Show Bullet As: Hollow Box.

You can also create ballot boxes with Ruling Box Around. For a square box at the front of a line choose a custom width equal to the inter-line spacing. Use a very thin Rule 1 height — 00.06 fractional pts., for instance. To push this box out into the margin, use the Alignment dialog box to create an outdent. The Ruling Box Around method, however, has a disadvantage if the paragraph is more than one line long. To keep the box only one line deep, assign it to an auto-numbering Z_Sec tag. Use Auto-Numbering from the Chapter menu to "number" the paragraph — but don't let the number appear. Now put a ruling box around this empty paragraph as described above. Every time you renumber the chapter, Ventura will automatically generate the ballot boxes.

You can also create hollow boxes with frames and graphics rectangles. Simply draw the shape and put a box around it. These methods, however, are rarely appropriate for ballot boxes. They do not move along with the text. Every time you move the text you must reposition the boxes.

See also "Bullets" below for suggestions on using filled boxes. See Chapter Three for more on entering bracket codes into text files. See Chapter Eight for more on using Auto-Numbering to create formatting effects.

Bullets

Use the Special Effects dialog box to create bullets. In addition to the common round bullet, you can also create a variety of other valuable effects.

For instance, you can have hollow or filled boxes. By using the Define Colors dialog box, you can assign shades of gray to different colors and thereby fill the box with gray instead of black:

□ A hollow box
■ A black filled box
▩ A gray filled box

Or you can signal special sections with symbols:

☛
☎
✉
✓
★
➥

Many of these symbols are only available in special *Pi* or *Dingbat* fonts. Many PostScript printers, for instance, can access the Zapf Dingbats font. To create a bullet character from a font that is different than the rest of the paragraph, choose Show Bullet As: Other. Then type the decimal equivalent on the Bullet Char line. Then use Set Font Properties to choose the font for this bullet character. This choice will affect only the bullet, not the rest of the paragraph. Unless you have special screen fonts, the symbol will not show properly on the screen, but it will print correctly.

You can also use Set Font to change the size of the bullet.

To enter bullet characters in the midst of a line (Figure 10-2),

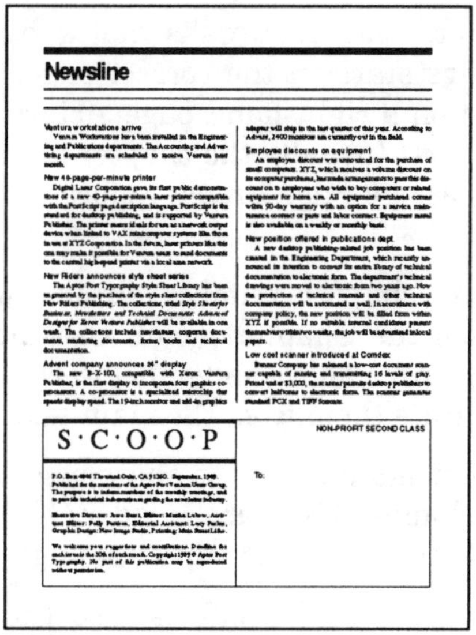
Newsline

Ventura workstations arrive

New 40-page-per-minute printer

New Riders announces style sheet series

Advent company announces 24" display

Employee discounts on equipment

New position offered in publications dept

Low cost scanner introduced at Comdex

S·C·O·O·P

NON-PROFIT SECOND CLASS

To:

Figure 10-2. Bullet characters were entered in between the letters of SCOOP to create the nameplate effect.

hold down the Alt key while typing their decimal equivalent on the numeric keypad. For instance, to place a round bullet character in the middle of a line, type Alt-195. To place a Dingbat character in the line, you must type its decimal equivalent, then change its font with Set Font in Text mode.

To push bullets into the margin, use the Alignment dialog box to create an outdent.

Chapter openings

Several of Ventura's functions will help you create easy, effective chapter openings If you keep each chapter in the document as a different Ventura chapter, you can use Page Size & Layout to make sure they all start on the correct side (traditionally, chapters start on a right-hand page). You can use Update Counters to set the Update Method to Previous Number + 1, which will automatically number across the chapter boundaries. (To set the page number manually, choose Update Method: Restart Number and type in the new starting number you want.)

If you put more than one document chapter inside a single

Ventura chapter, use the Breaks dialog box to make sure chapter openings start on the correct page. For instance, to force it to start on a right-hand page, determine which paragraph appears first (usually the chapter number or the chapter title). Then assign Page Break: Before/Until Right for that tag.

To generate the chapter number automatically, use Auto-Numbering from the Chapter menu. Use the Spacing dialog box to put extra space above and/or below the chapter title and number to separate them from the main text.

Many books and manuals don't show page numbers on the first page of a chapter. Use Turn Header Off from the Chapter menu to disable the header for the first page only.

For drop caps and similar effects, use the Special Effects dialog box. Usually you will want to have a "Body First" tag for the first paragraph. It will usually be similar to standard body text, except for a big first character and/or extra space above.

See also Page Numbers later in this section.

Coupons

Clip-out coupons are an important part of many brochures, flyers, and direct mail pieces (Figure 10-3).

Usually you will want to put the coupon in its own frame. Then you can reposition the coupon without affecting the rest of the document. Use Ruling Box Around from the Frame menu to put a line around the coupon. To create a dotted or dashed line, choose Dashes: On. Type in the width and spacing you want for the dashes.

If you have access to a Dingbat font you can place a scissors character (✂) on the line to indicate it should be clipped and mailed. Use Box Text to put the symbol at the precise point you want it.

You can use Frame Background to put a tint screen effect in the coupon. Be careful that the background pattern is not too dark, or it will obscure the type. If the standard patterns are too dark, create a lighter shade of gray with Define Colors. Assign the gray shade to a color, and make the Frame Background that color.

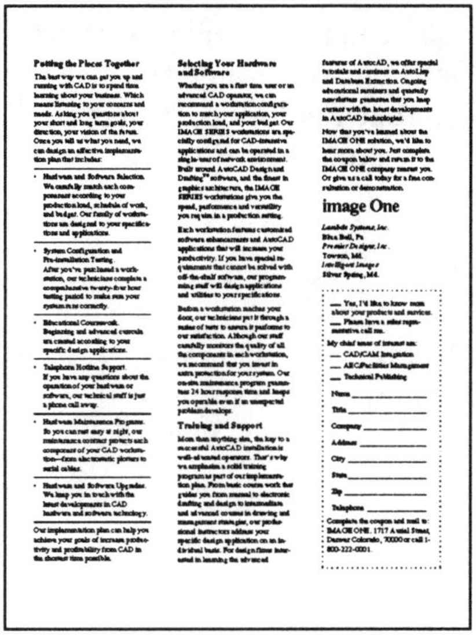

Figure 10-3. One example of a clip-out coupon.

Create a separate tag for fill-in lines. Make sure it is not justified, so tabs will take effect. Then use Tab Settings to create the lines. Choose Tab Shown As: Leader Char. Then select the underline as the Leader Character. For solid horizontal lines, make sure the leader spacing is 0. For dashed and dotted lines, pick a number from 1 to 8 from the Leader Spacing pop-up menu. Make sure the inter-line spacing is adequate so that readers have room to print or type in their names — not any smaller than 12 fractional pts.

Use hollow box characters for ballot boxes (see above in this section).

Fractions

Do not type fractions as you would on a typewriter, in the same size font separated by a full-size slash. Instead, use Ins Special Item from the Edit menu to create fractions in the correct typographic style. Select Fraction from the Insert Special Item dialog box. Type fractions with a front slash between numerator and denominator to create fractions with a slanted bar. Thus, you would type 13/32 to create $^{13}/_{32}$. Type fractions with the word over between numerator and denominator to create fractions with a horizontal bar. Thus, you would type 13 over 32 to create $\frac{13}{32}$.

To make fractions larger or smaller, select the fraction in Text mode and use Set Font to change the size. You can delete and copy fractions in Text mode like any other text. To edit fractions, however, you must use Edit Special Item from the Edit menu.

Frames and pictures

Chapter Six, "Building the Chapter," presented a number of basic frame techniques:

- drawing
- copying
- deleting
- margins
- padding
- captions
- Box Text for callouts

In this section we present some additional ideas and techniques.

Irregular text runarounds

To create an irregular text runaround, load the picture inside a frame as normal. At this point, the text flows around the frame (Figure 10-4).

With the frame still selected, open the Sizing & Scaling dialog box. Choose Flow Text Around: Off. Now the text flows underneath the frame (Figure 10-5).

Now use small, invisible frames to selectively push the text away from the parts of the picture that project into the text (Figure 10-6).

Shadow effects

Shadow effects are useful for setting off headlines, banners, pictures, callouts, tables of contents, and special notes (Figure

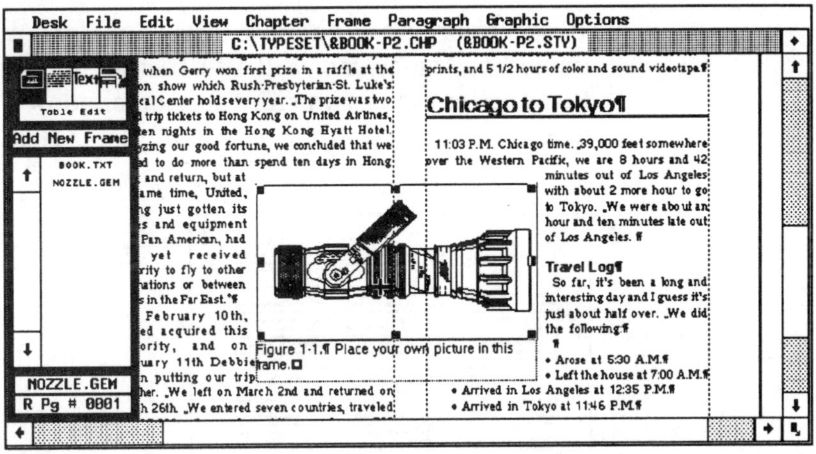

Figure 10-4. To create a text runaround, start by loading the picture into a frame as normal.

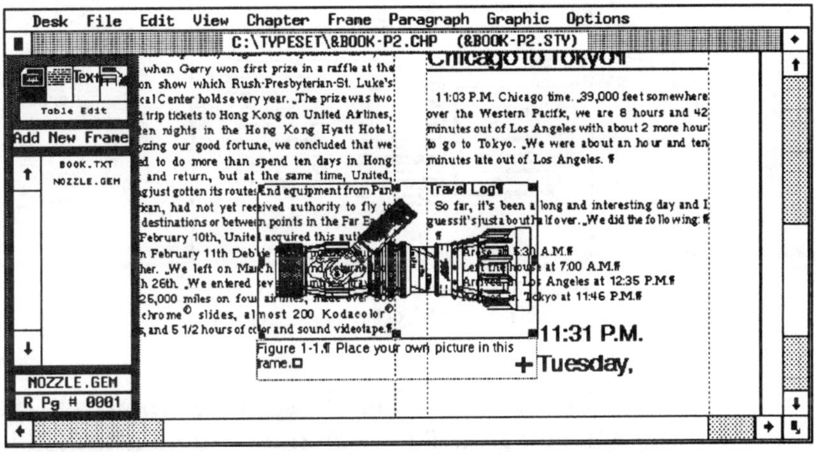

Figure 10-5. Then turn Flow Text Around to Off.

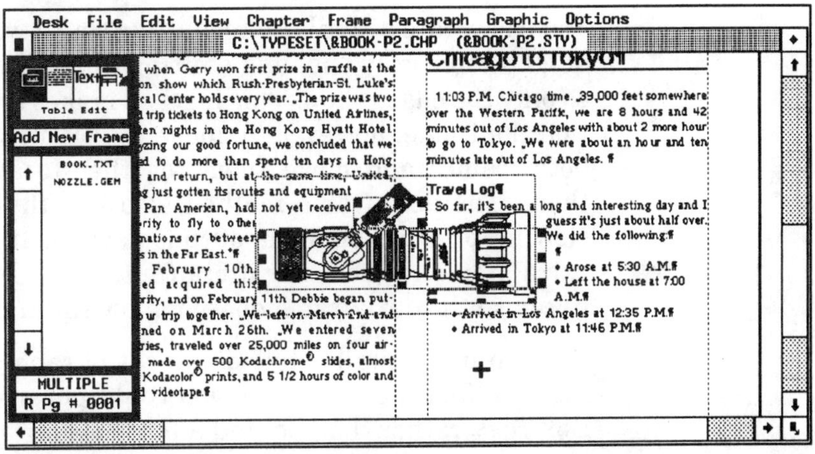

Figure 10-6. Then create a "stairstep" of small frames to push the text away.

10-7). To create a shadow effect, use graphic rectangles attached to the frame. Fill the rectangles with black or gray. Place them along two sides for the shadow effect. Or you can use thick graphic rules instead of rectangles.

Basic design for newsletters

DTP reduces editors' anxiety

MEMBER OF THE MONTH

Pattison involved in communication community

Imagemaker
The Orange County
Newsletter Association
P.O. Box 4846
Thousand Oaks, CA 91360
September, 1989

EDITOR Martha Lubow
Please send suggestions or contributions to the editorial address above.

Figure 10-7. The shadow effect sets off the notice in the lower left of this newsletter page.

Be sure the frame is selected when you create the graphic rectangles. That way they will be attached to the frame, and so they will move along with it.

You can create a similar effect by putting a white frame on top of a black or gray one, and shifting the darker frame slightly, so only the edges show. This method makes it harder to reposition the frame, however. To move it, you must carefully select both frames and move them together to avoid misaligning them. The dual-frame method also has the disadvantage of slowing printing on some output devices. It also requires an extra step with some printers (putting a third frame in between so the dark frame doesn't show through the light one).

You can use a similar technique with graphic shapes, including Box Text. For instance, you could put a shadow behind a Box Text, rather than behind a frame.

Tint blocks

Use Frame Background to put a light gray pattern inside a frame to separate it from the rest of the text. If the pattern is too dark and obscures the text, assign a color to the background instead of a pattern. Then use Define Colors to assign a light gray pattern to the color.

Frame templates

Although we mentioned frame templates in Chapter Six, they are so important we wanted to reinforce the notion. Once you create a valuable effect, there is no need to do it over again. Simply save the frame in a special chapter. You can save it together with its contents if it's the total effect you want to reproduce. Or you can save an empty frame if it's the settings (the margins, captions, padding, labels, etc.) that you want to reuse. Then you can use these frames over and over again by copying them from the "library" chapter to the document at hand.

Repeating frames

Repeating frames are a powerful tool for a variety of advanced formats. Under most circumstances, any text or graphics placed into a repeating frame will repeat identically throughout the document. Use this feature if you will want a frame with the same size and contents on all or most pages. The trick is to create the frame exactly the way you want it: size, position, and contents (text or picture). Then choose Repeating Frame from the Frame menu (Figure 10-8). The frame and everything in it will be reproduced throughout the document.

The dialog box permits you to choose if you want the frame to repeat just on left pages, just on right pages, or on all pages. You can also go to an individual page and turn off a repeating frame just for that page, while leaving it on in the rest of the document.

You can use repeating frames to make a logo appear throughout a document (Figure 10-9). You can use them to

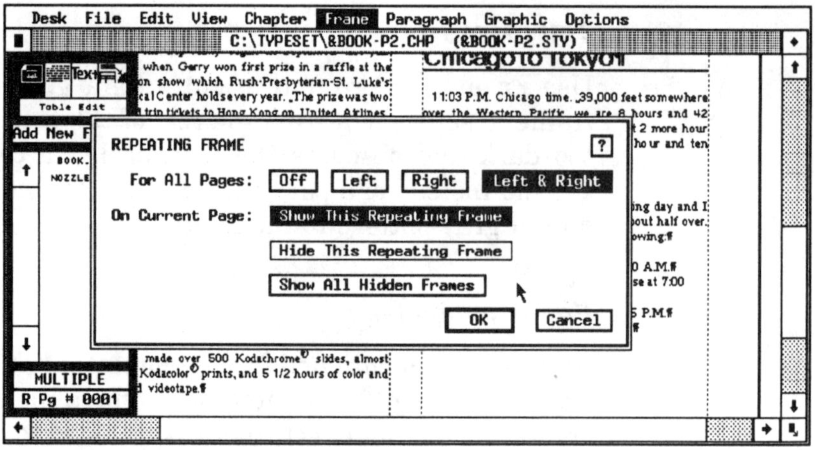

Figure 10-8. The Repeating Frame dialog box.

create thumb tabs and extra large headers, both of which are explained later in this section.

Under one special condition, however, text in a repeating frame is *not* cloned throughout the document. This occurs if you place text from a file that is also on the Underlying Page.

To understand how this works, you may want to review the

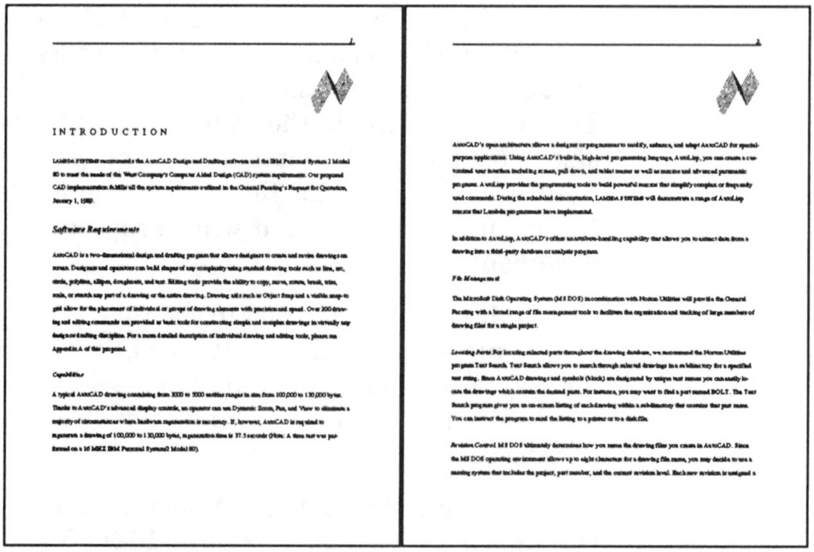

Figure 10-9. Because the logo is inside a repeating frame, it is duplicated on every page of the document.

discussions of frame-style documents in Chapter Six and further on in this chapter. In frame-style documents, text resides inside frames on top of the Underlying Page. If a file cannot fit entirely into a frame, Ventura remembers where it left off. You can select another frame and Ventura will take up where it left off, placing more of the text file in the new frame.

This same effect occurs with repeating frames, provided the text file also appears on the Underlying Page. Under those circumstances, clicking on the repeating frame and then on the name of the text file will cause Ventura to pour as much of that file into the repeating frame as it can fit. The balance of the text will automatically continue onto the following pages.

You can also build unusual columnar formats with repeating frames. Suppose, for example, that you want to create a three-column stairstep effect throughout the document. The left-most column could be created standard length on the Underlying Page. The next two shorter columns could be repeating frames. Using frame-style layout, you could flow text from column to column.

You can also use repeating frames for forms or repetitive letters. A repeating frame (or several repeating frames) holds the portions that do not change. The information that does change (for instance, the name and address in a form letter) goes on the Underlying Page. Make sure that the final tag on each page has Page Break: After from the Breaks dialog box. Each time Ventura Publisher encounters the page break command it will start a new Underlying Page and create a new repeating frame, thereby creating a new form.

With this technique you do not need to know how many forms are required. Ventura will build new ones as needed. It's easy to see how you could instruct a database or accounting program to dump, for example, the day's orders into a text file. The database could also insert the tags as part of the report process. All the forms for the day could then be created by bringing this file into Ventura Publisher.

Headers with Repeating Frames

Chapter Six, "Building the Chapter," delved into headers and how to build them. You will find Ventura's standard header (and footer) functions adequate for most applications. However, to create extra large headers and footers, use a repeating frame instead. We will discuss an extra large header, but the same principles apply to an extra large footer.

Draw a frame at the top of the page. Type in the header text as you want it to appear. To place chapter or page numbers in the header, position the text cursor where you want the number to appear and use Ins Special Item from the Edit menu.

Headings

Headings are signposts that guide readers through a document. Ventura has a variety of methods for making them more eye-catching and effective.

Headlines and main headings should be larger than the main text — usually 18 points or larger. Subheads should usually be slightly larger than the main text, although they can also be the same size if you use italics, bold, or small caps to set them apart. Don't let headings compete. Establish a clear hierarchy (Figure 10-10). Make the title larger than the main heading, which is larger than the second-level heading, which is larger than the third-level heading, and so on.

You can also establish a hierarchy with white space, ruling lines, indents, bold type, italics, and other formatting effects. Upper and lower case headings are easier to read than all caps.

Aligning headings

Centered headings impart a traditional look and feel to a document. In most cases, flush left headings are more effective. The eye travels naturally to the left side of the page. Centered headings divide the white space, making it less noticeable. Flush right alignment can be valuable for title pages, and for marginal headings, where you want the heading in the left column to be as close as possible to the related text in the right column.

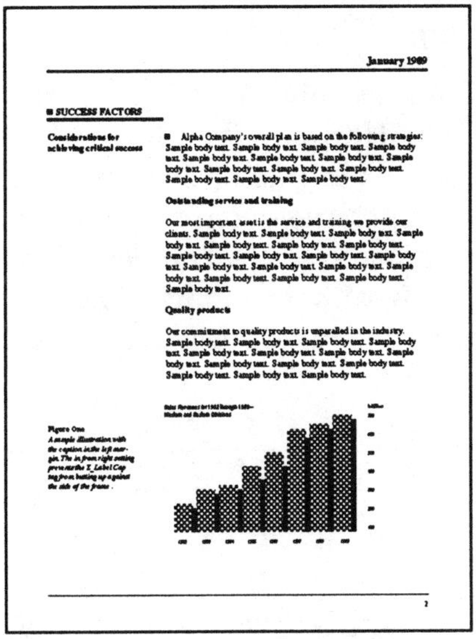

Figure 10-10. The subheadings in this document are subordinate to the main headings, as established by type size, ruling lines, spacing, and other typographic treatment.

Hanging or outdented headings

Many manuals and books (including this one) place headings in an extra wide left margin. This isolates the heading and makes it more noticeable. Usually the effect is created by leaving the heading at the left margin and using In From Left spacing to push the main text to the right. Conversely, you can use the margin to restrict the main text, then use First Line: Outdent from the Alignment dialog box to push the heading left past the margin.

Glance through a few pages of this book. You will see that first- and second-level headings start all the way to the left margin. Third-level headings start further in, even with the main text.

You can also create a similar effect with mirrored margins and headings. In a mirrored format, headings on the left page would be in the left margin, while headings on the right page would be in the right margin. You only need one heading tag to create this effect, but it must have different (opposite) In From Left and In From Right settings for left and right pages.

Marginal headings

Marginal headings are slightly different from hanging or outdented headings. Hanging headings, like the first- and second-level headings in this book, start at the left margin. If they are long enough, they continue on for the width of the column. Marginal headings, by contrast, are restricted entirely to the margin. If they are longer, the rest of the heading wraps down inside the margin to create a second or third line (Figure 10-11).

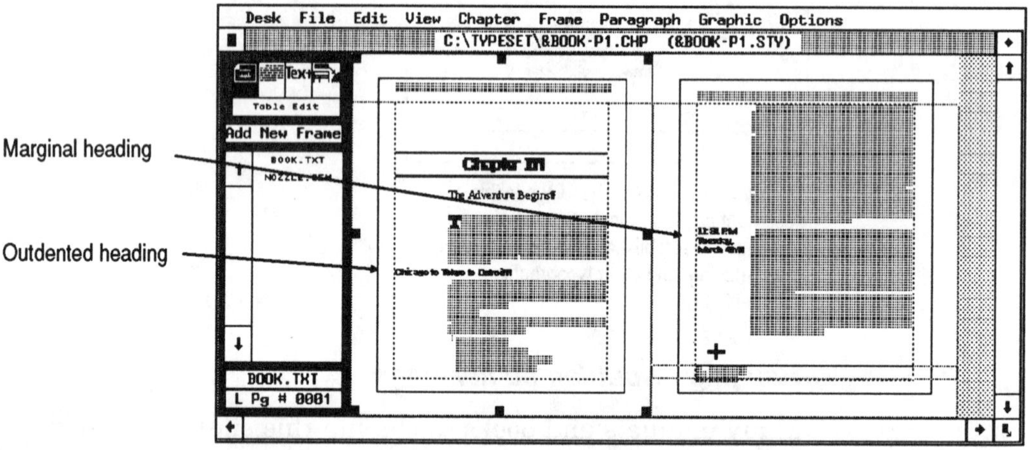

Figure 10-11. Marginal headings are restricted to the margin. They do not extend into the text area.

To achieve marginal headings you must (1) make sure that there are no line breaks between the heading and the main text, so they can reside on the same line and (2) use the Spacing dialog box to restrict the text to the margin.

Banner headlines

Banner headings occur in multi-column documents. They stretch across all the columns, not just a single column. To create a banner headline, select the headline paragraph and choose Overall Width: Frame-Wide from the Alignment dialog box. For single-column headlines, choose Column-Wide.

If you want banner headlines within the body of the main text (as for newspaper-style layouts), you must choose Column Balance: On from the Chapter Typography or Frame Typography dialog boxes. Otherwise, the text will not balance underneath the headlines, and headlines will overlap text.

What if you want a heading to stretch across some, but not all of the columns? You can put the headline into a separate frame, or you can restrict it with In From Right spacing.

See Chapter Six, "Building the Chapter," for more on Alignment options.

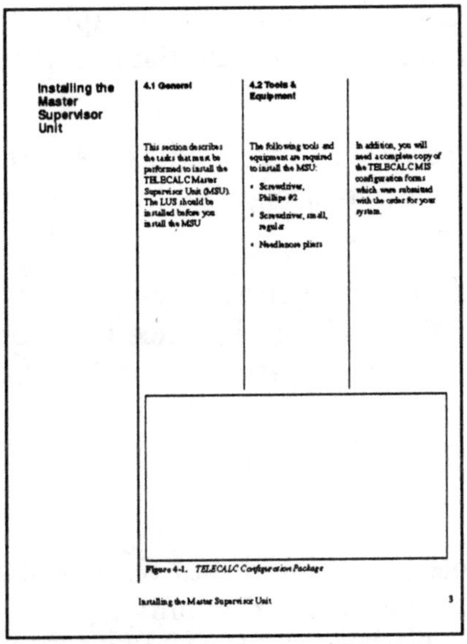

Figure 10-12. The heading in the upper left has been isolated by placing column breaks before and after.

Isolated headings

With the Breaks dialog box, you can force headings to appear first on a page or column (Page Break: Before or Column Break: Before) or be the only element in the column (Column Break: Before & After). Figure 10-12 shows an example of an isolated heading.

We have discussed line breaks and page breaks repeatedly in this book. Some users don't realize that you can also create column breaks. A column break forces text to the top of the next column, instead of the next page or line.

Numbered headings

Ventura's Auto-Numbering feature can generate military-style section numbering, traditional-style outlines, and other numbered headings. See Chapter Eight, "Advanced Functions," for more about this topic.

Run-in headings

Run-in headings reside on the same line with the text they describe. They carry a different typographic treatment to distinguish them from the main text. Sometimes they are partially outdented.

One easy way to create run-in headings is with text attributes. Simply use Text mode to assign bold, italics, small caps, and/or a larger font size.

You can also create two separate tags, one for the heading and one for the text that follows. To place them on the same line, use the relative indent feature described below under "Indents."

Indents

Indents are another special format worthy of extra consideration. Because of Ventura's flexibility, you can create some unusual and useful formats. Since the Alignment dialog box (Figure 10-13) can be confusing, let's start by reviewing a run-of-the-mill single-line fixed indent.

To indent the first line of a paragraph by, for example, 12 fractional pts., you would select:

```
First Line: Indent

Relative Indent: Off

In/Outdent Width: 12,00 fractional pts.

In/Outdent Height: 001 lines
```

To indent the first two lines, you would select In/Outdent Height: 002 lines.

Occasionally, you may want to create an outdent, whereby the first line of a paragraph is pushed to the left of the margin

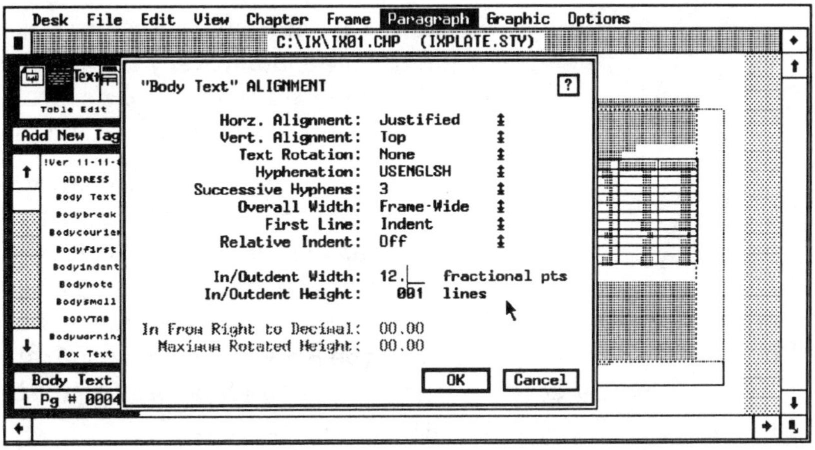

Figure 10-13. The Alignment dialog box.

(called *hanging indents*). Choose First Line: Outdent. Type in the amount of spacing in the In/Outdent Width line. To cancel an indent or an outdent, simply enter In/Outdent Width: 00,00.

Relative indents

Ventura also has a unique relative indent feature. Normally, Relative Indent is Off. By choosing Relative Indent: On instead, each new paragraph starts where the previous one left off. In other words, the first line of the new line is pushed right exactly the length of the preceding line (Figure 10-14).

Relative indent

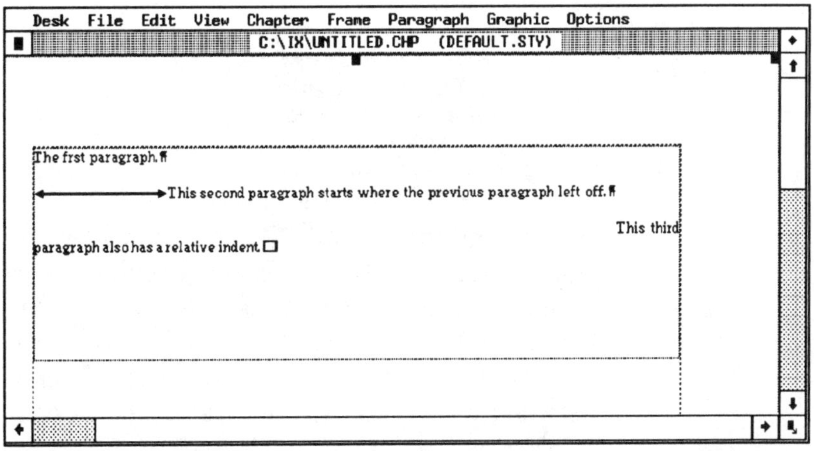

Figure 10-14. Because Relative Indent is On, each one of these paragraphs is indented to the spot where the previous paragraph left off.

In and of itself, this stairstep effect is not very useful. But Relative Indent does come in very handy if you combine it do two other things: (1) turn off the line break between paragraphs and (2) insert a small first-line indent.

Turning off the line break allows two paragraphs to reside on the same line. As you can see in Figure 10-15, this allows you to create such things as run-in heads. The bold heads are one paragraph; the normal text is a second paragraph. They reside on the same line because they do not have a line break between them. Use the Breaks dialog box. Most people create the effect by putting a line break before the first paragraph and a line break after the second one.

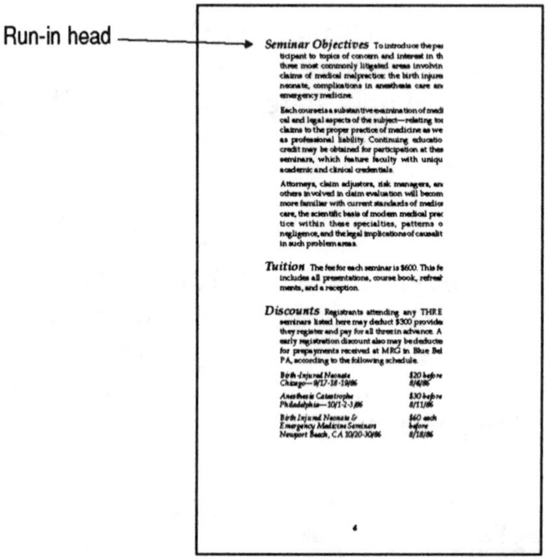

Figure 10-15. The run-in heads in this document reside on the same line as the paragraphs they describe. The following paragraphs have both a relative indent and a first-line indent.

If you combine a relative indent with two paragraphs on the same line, you still have one problem. A relative indent is *exactly* the same length as the previous line. Consequently, the text from the second paragraph will butt up flush against the last letter of the first paragraph. To create a small space between the two tags, use First Line: Indent.

Relative indents have many other applications:

- Putting a caption label and caption text on the same line, as with the figures in this book
- Question and Answer interview formats for magazines and newsletters
- Numbered section headings (see Chapter Eight's discussion of Auto-Numbering)

Jump text

Jump text is a small phrase telling the reader where to find the rest of an article. For instance, "Continued on page 17," or "See *Newsmakers*, p. 17."

Theoretically, you could type the jump phrase right in the text file at the right spot. In practice, it makes more sense to put it in a separate frame (Figure 10-16). That way, it will stay in place if you add or subtract text from the article. If you turn on the Line-Snap feature, you can easily draw small frames that are only one or two lines deep.

Figure 10-16. Jump text is best placed in a small frame.

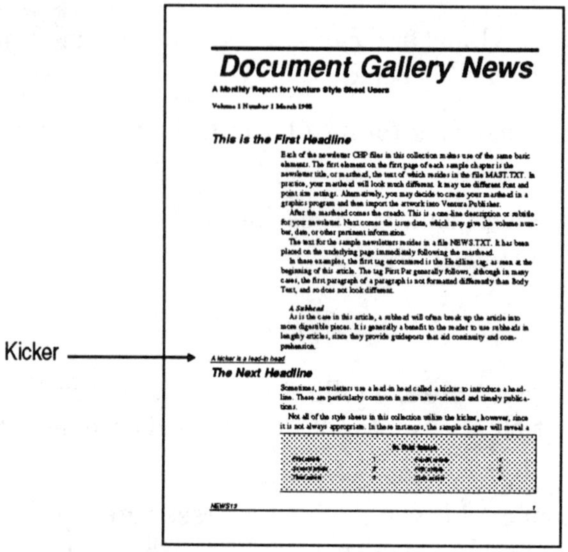

Document Gallery News

A Monthly Report for Venture Style Sheet Users

Volume 1 Number 1 March 1988

This is the First Headline

Each of the newsletter CHP files in this collection makes use of the same basic elements. The first element on the first page of each sample chapter is the newsletter title, or masthead, the text of which resides in the file MAST.TXT. In practice, your masthead will look much different. It may use different font and point size settings. Alternatively, you may decide to create your masthead in a graphics program and then import the artwork into Ventura Publisher.

After the masthead comes the creado. This is a one-line description or subtitle for your newsletter. Next comes the issue date, which may give the volume number, date, or other pertinent information.

The text for the sample newsletters resides in a file NEWS.TXT. It has been placed on the underlying page immediately following the masthead.

In these examples, the first tag encountered is the Headline tag, as seen at the beginning of this article. The tag First Par generally follows, although in many cases, the first paragraph of a paragraph is not formatted differently than Body Text, and so does not look different.

A Subhead

As is the case in this article, a subhead will often break up the article into more digestible pieces. It is generally a benefit to the reader to use subheads in lengthy articles, since they provide guideposts that aid continuity and comprehension.

A kicker is a lead-in head

The Next Headline

Sometimes, newsletters use a lead-in head called a kicker to introduce a headline. These are particularly common in more news-oriented and timely publications.

Not all of the style sheets in this collection utilize the kicker, however, since it is not always appropriate. In these instances, the sample chapter will reveal a

NEWS13 1

Figure 10-17. Kickers are short lead-ins for headlines.

Kickers

Kickers are small lines of text that precede a headline (Figure 10-17). Usually they act as a teaser, as a lead-in to the headline, or as amplification of the headline topic.

Type the kicker immediately ahead of the headline and give it its own tag. One good style is to set the kicker flush left above a headline that is slightly indented. Kickers are usually italic, or underlined, or both.

Labels

This section discusses two types of labels: creating labels inside a document, and printing peel-off labels.

Label space in documents

Label space can be built into the back sheet of a document to create a self-mailer. The most common applications are flyers, brochures, direct mail pieces, and newsletters. The size of the label depends on (1) how you plan to fold the document and (2) postal regulations. Figure 10-18 shows two examples.

Use a separate frame to create the space for the label. Box

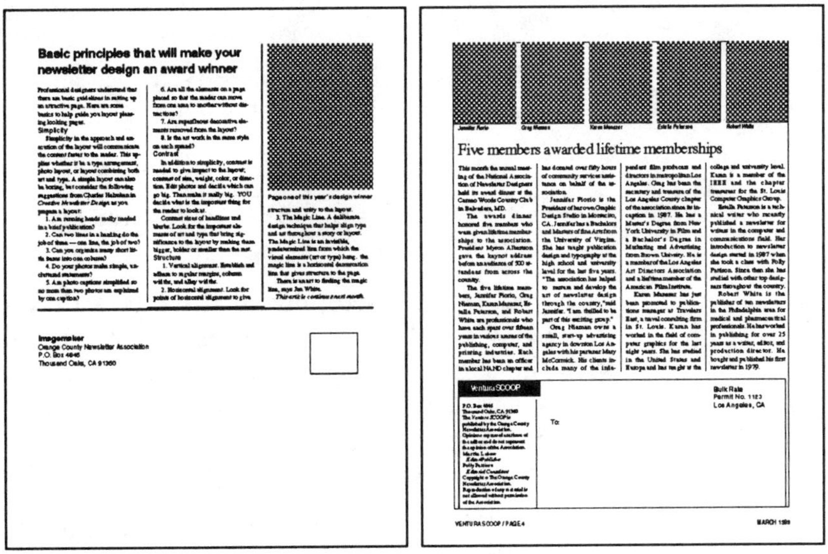

Figure 10-18. These newsletters have the mailing label designed into the back page so you can just fold and mail.

Text is a simple way to position a return address within the label area.

Peel-off labels

Creating peel-off labels with laser printers can be difficult with database programs or word processors. First, the programs may not support your laser printer. Second, you may have to do some programming to solve the problem of skipped lines. If an address doesn't have as many lines as the one before (for instance, if one person has no company name), it can throw off the spacing for all the labels that follow.

You can solve this problem in Ventura with a special Spacer tag. First create the addresses. Separate each line with a line-break code, not with a carriage return. Add a carriage return between each address. Pretag this empty paragraph as Spacer. The addresses don't need any tag, since you will treat them as Body Text. Put the addresses into a text file compatible with Ventura. Here's how two addresses might look in the file:

```
¶

John Doe<R>XYZ Company<R>123 Main
Street<R>Anytown, USA 00000 ¶

¶

Fred Freelance<R>456 Elm Avenue<R>Smalltown, USA
00000 ¶
```

Now you are ready to format the labels in Ventura. Bring in the text file with the addresses. Create an Underlying Page with the correct number of columns — one column for one-up labels, two columns for two-up, and so on. Set the top and bottom margins according to the space between the top of the sheet and the top of the first label.

It's easier if you format the Spacer first. Align it Right, so you can easily see the paragraph return against the right margin. Set Above, Inter-Line, and Inter-Paragraph to zero. Set the Below spacing to the height of your labels. For one-inch labels, then, you'd set the Below spacing to one inch. Now use the Breaks dialog box to select Line Break: Before.

You've just told Ventura to put exactly one inch of space below every Spacer paragraph. Now format the Body Text using any reasonable font and inter-line spacing. Make sure there is no space above or below the tag. Then use Breaks to choose Line Break: None.

Since the addresses don't have any line breaks after the paragraph, Ventura ignores their spacing and uses that of the Spacer paragraph — which is always exactly one inch, no matter how many or how few lines in the address label.

Logos and nameplates

Normally, a nameplate appears on the first page of a newsletter or similar publication. Many users refer to this as a logo. Technically, a logo is a special design identifying an entire company.

Ideally, a nameplate typeface should be decorative and strong. It should establish the correct image for your company and publication. If you don't have the font you need on your system, consider creating it with a drawing program, and bringing it into Ventura as a picture. As mentioned above, you can also cause a logo to repeat throughout a publication by putting it inside a repeating frame.

Ventura wasn't intended as a graphic design program for the creation of fancy logos and artwork. Nonetheless, it has a number of features you can use to dress up a logo or nameplate. Scan the rest of this section for ideas you can apply to logos and nameplates. Pay particular attention to "Ruling lines" and "Type effects."

Page numbers

Our discussion of headers and footers in Chapter Six explained how to put page numbers at the top or bottom of the page. We also mentioned that you can put page numbers (and/or chapter numbers) anywhere using Ins Special Item from the Edit menu.

For instance, here's how you would cause page numbers to appear at the outside center of each page.

- Move to a left page and enable Frame mode.
- Draw a small frame at the left center. Use the rulers to center it. Do not allow it to encroach upon the dead zone of your printer. Hold down the Alt key while drawing or resizing to force it to become a perfect square. Add a ruling box around and/or a frame background if desired.
- Enable Text mode. Place the text cursor inside the frame. Type any text you want to precede the page number (for instance, the word "Page").
- Use Ins Special Item to place a page number reference.
- Enable Frame mode and make the frame a repeating frame for left pages.
- Repeat the process for the right page.

Pull quotes

Pull quotes, also called *lift outs, call outs,* or *blurbs,* are enlarged excerpts used as teasers and decorative elements for magazine and newsletter articles (Figure 10-19).

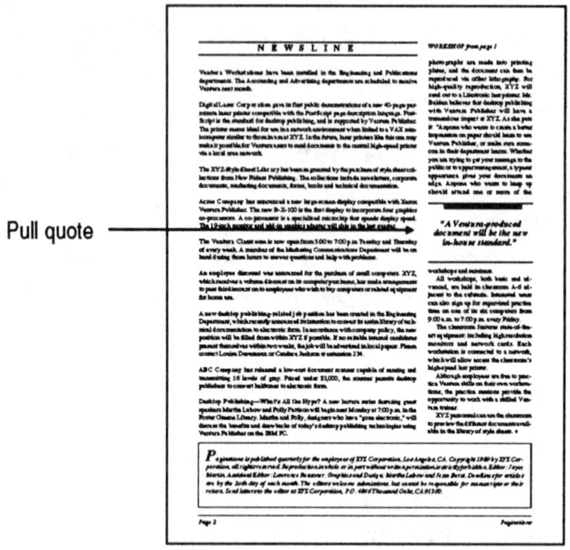

Figure 10-19. This pull quote is set off from the rest of the text with ruling lines and a larger type size.

You can separate pull quotes with boxes, ruling lines, or fill patterns. Make the font larger than the body text, but not so large that it overpowers the headings. You can create a separate tag, and leave the pull quotes in the normal text stream, but most people find it easier and more effective to put pull quotes inside their own small frame.

Ruling lines

Ventura has a wealth of ruling line effects. We can only touch on a few of them here. Table 10-1 lists the various ways to create ruling lines within Ventura. As you can see, you have an amazing assortment of methods to choose from.

When you consider that you can combine rules, and that you can also achieve dashed and patterned rules, you will understand that the number of variations is enormous.

There are dozens — if not hundreds — of ways to combine rules with type and artwork to create attractive logos and nameplates. If you can visualize it, Ventura can probably create it for you. Pay particular attention to the custom width option, which lets you draw a rule of any width and place it

Table 10-1. Options for creating ruling lines.

Horizontal rules	Frame mode	Ruling lines above or below frames
	Paragraph mode	Ruling lines above or below paragraphs
	Text mode	Underscore, overscore, and strike-through
		Tab settings with underscore as the leader character
	Graphic mode	Line drawing tool
Vertical rules	Any mode	Vertical Rules from the Chapter menu
	Frame mode	Ruling Box Around a frame that is so thin it looks like a line instead of a box
	Paragraph mode	Ruling box around a paragraph, with the custom width so thin it looks like a line instead of box
	Graphic mode	Line drawing tool
Boxes and borders	Frame mode	Ruling Boxes Around frames
	Paragraph mode	Ruling Boxes Around Paragraphs
	Graphic mode	Rectangles, circles, rounded rectangles, or Box Text

almost anywhere. We hope the samples below will give you a few ideas. We have included a few hints as well.

Custom width horizontal rules

The ruling line functions of the Paragraph menu permit rules to be the width of the text, the margin, the column, the frame, or a custom length. The last option provides many unique opportunities to the creative desktop publisher.

Special graphic effects are possible by varying the width and the vertical position. Don't forget the Space Below Rule 3 function that permits you to move a rule down into the text below. Read the "Type effects" section further in this chapter to see how this can create white type on a black rule.

By varying the width, the indent, and the space below a custom rule, you can make it part of a logo. Or you can create rules to set off headings that are always the same size regardless of the width of the text. We used that technique to create the thick portion of the double rule that accompanies our first-level headings.

Or you can make square bullets by creating a custom rule that is exactly as wide as it is tall. You can make these bullets very large and noticeable by indenting the first few lines of the paragraph, and creating a custom rule that fills the space left by the multi-line indent — similar to a big first character without the character. You can make these bullets dashed by selecting Dashes: On. Or you can fill these large square black bullets with a Big First Character whose color has been turned to white, as explained below in "Type effects."

A similar effect can be achieved by using the dashed rule option. In this example, we have moved the square into the margin by specifying a custom indent of negative 36 points for the rule.

A Thin Separator Rule

A thin, short rule can separate headlines from body text. Use the custom indent and width options from the Ruling Line Below dialog box.

Combining horizontal rules

Horizontal ruling lines can separate page elements while serving a decorative purpose at the same time. For instance, they can set off a logo, a nameplate, a header or footer, a warning, a sidebar, a pull quote, or a table of contents, to name just a few examples. Double or triple rules have extra impact if used with care. In addition, you may want to combine two rules of different widths and thicknesses (Figure 10-20).

Ventura doesn't allow two rules of different lengths in the same dialog box. To create this effect, you must use two tags.

Figure 10-20. The nameplate in this newsletter is set off by double rules of different widths and lengths.

Then use space above and below the rules to shift them until they touch. Sometimes you can create one rule with one tag, and the second one with the tag that follows it. In other cases, you must assign one of the rules to an empty paragraph, whose only job is to be a carrier for the ruling line. Or you can generate a paragraph with Auto-Numbering, and assign the second rule to the resulting Z_SEC paragraph.

You can also draw rules in Graphic mode, but you cannot be as precise by hand as you can with a dialog box. If you decide to draw the rules by hand, be sure to attach them to a frame (even if it's an invisible frame off to the side) so you can move the rules as one unit by moving the frame.

Text-wide horizontal rules

You can assign a text-wide rule to a paragraph tag. This is a useful way to ensure that you will have a ruling line underneath a paragraph no matter how long, or short, it is. For instance, you can use it to underline a kicker (see "Kickers" earlier in this chapter).

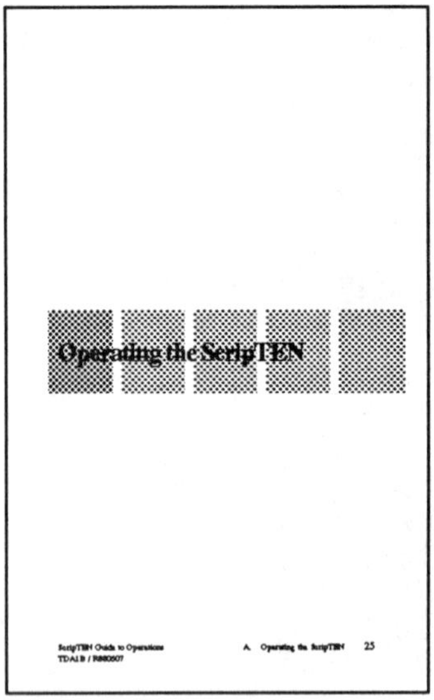

Figure 10-21. The decorative effect on this title page is actually a very wide dashed rule with a pattern.

Dashed and patterned horizontal rules

You cannot create dashed or patterned rules in Graphic mode. In Frame and Paragraph mode, however, you can create dashed rules by choosing Dashes: On from the dialog box. You can also control the width and spacing of the dashes. In addition, you can assign patterns to rules in the same dialog box. As you can see in Figure 10-21, you can combine dashes and patterns.

You can also create dashed horizontal lines in Text mode with tab settings. Use the underscore as the leader character for the tab stop. Then use the Leader Spacing line to make it a dashed line by inserting spaces between each underline.

Vertical rules

In Chapter Six we explained how to place inter-column rules using the Vertical Rules option from the Frame menu. You can also create vertical rules elsewhere on the page.

The Vertical Rules dialog box provides the ability to place up to two additional rules on the page (in addition to any inter-column rules you select). However, we advise against using this feature in most applications. Rules created here have several disadvantages:

- They extend all the way from the top to the bottom of the frame, even if you want less.
- They cannot be drawn in; they must be positioned by entering measurements.
- The rules remain stationary even if you move the frame.

It is usually better to create vertical rules with the line tool in Graphic mode. These rules have none of the limitations described above. They can be tied to the frame so they move with it. Hold down the Alt key while drawing to make the rules perfectly vertical. Choose Show On All Pages from the Graphic menu if you want the lines to appear on every page of the document.

Vertical rules for change bars

You can also create a vertical rule in Paragraph mode using Ruling Box Around. The trick is to choose a height for the box, but to give it a custom width of zero. The advantage of this method is that the vertical rule will always be the exact length of the paragraph. By manipulating the custom indent, you can cause the line to appear anywhere you want, although the left margin is the most common location.

You can, for instance, use this method to create change bars. Change bars are vertical lines placed in the margin to alert authors and editors that alterations have been made to the original manuscript. Certain legal, military, and technical documentation applications require change bars. To create a change bar, create a new tag identical to body text except for a ruling line around. Give the ruling line a small height, and select a Custom Width of 00,00 picas & points. To place the change bar in the margin, use the custom indent line — usually a negative indent of about 01,00 picas & points. Because the custom width is set to 0, the ruling line will not go around the text. It will appear as a vertical line in the margin next to the new text as the editor types it in.

To make change bars even more convenient, assign the tag to a function key. Now editors can press this key whenever they add new material and know that the change will be documented with a marginal change bar.

Dashed vertical rules

Dashed vertical rules are not available with the Graphic mode's line tool. If you need this effect, you can create it in Frame or Paragraph mode. In Paragraph mode, follow the instructions above for change bars, but select Dashes: On from the Ruling Box Around dialog box.

In Frame mode, create a frame with a dashed box around. Give it a width of zero to create a vertical dashed line. (By the way, if you give it a *height* of zero, you create a dashed *horizontal* line.) Be careful, however, since it can be difficult to select a thin frame. Usually it is best to leave it highlighted and to reposition it with the Sizing & Scaling dialog box.

Tables

As with most other formats, Ventura has a variety of ways to create tables:

1. with spaces and monospaced fonts

2. with tab settings

3. with Box Text

4. with side-by-side paragraphs

5. with the Table Edit mode in the Professional Extension

We explain the fifth option, Table Edit mode, in Chapter Eleven, "Specialized Functions." We explain the other four options in this section. We have listed them in approximate order of their difficulty for the beginning user. We wish to emphasize, however, that the side-by-side paragraphs method is the most versatile and useful. If you are trying to create tables without the benefit of the Professional Extension, we highly recommend that you become proficient with side-by-side paragraphs.

Tables with monospaced fonts

If you are working in a word processor, you can create simple tables with spaces. You simply tap the space bar the correct number of times to line up each column. Likewise, when you print a table from a spreadsheet, the program inserts spaces to make the columns line up.

Word processors and spreadsheets use *monospaced* fonts. Every character and every space has the same width. By contrast, most of the fonts used with Ventura are *proportionally* spaced. Different characters take up different amounts of room on the line. The letter *i*, for instance, is relatively thin, so it gets less space than the wider *m* character.

When you bring in a monospaced table, and format it with proportional fonts, the spacing is thrown off. For instance, notice what happens to this simple table when we switch it from a monospaced font (top example) to a proportional font (bottom example).

```
The First Column 1       First Column 2

Second Column 1          Second Column 2

Third Column 1           Third Column 2
```

The First Column 1 First Column 2

Second Column 1 Second Column 2

Third Column 1 Third Column 2

As you can see, a monospaced table doesn't look right when you bring it into Ventura *unless you choose a monospaced font.* A monospaced font is one that mimics the spacing system of a typewriter — that is, every character is assigned the same amount of space.

The good news is that you can bring in spaced tables without alteration and format them with a monospaced font such as Courier. The bad news is that monospaced fonts aren't very attractive. Since they usually imitate the look of a typewriter, they do not achieve a professional, typeset look. As if that weren't enough, it's actually harder to create a table with spaces than it is to build it with tabs or side-by-side paragraphs (see below).

For these reasons, we can't recommend monospaced tables for most applications. They may have some value for internal reports and studies, particularly if the tables have already been typed and you don't want to convert them. Otherwise, use one of the other methods described below.

If you find yourself building monospaced tables, be sure not to justify the lines. And don't forget that you can use fixed-width figure spaces to align columns. You can enter figure spaces in Ventura (Ctrl-Shift-F), or directly into a text file using bracket codes. See Chapter Three, "Creating Text," for an explanation of bracket codes.

Tables with tab settings

Those of you with word processing backgrounds probably associate tables with the use of tab stops. In Ventura Publisher, however, tab stops should be used only for simple tables with a single line per entry (Figure 10-22).

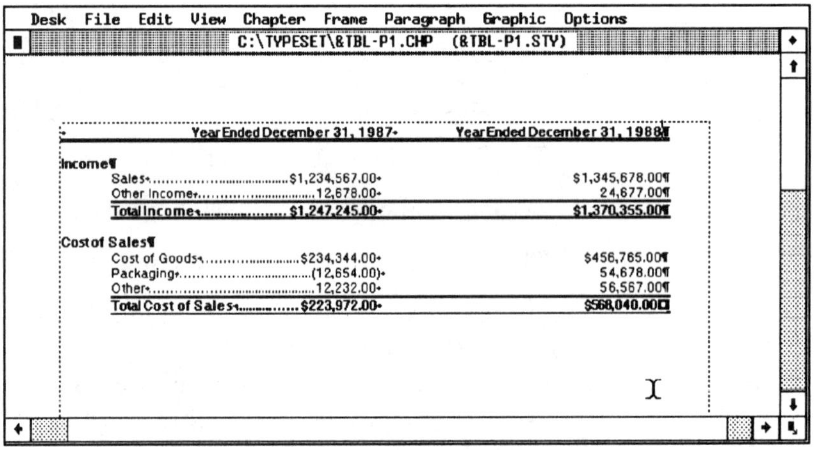

Figure 10-22. You can build simple, single-line tables like this one using tab settings.

Tabs permit decimal alignment and leader dots. (Version 3 of Ventura makes these same effects available with ordinary paragraphs as well.) Decimal columns are important to financial and scientific tables; they force all the entries to line up around a decimal point, like this:

A...123.456

B...12.3

C..................................12345

D 1.23

In addition, when you choose decimal alignment, Ventura automatically hangs parentheses outside the normal margin, so negative numbers in financial reports line up properly. If you look again at Figure 10-22, you will notice that the negative numbers align with the right-most numeral, *not* with the right-hand parenthesis. The parenthesis has been pushed to the right.

Leader dots are useful for product specifications, price lists, and directories, since they lead the reader's eye across the page:

John A. Doe.......555-1212

J. Q. Doe............555-0011

If you need either of these effects, you can use tab settings to create the table instead of separate tags *as long as the entries do not exceed one line in each column.* For multiple-line columns, use the side-by-side paragraph technique explained further below.

Proper use of tab stops in Ventura Publisher starts with your word processing program. Review Chapter Three for complete details on inserting tabs into text. The two key points: (1) make sure the word processor inserts actual tab characters, not merely a string of spaces and (2) make sure you have just one tab stop inserted between columns. The temptation is to insert extra tabs to line up the text in the word processor. Don't do it. As long as you have only one tab between columns, Ventura formats everything correctly once you load the file.

➡*NOTE: Hit the Tab key once to separate each column. Hit the Return key once to end each row in the table.*

Once the text file is loaded into Ventura, create a single tag and apply it to each row of the table. When choosing horizontal alignment, *do not select Justified.* Ventura's justification feature overrides tab settings. In multi-column pages, you may want to specify Overall Width: Frame-Wide so the table can spread across all columns. If you choose Overall Width: Column-Wide it will be confined to a single column.

Select Tab Settings from the Paragraph menu to specify the column widths and other characteristics. Chapter Eight, "Advanced Functions," explains the operation of the Tab Settings dialog box.

Tips on tabs for tables

TIP *Experiment with tab locations* until you get them right. If you fail to leave enough space for lengthy entries, the text wraps to the extreme left margin of the table, not the left edge of the column. As a result, you must adjust the tab locations to accommodate the longest entry in each column. You must also experiment to visually balance the table.

TIP *Consider using a line break* to separate the rows in a table. A line break is created by pressing Ctrl-Enter in text editing mode, or by typing <R> into the word processing file. *Advantage*: You do not have to tag each line separately. A line break tells Ventura to start a new line without starting a new paragraph. *Disadvantage*: The table is harder to enter and read in the word processor. The exception is Microsoft Word, which can not only enter line breaks that are read by Ventura, but also displays them on separate lines in the word processing screen.

TIP *A sans-serif font* (such as Helvetica or Swiss) and a point size smaller than body text are typical choices for tabular material.

TIP *To create lines* between each row, use the Ruling Lines dialog boxes from the Paragraph menu. To create vertical lines between columns, use Graphic mode to draw in the lines. If you plan to add vertical lines, make sure the table is in a separate frame. Select the frame before drawing the lines, so they are attached to the frame. Now you can move the table anywhere in the document and the lines will move with it.

➥ *NOTE: We recommend using the Box Text method instead for tables with vertical lines.*

Tables with Box Text

You can also use Ventura's Box Text feature to construct

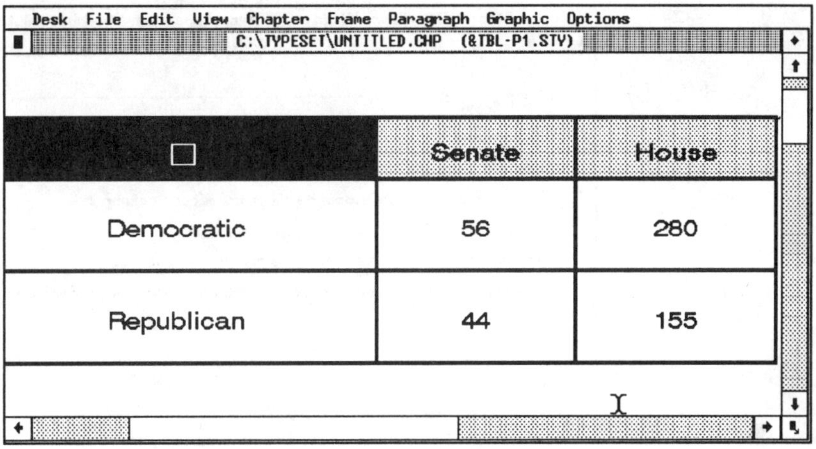

Figure 10-23. This table was created entirely with Ventura's Box Text function.

simple tables (Figure 10-23). This method is appropriate if (1) you want lines between rows and/or columns and (2) the table is small enough to type directly into Ventura.

Constructing a table with Box Text follows the same principles as building a free-form document (see the section later in this chapter). The secret is to construct the Grid Settings so each Box Text automatically snaps into alignment.

When you first type material into a Box Text, Ventura assigns it the Z_BOXTEXT tag. Many users do not realize that they can change this tag. If you create a series of tags called Center, Vertical Center, Left, Right, Justified, and Decimal, you will have the ability to align the text within the box in any fashion by assigning the correct tag.

Tables with side-by-side paragraphs

The most useful and versatile table creation option is the side-by-side paragraphs method (called *vertical tabbing* in the Ventura Reference Guide). With this method, your tables can have multi-line entries. Ventura automatically adjusts the spacing to fit.

Creating side-by-side paragraphs takes three steps:

- type each cell as a separate paragraph
- align the paragraphs into columns
- move the paragraphs side-by-side

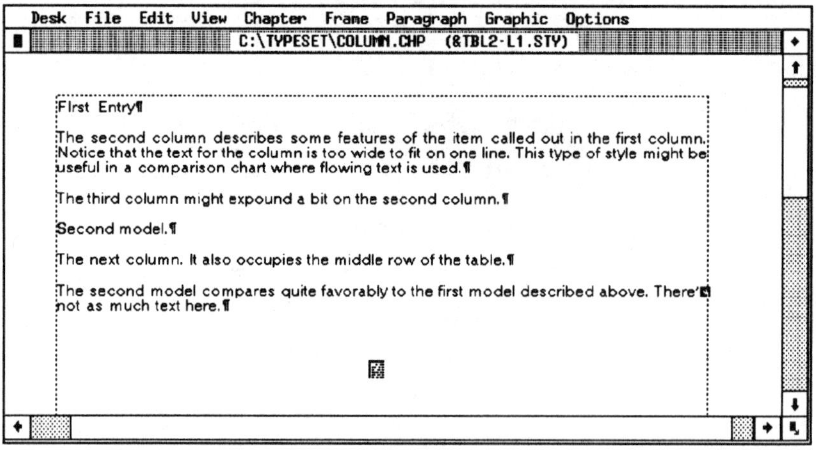

Figure 10-24. To create a table with side-by-side paragraphs, start by typing each cell as a separate paragraph.

First you type the paragraphs one after another (Figure 10-24). Each paragraph represents one cell in the table. Type them in the same order they occur when reading the table left to right. Create one tag for each column. Our example has three columns, so we might call these tags COL1, COL2, and COL3.

Your next step is to align the paragraphs into columns. To do this, you use In From Left and In From Right from the Spacing dialog box (Figure 10-25). Formerly, each paragraph was the full width of the margins. Now each paragraph is restricted into a narrow column.

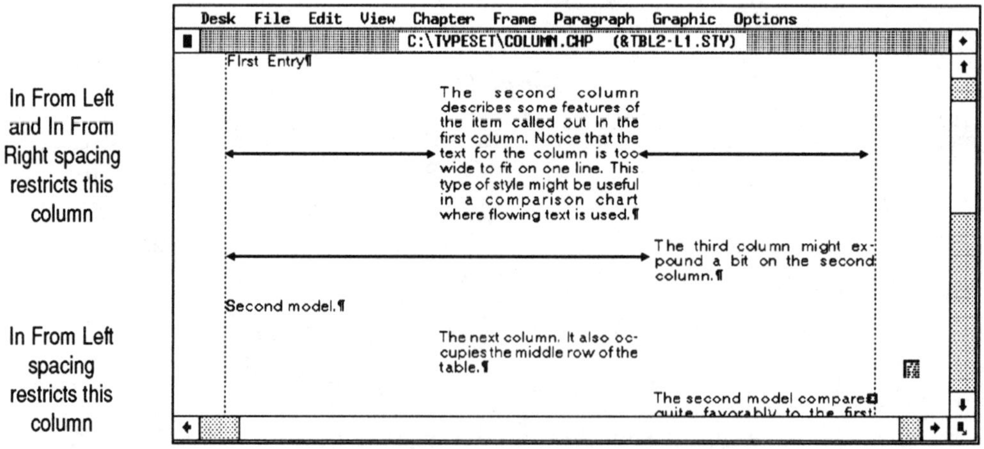

Figure 10-25. Give each column a separate tag. Restrict the text to narrow columns with In From Left and In From Right spacing.

Be sure to allow extra space for a gutter between columns to prevent the text from touching when you put the paragraphs side-by-side.

Now you are ready for the third and final step: moving the paragraphs side-by-side. To do this, remove the line breaks between the column tags. In our example, COL1 will get a line break *before.* COL2 will get a line break of *none.* And COL3 will get a line break *after* (Figure 10-26).

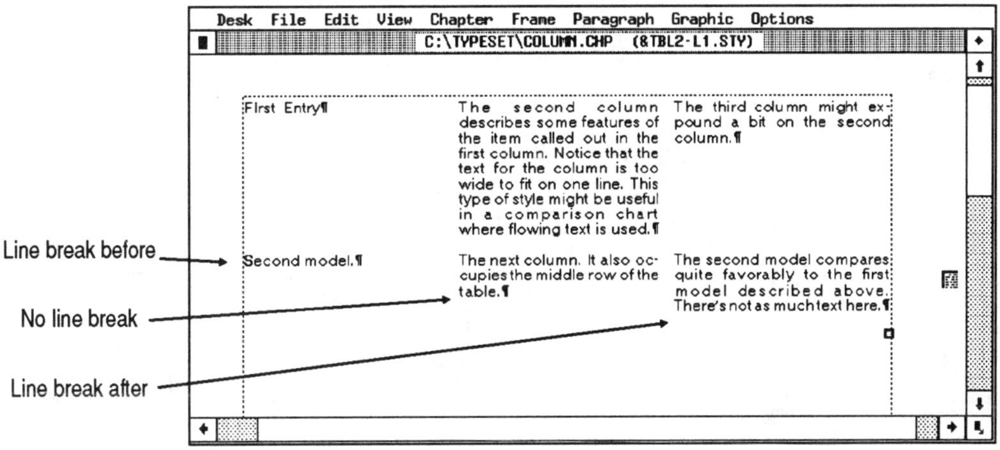

Figure 10-26. With the Breaks dialog box, remove any line breaks between the columns, so they can all reside on the same line.

To prevent a table from breaking across a page, use the Breaks dialog box to choose Allow Within: No and Keep With Next: Yes for all three column tags.

➡ *NOTE: If you set Keep With Next: Yes for the third column, you will need a separate tag for the last entry in the table. This last entry must have Keep With Next: No. Otherwise, Ventura will try to keep this final table entry on the same page with whatever paragraph follows.*

While in the Breaks dialog box, make sure the Next Y Position is set to Normal for each of the tags. In Ventura Publisher, the Y position refers to the vertical position of the upper left corner. A normal Y position puts the top line of each column even with the top line of the previous one. By contrast, Beside Last Line of Prev. Para puts the top of each column even with the *bottom* of the previous one.

Table 10-2 lists the key attributes for the example discussed above, should you want to duplicate it for practice.

Table 10-2. Key tag attributes for a three-column table with side-by-side paragraphs.

Attribute	COL1	COL2	COL3
Font	Helvetica 12	Helvetica 12	Helvetica 12
Alignment	Left	Justified	Justified
Above Spacing	12 pt	0	0
Below Spacing	0	0	0
Inter-Line Spacing	14 pt	14 pt	14 pt
In From Left Spacing	0	13 picas	26 picas
In from Right Spacing	27 picas	14 picas	0
Line Breaks	Before	No	After

Although we showed you a three-column example, you can use the same method to create as many columns as will fit on the page. Give the first column a line break before, the middle columns a line break of none, and the last column a line break after.

Lines around side-by-side paragraphs

To add rules to the table, use the Ruling Lines dialog boxes. You can put lines between each row, or boxes around each cell. For boxes, choose Ruling Box Around for each of the column tags. You must redo the spacing of the columns so there is no gutter between the columns. In other words, each column must start exactly where the other one left off. That way, the ruling lines will overlap exactly. To keep the text from touching the lines, put space below the rule.

For extra space between the text and the lines, or to create blank cells, use line breaks.

TAB

Thumb tabs

Thumb tabs are small dark marks at the edge of directories and similar publications. They make it easier to find specific parts of the document. They show up better if you print them on both sides of the paper, so use the Left & Right option in the Repeating Frame dialog box. Create a small frame with an opaque black fill pattern at the upper right of the first (right-hand) page and turn it into a repeating frame. Repeat the process for the next chapter, but place this repeating frame one notch lower. Use the rulers and enlarged view to get the size and position correct. If your printer cannot produce reverse text, use a gray box instead.

Use the text rotation feature from the Alignment dialog box to place text sideways in the thumb tab. To create vertical text, simply place a line break after each letter.

We have produced an example of a thumb tab in the upper righthand corner of this page.

➥ *NOTE: Most laser printers won't print to the edge of the page, so thumb tabs in laser-printed documents are only possible when creating pages smaller than the 8.5x11 in. page size.*

Title pages

Title pages for reports, proposals, and similar documents should be simple and uncluttered (Figure 10-27). Try to use design elements that relate to and foreshadow the design of the interior pages. Avoid extremely large display type, which is more appropriate for ads, flyers, and brochures.

You can use Ventura's page break features to isolate the title material on its own page.

Type effects

We reminded you earlier that you can treat a logo as a picture and bring it into a frame. There are several other ways to get unusual font effects.

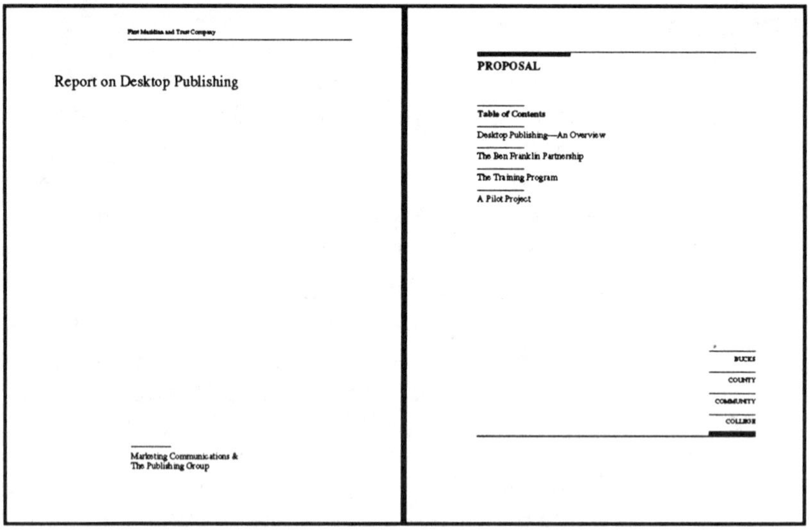

Figure 10-27. These simple, clean title pages echo the design elements used in the interior.

Reverse type

Reverse type is an effective technique that is available with some (but not all) laser printers. It is accomplished by putting white text onto a black background. You can accomplish a similar effect by putting either white or black type against a gray background. Figure 10-28 shows both effects.

The easiest way to get a black background is to create a frame and choose a black fill pattern (Frame Background from the Frame menu). Ventura automatically changes the font to white if you select a black background for a frame.

Likewise, you can put a black or gray fill pattern inside a Box Text. Frames and Box Texts are fine for one-time effects. For repetitive effects — for instance, for a heading that will repeat throughout the document — we recommend a second method instead. Frames and graphic shapes have to be drawn one by one. But if you use a ruling line to create the black or gray background, Ventura can generate it for you. Although it takes longer the first time around, it results in a tag that can be used over and over again.

The theory is simple: make the white text overlap a wide black rule. To create this effect, start in Paragraph mode. Add a new tag and call it Reverse (or something similar). Change the font

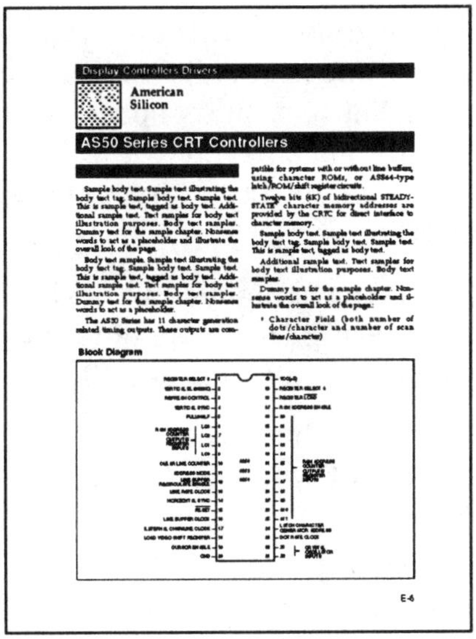

Figure 10-28. The title and heading of this sample page use reverse type.

characteristics until the text looks the way you want. Select white for the color. Now create a black ruling line above for this tag. Select a width at least 4 points bigger than the type size.

These steps give you everything you want except the overlap. The key to forcing the text to overlap the rule is found in the Ruling Line Above dialog box (Figure 10-29). Notice Space Below Rule 3 at the bottom left. As you may recall from an

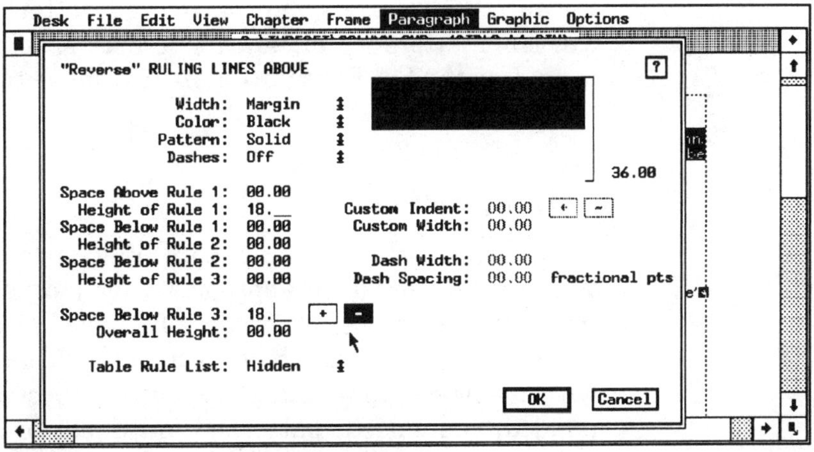

Figure 10-29. The Ruling Line Above dialog box.

earlier chapter, this number actually represents the space below the last ruling line (not just the third line). If you enter a positive number, Ventura adds space. But if you enter a negative number (by clicking on the minus sign), Ventura *subtracts* space. If you subtract enough space, the text moves up to overlap the rule.

How much negative space should you enter in Space Below Rule 3? Start by entering the same amount as the height of the rule. Then experiment until it looks the way you want.

We have described white text on a black rule. The same technique can be used to put white text onto a gray rule, or black text on a white rule.

➡*NOTE: Some printers cannot produce white text on a black background. In many cases, however, you can buy special fonts for these printers that achieve the same effect.*

Tracking

Many people use tracking (from the Paragraph Typography dialog box) to improve the appearance of display type by moving the letters closer together. You can also use tracking to move letters farther apart to create a special effect (Figure 10-30).

Baseline shifts

Because Ventura lets you control each letter individually, you can shift letters up or down to create special nameplate effects. Use the Set Font button in Text mode to shift individual letters.

Other type effects

Many type and printer vendors offer special display fonts. These typefaces are inappropriate for long stretches of text, but they can be useful for special purposes such as logos and headlines. You can also buy special effects packages that start with a normal font and transform it to create rotated, expanded, condensed, patterned, outlined, or shadowed type, among others. Ventura also comes with some type effects for

VENTURA SCOOP

Xerox introduces a new product
Will Ventura run on the Macintosh?
Xerox takes on Aldus in IBM market
Scanner produces 256 levels of grey

Xerox shows Ventura 1.1 at Spring conference

Board approves Ventura purchase

Ventura 1.1 takes on PageMaker in battle for IBM PC marketplace

Figure 10-30. This newsletter nameplate uses looser tracking to space the letters of the word "Ventura" further apart, so it aligns with the word "Scoop."

PostScript printers. See Chapter Seven, "Producing Output," for more on fonts.

Other type effects can be created using the drawing tools to lay a screen of white dots on top of large black type. Normally, when you select a fill pattern, the printer creates an arrangement of tiny black dots. If you select white for the color of the fill pattern, you have created a pattern of white dots. If you put that pattern on top of large black type, the result is patterned type. Only the very largest type sizes of 24 points and up are big enough to show this effectively. Not all printers can recreate this effect.

In a similar fashion, you can create a box with a series of closely spaced white lines. If you move the box over black type, the white lines become visible where they intersect with the type. The result is an interesting logo type effect similar to the one seen in logos from companies like IBM and Ventura Software.

Building frame-style chapters

In Chapter Six, we explained that Ventura can create three kinds of documents: page-style, frame-style, and free-form. This section explains how to build a frame-style chapter. Frame-style chapters are the most complex document type. If you can master this method, you can produce virtually any type of publication with Ventura.

Many of the skills and steps are the same ones described in Chapter Six for page-style documents. But there is a crucial difference. In a page-style chapter, you put text on the Underlying Page. That's the method of choice when all (or most) of the chapter is contained in a single file. By contrast, in frame-style documents, you first draw frames onto the page. Then you pour text into the frames.

Some documents contain many different text files. Newsletters and magazines are common examples. Theoretically, you could combine them all into one large file and place that file on the Underlying Page. In practice, it's usually easier to keep each article as a separate file. In frame-style chapters, you put those separate files into frames. The frames go on top of the Underlying Page. They act as containers for the text files.

How Ventura handles text in frames

Let's review how Ventura works with text in frames to better understand how to build this type of chapter. If you place a text file onto the Underlying Page, Ventura creates as many new pages as needed to fit the entire file. But if you place a file into a frame, *Ventura places text to the bottom of the frame and stops*. Then it waits for you to tell it where to put the rest of the file (Figure 10-31).

Frames create boundaries separating different files. For instance, you can use frames to place one text file into the left column, and a second, separate file into the right column (Figure 10-32).

Or you could leave the two files at the top of the page, and place a third file into a frame that stretches the full width of the margin (Figure 10-33). The possibilities are endless.

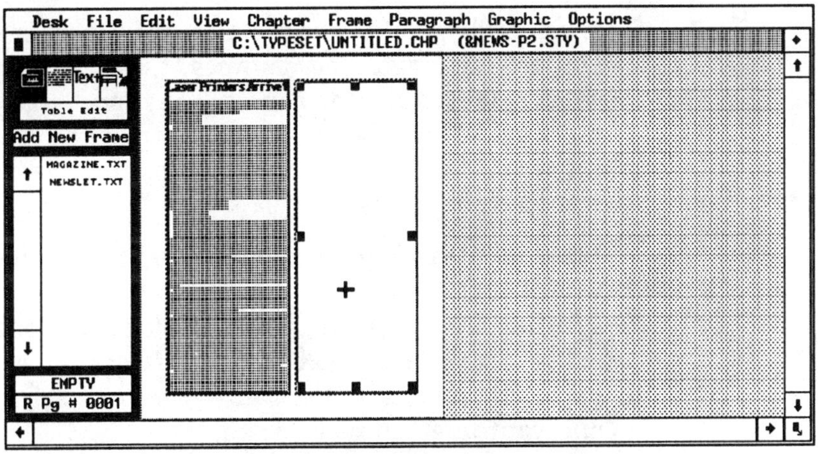

Figure 10-31. Text poured into the left frame stopped flowing at the bottom of the frame.

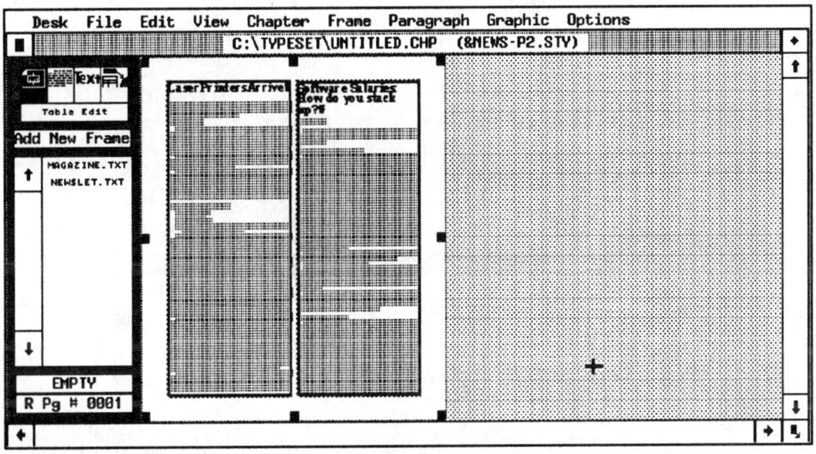

Figure 10-32. A new file has been poured into the right-hand frame.

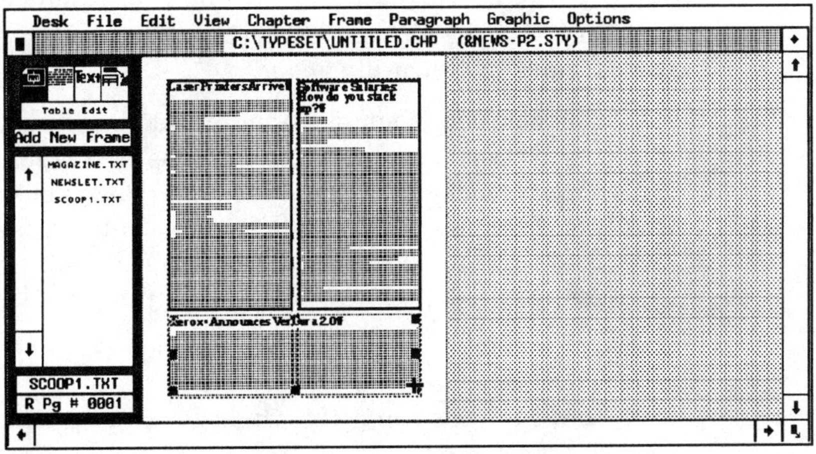

Figure 10-33. A third file has been poured into the wide frame at the bottom.

Incidentally, you can combine text in frames with text on the Underlying Page. For instance, that's how you would add a short sidebar to a long report. The report goes on the Underlying Page. The sidebar sits in a separate frame on top of the Page. In frame-style documents, however, all of the text resides in separate frames.

When Ventura puts part of a file into a frame, it remembers where it left off. You can then put the rest of the file into another frame (or frames). Best of all, the second frame doesn't have to be next to the first one, or even on the same page. For instance, you can put part of a file onto page one, and continue the rest of it on page two — or page three, or page four, or wherever you want. Consequently, articles can leap-frog one another. Many publishing professionals refer to this as *chaining* articles.

Ventura remembers the link between frames. As you make editing changes, text flows back and forth between frames, without your intervention. There's more good news. When you put a frame on top of the Underlying Page, you can choose to mimic the format and typography of the Page, or you can use a different format. As you saw above, you can put a single column frame at the bottom of a three-column page.

Using the Underlying Page as a snap-to grid

The first step in creating frame-style documents is to understand that frames act as containers for articles. The second step is to learn how to position the frames for an attractive look. Obviously, your newsletter won't look right if you scatter frames haphazardly about.

The solution is simple. You format the Underlying Page with the correct margins and columns *even though you are not going to place any text on the Page.* Then you use the Underlying Page as a framework — a snap-to guide for positioning frames. Thanks to Ventura's snap-to features, frames automatically align because they will jump to the column guides (Figure 10-34).

Those of you with a background in the graphic arts will realize that you are using the Underlying Page to set up a simple

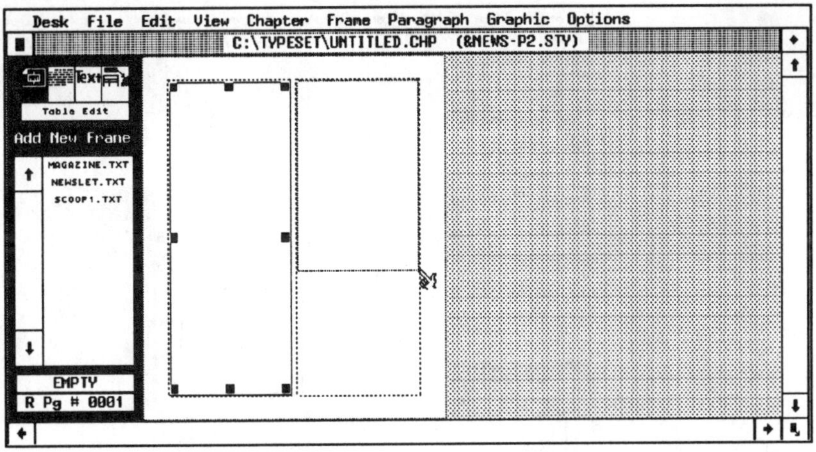

Figure 10-34. By formatting the Underlying Page in advance, you can draw frames by snapping them to the column guides.

grid. A grid is an underlying system of spacing page elements that gives form and structure to a design.

You need one more bit of theory before you are ready to start building a newsletter. Ventura can flow text only in a *forward* direction. To Ventura, forward refers to two different things. On a page-by-page basis, it means that Ventura cannot flow text to a previous page. You cannot start an article on page four and continue it on page two.

On a single page, forward refers to the order in which frames were drawn. You cannot flow backward from the second frame to the first one. Position makes no difference. Figure 10-35 illustrates the distinction.

Fortunately, Ventura provides a simple method for changing the order of frames. To make a frame the last one in Ventura's eyes, simply delete and insert it again.

Creating the Page grid

Now let's walk through the process of creating a frame-style chapter. You begin by establishing a format for the Underlying Page. This is the structure onto which you hang frames.

As with page-style documents, you can use the revised Ventura Formula as a general guideline. Table 10-3 summarizes the process.

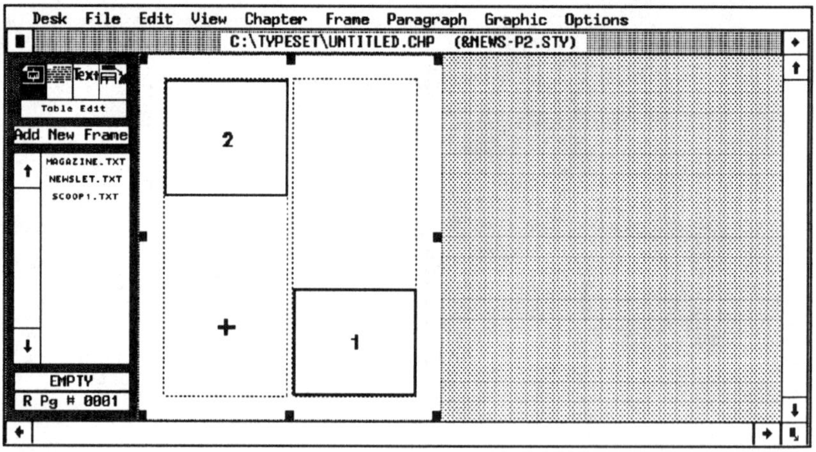

Figure 10-35. Frame #1 was drawn first. Ventura can flow text from #1 to #2, but not the reverse, no matter what their position on the page.

Table 10-3. Stages in building a frame-style chapter.

Style	Create the underlying structure
Text	Draw frames and put the text inside Edit the Pictures
Pictures	Draw frames and put the pictures inside Edit the pictures
Chapter	Save the chapter Create a chapter template

First determine the format you want. In the examples below, we show a three-column newsletter, but the same principles apply to other formats and document types. Build the style sheet. Be sure to choose margin and column settings that represent the correct spacing (Figure 10-36).

Then complete the structure by adding headers and/or footers (if desired). Now add frames for each separate article and page element on page one. Snap them to the column guides so they fit into the overall page design. Choose Show Column Guides from the Options menu so you can see what you're doing. Don't forget to draw frames for such things as the nameplate, the articles, the masthead, pictures, and the table of contents (Figure 10-37).

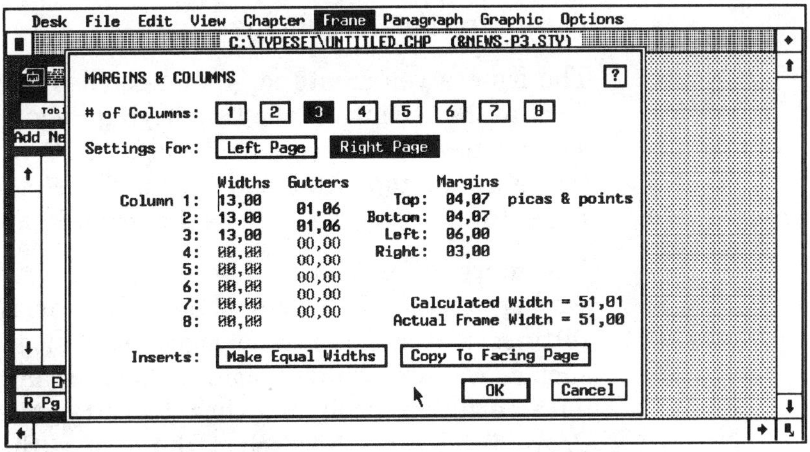

Figure 10-36. These margin and column settings create the Underlying Page.

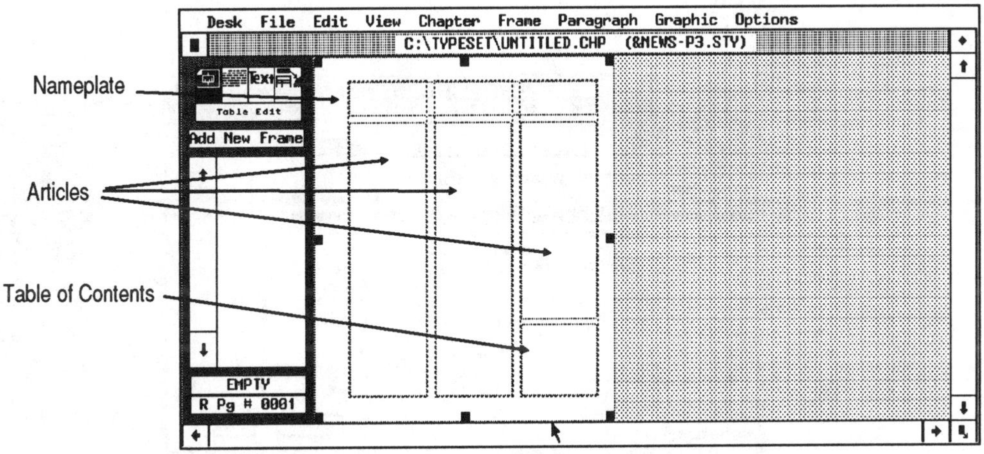

Figure 10-37. Draw frames for each of the major page elements. In this example, we have created frames for the nameplate, the articles, and the table of contents.

When you have blank frames drawn in for page one, use Insert/Remove Page from the Chapter menu to add a second page. Draw the frames for the articles and pictures on this page. You don't have to be exact — you can resize the frames later if necessary. Right now you just want to build the basic structure.

Continue with this process for the rest of the pages in the document. If you are not sure where you will need frames on a page, leave them off and add them later.

Overriding default settings

The frames you create for your text files do not have to conform to the settings of the Underlying Page. For instance, the sample newsletter page in Figure 10-37 has a one-column frame at the top, stretched over a three-column Underlying Page. In this case, we will use it to contain a masthead.

The margins and column settings of a frame override the settings of the Underlying Page. You can also override the settings in the Chapter Typography dialog box for features such as widows, orphans, column balance and so on. Normally a frame automatically matches the settings of the Underlying Page. To change this, select the frame, then select Frame Typography from the Frame menu (Figure 10-38). Change the settings and click OK. Your changes apply only to the selected frame.

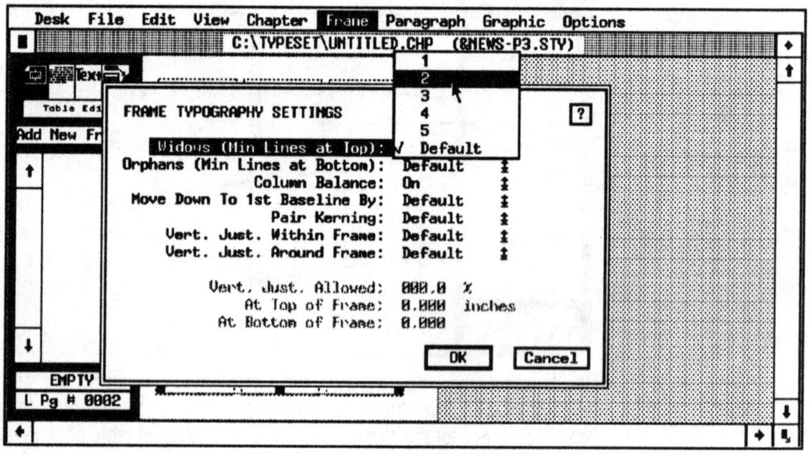

Figure 10-38. The Frame Typography dialog box can override the chapter settings for an individual frame.

Loading and placing the text

With a framework in place, you are ready to work on the text. Load the text files as a group, using the procedures outlined in Chapter Six. Now place them one by one into the proper frames.

To place a text file into a frame:

- Enable Frame mode.

- Select the frame.
- Select the file name from the Assignment List.

Ventura pours as much of the file as will fit into the frame and stops at the bottom. To continue placing this file, go to the frame where you want the rest of the text to appear and repeat the process: select the frame, then select the file name from the Assignment List. Ventura fills the new frame with the remaining text.

You can continue this process as many times as necessary until the text file has been completely placed. If you want, you can leave part of a file unplaced. Ventura won't lose the rest of the file, nor will it forget to save it. It simply won't display or print it. At any time, you can draw another frame and place the rest of the file.

➥*NOTE: If you choose Show Tabs & Returns from the Options menu, you will be able to tell when you have reached the end of the file by the square end-of-file symbol.*

You will be pleased to know that Ventura does not require you to place an entire file at one time. You can stop in the middle and begin another task, such as placing a different file in another frame. Whenever you are ready to put more of the first file somewhere else, Ventura continues where it left off.

This feature greatly speeds up the layout of frame-style documents like newsletters. You can start several articles on page one. When you are finished, move to page two and continue any or all of them onto that page. Then move to page three and so on.

Ventura remembers this path and dynamically adjusts the text. For instance, suppose you place a text file into frames on pages one, three, four, five, and eight. As you make changes to the text, Ventura flows text back and forth as necessary between these frames.

Jump text

When continuing articles onto following pages, most designers recommend a jump line — for instance, "Continued on page 4," or "See *Market Research*, page 4." You could add this jump text right in the text file. However, if you add or delete text, the jump phrase may be pushed out of position onto another page. A better solution is to place jump text into separate, very small frames.

➥ *NOTE: You can also insert cross-references so Ventura will automatically track which page the article jumps to and insert the correct number.*

Completing a frame-style chapter

The rest of the process of building a frame-style chapter duplicates the steps of a page-style chapter:

- draw frames for pictures
- load picture files inside
- edit the pictures
- save the chapter
- create a chapter template

See Chapter Six, "Building the Chapter," if you need to brush up on these skills.

Tips for frame-style chapters

TIP *Use Reduced View* when you first place text files in frames. This lets you see how much of the frame is filled and how much space remains. It also speeds text flow, assuming you have set Text to Greek: 6 in the Set Preferences dialog box. Once you've placed the text, return to Normal View to tag and edit it.

TIP *Use Go to Page* to jump quickly to the next page containing the continuation of an article. For instance, if you start an article on page one, and continue it to page eight, you can jump directly from one to the other. Enable Frame mode and select the frame containing the text file. Choose Go to Page from the Chapter menu (or press the shortcut Ctrl-G). Select Relative to: File and Which Page: Next. Ventura jumps you to the next page containing that text file, no matter how far it is from the current page. To jump backwards, select Which Page: Prev.

TIP *Save time constructing newsletters* and similar documents by using the same text file names for each issue. When you finish with an issue, back up the chapter and the text files under new names and in a new location. When you write stories for the next issue, use the same text file names as you did for the first issue. Put them in the same location, so Ventura's chapter file knows where to find them.

When you open the newsletter chapter, it will look for the previous file names in the previous location. Since you have put new text into the old file names, you have created a new issue without even loading new files. Obviously, you will have to do some fine-tuning to make the new text fit precisely. This technique is best for publications that use the same basic format from issue to issue. Typical file names might be NLLEAD.TXT for the newsletter's lead story, NLNEWS.TXT for the news section, and so on. The same concept works for picture files as well.

TIP *You can combine the previous technique with batch files* to further automate newsletter production. If you create a template that always looks for the same file names, you can then program a short batch file that not only loads Ventura, but opens the newsletter template as well. You could have separate batch files for all your major document types: NEWSLET.BAT, BROCHURE.BAT, RELEASE.BAT, etc. See Chapter Nine, "Special Tips and Techniques," for more on using batch files with Ventura.

Balanced columns in frame-style layout

Ventura can automatically balance columns. This feature is particularly useful for the last page of a multi-column book or manual. Without column balance, text fills the left-most column all the way to the bottom. Only then does it proceed to the next column(s), and only if it has sufficient text.

Column balance forces Ventura to place equal amounts of text in each column, creating a visually pleasing result. Although the most common application is the last page in a chapter or section, column balance also helps when illustrations or sidebars are stretched across the entire width of a multi-column layout.

The Column Balance button occurs in the Chapter Typography and Frame Typography dialog boxes. Choose On to force the columns to balance horizontally. Choose Off to allow them to be uneven. We recommend On for books and manuals and Off for most newsletters and magazines. (Choose On if you use banner headlines, however.) You can mix and match within the same document; for instance, you could have Column Balance: Off on the Underlying Page, but On for certain frames on top of the page. Column Balance is of no value for single-column formats (there's nothing to balance), so turn it off to increase text formatting speed.

Although a headline may extend across a frame, text subordinate to that headline does not necessarily line up in columns underneath the headline. Instead, it will jump to the top of the next column unless you have column balance on. Figures 10-39 and 10-40 show column balance on and off.

➥*NOTE: Column Balance has certain limitations. It balances columns as closely as possible, but you may be required to fine-tune the spacing on your own.*

Building free-form chapters

A free-form chapter is one where each page has a different format, and text is contained in Box Text or separate frames. Advertisements and forms are the most common examples (Figure 10-41). Although Ventura is widely known for its long-document power, it is also capable of creating short, free-form documents quickly and efficiently.

Chapter Four, "Creating Pictures," provides a complete course in the fundamentals of Graphic mode. Review this chapter to learn the basics. In this section, we will simply add a few comments on how to build documents with Box Text and other graphic shapes.

In our discussion earlier of frame-style chapters, we pointed

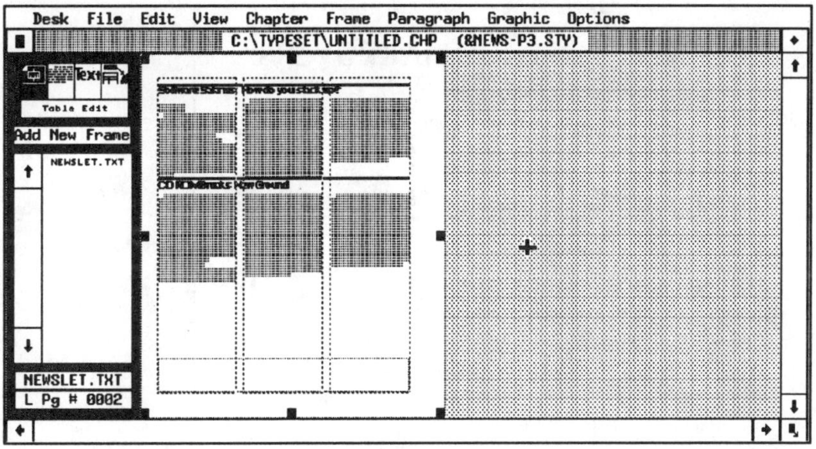

Figure 10-39. With column balance on, text in multi-column frames will align evenly under frame-wide tags such as the headings in this document.

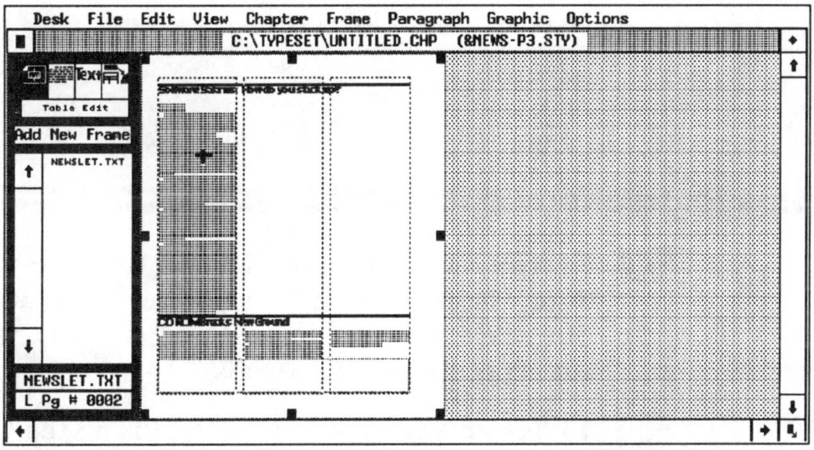

Figure 10-40. With column balance off, text in multi-column frames will not align itself evenly if frame-wide tags intervene. Choose Column Balance: On to avoid this problem.

out the importance of building the Underlying Page. The Page provides a structure for the frames. In the same fashion, the secret to building free-form documents is to construct a snap-to grid. The Grid Settings dialog box performs the same snap-to functions for Graphic mode as Column and Line Snap for frames.

Once you determine the correct grid settings, building a free-form document is extremely simple. Because the grid automatically snaps everything into position, it's hard to go wrong. Boxes and rules align automatically.

Figure 10-41. Use Box Text and frames to construct free-form documents such as ads and forms.

Tips for free-form documents

TIP *You can retag Box Text.* The first time you type inside a Box Text, Ventura automatically assigns the Z_BOXTEXT tag. You can retag this text to anything else you want to create a variety of styles and formats.

TIP *To link graphics* select them all (using the Graphic menu or the keyboard shortcut Ctrl-Q). Then when you move one graphic you move them all. If you don't want to move them all, deselect some of them. Graphics that are selected together move together.

TIP *To create several groups on the same page* assign all the graphics in one group to a frame, all the graphics in the other group to another frame and so on. These grouping frames can be small, invisible (no ruling lines), empty and off in the margin. Their only function is to link a group of graphics. To choose one group, select the proper frame in frame-setting mode, then switch to graphics drawing and press Ctrl-Q (select all).

TIP *To fine-tune the position* of a graphic, link the graphic to a frame, and place the upper left corner of the graphic at the upper left corner of that frame. Now you can use Sizing & Scaling from the Frame menu to adjust the upper left X,Y position of the frame — and, therefore, of the graphic.

TIP *To move a tiny line or box* that is difficult to position, surround it with a larger box, choose Select All and move the small graphic by dragging the larger one (you may have to deselect some of the other graphics on the page).

TIP *Don't forget that you can save line and fill attributes.* If you are building, for instance, a series of rectangles with the same attributes, click on the Save To buttons in Line Attributes and Fill Attributes. From then on, every box you draw will have the same attributes.

TIP *You can copy more than one graphic shape to the Graphic Clipboard.* For instance, to speed drawing, use Shift-Click to select an entire row of boxes. Copy all of them to the Clipboard. Then you can paste in the entire row at once to create a large form or calendar in moments.

TIP *Ventura's page and chapter numbering features* work anywhere on the page, not just in headers and footers. You can use it to create sequentially numbered forms.

Notes on document types

We wish to finish this chapter with some general comments on the major document types. Preceding sections of this chapter have provided tips on special formats. This section provides tips on which formats are appropriate for which documents.

Advertisements, flyers, and other marketing materials

We recommend that you build most marketing materials as free-form documents, provided they are only a page or two in length. For longer documents, such as brochures and proposals, you will probably want to put most of the text on the Underlying Page.

Though Ventura Publisher is known for its long-document power, it is admirably suited to one- and two-page documents as well. It is safe to say that anything you can do with another program, you can do with Ventura. For most free-form documents, you can type the text inside Ventura Publisher, since there is generally not too much to write. You will probably want to use individual frames or box text to hold the text within the ad. Logos and unusual typestyles (stretched, angled, pi fonts) can be created in outside graphics programs and then brought into Ventura as pictures.

Books, handbooks, manuals

Books are a prime application for Ventura Publisher. Its batch processing capabilities make it ideal for long documents that would be a headache with other desktop publishing programs. To make best use of this batch processing power, minimize the use of separate frames. Keep as much of the activity as possible on the Underlying Page.

Camera-ready art for book pages needs crop marks to show the printer where to line up the negatives on the masking sheets. These marks are reference points that keep the pages of the book from ending up crooked or off center. They also indicate the final size of the page. Crop marks are printed along with the rest of the page, then trimmed off when the book is bound.

Ventura has a built-in crop marks feature that is turned on and off in the To Print dialog box. To use this feature, you must make sure the Underlying Page is the same size as the final trim size. (Hint: Select on the Underlying Page, then use Sizing & Scaling to change its size.) If you are using anything larger than 7.5x10 in. pages, the crop marks will probably fall into the dead zone of a laser printer.

Catalogs, directories, listings

Perhaps no other type of document demonstrates the amazing power of Ventura Publisher as well as directories and listings. Most directories consist of repeating elements that are consistently formatted. For example, in a product directory, the product category names might always appear at the top of a column in 12-point Helvetica Bold and company names in 8-point Helvetica Light.

An intelligent approach to directories is to use a database management program such as dBASE III or DataFlex to generate both the text *and* the tags. It is then just a matter of loading the resulting ASCII file into Ventura Publisher. If you have previously created a style sheet for the directory, you will see the document instantly formatted according to your specifications.

The key to this technique is to devise a report format for your database that creates an ASCII file with Ventura Publisher tags inserted in it. For instance, you might instruct the program to print the character string "@PROD_CAT = " before outputting the contents of the Product Category field.

Forms

Forms are quick, easy, and simple to produce with Ventura Publisher. You can produce camera-ready masters for reproduction at a quick print shop. Or, by using Box Text for the rectangles and divisions, you can even fill in the forms on screen and print them out with Ventura.

And because of Ventura's style sheet approach, you may be able to merge data from another program into a Ventura file. In this fashion, you can print both the form and the data in one pass.

Simple, one-page forms that will be filled out by hand don't need much discussion here. Use any and all graphic drawing and frame techniques you need to get the right look. Box Text is the easiest way to create simple forms like invoices. Use grid snap to make sure the boxes line up with each other. Fill some of the boxes with a pattern to set them apart.

But if you want to merge the form with data from another computer application, use tags as much as possible to create graphic effects. If graphics are needed, put them on the Underlying Page so they'll be reproduced on every page. Separate logos and address information from the data by putting them into repeating frames that appear on every page. The idea is to create a format and style sheet that can reproduce as many forms as needed just by pouring in tagged text.

➡ *NOTE: Make sure that the last tag on the page includes a page break. This will force Ventura to a new page where it will start the next form.*

This method won't work, of course, unless you can get the other application to generate the tags. Many accounting programs, for instance, are limited in their reporting abilities. Others, however, are based around database management software, and may have the capabilities you need. And most popular database programs can do what you want — namely, pull out specified information, insert tags before it, and put them together into an ASCII file.

The preceding section about directory publishing gave additional thoughts on getting other software to generate tags. And the final section of Chapter Three, Creating Text, gave a full explanation of how to preformat files by inserting tags and other information.

Magazines and newsletters

Ventura Publisher can be a powerful tool for producing magazines, especially trade and technical magazines that follow a consistent format from month to month. Use frame-style chapters. The bulk of the work will come in building the first issue. Once that is done, you can use chapter templates as a starting point for each successive issue.

If there are advertisements in your magazine, you can use frames to indicate where they will be placed so that your lithographer can strip in the right negative from each client. Place a label in the empty frames to indicate which ad goes where, and any other pertinent information about the ad. Handle photographs within the editorial pages using the techniques described in Chapter Seven.

For short, simple newsletters, you can place all the articles into a single text file, and place that file onto the Underlying Page. This is the fastest technique, but it does not allow the design flexibility of the frame-style approach.

Letters, memos, and correspondence

Standardized memo formats can improve your image if they incorporate good design. They can cut costs if you are able to use the laser printer to put the company logo on the same page (without the need to reload the printer with letterhead). They can convey more information if graphics are combined with text on the page. And they can increase productivity if information is in a standard format, so readers always know where to look for the facts they need.

One approach to creating memos with Ventura Publisher is to put the logo/letterhead material into a separate frame at the top of the page. Use this as the document template as described above — load the template, then bring in the text file. Rename the document if you want to save an electronic version, or simply abandon it after printing if you do not.

A second approach uses a word processing file as a template. This standardized file can be handed out to all the people who write memos. (If they use different word processors, create it once and use Chapter Three's technique to convert it to different formats.) This file will have the correct tag names inserted. It can also include text that you want to appear in every memo. All the writers need to do is fill in the blanks.

Once you master this simple template technique for memos, you'll find ways to adapt it to other, more complex documents.

Proposals

Since proposals are usually intended to get business, they are vitally important. Appearance and readability are crucial. This is one application where it might pay to hire a professional to create a graphic design you can use over and over again. As an alternative, search for outstanding proposal samples you can imitate.

Consider using a repeating frame to place the company logo on every other page. You may want to include the date in the header or footer as well. Live headers can also be a good idea. Key them to the section heading, or even to the subtitles, so readers can glance at the top of the page to know exactly where they are.

Reports

The longer the report, the more important it is to use Ventura's table of contents and indexing capabilities. Consider adding live headers as well, to make reference easier.

Drawings and charts can be incorporated through the standard means: by saving the desired illustration to a file, then loading that file into a frame. Spreadsheets can be incorporated using the technique from Chapter Three for converting and inserting tab characters into spreadsheets.

Technical documentation

Organization is one key to usable, effective documentation, and Ventura has several features to aid organization, including table of contents, indexing, footnotes, and live headers.

You may also find that you can enforce a degree of standardization upon your authors by supplying them with template documents for their word processors. If they are given the organization in advance, their job becomes one of filling in the blanks. And if the template incorporates tags, the editor's job becomes one of simply loading the pretagged text files into Ventura and fine-tuning the end result.

Those who document software may be able to benefit from Software Carousel, DESQView, and other programs that provide the ability to switch back and forth from one application to another. The idea is to keep the word processing program in one partition. In another partition, the writer keeps the software being documented along with a screen capture utility like HotShot.

The writer works in tandem: He or she uses the software in one partition, switches to the word processor to write about it, switches back to the software again, and so on. When the writer needs a screen to illustrate a point, he or she invokes the capture utility to put the screen into a file. Then the writer jumps back to the word processor and inserts that file name at the spot where the illustration belongs. The writer can also insert the caption at the same time.

When laying out the document, the editor has merely to stop at each reference and load the screen file into a frame. If the screen illustrations are a standard size, the editor can keep a frame in temporary memory and paste it in as needed.

We hope the advice in the preceding section will serve as a starting point for bright ideas of your own.

Chapter Eleven

The Professional Extension

This chapter examines several specialized functions present in the Professional Extension of Ventura Publisher:

- how to create and edit tables
- how to create and edit equations
- how to insert and use cross-references
- how to use vertical justification
- how to use the advanced hyphenation dictionary

Let's take a quick overview of these functions before we explore them in detail.

Table editor

Ventura's table editor is a powerful tool for complex tables, matrices, and forms. It works as a fifth mode, augmenting the Frame, Text, Paragraph Tagging, and Graphic modes.

Equation editor

Similarly, Ventura's equation editor is a valuable function for technical publications. It easily creates mathematical expressions, scientific formulas, and Greek symbols.

Cross-references

With DOS Version 3 you can reference figures, tables, captions, or text passages that appear elsewhere in the publication. Thus, each time the page number, figure number, or other variable information changes, your text reference changes accordingly.

Vertical justification

The vertical justification feature ensures that text aligns vertically at the top and bottom of the page, just as text aligns horizontally at the left and right margins.

Edco hyphenation dictionary

The Edco hyphenation dictionary brings the quality of Ventura's hyphenation up to the level of dedicated typesetting systems. It requires 1.2 megabytes of EMS memory to run.

Table Edit mode

Table Edit mode is a valuable, frequently used function for people who produce technical documentation or similar publications. We have made extensive use of the table editor in this book. This section explains several facets of Table Edit mode:

- Creating tables in Ventura
- Entering text into tables
- Editing tables
- Creating tables in a word processor

How Table Edit mode works

Ventura's table features are set up as a fifth operating mode, in addition to the existing Frame, Text, Paragraph, and Graphic modes. When you load Ventura, you will see a fifth function button at the top of the Side-Bar (Figure 11-1). You access Table Edit mode by clicking on that button. You can also create a table in Text mode.

Creating a table does not require you to exit Ventura Publisher or your current chapter file. You enter table text using

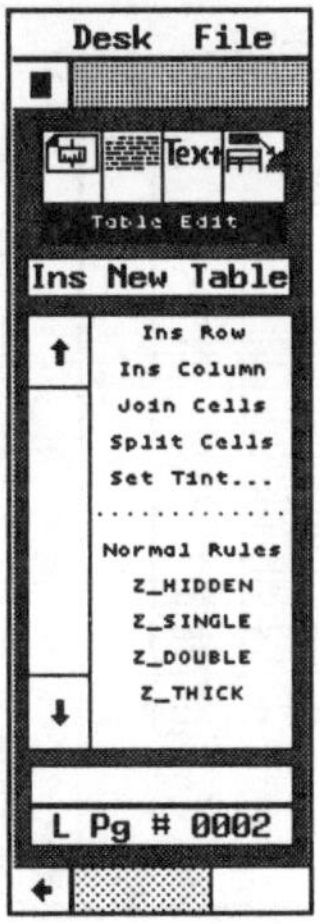

Figure 11-1.

Ventura's Text mode. As you do, you have access to all the normal editing, tagging, and text attribute tools. The only difference is that the text conforms to the boundaries of the current cell. In a sense, it is as if you were typing inside a tiny frame, or a small Box Text. However, text in a table *remains within the normal text stream.* If you look at the word processing file after creating a table, you will see the table text in the proper position in the text file (Figure 11-2).

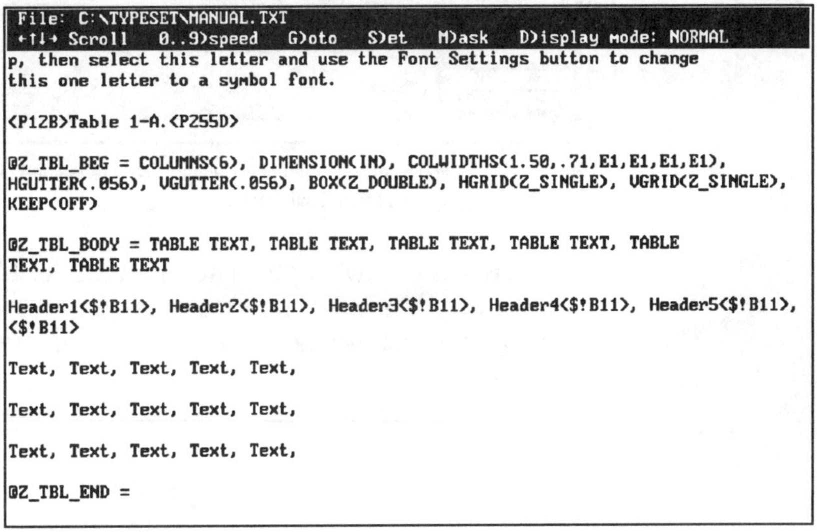

```
File: C:\TYPESET\MANUAL.TXT
←↑↓→ Scroll   0..9>speed   G>oto   S>et   M>ask   D>isplay mode: NORMAL
p, then select this letter and use the Font Settings button to change
this one letter to a symbol font.

<P12B>Table 1-A.<P255D>

@Z_TBL_BEG = COLUMNS(6), DIMENSION(IN), COLWIDTHS(1.50,.71,E1,E1,E1,E1),
HGUTTER(.056), VGUTTER(.056), BOX(Z_DOUBLE), HGRID(Z_SINGLE), VGRID(Z_SINGLE),
KEEP(OFF)

@Z_TBL_BODY = TABLE TEXT, TABLE TEXT, TABLE TEXT, TABLE TEXT, TABLE
TEXT, TABLE TEXT

Header1<$!B11>, Header2<$!B11>, Header3<$!B11>, Header4<$!B11>, Header5<$!B11>,
<$!B11>

Text, Text, Text, Text, Text,

Text, Text, Text, Text, Text,

Text, Text, Text, Text, Text,

@Z_TBL_END =
```

Figure 11-2. Although the text in a table is restricted inside cells, it appears in the word processor as part of the normal text stream.

You can place tables inside separate frames if you choose to do so. But one of the strengths of Ventura's Table Edit mode is that it makes this segregation unnecessary. If you so instruct it, Ventura will keep a table together on one page. Conversely, you can tell Ventura to break a table if necessary, and it will automatically repeat the header rows on the following page (Figure 11-3).

The uses of Table Edit mode

As explained in Chapter Nine, you can create simple tables with tab settings. You put each row into one paragraph and separate the columns with a tab stop. By defining the number, location, and alignment of the tabs, you create simple tables. This process is somewhat cumbersome, however, since you

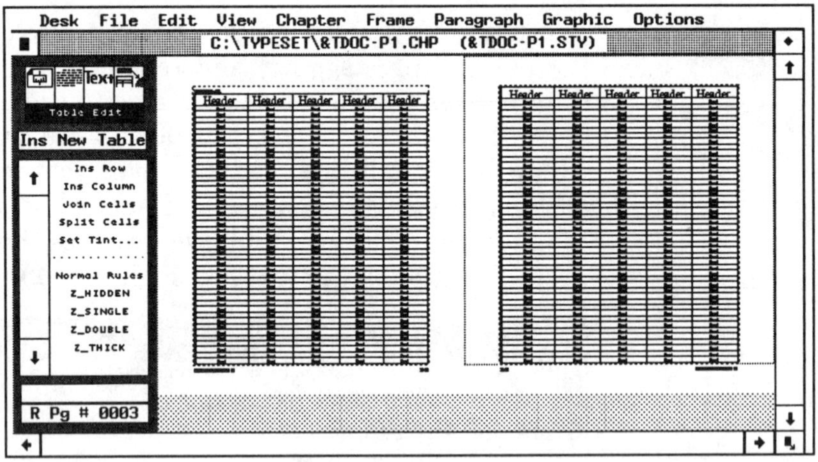

Figure 11-3. If you want it to, Ventura will automatically repeat the header row when it breaks a table across page or column boundaries.

must create a new tag for each new table. Moreover, you are limited to tables with short entries (short *cells*). Any cell requiring more than one line creates formatting problems (Figure 11-4).

Column 1 Column 2

Column one Column two

Column 1 The second column. Notice what happens if text in the cell becomes too long. It just jumps down to the next row without staying in the same column.

Another type of problem emerges when the first column is longer than a few words. The second column.

Figure 11-4. Tables created using tab settings can cause problems when any individual cell becomes too long.

But many tables need cells of variable length, sometimes several paragraphs long. For instance:

- Product comparison charts
- Procedural manuals and troubleshooting guides
- Business forms

The Ventura table editor is ideally suited for these applications. You do not need a different tag for each table you create.

Each cell in the table is a "minidocument" that can contain several lines or paragraphs of text. And you can easily modify the format of a table once it has been created. For instance, if you type more text into a cell, Ventura automatically enlarges it as needed. In addition, you can change column widths with a dialog box, or with the mouse.

Creating a table

You can create a new table in Table Edit mode, or in Text mode. Either way, you must have text in a frame or on the Underlying Page before you can create a table.

Creating a table in Table Edit mode

You can create a table between any two paragraphs with the following steps:

- Select Table Edit mode by clicking on Table Edit in the Function Selector.
- Position the table cursor between two paragraphs, where you want the table to appear.
- Click on Ins New Table in the Side-Bar. The Insert/Edit Table dialog box appears (Figure 11-5).
- Fill in the dialog box and click OK.

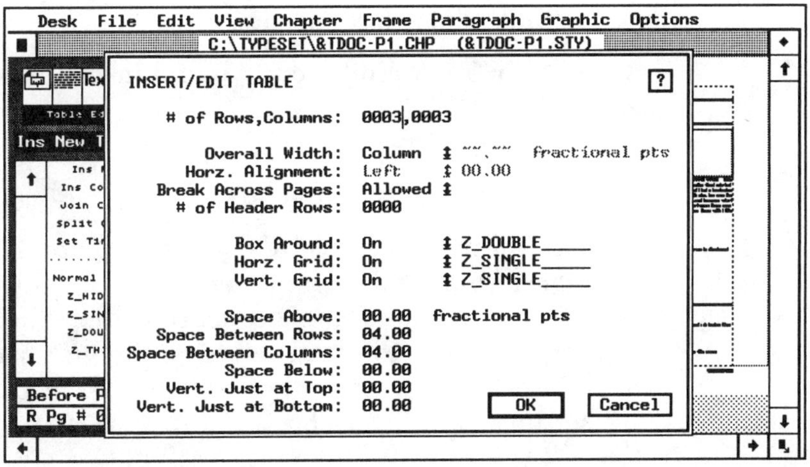

Figure 11-5. The Insert/Edit Table dialog box.

Creating a table in Text mode

Alternatively, you can create a table from Text mode:

- Position the text cursor at the very end of the paragraph preceding the spot where you want the table. You will see the words Paragraph End in the Current Selection Box at the bottom of the Side-Bar.
- Select Ins Special Item from the Edit menu (or press Ctrl-C). The secondary menu appears (Figure 11-6).

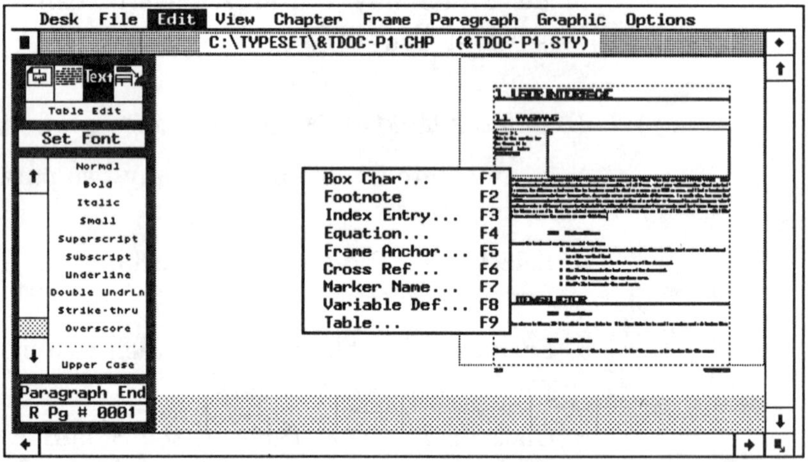

Figure 11-6. This secondary dialog box appears when you select Ins Special Item in Text mode.

- Select Table (or press function key F9). The Insert/Edit Table dialog box appears.
- As in Table Edit mode, you fill in the dialog box and click OK.

Insert/Edit Table dialog box

The Insert/Edit Table dialog box (Figure 11-5) controls the table format. It determines the width; the number of rows and columns; the number of header rows; the spacing above, below, and between rows and columns; the grid settings (the lines between cells); and other variables. You can change these settings later if you choose.

of Rows, Columns. You can enter any number of rows and

columns between 1 and 9999. The first number indicates the rows, the second the columns.

Overall Width can be set to the column width or a custom width. If you select Overall Width: Column, the table automatically adjusts itself to fit exactly into the width of the column. If you select Overall Width: Custom, you must select the horizontal alignment you want (see below). A custom width cannot be wider than the page. If you have a multi-column page, but you want the table to stretch the full width of the frame, choose Custom.

Horz. Alignment is active only if you choose Overall Width: Custom. In that case, you can specify how to align the table. If you choose Left, it will align flush against the left margin. If you choose Center, it will be centered inside the margins. If you choose Right, it will align flush-right. If you choose Indent, you can specify how far to move the table from the *left* margin.

Break Across Pages. In some cases, a table may be too long for a particular column or page. You can permit the table to spill over to the next page or column by setting Break Across Pages to Allowed. Otherwise, Ventura will force the entire table to stay on the same page together, even if it means creating a large white space at the bottom of the previous page. To keep the table together, choose Break Across Pages: No. Choose No only for tables that are shorter than a page.

# of Header Rows. If you do allow the table to break, you can set the number of rows to repeat at the top of the next page (or column). If you choose # of Header Rows: 0003, for example, Ventura will repeat the first three rows of the table after each page or column break. Ventura will not place a break between header rows. If you don't want to repeat any material, choose 0000.

The next three settings in the Insert/Edit Table dialog box determine whether ruling lines appear in the table. *Box Around* is a line around the entire table. *Horz. Grid* and *Vert. Grid* are ruling lines placed between rows and columns. To make the lines appear, turn the setting on. The words "Z_DOUBLE" and "Z_SINGLE" refer to the tags that Ventura automatically assigns to these ruling lines. You can change the settings of these tags, or use different tags instead.

The tags determine line attributes like width, style (dotted or solid, for example), and spacing. For each type of line, you can choose from among four automatically generated tags, or type a tag name of your own. The generated tags are Z_DOUBLE, Z_SINGLE, Z_THICK, and Z_HIDDEN. Z_SINGLE draws a single thin line, Z_THICK draws a single thick line, Z_DOUBLE draws two thin lines, and Z_HIDDEN hides the rule. Applying Z_THICK to Box Around, Z_SINGLE to Horizontal Grid, and Z_DOUBLE to Vertical Grid would place a thick rule around the table with thin horizontal grid lines and double vertical lines (Figure 11-7).

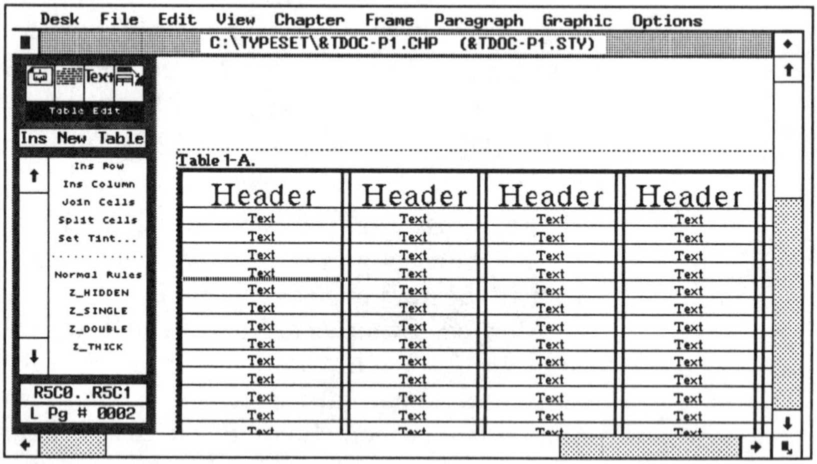

Figure 11-7. In this example, the ruling box around has the Z_THICK tag, the vertical lines are Z_DOUBLE and the horizontal lines are Z_SINGLE.

The spacing commands in the Insert/Edit Table dialog box work in a similar manner to Ventura's other spacing commands. *Space Above* and *Space Below* determine how much space to add between the table and the paragraphs above or below. In most cases, you should put extra space above and below your tables. We recommend an amount equal to or greater than the inter-line spacing of Body Text. If Body Text has an inter-line spacing of 12 points, then you might choose 12.00, 24.00, or 36.00 fractional pts. above and below the table.

Space Between Columns and *Space Between Rows* determine the spacing between entries in each cell. Space Between Columns adds space to the left of each column, preventing text from touching adjacent cells. Space Between Rows adds extra space between rows. In many cases, it is sufficient to add 25% to 50% of the inter-line spacing of your table tags. If Table Text has 12.00 fractional pts. of inter-line spacing, for example, you might choose, 03.00, 04.00, or 06.00 fractional points.

Vert. Just at Top and *Vert. Just at Bottom* determine the maximum amount of space that can be used for Vertical Justification. If Vert. Just at Top is set to 18.00 fractional pts., for example, Ventura's vertical justification feature will add no more than 18 points to the spacing above the table. If you are not using vertical justification, you can ignore these fields. Vertical Justification is explained later in this chapter.

When you have completed the settings in the dialog box, click OK. Ventura returns to the workspace. You will see a blank table that matches the specifications you entered.

At first, all the columns and rows are the same width and height. You can change this as you see fit. For instance, as you add text to a cell, the entire row grows to accommodate the new spacing requirements.

Entering text into a table

When you create a table, Ventura treats it as part of the text. It treats each cell as a separate paragraph. To type in text, enable Text mode, move the cursor to the first cell, and start

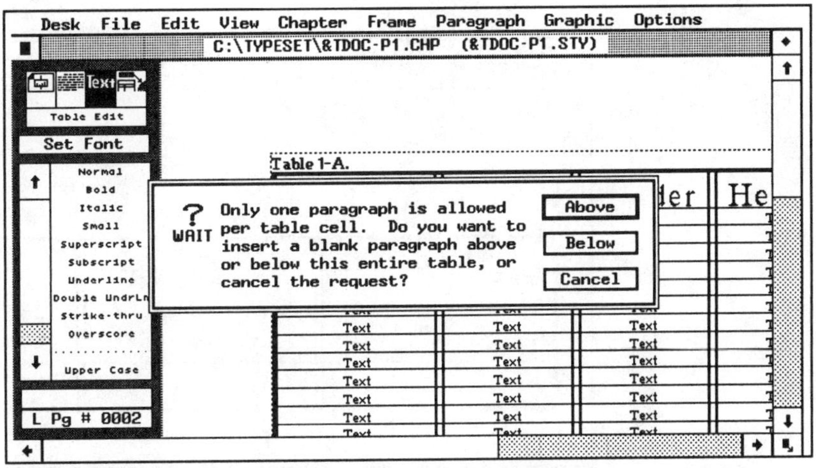

Figure 11-8. You cannot start a new line by pressing Enter within a cell. If you do, you will see the error message shown here.

typing. Once the cursor is inside a cell, you can enter as much text as desired. If you enter more than can fit on one line, the entire row expands to accommodate the extra.

You can skip from cell to cell with the arrow keys or the mouse. Pressing an arrow key when at the end of a paragraph *jumps* you to the next cell. You cannot use the Enter key to start a new paragraph. If you do, you will see an error message that prompts you to tell Ventura what you want (Figure 11-8). To start a new line within a cell, use a line break (Ctrl-Enter).

Formatting the table text

Ventura applies a default tag called Table Text to each entry in each cell. Ventura starts by assuming you want everything to be Table Text, but you can change some or all of the cells if you prefer. Initially, Table Text has the same attributes as Body Text. You can change the attributes as you see fit in Paragraph mode. You can also retag any or every cell with different tags. You add, assign, and modify these tags in Paragraph mode, just as any others.

You may prefer to create and name tags according to their alignment. Use the Alignment dialog box to create different combinations of horizontal and vertical alignment. As you can see in Figure 11-9, these combinations give you nine different positions within a cell.

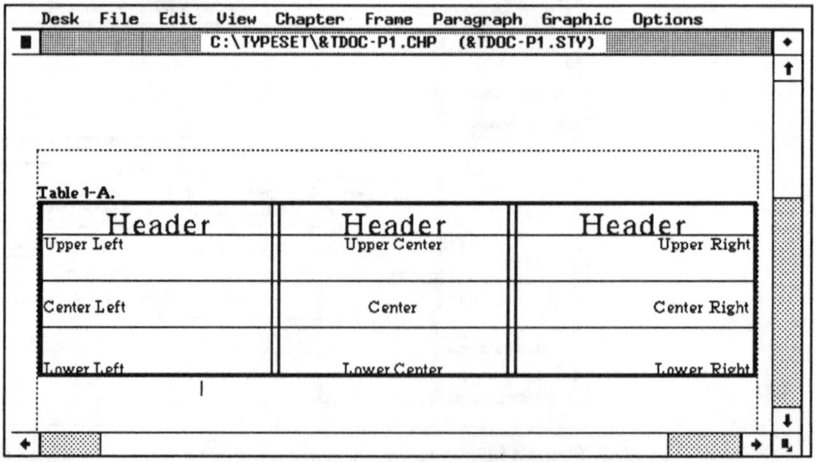

Figure 11-9. You can create tags to position text in any of nine positions within a cell.

In addition, you can choose decimal alignment, if your table includes numbers. The Alignment dialog box also provides the means to create rotated text, a useful effect for many tables (Figure 11-10).

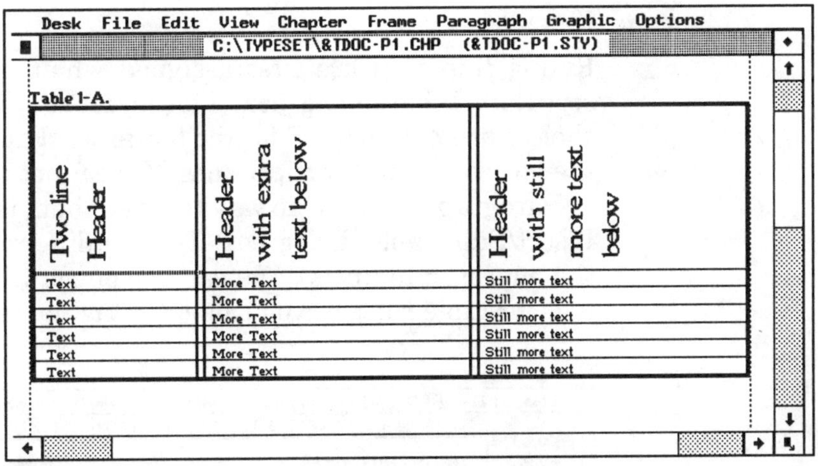

Figure 11-10. Rotated text is a valuable way to save space in complex tables.

You can place leader characters in your table by choosing Auto-Leader from the Tab Settings dialog box and selecting a desired leader character, such as a period or hyphen. Tagging a blank cell automatically fills one line with the leader characters. Tagging a cell containing text places leaders between the text and the right column margin. This "margin" is determined by the Space Between Columns line in the Insert/Edit Table dialog box. You can also use In From Right and In From Left from the Spacing dialog box to reduce the leader width within each cell.

As with any text, you can also affect the appearance by assigning attributes from the Assignment List, or by using Set Font in Text mode. You may find it easier to keep just a few tags and use the Set Font feature in Text mode to change typefaces or type size. Consider choosing Grow Interline to Fit: On from the Paragraph Typography dialog box for your table tags. That way, changes in font size will automatically increase the space between the lines.

Formatting the ruling lines

The ruling lines in Ventura's tables are separate paragraphs. Like other paragraphs, they have tags. Assigning, accessing and modifying these tags, however, is different from modifying text tags.

Ruling line tags are first assigned when you open the Insert/Edit Table dialog box (Figure 11-11). Ventura's default choices are Z_DOUBLE for the box around and Z_SINGLE for the horizontal and vertical lines. You cannot retag ruling lines in Paragraph mode. One way to retag them is to return to the Insert/Edit Table dialog box. Type in different tag names on the appropriate line(s). You can use one of the four generated tags for table rules or you can enter tag names of your own.

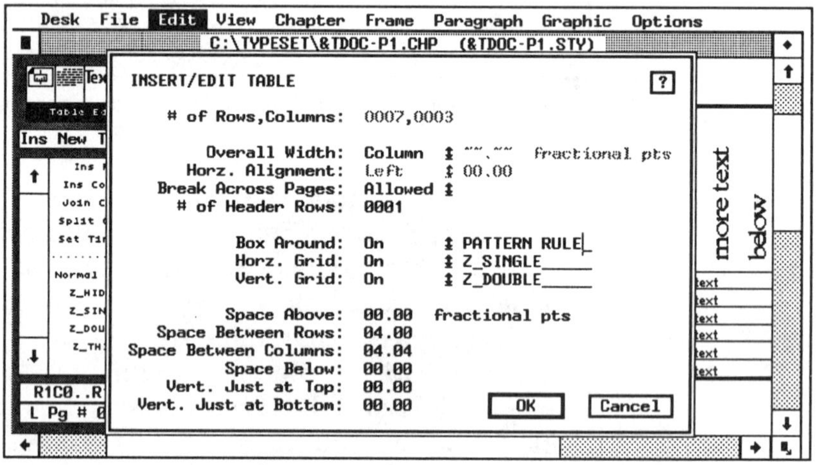

Figure 11-11. You can assign new tag names for ruling lines by entering them in the Insert/Edit Table dialog box.

Using the Insert/Edit Table dialog box is the only way to retag the box around a table. However, you can retag vertical and horizontal rules in Table mode. First select the rule(s) you want to retag. Then choose a new tag from the list at the bottom of the Assignment List.

To select a portion of a horizontal line, click once on the line while in Table Edit mode. To select more, drag the cursor over the line you wish to select. To select all or part of a vertical rule, drag the cursor over the rule.

With the rule selected, point to the tag you wish to assign from the Assignment List. The first time you use Table Edit mode, you will see the four generated tags on the list, plus the choice Normal Rules at the top. Normal Rules has the same effect as Normal in Text mode — that is, it resets the format to its previous, default condition. Use it if you want to undo your changes and start over. You can select adjacent line segments or the entire line. If you apply a new tag to a line segment, it overrides the tag applied to the entire line.

Adding ruling line tags to Table Edit mode

To add a tag to Table Edit mode's Assignment List, you must switch to Paragraph mode. Click on a paragraph. Now click on the tag whose name you wish to show up in Table Edit mode, or create a new one with the Add New Tag button. Select Ruling Line Above from the Paragraph menu (you may also choose Ruling Line Below or Ruling Box Around). Now select Table Rule List: Shown from the bottom left of the Ruling Lines Above dialog box (Figure 11-12).

Even though Ruling Line Above is disabled for this paragraph, you can define a ruling line for Table Edit mode.

Setting Table Rule List: Shown enables the ruling options in this dialog box.

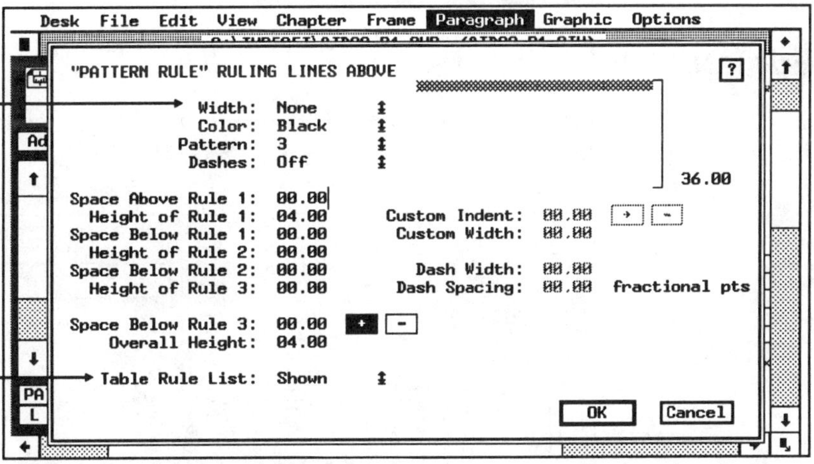

Figure 11-12. To make a tag's name appear on the Assignment List in Table mode, select Table Rule List: Shown from any ruling lines dialog box.

Selecting Table Rule List: Shown enables the ruling options of the dialog box — even if you have set Width: None. Any type of rule you can create in this dialog box can be used in Table Edit mode by selecting the tag from the Assignment List.

Once you choose Table Rule List: Shown from any ruling line dialog box, it affects the other two ruling line dialog boxes as well. This action causes a tag name to appear on the Assignment List in Table Edit mode.

A tag doesn't have any effect in Table mode unless you define settings for the ruling line. By typing the height and spacing choices you want, you determine the appearance of ruling lines in Table Edit mode. A tag can have ruling line settings that are active in Table Edit mode, but not in Paragraph mode. In practice, however, it is best not to use text paragraphs to carry rule settings for tables. Instead, create separate tags whose only function is ruling line effects.

Modifying ruling line tags

Modifying tags that apply to lines is a bit tricky and can be confusing. You *apply* ruling lines in Table Edit mode, but you *modify* them in Paragraph mode. To do so, enable Paragraph mode and apply the tag to any paragraph. Select the Ruling Lines Above or Below dialog box. Make sure Table Rule List is set to Shown. Now change the settings of the ruling lines.

Editing a table

Once you've set up your table, you can easily modify settings for individual cells, groups of cells, or the entire table. Some

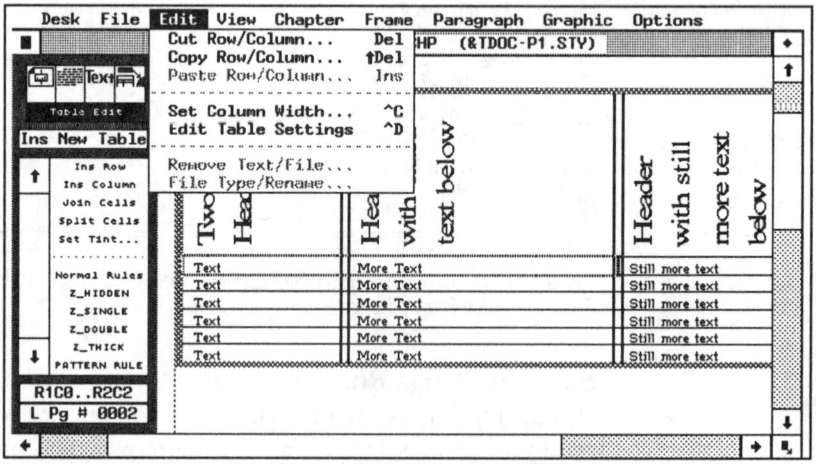

Figure 11-13. The Edit menu shows different choices in Table Edit mode.

editing commands are found in the Assignment List in Table Edit mode. You will find other editing commands in the Edit menu. As shown in Figure 11-13, the Edit menu options change when you are in Table Edit mode.

The first step in modifying a table is to select the cell, or group of cells, you want to adjust:

- Enable Table Edit mode.
- Place the cursor at the beginning of the section.
- Press and hold the mouse button as you drag to the end of the area you want to select.

When you release the mouse button, the selected area is highlighted with dotted lines. You can also see the range of cells selected in the Current Selection Box (Figure 11-14).

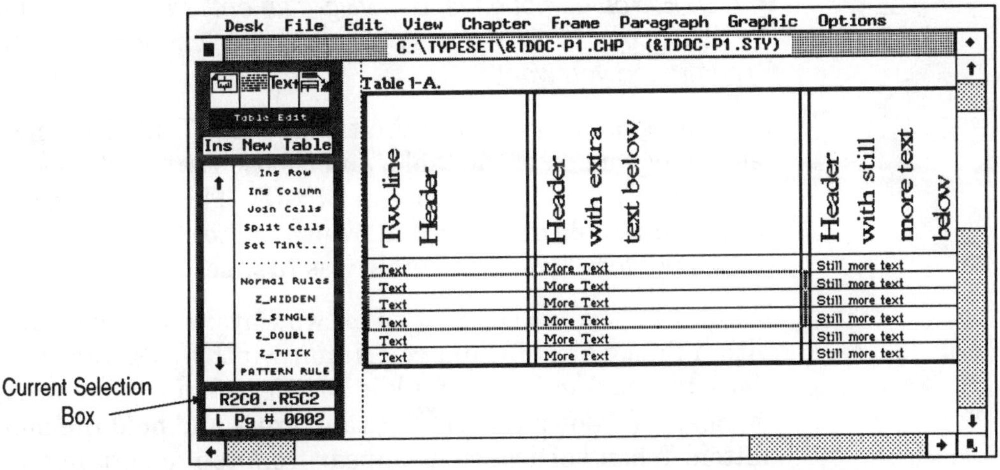

Figure 11-14. You can confirm your choice of cells by examining the range shown in the Current Selection Box.

The Shift-Click method works in Table Edit mode, too. To enlarge or reduce a selection, hold down the Shift key while you click again at the new ending point. Users of mouse-oriented spreadsheet programs such as Microsoft Excel should be immediately familiar with the table editor's method of selecting a range of cells.

Once you have selected a range of cells, you can insert rows or columns; cut, copy, and paste rows or columns; change column widths; apply cell attributes; apply tags to rules; and apply global changes to cells.

Cut, copy, and paste commands work the same way they do in other modes. Select any portion of a row or column, and choose Cut or Copy from the Edit menu. You will be asked if you wish to cut rows (cut everything on both sides of the selection) or columns (cut everything above and below the selection). You can also cancel the operation. The same keyboard shortcuts apply in Table mode as in all others.

After it is cut or copied, the row or column is placed in the Table Clipboard. It can then be pasted to a different area of the table or to another table altogether. If you select the entire table, Ventura asks you to verify that you want to go forward with the operation.

➥*NOTE: You do not have to highlight an entire row or column to cut or copy it. Select a single cell, then choose the editing command you want.*

To apply global changes to the table, enter Table Edit mode, select any portion of the table, and choose Edit Table Settings from the Edit menu (or press Ctrl-D). This brings up the Insert/Edit Table dialog box, allowing you to change any of the settings entered when the table was first set up.

Column widths can be changed in two ways: with the mouse or with a dialog box. To change column widths with the mouse, place the cursor in the middle of the column you want to change. Hold down the Alt key, then press and hold the mouse button. When vertical rules appear from top to bottom on the screen, move the cursor right or left to change the column width (Figure 11-15).

You can also change column widths by choosing the Set Column Width command from the Edit menu (or press Ctrl-C). The Table Column Widths dialog box appears (Figure 11-16). To set columns widths, first select the correct column number. Then choose whether you want Fixed or Variable widths, and enter the number. Repeat for each column you want to change.

Fixed-width columns are set at the measurement you enter. Variable-width columns use any space left over when fixed-

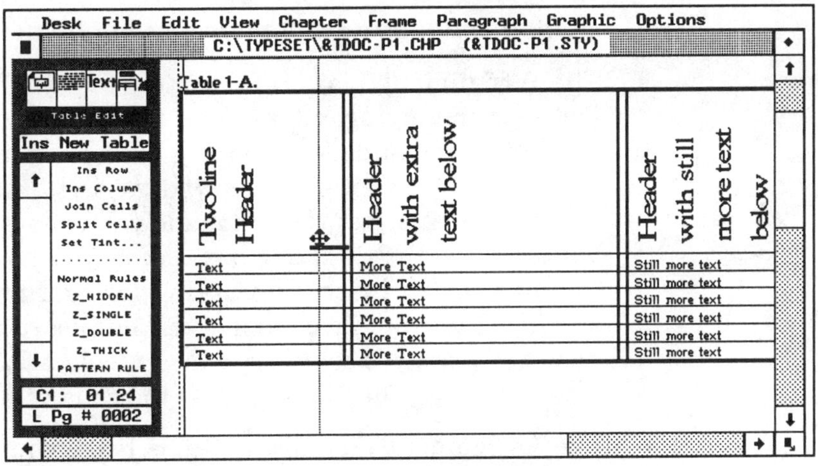

Figure 11-15. You can change column widths on screen by holding down the Alt key while dragging with the mouse.

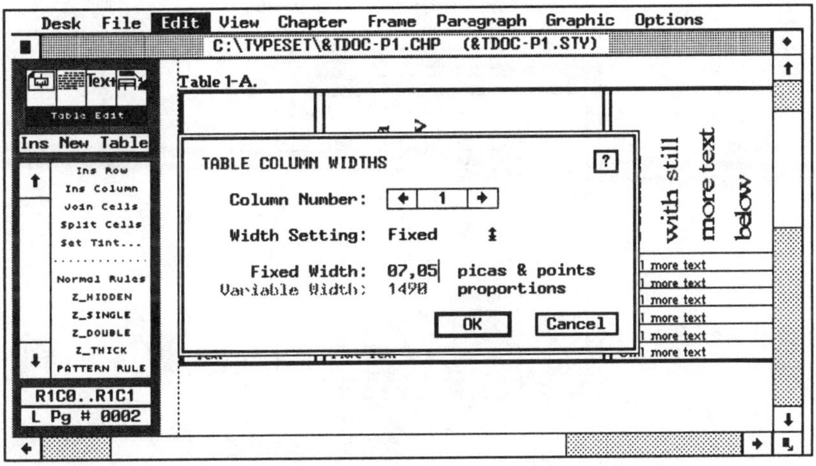

Figure 11-16. The Table Column Widths dialog box.

width columns have been set. The number you enter determines how the leftover space is allocated. If Column 1 is set at 3 and Column 2 at 1, the first column gets three times as much space as the second. You can also use percentages for the variable width. However, you must use percentages for all the variable columns, and the percentages must add up to 100.

Making changes with the Assignment List

The Assignment List in Table Edit mode offers a variety of tools for modifying tables. The top of the Assignment List contains commands for inserting rows or columns. Just select the cell or cells after which you want to insert the row or column. Then select the command from the Assignment List. Ventura presents a dialog box telling you how many rows or columns it will insert and asking for confirmation. Click on Yes and the rows or columns will be inserted. To determine how many rows or columns to insert, select that same number when you drag the mouse across the cells.

The Assignment List also contains two commands for joining and splitting cells. In some cases, you may want to create one large cell from two or more adjacent cells (Figure 11-17).

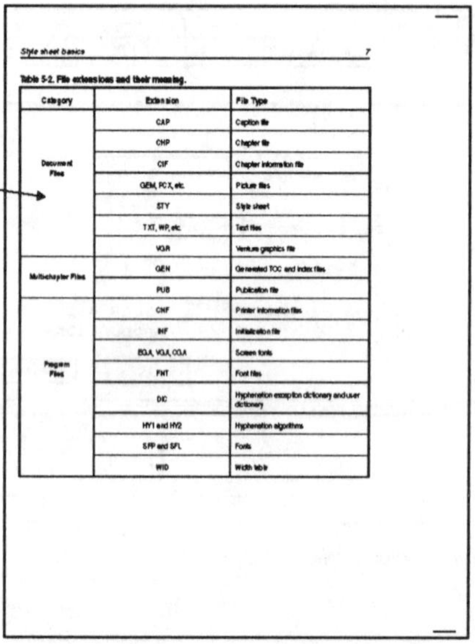

Style sheet basics 7

Table 5-2. File extensions and their meaning.

Category	Extension	File Type
Document Files	CAP	Caption file
	CHP	Chapter file
	CIF	Chapter information file
	GEM, PCX, etc.	Picture files
	STY	Style sheet
	TXT, WP, etc.	Text files
	VGR	Ventura graphics file
Multichapter Files	GEN	Generated TOC and index files
	PUB	Publication file
Program Files	CNF	Printer information files
	INF	Initialization file
	EGA, VGA, CGA	Screen fonts
	FNT	Font files
	DIC	Hyphenation exception dictionary and user dictionary
	HY1 and HY2	Hyphenation algorithms
	SFP and SFL	Fonts
	WID	Width table

Figure 11-17. The large white spaces in this table were created by joining cells.

First select the cells you want to combine. Then click on Join Cells in the Assignment List. If you change your mind, you can separate them again with the Split Cells command. If the joined cells have text, only the text from the upper left cell shows in the new large cell. However, if you split the cells, the original text reappears. Joining cells has the effect of hiding the rules and the text. Even though they are hidden, Ventura still treats each cell as a separate entity.

You can also apply a background pattern with the Assignment List. You can apply a tint — either a color or shade of gray — to any cell or group of cells. First select the range you want to change. Then choose Set Tint from the Assignment List. Ventura asks you for the color and pattern. If you do not like any of Ventura's predetermined shades of gray (patterns), you can create alternates. Tint the cell(s) with a color. Then use Define Colors from the Paragraph menu to redefine that color as a shade of gray instead.

Creating tables in a word processor

You can create tables in advance with a word processor, provided you take two steps. First, you must insert the proper tags to define the beginning and ending point of the table, and the number of columns. (If you like, you can specify other settings at the same time.) Second, you must type the text in a Special format that Ventura can interpret as table text.

Inserting table tags

To create a table within your word processor, you must observe several rules very carefully. At a minimum, Ventura requires the following four pieces of information:

- The table begin tag, @Z_TBL_BEG = . This tells Ventura that the text that follows should be placed in a table.
- The number of columns, using the COLUMNS(n) command. This should follow immediately after the table begin command, in the same paragraph.
- The data in each row of the table. Each row should be entered as a single paragraph, with a comma and space separating each column within the row. (If you want to use a comma within a cell, use a double comma (,,) to tell Ventura.
- The table end command, @Z_TBL_END = . This demarcates the end of the table data.

Figure 11-18 shows this minimum set of commands within a

Table 11-1. Table formatting commands.

Command	Description	Required?	Examples
@Z_TBL_BEG =	Defines beginning of table	Required (Must be the first item)	@Z_TBL_BEG =
COLUMNS(n)	Defines number of columns	Required. Comes immediately after @Z_TBL_BEG =	@Z_TBL_BEG = COLUMNS(3) @Z_TBL_BEG = COLUMNS(4)
DIMENSION( )	Defines dimensions used in table	Optional	DIMENSION(IN) DIMENSION(PT) DIMENSION(CM) DIMENSION(PI)
COLWIDTHS( )	Defines width of columns in dimensions specified above, or in number of proportions. E*n* specifies *n* proportions	Optional	COLWIDTHS(.5,1.5,2) COLWIDTHS(E2,E1,E1,E1) COLWIDTHS(12,E2,E1)
WIDTH( )	Defines overall width of custom table	Optional (if not specified, uses width of current text column)	WIDTH(4.5)
INDENT( )	Defines indent of table from text column for custom table	Optional	INDENT(1.00) INDENT(2IN)
ABOVE( )	Space above table	Optional	ABOVE(6.5) ABOVE(2PT)
BELOW( )	Space below table	Optional	BELOW(1.0) BELOW(13PT)
VJTOP( )	Amount of vertical justification allowed above table	Optional	VJTOP(2) VJTOP(15PT)
VJBOT( )	Amount of vertical justification allowed below table	Optional	VJBOT(6)
HGUTTER( )	Space allowed between columns of table	Optional	HGUTTER(12) HGUTTER(1PI)
VGUTTER( )	Space allowed between rows of table	Optional	VGUTTER(7) VGUTTER(1PI)
BOX( )	Specifies name of tag used for lines around table	Optional	BOX(Z_DOUBLE) BOX(Z_SINGLE)

Command	Description	Required?	Examples
HGRID( )	Specifies name of tag used for lines between rows	Optional	HGRID(Z_SINGLE) HGRID(Z_DOUBLE)
VGRID( )	Specifies name of tag used for lines between columns	Optional	VGRID(Z_THICK) VGRID(Z_SINGLE)
KEEP( )	Permits or disallows table to be broken	Optional	KEEP(ON) KEEP(OFF)
RULE( )	Defines alternative rule type for range in table	Optional	RULE(Z_THICK,R0C3...R2C5) RULE(Z_SINGLE,R5C5...R5C6)
@Z_TBL_HEAD =	Defines tag names for header rows	Optional	@Z_TBL_HEAD = Head2,Head3,Head3
@Z_TBL_BODY =	Defines tag names for nonheader rows	Optional Must precede row(s) that it modifies	@Z_TBL_BODY = TableLeft, TableCenter,TableCenter, TableRight
@Z_TBL_END =	Defines end of table	Required Must be last item	@Z_TBL_END =

text file. It is important that you follow these specifications to the letter; if not, Ventura may refuse to accept your table when you load the text file. Also, notice that the minimum commands given above will produce a very plain, unformatted table that you will need to modify in Ventura's Table Edit mode.

In addition to these commands, you may want to enter more detailed information about your table within the word processor. Table 11-1 shows the optional table formatting commands that can be inserted in your word processor.

Pretagging in the word processor

By default, Ventura assigns the tag Table Text to any text within your table. If you would like to change the tag name assigned to the columns or the headers in your table, use the @Z_TBL_HEAD = command or the @Z_TBL_BODY = command for header rows or table body, respectively. For example,

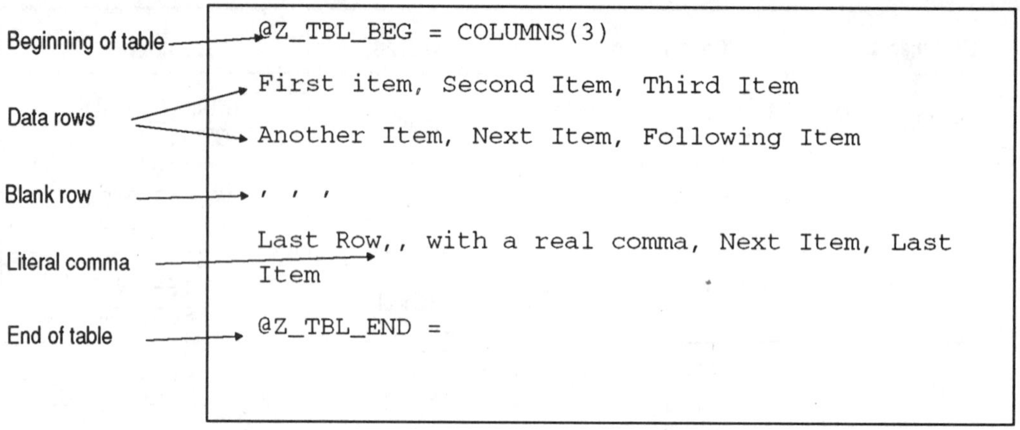

Figure 11-18. Example of minimum level of formatting required for creating a table in the word processor.

to assign different tag names to the four columns in a table, you would enter the command:

```
@Z_TBL_BODY = Table1, Table2, Table3, Table4
```

Similarly, you can predefine the ruling lines within your word processor by inserting the BOX(), HGRID(), VGRID(), or RULE() commands.

Creating tables with a spreadsheet program

Creating tables in a spreadsheet has two aspects: (1) working correctly inside the spreadsheet and (2) bringing the table into Ventura.

Creating the table

Text from a spreadsheet can be entered if first converted to PRN format or another ASCII format. To accomplish this, format your spreadsheet as desired, access the print range feature, and print to file rather than the printer. In Lotus 1-2-3, the command is:

```
/PRfile.prn
```

Specify the desired range and then select GO to produce the output file.

Be sure to make your column widths large enough, since

Ventura requires a minimum of two space characters between any two cells in the same row.

Bringing a spreadsheet table into Ventura

Once the spreadsheet has been correctly formatted and printed to disk, it is a simple matter to convert it to a Ventura table. Run Ventura and enter Text mode. Place the cursor at the position where you want the table to appear. Then select Load Text/Picture from the File menu, just as if you were importing a text file. One of the options in the dialog box is "PRN-to-Table." Select that, then select Text Cursor as the location (Figure 11-19). Click OK, then select the print file you created in your spreadsheet program. If it doesn't show up on the Item Selector, be sure that you are looking at the proper subdirectory and that the file filters display the PRN file extension.

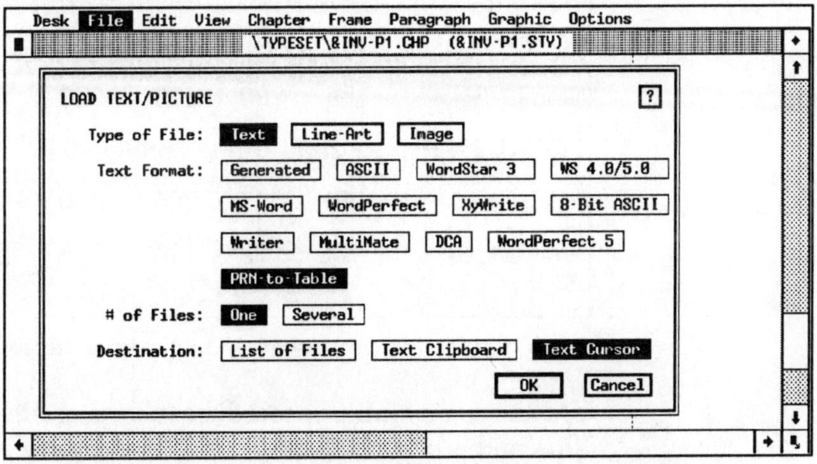

Figure 11-19. To load a spreadsheet print file into a Ventura table, select Text Format: PRN-to-Table and Destination: Text Cursor from the Load Text/Picture dialog box.

The PRN file is converted to a text file with the extension TBL, then pours onto the page following the text cursor. Any changes made to the table text will be reflected in the TBL file, not the original PRN file. Figure 11-20 shows an example of a table created from a spreadsheet file. Figure 11-21 shows how the same table would look if it had been loaded as a regular text file.

	1987 & prior	1988	1989	1990	1991
PC Users	14000	5000	6200	7000	8000
Mac Users	1500	850	1250	1550	1800
PC DTP	105	170	265	425	575
Mac DTP	185	280	415	520	620
TOTAL DTP	290	450	680	945	1195
PC LANs	450	215	285	350	460
Mac LANs	100	78	130	195	240

Figure 11-20. This table was imported using the PRN-to-Table file format.

```
             1987 & prior  1988   1989   1990   1991
PC Users        14000    5000   6200   7000   8000
Mac Users        1500     850   1250   1550   1800
PC DTP           105     170    265    425    575
Mac DTP           185     280    415    520    620
TOTAL DTP           290    450    680    945    1195
PC LANs           450     215    285    350    460
Mac LANs           100     78    130    195    240
```

Figure 11-21. How the table above would look if loaded as a regular text file.

You can use a similar procedure to import files from dBASE III Plus and other database management programs. Each row in the table will correspond to a record, while cells will constitute individual fields. The simplest way to do this is to create an SDF file from the database. The problem is that the SDF format does not place two spaces between each field; if any fields are completely filled, they will not show up correctly in the table. Two alternatives are available. You can set up a report format with two spaces between each field and print the report to disk. Or you can write a simple program that does the same thing.

Creating and editing equations

Ventura's equation editor can create complex scientific and mathematical equations, including true fractions, Greek characters, and mathematical symbols.

To create an equation:

- Enable Text mode.
- Select Ins Special Item from the Edit menu (or hit Ctrl-C).
- When the secondary menu appears, choose Equation (or press F4). The Equation Editing screen appears (Figure 11-22).

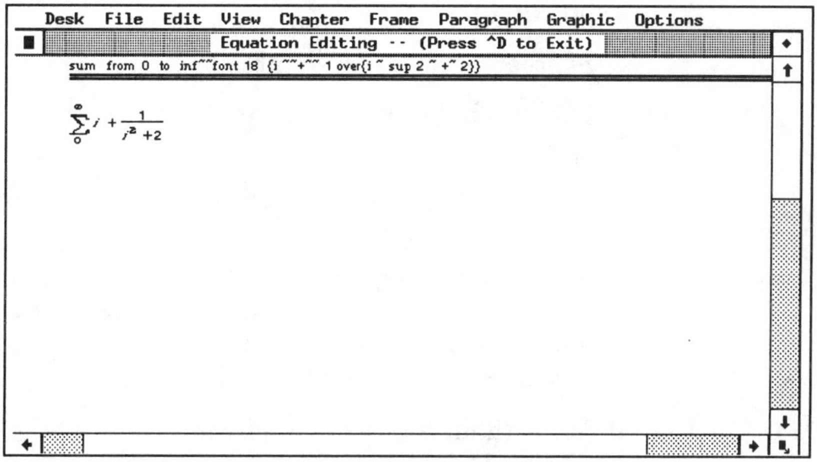

Figure 11-22. You enter codes into the top half of the equation editor. The results show in the bottom half, beneath the double lines.

The equation screen has two parts. In the top half, you enter the codes for the equation. In the bottom half, you preview the effect of those codes. The bottom half, in other words, shows what the equation will look like in text. An equation can appear anywhere in the text stream of a document.

When you return to text mode, whatever shows below the double lines appears in the text.

Creating the equation

You enter equations as abbreviations that describe the symbols to be included. After you enter the abbreviations, the actual equation appears below. Here's a simple example of an formula entered in the equation editor:

sqrt { x sup 2 ~ + ~ pi sup 2 }.

The result is:

$$\sqrt{x^2 + \pi^2}$$

Sqrt is the Equation editor's code for the square root symbol.

The brackets "{}" group part of the equation together.

Sup creates superscript "2" after x and pi.

The tilde (~) enters a space between items. You must use the tilde character to create a space. You cannot create a space by striking the space bar.

pi creates the Greek symbol π.

Note that characters in the final formula appear in italicized form. Except for mathematical operators like "sin" and "cos," all characters appear as italics.

The equation editor recognizes certain parts of an equation as an expression. An expression is any single character, a code such as "pi," a group of characters not separated with a space, and anything placed within brackets. In the example above, { x sup 2 ~ + ~ pi sup 2 } is an expression.

More than 100 codes and commands are recognized by the editor. The Ventura Publisher Reference Guide provides a complete list. *Codes* (or *special words*) are abbreviations that produce special characters or symbols, such as "pi," which produces the symbol "π." Codes can be further broken down into symbol codes and romanized codes. Symbol words such as "pi" are converted into their equivalent symbols. Romanized words, such as "sin," "cos," and "log," are printed in normal, rather than italicized type.

Commands modify codes, words or numbers. The code "sqrt," for example, creates a square root symbol that grows to fit the following expression. The code "bold" places the following expression in boldface. In most cases, commands modify the expression that follows (not the expression that precedes). Commands also fall into several categories. Some commands change the font for the expressions that follow. Some commands create math symbols or change the placement of the following expression. Typing X over Y produces the equation $\frac{X}{Y}$, for example. And some commands produce diacritical marks. Unlike other commands, diacritical marks modify the preceding characters. For example, "xyz" bar produces $\overline{xyz}$.

When entering equations, there are a few things to remember:

- Spaces must be placed before and after all codes. Otherwise, the code itself will be printed in the equation.
- Spaces are otherwise ignored in the equation editor. X+Y and X + Y both appear as $X+Y$. The tilde character (~) is used to insert a normal space and the caret character (^) is used for a thin space.
- In most cases, equation editor commands modify the expression that follows. Commands that produce diacritical marks are the exception to this.

Formatting equations

Although an equation may appear to be a long chain of separate elements, to Ventura each equation is a single, separate entity. When you move the cursor, and copy or delete equations, they behave as if they were a single text character. You can change the font size and other attributes as you would with any other text.

Equations can take up a lot of room on a line, both vertically and horizontally, so it's a good idea to set Grow Inter-Line to Fit: On in the Paragraph Typography menu. This way, line spacing will be adjusted to accommodate large formulas.

Entering equations in a word processor

By far the easiest way to use Ventura's equation function is to enter equations directly into Ventura. That way you can instantly see the results of your codes, and change them as necessary. Still, some companies may not have the luxury of a Ventura workstation for each and every author. In those cases, you may want authors to enter the equation into their word processing files. You can proof and correct these equations after you bring them into Ventura.

You can enter formulas directly in your word processor using the same codes and commands described above. Each equation must be preceded with <$E and followed with a close bracket >. In other words, you use the same command language as you do in the on-screen editor. The only difference is that you place the expression inside bracket codes. Thus, if the expression in the editor is *left {pile {x above y above z}* then the equivalent word processor code is <$Eleft {pile {x above y above z}>, which produces:

$$\left\{ \begin{matrix} x \\ y \\ z \end{matrix} \right.$$

See Chapter Three, "Creating Text," for a complete explanation of preformatting and bracket codes.

Creating and using cross-references

With Ventura's cross-reference feature, you can reference any figure, table, caption, or text passage within the text. If the page number, figure number, or other variable information changes, the text reference changes accordingly.

Suppose you're editing a book on the history of desktop publishing. On page 124, the author mentions the famous Acme Laser Printer, which was discussed earlier in Chapter Two. You can insert a sentence that says, "The Acme Printer, as discussed on page," leaving a blank after "page." The cross-reference feature causes Ventura to substitute the correct page number in place of the blank. If the first mention of the Acme Laser Printer is on page 20 in Chapter Two, the above sentence will read, "The Acme Printer, as discussed on page 20." Later, if you add enough illustrations to Chapters One and Two that the mention moves to page 25, the cross-reference feature causes the sentence to read, "The Acme Printer, as discussed on page 25." The page number changes as the book is expanded.

Cross-referencing is a powerful function, but it has some dangers. First, you must often know in advance what you want to reference. If you do not, you will have to return to previous chapters to insert markers. Returning to previous chapters negates some of the speed and efficiency advantages of cross referencing.

Second, the cross-reference does not appear in the text until you use the Multi-Chapter dialog box to renumber the chapters. Until that time, only a degree symbol (°) shows. Suppose you plan to insert a long phrase such as "Inside Xerox Ventura Publisher." You can see that the formatting of many lines and paragraphs will change when this long phrase is substituted in place of the degree symbol. Thus, to accurately format a series of chapters, you must use Multi-Chapter to renumber them *before* you format. Then, in case you moved any referenced items when you formatted, you must renumber and reformat again to catch any changes.

Despite these shortcomings, the cross-reference feature has numerous applications for professional publishers. Newsletters, newspapers, and magazines can use it to create Continued From and Continued To references that remain correct even if pagination changes. Book publishers can enter references to figures, tables, pages, and chapters without worrying about where the referenced text or graphics have moved. You can also use it for mail-merge functions, inserting variable information at reference points to create customized documents.

In this section, we explain the key applications of the cross-reference function, and provide some examples of its use.

The simplest application is inserting the current page or chapter number. But Ventura adds the ability to reference text or frames in other pages or chapters. To do this, you must create a link between the reference and the text or frame to which it refers.

Inserting the current page or chapter number

To insert a reference to the current page or chapter number, enter Text mode and:

- Place the cursor where you want the page or chapter number to be inserted.
- Select Ins Special Item from the Edit menu, or press Ctrl-C.

After the pop-up menu appears, select Cross Ref. or press the F6 key. The Insert/Edit Reference dialog box is displayed (Figure 11-23).

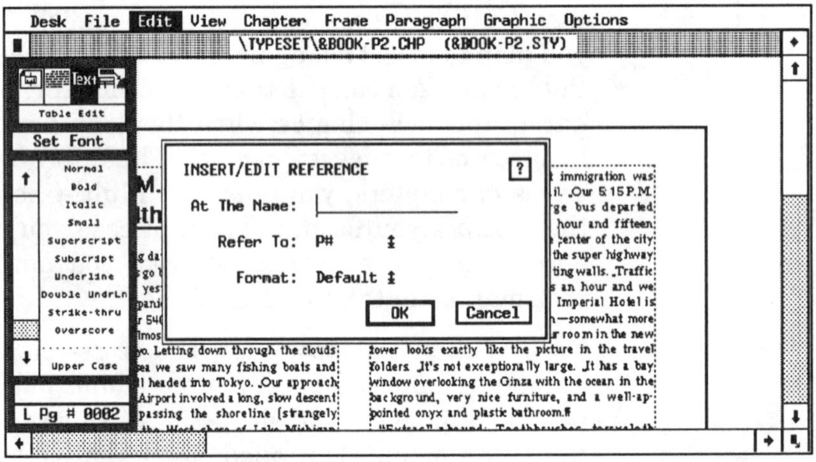

Figure 11-23. The Insert/Edit Reference dialog box.

- If you want to insert the page number, select Refer To: P#. To insert the chapter number, select Refer To: C#. Do not enter anything for At The Name. Choose the desired format for the page or chapter number if you want to change the default. The newly defined format then becomes the default for that type of counter.
- Click on OK.

Referencing other pages and chapters

The Ventura cross-reference feature can also be used to refer to text or graphics in other pages or chapters in the document. To do this, you must create a link between the original reference and the section to which it refers. This is done by marking the text or frame you want to refer to with a unique label. You then refer to this label when creating the cross-reference.

To place a marker label in text:

- Enter text mode.
- Place the cursor at the location you want to refer to.
- Select Ins Special Item from the Edit menu (or hit Ctrl C).
- Select Marker Name or hit F7 from the menu that pops up. The Insert/Edit Marker Name dialog box appears (Figure 11-24).

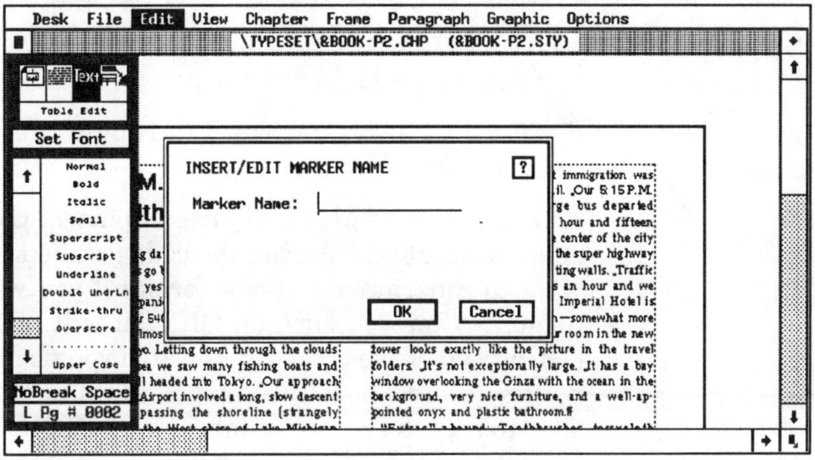

Figure 11-24. The Marker Name dialog box lets you mark a point in text that can later be referenced.

- Enter a marker name.

Ventura does not distinguish between uppercase and lowercase, so the word "SECTION" will be regarded as the same as "section." It's a good idea to write the marker name on a piece of paper so you can recall it when entering the reference.

To place a marker in a picture or text frame, go back to the familiar Anchors & Captions dialog box. If you recall, Anchors & Captions allows you to enter a label to anchor a frame to the text that refers to it. The same name used to anchor the frame to text is used for cross-referencing purposes. First, enter Frame mode, then:

- Select the frame you want to refer to.
- Select Anchors & Captions.
- Enter a unique label name in the Anchor Name field.

- Click on OK.

The marker names you've entered represent one end of the cross-reference link. Now you can refer to them by completing the link. You essentially follow the same procedure described above for inserting the current page or chapter number, with one additional step. Enter Text mode and place the cursor where you want the page or chapter number to be inserted. Then:

- Select Ins Special Item from the Edit menu, or press the Ctrl-C key
- Select Cross Ref. from the pop-up menu or enter F6.
- After At The Name:, enter the marker name for the text or frame you want to refer to.

Follow the same procedure used to insert the current page or chapter number, entering the code for the kind of counter you want to generate and a new format if you want to change the default. After you click on OK, you will see a degree symbol (°) instead of the cross-reference (if you do not, make sure you have selected Show Tabs and Returns in the Options menu). To generate the actual number, you must use the Multi-Chapter option in the Options menu to renumber the publication (See Chapter Eight). After adding each chapter to the file list, click on Renumber to produce the cross-references.

In addition to the page or chapter number, you can also create automatic references to other kinds of information: the section number in which the referenced text or picture appears, a figure number, a table number, caption text, or variable text. This is done by choosing the appropriate code from the Refer To: field in the Insert/Edit Reference dialog box. The choices are summarized below:

P#, for Page Number, inserts the page number of the text or frame marked earlier.

C# inserts the chapter number of the referenced text or frame.

F# inserts a figure number for a referenced frame. This is the same as the Figure number generated with the Anchors & Captions features in Frame mode.

T# inserts a table number for a referenced table. This does not apply to tables created with the Table Editor, but to tables placed into frames (see below).

*S** inserts the section number preceding the referenced text or frame.

*C** inserts the caption from a referenced frame if a caption has been entered under Anchors & Captions.

*V** inserts a variable text reference (see below).

In some cases, you may want to generate multiple references. The most common example is combining a chapter and page number, as in: "The Acme Laser Printer, as mentioned in Chapter Two, page 20." To do this, you must create two cross-references that refer to the same marker name in Chapter Two. One cross-reference would refer to the chapter number, using "One" for the format to indicate that the reference should be spelled out. The other cross-reference would refer to the page number, with "1" as the format to indicate that Arabic numerals should be used.

Cross-referencing tables

One confusing aspect of the cross-reference feature pertains to tables. Some tables used in Ventura publications are placed in frames. With the Anchors & Captions dialog box, you can use a table counter to label and caption table frames just as you use a figure counter to label and caption picture frames. The T# code applies only to these table frames. It will not work with tables created in text with the table editor.

There is a way to reference tables created in Table Edit mode, however. You must create a unique tag for table captions, and use Auto-Numbering to create section numbers. Each section corresponds to a table number. You can then place a text marker in the caption. When you create the cross-reference, enter S*, for section number, in the Refer To: field. At the Name: should refer to the marker name you just created for the frame. It's a somewhat cumbersome technique, but it will work. Remember to use just one of the two techniques — frame or table editor — to create the tables if you want to number them consistently.

Variable text references

Variable text references work in a similar manner to other cross-references. If you've ever used a merge-print program to generate form letters, this feature should be easy to grasp. In a merge-print application, you set up a form letter in which variable names are used for pieces of information that will be inserted from a database file. For example, the letter might begin "Dear &firstname&." When the merge-print function is invoked, the program prints a series of letters in which first names from a database are inserted in place of the variable "&firstname&."

With the variable text reference feature, you can insert variable names throughout your document and replace them with any desired text in a single operation. Unlike merge-print programs, however, Ventura does not show the actual variable name. Instead, you enter the variable name as a cross-reference. A degree symbol then appears in the text location to indicate the presence of the variable.

Suppose you want to create a "generic" proposal you will send to a number of companies. At certain places in the document, you want to refer to the particular company being addressed. To do this, place the text cursor at the location where you want to insert the variable, and go to the Ins/Edit Reference dialog box. Then:

- In the At the Name: field, enter your variable name, in this case "Company."
- In the Refer To: field, select V*. Notice that the format field is grayed.
- Click OK.

Repeat this process at each point in the generic document where you want to reference the company name. When you are ready to print a version of your generic chapter that is directed at a specific company, you must insert a variable definition in the chapter that instructs Ventura to replace each occurrence of the reference "company" with the actual company name.

The variable definition can be placed in any location in the document that precedes the reference. It's a good idea to insert your variable definitions at the beginning of the first chapter, since they'll be easy to locate and edit.

To insert the variable definition:

- Enter Text mode.
- Select Ins Special Item from the Edit menu.
- Choose Variable Def (or press F8) from the pop-up menu. The Insert/Edit Variable Definition dialog box appears (Figure 11-25).

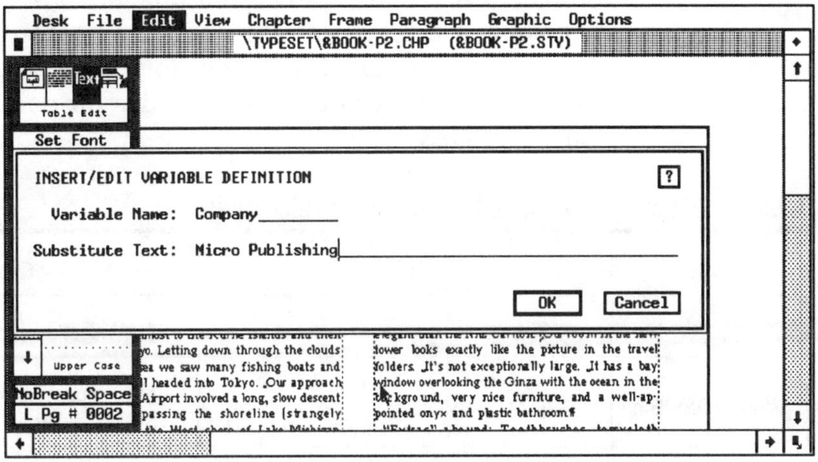

Figure 11-25. The Insert/Edit Variable Definition dialog box allows you to substitue new text for every occurrence of a reference (Company in this case).

- Enter the variable name and the text you want to substitute for it. If the document is addressed to a company called "Micro Publishing," enter "Company" for Variable Name and "Micro Publishing" for Substitute Text.
- Click on OK.

When the chapter is re-numbered, "Micro Publishing" will appear at each variable cross-reference. To change the company, enter new substitute text in the Insert/Edit Variable Definition dialog box. The new name will appear when you perform the renumbering operation in the Multi-Chapter dialog box.

Editing the cross-reference

As we have noted, a degree symbol is used to indicate the presence of a cross-reference or marker name in text (the symbol will not appear, however, if Tabs and Returns are hidden in the Options menu). When you place the text cursor just before the degree symbol, the Current Selection Box in the Side-Bar indicates whether the symbol refers to a reference, variable definition, or marker name. To delete the cross-reference, simply delete the degree symbol. To edit the reference, select Edit Special Item from the Edit menu.

In Chapter Three, we showed how bracket codes can be used in your word processor to achieve many effects otherwise created in Ventura Publisher. You can also enter cross-references in your word processor. Codes for doing this are shown in Table 11-2.

Table 11-2. Word processor codes for cross-references.

Type	Code	Example
Marker	<$M[label]>	<$M[Widget description]>
Variable Definition	<$V[label]definition>	<$V[Company]Micro Publishing> <$V[product]Model 123-Q>
Reference	<$R[type,label,format]string> Type = C#, P#, F#, T#, S*, C*, or V* Format = 1, A, a, I, i, ONE, One, or one string = Optional temporary value	<$R[C#,Intro,ONE]> <$R[F#,Widget photo,1]000> <$R[C*,map label,i]> <$R[V*,Company]XYZ Corp.>

In some cases, you may accidentally create a cross-reference that refers to a nonexistent marker name or frame anchor. If so, the mistake won't show up immediately. But when you try to renumber the publication, you'll get an error message indicating the mistake. Ventura generates a text file listing where the mistake occurred and the marker name it could not identify. You can load this file into a frame or study it with a word processor to see where the problem lies. The file uses the GEN extension for generated files. The file name consists of the first five characters of the publication name plus "ERR."

Cross-reference examples

Let's show some examples of using the cross-referencing feature to give you a better idea of how it works. We'll look at how a magazine might use the feature for "continued on" and "continued from" page references. Then we'll see how cross-references might be used in *History of Desktop Publishing*.

Magazine

Suppose you're a magazine editor who wants to continue an article from page 15 to page 52. You want to have a line at the bottom of the last column on Page 15 that says, "Continued on page 52." And on page 52, of course, you want a line that says, "Continued from page 15." But there's always the possibility that the magazine's advertising sales force will do a better than usual job and sell a few more ad pages. Depending on how the ads are placed, either section of the article might have to move.

Frames are placed on each page, with the article jumping from one to the other. Go into Frame mode, and give each frame an anchor name by means of the Anchors & Captions dialog box in the Frame menu. For example, you might use "Part One" for the first frame and "Part Two" for the second. Then place smaller frames at the bottom of the first frame and the top of the second frame. These will contain the "continued" text. You do not need to give them an anchor name, but for the purposes of discussion we'll call them "Part One Jump" and "Part Two Jump."

Enter Text mode, and type the following into the small "Part One Jump" frame we just created on page 15:

```
Continued on Page
```

Be sure to leave a space after the word "page." Select Ins Special Item from the Edit menu (or hit Ctrl-C), then Cross-Ref from the pop-up menu that appears (or hit F6). The Insert/Edit Reference dialog box is shown. After At The Name:, type in the anchor name for the "Part Two" frame. Select P# in the Refer To: field. You can also change the numeric format if you want to have it read "Continued on page Fifty-Two" instead of "Continued on page 52."

Now go to the "Part Two" frame on page 52. Enter "Continued from Page " in the jump frame, and follow the same procedure described above. Enter the anchor name "Part One" in the Insert/Edit Reference dialog box. As the pagination of the magazine changes, the "Continued To" and "Continued From" page references will change accordingly.

Book

Earlier, we described a book called the *History of Desktop Publishing*. If you recall, the author mentions the Acme Laser Printer, which was first described earlier in the book. The editor wants to add a cross-reference that will remain accurate even if the page number of the first reference changes.

The original mention of the printer is on page 20 in Chapter Two. The second mention is on page 124. It reads, in part, "The Acme Printer, as discussed on page x," with a blank left in place of the "x." To insert the cross-reference, follow the same general procedure described for the "continued" references. The difference is that instead of referring to a frame, we'll refer to a section of text. While in Text mode:

- Place the cursor at the point of the original mention in Chapter Two.
- Choose Ins Special Item from the Edit menu (or hit Ctrl-C).
- Select Marker Name from the pop-up menu (or press F7).
- Enter a marker name, such as "Laser Printer," in the Insert/Edit Marker Name dialog box.

Go back to Page 124, where you again refer to the printer. Type "The Acme Laser Printer, as discussed on page " leaving a space after the word "page." Then go to the Cross Reference dialog box as we did in our magazine example. Enter "Laser Printer" in the At The Name: field, and P# in the Refer To: field.

Variable Names

Suppose Acme Laser Printers is the target of a hostile corporate takeover bid by Discount Laser Printers. It is possible that the name "Acme" will have to be changed to "Discount," but you're not sure. One way out of this dilemma is to replace the brand name of the printer with a variable. You can then go back and replace the variable with "Acme" or "Discount" as the situation warrants.

The first step is to insert a cross-reference at each mention of the brand name "Acme." Enter a variable name, such as "Brand," in the At the Name field. Enter V* in the Refer To field. The V* code causes the Format field to be grayed.

Now you can record your variable definition. Go into Text mode and position the text cursor, preferably on the first page of the first chapter. Select Variable Def (or hit F8) from the Ins Special Item menu. Enter "Brand" in the variable name field. Enter the desired company name (either "Acme" or "Discount") in the substitution text field. When you renumber the publication, the chosen variable, "Discount" or "Acme," will appear at each cross-reference point. To change it again, return to the Insert/Edit Variable Definition dialog box and enter the new substitution text.

In some cases, this operation may be more easily performed with a word processor's search and replace function. But the variable name feature is helpful if:

- You don't want to go back to your word processor.
- You don't want to replace every mention of a phrase.
- You want to replace several variables at once.
- You want to make changes in multiple chapter files.

Vertical justification

This section details the functions and commands of Ventura's vertical justification feature. It covers the following areas:

- uses of vertical justification
- differences between feathering and carding
- applying vertical justification

Uses of vertical justification

Vertical justification is a handy feature that allows for more attractive page designs. Earlier, we discussed justification as an aspect of horizontal text alignment. Justified columns are evenly aligned on both sides, with spaces evenly inserted between characters and words to assure uniform *width.*

Vertical justification places spaces between lines and paragraphs to assure columns of uniform *height.* Figure 11-26 shows two versions of the same column, one justified and one not justified. Extra spacing is used in the justified column to make it reach the bottom of the page. The unjustified column, without any extra spacing, does not reach the bottom.

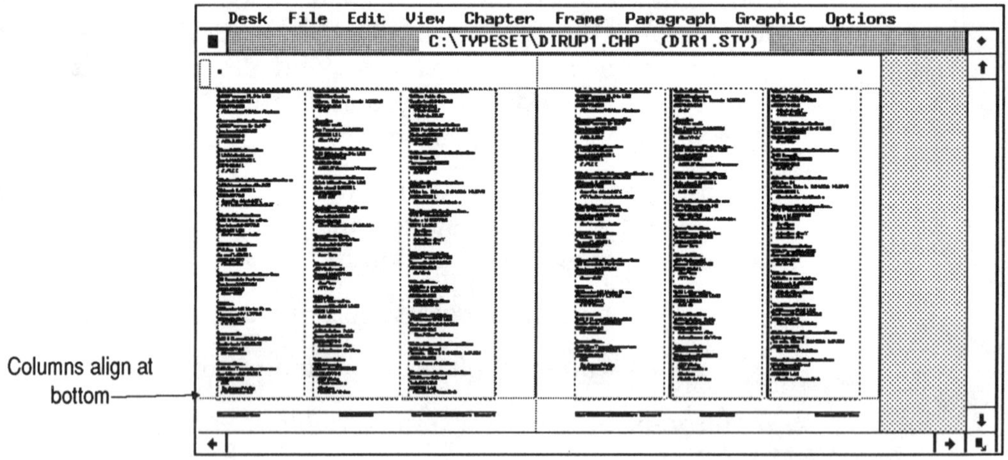

Figure 11-26. The page on the left has vertical justification on; the page on the right has vertical justification off.

The need for vertical justification can arise in many situations. You may be at the end of an article or section and don't have enough text to reach the bottom of the page. Or, if Keep With Next is used to link a headline with following text, the headline can be forced to a new column or page, again leaving space.

Widow and Orphan controls can also force text to a new column or page. It is possible to use spacing controls in Ventura to achieve uniform column length by placing extra gaps between frames, paragraphs or sections, but this is a time-consuming, trial-and-error effort. With vertical justification, the program can add spacing in an eye-pleasing manner according to rules that you specify.

The problem with vertical justification is that it can sometimes make a page look worse than it would if columns were unjustified. If too much space is added, gaps between lines and paragraphs can be so large that text blocks seem to be floating in the middle of a vacuum. On pages with multiple columns, spacing can move lines out of alignment with those in neighboring columns. Also, certain paragraphs or frames may not lend themselves to extra spacing.

Fortunately, Ventura lets you determine just how columns are vertically justified to avoid unattractive page designs. The order in which it performs justification also minimizes spacing problems. For each page element — frames, paragraphs, tables, and lines — you can define a maximum amount of space that can be added above or below. You can also set page elements so that no extra spacing can be added.

Carding versus feathering

Ventura uses two different forms of vertical justification: carding and feathering. They differ in the way they add space between frames, paragraphs and lines. Each has its pros and cons.

The carding option is related to Ventura's line snap feature

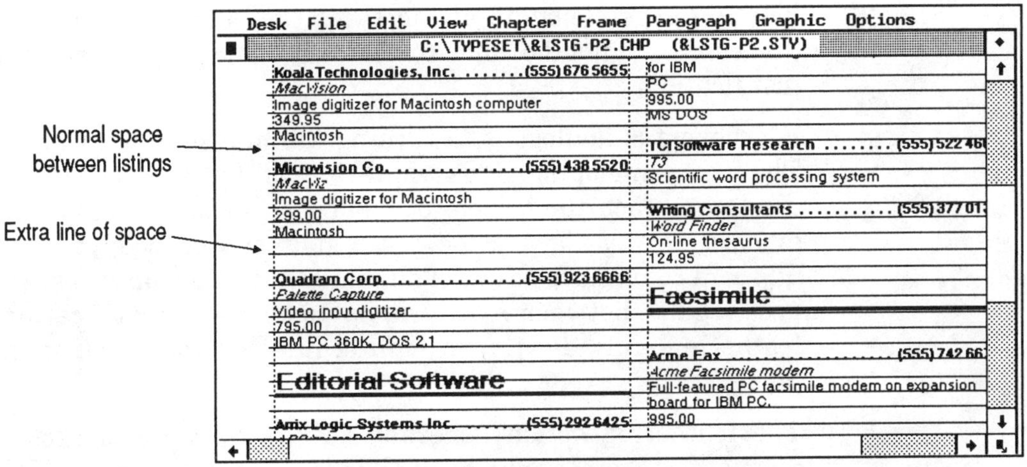

Figure 11-27. When carding, Ventura adds space in multiples of the line spacing.

(Figure 11-27). When it adds space between page elements, it uses exact multiples of inter-line spacing. If inter-line spacing is 12 points, carding will add spacing in units of 12, 24, 36 points — any multiple of 12.

The advantage of carding is that it allows even alignment of text across adjacent columns. If all spacing settings for paragraphs, frames, tables and other elements are set at multiples of inter-line spacing, text will be evenly aligned at its baseline. If any settings are not in multiples of inter-line spacing, alignment will be thrown off.

The disadvantage of carding is that it can sometimes lead to unattractive page designs, epecially if justification is permitted between lines in a paragraph. In this case, some lines will have extra spacing, others will not. Also, there are some cases where carding will not permit justification unless you allow unacceptably large amounts of space between frames and paragraphs.

As we'll see below, Ventura's vertical justification feature adds space according to a certain set of rules, adding space first between frames, then between paragraphs, and finally between lines. For each page element, you can set a maximum amount of space that can be added above or below. The program will try to add as much space as it can, up to the limits set by the user. If it cannot get the column to reach the bottom of the page, no justification takes place at all. And since carding further restricts the amount of space that can be added between page elements, it increases the possibility that the program will not be able to add enough space to achieve justification.

Feathering is analogous to turning the line snap feature off. The feathering option adds whatever space is needed to make a column reach the bottom of a page — up to the maximum amount set by the user — even if it causes body text in adjacent columns to go out of alignment. If 14.5 points of space are needed between paragraphs to achieve justification, feathering will add it even if inter-line spacing is set to 12 points.

The feathering option generally results in more attractive page designs, since spacing is added in an even manner. This is especially noticeable if you allow spacing between lines in a paragraph. The downside, of course, is that you cannot have multiple-column layouts with evenly aligned text baselines.

In general, you should use carding for:

- Newsletters
- Newspapers
- Magazines
- Any other document where even alignment across adjacent columns is important.

Use feathering for:

- books
- flyers
- brochures
- any other document where even alignment across adjacent columns is not important

Applying vertical justification

Vertical justification is controlled from several areas in Ventura:

- the Chapter Typography dialog box
- the Frame Typography dialog box (Frame mode)
- the Paragraph Typography dialog box (Paragraph mode)
- the Insert/Edit Table dialog box (Table Edit mode)

Global attributes for vertical justification are set in the Chapter Typography dialog box. They can be overridden in the Frame Typography dialog box, which has its own commands for setting justification within and around frames. The Paragraph Typography dialog box controls spacing above and below paragraphs and between lines within the paragraph. The Insert/Edit Table dialog box controls vertical justification above and below tables.

When Ventura performs justification, it does so in a certain order. Space is first added between frames and surrounding text, up to the maximum amount allowed by the user. If the column still does not reach the bottom of the page, space is added between paragraphs, again up to the maximum amount allowed. Space is then added between lines in a paragraph (tables are treated like paragraphs for the purpose of justification). If the column is not justified after all this space has been added, justification is canceled and the original amount of space at the bottom of the page remains.

Now we'll look at the specific steps you must take to use the justification feature:

- Turn it on globally for the entire document with the Chapter Typography dialog box.
- Override chapter settings for individual frames with the Frame Typography dialog box (if necessary).
- Specify paragraph settings with the Paragraph Typography dialog box.
- Specify table settings with the Insert/Edit Table dialog box.

Chapter Typography

Vertical justification is set globally for the entire chapter in the Chapter Typography dialog box in the Chapter menu (Figure 11-28). Here, you can turn on the vertical justification

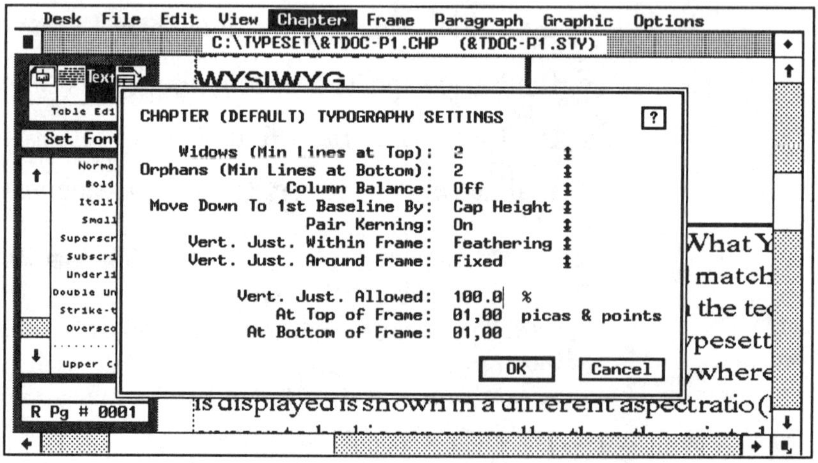

Figure 11-28. The Chapter Typography dialog box controls the amount and type of vertical justification.

feature and set the maximum amount of spacing allowable around frames in the chapter. It can be invoked from any of Ventura's program modes.

Your first choice in this dialog box is whether to use carding or feathering, which were described earlier. Whichever you choose, you can override it within individual frames. As mentioned, carding should be used when text must be evenly aligned across adjacent columns. Otherwise, use feathering.

Vert. Just. Allowed globally increases or decreases the maximum amount of justification set for each page element: lines, paragraphs, tables, and frames. If maximum spacing for a certain paragraph were set at 12 points, entering 200 percent for Vert. Just. Allowed would double this maximum to 24 points. Normally it should be set at 100 percent.

Three settings allow you to control how spacing is added around frames:

- Vert. Just. Around Frame
- At Top of Frame
- At Bottom of Frame

Vert. Just. Around Frame determines whether a frame can be moved from a fixed position. If you set it as Moveable, space can be added above or below a frame. If space is added between paragraphs or lines above the frame, of course, the frame will move down. If you set Vert. Just. Around Frame to Fixed, space cannot be added to any lines, paragraphs or tables above the frame. This keeps the frame a specified distance from the top of the page. Frames should be fixed if you want to keep them in the same location on a page.

At Top of Frame and *At Bottom of Frame* are used to enter a maximum amount of spacing for all frames in the chapter. These settings can be overridden in the Frame Typography dialog box. If you set each at 24 points, no more than 24 points of spacing can be added above or below any frame in the chapter, unless you override the setting in the Frame Typography dialog box.

Frame Typography

In many cases, you may need to override the frame settings used in the Chapter Typography dialog box. You may want to permit more or less maximum spacing above or below a particular frame. You may want to turn off justification within a frame, or use carding instead of feathering. In these cases, you need to go to the Frame Typography dialog box in the Frame menu (Figure 11-29). Here you can override chapter settings for any particular frame or inserted page.

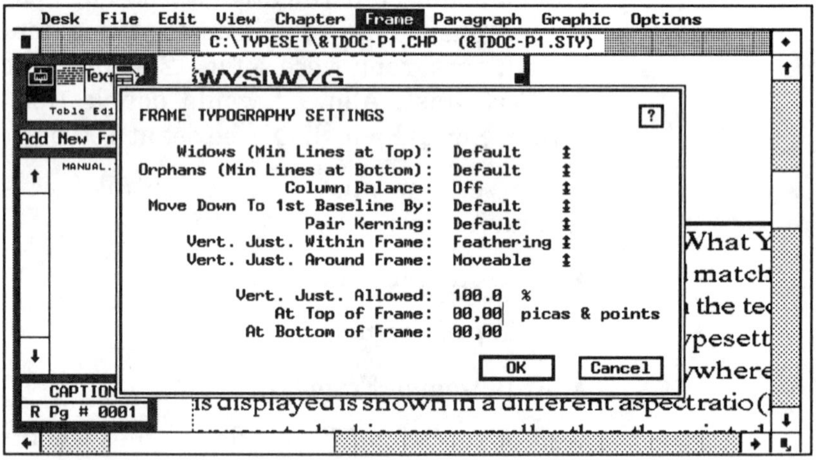

Figure 11-29. The Frame Typography dialog box.

The dialog box contains five settings that affect vertical justification:

- Vert. Just. Within Frame
- Vert. Just. Around Frame
- Vert. Just. Allowed
- At Top of Frame
- At Bottom of Frame

Vert. Just. Within Frame allows you to turn justification on or off for text within the frame. As with the equivalent Chapter Typography dialog box setting, you can choose between feathering and carding. If the global setting is for feathering, you can change it to carding within that particular frame.

Vert. Just. Around Frame allows you to override global settings for whether frames are fixed or moveable. In most cases, the global setting allows frames to be moveable. But in certain cases, it may be important to keep a frame in a fixed position on the page.

Vert. Just. Allowed permits you to change the maximum amount of spacing allowed between elements within the frame. Suppose you allow a maximum of 12 points of spacing above and below frames in the Chapter Typography dialog box. If you enter 200% for this setting, up to 24 points of spacing can be added between frames within this frame. This setting can be helpful if you add frames to an inserted page and you want to increase or decrease the allowable amount of spacing. You would select the frame and then change this setting.

At Top of Frame and *At Bottom of Frame* allow you to change the maximum amount of space that can be added above or below the frame.

Paragraph Typography

The Paragraph Typography dialog box (Figure 11-30) allows you to control maximum allowable spacing for lines and paragraphs. You can specify the amount of space that can be added

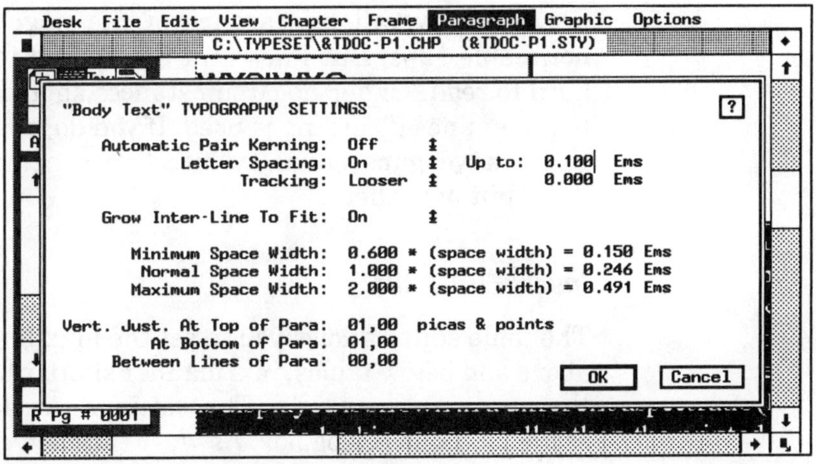

Figure 11-30. The Paragraph Typography dialog box.

above or below a particular paragraph, and how much can be added between lines within the paragraph. It is invoked from the Paragraph menu if a paragraph has been tagged. You can have different settings for each tag in your style sheet.

Use the Paragraph Typography settings if you want Ventura to add space between paragraphs or lines of text to achieve justification. In many cases, columns cannot be attractively justified if space is added only to frames. A large gap at the bottom of the page is usually less of an eyesore than large gaps between frames within the column. For this reason, it is often wise to allow some extra spacing between paragraphs to achieve justification.

The Paragraph Typography dialog box has three settings:

- Vert. Just. at Top of Para.
- At Bottom of Para.
- Between Lines of Para.

The first two settings allow you to specify the maximum amount of space permitted above or below paragraphs. They are similar to the equivalent settings in the Frame Typography and Chapter Typography dialog boxes.

Between Lines of Para. allows you to set a maximum amount of spacing between lines of text. Be careful when using this feature. If you permit a small amount of space, you can improve the overall appearance of the page without having noticeable gaps. But lines that are spaced too loosely can be hard to read. Under no circumstances should you allow space between lines if carding is used. If you do, you'll see that some pages have gaps equal to interline spacing between some lines, but not others.

Insert/Edit Table

The table editor allows you to set the maximum extra spacing above and below tables, in a manner similar to that allowed by the paragraph controls. The settings are found in the Insert/Edit Table dialog box. As we mentioned earlier, tables are treated the same as paragraphs for the purposes of justification. Each table can have its own unique justification settings.

How vertical justification works

Now let's look at an example of how vertical justification might work. Suppose the maximum amount of spacing allowed for frames and paragraphs is 12 points above and 12 points below. The maximum amount of spacing allowed for lines within a paragraph is 6 points above and below. A column on a particular page consists of one picture frame and three paragraphs. White space at the bottom of the page amounts to 72 points.

The vertical justification feature first adds 12 points of space above and below the frame. This leaves 48 points of white space at the bottom of the page. Ventura then adds 12 points below the first paragraph, above the third paragraph, and above and below the middle paragraph. That uses up the remaining 48 points. If more space were needed, the vertical justification feature would then add up to 6 points between each line. If space is still left at the bottom of the page when the maximum amount has been added to each page element, no vertical justification takes place.

Spacing between frames, paragraphs, and lines is added in proportion to the maximum amount of spacing permitted for each page element. Suppose we allowed 6 points of space above a frame and 12 points below. If an extra 15 points of spacing are needed to make the column reach page bottom, 5 points are added above the frame and 10 points below.

Edco hyphenation dictionary

The Edco hyphenation dictionary provided with Ventura improves on the standard hyphenation function. Containing 130,000 words, it brings hyphenation quality to the level of dedicated typesetting systems. It runs a little more slowly than the standard hyphenation feature, but provides more control over how hyphenation is performed and reduces the number of hyphenation errors. To run it, you need at least 1.2 MB of EMS memory, plus an extra 1.3 MB of hard disk storage.

The hyphenation feature actually contains three dictionaries.

The main dictionary contains whole words, while the other two dictionaries contain common prefixes and suffixes in the English language.

The prefix and suffix dictionaries are standard ASCII files that can be edited with most word processors.

Installing the Edco dictionary

To load the hyphenation dictionary, you must add two or three lines to the VPPROF.BAT file that launches Ventura. Ventura's installation program does this for you automatically, but you can modify its default choices. This can be done with any word processor that handles ASCII files. The extra lines will look something like this:

```
DRTLCFG -M6 -B2 E3 -AA -PC:\Ventura\DICT

DLOAD ENGLISH

DLOAD -U
```

The first line configures the hyphenation function according to the user's wishes. The second line actually loads the dictionary into memory. The third line, which is optional, removes the dictionary from memory, freeing up EMS for other uses. The first two lines should be at the beginning of the batch file. The third line should be at the end of the file.

Each of the arguments in the first line can be changed to reflect the user's wishes. They are as follows:

M. The minimum number of characters for a word to be hyphenated. If M is set to 6, words with fewer than six characters cannot be hyphenated. We recommend *-M6* for most applications.

B. The minimum number of characters that can be placed before the hyphen. If it is set at two, a hyphen cannot be inserted between the first two characters. We recommend *-B3* for most applications. However, if your publications have very narrow columns, you may prefer *-B2*.

E. The minimum number of characters that can be placed after the hyphen. If it is set at three, at least three characters must be placed on the next line after the hyphen. We recommend *E3* for most applications.

A. This determines how apostrophes are handled. AA is the default for the particular language in use. AE causes the dictionary to recognize an apostrophe as the end of a word. AC handles the apostrophe as a normal character. The English dictionary uses AE as a default, so entering AA and AE have the same effect.

P. The directory path for the dictionary. \Ventura\DICT is the default. The installation program automatically copies the dictionary to that subdirectory. If you wish to move it, type the new location here in the batch file so Ventura will know where to find it.

Enter all commands in the same format shown above. Do not add spaces between the hyphen and the letter, or the letter and the number. Place spaces between each option, however.

Once the dictionary is installed, it is activated when you select the USDICT option in the Alignment dialog box. If you install and load the Edco dictionary, but fail to specify USDICT for each tag, Ventura will continue to use its default hyphenation algorithm instead. If you make any changes to the Prefix or Suffix dictionaries, they will show up only if you exit Ventura, remove the dictionary from memory, then reload Ventura.

Changing the dictionaries

Typographically sophisticated users who wish to modify the Edco hyphenation dictionary may want to make use of two utility programs that come with Ventura. These are the DUPD and CHKWORD programs.

DUPD

DUPD allows you to update the Edco dictionary by adding words, deleting words, or changing hyphenation points for words. Before running this program, you must make a list of all the changes you wish to make. Use you word processor's ASCII or nondocument mode to put words, one per line, into the file. Each word should be preceded by one of three symbols:

- the equals sign (=) to change the hyphenation points

- the plus sign (+) to add the word to the dictionary
- the exclamation point (!) to delete the word from the dictionary

Use the hyphen character within words to indicate acceptable hyphenation points. Here's an example of what an update file might look like:

```
+micro-Publishing

+Laser-Jet

=Z-ebr-a

!Ventura
```

Once you have created and saved your update file in ASCII format, execute the program DUPD as follows:

```
CD\Ventura\DICT

DUPD UPDATE.LST
```

The program will then modify the Edco dictionary with your desired changes.

CHKWORD

The CHKWORD utility allows you to examine the contents of the Edco dictionary to see if certain words are present and, if so, what the hyphenation points are. To run this program, simply type CHKWORD from the DOS prompt. You will be asked for a word to check. Enter the word in question, followed by Enter.

If it finds the word, CHKWORD will display it on screen, with hyphen characters denoting the acceptable hyphenation points in the word. In addition, CHKWORD uses the tilde character (~) to indicate hyphenation points that would be acceptable if you used more liberal settings for the M, B, and E parameters in your VP.BAT file (see previous discussion of hyphenation controls).

Now that you have a familiarity with Ventura's specialized

functions, you are well on your way to producing sophisticated, complex, and attractive documents that would probably not be possible with any other desktop publishing program. But if you get stuck at some point in the future, remember that this book is here to help as a reference source or an applications guide.

Thank you for letting us be your guide to Ventura Publisher, and good luck in creating your own documents.

Appendix A

Glossary

A.

Align. To arrange letters along a vertical line (margin) or horizontal line (baseline).

Alley. See **Gutter**.

Anchoring. Attaching text or graphics to a fixed point in the file. The anchor point moves with the text to which it is anchored.

Ascender. The portion of a lowercase letter rising above its x-height, or body height. The long upper strokes in letters like "b" and "t."

ASCII. American Standard Code for Information Interchange. A standard coding system that assigns a numeric value to letters, numbers, and symbols. The lowest common denominator for exchanging text between word processing and page layout programs.

Aspect Ratio. The relationship between the height and width of a displayed object. A 1:1 aspect ratio means the object will appear undistorted.

Assignment List. A list of files, tags, or attributes that can be transferred to the selected frame, paragraph, or text. Shown in the Side-Bar on the left side of the screen.

Attribute. A physical characteristic of a typeface. The primary attributes for type are normal, bold, light, and italic. Other attributes are reverse, outline, shadow, uppercase, lowercase, small caps, subscript and superscript. Some attributes can be combined, for example, ***SMALL CAPS BOLD ITALIC.***

Auto Reformatting. A feature in which text insertion, deletion or reformatting causes text to flow as necessary to all linked pages.

Auto Text Flow (Autoflow). A feature in which text flows automatically from page to page when text is first placed.

B.

Backup Button. A small black box in Ventura file-selection boxes that allows access to another directory.

Baseline. The imaginary horizontal line on which type is placed. Line spacing is measured from baseline to baseline.

Bastard Title. A page, usually the first page in a book, containing only the title. If it appears after the contents and just before the text it is a *half title*. Many people use the two terms interchangeably.

Batch File. A file used with DOS to group DOS commands and execute them in a specific order.

Binding. Securing pages together and attaching a cover. Popular methods include *case*, *hard*, or *perfect* binding, and *saddle stitching*.

Bit-Map. Type and images formed by patterns of dots, as opposed to *object-oriented* images, where shapes are formed from mathematical descriptions.

Bleed. Extending an image to the edge of a page without leaving a margin.

Block. A unit of text or graphics that can be manipulated as a whole.

Board. A synonym for *camera-ready copy* and *mechanicals* from the days when text and illustrations were pasted onto stiff pieces of artboard.

Body Text. The main text of a document. Ventura treats any untagged paragraph as Body Text.

Bold. Type with a heavier, darker appearance than regular type.

Box Text. A feature found in Ventura's Graphics mode that allows creation of text associated with graphic elements.

Break. The beginning or ending point for a line, column, or page.

Bullet. A bold dot or other symbol used to emphasize or set off items in a list.

C.

Callout. Words describing portions of an illustration, often with arrows pointing to the described object.

Camera-Ready Copy. Text and illustrations laid out on a page in the proper size and position, and ready to be photographed for a printing plate. See **Mechanicals**.

Caption. Traditionally, a title or explanation above an illustration, as compared to a *legend*, which appeared below. Today used interchangeably for any accompanying text whether above, below or to the side.

Carding. A form of vertical justification that adds space only between user-defined elements such as paragraphs and illustrations. See **Feathering** and **Vertical Justification**.

Chapter. A Ventura Publisher file containing references to constituent text, graphics, and style sheet files.

Cicero. A European unit of measurement for type. One Cicero is 4.55 millimeters.

Clipboard. A temporary electronic storage area where text or graphics can be held for reuse.

Code-Based. Desktop publishing software that does not provide an interactive screen preview of the printed page. Code-based programs use embedded codes to signal changes in typestyle, spacing, and other specifications.

Collate. To sort multiple reproductions of pages into corrrectly ordered sets.

Color Separations. Set of four halftone transparencies for making plates in four-color process printing.

Commercial Printer. A printing company that emphasizes quality and longer print runs. Usually uses metal printing plates. Most books and magazines are produced by commercial printers. See **Quick Printer**.

Condensed Font. A version of a typeface with a narrow, compressed appearance.

Continuous Tone. A photograph or illustration containing shades of gray. Must be converted to a *halftone* for printing. See **Line Art**.

CPU. The Central Processing Unit. A microchip that acts as the "brains" of a computer, controlling most processing functions.

Crop. To cut or trim an illustration or other graphic element.

Crop Marks. Traditionally, tiny marks on the corners or edges of drawings and photographs that tell the camera operator which portions of the illustration to include and which to eliminate (crop out). Often used today to mean any corner, trim or registration mark, including those on text pages.

CRT. Cathode Ray Tube. An abbreviation for a computer display.

Current Selection Box. An area in the lower left corner of the Ventura Publisher display showing useful information, which varies depending on the selected mode.

Cursor. An on-screen position indicator. Usually a blinking square or line.

D.

Default. A specification that takes effect in the absence of any other. Most programs have default settings for variables like margins and type sizes that apply unless the user requests something else.

Descender. The portion of a lowercase letter falling below the baseline. The long lower portion of letters like "g" and "p."

Dialog Box. A pop-up window that allows the user to choose among different options.

Digitize. To convert information to the digital format useable by a computer. For instance, an illustration can be digitized by a scanner. See **Scanner**.

Dingbats. Symbols used for emphasis or decoration. Some desktop publishing systems have access to special dingbat fonts.

Discretionary Hyphen. A hyphen indicating where a word may be broken if necessary. The hyphen will not appear unless the word must be broken at the end of a line.

Display Type. Type large enough for headlines and other display purposes. Usually considered to be 14 points or larger.

Dithering. A process by which continuous-tone photographs are converted into bit-mapped images simulating varying shades of gray.

Draw Program. A program used to create object-oriented graphics. See **Object-Oriented Graphics**.

Drop Cap. An oversized first letter, usually used at the beginning of a chapter or section. The first letter is top-aligned with the remainder of the first line of text; the bottom portion of the initial letter extends downward into one or more lines of text.

Dummy. A mock-up or preview of a book. Sometimes it is a rough preliminary layout. Other times it is made from blank pages or photocopies of galley pages.

E.

Ellipsis. Equally spaced periods (usually three) indicating the omission of a section of text.

Em. A printing measurement unit equal to the point size of the current font.

Em Space. A space equal to the width of the letter M in the current point size. It is created by pressing and holding both the Crtl and Shift keys and then pressing "M." (Ventura actually uses the width of the @ character.)

En. A printing measurement unit equal to half the em, or half the point size of the type.

End Paper. Blank paper attached to the first and last pages and then glued to the cover of a hardbound book.

Expanded Font. A version of a typeface with a stretched, wide appearance.

Export. To copy text or graphics from one program to another.

F.

Feathering. A form of vertical justification that adds spaces evenly between all lines in a column. See **Carding** and **Vertical Justification**.

Five-Color Printing. A printing process in which a fifth tone, such as gold or silver, is added to the four process colors normally used in color reproduction. Often seen on mass-market book covers. See **Four-Color Printing**.

Flush. Absence of indentation. *Flush-left* text is butted up even with the left margin, *flush-right* with the right margin.

Font. All letters, numbers and symbols in one size and typeface. Helvetica Bold Italic is a typeface. For example, 12-point Helvetica bold italic is a font. *Font* is sometimes used interchangeably with typeface.

Footer. One or more lines of type that appear at the bottom of every page.

Format. The appearance of a document, especially its design elements like margins, columns, spacing and page layout. In this book, also used to indicate a precoded software style sheet or template containing the specifications for one particular page style.

Format File. See **Style Sheet**.

Four-Color Printing. Enables a printer to reproduce most colors by mixing the three primary colors (cyan, yellow, magenta) and black. Also known as *process* color printing. See **Five-Color Printing**.

Frame. A block positioned on a page into which the user can place text or graphics.

Frame Mode. A mode in Ventura Publisher in which frames can be created, positioned, and manipulated.

Front Matter. The pages that precede the main text of a book, including the title page, copyright page and contents page(s).

G.

Galley. In typesetting terminology, a reproduction of a column of type, usually printed on a long paper sheet.

Generic Font. A screen font used to represent many different similar fonts. It provides only a representation of the font, but allows the user to see the proper line endings.

Graphic. Any drawing, chart, graph, illustration, design element or photograph used in a publication.

Graphic Mode. A mode in Ventura Publisher in which simple graphics, such as lines and boxes, can be created and edited.

Gray Scale. The number of gradations of gray between white and black that can be generated by a particular scanner or software package.

Greeking. Conversion of text to lines that show approximate position but not the actual characters. Used when drawing the actual text would slow down the display unacceptably.

Grid. A matrix of horizontal and vertical lines used by designers and pasteup artists to organize and align the elements of a page. Some desktop publishing programs use an electronic version of a grid, consisting of light-gray lines on the screen.

Gutter. The inner margin between two columns or facing pages of text.

H.

Hairline. Very thin rule of about 1/100 of an inch. Many laser printers are not capable of reproducing a true hairline rule.

Halftone. A special version of a photograph that can be reproduced by a printing press. A halftone breaks a continuous-tone photo into tiny dots, which the press can reconstruct with ink. The eye interprets the dots as tones and shades. The density of the dot pattern, called a *screen*, determines the ultimate quality of the printed reproduction. A halftone can be a positive or a negative. See **Screen**.

Hanging Indent. Text with the first line flush-left and the rest of the paragraph indented. This glossary is set with a hanging indent.

Head or Heading. A word or phrase used to divide a chapter into sections. Usually printed on a line by itself in boldface.

Header. A title repeated on consecutive pages. For most books, the header contains the book title on left-hand pages and the chapter title on right-hand pages.

I.

Import. To copy text or graphics into one program from another.

Imposition. The arrangement of pages on a large sheet of paper so that when printed and folded the pages will be in the correct order. See **Signature**.

Indent. A specified space at the beginning of a line or paragraph of text.

Initial Caps. Text in which the first letter of each word is capitalized.

Inter-Line Spacing. See **Leading**.

Italic. A slanted typeface. Previously, italic typefaces were separately designed and had their own letterforms, whereas *oblique* typefaces were obtained by taking a vertical face and giving it a slant. Today, most desktop publishing programs produce oblique typefaces but call them italics.

J.

Justify. To place spaces between words or characters in a column so that one or both margins are even.

K.

Kerning. The reduction of space between characters to make them fit more tightly. When performed for all characters, it may be called *negative letter spacing*. When performed for individual letters, it may be called *manual kerning*.

Keyline. An outline to indicate the size and position of photos or other page elements that will be placed separately.

L.

Landscape. Horizontal orientation of pages or screen displays. See **Portrait**.

Laser Printer. A non-impact output device that fuses toner to paper to create near-typeset-quality text and graphics. The basic technology is similar to that of a photocopier.

Layout. The arrangement of a page, especially the spacing and position of text and graphics. Often used to describe a rough sketch. As a verb, the process of placing text and graphics in their proper position on the page.

Leader Dots. Evenly spaced dots or dashes to guide the eye across a page. Especially useful in tables, lists, catalogs and directories.

Leading. Vertical spacing between lines of type, specified in points. Pronounced *ledding*.

Left-Justified. See **Ragged-Right**.

Letter Spacing. Adjusting the normal space between letters. Usually assumed to be positive (adding space) unless otherwise noted. Negative letter spacing is usually called *kerning*.

Ligatures. Two or more letters that touch to form a single unit when placed next to each other. Traditional phototypesetters accommodate ligatures for special letter pairs such as fi, ff and others.

Line Art. A drawing that contains no grays or middle tones. Even when cross-hatching and other techniques are used to simulate shading, line art is made up exclusively of black (lines) and white (paper).

Lithography. See **Offset Printing**.

Lowercase. Small letters, as opposed to capital letters.

M.

Macro. A feature that assigns a command or string of characters to one key so an entire command can be entered with a single keystroke.

Make-Up. The physical assembly of page components, usually on stiff paper called artboards or flats. Also known as *paste-up*.

Margin. The blank border along the edge of a page.

Measure. The length of a line.

Mechanicals. Camera-ready pages on artboards or flats, with text and art in position. See **Camera-Ready Copy**.

Modem. A device that allows computers to send information over phone lines.

Monospaced Font. A type style with an equal amount of space allotted for each character. Most typewriters produce monospaced characters.

Mouse. A small, hand-held device for positioning the cursor on the screen. When the mouse is rolled across the surface of the desk, the cursor moves a corresponding distance on the screen.

N.

Numerals. Symbolic representations of numbers, such as Arabic numerals (1, 2, 3, 4, etc.) or Roman numerals (I, II, III, IV, etc.).

O.

Object-Oriented Graphics. Graphic images created by means of mathematical descriptions. They can usually be displayed or printed at the full resolution of the monitor or output device.

Oblique. See **Italic**.

Offset Printing. A widely used printing process in which a page is reproduced photographically on a metal plate attached to a revolving cylinder. Ink is transferred from the plate to a rubber blanket from which it is transferred to paper.

Orphan. The first line of a paragraph isolated at the bottom of a page. See **Widow**.

Overlay. A sheet laid on top of a page for spot-color printing.

P.

Page Description Language. A programming language, such as PostScript, that gives precise instructions to an output device for how a page should look. See **PostScript**.

Pagination. The process of numbering pages in a book. In desktop publishing, often extended to mean the process of laying out or flowing text onto all pages of a document.

Paint Program. A program used to create bit-mapped graphics. See **Bit-Map**.

Panning. Moving a graphic image inside a frame to see its various sections.

Pantone Matching System. A popular system for specifying spot colors. Each color has its own PMS number by which it can be selected. See **Spot Color**.

Paragraph. In Ventura Publisher, a distinct section of text. Can be a single word or sentence.

Paragraph mode. The mode in Ventura Publisher in which style sheet tags are created and applied to text elements.

Pasteup. The act of assembling all page elements, such as type and illustrations, into position. Traditionally done by attaching the separate elements with glue or wax. In desktop publishing, accomplished electronically on screen.

Phototypesetting. The process by which pages are composed and/or produced on a phototypesetter, which generally permits very high resolution compared with a laser printer.

Pi Font. A special font with math symbols, dingbats or other special characters.

Pica. A printing measurement unit used to specify line lengths, margins, columns, gutters and so on. Equivalent to 12 points, or about 1/6 of an inch.

Pixel. A picture element, or the smallest possible unit on a page or screen. Used to describe resolution.

Plate. A thin, flexible sheet of metal, paper or plastic used in offset printing. It contains a photographic reproduction of the page.

Point. A printing measurement unit equivalent to 1/12 of a pica, or about 1/72 of an inch. Used to specify type sizes, line spacing, and rule widths.

Point Size. The vertical measurement of type, roughly equivalent to the distance between the highest ascender and lowest descender, plus a small bit of breathing room on top and bottom.

Portrait. Vertical orientation of a page or display. See **Landscape**.

Position Stat. A photocopy or other reproduction of a halftone that is pasted onto a mechanical to show the printer how to crop and position the final image.

PostScript. A page description language developed by Adobe Systems and used by many laser printers and phototypesetters. See **Page Description Language**.

Process Camera. A camera used in graphic arts to photograph mechanicals and create printing plates.

Process Colors. The four colors needed for four-color printing: yellow, magenta, cyan and black. See **Four-Color Printing**.

Proof. A trial copy of a page or publication used to check accuracy. Also short for proofread, meaning to check for mistakes.

Publication. A file in Ventura Publisher containing references to related chapters.

Q.

Quick Printer. A print shop that emphasizes speed, short print runs and acceptable quality. Not widely used for book or magazine publishing except by short-run self-publishers. See **Commercial Printer**.

R.

Ragged-Left. See **Right-Justified**.

Ragged-Right. Used to describe columns of text in which the left side lines up evenly and the right side varies. Also known as *left-justified* type.

Recto. A right-hand page.

Register. Precise alignment of printing plates or negatives.

Register Marks. Marks used to permit exact alignment of pages. Usually printed just outside the live area and then trimmed off. The standard register mark is a small circle with a cross inside.

Resolution. The density of dots or pixels on a page or display, usually measured in dots per inch. The higher the resolution, the smoother the appearance of text or graphics.

Reverse Type. Light letters on a dark background.

Right-Justified. Used to describe columns of text in which the right side lines up evenly and the left side varies. Also known as *ragged left*.

Roman. The traditional name for upright (unslanted) type, as distinguished from oblique, backslant or italic type.

Rule. A straight line whose width is normally specified in points.

Ruler. In a desktop publishing program, a measuring guide on the edge of the screen.

Runaround. When text deviates from its normal margins to fit around an illustration that projects into the text area.

Running Head. See **Header**.

S.

Sans-Serif. Typestyles without little strokes known as *serifs*, such as Helvetica and Avant Garde. Sometimes called *block* or *gothic*. This sentence is set in a sans-serif typestyle.

Scale. To change the size of a piece of artwork.

Scanner. A digitizing device that converts a piece of artwork into an electronic bit-map that can be loaded and manipulated by a software program. A means of converting hand-drawn art or photos into electronic form.

Screen. The pattern of dots used to make a halftone or tint. Halftone screens are measured in *lines*, equivalent to dots per inch. Tint screens are measured in percentages, with a 10-percent screen being very light and a 100-percent screen being totally black.

Separations. Transparencies or pages used for color reproduction. Each separation is used to reproduce a particular color. See **Process Colors**, **Four-Color Process**, and **Five-Color Process**.

Serif. A tiny decorative stroke in character designs. Serif typefaces, such as Times or Palatino, use serifs in their designs. The type you are reading is a serif typeface. See **Sans-Serif**.

Signature. A section of a book or magazine consisting of a large piece of paper folded into the smaller size used in the publication. Most printers use signatures of 16 or 32 pages. See **Imposition**.

Size. To change the size of a piece of artwork.

Small Caps. Letters with the shape of capital letters, but smaller than normal. Often, small caps are equal to the x-height of the typeface. THIS SENTENCE IS SET IN SMALL CAPS.

Snap-To. A feature in which a page element is pulled into alignment when placed close to prespecified guidelines.

Solid. A line of type set with no extra line spacing.

Spine. The bound edge of a book visible when books are stored side-by-side on a shelf.

Spot Color. The use of one or more extra colors on a page, used to highlight specified page elements. Colors are usually specified as PMS codes. See **Pantone Matching System**.

Strip. To paste one piece of film, usually a halftone, into a piece of film containing a page to produce a printing plate.

Style Sheet. Format and type specifications for a page design that can be stored and reused in desktop publishing programs.

Subhead. A heading, usually set in smaller type than a main headline, used to break up chapters or articles into smaller sections.

Subscript. A number, letter, or symbol that is smaller than the standard text and aligned below the baseline. Often used in mathematical and scientific notation, such as H_2O.

Superscript. A number, letter, or symbol that is smaller than the standard text and aligned above the baseline. Often used in mathematical notation or to indicate footnotes.

T.

Tags. Style sheet elements that specify font, type size, line spacing, and other attributes for sections of text. Can be applied while text is created in a word processor or in Ventura Publisher's Paragraph mode. See **Style Sheet**.

Template. A predesigned page with specified areas for text, heads and illustrations.

Text Flow-Through. A feature in which text flows freely between columns and pages as changes are made. Changes on one page automatically cause reformatting on other affected pages.

Text Mode. A mode in Ventura Publisher in which text can be created or edited.

Tint. A light color or shade obtained by printing a fine pattern of dots on the page. See **Screen**.

Tint Block. An area printed with a color or shade (screened) to lower its intensity. Tint blocks are used to distinguish a section of text from the main body and to provide a color or shaded background for line drawings.

Tracking. Reduction or enlargement of space between characters and words. See **Kerning** and **Letter Spacing**.

Trim Size. The size of a finished book after all the edges have been trimmed. Typically specified in inches with the horizontal measurement first.

Turnkey System. A desktop publishing system sold as a package with all necessary software and hardware components.

Typeface. A particular type design, such as Helvetica Bold. See **Font**, **Typeface Family.**

Typeface Family. A set of all the different variations — wide, narrow, italic, bold, bold italic — of a given type design. Helvetica is a type family. See **Font, Typeface.**

U.

Underlying Page. The frame that automatically appears on each page in Ventura Publisher.

Upper and Lower. Text that uses upper- and lowercase letters. Abbreviated u&lc.

Uppercase. Capital letters.

V.

Verso. A left-hand page.

Vertical Justification. A feature in which a column of text is spaced so that it spans an entire page or section from top to bottom.

W.

Weight. Variations in the thickness of letter strokes in a family of type, such as light, medium, bold and extra bold.

Widow. The last line of a paragraph isolated at the top of a page. See **Orphan**.

Wrap. A typesetting feature in which text runs around a graphic element.

WYSIWYG. An acronym for What You See Is What You Get, meaning that text and graphics on a screen correspond closely to final printed output. Pronounced wizzy-wig.

X.

X-Height. The height of a lowercase letter in a particular font without ascenders or descenders, equivalent to the height of the letter x.

Z.

Zoom. To view an enlarged (zoom in) or reduced (zoom out) portion of a page on screen.

Appendix B

Ventura Character Sets

Decimal	International	Symbol	Dingbat
32			
33	!	!	✁
34	"	⊇	✂
35	#	#	✃
36	$	∃	✄
37	%	%	☎
38	&	&	✆
39	'	∋	✇
40	(	(	✈
41	)	)	✉
42	*	*	☛
43	+	+	☞
44	,	,	✌
45	-	−	✍
46	.	.	✎
47	/	/	✏
48	0	0	✐
49	1	1	✑
50	2	2	✒
51	3	3	✓
52	4	4	✔
53	5	5	✕
54	6	6	✖
55	7	7	✗
56	8	8	✘
57	9	9	✙
58	:	:	✚
59	;	;	✛

Decimal	International	Symbol	Dingbat
60	<	<	✜
61	=	=	✝
62	>	>	✞
63	?	?	✟
64	@	≅	✠
65	A	Α	✡
66	B	Β	✢
67	C	Χ	✣
68	D	Δ	✤
69	E	Ε	✥
70	F	Φ	✦
71	G	Γ	✧
72	H	Η	★
73	I	Ι	✩
74	J	ϑ	✪
75	K	Κ	✫
76	L	Λ	✬
77	M	Μ	✭
78	N	Ν	✮
79	O	Ο	✯
80	P	Π	✰
81	Q	Θ	✱
82	R	Ρ	✲
83	S	Σ	✳
84	T	Τ	✴
85	U	Υ	✵
86	V	ς	✶
87	W	Ω	✷

Decimal	International	Symbol	Dingbat	Decimal	International	Symbol	Dingbat
88	X	Ξ	✸	122	z	ζ	❚
89	Y	Ψ	✹	123	{	{	❛
90	Z	Z	✺	124	|	|	❜
91	[	[	✻	125	}	}	❝
92	\	∴	✼	126	~	~	❞
93	]	]	✽	127			
94	^	⊥	✾	128	Ç		
95	_	_	✿	129	ü	ϒ	❡
96	‘	‾	❀	130	é	′	❢
97	a	α	❁	131	â	≤	❣
98	b	β	❂	132	ä	⁄	❤
99	c	χ	❃	133	à	∞	❥
100	d	δ	❄	134	å	ƒ	❦
101	e	ε	❅	135	ç	♣	❧
102	f	ϕ	❆	136	ê	♦	♣
103	g	γ	❇	137	ë	♥	♦
104	h	η	❈	138	è	♠	♥
105	i	ι	❉	139	ï	↔	♠
106	j	φ	❊	140	î	←	①
107	k	κ	❋	141	ì	↑	②
108	l	λ	●	142	Ä	→	③
109	m	μ	❍	143	Å	↓	④
110	n	ν	■	144	É	°	⑤
111	o	ο	❏	145	æ	±	⑥
112	p	π	❐	146	Æ	″	⑦
113	q	θ	❑	147	ô	≥	⑧
114	r	ρ	❒	148	ö	×	⑨
115	s	σ	▲	149	ò	∝	⑩
116	t	τ	▼	150	û	∂	❶
117	u	υ	◆	151	ù	•	❷
118	v	ϖ	❖	152	ÿ	÷	❸
119	w	ω	◗	153	Ö	≠	❹
120	x	ξ	❘	154	Ü	≡	❺
121	y	ψ	❙	155	¢	≈	❻

Decimal	International	Symbol	Dingbat
156	£	…	❼
157	¥	|	❽
158	¤	—	❾
159	ƒ	↵	❿
160	á	ℵ	①
161	í	ℑ	②
162	ó	ℜ	③
163	ú	℘	④
164	ñ	⊗	⑤
165	Ñ	⊕	⑥
166	ª	∅	⑦
167	º	∩	⑧
168	¿	∪	⑨
169	“	⊃	⑩
170	”	⊇	❶
171	‹	⊄	❷
172	›	⊂	❸
173	¡	⊆	❹
174	«	∈	❺
175	»	∉	❻
176	ã	∠	❼
177	õ	∇	❽
178	Ø	®	❾
179	ø	©	❿
180	œ	™	➔
181	Œ	∏	→
182	À	√	↔
183	Ã	·	↕
184	Õ	¬	➘
185	§	∧	➙
186	‡	∨	➚
187	†	⇔	➛
188	¶	⇐	➜
189	©	⇑	➝
190	®	⇒	➞
191	™	⇓	➟
192	„	◊	➠
193	…	〈	➡
194	‰	®	➢
195	•	©	➣
196	–	™	➤
197	—	∑	➥
198	°	⎛	➦
199	Á	⎜	➧
200	Â	⎝	➨
201	È	⎡	➩
202	Ê	⎢	➪
203	Ë	⎣	➫
204	Ì	⎧	➬
205	Í	⎨	➭
206	Î	⎩	➮
207	Ï	⎪	➯
208	Ò		
209	Ó	〉	➱
210	Ô	∫	➲
211	Š	⌠	➳
212	š	⎮	➴
213	Ù	⌡	➵
214	Ú	⎞	➶
215	Û	⎟	➷
216	Ÿ	⎠	➸
217	ß	⎤	➹
218	Ž	⎥	➺
219	ž	⎦	➻
220	/	⎫	➼
221		⎬	➽
222		⎭	➾

Index

A

B

C

E

F

G

H

I

N

O

Q

R

S

T

U

V

W

X

Z

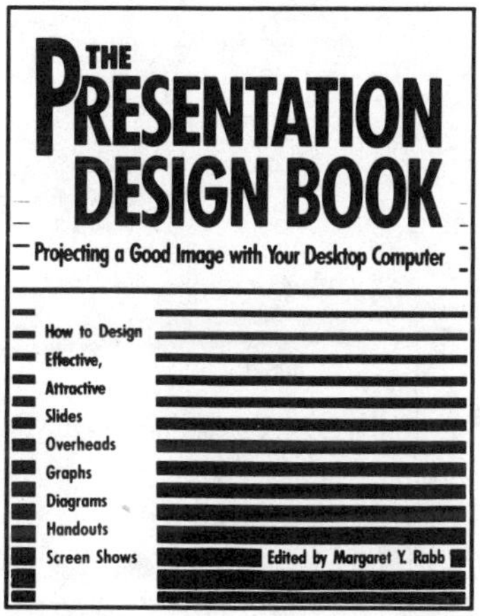

Looking Good in Print, Second Edition
$23.95
410 pages, Illustrated
ISBN: 0-940087-32-4

With over 100,000 in print, **Looking Good in Print** is looking even better. More makeovers, a new section on designing newsletters and a wealth of new design tips and techniques to broaden the design skills of the ever-growing number of desktop publishers.

Newsletters from the Desktop
$23.95
306 pages, Illustrated
ISBN: 0-940087-40-5

Now the millions of desktop publishers who produce newsletters can learn how to improve the design of their publications.

The Makeover Book: 101 Design Solutions for Desktop Publishing
$17.95
282 pages, Illustrated
ISBN: 0-940087-20-0

"Before-and-after" desktop publishing examples demonstrate how basic design revisions can dramatically improve a document.

Type from the Desktop
$23.95
226 pages, Illustrated
ISBN: 0-940087-45-6

Learn the basics of designing with type from a desktop publisher's perspective.

The Gray Book: Designing in Black and White on Your Computer
$22.95
210 pages, Illustrated
ISBN: 0-940087-50-2

This "idea gallery" for desktop publishers offers a lavish variety of the most interesting black, white and gray graphic effects that can be achieved with laser printers, scanners and high-resolution output devices.

The Presentation Design Book
$24.95
258 pages, Illustrated
ISBN: 0-940087-37-5

How to design effective, attractive slides, overheads, graphs, diagrams, handouts and screen shows with your desktop computer.

Desktop Publishing with WordPerfect, Second Edition (For 5.0 and 5.1)
$21.95
325 pages, Illustrated
ISBN: 0-940087-47-2

WordPerfect offers graphics capabilities that can save users thousands of dollars in design and typesetting costs. Includes invaluable information on creating style sheets for consistency and speed.